C000228441

# BRITISH RAILWAYS
# LOCOMOTIVES & COACHING STOCK
# 2021

The Complete Guide to all Locomotives & Coaching Stock which operate on the National Rail network and Eurotunnel

## Robert Pritchard

Published by Platform 5 Publishing Ltd,
52 Broadfield Road, Sheffield, S8 0XJ, England.

Printed in England by The Lavenham Press, Lavenham, Suffolk.

ISBN 978 1 909431 86 7

# CONTENTS

## SECTION 1 – LOCOMOTIVES

## SECTION 2 – LOCO-HAULED COACHING STOCK

## SECTION 3 – DIESEL MULTIPLE UNITS

# CONTENTS

## SECTION 4 – ELECTRIC MULTIPLE UNITS

## SECTION 5 – ON-TRACK MACHINES

## SECTION 6 – CODES

## COVER PHOTOGRAPHS

**Front Cover:** Colas Rail-liveried 67027 "Charlotte" and 67023 "Stella" top-and-tail a Tyseley–Weymouth Network Rail test train at Wyke Champflower, near Bruton, on 12/08/20. **Glen Batten**

**Back Cover:** New West Midlands Trains 3-car Aventra 730 001 is seen on test at Velim in the Czech Republic on 09/08/20. **Vladimír Fišar**

# BRITAIN'S RAILWAY SYSTEM

The structure of Britain's railway system changed significantly during 2020, following the ongoing Covid-19 pandemic which saw passenger numbers drop by around 60–70% across the country. This drop in passenger numbers meant that franchises were no longer profitable and the Government was forced to step in and provide financial support to operators. Initially, in March 2020, the Transport Secretary suspended rail franchising and operators transitioned to "Emergency Measures Agreements". These EMAs suspended the normal financial agreements, instead transferring all revenue and cost risk to the Government. The existing operators in England all accepted these new arrangements and continued to operate trains (initially with reduced service frequencies) for a small management fee. Similar arrangements were put in place by the Scottish and Welsh Governments for ScotRail, Caledonian Sleeper and Transport for Wales.

The EMAs initially lasted for six months until September 2020, from which time longer "Emergency Recovery Management Agreements" (ERMAs) were put in place in most cases. These were similar management contracts which continued to see operators run services for a management fee. In the longer term the franchise model is expected to be changed to one of concessions, although this is expected to take several years to fully implement.

In London and on Merseyside concessions were already in place. Concessions see the operator paid a fee to run the service, usually within tightly specified guidelines. Operators running a concession would not normally take commercial risks, although there are usually penalties and rewards in the contract.

Britain's national railway infrastructure is owned by a "not for dividend" company, Network Rail. In 2014 Network Rail was reclassified as a public sector company, being described by the Government as a "public sector arm's-length body of the Department for Transport".

Most stations and maintenance depots are leased to and operated by Train Operating Companies (TOCs), but some larger stations are controlled by Network Rail. The only exception is the infrastructure on the Isle of Wight: The Island Line franchise uniquely included maintenance of the infrastructure as well as the operation of passenger services. As Island Line is now part of South Western Railway, both the infrastructure and trains are operated by SWR.

Trains are operated by TOCs over Network Rail tracks (the National Network), regulated by access agreements between the parties involved. In general, TOCs are responsible for the provision and maintenance of the trains and staff necessary for the direct operation of services, whilst Network Rail is responsible for the provision and maintenance of the infrastructure and also for staff to regulate the operation of services.

The Department for Transport (DfT) is the franchising authority for the national network, with Transport Scotland overseeing the award of the ScotRail and Caledonian Sleeper franchises and the Welsh Government overseeing the Wales & Borders franchise. From February 2021 the Welsh Government will take over the direct operation of the Wales & Borders franchise from KeolisAmey, with the operation of day-to-day rail services becoming the responsibility of a new publicly owned subsidiary of Transport for Wales.

Now superseded by the ERMAs, each franchise was set up with the right to run specified services within a specified area for a period of time, in return for the right to charge fares and, where appropriate, to receive financial support from the Government. Subsidy was payable in respect of socially necessary services. Service standards are monitored by the DfT throughout the duration of the franchise. Franchisees earned revenue primarily from fares and from subsidy. They generally leased stations from Network Rail and earned rental income by sub-letting parts of them, for example to retailers.

TOC's and open access operator's main costs are the track access charges they pay to Network Rail, the costs of leasing stations and rolling stock and of employing staff. Franchisees may do light maintenance work on rolling stock or contract it out to other companies. Heavy maintenance is normally carried out by the Rolling Stock Leasing Companies, according to contracts.

# DOMESTIC PASSENGER TRAIN OPERATORS

The majority of passenger trains are operated by Train Operating Companies, now supported by the Government through the Emergency Recovery Management Agreements, which have replaced franchises. These generally run for between six and 18 months and many have options in place for extensions of up to 12 months. Caledonian Sleeper, Great Western Railway, ScotRail, Southeastern and Transport for Wales are still operating under Emergency Measures Agreements (EMAs) pending longer support deals being signed or because the original franchise ran out shortly after the onset of Covid-19. For reference the date of the expiry of the original franchise is also shown here.

*Name of franchise*     *Operator*     *Trading Name*
**Caledonian Sleeper**     Serco     **Caledonian Sleeper**
*EMA until 31 March 2021; original franchise was until 31 March 2030*

The Sleeper franchise started in April 2015 when operation of the ScotRail and ScotRail Sleeper franchises was separated. Abellio won the ScotRail franchise and Serco the Caledonian Sleeper franchise. Caledonian Sleeper operates four trains nightly between London Euston and Scotland using locomotives hired from GBRf. New CAF Mark 5 rolling stock was introduced during 2019.

**Chiltern**     Arriva (Deutsche Bahn)     **Chiltern Railways**
*EMRA until 11 December 2021, the original franchise expiry date*

Chiltern Railways operates a frequent service between London Marylebone, Oxford, Banbury and Birmingham Snow Hill, with some peak trains extending to Kidderminster. There are also regular services from Marylebone to Stratford-upon-Avon and to Aylesbury Vale Parkway via Amersham (along the London Underground Metropolitan Line). The fleet consists of DMUs of Classes 165, 168 and 172 plus a number of locomotive-hauled rakes used on some of the Birmingham and Oxford route trains, worked by Class 68s hired from DRS.

**Cross Country**     Arriva (Deutsche Bahn)     **CrossCountry**
*ERMA until 15 October 2023; original franchise expired on 17 October 2020*

CrossCountry operates a network of long distance services between Scotland, the North-East of England and Manchester to the South-West of England, Reading, Southampton, Bournemouth and Guildford, centred on Birmingham New Street. These trains are mainly formed of diesel Class 220/221 Voyagers, supplemented by a small number of HSTs on the NE–SW route. Inter-urban services also link Nottingham, Leicester and Stansted Airport with Birmingham and Cardiff. These trains use Class 170 DMUs.

**Crossrail**     MTR     **TfL Rail**
*Concession until 27 May 2023 (with an option to extend the concession by 2 years to May 2025)*

This concession started in May 2015. Initially Crossrail took over the Liverpool Street–Shenfield stopping service from Greater Anglia, using a fleet of Class 315 EMUs, with the service branded "TfL Rail". New Class 345 EMUs are being introduced on this route and are also now used between Paddington and Hayes & Harlington, Heathrow Airport and Reading. TfL Rail currently also operates the former Heathrow Connect stopping service that now also uses Class 345s. The opening of Crossrail through central London has been delayed and operation through new tunnels beneath central London, from Shenfield and Abbey Wood in the east to Reading and Heathrow Airport in the west is now expected in 2022. It will then be branded the "Elizabeth Line".

**East Coast**     DfT     **London North Eastern Railway**
*Operated by DfT's "Operator of Last Resort" until June 2023 (with an option to extend by 2 years to June 2025)*

LNER operates frequent long distance trains on the East Coast Main Line between London King's Cross, Leeds, Lincoln, Harrogate, York, Newcastle-upon-Tyne and Edinburgh, with less frequent services to Bradford, Skipton, Hull, Glasgow, Stirling, Aberdeen and Inverness. A new fleet of 65 Hitachi Class 800 and 801 "Azuma" trains have all now been introduced (these are a mix of bi-mode and electric, 5- and 9-car units) and operate the majority of services. A small number of Class 91 + Mark 4 sets have been retained until at least 2023 and are mainly used on Leeds and York services.

**East Midlands**     Abellio     **East Midlands Railway**
*ERMA until 31 March 2022; original franchise was until 21 August 2027*

EMR operates a mix of long distance high speed services on the Midland Main Line (MML), from London St Pancras to Sheffield (to Leeds at peak times and with some extensions to York), Nottingham (plus peak-hour trains to Lincoln) and Corby, and local and regional services ranging from the long distance Norwich–Liverpool route to Nottingham–Skegness, Nottingham–Mansfield–Worksop, Newark–Matlock and Derby–Crewe. It also operates local services across Lincolnshire. Trains on the MML are worked by a fleet of Class 180 and 222 DMUs and HSTs, whilst the local and regional fleet consists of DMU Classes 153, 156 and 158. Class 360 EMUs will operate services on the newly electrified St Pancras–Corby route from May 2021.

**East Anglia**     Abellio (Netherlands Railways) (60%)/Mitsui Group (40%)     **Greater Anglia**
*ERMA until 18 September 2021; original franchise was until 11 October 2025*

Greater Anglia operates main line trains between London Liverpool Street, Ipswich and Norwich and local trains across Norfolk, Suffolk and parts of Cambridgeshire. It also runs local and commuter services into Liverpool Street from the Great Eastern (including Southend, Braintree and Clacton) and West Anglia (including Ely/Cambridge and Stansted Airport) routes. In 2019–20 a new fleet of Stadler EMUs and bi-mode units (Classes 745 and 755) was introduced on the

GEML and in East Anglia, replacing older DMUs and loco-hauled trains. Classes 317, 321, 322, 360 and 379 EMUs are still operated out of Liverpool Street and during 2020–22 are being replaced by a large fleet of new Class 720 Aventras.

| **Essex Thameside** | Trenitalia | **c2c** |
|---|---|---|

*ERMA until 31 March 2021; original franchise was until 10 November 2029*

c2c operates an intensive, principally commuter, service from London Fenchurch Street to Southend and Shoeburyness, via both Upminster and Tilbury. The fleet consists of 74 Class 357 EMUs, plus six Class 387s.

| **Great Western** | First Group | **Great Western Railway** |
|---|---|---|

*EMA until 26 June 2021; original franchise was until 31 March 2023*

Great Western Railway operates long distance trains from London Paddington to South Wales, the West Country and Worcester and Hereford. In addition there are frequent trains along the Thames Valley corridor to Newbury/Bedwyn and Oxford, plus local and regional trains throughout the South-West including the Cornish, Devon and Thames Valley branches, the Reading–Gatwick North Downs Line and Cardiff–Portsmouth Harbour and Bristol–Weymouth regional routes. Long distance services are now in the hands of a new fleet of Class 800/802 bi-mode InterCity Express Trains. DMUs of Classes 165 and 166 are used on the Thames Valley branches and North Downs routes as well as on local services around Bristol and Exeter and across to Cardiff. Class 387 EMUs are used between Paddington, Reading, Didcot Parkway and Newbury. Classes 150 and 158 and a fleet of short 4-car HSTs are used on local and regional trains in the South-West. A small fleet of Class 57s is maintained to work the overnight "Cornish Riviera" Sleeper service between London Paddington and Penzance formed of Mark 3 coaches. In 2021 tri-mode Class 769 units will be introduced on some routes around Reading.

| **London Rail** | Arriva (Deutsche Bahn) | **London Overground** |
|---|---|---|

*Concession until 25 May 2024 (with an option to extend the concession by 2 years to May 2026)*

London Overground operates services on the Richmond–Stratford North London Line and the Willesden Junction–Clapham Junction West London Line, plus the East London Line from Highbury & Islington to New Cross and New Cross Gate, with extensions to Clapham Junction (via Denmark Hill), Crystal Palace and West Croydon. It also runs services from London Euston to Watford Junction. All these use Class 378 EMUs, with new Class 710s also recently introduced onto the Watford Junction route. Class 710s also operate services on the Gospel Oak–Barking line. London Overground also operates some suburban services from London Liverpool Street – to Chingford, Enfield Town and Cheshunt. From autumn 2020 these services all use Class 710s, with one unit also used on the Romford–Upminster shuttle.

| **Merseyrail Electrics** | Serco (50%)/Abellio (Netherlands Railways) (50%) | **Merseyrail** |
|---|---|---|

*Concession until 22 July 2028. Under the control of Merseytravel PTE instead of the DfT*
*Due to be reviewed every five years to fit in with the Merseyside Local Transport Plan*

Merseyrail operates services between Liverpool and Southport, Ormskirk, Kirkby, Hunts Cross, New Brighton, West Kirby, Chester and Ellesmere Port, using Class 507 and 508 EMUs. A new fleet of Class 777 EMUs will be introduced in 2021–22.

| **Northern** | DfT | **Northern** |
|---|---|---|

*Operated by DfT's "Operator of Last Resort" until further notice*

Northern operates a range of inter-urban, commuter and rural services throughout the North of England, including those around the cities of Leeds, Manchester, Sheffield, Liverpool and Newcastle. The network extends from Chathill in the north to Nottingham in the south, and Cleethorpes in the east to St Bees in the west. Long distance services include Leeds–Carlisle,

Morpeth–Carlisle and York–Blackpool North. The operator uses a large fleet of DMUs of Classes 150, 153, 155, 156, 158, 170 and 195 plus EMU Classes 319, 323, 331 and 333. The new fleets of DMUs (Class 195) and EMUs (Class 331) have now been introduced on a number of routes, and will be followed by Class 769 bi-mode diesel electric units (converted from Class 319s) in 2021. All of the remaining Class 142 and 144 "Pacer" units had been withdrawn by November 2020.

**ScotRail**                      Abellio (Netherlands Railways)                      **ScotRail**
*EMA until 31 March 2021; original franchise was until 31 March 2022*

ScotRail provides almost all passenger services within Scotland and also trains from Glasgow to Carlisle via Dumfries, some of which extend to Newcastle-upon-Tyne (jointly operated with Northern). The company operates a large fleet of DMUs of Classes 156, 158 and 170 and EMU Classes 318, 320, 334, 380 and 385. A fleet of 26 refurbished HSTs are being introduced onto InterCity services between Edinburgh/Glasgow and Aberdeen and Inverness and also between Inverness and Aberdeen. In 2021 five Class 153s are also due to be introduced on the West Highland Line to provide more capacity and space for bikes and other luggage.

**South Eastern**                      Govia (Go-Ahead/Keolis)                      **Southeastern**
*EMA until 16 October 2021; original franchise expired on 1 April 2020*

Southeastern operates all services in the south-east London suburbs, the whole of Kent and part of Sussex, which are primarily commuter services to London. It also operates domestic High Speed trains on HS1 from London St Pancras to Ashford, Ramsgate, Dover and Faversham with additional peak services on other routes. EMUs of Classes 375, 376, 377, 465 and 466 are used, along with Class 395s on the High Speed routes. From 2021 the 30 Class 707 EMUs, sub-leased from South Western Railway, will also be introduced.

**South Western**                      First Group (70%)/MTR (30%)                      **South Western Railway**
*ERMA until 31 March 2021; original franchise ran until 17 August 2024*

South Western Railway operates trains from London Waterloo to destinations across the South and South-West including Woking, Basingstoke, Southampton, Portsmouth, Salisbury, Exeter, Reading and Weymouth, as well as suburban services from Waterloo. SWR also runs services between Ryde and Shanklin on the Isle of Wight, with the former London Underground 1938 stock (Class 483s) being withdrawn at the start of 2021 and a fleet of five third rail Vivarail units (converted former LU D78 stock) due to be introduced in spring 2021. The rest of the fleet consists of DMU Classes 158 and 159 and EMU Classes 442, 444, 450, 455, 456, 458 and 707. A new fleet of Bombardier Class 701s are being delivered to replace Classes 455, 456, 458 and 707 in 2021–22.

**Thameslink, Southern &**                      Govia (Go-Ahead/Keolis)                      **Govia Thameslink Railway**
**Great Northern (TSGN)**
*ERMA until 18 September 2021, the original franchise expiry date*

TSGN is the largest operator in Great Britain (the former Southern franchise was combined with Thameslink/Great Northern in 2015). GTR uses four brands: "Thameslink" for trains between Cambridge North, Peterborough, Bedford and Rainham, Sevenoaks, East Grinstead, Brighton, Littlehampton and Horsham via central London and also on the Sutton/Wimbledon loop using Class 700 EMUs. "Great Northern" comprises services on London King's Cross and Moorgate to Welwyn Garden City, Hertford North, Peterborough, Cambridge and King's Lynn using Class 365, 387 and 717 EMUs. "Southern" operates predominantly commuter services between London, Surrey and Sussex and "metro" services in South London, as well as services along the south Coast between Southampton, Brighton, Hastings and Ashford, plus the cross-London service from South Croydon to Milton Keynes. Class 171 DMUs are used on Ashford–Eastbourne and London Bridge–Uckfield services, whilst all other services are in the hands of Class 313, 377, 455 and 700 EMUs. Finally, Gatwick Express operates non-stop trains between London Victoria, Gatwick Airport and Brighton using Class 387/2 EMUs.

**Trans-Pennine Express**    First Group    **TransPennine Express**
*ERMA until 31 March 2021; original franchise ran until 31 March 2023*

TransPennine Express operates predominantly long distance inter-urban services linking major cities across the North of England, along with Edinburgh and Glasgow in Scotland. The main services are Manchester Airport/Manchester Piccadilly–Newcastle/Redcar Central/Hull plus Liverpool–Scarborough and Liverpool–Newcastle–Edinburgh along the North Trans-Pennine route via Huddersfield, Leeds and York, and Manchester Airport–Cleethorpes along the South Trans-Pennine route via Sheffield. TPE also operates Manchester Airport–Edinburgh/Glasgow and Liverpool–Glasgow. The fleet consists of Class 185 DMUs, plus three new fleets: Class 68s + Mark 5A sets being used, or to be used, on Liverpool–Scarborough and Manchester Airport–Redcar Central, Class 397s used on Manchester Airport/Liverpool–Scotland and Class 802 bi-mode units used on Liverpool–Edinburgh and Manchester Airport–Newcastle.

**Wales & Borders**    KeolisAmey    **Transport for Wales**
*EMA until 6 February 2021; original franchise ran until 15 October 2033. From 7 February 2021 the Welsh Government will take direct control of rail service operation. Infrastructure management will continue to be managed by KeolisAmey.*

Transport for Wales was procured by the Welsh Government and operates a mix of long distance, regional and local services throughout Wales, including the Valley Lines network of lines around Cardiff, and also through services to the English border counties and to Manchester and Birmingham. The fleet consists of DMUs of Classes 143, 150, 153, 158, 170 and 175 and three locomotive-hauled Mark 4 sets, to be introduced in 2021 on the Cardiff–Holyhead route. Rebuilt Class 230 D-Trains are to be introduced on the Wrexham–Bidston line from 2021 and new Stadler and CAF fleets will be introduced across other routes from 2022.

**West Coast Partnership**    First Group (70%)/Trenitalia (30%)    **Avanti West Coast**
*ERMA until 31 March 2022; original franchise ran until 31 March 2031*

Avanti West Coast operates long distance services along the West Coast Main Line from London Euston to Birmingham/Wolverhampton, Manchester, Liverpool, Blackpool North and Glasgow using Class 390 Pendolino EMUs. It also operates Class 221 Voyagers on the Euston–Chester–Holyhead route and a small number of trains from Wolverhampton to Shrewsbury and to Wrexham, whilst a mix of Class 221s and 390s are used on the Euston–Birmingham–Glasgow/Edinburgh route.

**West Midlands Trains**    Abellio (70%)/JR East (15%)/Mitsui (15%)    **West Midlands Railway/London Northwestern**
*ERMA until 18 September 2021; original franchise ran until 31 March 2026*

West Midlands Trains operates services under two brand names. West Midlands Railway trains are local and regional services around Birmingham, including to Stratford-upon-Avon, Worcester, Hereford, Redditch, Rugeley and Shrewsbury. WMR is managed by a consortium of 16 councils and the Department for Transport. London Northwestern is the brand used for long distance and regional services from London Euston to Northampton and Birmingham/Crewe and also between Birmingham and Liverpool, Bedford–Bletchley and Watford Junction–St Albans Abbey. The fleet consists of DMU Classes 139, 170 and 172 and EMU Classes 319, 323 and 350. Class 230 D-Trains were introduced onto the Bedford–Bletchley route in 2019 and a new fleet CAF Class 196 DMUs and Bombardier Class 730 EMUs will be introduced on a number of routes in 2021–22.

# NON-FRANCHISED SERVICES

The following operators run non-franchised, or "open access" services (* special seasonal services):

| Operator | Trading Name | Route |
|---|---|---|
| Heathrow Airport Holdings | Heathrow Express | London Paddington–Heathrow Airport |

Heathrow Express is a frequent express passenger service between London Paddington and Heathrow Airport. From late 2020 it started using Class 387 EMUs which have replaced the dedicated Class 332 units. HEx is now operated by GWR as part of its franchise.

| Hull Trains (part of First) | Hull Trains | London King's Cross–Hull |
|---|---|---|

Before the Covid-19 pandemic Hull Trains operated seven trains a day on weekdays from Hull to London King's Cross via the East Coast Main Line. New bi-mode Class 802s were introduced in late 2019/early 2020, replacing the Class 180 DMUs. One train in each direction starts back from and extends to Beverley. During the Covid-19 lockdown HT stopped running services, but reintroduced a limited timetable from August 2020 only to pause operation again in early 2021.

| Grand Central (part of Arriva) | Grand Central | London King's Cross–Sunderland/ Bradford Interchange |
|---|---|---|

Grand Central operates five trains a day from Sunderland and four trains a day from Bradford Interchange to London King's Cross using Class 180 DMUs. Grand Central also planned to introduce a service between King's Cross and Blackpool in 2020, but in the light of drop in passengers caused by the Covid-19 pandemic these plans were dropped – but not before four sets of Mark 4s had been refurbished and repainted into GC livery. Grand Central also paused operation during the Covid-19 lockdowns.

| Locomotive Services (TOC) | Locomotive Services |
|---|---|

Locomotive Services runs various excursions across the network using diesel, electric and steam locomotives operating under the brands Saphos Trains (principally steam-hauled trips), Statesman Rail (diesel-locomotive hauled trips and land cruises), Rail Charter Services (regular summer diesel-hauled trips over the Settle & Carlisle Line), Midland Pullman (HST tours) and Intercity (electric locomotive-hauled tours).

| North Yorkshire Moors Railway Enterprises | North Yorkshire Moors Railway | Pickering–Grosmont–Whitby/ Battersby, Sheringham–Cromer* |
|---|---|---|

The North Yorkshire Moors Railway operates services on the national network between Grosmont and Whitby or Grosmont and Battersby as an extension of its Pickering–Grosmont services and also operates services between Sheringham and Cromer on behalf of the North Norfolk Railway.

| South Yorkshire Supertram | Stagecoach Supertram | Meadowhall South–Rotherham Parkgate |
|---|---|---|

South Yorkshire Supertram holds a passenger licence to allow the operation of the pilot tram-train service linking Sheffield city centre with Rotherham Central and Rotherham Parkgate.

| Tyne & Wear PTE | Tyne & Wear Metro | Pelaw–Sunderland |

Tyne & Wear Passenger Transport Executive holds a passenger license to allow the operation of its Metro service over Network Rail tracks between Pelaw and Sunderland.

| Vintage Trains | Vintage Trains | Birmingham Snow Hill–Stratford-upon-Avon* |

Vintage Trains operates steam-hauled services on a seasonal basis.

| West Coast Railway Company | West Coast Railway Company | Fort William–Mallaig* York–Settle–Carlisle* Carnforth–York–Scarborough* |

WCRC operates steam-hauled services on these routes on a seasonal basis and a range of other excursions across the network, including the Northern Belle luxury train.

# INTERNATIONAL PASSENGER OPERATORS

Eurostar International operates passenger services between London St Pancras and mainland Europe. The company, established in 2010, is jointly owned by SNCF (the national operator of France): 55%, SNCB (the national operator of Belgium): 5% and Patina Rail: 40%. Patina Rail is made up of Canadian-based Caisse de dépôt et placement du Québec (CDPG) and UK-based Hermes Infrastructure (owning 30% and 10% respectively). This 40% was previously owned by the UK Government until it was sold in 2015.

In addition, a service for the conveyance of accompanied road vehicles through the Channel Tunnel is provided by the tunnel operating company, Eurotunnel. All Eurotunnel services are operated in top-and-tail mode by the powerful Class 9 Bo-Bo-Bo locomotives.

# FREIGHT TRAIN OPERATORS

The following operators operate freight services or empty passenger stock workings under "Open Access" arrangements:

**Colas Rail:** Colas Rail operates a number of On-Track Machines and also supplies infrastructure monitoring trains for Network Rail. It also operates a number of different freight flows, including oil and timber. Colas Rail has a small but varied fleet consisting of Class 37s, 56s, 66s, 67s and 70s. From 2020 it started using HST power cars (Class 43) on Network Rail test trains.

**DB Cargo (UK):** Still the biggest freight operator in the country, DBC (EWS until bought by Deutsche Bahn, when it was initially called DB Schenker) provides a large number of infrastructure trains to Network Rail and also operates coal, steel, intermodal and aggregate trains nationwide. The core fleet is Class 66s. Of the original 250 ordered, 79 have moved to DB's French and Polish operations, although some of the French locos do return to the UK when major maintenance is required. Around 22 Class 60s are also used on heavier trains, the remainder of the fleet having been stored or sold, although DB Cargo is still responsible for the maintenance of GBRf and DCR Class 60s at Toton.

DBC's fleet of Class 67s are used on passenger or standby duties for Transport for Wales and LNER and also on excursions or special trains. Class 90s see some use on West Coast Main Line freight traffic. The Class 92s are mainly used on a limited number of overnight freights on High Speed 1.

DBC also operates the Class 325 EMUs for Royal Mail and a number of excursion trains.

**Devon & Cornwall Railways** (part of Cappagh Construction Contractors (London)): DCRail specialises in short-term freight haulage contracts, using Class 56s or four Class 60s acquired from DB Cargo.

**Direct Rail Services:** DRS has built on its original nuclear flask traffic to operate a number of different services. The main flows are intermodal plus the provision of crews and locomotives to Network Rail for autumn RailHead Treatment Trains and also infrastructure trains. DRS has a varied fleet of locomotives, with Class 20s, 37s, 57s and 66s working alongside new Class 68s and diesel-electric Class 88s. Class 68s are hired to Chiltern Railways and TransPennine Express for passenger work. Its Class 68s are also used on some excursion work.

**Freightliner:** Freightliner (owned by Genesee & Wyoming) operates container trains from the main Ports at Southampton, Felixstowe, Tilbury and Thamesport to major cities including London, Manchester, Leeds and Birmingham. It also operates trains of coal, cement, infrastructure and aggregates. Most services are worked by Class 66s, with Class 70s mainly used on some of the heavier intermodal flows and cement trains from the Peak District. A small fleet of Class 90 electrics are used on intermodal trains on the Great Eastern and West Coast Main Lines, the fleet of Class 86s having been almost completely withdrawn by early 2021. The Class 90 fleet includes 13 locomotives previously operated by Greater Anglia.

The six Class 59/2s were purchased from DBC and are used alongside the Mendip Rail 59/0s and 59/1s on stone traffic from the Mendip quarries and around the South-East.

**GB Railfreight:** GBRf (owned by Infracapital) operates a mixture of traffic types, mainly using Class 66s together with a small fleet of Class 73s on infrastructure duties and test trains in the South-East and ten Class 60s acquired from Colas Rail in 2018. The company has also now purchased a number of Class 56s and owns a single Class 59, 59003. Some of the Class 56s are being rebuilt as Class 69s with a new GM engine. A fleet of Class 92s is also used on some intermodal flows to and from Dollands Moor or through the Channel Tunnel to Calais. Traffic includes coal, intermodal, biomass, aggregates and gypsum as well as infrastructure services for

Network Rail and London Underground. GBRf also supplies Class 73/9s and Class 92s to Caledonian Sleeper and owns the three former Colas Rail Class 47s.

GBRf also operates some excursion trains, including those using the preserved Class 201 "Hastings" DEMU.

**LORAM (UK):** LORAM has a freight license and operates a limited number of trains, most hauling On-Track Machines using hired-in locomotives.

**Rail Operations Group:** This company mainly facilitates rolling stock movements by providing drivers or using locomotives hired from other companies or by using its own fleet of Class 47s or Class 37s hired from Europhoenix or Class 57s hired from DRS.

**West Coast Railway Company:** WCRC has a freight licence but doesn't operate any freight as such – only empty stock movements. Its fleet of Class 47s, supplemented by a smaller number of Class 33s, 37s and 57s, is used on excursion work nationwide.

In addition, Amey, Balfour Beatty Rail, Harsco Rail, Swietelsky Babcock Rail (SB Rail) and VolkerRail operate trains formed of On-Track Machines.

# PROVISION OF INFORMATION

This book has been compiled with care to be as accurate as possible, but some information is not easily available and the publisher cannot be held responsible for any errors or omissions. We would like to thank the companies and individuals who have been helpful in supplying information to us. The authors of this series of books are always pleased to receive notification of any inaccuracies that may be found, to enhance future editions. Please send comments to:

Robert Pritchard, Platform 5 Publishing Ltd, 52 Broadfield Road, Sheffield, S8 0XJ, England.

**e-mail:** robert.pritchard@platform5.com  **Tel:** 0114 255 2625.

# UPDATES

This book is updated to the start of January 2021. The Platform 5 railway magazine "Today's Railways UK" publishes Stock Changes every month to update this book. The magazine also contains news and rolling stock information on the railways of Great Britain and Ireland and is published on the second Monday of every month. For further details of **Today's Railways UK**, please contact Platform 5 Publishing Ltd or visit our website **www.platform5.com**.

# 1. LOCOMOTIVES

# INTRODUCTION

This section contains details of all locomotives which can run on Britain's national railway network, plus those of Eurotunnel.

Locomotives currently approved for use on the national railway network fall into four broad types: passenger, freight, mixed traffic and shunting.

### Passenger
The number of dedicated passenger locomotives has not changed significantly in recent years. Classes 43 (HST) and 91 and some members of Classes 57, 67, 68, 73/9 and 92 are dedicated to franchised and Open Access passenger operations. Excursion trains have a few dedicated locomotives but mainly use locomotives that are best described as mixed traffic.

### Freight
By far the most numerous locomotives are those used solely for bulk commodity and intermodal freight. Since 1998 a large number of new Class 66 locomotives have replaced many former BR designs and in more recent years smaller numbers of Class 70s have also been introduced. There are however a significant number of BR era Class 20, 37, 47, 56, 60, 73/1, 86, 90 and 92 locomotives still in use; their number has increased slightly as some locomotives have been reinstated to cope with demand. In addition there is a small fleet of Class 59s acquired privately in the 1980s and 1990s and a small number of re-engined Class 57s in use.

### Mixed Traffic
In addition to their use on passenger and commodity freight workings these locomotives are used for stock movements and specialist infrastructure and test trains. The majority, but not all, are fitted with Electric Train Supply. Locomotives from Classes 20, 33, 37, 47, 57, 67, 68, 73/9, 88 and 90 fall into this category. Also included under this heading are preserved locomotives permitted to operate on the national railway network. Although these have in the past solely operated excursion trains they are increasingly seeing occasional use on other types of trains. Some, such as Class 50s with GB Railfreight, are frequently used by the main freight companies.

### Shunting
Very few shunting locomotives are now permitted to operate freely on the National Railway network. The small number that are have to be fitted with a plethora of safety equipment in order to have engineering acceptance. They are mainly used for local workings such as trips between yards or stock movements between depots and stations. Otherwise, shunting locomotives are not permitted to venture from depots or yards onto the National Railway network other than into defined limits within interface infrastructure. Remotely-controlled driverless shunters are not included in this book. However, all ex-BR shunting locomotives are listed under Section 1.1 "Diesel Shunting Locomotives".

Locomotives which are owned by, for example, DB Cargo or Freightliner, which have been withdrawn from service and are awaiting disposal are listed in the main part of the book. Locomotives which are awaiting disposal at scrapyards are listed in the "Locomotives Awaiting Disposal" section.

Only preserved locomotives which are currently used on the National Railway network are included. Others, which may still be Network Rail registered but not at present certified for use, are not included, but can be found in the Platform 5 book, "Preserved Locomotives of British Railways".

# LAYOUT OF INFORMATION

Locomotive classes are listed in numerical order of class. Principal details and dimensions are quoted for each class in metric and/or imperial units as considered appropriate bearing in mind common UK usage.

The heading "Total" indicates how many of that particular class are listed in this book.

Where numbers actually carried are different from those officially allocated, these are noted in class headings where appropriate. Where locomotives have been recently renumbered, the most immediate previous number is shown in parentheses. Each entry is laid out as in the following example:

| No. | Detail | Livery | Owner | Pool | Allocn. | Name |
|-----|--------|--------|-------|------|---------|------|
| 60091 +* | **DB** | DB | WCBT | TO | Barry Needham |

**Detail Differences.** Only detail differences which currently affect the areas and types of train which locomotives may work are shown. Where such differences occur within a class or part class, they are shown in the "Detail" column alongside the individual locomotive number.

**Codes:** Codes are used to denote the livery, owner, pool and depot of each locomotive. Details of these will be found in section 6 of this book.

The owner is the responsible custodian of the locomotive and this may not always be the legal owner. Actual ownership can be very complicated. Some vehicles are owned by finance/leasing companies. Others are owned by subsidiary companies of a holding company or by an associate company of the responsible custodian or operator.

Depot allocation codes for all locomotives are shown in this book (apart from shunting locomotives where the actual location of each is shown). It should be noted that today much locomotive maintenance is undertaken away from these depots. This may be undertaken at fuelling points, berthing sidings or similar, or by mobile maintenance teams. Therefore locomotives in particular may not return to their "home" depots as often as in the past.

(S) denotes that the locomotive is stored (the actual location is shown).

**Names:** Only names carried with official sanction are listed. Names are shown in UPPER/lower case characters as actually shown on the name carried on the locomotive.

**Builders:** These are shown in the class headings. More details and a full list of builders can be found in section 6.7.

# GENERAL INFORMATION

## CLASSIFICATION AND NUMBERING

All locomotives are classified and allocated numbers under the TOPS numbering system, introduced in 1972. This comprises a two-digit class number followed by a three-digit serial number.

For diesel locomotives, class numbers offer an indication of engine horsepower as shown in the table below.

| Class No. Range | Engine hp |
|---|---|
| 01–14 | 0–799 |
| 15–20 | 800–1000 |
| 21–31 | 1001–1499 |
| 32–39 | 1500–1999 |
| 40–54, 57 | 2000–2999 |
| 55–56, 58–70 | 3000+ |

For electric locomotives class numbers are allocated in ascending numerical order under the following scheme:

Class 71–80      Direct current and DC/diesel dual system locomotives.
Class 81 onwards   Alternating current and AC/DC dual system locomotives.

Numbers in the 89101–89999 series are allocated to locomotives which have been deregistered but subsequently re-registered for use on the national railway network and whose original number has already been reused. These numbers are normally only carried inside locomotive cabs and are not carried externally in normal circumstances.

## WHEEL ARRANGEMENT

For main line locomotives the number of driven axles on a bogie or frame is denoted by a letter (A = 1, B = 2, C = 3 etc) and the number of non-powered axles is denoted by a number. The use of the letter "o" after a letter indicates each axle is individually powered, whilst the "+" symbol indicates bogies are inter-coupled.

For shunting locomotives, the Whyte notation is used. In this notation the number of leading wheels are given, followed by the number of driving wheels and then the trailing wheels.

## UNITS OF MEASUREMENT

All dimensions and weights are quoted for locomotives in an "as new" condition with all necessary supplies (eg oil, water and sand) on board. Dimensions are quoted in the order length x width. Lengths quoted are over buffers or couplers as appropriate. All widths quoted are maxima. Where two different wheel diameter dimensions are shown, the first refers to powered wheels and the second refers to non-powered wheels. All weights are shown as metric tonnes (t = tonnes).

# HAULAGE CAPABILITY OF DIESEL LOCOMOTIVES

The haulage capability of a diesel locomotive depends upon three basic factors:

1. Adhesive weight. The greater the weight on the driving wheels, the greater the adhesion and more tractive power can be applied before wheelslip occurs.

2. The characteristics of its transmission. To start a train the locomotive has to exert a pull at standstill. A direct drive diesel engine cannot do this, hence the need for transmission. This may be mechanical, hydraulic or electric. The present British Standard for locomotives is electric transmission. Here the diesel engine drives a generator or alternator and the current produced is fed to the traction motors. The force produced by each driven wheel depends on the current in its traction motor. In other words, the larger the current, the harder it pulls. As the locomotive speed increases, the current in the traction motor falls, hence the *Maximum Tractive Effort* is the maximum force at its wheels the locomotive can exert at a standstill. The electrical equipment cannot take such high currents for long without overheating. Hence the *Continuous Tractive Effort* is quoted which represents the current which the equipment can take continuously.

3. The power of its engine. Not all power reaches the rail, as electrical machines are approximately 90% efficient. As the electrical energy passes through two such machines (the generator or alternator and the traction motors), the *Power at Rail* is approximately 81% (90% of 90%) of the engine power, less a further amount used for auxiliary equipment such as radiator fans, traction motor blowers, air compressors, battery charging, cab heating, Electric Train Supply (ETS) etc. The power of the locomotive is proportional to the tractive effort times the speed. Hence when on full power there is a speed corresponding to the continuous tractive effort.

# HAULAGE CAPABILITY OF ELECTRIC LOCOMOTIVES

Unlike a diesel locomotive, an electric locomotive does not develop its power on board and its performance is determined only by two factors, namely its weight and the characteristics of its electrical equipment. Whereas a diesel locomotive tends to be a constant power machine, the power of an electric locomotive varies considerably. Up to a certain speed it can produce virtually a constant tractive effort. Hence power rises with speed according to the formula given in section three above, until a maximum power is reached at which tractive effort falls, such that the power also falls. Hence the power at the speed corresponding to the maximum tractive effort is lower than the maximum speed.

## BRAKE FORCE

Brake Force (also known as brake power) is a measure of the braking power of a locomotive. The Brake Force available is dependant on the adhesion between the rail and the wheels being braked and the normal reaction of the rail on the wheels being braked (and hence on the weight per braked wheel). A locomotive's Brake Force is shown on its data panels so operating staff can ensure sufficient brake power is available for specific trains.

## ELECTRIC TRAIN SUPPLY (ETS)

A number of locomotives are equipped to provide a supply of electricity to the train being hauled to power auxiliaries such as heating, cooling fans, air conditioning and kitchen equipment. ETS is provided from the locomotive by means of a separate alternator (except Class 33 locomotives, which have a DC generator). The ETS index of a locomotive is a measure of the electrical power available for train supply. Class 55 locomotives provide an ETS directly from one of their traction generators into the train supply.

Similarly, most locomotive-hauled carriages also have an ETS index, which in this case is a measure of the power required to operate equipment mounted in the carriage. The sum of the ETS indices of all the hauled vehicles in a train must not exceed the ETS index of the locomotive.

ETS is commonly (but incorrectly) known as ETH (Electric Train Heating), which is a throwback to the days before locomotive-hauled carriages were equipped with electrically powered auxiliary equipment other than for train heating.

## ROUTE AVAILABILITY (RA)

This is a measure of a railway vehicle's axle load. The higher the axle load of a vehicle, the higher the RA number on a scale from 1 to 10. Each Network Rail route has a RA number and in general no vehicle with a higher RA number may travel on that route without special clearance.

## MULTIPLE WORKING

Multiple working between vehicles (ie two or more powered vehicles being driven from one cab) is facilitated by jumper cables connecting the vehicles. However, not all types of locomotive are compatible with each other, and a number of different systems are in use. Some are compatible with others, some are not. BR used "multiple working codes" to designate which locomotives were compatible. The list below shows which classes of locomotives are compatible with each other – the former BR multiple working code being shown in brackets. It should be noted that some locomotives have had the equipment removed or made inoperable.

**With other classes:**
Classes 20, 25, 31, 33, 37 40 & 73/1*. (Blue Star)
Classes 56 & 58. (Red Diamond)
Classes 59, 66, 67, 68, 70, 73/9 & 88.
* DRS has since adapted the systems so its Classes 20/3, 37 & 57 can work with each other only.

**With other members of same class only:**
Class 43, Class 47 (Green Circle), Class 50 (Orange Square), Class 60.

# PUSH-PULL OPERATION

Some locomotives are modified to operate passenger and service (formed of laboratory, test and inspection carriages) trains in "push-pull" mode – which allows the train to be driven from either end – either with locomotives at each end (both under power) or with a driving brake van at one end and a locomotive at the other. Various different systems are now in use. Electric locomotive Classes 86, 87, 90 & 91 use a time-division multiplex (TDM) system for push-pull working which utilises the existing Railway Clearing House (RCH) jumper cables fitted to carriages. Previously these cables had only been used to control train lighting and public address systems.

More recently locomotives of Classes 67 and 68 have used the Association of American Railroads (AAR) system.

# ABBREVIATIONS

Standard abbreviations used in this section of the book are:

| | |
|---|---|
| a | Train air brake equipment only. |
| b | Drophead buckeye couplers. |
| c | Scharfenberg couplers. |
| d | Fitted with retractable Dellner couplers. |
| e | European Railway Traffic Management System (ERTMS) signalling equipment fitted. |
| k | Fitted with Swinghead Automatic "buckeye" combination couplers. |
| p | Train air, vacuum and electro-pneumatic brakes. |
| r | Radio Electric Token Block signalling equipment fitted. |
| s | Slow Speed Control equipment. |
| v | Train vacuum brake only. |
| x | Train air and vacuum brakes ("Dual brakes"). |
| + | Additional fuel tank capacity. |
| § | Sandite laying equipment. |

In all cases use of the above abbreviations indicates the equipment in question is normally operable. The definition of non-standard abbreviations and symbols is detailed in individual class headings.

# 1.1. DIESEL SHUNTING LOCOMOTIVES

All BR design shunting locomotives still in existence, apart from those considered to be preserved, are listed together in this section. Preserved shunting locomotives are listed in the Platform 5 publication "Preserved Locomotives of British Railways" (a small number are listed in both that book and in this publication).

Few shunting locomotives have engineering acceptance and are equipped to operate on Network Rail infrastructure (beyond interface infrastructure), but those that are known to be permitted are indicated here.

For shunting locomotives, instead of the two-letter depot code, actual locations at the time of publication are given. Pool codes for shunting locomotives are not shown.

## CLASS 03           BR/GARDNER           0-6-0

**Built:** 1958–62 by BR at Swindon or Doncaster Works.
**Engine:** Gardner 8L3 of 152 kW (204 hp) at 1200 rpm.
**Transmission:** Mechanical. Fluidrive type 23 hydraulic coupling to Wilson-Drewry CA5R7 gearbox with SCG type RF11 final drive.
**Maximum Tractive Effort:** 68 kN (15300 lbf).
**Continuous Tractive Effort:** 68 kN (15300 lbf) at 3.75 mph.
**Train Brakes:** Air & vacuum.

| | |
|---|---|
| **Brake Force:** 13 t. | **Dimensions:** 7.93 x 2.59 m. |
| **Weight:** 31.3 t. | **Wheel Diameter:** 1092 mm. |
| **Design Speed:** 28.5 mph. | **Maximum Speed:** 28.5 mph. |
| **Fuel Capacity:** 1364 litres. | **Route Availability:** 1. |
| **Train Supply:** Not equipped. | **Total:** 3. |

| Number | Notes | Livery | Owner | Location |
|--------|-------|--------|-------|----------|
| 03084 | | G | WC | West Coast Railway Company, Carnforth Depot |
| 03196 | | B | WC | West Coast Railway Company, Carnforth Depot |
| D2381 | v | G | WC | West Coast Railway Company, Carnforth Depot |

## CLASS 07           BR/RUSTON & HORNSBY           0-6-0

**Built:** 1962 by Ruston & Hornsby, Lincoln.
**Engine:** Paxman 6RPHL Mk III of 205 kW (275 hp) at 1360 rpm.
**Transmission:** Electric. One AEI RTB 6652 traction motor.
**Maximum Tractive Effort:** 126 kN (28240 lbf).
**Continuous Tractive Effort:** 71 kN (15950 lbf) at 4.38 mph.
**Train Brakes:** Vacuum.

| | |
|---|---|
| **Brake Force:** | **Dimensions:** 8.17 x 2.59 m. |
| **Weight:** 43.6 t. | **Wheel Diameter:** 1067 mm. |
| **Design Speed:** 20 mph. | **Maximum Speed:** 20 mph. |
| **Fuel Capacity:** 1400 litres. | **Train Supply:** Not equipped. |
| **Total:** 1. | |

| Number | Notes | Livery | Owner | Location |
|--------|-------|--------|-------|----------|
| 07007 | v | B | AF | Arlington Fleet Services, Eastleigh Works, Hants |

# CLASS 08     BR/ENGLISH ELECTRIC     0-6-0

**Built:** 1955–62 by BR at Crewe, Darlington, Derby Locomotive, Doncaster or Horwich Works.
**Engine:** English Electric 6KT of 298 kW (400 hp) at 680 rpm.
**Main Generator:** English Electric 801.
**Traction Motors:** Two English Electric 506.
**Maximum Tractive Effort:** 156 kN (35000 lbf).
**Continuous Tractive Effort:** 49 kN (11100 lbf) at 8.8 mph.
**Power at Rail:** 194 kW (260 hp).    **Train Brakes:** Air & vacuum.
**Brake Force:** 19 t.    **Dimensions:** 8.92 x 2.59 m.
**Weight:** 49.6–50.4 t.    **Wheel Diameter:** 1372 mm.
**Design Speed:** 20 mph.    **Maximum Speed:** 15 mph.
**Fuel Capacity:** 3037 litres.    **Route Availability:** 5.
**Train Supply:** Not equipped.    **Total:** 170.

\* Locomotives with engineering acceptance to operate on Network Rail infrastructure. 08850 has acceptance for use between Battersby and Whitby only, for rescue purposes.

† – Fitted with remote control equipment.

**Non-standard liveries:**

| | |
|---|---|
| 08308 | All over ScotRail Caledonian Sleeper purple. |
| 08401 | Dark green. |
| 08442 | Dark grey lower bodyside & light grey upper bodyside. |
| 08445 | Yellow, blue & green. |
| 08447 | Lilac. |
| 08502 | Mid blue. |
| 08568 | Dark grey lower bodyside & light grey upper bodyside. Red solebar stripe. |
| 08598 | Yellow. |
| 08600 | Red with a light grey roof. |
| 08630 | Black with red cabsides and solebar stripe. |
| 08645 | All over black with a white cross. |
| 08682 | Multi-coloured. |
| 08730 | ABP Ports blue |
| 08774 | Red with a light grey roof. |
| 08870 | Light grey. |
| 08899 | Crimson lake. |
| 08956 | Serco Railtest green. |

| Number | Notes | Livery | Owner | Location |
|---|---|---|---|---|
| 08220 | v | B | EE | Nottingham Transport Heritage Centre, Ruddington |
| 08308 | a | 0 | RL | Weardale Railway, Wolsingham, County Durham |
| 08331 | | K | 20 | Midland Railway-Butterley, Derbyshire |
| 08375 | a | RL | RL | Victoria Group, Port of Boston, Boston |
| 08389 | a† | E | HN | Celsa Steel UK, Tremorfa Steelworks, Cardiff |
| 08401 | a | 0 | HU | LH Group, Barton-under-Needwood, Staffordshire (S) |
| 08405 | a† | E | RS | East Midlands Railway, Neville Hill Depot, Leeds |
| 08410 | * a | GW | AD | AV Dawson, Ayrton Rail Terminal, Middlesbrough |
| 08411 | a | B | RS | RSS, Rye Farm, Wishaw, Sutton Coldfield (S) |
| 08417 | * a | Y | NR | Loram (UK), RTC Business Park, Derby |

| 08418 | a | E | WC | West Coast Railway Company, Carnforth Depot |
| 08423 | a | RL | RL | PD Ports, Teesport, Grangetown, Middlesbrough |
| 08428 | ak | E | HN | Barrow Hill Roundhouse, Chesterfield, Derbys (S) |
| 08441 | * a | RS | RS | Hitachi, Bounds Green Depot, London |
| 08442 | a | 0 | AV | Arriva TrainCare, Eastleigh Depot, Hampshire (S) |
| 08445 | a | 0 | HU | Daventry International Railfreight Terminal, Crick |
| 08447 | a | 0 | RU | Assenta Rail, Hamilton, Glasgow (S) |
| 08451 | * | B | AM | Alstom, Longsight Depot, Manchester |
| 08454 | * | B | AM | Alstom, Widnes Technology Centre, Merseyside |
| 08460 | a | RS | RS | GB Railfreight, Eastleigh East Yard |
| 08472 | * a | WA | WA | Hitachi, Craigentinny Depot, Edinburgh |
| 08480 | * a | RS | RS | Gemini Rail Group, Wolverton Works, Milton Keynes |
| 08483 | * a | K | LS | L&NWR Heritage Company, Crewe Diesel Depot |
| 08484 | a | RS | RS | Greater Anglia, Crown Point Depot, Norwich |
| 08485 | a | B | WC | West Coast Railway Company, Carnforth Depot |
| 08499 | a | B | CS | Colas Rail, Canton Depot, Cardiff |
| 08500 | | E | HN | Nemesis Rail, Burton-upon-Trent, Staffordshire (S) |
| 08502 | | 0 | HN | East Kent Light Railway, Shepherdswell, Kent (S) |
| 08507 | a | RB | RV | Arlington Fleet Services, Eastleigh Works |
| 08511 | a | RS | RS | GB Railfreight, Eastleigh East Yard |
| 08516 | a | LW | RS | Arriva TrainCare, Bristol Barton Hill Depot |
| 08523 | * | B | RL | Weardale Railway, Wolsingham, County Durham |
| 08525 | | ST | EM | East Midlands Railway, Neville Hill Depot, Leeds (S) |
| 08527 | | FA | HN | Attero Recycling, Rossington, Doncaster |
| 08530 | * | FL | FL | Freightliner, Trafford Park FLT |
| 08531 | * a | FH | FL | Freightliner, Felixstowe FLT |
| 08536 | | B | RS | RSS, Rye Farm, Wishaw, Sutton Coldfield (S) |
| 08567 | | E | AF | Arlington Fleet Services, Eastleigh Works |
| 08568 | | 0 | RS | RSS, Rye Farm, Wishaw, Sutton Coldfield (S) |
| 08571 | * a | WA | WA | Daventry International Railfreight Terminal, Crick |
| 08573 | | K | RL | Weardale Railway, Wolsingham, County Durham |
| 08575 | | FL | FL | Nemesis Rail, Burton-upon-Trent, Staffordshire (S) |
| 08578 | | E | HN | Quinton Rail Technology Centre, Long Marston, Warks (S) |
| 08580 | * | RS | RS | Hitachi, Bounds Green Depot, London |
| 08585 | * | FH | FL | Freightliner, Southampton Maritime FLT |
| 08588 | | RL | RL | Loram (UK), RTC Business Park, Derby |
| 08593 | | E | RS | RSS, Rye Farm, Wishaw, Sutton Coldfield (S) |
| 08596 | * a† | WA | WA | Hitachi, Craigentinny Depot, Edinburgh |
| 08598 | | 0 | AD | AV Dawson, Ayrton Rail Terminal, Middlesbrough |
| 08600 | a | 0 | AD | AV Dawson, Ayrton Rail Terminal, Middlesbrough |
| 08602 | | B | BT | Bombardier Transportation, Derby Works (S) |
| 08605 | † | DB | RV | DB Cargo UK, Knottingley Depot |
| 08611 | * | B | AM | Alstom, Wembley Depot, London |
| 08613 | | RL | RL | Weardale Railway, Wolsingham, County Durham |
| 08615 | * | HU | WA | Tata Steel, Shotton Works, Deeside |
| 08616 | | LM | WM | West Midlands Trains, Tyseley Depot, Birmingham |
| 08617 | * | B | AM | Alstom, Oxley Depot, Wolverhampton |
| 08622 | | K | RL | Hanson Cement, Ketton Cement Works, nr Stamford |
| 08623 | | DB | HN | Breedon, Hope Cement Works, Derbys (S) |
| 08624 | * | FH | FL | Freightliner, Southampton Maritime FLT |
| 08630 | † | K | HN | Celsa Steel UK, Tremorfa Steelworks, Cardiff |

| 08631 |     | B   | LS | Weardale Railway, Wolsingham, County Durham |
| 08632 | †   | RS  | RS | Loram (UK), RTC Business Park, Derby |
| 08641 | *   | B   | GW | Great Western Railway, Laira Depot, Plymouth |
| 08643 |     | B   | MR | Aggregate Industries, Merehead Rail Terminal |
| 08644 | *   | B   | GW | Great Western Railway, Laira Depot, Plymouth |
| 08645 | *   | O   | GW | Great Western Railway, Long Rock Depot, Penzance |
| 08648 | *   | K   | RL | ScotRail, Inverness Depot |
| 08649 |     | KB  | ME | Meteor Power, Silverstone |
| 08650 |     | B   | MR | RSS, Rye Farm, Wishaw, Sutton Coldfield |
| 08652 |     | B   | RS | RSS, Rye Farm, Wishaw, Sutton Coldfield (S) |
| 08653 |     | E   | HN | Quinton Rail Technology Centre, Long Marston, Warks (S) |
| 08663 | * a | B   | HH | Chrysalis Rail, Landore Depot, Swansea |
| 08669 | * a | WA  | WA | Wabtec Rail, Doncaster Works |
| 08670 | * a | RS  | RS | GB Railfreight, Bescot Yard |
| 08676 |     | E   | HN | East Kent Light Railway, Shepherdswell, Kent (S) |
| 08678 | a   | WC  | WC | West Coast Railway Company, Carnforth Depot |
| 08682 |     | O   | BT | Bombardier Transportation, Derby Works (S) |
| 08683 | *   | RS  | RS | Greater Anglia, Crown Point Depot, Norwich |
| 08685 |     | E   | HN | East Kent Light Railway, Shepherdswell, Kent (S) |
| 08690 |     | ST  | EM | East Midlands Railway, Neville Hill Depot, Leeds (S) |
| 08691 | *   | FL  | FL | Freightliner, Crewe Basford Hall Yard, Cheshire |
| 08696 | * a | B   | AM | Alstom, Wembley Depot, London |
| 08700 |     | B   | RL | Bombardier Transportation, Ilford Works, London |
| 08701 | a   | RX  | HN | Quinton Rail Technology Centre, Long Marston, Warks (S) |
| 08703 | a   | E   | RS | Chasewater Railway, Staffordshire |
| 08704 |     | RB  | RV | Ecclesbourne Valley Railway, Wirksworth, Derbys |
| 08706 | †   | E   | HN | RSS, Rye Farm, Wishaw, Sutton Coldfield (S) |
| 08709 |     | E   | RS | RSS, Rye Farm, Wishaw, Sutton Coldfield (S) |
| 08711 | k   | RX  | HN | Nemesis Rail, Burton-upon-Trent, Staffordshire (S) |
| 08714 |     | E   | HN | Breedon, Hope Cement Works, Derbys (S) |
| 08721 | *   | B   | AM | Alstom, Widnes Technology Centre, Merseyside |
| 08724 | *   | WA  | WA | Wabtec Rail, Doncaster Works |
| 08730 |     | O   | RS | GB Railfreight, Whitemoor Yard, March, Cambs |
| 08735 | †   | AW  | AV | Arriva TrainCare, Eastleigh Depot |
| 08737 |     | G   | LS | L&NWR Heritage Company, Crewe Diesel Depot |
| 08738 |     | RS  | RS | Felixstowe FLT |
| 08742 | †   | RX  | HN | Barrow Hill Roundhouse, Chesterfield, Derbys (S) |
| 08743 |     | B   | SU | SembCorp Utilities UK, Wilton, Middlesbrough |
| 08752 | †   | RS  | RS | Gemini Rail Group, Wolverton Works, Milton Keynes |
| 08754 | *   | B   | RL | Gemini Rail Group, Wolverton Works, Milton Keynes |
| 08756 |     | DG  | RL | Weardale Railway, Wolsingham, County Durham |
| 08757 |     | RG  | PO | Telford Steam Railway, Shropshire |
| 08762 |     | RL  | RL | Eastern Rail Services, Great Yarmouth |
| 08764 | *   | B   | AM | Alstom, Polmadie Depot, Glasgow |
| 08765 |     | HN  | HN | Barrow Hill Roundhouse, Chesterfield, Derbys (S) |
| 08774 | a   | O   | AD | AV Dawson, Ayrton Rail Terminal, Middlesbrough |
| 08780 |     | G   | LS | L&NWR Heritage Company, Crewe Diesel Depot |
| 08782 | a†  | CU  | HN | Barrow Hill Roundhouse, Chesterfield, Derbys (S) |
| 08783 |     | E   | HN | European Metal Recycling, Kingsbury, nr Tamworth |
| 08784 |     | DG  | PO | EMD, Longport Works, Stoke-on-Trent |
| 08785 | * a | FL  | FL | Freightliner, Southampton FLT |

| 08786 | a | DG | HN | Barrow Hill Roundhouse, Chesterfield, Derbys (S) |
|---|---|---|---|---|
| 08787 | | B | MR | Hanson Aggregates, Whatley Quarry, near Frome |
| 08788 | * | RL | RL | PD Ports, Teesport, Grangetown, Middlesbrough |
| 08790 | * | B | AM | Alstom, Edge Hill Depot, Liverpool |
| 08798 | | E | HN | Barrow Hill Roundhouse, Chesterfield, Derbys (S) |
| 08799 | a | E | HN | East Kent Light Railway, Shepherdswell, Kent (S) |
| 08802 | † | E | HN | RSS, Rye Farm, Wishaw, Sutton Coldfield (S) |
| 08804 | † | E | HN | East Kent Light Railway, Shepherdswell, Kent (S) |
| 08805 | | FO | WM | West Midlands Trains, Soho Depot, Birmingham |
| 08809 | | RL | RL | Hanson Cement, Ketton Cement Works, nr Stamford |
| 08810 | a | LW | AV | Arriva TrainCare, Eastleigh Depot, Hampshire |
| 08818 | | GB | HN | HNRC, Worksop Depot, Nottinghamshire |
| 08822 | * | IC | GW | Great Western Railway, St Philip's Marsh Depot, Bristol |
| 08823 | a | HU | HU | Tata Steel, Shotton Works, Deeside |
| 08824 | ak | K | HN | Barrow HIll Roundhouse, Chesterfield, Derbys (S) |
| 08834 | | HN | HN | Northern, Allerton Depot, Liverpool |
| 08836 | * | GW | GW | Great Western Railway, Reading Depot |
| 08846 | | B | RS | East Midlands Railway, Neville Hill Depot, Leeds |
| 08847 | * | CD | RL | PD Ports, Teesport, Grangetown, Middlesbrough |
| 08850 | * | B | NY | North Yorkshire Moors Railway, Grosmont Depot |
| 08853 | * a | WA | WA | Wabtec Rail, Doncaster Works |
| 08865 | | E | HN | Bombardier Transportation, Central Rivers Depot, Barton-under-Needwood |
| 08868 | | AW | HN | Arriva TrainCare, Crewe Depot, Cheshire |
| 08870 | | 0 | RL | Weardale Railway, Wolsingham, County Durham |
| 08871 | | CD | RL | Bombardier Transportation, Ilford Works, London |
| 08872 | | E | HN | European Metal Recycling, Attercliffe, Sheffield (S) |
| 08873 | * | RX | HU | LH Group, Barton-under-Needwood, Staffordshire (S) |
| 08874 | * | SL | RL | Weardale Railway, Wolsingham, County Durham |
| 08877 | | DG | HN | Celsa Steel UK, Tremorfa Steelworks, Cardiff |
| 08879 | | E | HN | Breedon, Hope Cement Works, Derbys (S) |
| 08885 | | B | RL | Weardale Railway, Wolsingham, County Durham |
| 08887 | * a | B | AM | Alstom, Polmadie Depot, Glasgow |
| 08891 | * | FL | FL | LH Group, Barton-under-Needwood, Staffordshire (S) |
| 08892 | | DR | HN | Bombardier Transportation, Old Dalby Test Centre, Asfordby |
| 08899 | | 0 | EM | East Midlands Railway, Derby Etches Park Depot |
| 08903 | | B | SU | SembCorp Utilities UK, Wilton, Middlesbrough |
| 08904 | d | E | HN | HNRC, Worksop Depot, Nottinghamshire |
| 08905 | | E | HN | Breedon, Hope Cement Works, Derbys (S) |
| 08908 | | ST | EM | East Midlands Railway, Neville Hill Depot, Leeds (S) |
| 08912 | | B | AD | AV Dawson, Ayrton Rail Terminal, Middlesbrough (S) |
| 08918 | | DG | HN | Nemesis Rail, Burton-upon-Trent, Staffordshire (S) |
| 08921 | | E | RS | RSS, Rye Farm, Wishaw, Sutton Coldfield (S) |
| 08922 | | DG | PO | EMD, Longport Works, Stoke-on-Trent |
| 08924 | † | GB | HN | Celsa Steel UK, Tremorfa Steelworks, Cardiff |
| 08925 | | G | GB | HNRC, Worksop Depot, Nottinghamshire |
| 08927 | | G | RS | GB Railfreight, Bescot Yard |
| 08933 | | B | MR | Hanson Aggregates, Whatley Quarry, near Frome |
| 08934 | a | VP | GB | GB Railfreight, Whitemoor Yard, March, Cambs |
| 08936 | | B | RL | Weardale Railway, Wolsingham, County Durham |
| 08937 | | G | BD | Dartmoor Railway, Meldon Quarry, nr Okehampton |

| 08939 |   | ECR | RS | DB Cargo UK, Springs Branch Depot, Wigan |
|-------|---|-----|-----|------|
| 08943 |   | HN | HN | Barrow Hill Roundhouse, Chesterfield, Derbys |
| 08947 |   | B | MR | Hanson Aggregates, Whatley Quarry, near Frome |
| 08948 | c | EP | EU | Eurostar, Temple Mills Depot, London |
| 08950 |   | ST | EM | East Midlands Railway, Neville Hill Depot, Leeds (S) |
| 08954 | * | B | AM | Alstom, Longsight Depot, Manchester |
| 08956 |   | 0 | LO | Bombardier Transportation, Old Dalby Test Centre, Asfordby |

**Class 08/9. Reduced height cab.** Converted 1985–87 by BR at Landore.

| 08994 | a | E | HN | Nemesis Rail, Burton-upon-Trent, Staffordshire (S) |
|-------|---|---|----|------|

**Other numbers or names carried:**

| 08308 | "23" |
|-------|------|
| 08423 | "LOCO 2" / "14" |
| 08451 | LONGSIGHT TMD |
| 08460 | SPIRIT OF THE OAK |
| 08483 | Bungle |
| 08484 | CAPTAIN NATHANIEL DARELL |
| 08499 | REDLIGHT |
| 08525 | DUNCAN BEDFORD |
| 08568 | St. Rollox |
| 08585 | Vicky |
| 08588 | "H047" |
| 08602 | "004" |
| 08605 | "WIGAN 2" |
| 08613 | "H064" |
| 08615 | UNCLE DAI |
| 08616 | TYSELEY 100 / 3783 |
| 08617 | Steve Purser |
| 08622 | "H028" / "19" |
| 08624 | Rambo PAUL RAMSEY |
| 08629 | Wolverton |
| 08630 | "CELSA 3" |
| 08641 | Pride of Laira |
| 08644 | Laira Diesel Depot 50 Years 1962–2012 |
| 08645 | St. Piran |
| 08649 | Bradwell |
| 08669 | Bob Machin |
| 08678 | "555" |
| 08682 | Lionheart |
| 08690 | DAVID THIRKILL |
| 08691 | Terri |
| 08735 | Geoff Hobbs 42 |
| 08737 | D3905 |

| 08743 | Bryan Turner |
|-------|------|
| 08754 | "H041" |
| 08757 | EAGLE C.U.R.C. |
| 08762 | "H067" |
| 08774 | ARTHUR VERNON DAWSON |
| 08780 | Zippy / D3948 |
| 08787 | "08296" |
| 08790 | M.A. SMITH |
| 08805 | Robin Jones 40 YEARS SERVICE |
| 08809 | "24" |
| 08810 | RICHARD J. WENHAM EASTLEIGH DEPOT DECEMBER 1989 – JULY 1999 |
| 08818 | MOLLY / "4" |
| 08822 | Dave Mills |
| 08823 | KEVLA |
| 08824 | "IEMD 01" |
| 08846 | "003" |
| 08847 | "LOCO 1" |
| 08865 | GILLY |
| 08870 | "H024" |
| 08871 | "H074" |
| 08885 | "H042" / "18" |
| 08899 | Midland Counties Railway 175 1839–2014 |
| 08903 | John W Antill |
| 08924 | "CELSA 2" |
| 08927 | D4157 |
| 08934 | D4164 |
| 08937 | D4167 |
| 08950 | DAVID LIGHTFOOT |

# CLASS 09        BR/ENGLISH ELECTRIC      0-6-0

**Built:** 1959–62 by BR at Darlington or Horwich Works.
**Engine:** English Electric 6KT of 298 kW (400 hp) at 680 rpm.
**Main Generator:** English Electric 801.
**Traction Motors:** English Electric 506.
**Maximum Tractive Effort:** 111 kN (25000 lbf).
**Continuous Tractive Effort:** 39 kN (8800 lbf) at 11.6 mph.
**Power at Rail:** 201 kW (269 hp).     **Train Brakes:** Air & vacuum.
**Brake Force:** 19 t.                 **Dimensions:** 8.92 x 2.59 m.
**Weight:** 49 t.                   **Wheel Diameter:** 1372 mm.
**Design Speed:** 27 mph.         **Maximum Speed:** 27 mph.
**Fuel Capacity:** 3037 litres.      **Route Availability:** 5.
**Train Supply:** Not equipped.     **Total:** 10.

**Class 09/0. Built as Class 09.**

| | | | |
|---|---|---|---|
| 09002 | G | GB | HNRC, Worksop Depot, Nottinghamshire |
| 09006 | E | HN | Nemesis Rail, Burton-upon-Trent, Staffordshire (S) |
| 09007 | G | LN | London Overground, Willesden Depot, London |
| 09009 | G | GB | Miles Platting Stone Terminal, Greater Manchester |
| 09014 | DG | HN | Nemesis Rail, Burton-upon-Trent, Staffordshire (S) |
| 09022 | B | VG | Victoria Group, Port of Boston, Boston |
| 09023 | E | EY | European Metal Recycling, Attercliffe, Sheffield (S) |

**Class 09/1. Converted from Class 08 1992–93 by RFS Industries, Kilnhurst.**
110 V electrical equipment.

| | | | |
|---|---|---|---|
| 09106 | **HN** | HN | Celsa Steel UK, Tremorfa Steelworks, Cardiff |

**Class 09/2. Converted from Class 08 1992 by RFS Industries, Kilnhurst.**
90 V electrical equipment.

| | | | |
|---|---|---|---|
| 09201 | **DG** | HN | Breedon, Hope Cement Works, Derbys (S) |
| 09204 | **AW** | AV | Arriva TrainCare, Crewe Depot, Cheshire |

**Other numbers or names carried:**

| | |
|---|---|
| 09007 | D3671 |
| 09106 | "6" |

# 1.2. MAIN LINE DIESEL LOCOMOTIVES

## CLASS 19

Experimental locomotive being rebuilt by Artemis Intelligent Power from a Mark 3B Driving Brake Van. Part of a project funded by the Rail Safety & Standards Board (RSSB) to test the viability of combining hydrostatic transmission to reduce engine emissions. Conversion work is taking place at the Bo'ness & Kinneil Railway. Full details awaited.

**Built:** 1988 by BR Derby Works.
**Engine:** 2 x JCB diesel engines.
**Main Generator:**
**Traction Motors:**
**Maximum Tractive Effort:**
**Continuous Tractive Effort:**          **Train Brakes:**
**Power at Rail:**                        **Dimensions:** 18.83 x 2.71 m.
**Brake Force:**                          **Weight:**
**Design Speed:**                         **Maximum Speed:**
**Fuel Capacity:**                        **Route Availability:**
**Train Supply:**                         **Total:** 1.

| | | | | | |
|---|---|---|---|---|---|
| 19001 | (82113) | **B** | AV | | BO |

## CLASS 20          ENGLISH ELECTRIC          Bo-Bo

**Built:** 1957–68 by English Electric at Vulcan Foundry, Newton-le-Willows or by Robert Stephenson & Hawthorns at Darlington.
**Engine:** English Electric 8SVT Mk II of 746 kW (1000 hp) at 850 rpm.
**Main Generator:** English Electric 819/3C.
**Traction Motors:** English Electric 526/5D or 526/8D.
**Maximum Tractive Effort:** 187 kN (42000 lbf).
**Continuous Tractive Effort:** 111 kN (25000 lbf) at 11 mph.
**Power at Rail:** 574 kW (770 hp).         **Train Brakes:** Air & vacuum.
**Brake Force:** 35 t.                       **Dimensions:** 14.25 x 2.67 m.
**Weight:** 73.4–73.5 t.                     **Wheel Diameter:** 1092 mm.
**Design Speed:** 75 mph.                    **Maximum Speed:** 75 mph.
**Fuel Capacity:** 1727 litres.              **Route Availability:** 5.
**Train Supply:** Not equipped.              **Total:** 29.

**Non-standard liveries/numbering:**

| | |
|---|---|
| 20056 | Yellow with grey cabsides and red solebar. Carries No. "81". |
| 20066 | Dark blue with yellow stripes. Carries No. "82". |
| 20096 | Carries original number D8096. |
| 20107 | Carries original number D8107. |
| 20110 | Carries original number D8110. |
| 20142 | LUL Maroon. |
| 20168 | White with green cabsides and solebar. Carries No. "2". |
| 20227 | LUL Maroon. |
| 20906 | White. Carries No. "3". |

**Class 20/0. Standard Design.**

| | | | | | |
|---|---|---|---|---|---|
| 20007 | **G** | EE | MOLO | SK | |
| 20056 | **0** | HN | HNRL | SC (S) | |
| 20066 | **0** | HN | HNRL | HO | |
| 20096 | **G** | LS | LSLO | CL | |
| 20107 | **G** | LS | LSLO | CL | Jocelyn Feilding 1940–2020 |
| 20110 | **G** | HN | HNRS | WS (S) | |
| 20118 | **FO** | HN | HNRL | WS | Saltburn-by-the-Sea |
| 20121 | **HN** | HN | HNRL | BH (S) | |
| 20132 | **FO** | HN | HNRL | WS | Barrow Hill Depot |
| 20142 | **0** | 20 | MOLO | SK | SIR JOHN BETJEMAN |
| 20168 | **0** | HN | HNRL | HO | SIR GEORGE EARLE |
| 20189 | **B** | 20 | MOLO | SK | |
| 20205 | **B** | 2L | MOLO | SK | |
| 20227 | **0** | 2L | MOLO | SK | SHERLOCK HOLMES |

**Class 20/3. Direct Rail Services refurbished locomotives.** Details as Class 20/0 except:

**Refurbished:** 15 locomotives were refurbished 1995–96 by Brush Traction at Loughborough (20301–305) or 1997–98 by RFS(E) at Doncaster (20306–315). Disc indicators or headcode panels removed.

**Train Brakes:** Air.      **Maximum Speed:** 60 mph (+ 75 mph).
**Weight:** 73 t (+ 76 t).      **Fuel Capacity:** 2909 (+ 4909) litres.
**Brake Force:** 35 t (+ 31 t).      **RA:** 5 (+ 6).

| | | | | | |
|---|---|---|---|---|---|
| 20301 (20047) r | **DS** | DR | XHSS | BH (S) | |
| 20302 (20084) r | **DS** | DR | XHSS | BO (S) | |
| 20303 (20127) r | **DS** | DR | XHSS | CR (S) | Max Joule 1958–1999 |
| 20304 (20120) r | **DS** | DR | XHHP | BH (S) | |
| 20305 (20095) r | **DS** | DR | XHSS | BO (S) | |
| 20308 (20187) r+ | **DS** | DR | XHHP | BH (S) | |
| 20309 (20075) r+ | **DS** | DR | XHHP | BH (S) | |
| 20311 (20102) r+ | **HN** | HN | HNRL | WS | |
| 20312 (20042) r+ | **DS** | DR | XHHP | BH (S) | |
| 20314 (20117) r+ | **HN** | HN | HNRL | WS | |

**Class 20/9. Harry Needle Railroad Company (former Hunslet-Barclay/DRS) locomotives.** Details as Class 20/0 except:

**Refurbished:** 1989 by Hunslet-Barclay at Kilmarnock.
**Train Brakes:** Air.      **Fuel Capacity:** 1727 (+ 4727) litres.
**RA:** 5 (+ 6).

| | | | | | |
|---|---|---|---|---|---|
| 20901 (20101) | **GB** | HN | HNRL | WS | |
| 20903 (20083) + | **DR** | HN | HNRS | BU (S) | |
| 20904 (20041) | **DR** | HN | HNRS | BU (S) | |
| 20905 (20225) + | **GB** | HN | HNRL | WS | Dave Darwin |
| 20906 (20219) | **0** | HN | HNRL | HO | |

## CLASS 25   BR/BEYER PEACOCK/SULZER   Bo-Bo

**Built:** 1965 by Beyer Peacock at Gorton.
**Engine:** Sulzer 6LDA28-B of 930 kW (1250 hp) at 750 rpm.
**Main Generator:** AEI RTB15656.   **Traction Motors:** AEI 253AY.
**Maximum Tractive Effort:** 200 kN (45000 lbf).
**Continuous Tractive Effort:** 93 kN (20800 lbf) at 17.1 mph.
**Power at Rail:** 708 kW (949 hp).   **Train Brakes:** Air & vacuum.
**Brake Force:** 38 t.   **Dimensions:** 15.39 x 2.73 m.
**Weight:** 71.5 t.   **Wheel Diameter:** 1143 mm.
**Design Speed:** 90 mph.   **Maximum Speed:** 60 mph.
**Fuel Capacity:** 2270 litres.   **Route Availability:** 5.
**Train Supply:** Not equipped.   **Total:** 1.

Carries original number D7628.

Only certified for use on Network Rail tracks between Whitby and Battersby, as an extension of North Yorkshire Moors Railway services.

| 25278 | **GG** | NY | MBDL | NY | SYBILLA |
|---|---|---|---|---|---|

## CLASS 31   BRUSH/ENGLISH ELECTRIC   A1A-A1A

**Built:** 1958–62 by Brush Traction at Loughborough.
**Engine:** English Electric 12SVT of 1100 kW (1470 hp) at 850 rpm.
**Main Generator:** Brush TG160-48.   **Traction Motors:** Brush TM73-68.
**Maximum Tractive Effort:** 160 kN (35900 lbf).
**Continuous Tractive Effort:** 83 kN (18700 lbf) at 23.5 mph.
**Power at Rail:** 872 kW (1170 hp).   **Train Brakes:** Air & vacuum.
**Brake Force:** 49 t.   **Dimensions:** 17.30 x 2.67 m.
**Weight:** 106.7–111 t.   **Wheel Diameter:** 1092/1003 mm.
**Design Speed:** 90 mph.   **Maximum Speed:** 90 mph.
**Fuel Capacity:** 2409 litres.   **Route Availability:** 5.
**Train Supply:** Not equipped.   **Total:** 2.

| 31106 | **B** | HH | | BQ | |
|---|---|---|---|---|---|
| 31128 | **B** | NS | NRLO | BU | CHARYBDIS |

## CLASS 33   BRCW/SULZER   Bo-Bo

**Built:** 1959–62 by the Birmingham Railway Carriage & Wagon Company at Smethwick.
**Engine:** Sulzer 8LDA28 of 1160 kW (1550 hp) at 750 rpm.
**Main Generator:** Crompton Parkinson CG391B1.
**Traction Motors:** Crompton Parkinson C171C2.
**Maximum Tractive Effort:** 200 kN (45000 lbf).
**Continuous Tractive Effort:** 116 kN (26000 lbf) at 17.5 mph.
**Power at Rail:** 906 kW (1215 hp).   **Train Brakes:** Air & vacuum.
**Brake Force:** 35 t.   **Dimensions:** 15.47 x 2.82 (2.64 m 33/2).
**Weight:** 76-78 t.   **Wheel Diameter:** 1092 mm.
**Design Speed:** 85 mph.   **Maximum Speed:** 85 mph.

**Fuel Capacity:** 3410 litres.          **Route Availability:** 6.
**Train Supply:** Electric, index 48 (750 V DC only).
**Total:** 5.

**Non-standard numbering:** 33012 Carries original number D6515.

**Class 33/0. Standard Design.**

| 33012 | **G** | 71 | MBDL | SW | Lt Jenny Lewis RN |
|---|---|---|---|---|---|
| 33025 | **WC** | WC | AWCA | CS | |
| 33029 | **WC** | WC | AWCA | CS | |
| 33030 | **DR** | WC | AWCX | CS (S) | |

**Class 33/2. Built to former Loading Gauge of Tonbridge–Battle Line.**
Equipped with slow speed control.

| 33207 | **WC** | WC | AWCA | CS | Jim Martin |
|---|---|---|---|---|---|

# CLASS 37      ENGLISH ELECTRIC      Co-Co

**Built:** 1960–66 by English Electric at Vulcan Foundry, Newton-le-Willows or by Robert Stephenson & Hawthorns at Darlington.
**Engine:** English Electric 12CSVT of 1300 kW (1750 hp) at 850 rpm.
**Main Generator:** English Electric 822/10G.
**Traction Motors:** English Electric 538/A.
**Maximum Tractive Effort:** 247 kN (55500 lbf).
**Continuous Tractive Effort:** 156 kN (35000 lbf) at 13.6 mph.
**Power at Rail:** 932 kW (1250 hp).          **Train Brakes:** Air & vacuum.
**Brake Force:** 50 t.                         **Dimensions:** 18.75 x 2.74 m.
**Weight:** 102.8–108.4 t.                     **Wheel Diameter:** 1092 mm.
**Design Speed:** 90 mph.                      **Maximum Speed:** 80 mph.
**Fuel Capacity:** 4046 (+ 7683) litres.       **Route Availability:** 5 (§ 6).
**Train Supply:** Not equipped.                **Total:** 68.

**Non-standard numbering:**

37424 Also carries the number 37558.
37521 Carries original number D6817.
37667 Carries original number D6851.
37703 Carries the number 37067.
37905 Also carries original number D6838.

**Class 37/0. Standard Design.**

| 37025 | **BL** | 37 | COTS | NM | Inverness TMD |
|---|---|---|---|---|---|
| 37038 a | **DI** | DR | XHNC | KM | |
| 37057 | **CS** | CS | COTS | NM | |
| 37059 ar+ | **DI** | DR | XHNC | KM | |
| 37069 ar+ | **DI** | DR | XHNC | KM | |
| 37099 | **CS** | CS | COTS | NM | MERL EVANS 1947–2016 |
| 37116 + | **CS** | CS | COTS | NM | |
| 37146 | **CE** | EP | EPUK | LR (S) | |
| 37165 a+ | **CE** | WC | AWCX | CS (S) | |
| 37175 a | **CS** | CS | COTS | NM | |
| 37190 | **B** | LS | MBDL | CL | |

| 37198 | + | **Y** | NR | MBDL | ZA (S) | |
| 37207 | | **B** | EP | MBDL | LR (S) | |
| 37218 | ar+ | **DI** | DR | XHNC | KM | |
| 37219 | | **CS** | CS | COTS | NM | Jonty Jarvis 8-12-1998 to 18-3-2005 |
| 37240 | | **F** | NB | COFS | NM | |
| 37254 | | **CS** | CS | COTS | NM | Cardiff Canton |
| 37259 | ar | **DS** | DR | XHSS | KM (S) | |

**Class 37/4. Refurbished with electric train supply equipment.** Main generator replaced by alternator. Regeared (CP7) bogies. Details as Class 37/0 except:
**Main Alternator:** Brush BA1005A.          **Power At Rail:** 935 kW (1254 hp).
**Traction Motors:** English Electric 538/5A.
**Maximum Tractive Effort:** 256 kN (57440 lbf).
**Continuous Tractive Effort:** 184 kN (41250 lbf) at 11.4 mph.
**Weight:** 107 t.                          **Design Speed:** 80 mph.
**Fuel Capacity:** 7683 litres.
**Train Supply:** Electric, index 30.

| 37401 | ar | **BL** | DR | XHAC | KM | Mary Queen of Scots |
| 37402 | a | **BL** | DR | XHAC | KM | Stephen Middlemore 23.12.1954–8.6.2013 |
| 37403 | | **BL** | SP | RAJV | BO | Isle of Mull |
| 37405 | ar | **DS** | DR | XHAC | KM | |
| 37407 | | **BL** | DR | XHAC | KM | Blackpool Tower |
| 37409 | ar | **BL** | DR | XHSS | KM (S) | Lord Hinton |
| 37418 | | **BL** | SB | COTS | NM | An Comunn Gaidhealach |
| 37419 | ar | **IC** | DR | XHAC | KM | Carl Haviland 1954–2012 |
| 37421 | | **CS** | CS | COTS | NM | |
| 37422 | ar | **DR** | DR | XHAC | KM | |
| 37423 | ar | **DR** | DR | XHAC | KM | Spirit of the Lakes |
| 37424 | | **BL** | DR | XHAC | KM | Avro Vulcan XH558 |
| 37425 | ar | **RR** | DR | XHAC | KM | Sir Robert McAlpine/Concrete Bob |

**Class 37/5. Refurbished without train supply equipment.** Main generator replaced by alternator. Regeared (CP7) bogies. Details as Class 37/4 except:
**Power At Rail:** 932 kW (1250 hp).
**Maximum Tractive Effort:** 248 kN (55590 lbf).
**Weight:** 106.1–110.0 t.
**Train Supply:** Not equipped.

| 37510 | a | **EX** | EP | GROG | LR | Orion |
| 37516 | s | **WC** | WC | AWCA | CS | Loch Laidon |
| 37517 | as | **LH** | WC | AWCX | CS (S) | |
| 37518 | ar | **WC** | WC | AWCA | CS | Fort William/An Gearasdan |
| 37521 | | **G** | LS | LSLO | CL | |

**Class 37/6. Originally refurbished for Nightstar services.** Main generator replaced by alternator. UIC jumpers. Details as Class 37/5 except:
**Maximum Speed:** 90 mph.          **Train Brake:** Air.
**Train Supply:** Not equipped, but electric through wired.

| 37601 | ad | **EX** | EP | GROG | LR | Perseus |
| 37602 | ar | **DS** | DR | XHHP | ZG (S) | |
| 37603 | a | **DS** | DR | XHHP | LW (S) | |

| 37604 | a   | **DS** | DR | XHHP  | LW (S) |                |
|-------|-----|--------|----|-------|--------|----------------|
| 37605 | ar  | **DS** | DR | XHHP  | ZA (S) |                |
| 37606 | a   | **DS** | DR | XHHP  | CR (S) |                |
| 37607 | ar  | **DR** | HN | COTS  | BH     |                |
| 37608 | ard | **EX** | EP | GROG  | LR     | Andromeda      |
| 37609 | a   | **DI** | DR | XHHP  | LW (S) |                |
| 37610 | ar  | **BL** | HN | COTS  | BH     |                |
| 37611 | ad  | **EX** | EP | GROG  | LR     | Pegasus        |
| 37612 | a   | **DR** | HN | COTS  | BH     |                |

**Class 37/5 continued.**

| 37667 | ars | **G**  | LS | LSLO  | CL     |               |
|-------|-----|--------|----|-------|--------|---------------|
| 37668 | e   | **WC** | WC | AWCA  | CS     |               |
| 37669 | e   | **WC** | WC | AWCA  | CS     |               |
| 37676 | a   | **WC** | WC | AWCA  | CS (S) | Loch Rannoch  |
| 37685 | a   | **WC** | WC | AWCA  | CS     | Loch Arkaig   |
| 37688 |     | **IC** | D0 | MBDL  | CL     | Great Rocks   |

**Class 37/7. Refurbished locomotives.** Main generator replaced by alternator. Regeared (CP7) bogies. Ballast weights added. Details as Class 37/5 except:
**Main Alternator:** GEC G564AZ (37800) Brush BA1005A (others).
**Maximum Tractive Effort:** 276 kN (62000 lbf).
**Weight:** 120 t.                              **Route Availability:** 7.

| 37703 |   | **DR** | DR | XHHP  | BO (S) |           |
|-------|---|--------|----|-------|--------|-----------|
| 37706 |   | **WC** | WC | AWCA  | CS     |           |
| 37710 |   | **LH** | WC | AWCX  | CS (S) |           |
| 37712 | a | **WC** | WC | AWCX  | CS (S) |           |
| 37716 |   | **DI** | DR | XHNC  | KM     |           |
| 37800 | d | **EX** | EP | GROG  | LR     | Cassiopeia |
| 37884 | d | **EX** | EP | GROG  | LR     | Cepheus   |

**Class 37/9. Refurbished locomotives.** New power unit. Main generator replaced by alternator. Ballast weights added. Details as Class 37/4 except:
**Engine:** * Mirrlees 6MB275T of 1340 kW (1800 hp) or † Ruston 6RK270T of 1340 kW (1800 hp) at 900 rpm.
**Main Alternator:** Brush BA15005A.
**Maximum Tractive Effort:** 279 kN (62680 lbf).
**Weight:** 120 t.                              **Route Availability:** 7.
**Train Supply:** Not equipped.

| 37901 | * | **EX** | EP | EPUK  | LR     | Mirrlees Pioneer |
|-------|---|--------|----|-------|--------|------------------|
| 37905 | † | **G**  | UR | UKRM  | LR (S) |                  |
| 37906 | † | **FO** | UR | UKRM  | BL (S) |                  |

**Class 97/3. Class 37s refurbished for use on the Cambrian Lines which are signalled by ERTMS.** Details as Class 37/0.

| 97301 | (37100) e | **Y** | NR | QETS  | ZA |                                                                          |
|-------|-----------|-------|----|-------|----|--------------------------------------------------------------------------|
| 97302 | (37170) e | **Y** | NR | QETS  | ZA | Ffestiniog & Welsh Highland Railways/Rheilffyrdd Ffestiniog ac Eryri     |
| 97303 | (37178) e | **Y** | NR | QETS  | ZA |                                                                          |
| 97304 | (37217) e | **Y** | NR | QETS  | ZA | John Tiley                                                               |

## CLASS 40　　　ENGLISH ELECTRIC　　　1Co-Co1

**Built:** 1961 by English Electric at Vulcan Foundry, Newton-le-Willows.
**Engine:** English Electric 16SVT Mk2 of 1492 kW (2000 hp) at 850 rpm.
**Main Generator:** English Electric 822/4C.
**Traction Motors:** English Electric 526/5D or EE526/7D.
**Maximum Tractive Effort:** 231 kN (52000 lbf).
**Continuous Tractive Effort:** 137 kN (30900 lbf) at 18.8 mph.

| | |
|---|---|
| **Power at Rail:** 1160 kW (1550 hp). | **Train Brakes:** Air & vacuum. |
| **Brake Force:** 51 t. | **Dimensions:** 21.18 x 2.78 m. |
| **Weight:** 132 t. | **Wheel Diameter:** 914/1143 mm. |
| **Design Speed:** 90 mph. | **Maximum Speed:** 90 mph. |
| **Fuel Capacity:** 3250 litres. | **Route Availability:** 6. |
| **Train Supply:** Steam heating. | **Total:** 2. |

40013 Carries original number D213
40145 Carries original number 345.

| 40013 | G | ST | LSLO | CL | Andania |
|---|---|---|---|---|---|
| 40145 | B | 40 | CFSL | CL | |

## CLASS 43　　　BREL/PAXMAN　　　Bo-Bo

**Built:** 1975–82 by BREL at Crewe Works.
**Engine:** MTU 16V4000R41R of 1680kW (2250 hp) at 1500 rpm.
(* Paxman 12VP185 of 1680 kW (2250 hp) at 1500 rpm.)
**Main Alternator:** Brush BA1001B.
**Traction Motors:** Brush TMH68–46 or GEC G417AZ (43124–152); frame mounted.
**Maximum Tractive Effort:** 80 kN (17980 lbf).
**Continuous Tractive Effort:** 46 kN (10340 lbf) at 64.5 mph.

| | |
|---|---|
| **Power at Rail:** 1320 kW (1770 hp). | **Train Brakes:** Air. |
| **Brake Force:** 35 t. | **Dimensions:** 17.79 x 2.74 m. |
| **Weight:** 70.25–75.0 t. | **Wheel Diameter:** 1020 mm. |
| **Design Speed:** 125 mph. | **Maximum Speed:** 125 mph. |
| **Fuel Capacity:** 4500 litres. | **Route Availability:** 5. |
| **Train Supply:** Three-phase electric. | **Total:** 191. |

† Buffer fitted.
§ Modified Great Western Railway power cars that can operate with power door fitted short sets.

43013, 43014 & 43062 are fitted with measuring apparatus & front-end cameras.

Power cars 43013 and 43321 carry small commemorative plates to celebrate 40 years of the HST, reading "40 YEARS 1976–2016".

**Non-standard liveries:**

43206 and 43312　Original HST blue & yellow. Carry the numbers 43006 and
　　　　　　　　　　43112
43238 and 43274　Red

| 43003 |   | **SI** | A | HAPC | HA | |
|-------|---|--------|------|------|------|---|
| 43004 | § | **GW** | A | EFPC | LA | Caerphilly Castle |
| 43005 | § | **GW** | A | EFPC | LA | |
| 43009 | § | **GW** | GW | EFPC | LA | |
| 43010 | § | **GW** | GW | EFPC | LA | |
| 43012 |   | **SI** | A | HAPC | HA | |
| 43013 | † | **Y** | P | QCAR | ZA | Mark Carne CBE |
| 43014 | † | **Y** | P | QCAR | ZA | The Railway Observer |
| 43015 |   | **SI** | A | HAPC | HA | |
| 43016 | § | **GW** | A | EFPC | LA | |
| 43017 |   | **FB** | A | SCEL | EP (S) | |
| 43020 |   | **FB** | A | EFPC | EP (S) | MTU Power. Passion. Partnership |
| 43021 |   | **SI** | A | HAPC | HA | |
| 43022 | § | **GW** | GW | EFPC | LA | |
| 43023 |   | **FB** | A | EFPC | EP (S) | |
| 43024 |   | **FB** | A | SCEL | EP (S) | |
| 43025 |   | **FB** | A | SCEL | EP (S) | |
| 43026 |   | **SI** | A | HAPC | HA | |
| 43027 | § | **GW** | GW | EFPC | LA | |
| 43028 |   | **SI** | A | HAPC | HA | |
| 43029 | § | **GW** | GW | EFPC | LA | |
| 43030 |   | **SI** | A | HAPC | ZH (S) | |
| 43031 |   | **SI** | A | HAPC | HA | |
| 43032 |   | **SI** | A | HAPC | HA | |
| 43033 |   | **SI** | A | HAPC | HA | |
| 43034 |   | **SI** | A | HAPC | HA | |
| 43035 |   | **SI** | A | HAPC | HA | |
| 43036 |   | **SI** | A | HAPC | HA | |
| 43037 |   | **SI** | A | HAPC | HA | |
| 43040 | § | **GW** | A | EFPC | LA | |
| 43041 | § | **GW** | A | EFPC | LA | St Catherine's Castle |
| 43042 | § | **GW** | A | EFPC | LA | Tregenna Castle |
| 43043 | * | **ST** | P | SBXL | BU (S) | |
| 43044 | * | **ST** | P | SBXL | NL (S) | |
| 43045 | * | **ST** | P | COTS | ZA | |
| 43046 | * | **MP** | LS | MBDL | CL | |
| 43047 | * | **ST** | P | EMPC | BU (S) | |
| 43049 | * | **ST** | P | EMPC | BU (S) | |
| 43050 | * | **ST** | P | COTS | ZA | |
| 43052 | * | **ST** | DA | MBDL | RJ | |
| 43053 |   | **FB** | P | SBXL | LM (S) | |
| 43054 | * | **ST** | DA | MBDL | RJ | |
| 43055 | * | **MP** | LS | MBDL | CL | |
| 43056 |   | **FB** | P | SBXL | LM (S) | |
| 43058 | * | **ST** | LS | MBDL | CL | |
| 43059 | * | **ST** | LS | MBDL | CL | |
| 43060 | * | **ST** | P | COTS | ZA | |
| 43061 | * | **ST** | P | SBXL | BU (S) | |
| 43062 |   | **Y** | P | QCAR | ZA | John Armitt |
| 43063 |   | **FB** | GW | SBXL | LA (S) | |
| 43064 | * | **ST** | P | SBXL | BU (S) | |

| 43066 | * | **ST** | DA  | MBDL | RJ      |                          |
|-------|---|--------|-----|------|---------|--------------------------|
| 43069 |   | **FB** | P   | SBXL | LM (S)  |                          |
| 43070 |   | **FB** | P   | SBXL | LM (S)  |                          |
| 43071 |   | **FB** | P   | EFPC | BU (S)  |                          |
| 43073 | * | **ST** | P   | EMPC | BU (S)  |                          |
| 43075 | * | **ST** | P   | SBXL | BU (S)  |                          |
| 43076 | * | **ST** | DA  | MBDL | RJ      |                          |
| 43078 |   | **FB** | P   | SBXL | LM (S)  |                          |
| 43079 |   | **FB** | P   | SBXL | BU (S)  |                          |
| 43081 | * | **ST** | P   | EMPC | BU (S)  |                          |
| 43082 | * | **ST** | P   | SBXL | BU (S)  |                          |
| 43083 | * | **ST** | LS  | SBXL | ZG (S)  |                          |
| 43086 |   | **FB** | P   | EFPC | BU (S)  |                          |
| 43087 |   | **FB** | P   | SBXL | LM (S)  |                          |
| 43088 | § | **GW** | FG  | EFPC | LA      |                          |
| 43089 | * | **ST** | 125 | ICHP | RJ      |                          |
| 43091 |   | **FB** | GW  | SBXL | LA (S)  |                          |
| 43092 | § | **GW** | FG  | EFPC | LA      | Cromwell's Castle        |
| 43093 | § | **GW** | FG  | EFPC | LA      | Old Oak Common HST Depot 1976–2018 |
| 43094 | § | **GW** | FG  | EFPC | LA      | St Mawes Castle          |
| 43097 | § | **GW** | FG  | EFPC | LA      | Castle Drogo             |
| 43098 | § | **GW** | FG  | EFPC | LA      | Walton Castle            |
| 43122 | § | **GW** | FG  | EFPC | LA      | Dunster Castle           |
| 43124 |   | **SI** | A   | HAPC | HA      |                          |
| 43125 |   | **SI** | A   | HAPC | HA      |                          |
| 43126 |   | **SI** | A   | HAPC | HA      |                          |
| 43127 |   | **SI** | A   | HAPC | HA      |                          |
| 43128 |   | **SI** | A   | HAPC | HA      |                          |
| 43129 |   | **SI** | A   | HAPC | HA      |                          |
| 43130 |   | **SI** | A   | HAPC | HA      |                          |
| 43131 |   | **SI** | A   | HAPC | HA      |                          |
| 43132 |   | **SI** | A   | HAPC | HA      |                          |
| 43133 |   | **SI** | A   | HAPC | HA      |                          |
| 43134 |   | **SI** | A   | HAPC | HA      |                          |
| 43135 |   | **SI** | A   | HAPC | HA      |                          |
| 43136 |   | **SI** | A   | HAPC | HA      |                          |
| 43137 |   | **SI** | A   | HAPC | HA      |                          |
| 43138 |   | **SI** | A   | HAPC | HA      |                          |
| 43139 |   | **SI** | A   | HAPC | HA      |                          |
| 43140 |   | **SI** | A   | HAPC | ZH (S)  |                          |
| 43141 |   | **SI** | A   | HAPC | HA      |                          |
| 43142 |   | **SI** | A   | HAPC | HA      |                          |
| 43143 |   | **SI** | A   | HAPC | HA      |                          |
| 43144 |   | **SI** | A   | HAPC | HA      |                          |
| 43145 |   | **SI** | A   | HAPC | HA      |                          |
| 43146 |   | **SI** | A   | HAPC | HA      |                          |
| 43147 |   | **SI** | A   | HAPC | HA      |                          |
| 43148 |   | **SI** | A   | HAPC | HA      |                          |
| 43149 |   | **SI** | A   | HAPC | HA      |                          |
| 43150 |   | **SI** | A   | HAPC | HA      |                          |

| 43151 | **SI** | A | HAPC | HA | |
| 43152 | **SI** | A | HAPC | HA | |
| 43153 § | **GW** | FG | EFPC | LA | Chûn Castle |
| 43154 § | **GW** | FG | EFPC | LA | Compton Castle |
| 43155 § | **GW** | FG | EFPC | LA | Rougemont Castle |
| 43156 § | **GW** | FG | EFPC | LA | |
| 43158 § | **GW** | FG | EFPC | LA | Kingswear Castle |
| 43159 | **FB** | P | SBXL | BU (S) | |
| 43160 § | **GW** | FG | EFPC | LA | |
| 43161 | **FB** | GW | SBXL | LA (S) | |
| 43162 § | **GW** | FG | EFPC | LA | |
| 43163 | **SI** | A | HAPC | HA | |
| 43164 | **SI** | A | HAPC | HA | |
| 43165 | **FB** | A | SCEL | EP (S) | |
| 43168 | **SI** | A | HAPC | HA | |
| 43169 | **SI** | A | HAPC | HA | |
| 43170 § | **GW** | A | EFPC | LA | Chepstow Castle |
| 43171 | **GW** | GW | EFPC | LA | |
| 43172 | **GW** | GW | EFPC | LA | |
| 43174 | **FB** | A | SCEL | EP (S) | |
| 43175 | **SI** | A | HAPC | HA | |
| 43176 | **SI** | A | HAPC | HA | |
| 43177 | **SI** | A | HAPC | HA | |
| 43179 | **SI** | A | HAPC | HA | |
| 43180 | **FB** | P | EFPC | LA (S) | |
| 43181 | **SI** | A | HAPC | HA | |
| 43182 | **SI** | A | HAPC | HA | |
| 43183 | **SI** | A | HAPC | HA | |
| 43185 | **IC** | A | SCEL | HA (S) | |
| 43186 § | **GW** | A | EFPC | LA | Taunton Castle |
| 43187 § | **GW** | A | EFPC | LA | |
| 43188 § | **GW** | A | EFPC | LA | Newport Castle |
| 43189 § | **GW** | A | EFPC | LA | Launceston Castle |
| 43190 | **FB** | A | SCEL | EP (S) | |
| 43191 | **FB** | A | EFPC | EP (S) | |
| 43192 § | **GW** | A | EFPC | LA | Trematon Castle |
| 43193 | **FB** | P | SBXL | LM (S) | |
| 43194 § | **GW** | FG | EFPC | LA | Okehampton Castle |
| 43195 | **FB** | FG | EFPC | LA (S) | |
| 43196 | **FB** | P | EFPC | BU (S) | |
| 43197 | **FB** | P | SBXL | LM (S) | |
| 43198 § | **GW** | FG | EFPC | LA | Driver Stan Martin 25 June 1950 – 6 November 2004/Driver Brian Cooper 15 June 1947 – 5 October 1999 |

**Class 43/2. Rebuilt CrossCountry and East Midlands Railway or stored former Grand Central power cars.** Power cars were renumbered by adding 200 to their original number or 400 to their original number (former Grand Central), except 43123 which became 43423.

| | | | | | |
|---|---|---|---|---|---|
| 43206 (43006) | **0** | A | IECP | EP (S) | |
| 43207 (43007) | **XC** | A | EHPC | LA | |
| 43208 (43008) | **XC** | A | EHPC | LA | |
| 43238 (43038) | **0** | A | EMPC | NL | |
| 43239 (43039) | **XC** | A | EHPC | LA | |
| 43251 (43051) | **VE** | P | EMPC | NL | |
| 43257 (43057) | **VE** | P | EMPC | NL | |
| 43272 (43072) | **VE** | P | EMPC | NL | |
| 43274 (43074) | **0** | P | EMPC | NL | |
| 43277 (43077) | **VE** | P | EMPC | BU (S) | |
| 43285 (43085) | **XC** | P | EHPC | LA | |
| 43290 (43090) | **VE** | P | EMPC | ZA (S) | |
| 43295 (43095) | **VE** | A | EMPC | NL | |
| 43296 (43096) | **VE** | A | EMPC | EP (S) | |
| 43299 (43099) | **VE** | P | SBXL | ZA (S) | |
| 43300 (43100) | **VE** | P | IECP | NL (S) | |
| 43301 (43101) | **XC** | P | EHPC | LA | |
| 43302 (43102) | **VE** | P | EMPC | NL | |
| 43303 (43103) | **XC** | P | EHPC | LA | |
| 43304 (43104) | **XC** | A | EHPC | LA | |
| 43305 (43105) | **VE** | A | EMPC | NL | |
| 43306 (43106) | **VE** | A | EMPC | NL | |
| 43307 (43107) | **VE** | A | EMPC | NL | |
| 43308 (43108) | **VE** | A | EMPC | EP (S) | |
| 43309 (43109) | **VE** | A | EMPC | NL | |
| 43310 (43110) | **VE** | A | EMPC | NL | |
| 43311 (43111) | **VE** | A | IECP | EP (S) | |
| 43312 (43112) | **0** | A | IECP | EP (S) | |
| 43313 (43113) | **VE** | A | IECP | LA (S) | |
| 43314 (43114) | **VE** | A | EMPC | EP (S) | |
| 43315 (43115) | **VE** | A | IECP | EP (S) | |
| 43316 (43116) | **VE** | A | EMPC | NL | |
| 43317 (43117) | **VE** | A | EMPC | NL | |
| 43318 (43118) | **VE** | A | EMPC | EP (S) | |
| 43319 (43119) | **VE** | A | EMPC | NL | |
| 43320 (43120) | **VE** | A | EMPC | NL | |
| 43321 (43121) | **XC** | P | EHPC | LA | |
| 43357 (43157) | **XC** | P | EHPC | LA | |
| 43366 (43166) | **XC** | A | EHPC | LA | |
| 43367 (43167) | **VE** | A | IECP | EP (S) | |
| 43378 (43178) | **XC** | A | EHPC | LA | |
| 43384 (43184) | **XC** | A | EHPC | LA | |
| 43423 (43123) † | **EA** | A | EMPC | EP (S) | 'VALENTA' 1972–2010 |
| 43465 (43065) † | **EA** | A | EMPC | EP (S) | |

| 43467 | (43067) | † | **EA** | A | EMPC | EP (S) | Nottinghamshire Fire and Rescue Service/ British Transport Police Nottingham |
|---|---|---|---|---|---|---|---|
| 43468 | (43068) | † | **EA** | A | EMPC | EP (S) | |
| 43480 | (43080) | † | **EA** | A | EMPC | EP (S) | West Hampstead PSB |
| 43484 | (43084) | † | **EA** | A | EMPC | EP (S) | |

# CLASS 47     BR/BRUSH/SULZER     Co-Co

**Built:** 1963–67 by Brush Traction, at Loughborough or by BR at Crewe Works.
**Engine:** Sulzer 12LDA28C of 1920 kW (2580 hp) at 750 rpm.
**Main Generator:** Brush TG160-60 Mk4 or TM172-50 Mk1.
**Traction Motors:** Brush TM64-68 Mk1 or Mk1A.
**Maximum Tractive Effort:** 267 kN (60000 lbf).
**Continuous Tractive Effort:** 133 kN (30000 lbf) at 26 mph.
**Power at Rail:** 1550 kW (2080 hp).     **Train Brakes:** Air.
**Brake Force:** 61 t.     **Dimensions:** 19.38 x 2.79 m.
**Weight:** 111.5–120.6 t.     **Wheel Diameter:** 1143 mm.
**Design Speed:** 95 mph.     **Maximum Speed:** 95 mph.
**Fuel Capacity:** 3273 (+ 5887).     **Route Availability:** 6 or 7.
**Train Supply:** Not equipped.     **Total:** 49.

Class 47s exported for use abroad are listed in section 1.6 of this book.

**Non-standard liveries/numbering:**

| | |
|---|---|
| 47270 | Also carries original number 1971. |
| 47501 | Carries original number D1944. |
| 47614 | Carries original number 1733. |
| 47739 | GBRf dark blue. |
| 47773 | Also carries original number D1755. |
| 47798 | Royal Train claret with Rail Express Systems markings. |
| 47805 | Carries original number D1935. |
| 47810 | Carries original number D1924. |
| 47830 | Also carries original number D1645. |

**Recent renumbering:**

47593 was renumbered from 47790 in 2019.
47614 was renumbered from 47853 in 2019.

**Class 47/0. Standard Design.** Built with train air and vacuum brakes.

| 47194 | + | **F** | WC | AWCX | CS (S) | |
|---|---|---|---|---|---|---|
| 47237 | x+ | **WC** | WC | AWCA | CS | |
| 47245 | x+ | **WC** | WC | AWCA | CS | V.E. Day 75th Anniversary |
| 47270 | + | **B** | WC | AWCA | CS | SWIFT |

**Class 47/3.** Built with train air and vacuum brakes. Details as Class 47/0 except: **Weight:** 113.7 t.

| 47355 | a+ | **K** | WC | AWCX | CS (S) | |
|---|---|---|---|---|---|---|
| 47368 | | **F** | WC | AWCX | CS (S) | |

**Class 47/4. Electric Train Supply equipment.**
Details as Class 47/0 except:

**Weight:** 120.4–125.1 t.          **Fuel Capacity:** 3273 (+ 5537) litres.
**Train Supply:** Electric, index 66.          **Route Availability:** 7.

| | | | | | |
|---|---|---|---|---|---|
| 47492 | x | **RX** | WC | AWCX | CS (S) |
| 47501 | x+ | **GG** | LS | LSLO | CL | CRAFTSMAN |
| 47526 | x | **BL** | WC | AWCX | CS (S) |
| 47580 | x | **BL** | 47 | MBDL | TM | County of Essex |
| 47593 | | **BL** | LS | LSLO | CL | Galloway Princess |
| 47614 | + | **B** | LS | LSLO | CL |

**Class 47/7. Previously fitted with an older form of TDM.**
Details as Class 47/4 except:

**Weight:** 118.7 t.          **Fuel Capacity:** 5887 litres.
**Maximum Speed:** 100 mph.

| | | | | | |
|---|---|---|---|---|---|
| 47703 | **FR** | HN | HNRL | ZB |
| 47712 | **IC** | CD | LSLO | CL |
| 47714 | **AR** | HN | HNRL | Old Dalby |
| 47715 | **N** | HN | HNRL | WS |

**Class 47/7. Former Railnet dedicated locomotives.**
Details as Class 47/0 except:

**Fuel Capacity:** 5887 litres.

| | | | | | |
|---|---|---|---|---|---|
| 47727 | **CA** | GB | GBDF | LR | Edinburgh Castle/ Caisteal Dhùn Èideann |
| 47739 | **O** | GB | GBDF | LR |
| 47746 | x | **WC** | WC | AWCA | CS | Chris Fudge 29.7.70 – 22.6.10 |
| 47749 | d | **B** | GB | GBDF | LR | CITY OF TRURO |
| 47760 | x | **WC** | WC | AWCA | CS |
| 47768 | | **RX** | WC | AWCX | CS (S) |
| 47769 | | **V** | HN | HNRS | BH (S) | Resolve |
| 47772 | x | **WC** | WC | AWCA | CS | Carnforth TMD |
| 47773 | x | **GG** | 70 | MBDL | TM |
| 47776 | x | **RX** | WC | AWCX | CS (S) |
| 47786 | | **WC** | WC | AWCA | CS | Roy Castle OBE |
| 47787 | | **WC** | WC | AWCX | CS (S) |

**Class 47/4 continued. Route Availability: 6.**

| | | | | | |
|---|---|---|---|---|---|
| 47798 | x | **O** | NM | MBDL | YK | Prince William |
| 47802 | + | **WC** | WC | AWCA | CS |
| 47804 | + | **WC** | WC | AWCA | CS |
| 47805 | + | **GG** | LS | LSLO | CL | Roger Hosking MA 1925–2013 |
| 47810 | + | **GG** | LS | LSLO | CL | Crewe Diesel Depot |
| 47811 | + | **GL** | LS | DHLT | CL (S) |
| 47812 | + | **RO** | RO | GROG | LR |
| 47813 | + | **RO** | RO | GROG | LR | Jack Frost |
| 47815 | + | **RO** | RO | GROG | LR | Lost Boys 68–88 |
| 47816 | + | **GL** | LS | DHLT | CL (S) |
| 47818 | + | **DS** | AF | MBDL | ZG (S) |

| 47826 | + | **WC** | WC | AWCA | CS |  |
|-------|---|--------|----|------|-----|--|
| 47828 | + | **IC** | D0 | AWCA | CL |  |
| 47830 | + | **GG** | FL | DFLH | CB | BEECHING'S LEGACY |
| 47832 | + | **WC** | WC | AWCA | CS |  |
| 47841 | + | **IC** | LS | LSLS | Margate (S) | The Institution of Mechanical Engineers |
| 47843 | + | **RB** | RO | SROG | LR (S) |  |
| 47847 | + | **BL** | RO | SROG | LR (S) |  |
| 47848 | + | **RB** | RO | GROG | LR |  |
| 47851 | + | **WC** | WC | AWCA | CS |  |
| 47854 | + | **WC** | WC | AWCA | CS | Diamond Jubilee |

# CLASS 50    ENGLISH ELECTRIC    Co-Co

**Built:** 1967–68 by English Electric at Vulcan Foundry, Newton-le-Willows.
**Engine:** English Electric 16CVST of 2010 kW (2700 hp) at 850 rpm.
**Main Generator:** English Electric 840/4B.
**Traction Motors:** English Electric 538/5A.
**Maximum Tractive Effort:** 216 kN (48500 lbf).
**Continuous Tractive Effort:** 147 kN (33000 lbf) at 23.5 mph.
**Power at Rail:** 1540 kW (2070 hp).    **Train Brakes:** Air & vacuum.
**Brake Force:** 59 t.    **Dimensions:** 20.88 x 2.78 m.
**Weight:** 116.9 t.    **Wheel Diameter:** 1092 mm.
**Design Speed:** 105 mph.    **Maximum Speed:** 90 mph.
**Fuel Capacity:** 4796 litres.    **Route Availability:** 6.
**Train Supply:** Electric, index 61.    **Total:** 5.

**Non-standard numbering:**

50007   Running with the number 50014 on one side.
50050   Also carries original number D400.

| 50007 | **GB** | 50 | CFOL | KR | Hercules |
|-------|--------|----|------|-----|---------|
| 50008 | **B** | HH | DCRO | LR | Thunderer |
| 50044 | **B** | 50 | CFOL | KR | Exeter |
| 50049 | **GB** | 50 | CFOL | KR | Defiance |
| 50050 | **B** | NB | COFS | NM | Fearless |

# CLASS 52      BR/MAYBACH      C-C

**Built:** 1961–64 by BR at Swindon Works.
**Engine:** Two Maybach MD655 of 1007 kW (1350 hp) each at 1500 rpm.
**Transmission:** Hydraulic. Voith L630rV.
**Maximum Tractive Effort:** 297 kN (66700 lbf).
**Continuous Tractive Effort:** 201 kN (45200 lbf) at 14.5 mph.

**Power at Rail:** 1490 kW (2000 hp).    **Train Brakes:** Air & vacuum.
**Brake Force:** 83 t.    **Dimensions:** 20.70 m x 2.78 m.
**Weight:** 110 t.    **Wheel Diameter:** 1092 mm.
**Design Speed:** 90 mph.    **Maximum Speed:** 90 mph.
**Fuel Capacity:** 3900 litres.    **Route Availability:** 6.
**Train Supply:** Steam heating.    **Total:** 1.

Never allocated a number in the 1972 number series.

| | | | | | |
|---|---|---|---|---|---|
| D1015 | **B** | DT | MBDL | KR | WESTERN CHAMPION |

# CLASS 55      ENGLISH ELECTRIC      Co-Co

**Built:** 1961 by English Electric at Vulcan Foundry, Newton-le-Willows.
**Engine:** Two Napier-Deltic D18-25 of 1230 kW (1650 hp) each at 1500 rpm.
**Main Generators:** Two English Electric 829/1A.
**Traction Motors:** English Electric 538/A.
**Maximum Tractive Effort:** 222 kN (50000 lbf).
**Continuous Tractive Effort:** 136 kN (30500 lbf) at 32.5 mph.

**Power at Rail:** 1969 kW (2640 hp).    **Train Brakes:** Air & vacuum.
**Brake Force:** 51 t.    **Dimensions:** 21.18 x 2.68 m.
**Weight:** 100 t.    **Wheel Diameter:** 1092 mm.
**Design Speed:** 105 mph.    **Maximum Speed:** 100 mph.
**Fuel Capacity:** 3755 litres.    **Route Availability:** 5.
**Train Supply:** Electric, index 66.    **Total:** 4.

**Non-standard numbering:**

| | |
|---|---|
| 55002 | Carries original number D9002. |
| 55009 | Carries original number D9009. |
| 55016 | Carries original number D9016. |

| | | | | | |
|---|---|---|---|---|---|
| 55002 | **GG** | NM | MBDL | YK | THE KING'S OWN YORKSHIRE LIGHT INFANTRY |
| 55009 | **B** | DP | MBDL | BH | ALYCIDON |
| 55016 | **GG** | LS | MBDL | CL (S) | GORDON HIGHLANDER |
| 55022 | **B** | LS | MBDL | CL | ROYAL SCOTS GREY |

# CLASS 56     BRUSH/BR/RUSTON     Co-Co

**Built:** 1976–84 by Electroputere at Craiova, Romania (as sub-contractors for Brush) or BREL at Doncaster or Crewe Works.
**Engine:** Ruston Paxman 16RK3CT of 2460 kW (3250 hp) at 900 rpm.
**Main Alternator:** Brush BA1101A.
**Traction Motors:** Brush TM73-62.
**Maximum Tractive Effort:** 275 kN (61800 lbf).
**Continuous Tractive Effort:** 240 kN (53950 lbf) at 16.8 mph.
**Power at Rail:** 1790 kW (2400 hp).     **Train Brakes:** Air.
**Brake Force:** 60 t.     **Dimensions:** 19.36 x 2.79 m.
**Weight:** 126 t.     **Wheel Diameter:** 1143 mm.
**Design Speed:** 80 mph.     **Maximum Speed:** 80 mph.
**Fuel Capacity:** 5228 litres.     **Route Availability:** 7.
**Train Supply:** Not equipped.     **Total:** 29.

All equipped with Slow Speed Control.

Class 56s exported for use abroad are listed in section 1.6 of this book.

Most of the locomotives at Longport are being rebuilt as Class 69.

**Non-standard liveries:**

56009 All over blue.
56303 All over dark green.

| 56007 | **B** | GB | UKRS | LT (S) | |
| 56009 | **0** | EO | UKRS | LT (S) | |
| 56032 | **FER** | GB | GBGS | LT (S) | |
| 56037 | **E** | GB | GBGS | LT (S) | |
| 56038 | **FER** | GB | GBGS | LT (S) | |
| 56049 | **CS** | CS | COFS | NM | Robin of Templecombe 1938–2013 |
| 56051 | **CS** | CS | COLS | NM (S) | Survival |
| 56060 | **FER** | GB | UKRS | LT (S) | |
| 56065 | **FER** | GB | UKRS | LT (S) | |
| 56069 | **FER** | GB | GBGS | LT (S) | |
| 56077 | **LH** | GB | UKRS | LT (S) | |
| 56078 | **CS** | CS | COFS | NM | |
| 56081 | **FO** | GB | GBGD | LR | |
| 56087 | **CS** | BN | COFS | NM | |
| 56090 | **CS** | BN | COFS | NM | |
| 56091 | **DC** | DC | DCRO | LR | Driver Wayne Gaskell |
| | | | | | The Godfather |
| 56094 | **CS** | CS | COFS | NM | |
| 56096 | **CS** | BN | COFS | NM | |
| 56098 | **FO** | GB | GBGD | LR | |
| 56103 | **DC** | DC | DCRO | LR | |
| 56104 | **FO** | GB | UKRL | LR (S) | |
| 56105 | **CS** | BN | COFS | NM | |
| 56106 | **FER** | GB | UKRS | LR (S) | |
| 56113 | **CS** | BN | COFS | NM | |
| 56128 | **F** | GB | | LT (S) | |

| 56301 | (56045) | **FA** | 56 | UKRL | LR | |
| 56302 | (56124) | **CS** | CS | COFS | NM | PECO The Railway Modeller |
| | | | | | | 2016 70 Years |
| 56303 | (56125) | **O** | GB | HTLX | LR | |
| 56312 | (56003) | **DC** | GB | GBGD | LR | |

# CLASS 57             BRUSH/GM                    Co-Co

**Built:** 1964–65 by Brush Traction at Loughborough or BR at Crewe Works as Class 47. Rebuilt 1997–2004 by Brush Traction at Loughborough.
**Engine:** General Motors 12 645 E3 of 1860 kW (2500 hp) at 904 rpm.
**Main Alternator:** Brush BA1101D (recovered from Class 56).
**Traction Motors:** Brush TM64-68 Mark 1 or Mark 1A.
**Maximum Tractive Effort:** 244.5 kN (55000 lbf).
**Continuous Tractive Effort:** 140 kN (31500 lbf) at ?? mph.
**Power at Rail:** 1507 kW (2025 hp).      **Train Brakes:** Air.
**Brake Force:** 80 t.                      **Dimensions:** 19.38 x 2.79 m.
**Weight:** 120.6 t.                        **Wheel Diameter:** 1143 mm.
**Design Speed:** 75 mph.                   **Maximum Speed:** 75 mph.
**Fuel Capacity:** 5550 litres.            **Route Availability:** 6
**Train Supply:** Not equipped.            **Total:** 33.

**Non-standard livery:** 57604 Original Great Western Railway green.

**Class 57/0. No Train Supply Equipment. Rebuilt 1997–2000.**

| 57001 | (47356) | **WC** | WC | AWCA | CS (S) | |
| 57002 | (47322) | **DI** | DR | XHCK | KM | RAIL EXPRESS |
| 57003 | (47317) | **DI** | DR | XHCK | KM | |
| 57004 | (47347) | **DS** | DR | XHHP | LW (S) | |
| 57005 | (47350) | **AZ** | WC | AWCX | CS (S) | |
| 57006 | (47187) | **WC** | WC | AWCX | CS (S) | |
| 57007 | (47332) | **DI** | DR | XHSS | KM (S) | John Scott 12.5.45–22.5.12 |
| 57008 | (47060) | **DS** | DR | XHHP | LW (S) | |
| 57009 | (47079) | **DS** | DR | XHHP | LW (S) | |
| 57010 | (47231) | **DI** | DR | XHHP | LW (S) | |
| 57011 | (47329) | **DS** | DR | XHHP | LW (S) | |
| 57012 | (47204) | **DS** | DR | XHHP | LW (S) | |

**Class 57/3. Electric Train Supply Equipment. Former Virgin Trains locomotives fitted with retractable Dellner couplers. Rebuilt 2002–04.** Details as Class 57/0 except:

**Engine:** General Motors 12645F3B of 2050 kW (2750 hp) at 954 rpm.
**Main Alternator:** Brush BA1101F (recovered from Class 56) or Brush BA1101G.
**Fuel Capacity:** 5887 litres.            **Train Supply:** Electric, index 100.
**Design Speed:** 95 mph.                   **Maximum Speed:** 95 mph.
**Brake Force:** 60 t.                      **Weight:** 117 t.

| 57301 | (47845) | d | **DI** | P | GROG | LR | Goliath |
| 57302 | (47827) | d | **DS** | DR | XHSS | ZG (S) | Chad Varah |
| 57303 | (47705) | d | **DI** | P | GROG | LR | Pride of Carlisle |
| 57304 | (47807) | d | **DI** | DR | XHVT | KM | Pride of Cheshire |

| 57305 | (47822) | d | RO | P | GROG | LR | |
| 57306 | (47814) | d | DI | P | XHAC | KM | Her Majesty's Railway Inspectorate 175 |
| 57307 | (47225) | d | DI | DR | XHVT | KM | LADY PENELOPE |
| 57308 | (47846) | d | DI | DR | XHVT | KM | Jamie Ferguson |
| 57309 | (47806) | d | DI | DR | XHVT | KM | Pride of Crewe |
| 57310 | (47831) | d | DR | P | GROG | LR | Pride of Cumbria |
| 57311 | (47817) | d | DS | DR | XHSS | KM (S) | Thunderbird |
| 57312 | (47330) | d | RO | P | GROG | LR | |
| 57313 | (47371) | | PC | WC | AWCA | CS | Scarborough Castle |
| 57314 | (47372) | | WC | WC | AWCA | CS | |
| 57315 | (47234) | | WC | WC | AWCA | CS | |
| 57316 | (47290) | | WC | WC | AWCA | CS | |

**Class 57/6. Electric Train Supply Equipment. Prototype ETS loco. Rebuilt 2001.** Details as Class 57/0 except:

**Main Alternator:** Brush BA1101E.  
**Train Supply:** Electric, index 95.  
**Design Speed:** 95 mph.  
**Brake Force:** 60 t.  
**Fuel Capacity:** 3273 litres.  
**Weight:** 113t.  
**Maximum Speed:** 95 mph.

| 57601 | (47825) | | PC | WC | AWCA | CS | Windsor Castle |

**Class 57/6. Electric Train Supply Equipment. Great Western Railway locomotives. Rebuilt 2004.** Details as Class 57/3.

| 57602 | (47337) | | GW | P | EFOO | PZ | Restormel Castle |
| 57603 | (47349) | | GW | P | EFOO | PZ | Tintagel Castle |
| 57604 | (47209) | | 0 | P | EFOO | PZ | PENDENNIS CASTLE |
| 57605 | (47206) | | GW | P | EFOO | PZ | Totnes Castle |

# CLASS 58    BREL/RUSTON    Co-Co

**Built:** 1983–87 by BREL at Doncaster Works.  
**Engine:** Ruston Paxman 12RK3ACT of 2460 kW (3300 hp) at 1000 rpm.  
**Main Alternator:** Brush BA1101B.  
**Traction Motors:** Brush TM73-62.  
**Maximum Tractive Effort:** 275 kN (61800 lbf).  
**Continuous Tractive Effort:** 240 kN (53950 lbf) at 17.4 mph.  
**Power at Rail:** 1780 kW (2387 hp).    **Train Brakes:** Air.  
**Brake Force:** 60 t.                 **Dimensions:** 19.13 x 2.72 m.  
**Weight:** 130 t.                     **Wheel Diameter:** 1120 mm.  
**Design Speed:** 80 mph.              **Maximum Speed:** 80 mph.  
**Fuel Capacity:** 4214 litres.        **Route Availability:** 7.  
**Train Supply:** Not equipped.        **Total:** 2.

All equipped with Slow Speed Control.

Class 58s exported for use abroad are listed in section 1.6 of this book.

| 58012 | | F | PO | BL (S) | |
| 58023 | | ML | PO | LR (S) | |

# CLASS 59     GENERAL MOTORS     Co-Co

**Built:** 1985 (59001–004) or 1989 (59005) by General Motors, La Grange, Illinois, USA or 1990 (59101–104), 1994 (59201) and 1995 (59202–206) by General Motors, London, Ontario, Canada.
**Engine:** General Motors 16-645E3C two stroke of 2460 kW (3300 hp) at 904 rpm.
**Main Alternator:** General Motors AR11 MLD-D14A.
**Traction Motors:** General Motors D77B.
**Maximum Tractive Effort:** 506 kN (113550 lbf).
**Continuous Tractive Effort:** 291 kN (65300 lbf) at 14.3 mph.
**Power at Rail:** 1889 kW (2533 hp).

| | |
|---|---|
| **Brake Force:** 69 t. | **Train Brakes:** Air. |
| **Weight:** 121 t. | **Dimensions:** 21.35 x 2.65 m. |
| **Design Speed:** 60 (* 75) mph. | **Wheel Diameter:** 1067 mm. |
| **Fuel Capacity:** 4546 litres. | **Maximum Speed:** 60 (* 75) mph. |
| **Train Supply:** Not equipped. | **Route Availability:** 7. |
| | **Total:** 15. |

**Class 59/0. Owned by Freightliner and GB Railfreight.**

| 59001 | **AI** | FL | DFHG | MD | YEOMAN ENDEAVOUR |
|---|---|---|---|---|---|
| 59002 | **AI** | FL | DFHG | MD | ALAN J DAY |
| 59003 | **GB** | GB | GBYH | RR | YEOMAN HIGHLANDER |
| 59004 | **AI** | FL | DFHG | MD | PAUL A HAMMOND |
| 59005 | **AI** | FL | DFHG | MD | KENNETH J PAINTER |

**Class 59/1. Owned by Freightliner,**

| 59101 | **HA** | FL | DFHG | MD | Village of Whatley |
|---|---|---|---|---|---|
| 59102 | **HA** | FL | DFHG | MD | Village of Chantry |
| 59103 | **HA** | FL | DFHG | MD | Village of Mells |
| 59104 | **HA** | FL | DFHG | MD | Village of Great Elm |

**Class 59/2. Owned by DB Cargo.**

| 59201 | * | **DB** | FL | DFHG | MD | |
|---|---|---|---|---|---|---|
| 59202 | * | **DB** | FL | DFHG | MD | Alan Meddows Taylor |
| | | | | | | MD Mendip Rail Limited |
| 59203 | * | **FG** | FL | DFHG | MD | |
| 59204 | * | **DB** | FL | DFHG | MD | |
| 59205 | *b | **DB** | FL | DFHG | MD | |
| 59206 | *b | **FG** | FL | DFHG | MD | John F. Yeoman Rail Pioneer |

# CLASS 60     BRUSH/MIRRLEES     Co-Co

**Built:** 1989–93 by Brush Traction at Loughborough.
**Engine:** Mirrlees 8MB275T of 2310 kW (3100 hp) at 1000 rpm.
**Main Alternator:** Brush BA1006A.
**Traction Motors:** Brush TM2161A.
**Maximum Tractive Effort:** 500 kN (106500 lbf).
**Continuous Tractive Effort:** 336 kN (71570 lbf) at 17.4 mph.
**Power at Rail:** 1800 kW (2415 hp).

| | |
|---|---|
| **Brake Force:** 74 t (+ 62 t). | **Train Brakes:** Air. |
| | **Dimensions:** 21.34 x 2.64 m. |

| **Weight:** 129 t (+ 131 t). | **Wheel Diameter:** 1118 mm. |
| **Design Speed:** 62 mph. | **Maximum Speed:** 60 mph. |
| **Fuel Capacity:** 4546 (+ 5225) litres. | **Route Availability:** 8. |
| **Train Supply:** Not equipped. | **Total:** 99. |

All equipped with Slow Speed Control.

\* Refurbished locomotives.

60034, 60064, 60070, 60072, 60073, 60077, 60084 and 60090 carry their names on one side only.

60500 originally carried the number 60016.

**Non-standard and Advertising liveries:**

60026 Beacon Rail (blue).
60028 Cappagh (blue).
60066 Powering Drax (silver).
60074 Puma Energy (grey).
60081 Original Great Western Railway green.
60099 Tata Steel (silver).

| 60001 | \* | **DB** | DB | WCAT | TO | |
| 60002 | +\* | **CS** | BN | GBTG | TO | |
| 60003 | + | **E** | DB | WQCA | TO (S) | FREIGHT TRANSPORT ASSOCIATION |
| 60004 | + | **E** | GB | WQCA | TO (S) | |
| 60005 | + | **E** | DB | WQDA | TO (S) | |
| 60007 | +\* | **DB** | DB | WCBT | TO | The Spirit of Tom Kendell |
| 60008 | | **E** | GB | WQCA | TO (S) | Sir William McAlpine |
| 60009 | + | **E** | DB | WQCA | TO (S) | |
| 60010 | +\* | **DB** | DB | WCBT | TO | |
| 60011 | | **DB** | DB | WCAT | TO | |
| 60012 | + | **E** | DB | WQCA | TO (S) | |
| 60013 | | **EG** | DB | WQCA | TO (S) | Robert Boyle |
| 60014 | | **EG** | GB | WQCA | TO (S) | |
| 60015 | +\* | **DB** | DB | WCBT | TO | |
| 60017 | +\* | **DB** | DB | WCBT | TO | |
| 60018 | | **E** | GB | WQCA | TO (S) | |
| 60019 | \* | **DB** | DB | WCAT | TO | Port of Grimsby & Immingham |
| 60020 | +\* | **DB** | DB | WCBT | TO | The Willows |
| 60021 | +\* | **GB** | BN | GBTG | TO | PENYGHENT |
| 60022 | + | **E** | DB | WQCA | TO (S) | |
| 60023 | + | **E** | DB | WQCA | TO (S) | |
| 60024 | \* | **DB** | DB | WCAT | TO | Clitheroe Castle |
| 60025 | + | **E** | DB | WQCA | TO (S) | |
| 60026 | +\* | **O** | BN | GBTG | TO | HELVELLYN |
| 60027 | + | **E** | DB | WQCA | TO (S) | |
| 60028 | + | **O** | DC | DCRS | TO | |
| 60029 | | **DC** | DC | DCRS | TO | Ben Nevis |
| 60030 | + | **E** | DB | WQCA | TO (S) | |
| 60031 | | **E** | DB | WQCA | TO (S) | |
| 60032 | | **F** | DB | WQCA | TO (S) | |
| 60033 | + | **CU** | DB | WQCA | TO (S) | Tees Steel Express |

| | | | | | |
|---|---|---|---|---|---|
| 60034 | **EG** | DB | WQCA | TO (S) | Carnedd Llewelyn |
| 60035 | **E** | DB | WQBA | TO (S) | |
| 60036 | **E** | DB | WQCA | TO (S) | GEFCO |
| 60037 + | **E** | DB | WQCA | TO (S) | |
| 60038 + | **E** | DB | WQCA | TO (S) | |
| 60039 * | **DB** | DB | WCAT | TO | Dove Holes |
| 60040 * | **DB** | DB | WCAT | TO | The Territorial Army Centenary |
| 60041 + | **E** | DB | WQCA | TO (S) | |
| 60042 | **E** | DB | WQCA | TO (S) | |
| 60043 | **E** | DB | WQCA | TO (S) | |
| 60044 * | **DB** | DB | WCAT | TO | Dowlow |
| 60045 | **E** | DB | WQBA | TO (S) | The Permanent Way Institution |
| 60046 + | **DC** | DC | DCRC | TO | William Wilberforce |
| 60047 * | **CS** | BN | GBTG | TO | |
| 60048 | **E** | DB | WQCA | TO (S) | |
| 60049 | **E** | DB | WQBA | TO (S) | |
| 60051 + | **E** | DB | WQCA | TO (S) | |
| 60052 + | **E** | DB | WQCA | TO (S) | Glofa Twr – The last deep mine in Wales – Tower Colliery |
| 60053 | **E** | DB | WQCA | TO (S) | |
| 60054 +* | **DB** | DB | WCBT | TO | |
| 60055 + | **DC** | DC | DCRS | TO | Thomas Barnardo |
| 60056 +* | **CS** | BN | GBTG | TO | |
| 60057 | **EG** | DB | WQCA | TO (S) | Adam Smith |
| 60058 + | **E** | DB | WQCA | TO (S) | |
| 60059 +* | **DB** | DB | WCBT | TO | Swinden Dalesman |
| 60060 | **EG** | PO | WQCA | TO (S) | |
| 60061 | **F** | DB | WQCA | TO (S) | |
| 60062 * | **DB** | DB | WCAT | TO | Stainless Pioneer |
| 60063 * | **DB** | DB | WCAT | TO | |
| 60064 + | **EG** | DB | WQCA | TO (S) | Back Tor |
| 60065 | **E** | DB | WCAT | TO | Spirit of JAGUAR |
| 60066 * | **AL** | DB | WCAT | TO | |
| 60067 | **EG** | DB | WQCA | TO (S) | |
| 60068 | **EG** | DB | WQCA | TO (S) | |
| 60069 | **E** | DB | WQCA | TO (S) | Slioch |
| 60070 + | **F** | DB | WQCA | TO (S) | John Loudon McAdam |
| 60071 + | **E** | DB | WQBA | TO (S) | Ribblehead Viaduct |
| 60072 | **EG** | DB | WQCA | TO (S) | Cairn Toul |
| 60073 | **EG** | DB | WQCA | TO (S) | Cairn Gorm |
| 60074 * | **AL** | DB | WCAT | TO | Luke |
| 60075 | **E** | DB | WQCA | TO (S) | |
| 60076 * | **CS** | BN | GBTG | TO | Dunbar |
| 60077 + | **EG** | DB | WQCA | TO (S) | Canisp |
| 60078 | **ML** | DB | WQCA | TO (S) | |
| 60079 * | **DB** | DB | WQBA | TO (S) | |
| 60080 + | **E** | DB | WQCA | TO (S) | |
| 60081 + | **O** | LS | WQDA | TO (S) | |
| 60082 | **EG** | DB | WQCA | CE (S) | |
| 60083 | **E** | DB | WQCA | TO (S) | |
| 60084 | **EG** | DB | WQCA | TO (S) | Cross Fell |

| 60085 | * | CS | BN | GBTG | TO | |
| 60087 | * | CS | BN | GBTG | TO | |
| 60088 | | F | DB | WQCA | TO (S) | |
| 60089 | + | E | DB | WQCA | TO (S) | |
| 60090 | + | EG | DB | WQCA | TO (S) | Quinag |
| 60091 | +* | DB | DB | WCBT | TO | Barry Needham |
| 60092 | +* | DB | DB | WCBT | TO | |
| 60093 | | E | DB | WQCA | TO (S) | |
| 60094 | | E | DB | WQCA | TO (S) | Rugby Flyer |
| 60095 | * | GB | BN | GBTG | TO | |
| 60096 | +* | CS | BN | GBTG | TO | |
| 60097 | + | E | DB | WQCA | TO (S) | |
| 60098 | + | E | DB | WQCA | TO (S) | |
| 60099 | | AL | DB | WQCA | TO (S) | |
| 60100 | * | DB | DB | WCAT | TO | Midland Railway - Butterley |
| 60500 | | E | DB | WQCA | TO (S) | |

## CLASS 66    GENERAL MOTORS/EMD    Co-Co

**Built:** 1998–2008 by General Motors/EMD, London, Ontario, Canada (Model JT42CWR (low emission locomotives Model JT42CWRM)) or 2013–16 by EMD/Progress Rail, Muncie, Indiana (66752–779).
**Engine:** General Motors 12N-710G3B-EC two stroke of 2385 kW (3200 hp) at 904 rpm. 66752–779 GM 12N-710G3B-T2.
**Main Alternator:** General Motors AR8/CA6.
**Traction Motors:** General Motors D43TR.
**Maximum Tractive Effort:** 409 kN (92000 lbf).
**Continuous Tractive Effort:** 260 kN (58390 lbf) at 15.9 mph.

| | |
|---|---|
| **Power at Rail:** 1850 kW (2480 hp). | **Train Brakes:** Air. |
| **Brake Force:** 68 t. | **Dimensions:** 21.35 x 2.64 m. |
| **Weight:** 127 t. | **Wheel Diameter:** 1120 mm. |
| **Design Speed:** 87.5 mph. | **Maximum Speed:** 75 mph. |
| **Fuel Capacity:** 6550 litres. | **Route Availability:** 7. |
| **Train Supply:** Not equipped. | **Total:** 393. |

All equipped with Slow Speed Control.

Class 66s previously used in the UK but now in use abroad are listed in section 1.6 of this book. Some of the DBC 66s moved to France return to Great Britain from time to time for maintenance or operational requirements.

**Class 66 delivery dates.** The Class 66 design and delivery evolved over an 18-year period, with more than 400 locomotives delivered. For clarity the delivery dates (by year) for each batch of locomotives is as follows:

| | |
|---|---|
| 66001–250 | EWS (now DB Cargo). 1998–2000 (some now in use in France or Poland, ten sold to GB Railfreight and five on long-term hire to DRS). |
| 66301–305 | Fastline. 2008. Now used by DRS. |
| 66401–410 | DRS. 2003. Now in use with GB Railfreight or Colas Rail and renumbered 66733–737 and 66742–746 (66734 since scrapped). |
| 66411–420 | DRS. 2006. Now leased by Freightliner (66411/412/417 exported to Poland). |

| 66421–430 | DRS. 2007 |
|---|---|
| 66431–434 | DRS. 2008 |
| 66501–505 | Freightliner. 1999 |
| 66506–520 | Freightliner. 2000 |
| 66521–525 | Freightliner. 2000 (66521 since scrapped). |
| 66526–531 | Freightliner. 2001 |
| 66532–537 | Freightliner. 2001 |
| 66538–543 | Freightliner. 2001 |
| 66544–553 | Freightliner. 2001 |
| 66554 | Freightliner. 2002† |
| 66555–566 | Freightliner. 2002 |
| 66567–574 | Freightliner. 2003. 66573–574 now used by Colas Rail and renumbered 66846–847. |
| 66575–577 | Freightliner. 2004. Now used by Colas Rail and renumbered 66848–850. |
| 66578–581 | Freightliner. 2005. Now used by GBRf and renumbered 66738–741. |
| 66582–594 | Freightliner. 2007 (66582/583/584/586 exported to Poland). |
| 66595–599 | Freightliner. 2008 (66595 exported to Poland). |
| 66601–606 | Freightliner. 2000 |
| 66607–612 | Freightliner. 2002 (66607/609/611/612 exported to Poland) |
| 66613–618 | Freightliner. 2003 |
| 66619–622 | Freightliner. 2005 |
| 66623–625 | Freightliner. 2007 (66624/625 exported to Poland). |
| 66701–707 | GB Railfreight. 2001 |
| 66708–712 | GB Railfreight. 2002 |
| 66713–717 | GB Railfreight. 2003 |
| 66718–722 | GB Railfreight. 2006 |
| 66723–727 | GB Railfreight. 2006 |
| 66728–732 | GB Railfreight. 2008 |
| 66747–749 | Built in 2008 as 20078968-004/006/007 (DE 6313/15/16) for Crossrail AG in the Netherlands but never used. Sold to GB Railfreight in 2012. |
| 66750–751 | Built in 2003 as 20038513-01/04 and have worked in the Netherlands, Germany and Poland. GBRf secured these two locomotives on lease in 2013. |
| 66752–772 | GB Railfreight. 2014 |
| 66773–779 | GB Railfreight. 2016 |
| 66780–789 | GB Railfreight. 1998–2000. Former DBC locomotives acquired in 2017 that have been renumbered in the GBRf number series. |
| 66790–792 | Built in 2002 as 20018352-3/4/5 (T66403–405) for CargoNet, Norway. Sold to Beacon Rail and leased to GBRf from 2019. |
| 66793–797 | Second-hand locos being imported from Germany. 66793/794 ex-HHPI 29004/005 built 2003. 66797 ex-MRCE 513-09 built 2004 (works No. 20038513-9). Full details of others awaited. |
| 66951–952 | Freightliner. 2004 |
| 66953–957 | Freightliner. 2008 (66954 exported to Poland). |

**Advertising and non-standard liveries:**

| 66109 | PD Ports (dark blue). |
|---|---|
| 66587 | Ocean Network Express (pink with white stripes). |
| 66709 | MSC – blue with images of a container ship. |

| 66718 | London Underground 150, (black). |
| 66720 | Day and night (various colours, different on each side). |
| 66721 | London Underground 150 (white with tube map images). Also carries the numbers 1933 and 2013. |
| 66723 | Also carries the number ZA723. |
| 66731 | Thank you NHS (blue with orange cabsides). |
| 66747 | Newell & Wright (blue, white & red). |
| 66775 | Also carries the number F231. |
| 66779 | BR dark green. |
| 66780 | Cemex (grey, blue & red). |
| 66783 | Biffa (red & orange). |
| 66791, 66793, 66794, 66797 Beacon Rail (blue). |

**Class 66/0. DB Cargo-operated locomotives.**

All fitted with Swinghead Automatic "Buckeye" Combination Couplers except 66001 and 66002.

66031, 66091, 66108, 66122 and 66126 are on long-term hire to DRS.

† Fitted with additional lights and drawgear for Lickey banking duties.

t Fitted with tripcocks for working over London Underground tracks between Harrow-on-the-Hill and Amersham.

| 66001 t | **DB** | DB | WBAE | TO | |
| 66002 | **E** | DB | WBAE | TO | |
| 66003 | **E** | DB | WBAE | TO | |
| 66004 | **E** | DB | WBAR | TO | |
| 66005 | **MT** | DB | WBAE | TO | Maritime Intermodal One |
| 66006 | **E** | DB | WBAR | TO | |
| 66007 | **E** | DB | WBAR | TO | |
| 66009 | **DB** | DB | WBAE | TO | |
| 66011 | **E** | DB | WBAE | TO | |
| 66012 | **E** | DB | WBAE | TO | |
| 66013 | **E** | DB | WBAE | TO | |
| 66014 | **E** | DB | WBAR | TO | |
| 66015 | **E** | DB | WBAR | TO | |
| 66017 t | **DB** | DB | WBAR | TO | |
| 66018 | **DB** | DB | WBAE | TO | |
| 66019 t | **DB** | DB | WBAR | TO | |
| 66020 | **DB** | DB | WBAE | TO | |
| 66021 | **DB** | DB | WBAE | TO | |
| 66023 | **E** | DB | WBAT | TO | |
| 66024 | **E** | DB | WBAE | TO | |
| 66025 | **E** | DB | WBAR | TO | |
| 66027 | **DB** | DB | WBAE | TO | |
| 66030 | **E** | DB | WBAR | TO | |
| 66031 | **E** | DB | XHIM | KM | |
| 66034 | **DB** | DB | WBAE | TO | |
| 66035 | **DB** | DB | WBAE | TO | Resourceful |
| 66037 | **E** | DB | WBAR | TO | |
| 66039 | **E** | DB | WBAE | TO | |
| 66040 | **E** | DB | WBAR | TO | |

| | | | | | |
|---|---|---|---|---|---|
| 66041 | **DB** | DB | WBAR | TO | |
| 66043 | **E** | DB | WQBA | TO (S) | |
| 66044 | **DB** | DB | WBAE | TO | |
| 66047 | **MT** | DB | WBAE | TO | Maritime Intermodal Two |
| 66050 | **E** | DB | WBAE | TO | EWS Energy |
| 66051 | **MT** | DB | WBAR | TO | Maritime Intermodal Four |
| 66053 | **E** | DB | WBAE | TO | |
| 66054 | **E** | DB | WBAR | TO | |
| 66055 † | **DB** | DB | WBLT | TO | Alain Thauvette |
| 66056 † | **E** | DB | WBLE | TO | |
| 66057 † | **E** | DB | WBLE | TO | |
| 66059 † | **E** | DB | WBLE | TO | |
| 66060 | **E** | DB | WBAR | TO | |
| 66061 | **E** | DB | WBAE | TO | |
| 66063 | **E** | DB | WBAE | TO | |
| 66065 | **DB** | DB | WBAE | TO | |
| 66066 | **DB** | DB | WBAR | TO | Geoff Spencer |
| 66067 | **E** | DB | WBAR | TO | |
| 66068 | **E** | DB | WBAR | TO | |
| 66069 | **E** | DB | WBAR | TO | |
| 66070 | **DB** | DB | WBAE | TO | |
| 66074 | **DB** | DB | WBAE | TO | |
| 66075 | **E** | DB | WBAE | TO | |
| 66076 | **E** | DB | WBAE | TO | |
| 66077 | **DB** | DB | WBAE | TO | Benjamin Gimbert G.C. |
| 66078 | **DB** | DB | WBAE | TO | |
| 66079 | **E** | DB | WBAR | TO | James Nightall G.C. |
| 66080 | **E** | DB | WBAE | TO | |
| 66082 | **DB** | DB | WBAE | TO | |
| 66083 | **E** | DB | WBAR | TO | |
| 66084 | **E** | DB | WBAE | TO | |
| 66085 | **DB** | DB | WBAR | TO | |
| 66086 | **E** | DB | WBAE | TO | |
| 66087 | **E** | DB | WBAE | TO | |
| 66088 | **E** | DB | WBAE | TO | |
| 66089 | **E** | DB | WBAR | TO | |
| 66090 | **MT** | DB | WBAE | TO | Maritime Intermodal Six |
| 66091 | **DR** | DB | XHIM | KM | |
| 66092 | **E** | DB | WBAE | TO | |
| 66093 | **E** | DB | WBAE | TO | |
| 66094 | **DB** | DB | WBAE | TO | |
| 66095 | **E** | DB | WBAE | TO | |
| 66096 | **E** | DB | WBAE | TO | |
| 66097 | **DB** | DB | WBAE | TO | |
| 66098 | **E** | DB | WBAE | TO | |
| 66099 r | **E** | DB | WBBE | TO | |
| 66100 r | **DB** | DB | WBBE | TO | Armistice 100 1918–2018 |
| 66101 r | **DB** | DB | WBBE | TO | |
| 66102 r | **E** | DB | WBBE | TO | |
| 66103 r | **E** | DB | WBBE | TO | |
| 66104 r | **DB** | DB | WBBT | TO | |

| 66105 r | **DB** | DB | WBAR | TO |                              |
|---------|--------|----|------|----|------------------------------|
| 66106 r | **E**  | DB | WBBE | TO |                              |
| 66107 r | **DB** | DB | WBBT | TO |                              |
| 66108 r | **E**  | DB | XHIM | KM |                              |
| 66109   | **AL** | DB | WBAR | TO | Teesport Express             |
| 66110 r | **E**  | DB | WBBE | TO |                              |
| 66111 r | **E**  | DB | WBAE | TO |                              |
| 66112 r | **E**  | DB | WBBE | TO |                              |
| 66113 r | **DB** | DB | WBBE | TO |                              |
| 66114 r | **DB** | DB | WBBT | TO |                              |
| 66115   | **DB** | DB | WBAE | TO |                              |
| 66116   | **E**  | DB | WBAE | TO |                              |
| 66117   | **DB** | DB | WBAE | TO |                              |
| 66118   | **DB** | DB | WBAE | TO |                              |
| 66119   | **E**  | DB | WBAE | TO |                              |
| 66120   | **E**  | DB | WBAE | TO |                              |
| 66121   | **E**  | DB | WBAE | TO |                              |
| 66122   | **E**  | DB | XHIM | KM |                              |
| 66124   | **DB** | DB | WBAR | TO |                              |
| 66125   | **E**  | DB | WBAE | TO |                              |
| 66126   | **E**  | DB | XHIM | KM |                              |
| 66127   | **E**  | DB | WBAT | TO |                              |
| 66128   | **DB** | DB | WBAE | TO |                              |
| 66129   | **E**  | DB | WBAR | TO |                              |
| 66130   | **DB** | DB | WBAR | TO |                              |
| 66131   | **DB** | DB | WBAE | TO |                              |
| 66133   | **E**  | DB | WBAE | TO |                              |
| 66134   | **DB** | DB | WBAE | TO |                              |
| 66135   | **DB** | DB | WBAE | TO |                              |
| 66136   | **DB** | DB | WBAE | TO |                              |
| 66137   | **DB** | DB | WBAE | TO |                              |
| 66138   | **E**  | DB | WQBA | TO (S) |                           |
| 66139   | **E**  | DB | WBAE | TO |                              |
| 66140   | **E**  | DB | WBAE | TO |                              |
| 66142   | **MT** | DB | WBAR | TO | Maritime Intermodal Three    |
| 66143   | **E**  | DB | WBAE | TO |                              |
| 66144   | **E**  | DB | WBAR | TO |                              |
| 66145   | **E**  | DB | WQBA | TO (S) |                           |
| 66147   | **E**  | DB | WBAE | TO |                              |
| 66148   | **MT** | DB | WBAE | TO | Maritime Intermodal Seven    |
| 66149   | **DB** | DB | WBAE | TO |                              |
| 66150   | **DB** | DB | WBAE | TO |                              |
| 66151   | **E**  | DB | WBAE | TO |                              |
| 66152   | **DB** | DB | WBAE | TO | Derek Holmes Railway Operator |
| 66154   | **E**  | DB | WBAE | TO |                              |
| 66155   | **E**  | DB | WBRT | TO |                              |
| 66156   | **E**  | DB | WBAE | TO |                              |
| 66158   | **E**  | DB | WBAE | TO |                              |
| 66160   | **E**  | DB | WBAR | TO |                              |
| 66161   | **E**  | DB | WBAE | TO |                              |
| 66162   | **MT** | DB | WBAR | TO | Maritime Intermodal Five     |

| 66164 | **E**  | DB | WBAE | TO     |                              |
|-------|--------|----|------|--------|------------------------------|
| 66165 | **DB** | DB | WBAR | TO     |                              |
| 66167 | **DB** | DB | WBAE | TO     |                              |
| 66168 | **E**  | DB | WBAR | TO     |                              |
| 66169 | **E**  | DB | WBAR | TO     |                              |
| 66170 | **E**  | DB | WBAE | TO     |                              |
| 66171 | **E**  | DB | WBAR | TO     |                              |
| 66172 | **E**  | DB | WBAE | TO     | PAUL MELLENEY                |
| 66174 | **E**  | DB | WBAE | TO     |                              |
| 66175 | **DB** | DB | WBAE | TO     | Rail Riders Express          |
| 66176 | **E**  | DB | WBAR | TO     |                              |
| 66177 | **E**  | DB | WBAT | TO     |                              |
| 66181 | **E**  | DB | WBAR | TO     |                              |
| 66182 | **DB** | DB | WQAB | TO (S) |                              |
| 66183 | **E**  | DB | WBAE | TO     |                              |
| 66185 | **DB** | DB | WBAE | TO     | DP WORLD London Gateway      |
| 66186 | **E**  | DB | WBAR | TO     |                              |
| 66187 | **E**  | DB | WBAE | TO     |                              |
| 66188 | **E**  | DB | WBAR | TO     |                              |
| 66192 | **DB** | DB | WBAR | TO     |                              |
| 66194 | **E**  | DB | WBAR | TO     |                              |
| 66197 | **E**  | DB | WBAE | TO     |                              |
| 66198 | **E**  | DB | WBAR | TO     |                              |
| 66199 | **E**  | DB | WBAE | TO     |                              |
| 66200 | **E**  | DB | WBAR | TO     |                              |
| 66206 | **DB** | DB | WBAR | TO     |                              |
| 66207 | **E**  | DB | WBAE | TO     |                              |
| 66221 | **E**  | DB | WBAR | TO     |                              |
| 66230 | **DB** | DB | WQBA | TO (S) |                              |

**Class 66/3. Former Fastline-operated locomotives now operated by DRS.
Low emission.** Details as Class 66/0 except:

**Engine:** EMD 12N-710G3B-T2 two stroke of 2420 kW (3245 hp) at 904 rpm.
**Traction Motors:** General Motors D43TRC.
**Fuel Capacity:** 5150 litres.

| 66301 | **DR** | BN | XHIM | KM | Kingmoor TMD |
|-------|--------|----|------|----|--------------|
| 66302 | **DR** | BN | XHIM | KM | Endeavour    |
| 66303 | **DR** | BN | XHIM | KM |              |
| 66304 | **DR** | BN | XHIM | KM |              |
| 66305 | **DR** | BN | XHIM | KM |              |

**Class 66/4. Low emission. Akiem-owned.** Details as Class 66/3.

| 66413 | **FG** | AK | DFIN | LD | Lest We Forget                                            |
|-------|--------|----|------|----|-----------------------------------------------------------|
| 66414 | **FH** | AK | DFIN | LD |                                                           |
| 66415 | **FG** | AK | DFIN | LD | You Are Never Alone                                       |
| 66416 | **FH** | AK | DFIN | LD |                                                           |
| 66418 | **FH** | AK | DFIN | LD | PATRIOT – IN MEMORY OF<br>FALLEN RAILWAY EMPLOYEES        |
| 66419 | **FG** | AK | DFIN | LD |                                                           |
| 66420 | **FH** | AK | DFIN | LD |                                                           |
| 66421 | **DR** | AK | XHIM | KM | Gresty Bridge TMD                                         |

| 66422 | **DR** | AK | XHIM | KM | |
| 66423 | **DR** | AK | XHIM | KM | |
| 66424 | **DR** | AK | XHIM | KM | |
| 66425 | **DR** | AK | XHIM | KM | |
| 66426 | **DR** | AK | XHIM | KM | |
| 66427 | **DR** | AK | XHIM | KM | |
| 66428 | **DR** | AK | XHIM | KM | Carlisle Eden Mind |
| 66429 | **DR** | AK | XHIM | KM | |
| 66430 | **DR** | AK | XHIM | KM | |
| 66431 | **DR** | AK | XHIM | KM | |
| 66432 | **DR** | AK | XHIM | KM | |
| 66433 | **DR** | AK | XHIM | KM | |
| 66434 | **DR** | AK | XHIM | KM | |

**Class 66/5. Standard design. Freightliner-operated locomotives.** Details as Class 66/0.

| 66501 | **FL** | P | DFIM | LD | Japan 2001 |
| 66502 | **FL** | P | DFIM | LD | Basford Hall Centenary 2001 |
| 66503 | **FG** | P | DFIM | LD | The RAILWAY MAGAZINE |
| 66504 | **FH** | P | DFIM | LD | |
| 66505 | **FL** | P | DFIM | LD | |
| 66506 | **FL** | E | DFIM | LD | Crewe Regeneration |
| 66507 | **FL** | E | DFIM | LD | |
| 66508 | **FL** | E | DFIM | LD | |
| 66509 | **FL** | E | DFIM | LD | |
| 66510 | **FL** | E | DFIM | LD | |
| 66511 | **FL** | E | DFIM | LD | |
| 66512 | **FL** | E | DFIM | LD | |
| 66513 | **FL** | E | DFIM | LD | |
| 66514 | **FL** | E | DFIM | LD | |
| 66515 | **FL** | E | DFIM | LD | |
| 66516 | **FL** | E | DFIM | LD | |
| 66517 | **FL** | E | DFIM | LD | |
| 66518 | **FL** | E | DFIM | LD | |
| 66519 | **FL** | E | DFIM | LD | |
| 66520 | **FL** | E | DFIM | LD | |
| 66522 | **FL** | E | DFIM | LD | |
| 66523 | **FL** | E | DFIM | LD | |
| 66524 | **FL** | E | DFIM | LD | |
| 66525 | **FL** | E | DFIM | LD | |
| 66526 | **FL** | P | DFIM | LD | Driver Steve Dunn (George) |
| 66528 | **FH** | P | DFIM | LD | Madge Elliot MBE |
|       |        |   |      |    | Borders Railway Opening 2015 |
| 66529 | **FL** | P | DFIM | LD | |
| 66531 | **FL** | P | DFIM | LD | |
| 66532 | **FL** | P | DFIM | LD | P&O Nedlloyd Atlas |
| 66533 | **FL** | P | DFIM | LD | Hanjin Express/Senator Express |
| 66534 | **FL** | P | DFIM | LD | OOCL Express |
| 66536 | **FL** | P | DFIM | LD | |
| 66537 | **FL** | P | DFIM | LD | |
| 66538 | **FL** | E | DFIM | LD | |

| 66539 | **FL** | E  | DFIM | LD     |                                      |
|-------|--------|----|------|--------|--------------------------------------|
| 66540 | **FL** | E  | DFIM | LD     | Ruby                                 |
| 66541 | **FL** | E  | DFIM | LD     |                                      |
| 66542 | **FL** | E  | DFIM | LD     |                                      |
| 66543 | **FL** | E  | DFIM | LD     |                                      |
| 66544 | **FL** | P  | DFIM | LD     |                                      |
| 66545 | **FL** | P  | DFIM | LD     |                                      |
| 66546 | **FL** | P  | DFIM | LD     |                                      |
| 66547 | **FL** | P  | DFIM | LD     |                                      |
| 66548 | **FL** | P  | DFIM | LD     |                                      |
| 66549 | **FL** | P  | DFIM | LD     |                                      |
| 66550 | **FL** | P  | DFIM | LD     |                                      |
| 66551 | **FL** | P  | DFIM | LD     |                                      |
| 66552 | **FL** | P  | DFIM | LD     | Maltby Raider                        |
| 66553 | **FL** | P  | DFIM | LD     |                                      |
| 66554 | **FL** | E  | DFIM | LD     |                                      |
| 66555 | **FL** | E  | DFIM | LD     |                                      |
| 66556 | **FL** | E  | DFIM | LD     |                                      |
| 66557 | **FL** | E  | DFIM | LD     |                                      |
| 66558 | **FL** | E  | DFIM | LD     |                                      |
| 66559 | **FL** | E  | DFIM | LD     |                                      |
| 66560 | **FL** | E  | DFIM | LD     |                                      |
| 66561 | **FL** | E  | DFIM | LD     |                                      |
| 66562 | **FL** | E  | DFIM | LD     |                                      |
| 66563 | **FL** | E  | DFIM | LD     |                                      |
| 66564 | **FL** | E  | DFIM | LD     |                                      |
| 66565 | **FL** | E  | DFIM | LD     |                                      |
| 66566 | **FL** | E  | DFIM | LD     |                                      |
| 66567 | **FL** | E  | DFIM | LD     |                                      |
| 66568 | **FL** | E  | DFIM | LD     |                                      |
| 66569 | **FL** | E  | DFIM | LD     |                                      |
| 66570 | **FL** | E  | DFIM | LD     |                                      |
| 66571 | **FL** | E  | DFIM | LD     |                                      |
| 66572 | **FL** | E  | DFIM | LD     |                                      |

**Class 66/5. Freightliner-operated low emission locomotives.** Details as Class 66/3.

| 66585 | **FL** | E  | DFIN | LD     |                                      |
|-------|--------|----|------|--------|--------------------------------------|
| 66587 | **AL** | E  | DFIN | LD     | AS ONE, WE CAN                       |
| 66588 | **FL** | E  | DFIN | LD     |                                      |
| 66589 | **FL** | E  | DHLT | LD (S) |                                      |
| 66590 | **FL** | E  | DFIN | LD     |                                      |
| 66591 | **FL** | E  | DFIN | LD     |                                      |
| 66592 | **FL** | E  | DFIN | LD     | Johnson Stevens Agencies             |
| 66593 | **FL** | E  | DFIN | LD     | 3MG MERSEY MULTIMODAL GATEWAY        |
| 66594 | **FL** | E  | DFIN | LD     | NYK Spirit of Kyoto                  |
| 66596 | **FL** | BN | DFIN | LD     |                                      |
| 66597 | **FL** | BN | DFIN | LD     | Viridor                              |
| 66598 | **FL** | BN | DFIN | LD     |                                      |
| 66599 | **FL** | BN | DFIN | LD     |                                      |

**Class 66/6. Freightliner-operated locomotives with modified gear ratios.**
Details as Class 66/0 except:

**Maximum Tractive Effort:** 467 kN (105080 lbf).
**Continuous Tractive Effort:** 296 kN (66630 lbf) at 14.0 mph.
**Design Speed:** 65 mph.                    **Maximum Speed:** 65 mph.

| | | | | |
|---|---|---|---|---|
| 66601 | **FL** | P | DFHH | LD | The Hope Valley |
| 66602 | **FL** | P | DFHH | LD | |
| 66603 | **FL** | P | DFHH | LD | |
| 66604 | **FL** | P | DFHH | LD | |
| 66605 | **FL** | P | DFHH | LD | |
| 66606 | **FL** | P | DFHH | LD | |
| 66607 | **FL** | P | DFHH | LD | |
| 66610 | **FL** | P | DFHH | LD | |
| 66613 | **FL** | E | DFHH | LD | |
| 66614 | **FL** | E | DFHH | LD | 1916 POPPY 2016 |
| 66615 | **FL** | E | DFHH | LD | |
| 66616 | **FL** | E | DFHH | LD | |
| 66617 | **FL** | E | DFHH | LD | |
| 66618 | **FL** | E | DFHH | LD | Railways Illustrated Annual |
| | | | | | Photographic Awards Alan Barnes |
| 66619 | **FL** | E | DFHH | LD | Derek W. Johnson MBE |
| 66620 | **FL** | E | DFHH | LD | |
| 66621 | **FL** | E | DFHH | LD | |
| 66622 | **FL** | E | DFHH | LD | |

**Class 66/6. Freightliner-operated low emission locomotive with modified gear ratios.** Details as Class 66/6 except:

**Fuel Capacity:** 5150 litres.

| | | | | |
|---|---|---|---|---|
| 66623 | **FG** | AK | DFHH | LD | |

**Class 66/7. Standard design. GB Railfreight-operated locomotives.** Details as Class 66/0 except 66793 and 66794 which are as Class 66/6.

| | | | | |
|---|---|---|---|---|
| 66701 | **GB** | E | GBBT | RR | |
| 66702 | **GB** | E | GBBT | RR | Blue Lightning |
| 66703 | **GB** | E | GBBT | RR | Doncaster PSB 1981–2002 |
| 66704 | **GB** | E | GBBT | RR | Colchester Power Signalbox |
| 66705 | **GB** | E | GBBT | RR | Golden Jubilee |
| 66706 | **GB** | E | GBBT | RR | Nene Valley |
| 66707 | **GB** | E | GBBT | RR | Sir Sam Fay GREAT CENTRAL RAILWAY |
| 66708 | **GB** | E | GBBT | RR | Jayne |
| 66709 | **AL** | E | GBBT | RR | Sorrento |
| 66710 | **GB** | E | GBBT | RR | Phil Packer BRIT |
| 66711 | **AI** | E | GBBT | RR | Sence |
| 66712 | **GB** | E | GBBT | RR | Peterborough Power Signalbox |
| 66713 | **GB** | E | GBBT | RR | Forest City |
| 66714 | **GB** | E | GBBT | RR | Cromer Lifeboat |
| 66715 | **GB** | E | GBBT | RR | VALOUR – IN MEMORY OF ALL RAILWAY |
| | | | | | EMPLOYEES WHO GAVE THEIR LIVES |
| | | | | | FOR THEIR COUNTRY |

| 66716 | **GB** E | GBBT | RR | LOCOMOTIVE & CARRIAGE INSTITUTION CENTENARY 1911–2011 |
| 66717 | **GB** E | GBBT | RR | Good Old Boy |

**66718–751. GB Railfreight locomotives.**

Details as Class 66/0 except 66718–732/747–749 as below:

**Engine:** EMD 12N-710G3B-T2 two stroke of 2420 kW (3245 hp) at 904 rpm.
**Traction Motors:** General Motors D43TRC.
**Fuel Capacity:** 5546 litres (66718–722) or 5150 litres (66723–732/747–749).

66747–749 were originally built for Crossrail AG in the Netherlands.

66750/751 were originally built for mainland Europe in 2003.

| 66718 | **AL** E | GBLT | RR | Sir Peter Hendy CBE |
| 66719 | **GB** E | GBLT | RR | METRO-LAND |
| 66720 | **O** E | GBLT | RR | |
| 66721 | **AL** E | GBLT | RR | Harry Beck |
| 66722 | **GB** E | GBLT | RR | Sir Edward Watkin |
| 66723 | **GB** E | GBLT | RR | Chinook |
| 66724 | **GB** E | GBLT | RR | Drax Power Station |
| 66725 | **GB** E | GBLT | RR | SUNDERLAND |
| 66726 | **GB** E | GBLT | RR | SHEFFIELD WEDNESDAY |
| 66727 | **MT** E | GBLT | RR | Maritime One |
| 66728 | **GB** P | GBLT | RR | Institution of Railway Operators |
| 66729 | **GB** P | GBLT | RR | DERBY COUNTY |
| 66730 | **GB** P | GBLT | RR | Whitemoor |
| 66731 | **AL** P | GBLT | RR | Capt. Tom Moore A True British Inspiration |
| 66732 | **GB** P | GBLT | RR | GBRf The First Decade 1999–2009 John Smith – MD |

| 66733 | (66401) r | **GB** P | GBFM | RR | Cambridge PSB |
| 66735 | (66403) | **GB** P | GBBT | RR | PETERBOROUGH UNITED |
| 66736 | (66404) r | **GB** P | GBFM | RR | WOLVERHAMPTON WANDERERS |
| 66737 | (66405) r | **GB** P | GBFM | RR | Lesia |
| 66738 | (66578) | **GB** BN | GBBT | RR | HUDDERSFIELD TOWN |
| 66739 | (66579) r | **GB** BN | GBFM | RR | Bluebell Railway |
| 66740 | (66580) r | **GB** BN | GBFM | RR | Sarah |
| 66741 | (66581) | **GB** BN | GBBT | RR | Swanage Railway |
| 66742 | (66406, 66841) | **GB** BN | GBBT | RR | ABP Port of Immingham Centenary 1912–2012 |
| 66743 | (66407, 66842) r | **M** BN | GBFM | RR | |
| 66744 | (66408, 66843) | **GB** BN | GBBT | RR | Crossrail |
| 66745 | (66409, 66844) | **GB** BN | GBRT | RR | Modern Railways The first 50 years |
| 66746 | (66410, 66845) r | **M** BN | GBFM | RR | |
| 66747 | (20078968-007) | **AL** BN | GBEB | RR | Made in Sheffield |
| 66748 | (20078968-004) | **GB** BN | GBEB | RR | West Burton 50 |
| 66749 | (20078968-006) | **GB** BN | GBEB | RR | Christopher Hopcroft MBE 60 Years Railway Service |

| 66750 | (20038513-01) | | **GB** | BN | GBEB | | RR | Bristol Panel Signal Box |
| 66751 | (20038513-04) c | | **GB** | BN | GBEB | | RR | Inspiration Delivered |
| | | | | | | | | Hitachi Rail Europe |

**66752–779. Low emission.** New build locomotives. Details as Class 66/3.

| 66752 | **GB** | GB | GBEL | RR | The Hoosier State |
| 66753 | **GB** | GB | GBEL | RR | EMD Roberts Road |
| 66754 | **GB** | GB | GBEL | RR | Northampton Saints |
| 66755 | **GB** | GB | GBEL | RR | Tony Berkeley OBE |
| | | | | | RFG Chairman 1997–2018 |
| 66756 | **GB** | GB | GBEL | RR | Royal Corps of Signals |
| 66757 | **GB** | GB | GBEL | RR | West Somerset Railway |
| 66758 | **GB** | GB | GBEL | RR | The Pavior |
| 66759 | **GB** | GB | GBEL | RR | Chippy |
| 66760 | **GB** | GB | GBEL | RR | David Gordon Harris |
| 66761 | **GB** | GB | GBEL | RR | Wensleydale Railway Association |
| | | | | | 25 Years 1990–2015 |
| 66762 | **GB** | GB | GBEL | RR | |
| 66763 | **GB** | GB | GBEL | RR | Severn Valley Railway |
| 66764 | **GB** | GB | GBEL | RR | |
| 66765 | **GB** | GB | GBEL | RR | |
| 66766 | **GB** | GB | GBEL | RR | |
| 66767 | **GB** | GB | GBEL | RR | |
| 66768 | **GB** | GB | GBEL | RR | |
| 66769 | **GB** | GB | GBEL | RR | |
| 66770 | **GB** | GB | GBEL | RR | |
| 66771 | **GB** | GB | GBEL | RR | Amanda |
| 66772 | **GB** | GB | GBEL | RR | Maria |
| 66773 | **GB** | GB | GBNB | RR | Pride of GB Railfreight |
| 66774 | **GB** | GB | GBNB | RR | |
| 66775 | **GB** | GB | GBNB | RR | HMS Argyll |
| 66776 | **GB** | GB | GBNB | RR | Joanne |
| 66777 | **GB** | GB | GBNB | RR | Annette |
| 66778 | **GB** | GB | GBNB | RR | Cambois Depot 25 Years |
| 66779 | **0** | GB | GBEL | RR | EVENING STAR |

**66780–789. Standard design.** Former DB Cargo locomotives acquired by GB Railfreight in 2017. Details as Class 66/0. Fitted with Swinghead Automatic "Buckeye" Combination Couplers.

† Fitted with additional lights and drawgear formerly used for Lickey banking duties.

| 66780 | (66008) | | **AL** | GB | GBOB | RR | The Cemex Express |
| 66781 | (66016) | | **GB** | GB | GBOB | RR | |
| 66782 | (66046) | | **GB** | GB | GBOB | RR | |
| 66783 | (66058) † | | **AL** | GB | GBOB | RR | The Flying Dustman |
| 66784 | (66081) | | **GB** | GB | GBOB | RR | Keighley & Worth Valley |
| | | | | | | | Railway 50th Anniversary |
| | | | | | | | 1968–2018 |
| 66785 | (66132) | | **GB** | GB | GBOB | RR | |
| 66786 | (66141) | | **GB** | GB | GBOB | RR | |

| 66787 | (66184) | **GB** | GB | GBOB | RR | |
| 66788 | (66238) | **GB** | GB | GBOB | RR | LOCOMOTION 15 |
| 66789 | (66250) | **BL** | GB | GBOB | RR | British Rail 1948–1997 |

**66790–797.** Locomotives sourced from mainland Europe. 66795–797 due to arrive during 2021.

| 66790 | (T66403) | **GB** | BN | GBBT | RR | |
| 66791 | (T66404) | **O** | BN | GBBT | RR | Neil Bennett |
| 66792 | (T66405) | **GB** | BN | GBBT | RR | |
| 66793 | (29004) | **O** | BN | MBDL | RR (S) | Dave Meehan |
| 66794 | (29005) | **O** | BN | MBDL | LT (S) | Ted Gaffney |
| 66795 | | | BN | | | |
| 66796 | | | BN | | | |
| 66797 | (513-09) | **O** | BN | | | |

**Class 66/8. Standard design. Colas Rail locomotives.** Details as Class 66/0.

| 66846 | (66573) | **CS** | BN | COLO | HJ | |
| 66847 | (66574) | **CS** | BN | COLO | HJ | Terry Baker |
| 66848 | (66575) | **CS** | BN | COLO | HJ | |
| 66849 | (66576) | **CS** | BN | COLO | HJ | Wylam Dilly |
| 66850 | (66577) | **CS** | BN | COLO | HJ | David Maidment OBE |

**Class 66/9. Freightliner locomotives. Low emission "demonstrator" locomotives.** Details as Class 66/3. * **Fuel Capacity:** 5905 litres.

| 66951 | * | **FL** | E | DFIN | LD | |
| 66952 | | **FL** | E | DFIN | LD | |

**Class 66/5. Freightliner-operated low emission locomotives.** Owing to the 665xx number range being full, subsequent deliveries of 66/5s were numbered from 66953 onwards. Details as Class 66/5 (low emission).

| 66953 | **FL** | BN | DFIN | LD | |
| 66955 | **FL** | BN | DFIN | LD | |
| 66956 | **FL** | BN | DFIN | LD | |
| 66957 | **FL** | BN | DFIN | LD | Stephenson Locomotive Society 1909–2009 |

# CLASS 67    ALSTOM/GENERAL MOTORS    Bo-Bo

**Built:** 1999–2000 by Alstom at Valencia, Spain, as sub-contractors for General Motors (General Motors model JT42 HW-HS).
**Engine:** GM 12N-710G3B-EC two stroke of 2385 kW (3200 hp) at 904 rpm.
**Main Alternator:** General Motors AR9A/HEP7/CA6C.
**Traction Motors:** General Motors D43FM.
**Maximum Tractive Effort:** 141 kN (31770 lbf).
**Continuous Tractive Effort:** 90 kN (20200 lbf) at 46.5 mph.

| **Power at Rail:** 1860 kW. | **Train Brakes:** Air. |
| **Brake Force:** 78 t. | **Dimensions:** 19.74 x 2.72 m. |
| **Weight:** 90 t. | **Wheel Diameter:** 965 mm. |
| **Design Speed:** 125 mph. | **Maximum Speed:** 125 mph. |
| **Fuel Capacity:** 4927 litres. | **Route Availability:** 8. |

**Train Supply:** Electric, index 66.      **Total:** 30.

All equipped with Slow Speed Control and Swinghead Automatic "Buckeye" Combination Couplers.

The following locomotives have been modified to operate with TfW Mark 4 stock: 67008, 67010, 67014, 67015, 67017, 67025.

**Non-standard liveries:**

67026 Diamond Jubilee silver.
67029 All over silver with DB logos.

| | | | | |
|---|---|---|---|---|
| 67001 | **AB** | DB | WAAC | CE |
| 67002 | **AB** | DB | WAAC | CE |
| 67003 | **AB** | DB | WQBA | TO (S) |
| 67004 r | **DB** | DB | WQAB | TO (S) |
| 67005 | **RZ** | DB | WAAC | CE | Queen's Messenger |
| 67006 | **RZ** | DB | WAAC | CE | Royal Sovereign |
| 67007 r | **E** | DB | WAAC | CE |
| 67008 | **TW** | DB | WAWC | CE |
| 67009 r | **E** | DB | WQBA | CE (S) |
| 67010 | **DB** | DB | WAWC | CE |
| 67011 r | **E** | DB | WQBA | CE (S) |
| 67012 | **CM** | DB | WAAC | CE |
| 67013 | **DB** | DB | WAAC | CE |
| 67014 | **TW** | DB | WAWC | CE |
| 67015 | **DB** | DB | WAWC | CE |
| 67016 | **E** | DB | WAAC | CE |
| 67017 | **TW** | DB | WAWC | CE |
| 67018 | **DB** | DB | WQBA | CE (S) | Keith Heller |
| 67019 | **E** | DB | WQBA | TO (S) |
| 67020 | **E** | DB | WAAC | CE |
| 67021 | **PC** | DB | WAAC | CE |
| 67022 | **E** | DB | WQBA | CE (S) |
| 67023 | **CS** | BN | COTS | RU | Stella |
| 67024 | **PC** | DB | WAAC | CE |
| 67025 | **TW** | DB | WAWC | TO |
| 67026 | **O** | DB | WQBA | CE (S) | Diamond Jubilee |
| 67027 | **CS** | BN | COTS | RU | Charlotte |
| 67028 | **DB** | DB | WAAC | CE |
| 67029 | **O** | DB | WQAA | CE (S) | Royal Diamond |
| 67030 r | **E** | DB | WQAA | CE (S) |

---

# CLASS 68      VOSSLOH/STADLER      Bo-Bo

New Vossloh/Stadler mixed-traffic locomotives operated by DRS.

**Built:** 2012–16 by Vossloh/Stadler, Valencia, Spain.
**Engine:** Caterpillar C175-16 of 2800 kW (3750 hp) at 1740 rpm.
**Main Alternator:** ABB WGX560.
**Traction Motors:** 4 x AMXL400 AC frame mounted ABB 4FRA6063.
**Maximum Tractive Effort:** 317 kN (71260 lbf).

**Continuous Tractive Effort**: 258 kN (58000 lbf) at 20.5 mph.
**Power at Rail**:                          **Train Brakes**: Air & rheostatic.
**Brake Force**: 73 t.                      **Dimensions**: 20.50 x 2.69 m.
**Weight**: 85 t.                           **Wheel Diameter**: 1100 mm.
**Design Speed**: 100 mph.                  **Maximum Speed**: 100 mph.
**Fuel Capacity**: 5600 litres.             **Route Availability**: 7.
**Train Supply**: Electric, index 96.       **Total**: 34.

68008–015 have been modified to operate in push-pull mode on the Chiltern Railways locomotive-hauled sets.

68019–034 have been modified to operate in push-pull mode with the TransPennine Express Mark 5A stock.

| | | | | | |
|---|---|---|---|---|---|
| 68001 | **DI** | BN | XHVE | CR | Evolution |
| 68002 | **DI** | BN | XHVE | CR | Intrepid |
| 68003 | **DI** | BN | XHVE | CR | Astute |
| 68004 | **DI** | BN | XHVE | CR | Rapid |
| 68005 | **DI** | BN | XHVE | CR | Defiant |
| 68006 | **SR** | BN | XHVE | CR | Daring |
| 68007 | **SR** | BN | XHVE | CR | Valiant |
| 68008 | **DI** | BN | XHVE | CR | Avenger |
| 68009 | **DI** | BN | XHVE | CR | Titan |
| 68010 | **CM** | BN | XHCE | CR | Oxford Flyer |
| 68011 | **CM** | BN | XHCE | CR | |
| 68012 | **CM** | BN | XHCE | CR | |
| 68013 | **CM** | BN | XHCE | CR | |
| 68014 | **CM** | BN | XHCE | CR | |
| 68015 | **CM** | BN | XHCE | CR | |
| 68016 | **DI** | BN | XHVE | CR | Fearless |
| 68017 | **DI** | BN | XHVE | CR | Hornet |
| 68018 | **DI** | BN | XHVE | CR | Vigilant |
| 68019 | **TP** | BN | TPEX | CR | Brutus |
| 68020 | **TP** | BN | TPEX | CR | Reliance |
| 68021 | **TP** | BN | TPEX | CR | Tireless |
| 68022 | **TP** | BN | TPEX | CR | Resolution |
| 68023 | **TP** | BN | TPEX | CR | Achilles |
| 68024 | **TP** | BN | TPEX | CR | Centaur |
| 68025 | **TP** | BN | TPEX | CR | Superb |
| 68026 | **TP** | BN | TPEX | CR | Enterprise |
| 68027 | **TP** | BN | TPEX | CR | Splendid |
| 68028 | **TP** | BN | TPCF | CR | Lord President |
| 68029 | **TP** | BN | TPEX | CR | Courageous |
| 68030 | **TP** | BN | TPEX | CR | Black Douglas |
| 68031 | **TP** | BN | TPEX | CR | Felix |
| 68032 | **TP** | BN | TPEX | CR | Destroyer |
| 68033 | **DI** | DR | XHVE | CR | |
| 68034 | **DI** | DR | XHVE | CR | |

## CLASS 69          BRUSH/BR/RUSTON/EMD          Co-Co

These locomotives are heavy rebuilds of Class 56s for GB Railfreight, with new General Motors engines, the same type as used in the Class 66s. The first rebuild is due to be completed in early 2021 and it is planned that a total of 16 locomotives will be rebuilt. Full details awaited. Donor locomotives are provisional.

**Built:** 1976–84 by Electroputere at Craiova, Romania (as sub-contractors for Brush) or BREL at Doncaster or Crewe Works. Rebuilt 2019–22 by ElectroMotive Diesel Services, Longport.
**Engine:** General Motors 12N-710G3B-T2 two stroke of 2385 kW (3200 hp) at 904 rpm.
**Main Alternator:**
**Traction Motors:**
**Maximum Tractive Effort:**
**Continuous Tractive Effort:**
**Power at Rail:**                          **Train Brakes:** Air.
**Brake Force:**                            **Dimensions:** 19.36 x 2.79 m.
**Weight:**                                 **Wheel Diameter:**
**Design Speed:**                           **Maximum Speed:**
**Fuel Capacity:** 5200 litres.             **Route Availability:** 7.
**Train Supply:** Not equipped.             **Total:** 16.

69001 (56031)
69002 (56311)
69003 (56018)
69004 (56069)
69005 (56007)
69006
69007
69008
69009
69010
69011
69012
69013
69014
69015
69016

## CLASS 70          GENERAL ELECTRIC          Co-Co

GE "PowerHaul" locomotives. 70012 was badly damaged whilst being unloaded in 2011 and was returned to Pennsylvania.

70801 (built as 70099) is a Turkish-built demonstrator that arrived in Britain in 2012. Colas Rail leased this locomotive and then in 2013 ordered a further nine locomotives (70802–810) that were delivered in 2014. 70811–817 followed in 2017.

**Built:** 2009–17 by General Electric, Erie, Pennsylvania, USA or by TÜLOMSAS, Eskişehir, Turkey (70801).

▲ 08598 and 08600 are seen at AV Dawson's rail terminal in Middlesbrough on 25/07/20. **Andrew Mason**

▼ HNRC-liveried 09106 / "6" shunts at the Celsa Steel UK terminal in Cardiff on 25/06/20. **Martin Turner**

▲ In white livery and carrying internal No. "3", 20906 is seen at Earles Sidings having hauled a train from Hope Cement Works on 22/08/20.  **Ian Beardsley**

▼ BR blue-liveried 31128 passes Barrow-on-Trent with 5Z34 12.50 Barrow Hill–Lichfield TV Sidings empty stock on 18/11/19.  **John Coleman**

▲ West Coast Railway Company maroon-liveried 33029 leads a London Paddington–Lancaster Branch Line Society railtour at Coventry on 09/03/20.
**Brad Joyce**

▼ Europhoenix-liveried 37608 "Andromeda" passes Hodthorpe, near Whitwell, with a 11.01 Worksop Down Yard–Old Dalby hauling Elizabeth Line EMU 345 045 on 18/05/20.
**Ian Beardsley**

▲ BR Blue-liveried 40145 passes Blea Moor, near Ribblehead, with the 14.38 Appleby–Skipton Rail Charter Services train on 12/09/20.　**Dave Gommersall**

▼ Great Western Railway-liveried "Castle Class" four-coach HST 43016+43160 passes Bethany, near Saltash, with the 13.11 Penzance–Plymouth on 13/09/20.
**Tony Christie**

▲ CrossCountry HST 43301+43357 is seen at Woodhouse with the diverted 09.27 Plymouth–Glasgow Central on 12/07/20. **Ian Beardsley**

▼ BR two-tone green-liveried 47805 passes Besford, Worcestershire with 5Z47 11.31 Long Marston–Eastleigh Works stock movement on 12/03/20. **Dave Gommersall**

▲ BR blue-liveried 50008 is seen at Besford hauling 20132, 20118 and 56091 from Leicester to Bristol Barton Hill on 03/12/19. **Dave Gommersall**

▼ Devon & Cornwall Railways-liveried 56103 passes Loughborough with 4Z20 17.58 Leicester Humberstone Road–Chaddesden Sidings box wagons on 13/06/20. **Paul Biggs**

▲ Pullman-liveried 57313 and 57601 pass Stafford with a 5M43 Southall–Carnforth stock movement on 16/03/20
**Brad Joyce**

▼ New Freightliner-liveried 59206 passes Hungerford Common with 7C64 15.25 Acton–Merehead stone empties on 17/09/20.
**Tony Bartlett**

▲ GBRf-liveried 60021 is seen at Marcheys House Junction on the Blyth & Tyne line with 6N85 08.41 Lynemouth Power Station–Tyne Dock biomass empties on 04/09/20. **Jamie Squibbs**

▼ Cappagh-liveried and DC Rail-operated 60028 passes Saxilby with 6Z63 15.00 Rossington–Chaddesden Sidings (Derby) empty box wagons on 08/08/20. **Robert Pritchard**

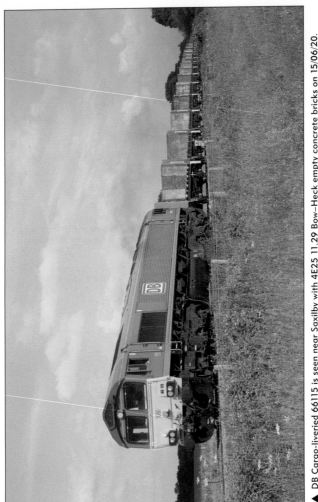

▲ DB Cargo-liveried 66115 is seen near Saxilby with 4E25 11.29 Bow–Heck empty concrete bricks on 15/06/20. **Robert Pritchard**

▲ GBRf-liveried 66769 is seen near Saxilby with 4Z81 11.34 Rotherham Masborough–Felixstowe intermodal on 16/04/20. **Robert Pritchard**

▼ Colas Rail-liveried 67027 and 67023 top-and-tail a Tyseley–Weymouth Network Rail test train at Wyke Champflower, near Bruton, on 12/08/20. **Glen Batten**

▲ TransPennine Express-liveried 68032 "Destroyer" leaves Seamer hauling a set of Mark 5A coaches on the 09.57 Scarborough–York on 08/08/20 (terminating at York due to engineering works). **Andrew Mason**

▲ Colas Rail-liveried 70805 passes Saxilby with 6E98 20.45 Aberdeen–Spalding china clay slurry on 02/06/20. **Robert Pritchard**

▼ Network Rail yellow-liveried 73952 is seen on display at the Locomotive Services Crewe open day on 08/06/19. **Robert Pritchard**

▲ Freightliner-liveried 86639+86609 pass Grendon, Northamptonshire with 4L97 06.15 Trafford Park–Felixstowe intermodal on 07/08/20.
**Andrew Mason**

▲ New DRS-liveried 88005 passes Carluke with 4S44 12.16 Daventry–Mossend intermodal on 20/05/20. **Robin Ralston**

▼ InterCity-liveried 90002 leads DVT 82139 and a set of Mark 3 coaches through Winwick with 5Z92 12.33 Preston–Crewe test run on 21/09/20. **Alan Hart**

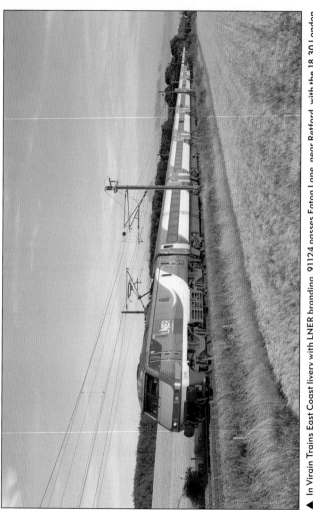

▲ In Virgin Trains East Coast livery with LNER branding, 91124 passes Eaton Lane, near Retford, with the 18.30 London King's Cross–Edinburgh on 06/08/20. **Ian Beardsley**

▲ GBRf-liveried 92043 passes Leggatfoot, south of Carstairs, with the previous evening's 23.50 London Euston–Glasgow Central/Edinburgh Lowland Sleeper on 28/06/19. **Robin Ralston**

▼ Eurotunnel Class 9/8 9809 leaves the Cheriton terminal before entering the Channel Tunnel with a car shuttle on 05/08/18. **Robert Pritchard**

**Engine:** General Electric PowerHaul P616LDA1 of 2848 kW (3820 hp) at 1500 rpm.
**Main Alternator:** General Electric GTA series.
**Traction Motors:** AC-GE 5GEB30.
**Maximum Tractive Effort:** 544 kN (122000 lbf).
**Continuous Tractive Effort:** 427 kN (96000 lbf) at 11 mph.

| | |
|---|---|
| **Power at Rail:** | **Train Brakes:** Air. |
| **Brake Force:** 96.7 t. | **Dimensions:** 21.71 x 2.64 m. |
| **Weight:** 129 t. | **Wheel Diameter:** 1066 mm. |
| **Design Speed:** 75 mph. | **Maximum Speed:** 75 mph. |
| **Fuel Capacity:** 6000 litres. | **Route Availability:** 7. |
| **Train Supply:** Not equipped. | **Total:** 36. |

## Class 70/0. Freightliner locomotives.

| | | | | | |
|---|---|---|---|---|---|
| 70001 | **FH** | AK | DFGI | LD | PowerHaul |
| 70002 | **FH** | AK | DFGI | LD | |
| 70003 | **FH** | AK | DFGI | LD | |
| 70004 | **FH** | AK | DFGI | LD | The Coal Industry Society |
| 70005 | **FH** | AK | DFGI | LD | |
| 70006 | **FH** | AK | DFGI | LD | |
| 70007 | **FH** | AK | DFGI | LD | |
| 70008 | **FH** | AK | DFGI | LD | |
| 70009 | **FH** | AK | DHLT | LD (S) | |
| 70010 | **FH** | AK | DFGI | LD | |
| 70011 | **FH** | AK | DFGI | LD | |
| 70013 | **FH** | AK | DHLT | LD (S) | |
| 70014 | **FH** | AK | DFGI | LD | |
| 70015 | **FH** | AK | DFGI | LD | |
| 70016 | **FH** | AK | DFGI | LD | |
| 70017 | **FH** | AK | DFGI | LD | |
| 70018 | **FH** | AK | DHLT | LD (S) | |
| 70019 | **FH** | AK | DFGI | LD | |
| 70020 | **FH** | AK | DFGI | LD | |

## Class 70/8. Colas Rail locomotives.

| | | | | |
|---|---|---|---|---|
| 70801 | **CS** | LF | COLO | CF |
| 70802 | **CS** | LF | COLO | CF |
| 70803 | **CS** | LF | COLO | CF |
| 70804 | **CS** | LF | COLO | CF |
| 70805 | **CS** | LF | COLO | CF |
| 70806 | **CS** | LF | COLO | CF |
| 70807 | **CS** | LF | COLO | CF |
| 70808 | **CS** | LF | COLO | CF |
| 70809 | **CS** | LF | COLO | CF |
| 70810 | **CS** | LF | COLO | CF |
| 70811 | **CS** | BN | COLO | CF |
| 70812 | **CS** | BN | COLO | CF |
| 70813 | **CS** | BN | COLO | CF |
| 70814 | **CS** | BN | COLO | CF |
| 70815 | **CS** | BN | COLO | CF |
| 70816 | **CS** | BN | COLO | CF |
| 70817 | **CS** | BN | COLO | CF |

# 1.3. ELECTRO-DIESEL & ELECTRIC LOCOMOTIVES

## CLASS 73/1          BR/ENGLISH ELECTRIC          Bo-Bo

Electro-diesel locomotives which can operate either from a DC supply or using power from a diesel engine.

**Built:** 1965–67 by English Electric Co. at Vulcan Foundry, Newton-le-Willows.
**Engine:** English Electric 4SRKT of 447 kW (600 hp) at 850 rpm.
**Main Generator:** English Electric 824/5D.
**Electric Supply System:** 750 V DC from third rail.
**Traction Motors:** English Electric 546/1B.
**Maximum Tractive Effort (Electric):** 179 kN (40000 lbf).
**Maximum Tractive Effort (Diesel):** 160 kN (36000 lbf).
**Continuous Rating (Electric):** 1060 kW (1420 hp) giving a tractive effort of 35 kN (7800 lbf) at 68 mph.
**Continuous Tractive Effort (Diesel):** 60 kN (13600 lbf) at 11.5 mph.
**Maximum Rail Power:** 2350 kW (3150 hp) at 42 mph.
**Train Brakes:** Air, vacuum & electro-pneumatic († Air & electro-pneumatic).
**Brake Force:** 31 t.                    **Dimensions:** 16.36 x 2.64 m.
**Weight:** 77 t.                         **Wheel Diameter:** 1016 mm.
**Design Speed:** 90 mph.                 **Maximum Speed:** 90 mph.
**Fuel Capacity:** 1409 litres.           **Route Availability:** 6.
**Train Supply:** Electric, index 66 (on electric power only). **Total:** 30.

Formerly numbered E6007–E6020/E6022–E6026/E6028–E6049 (not in order).

Locomotives numbered in the 732xx series are classed as 73/2 and were originally dedicated to Gatwick Express services.

There have been two separate Class 73 rebuild projects. For GBRf 11 locomotives were rebuilt at Brush, Loughborough with a 1600 hp MTU engine (renumbered 73961–971). For Network Rail 73104/211 were rebuilt at RVEL Derby (now LORAM) with 2 x QSK19 750 hp engines (73951/952).

**Non-standard liveries and numbering:**

73110   Carries original number E6016.
73128   Two-tone grey.
73139   Light blue & light grey.
73235   Plain dark blue.

| 73101 | **PC** | GB | GBSD | ZG (S) | |
| 73107 | **GB** | GB | GBED | SE | Tracy |
| 73109 | **GB** | GB | GBED | SE | Battle of Britain 80th Anniversary |
| 73110 | **B** | GB | GBBR | ZG (S) | |
| 73119 | **GB** | GB | GBED | SE | Borough of Eastleigh |
| 73128 | **GB** | GB | GBED | SE | O.V.S. BULLEID C.B.E. |
| 73133 | **TT** | TT | MBED | ZG | |
| 73134 | **IC** | GB | GBBR | LB (S) | Woking Homes 1885–1985 |

| 73136 | **GB** | GB | GBED | SE | Mhairi |
|--------|--------|----|------|-----|--------|
| 73138 | **Y** | NR | QADD | ZA | |
| 73139 | **O** | GB | GBSD | ZG (S) | |
| 73141 | **GB** | GB | GBED | SE | Charlotte |
| 73201 † | **B** | GB | GBED | SE | Broadlands |
| 73202 † | **SN** | P | MBED | SL | Graham Stenning |
| 73212 † | **GB** | GB | GBED | SE | Fiona |
| 73213 † | **GB** | GB | GBED | SE | Rhodalyn |
| 73235 † | **O** | P | HYWD | BM | |

## CLASS 73/9 (RVEL)   BR/RVEL                          Bo-Bo

The 7395x number series was used for rebuilt Network Rail locomotives.

**Rebuilt:** Re-engineered by RVEL Derby 2013–15.
**Engine:** 2 x QSK19 of 560 kW (750 hp) at 1800 rpm (total 1120 kW (1500 hp)).
**Main Alternator:** 2 x Marathon Magnaplus.
**Electric Supply System:** 750 V DC from third rail.
**Traction Motors:** English Electric 546/1B.
**Maximum Tractive Effort (Electric):** 179 kN (40000 lbf).
**Maximum Tractive Effort (Diesel):** 179 kN (40000 lbf).
**Continuous Rating (Electric):** 1060 kW (1420 hp) giving a tractive effort of 35 kN (7800 lbf) at 68 mph.
**Continuous Tractive Effort (Diesel):** 990 kW (1328 hp) giving a tractive effort of 33 kN (7420 lbf) at 68 mph.
**Maximum Rail Power (Electric):** 2350 kW (3150 hp) at 42 mph.
**Train Brakes:** Air.                    **Brake Force:** 31 t.
**Weight:** 77 t.                         **Dimensions:** 16.36 x 2.64 m.
**Maximum Speed:** 90 mph.                **Wheel Diameter:** 1016 mm.
**Fuel Capacity:** 2260 litres.           **Route Availability:** 6.
**Train Supply:** Not equipped.

| 73951 | (73104) | **Y** | LO | QADD | ZA | Malcolm Brinded |
|--------|---------|-------|----|------|-----|------------------|
| 73952 | (73211) | **Y** | LO | QADD | ZA | Janis Kong |

## CLASS 73/9 (GBRf)   BR/BRUSH                         Bo-Bo

GBRf Class 73s rebuilt at Brush Loughborough. 73961–965 are normally used on Network Rail contracts and 73966–971 are used by Caledonian Sleeper.

**Rebuilt:** Re-engineered by Brush, Loughborough 2014–16.
**Engine:** MTU 8V4000 R43L of 1195 kW (1600 hp) at 1800 rpm.
**Main Alternator:** Lechmotoren SDV 87.53-12.
**Electric Supply System:** 750 V DC from third rail (73961–965 only).
**Traction Motors:** English Electric 546/1B.
**Maximum Tractive Effort (Electric):** 179 kN (40000 lbf).
**Maximum Tractive Effort (Diesel):** 179 kN (40000 lbf).
**Continuous Rating (Electric):** 1060 kW (1420 hp) giving a tractive effort of 35 kN (7800 lbf) at 68 mph.
**Continuous Tractive Effort (Diesel):**

**Maximum Rail Power (Electric):** 2350 kW (3150 hp) at 42 mph.
**Train Brakes:** Air.                          **Brake Force:** 31 t.
**Weight:** 77 t.                               **Dimensions:** 16.36 x 2.64 m.
**Maximum Speed:** 90 mph.                      **Wheel Diameter:** 1016 mm.
**Fuel Capacity:** 1409 litres.                 **Route Availability:** 6.
**Train Supply:** Electric, index 38 (electric & diesel).

| | | | | | |
|---|---|---|---|---|---|
| 73961 | (73209) | **GB** GB | GBNR | SE | Alison |
| 73962 | (73204) | **GB** GB | GBNR | SE | Dick Mabbutt |
| 73963 | (73206) | **GB** GB | GBNR | SE | Janice |
| 73964 | (73205) | **GB** GB | GBNR | SE | Jeanette |
| 73965 | (73208) | **GB** GB | GBNR | SE | |

73966–971 have been rebuilt for Caledonian Sleeper but their third rail
electric capability has been retained. They have a higher Train Supply index
and a slightly higher fuel capacity. Details as 73961–965 except:
**Fuel Capacity:** 1509 litres.               **Train Supply:** Electric, index 96.

73005 and 73006 were originally assembled at Eastleigh Works.

| | | | | |
|---|---|---|---|---|
| 73966 | (73005) d | **CA** GB | GBCS | EC |
| 73967 | (73006) d | **CA** GB | GBCS | EC |
| 73968 | (73117) d | **CA** GB | GBCS | EC |
| 73969 | (73105) d | **CA** GB | GBCS | EC |
| 73970 | (73103) d | **CA** GB | GBCS | EC |
| 73971 | (73207) d | **CA** GB | GBCS | EC |

# CLASS 86          BR/ENGLISH ELECTRIC          Bo-Bo

**Built:** 1965–66 by English Electric Co at Vulcan Foundry, Newton-le-Willows
or by BR at Doncaster Works.
**Electric Supply System:** 25 kV AC 50 Hz overhead.
**Traction Motors:** AEI 282BZ axle hung.
**Maximum Tractive Effort:** 207 kN (46500 lbf).
**Continuous Rating:** 3010 kW (4040 hp) giving a tractive effort of 85 kN
(19200 lbf) at 77.5 mph.
**Maximum Rail Power:** 4550 kW (6100 hp) at 49.5 mph.
**Train Brakes:** Air.                          **Brake Force:** 40 t.
**Dimensions:** 17.83 x 2.65 m.                 **Weight:** 83–86.8 t.
**Wheel Diameter:** 1156 mm.                    **Train Supply:** Electric, index 74.
**Design Speed:** 110–125 mph.                  **Maximum Speed:** 100 mph.
**Route Availability:** 6.                      **Total:** 21.

Formerly numbered E3101–E3200 (not in order).

Class 86s exported for use abroad are listed in section 1.6 of this book.

**Class 86/1. Class 87-type bogies & motors.** Details as above except:

**Traction Motors:** GEC 412AZ frame mounted.
**Maximum Tractive Effort:** 258 kN (58000 lbf).
**Continuous Rating:** 3730 kW (5000 hp) giving a tractive effort of 95 kN
(21300 lbf) at 87 mph.
**Maximum Rail Power:** 5860 kW (7860 hp) at 50.8 mph.

**Wheel Diameter:** 1150 mm.
**Design Speed:** 110 mph.          **Maximum Speed:** 110 mph.

| 86101 | **IC** | LS | LSLO | CL | Sir William A Stanier FRS |

**Class 86/2. Standard design rebuilt with resilient wheels & Flexicoil suspension.** Details as in main class heading.

**Non-standard livery:**

86259 BR "Electric blue". Also carries number E3137.

| 86251 | **V** | FL | EPEX | CB (S) | |
| 86259 x | **0** | PP | MBEL | WN | Les Ross/Peter Pan |

**Class 86/4.** Details as Class 86/2 except:

**Traction Motors:** AEI 282AZ axle hung.
**Maximum Tractive Effort:** 258 kN (58000 lbf).
**Continuous Rating:** 2680 kW (3600 hp) giving a tractive effort of 89 kN (20000 lbf) at 67 mph.
**Maximum Rail Power:** 4400 kW (5900 hp) at 38 mph.
**Weight:** 83–83.9 t.
**Design Speed:** 100 mph.          **Maximum Speed:** 100 mph.

| 86401 | **CA** | WC | MBEL | CS | Mons Meg |

**Class 86/6. Freightliner-operated locomotives.**

Previously numbered in the Class 86/0 and 86/4 series'. 86608 was also regeared and renumbered 86501 between 2000 and 2016.

Details as Class 86/4 except:
**Traction Motors:** AEI 282AZ axle hung.
**Maximum Speed:** 75 mph.          **Train Supply:** Electric, isolated.

| 86604 | **FL** | FL | DHLT | CB (S) |
| 86605 | **FL** | FL | DHLT | CB (S) |
| 86607 | **FL** | FL | DHLT | CB (S) |
| 86608 | **FL** | FL | DFNC | CB |
| 86609 | **FL** | FL | DFNC | CB |
| 86610 | **FL** | FL | DHLT | CB (S) |
| 86612 | **FL** | FL | DHLT | CB (S) |
| 86613 | **FL** | FL | DFNC | CB |
| 86614 | **FL** | FL | DHLT | CB (S) |
| 86622 | **FH** | FL | DHLT | CB (S) |
| 86627 | **FL** | FL | DHLT | CB (S) |
| 86628 | **FL** | FL | DHLT | CB (S) |
| 86632 | **FL** | FL | DFNC | CB |
| 86637 | **FH** | FL | DHLT | CB (S) |
| 86638 | **FL** | FL | DFNC | CB |
| 86639 | **FL** | FL | DFNC | CB |

# CLASS 87        BREL/GEC        Bo-Bo

**Built:** 1973–75 by BREL at Crewe Works.
**Electric Supply System:** 25 kV AC 50 Hz overhead.
**Traction Motors:** GEC G412AZ frame mounted.
**Maximum Tractive Effort:** 258 kN (58000 lbf).
**Continuous Rating:** 3730 kW (5000 hp) giving a tractive effort of 95 kN (21300 lbf) at 87 mph.
**Maximum Rail Power:** 5860 kW (7860 hp) at 50.8 mph.

| | |
|---|---|
| **Train Brakes:** Air. | **Brake Force:** 40 t. |
| **Dimensions:** 17.83 x 2.65 m. | **Weight:** 83.3 t. |
| **Wheel Diameter:** 1150 mm. | **Train Supply:** Electric, index 95. |
| **Design Speed:** 110 mph. | **Maximum Speed:** 110 mph. |
| **Route Availability:** 6. | **Total:** 1. |

Class 87s exported for use abroad are listed in section 1.6 of this book.

87002    **IC**  LS   LSLO         CL       Royal Sovereign

# CLASS 88        VOSSLOH/STADLER        Bo-Bo

New Vossloh/Stadler bi-mode DRS locomotives.

**Built:** 2015–16 by Vossloh/Stadler, Valencia, Spain.
**Electric Supply System:** 25 kV AC 50 Hz overhead.
**Engine:** Caterpillar C27 12-cylinder of 708 kW (950 hp) at 1750 rpm.
**Main Alternator:** ABB AMXL400.
**Traction Motors:** ABB AMXL400.
**Maximum Tractive Effort (Electric):** 317 kN (71 260 lbf).
**Maximum Tractive Effort (Diesel):** 317 kN (71 260 lbf).
**Continuous Rating:** 4000 kW (5360 hp) giving a tractive effort of 258 kN (58000 lbf) at 28 mph (electric).
**Maximum Rail Power:**
**Train Brakes:** Air, regenerative & rheostatic.

| | |
|---|---|
| **Brake Force:** 73 t. | **Dimensions:** 20.50 x 2.69 m. |
| **Weight:** 85 t. | **Wheel Diameter:** 1100 mm. |
| **Fuel Capacity:** 1800 litres. | **Train Supply:** Electric, index 96. |
| **Design Speed:** 100 mph. | **Maximum Speed:** 100 mph. |
| **Route Availability:** 7. | **Total:** 10. |

| | | | | | |
|---|---|---|---|---|---|
| 88001 | **DI** | BN | XHVE | KM | Revolution |
| 88002 | **DI** | BN | XHVE | KM | Prometheus |
| 88003 | **DI** | BN | XHVE | KM | Genesis |
| 88004 | **DI** | BN | XHVE | KM | Pandora |
| 88005 | **DI** | BN | XHVE | KM | Minerva |
| 88006 | **DI** | BN | XHVE | KM | Juno |
| 88007 | **DI** | BN | XHVE | KM | Electra |
| 88008 | **DI** | BN | XHVE | KM | Ariadne |
| 88009 | **DI** | BN | XHVE | KM | Diana |
| 88010 | **DI** | BN | XHVE | KM | Aurora |

# CLASS 90     GEC     Bo-Bo

**Built:** 1987–90 by BREL at Crewe Works (as sub-contractors for GEC).
**Electric Supply System:** 25 kV AC 50 Hz overhead.
**Traction Motors:** GEC G412CY frame mounted.
**Maximum Tractive Effort:** 258 kN (58000 lbf).
**Continuous Rating:** 3730 kW (5000 hp) giving a tractive effort of 95 kN (21300 lbf) at 87 mph.
**Maximum Rail Power:** 5860 kW (7860 hp) at 68.3 mph.

| | |
|---|---|
| **Train Brakes:** Air. | **Dimensions:** 18.80 x 2.74 m. |
| **Brake Force:** 40 t. | **Wheel Diameter:** 1150 mm. |
| **Weight:** 84.5 t. | **Maximum Speed:** 110 mph. |
| **Design Speed:** 110 mph. | **Route Availability:** 7. |
| **Train Supply:** Electric, index 95. | **Total:** 50. |

**Advertising liveries:**

90024    Malcolm Logistics (blue).
90039    I am the backbone of the economy (black).

| | | | | | |
|---|---|---|---|---|---|
| 90001 | b | **IC** | LS | LSLO | CL | Royal Scot |
| 90002 | b | **IC** | LS | LSLO | CL | Wolf of Badenoch |
| 90003 | b | **GA** | FL | DFLC | CB | |
| 90004 | b | **GA** | FL | DFLC | CB | City of Chelmsford |
| 90005 | b | **GA** | FL | DFLC | CB | Vice-Admiral Lord Nelson |
| 90006 | b | **GA** | FL | DFLC | CB | Modern Railways Magazine/ Roger Ford |
| 90007 | b | **GA** | FL | DFLC | CB | Sir John Betjeman |
| 90008 | b | **GA** | FL | DFLC | CB | The East Anglian |
| 90009 | b | **GA** | FL | DFLC | CB | |
| 90010 | b | **GA** | FL | DFLC | CB | |
| 90011 | b | **GA** | FL | DFLC | CB | East Anglian Daily Times Suffolk & Proud |
| 90012 | b | **GA** | FL | DFLC | CB | Royal Anglian Regiment |
| 90013 | b | **GA** | FL | DFLC | CB | |
| 90014 | b | **FG** | FL | DFLC | CB | Over the Rainbow |
| 90015 | b | **GA** | FL | DFLC | CB | Colchester Castle |
| 90016 | | **FL** | FL | DFLC | CB | |
| 90017 | | **E** | DB | WQAB | CE (S) | |
| 90018 | | **DB** | DB | WQAB | CE (S) | The Pride of Bellshill |
| 90019 | | **DB** | DB | WEDC | CE | Multimodal |
| 90020 | | **GC** | DB | WEDC | CE | |
| 90021 | | **FS** | DB | WQAA | CE (S) | |
| 90022 | | **EG** | DB | WQBA | CE (S) | Freightconnection |
| 90023 | | **E** | DB | WQBA | CE (S) | |
| 90024 | | **AL** | DB | WEAC | CE | |
| 90025 | | **F** | DB | WQBA | CE (S) | |
| 90026 | | **GC** | DB | WEDC | CE | |
| 90027 | | **F** | DB | WQBA | CE (S) | Allerton T&RS Depot |
| 90028 | | **DB** | DB | WEDC | CE | Sir William McAlpine |
| 90029 | | **GC** | DB | WEDC | CE | |
| 90030 | | **E** | DB | WQBA | CE (S) | |

| 90031 | E | DB | WQBA | CE (S) | The Railway Children Partnership Working For Street Children Worldwide |
|---|---|---|---|---|---|
| 90032 | E | DB | WQBA | CE (S) | |
| 90033 | FE | DB | WQBA | CE (S) | |
| 90034 | DR | DB | WEDC | CE | |
| 90035 | DB | DB | WEAC | CE | |
| 90036 | DB | DB | WEDC | CE | Driver Jack Mills |
| 90037 | DB | DB | WEAC | CE | Christine |
| 90038 | FE | DB | WQBA | CE (S) | |
| 90039 | AL | DB | WQAA | CE (S) | |
| 90040 | DB | DB | WQAA | CE (S) | |
| 90041 | FL | FL | DFLC | CB | |
| 90042 | FH | FL | DFLC | CB | |
| 90043 | FH | FL | DFLC | CB | |
| 90044 | FG | FL | DFLC | CB | |
| 90045 | FH | FL | DFLC | CB | |
| 90046 | FL | FL | DFLC | CB | |
| 90047 | FG | FL | DFLC | CB | |
| 90048 | FF | FL | DFLC | CB | |
| 90049 | FH | FL | DFLC | CB | |
| 90050 | FF | AV | DHLT | CB (S) | |

# CLASS 91                 GEC                          Bo-Bo

**Built:** 1988–91 by BREL at Crewe Works (as sub-contractors for GEC).
**Electric Supply System:** 25 kV AC 50 Hz overhead.
**Traction Motors:** GEC G426AZ.
**Maximum Tractive Effort:** 190 kN (43 000 lbf).
**Continuous Rating:** 4540 kW (6090 hp) giving a tractive effort of 170 kN at 96 mph.
**Maximum Rail Power:** 4700 kW (6300 hp) at ?? mph.

| | |
|---|---|
| **Train Brakes:** Air. | **Dimensions:** 19.41 x 2.74 m. |
| **Brake Force:** 45 t. | **Wheel Diameter:** 1000 mm. |
| **Weight:** 84 t. | **Maximum Speed:** 125 mph. |
| **Design Speed:** 140 mph. | **Route Availability:** 7. |
| **Train Supply:** Electric, index 95. | **Total:** 31. |

Locomotives were originally numbered in the 910xx series, but were renumbered upon completion of overhauls at Bombardier, Doncaster by the addition of 100 to their original number. The exception to this rule was 91023 which was renumbered 91132.

**Advertising liveries:**

91101 Flying Scotsman (red, white & purple).
91110 Battle of Britain (black and grey).
91111 For the fallen (various with poppy and Union Jack vinyls).

| 91101 | AL | E | IECA | BN | FLYING SCOTSMAN |
|---|---|---|---|---|---|
| 91102 | VE | E | SAXL | DR (S) | City of York |
| 91103 | VE | E | SAXL | ZB (S) | |
| 91104 | VE | E | SAXL | DR (S) | |

| 91105 | **VE** | E  | IECA | BN     |                                      |
|-------|--------|----|------|--------|--------------------------------------|
| 91106 | **VE** | E  | IECA | BN     |                                      |
| 91107 | **VE** | E  | IECA | BN     | SKYFALL                              |
| 91108 | **VE** | E  | SAXL | ZB (S) |                                      |
| 91109 | **VE** | E  | IECA | BN     | Sir Bobby Robson                     |
| 91110 | **AL** | E  | IECA | BN     | BATTLE OF BRITAIN MEMORIAL FLIGHT    |
| 91111 | **AL** | E  | IECA | BN     | For the Fallen                       |
| 91112 | **VE** | E  | SAXL | DR (S) |                                      |
| 91113 | **VE** | E  | SAXL | DR (S) |                                      |
| 91114 | **VE** | E  | IECA | BN     | Durham Cathedral                     |
| 91115 | **VE** | E  | SAXL | DR (S) | Blaydon Races                        |
| 91116 | **VE** | E  | SAXL | DR (S) |                                      |
| 91117 | **EX** | EP | EPEX | DR (S) |                                      |
| 91118 | **VE** | E  | SAXL | DR (S) | The Fusiliers                        |
| 91119 | **IC** | E  | IECA | BN     | Bounds Green INTERCITY Depot 1977–2017 |
| 91120 | **EX** | EP | EPEX | DR (S) |                                      |
| 91121 | **VE** | E  | SAXL | DR (S) |                                      |
| 91122 | **VE** | E  | EROG | LR     |                                      |
| 91124 | **VE** | E  | IECA | BN     |                                      |
| 91125 | **VE** | E  | SAXL | DR (S) |                                      |
| 91126 | **VE** | E  | SAXL | DR (S) | Darlington Hippodrome                |
| 91127 | **VE** | E  | IECA | BN     |                                      |
| 91128 | **VE** | E  | EROG | LR     | INTERCITY 50                         |
| 91129 | **VE** | E  | SAXL | DR (S) |                                      |
| 91130 | **VE** | E  | IECA | BN     | Lord Mayor of Newcastle              |
| 91131 | **VE** | E  | SAXL | DR (S) |                                      |
| 91132 | **VE** | E  | SAXL | DR (S) |                                      |

---

# CLASS 92     BRUSH     Co-Co

**Built:** 1993–96 by Brush Traction at Loughborough.
**Electric Supply System:** 25 kV AC 50 Hz overhead or 750 V DC third rail.
**Traction Motors:** Asea Brown Boveri design. Model 6FRA 7059B (Asynchronous 3-phase induction motors).
**Maximum Tractive Effort:** 400 kN (90 000 lbf).
**Continuous Rating:** 5040 kW (6760 hp) on AC, 4000 kW (5360 hp) on DC.

| | |
|---|---|
| **Maximum Rail Power:** | **Train Brakes:** Air. |
| **Brake Force:** 63 t. | **Dimensions:** 21.34 x 2.67 m. |
| **Weight:** 126 t. | **Wheel Diameter:** 1070 mm. |
| **Design Speed:** 140 km/h (87 mph). | **Maximum Speed:** 140 km/h (87 mph). |

**Train Supply:** Electric, index 180 (AC), 108 (DC).
**Route Availability:** 7.       **Total:** 33.

* Fitted with TVM430 signalling equipment to operate on High Speed 1.

Class 92s exported for use abroad are listed in section 1.6 of this book.

**Advertising livery:** 92017 Stobart Rail (two-tone blue & white).

| 92004 |      | **EG** | DB | WQBA | CE (S) | Jane Austen |
| 92006 | d    | **CA** | GB | GBSL | WB     |             |
| 92007 |      | **EG** | DB | WQBA | CE (S) | Schubert    |
| 92008 |      | **EG** | DB | WQBA | CE (S) | Jules Verne |
| 92009 | *    | **DB** | DB | WQBA | CE (S) | Marco Polo  |
| 92010 | *d   | **CA** | GB | GBST | WB     |             |
| 92011 | *    | **EG** | DB | WFBC | CE     | Handel      |
| 92013 |      | **EG** | DB | WQBA | CE (S) | Puccini     |
| 92014 | d    | **CA** | GB | GBSL | WB     |             |
| 92015 | *    | **DB** | DB | WFBC | CE     |             |
| 92016 | *    | **DB** | DB | WQBA | CE (S) |             |
| 92017 |      | **AL** | DB | WQBA | CE (S) | Bart the Engine |
| 92018 | *d   | **CA** | GB | GBST | WB     |             |
| 92019 | *    | **EG** | DB | WFBC | CE     | Wagner      |
| 92020 | d    | **GB** | GB | GBSL | WB     |             |
| 92021 |      | **EP** | GB | GBSD | LB (S) | Purcell     |
| 92023 | *d   | **CA** | GB | GBSL | WB     |             |
| 92028 | d    | **GB** | GB | GBST | WB     |             |
| 92029 |      | **EG** | DB | WQAB | CE (S) | Dante       |
| 92031 | *    | **DB** | DB | WQBA | CE (S) |             |
| 92032 | *d   | **GB** | GB | GBCT | WB     | IMechE Railway Division |
| 92033 | d    | **CA** | GB | GBSL | WB     |             |
| 92035 |      | **EG** | DB | WQBA | CE (S) | Mendelssohn |
| 92036 | *    | **EG** | DB | WFBC | CE     | Bertolt Brecht |
| 92037 |      | **EG** | DB | WQBA | CE (S) | Sullivan    |
| 92038 | *d   | **CA** | GB | GBST | WB     |             |
| 92040 |      | **EP** | GB | GBSD | LB (S) | Goethe      |
| 92041 | *    | **EG** | DB | WFBC | CE     | Vaughan Williams |
| 92042 | *    | **DB** | DB | WFBC | CE     |             |
| 92043 | *d   | **GB** | GB | GBST | WB     |             |
| 92044 | *    | **EP** | GB | GBCT | WB     | Couperin    |
| 92045 |      | **EP** | GB | GBSD | LB (S) | Chaucer     |
| 92046 |      | **EP** | GB | GBSD | LB (S) | Sweelinck   |

# CLASS 93    STADLER    Bo-Bo

In January 2021 Rail Operations Group placed an order with Stadler for an initial ten Class 93 mixed-traffic tri-mode locomotives, as part of a framework agreement for up to 30 of the type. The locomotive is a development of the DRS Class 88 and as well as having a more powerful diesel engine and electric capability will be fitted with batteries and a slightly higher maximum speed of 110 mph. The locomotives are due to be delivered in early 2023 and are being funded by Beacon Rail. Full details awaited.

**Built:** 2021–23 by Stadler, Valencia, Spain.
**Electric Supply System:** 25 kV AC 50 Hz overhead.
**Engine:** Caterpillar C32 12-cylinder of 900 kW (1205 hp) at      rpm.
**Batteries:** Two LTO battery packs providing 400 kW (535 hp).
**Main Alternator:**
**Traction Motors:**
**Maximum Tractive Effort (Electric):**
**Maximum Tractive Effort (Diesel):**
**Continuous Rating:** 4000 kW (5360 hp).
**Maximum Rail Power:**
**Train Brakes:**

**Brake Force:**                           **Dimensions:**
**Weight:**                                **Wheel Diameter:**
**Fuel Capacity:**                         **Train Supply:**
**Design Speed:** 110 mph.                 **Maximum Speed:** 110 mph.
**Route Availability:**                    **Total:** 10.

| | |
|---|---|
| 93001 | BN |
| 93002 | BN |
| 93003 | BN |
| 93004 | BN |
| 93005 | BN |
| 93006 | BN |
| 93007 | BN |
| 93008 | BN |
| 93009 | BN |
| 93010 | BN |

# 1.4. EUROTUNNEL LOCOMOTIVES

## DIESEL LOCOMOTIVES

0001–10 are registered on TOPS as 21901–910.

### 0001–0005         Krupp MaK                    Bo-Bo

Channel Tunnel maintenance and rescue train locomotives.
**Built:** 1991–92 by MaK at Kiel, Germany (Model DE 1004).
**Engine:** MTU 12V396 TC 13 of 950 kW (1275 hp) at 1800 rpm.
**Main Alternator:** ABB.              **Traction Motors:** ABB.
**Maximum Tractive Effort:** 305 kN (68600 lbf).
**Continuous Tractive Effort:** 140 kN (31500 lbf) at 20 mph.
**Power At Rail:** 750 kW (1012 hp).   **Dimensions:** 14.40 x ?? m.
**Brake Force:** 120 kN.               **Wheel Diameter:** 1000 mm.
**Train Brakes:** Air.                 **Weight:** 90 t.
**Maximum Speed:** 100 km/h.           **Design Speed:** 120 km/h.
**Fuel Capacity:** 3500 litres.        **Multiple Working:** Within class.
**Train Supply:** Not equipped.        **Signalling System:** TVM430 cab signalling.

| 0001 | **GY** | ET | CT | | 0004 | **GY** | ET | CT |
|------|--------|----|----|-|------|--------|----|----|
| 0002 | **GY** | ET | CT | | 0005 | **GY** | ET | CT |
| 0003 | **GY** | ET | CT | | | | | |

### 0006–0010         Krupp MaK                    Bo-Bo

Channel Tunnel maintenance and rescue locomotives. Rebuilt from
Netherlands Railways/DB Cargo Nederland Class 6400. 0006/07 were
added to the ET fleet in 2011, and 0008–10 in 2016. 0010 is used for shunting
at Coquelles.

**Built:** 1990–91 by MaK at Kiel, Germany (Model DE 6400).
**Engine:** MTU 12V396 TC 13 of 1180 kW (1580 hp) at 1800 rpm.
**Main Alternator:** ABB.              **Traction Motors:** ABB.
**Maximum Tractive Effort:** 290 kN (65200 lbf).
**Continuous Tractive Effort:** 140 kN (31500 lbf) at 20 mph.
**Power At Rail:** 750 kW (1012 hp).   **Dimensions:** 14.40 x ?? m.
**Brake Force:** 120 kN.               **Wheel Diameter:** 1000 mm.
**Train Brakes:** Air.                 **Weight:** 80 t.
**Maximum Speed:** 120 km/h.           **Design Speed:** 120 km/h.
**Fuel Capacity:** 2900 litres.        **Multiple Working:** Within class.
**Train Supply:** Not equipped.

Not fitted with TVM 430 cab signalling so have to operate with another
locomotive/s when used on HS1.

| 0006 | (6456) | **GY** | ET | CT | | 0009 | (6451) | **GY** | ET | CT |
|------|--------|--------|----|----|-|------|--------|--------|----|----|
| 0007 | (6457) | **GY** | ET | CT | | 0010 | (6447) | **EB** | ET | CO |
| 0008 | (6450) | **GY** | ET | CT | | | | | | |

## 0031–0042      HUNSLET/SCHÖMA      0-4-0

**Built:** 1989–90 by Hunslet Engine Company at Leeds as 900 mm gauge.
**Rebuilt:** 1993–94 by Schöma in Germany to 1435 mm gauge as Type CFL 200 DCL-R.
**Engine:** Deutz F10L 413 FW of 170 kW (230 hp) at 2300 rpm.
**Transmission:** Mechanical Clark 5421-179 type.
**Maximum Tractive Effort:** 68 kN (15300 lbf).
**Continuous Tractive Effort:** 47 kN (10570 lbf) at 5 mph.
**Power At Rail:** 130.1 kW (175 hp).

| | |
|---|---|
| **Brake Force:** | **Dimensions:** 7.87 (* 10.94) x 2.69 m. |
| **Weight:** 25 t. (* 28 t.) | **Wheel Diameter:** 1010 mm. |

**Maximum Speed:** 48 km/h (* 75 km/h).

| | |
|---|---|
| **Fuel Capacity:** 450 litres. | **Train Brakes:** Air. |
| **Train Supply:** Not equipped. | **Multiple Working:** Not equipped. |

\* Rebuilt with inspection platforms to check overhead catenary (Type CS 200).

| | | | | |
|------|---|-----|-----|----------|
| 0031 |   | **GY** | ET | CT | FRANCES |
| 0032 |   | **GY** | ET | CT | ELISABETH |
| 0033 |   | **GY** | ET | CT | SILKE |
| 0034 |   | **GY** | ET | CT | AMANDA |
| 0035 |   | **GY** | ET | CT | MARY |
| 0036 |   | **GY** | ET | CT | LAURENCE |
| 0037 |   | **GY** | ET | CT | LYDIE |
| 0038 |   | **GY** | ET | CT | JENNY |
| 0039 | * | **GY** | ET | CT | PACITA |
| 0040 |   | **GY** | ET | CT | JILL |
| 0041 | * | **GY** | ET | CT | KIM |
| 0042 |   | **GY** | ET | CT | NICOLE |

# ELECTRIC LOCOMOTIVES

## 9005–9840      BRUSH/ABB      Bo-Bo-Bo

**Built:** 1993–2002 by Brush Traction, Loughborough.
**Electric Supply System:** 25 kV AC 50 Hz overhead.
**Traction Motors:** Asea Brown Boveri design. Asynchronous 3-phase motors. Model 6FHA 7059 (as built). Model 6FHA 7059C (7000 kW rated locos).
**Maximum Tractive Effort:** 400kN (90 000 lbf).
**Continuous Rating:** Class 9/0: 5760 kW (7725 hp). Class 9/7 and 9/8: 7000 kW (9387 hp).

| | |
|---|---|
| **Maximum Rail Power:** | **Multiple Working:** TDM system. |
| **Brake Force:** 50 t. | **Dimensions:** 22.01 x 2.97 x 4.20 m. |
| **Weight:** 136 t. | **Wheel Diameter:** 1250 mm. |
| **Maximum Speed:** 140 km/h. | **Design Speed:** 140 km/h. |
| **Train Supply:** Electric. | **Train Brakes:** Air. |

**Class 9/0 Original build locos.** Built 1993–94.

| | | | | |
|------|------|----|----|----------------|
| 9005 | **EB** | ET | CO | JESSYE NORMAN |

| 9007 | **EB** | ET | CO | DAME JOAN SUTHERLAND[1] |
|------|--------|----|----|------------------------|
| 9011 | **EB** | ET | CO | JOSÉ VAN DAM[1] |
| 9013 | **EB** | ET | CO | MARIA CALLAS[1] |
| 9015 | **EB** | ET | CO | LÖTSCHBERG 1913[1] |
| 9018 | **EB** | ET | CO | WILHELMENIA FERNANDEZ |
| 9022 | **EB** | ET | CO | DAME JANET BAKER |
| 9024 | **EB** | ET | CO | GOTTHARD 1882 |
| 9026 | **EB** | ET | CO | FURKATUNNEL 1982 |
| 9029 | **EB** | ET | CO | THOMAS ALLEN |
| 9033 | **EB** | ET | CO | MONTSERRAT CABALLE |
| 9036 | **EB** | ET | CO | ALAIN FONDARY[1] |
| 9037 | **EB** | ET | CO | |

**Class 9/7. Increased power freight shuttle locos.** Built 2001–02 (9711–23 built 1998–2001 as 9101–13 and rebuilt as 9711–23 2010–12).

| 9701 | **EB** | ET | CO |
|------|--------|----|----|
| 9702 | **EB** | ET | CO |
| 9703 | **EB** | ET | CO |
| 9704 | **EB** | ET | CO |
| 9705 | **EB** | ET | CO |
| 9706 | **EB** | ET | CO |
| 9707 | **EB** | ET | CO |

| 9711 | (9101) | **EB** | ET | CO |
|------|--------|--------|----|----|
| 9712 | (9102) | **EB** | ET | CO |
| 9713 | (9103) | **EB** | ET | CO |
| 9714 | (9104) | **EB** | ET | CO |
| 9715 | (9105) | **EB** | ET | CO |
| 9716 | (9106) | **EB** | ET | CO |
| 9717 | (9107) | **EB** | ET | CO |
| 9718 | (9108) | **EB** | ET | CO |
| 9719 | (9109) | **EB** | ET | CO |
| 9720 | (9110) | **EB** | ET | CO |
| 9721 | (9111) | **EB** | ET | CO |
| 9722 | (9112) | **EB** | ET | CO |
| 9723 | (9113) | **EB** | ET | CO |

**Class 9/8 Locos rebuilt from Class 9/0 by adding 800 to the loco number. Uprated to 7000 kW.**

90xx and 98xx locomotives have a cab in the blunt end for shunting, except 9840 which does not have this feature.

| 9801 | **EB** | ET | CO | LESLEY GARRETT |
|------|--------|----|----|----------------|
| 9802 | **EB** | ET | CO | STUART BURROWS |
| 9803 | **EB** | ET | CO | BENJAMIN LUXON |
| 9804 | **EB** | ET | CO | |
| 9806 | **EB** | ET | CO | REGINE CRESPIN |
| 9808 | **EB** | ET | CO | ELISABETH SODERSTROM |
| 9809 | **EB** | ET | CO | |
| 9810 | **EB** | ET | CO | |
| 9812 | **EB** | ET | CO | |
| 9814 | **EB** | ET | CO | LUCIA POPP |

| 9816 | **EB** | ET | CO | |
|------|--------|-----|-----|--------------------------------------|
| 9819 | **EB** | ET | CO | MARIA EWING[1] |
| 9820 | **EB** | ET | CO | NICOLAI GHIAROV |
| 9821 | **EB** | ET | CO | |
| 9823 | **EB** | ET | CO | DAME ELISABETH LEGGE-SCHWARZKOPF |
| 9825 | **EB** | ET | CO | |
| 9827 | **EB** | ET | CO | BARBARA HENDRICKS |
| 9828 | **EB** | ET | CO | |
| 9831 | **EB** | ET | CO | |
| 9832 | **EB** | ET | CO | RENATA TEBALDI |
| 9834 | **EB** | ET | CO | MIRELLA FRENI |
| 9835 | **EB** | ET | CO | NICOLAI GEDDA |
| 9838 | **EB** | ET | CO | HILDEGARD BEHRENS |
| 9840 | **EB** | ET | CO | |

[1] nameplates carried on one side only.

# 1.5. LOCOMOTIVES AWAITING DISPOSAL

Locomotives that are still extant but best classed as awaiting disposal are listed here.

66048    EMD, Longport Works

# 1.6. **LOCOMOTIVES EXPORTED FOR USE ABROAD**

This section details former British Railways (plus privatisation era) diesel and electric locomotives that have been exported from Great Britain for use in industrial locations or with a main line operator abroad. Not included are locos that are classed as "preserved" abroad. These are included in the Platform 5 "Preserved Locomotives of British Railways" publication.

(S) denotes locomotives that are stored.

*Number Other no./name    Location*

**Class 03**

| | | |
|---|---|---|
| 03156 | | Ferramenta Pugliese, Terlizzi, Bari, Italy |

**Class 47**

| | | |
|---|---|---|
| 47375 | 92 70 00 47375-5 | Continental Railway Solution, Hungary |

**Class 56**

| | | |
|---|---|---|
| 56101 | 92 55 0659 001-5 | FLOYD, Hungary |
| 56115 | 92 55 0659 002-3 | FLOYD, Hungary |
| 56117 | 92 55 0659 003-1 | FLOYD, Hungary (S) Budapest Keleti |

**Class 58**

| | | |
|---|---|---|
| 58001 | | DB, France, (S) Alizay |
| 58004 | | DB, France, (S) Alizay |
| 58005 | | DB, France, (S) Alizay |
| 58006 | | DB, France, (S) Alizay |
| 58007 | | DB, France, (S) Alizay |
| 58009 | | DB, France, (S) Alizay |
| 58010 | | DB, France, (S) Alizay |
| 58011 | | DB, France, (S) Alizay |
| 58013 | | DB, France, (S) Alizay |
| 58018 | | DB, France, (S) Alizay |
| 58021 | | DB, France, (S) Alizay |
| 58025 | | DB, Spain, (S) Albacete |
| 58026 | | DB, France, (S) Alizay |
| 58027 | L52 | DB, Spain, (S) Albacete |
| 58032 | | DB, France, (S) Alizay |
| 58033 | | DB, France, (S) Alizay |
| 58034 | | DB, France, (S) Alizay |
| 58035 | | DB, France, (S) Alizay |
| 58036 | | DB, France, (S) Alizay |
| 58038 | | DB, France, (S) Alizay |
| 58039 | | DB, France, (S) Alizay |
| 58040 | | DB, France, (S) Alizay |
| 58041 | L36 | Transfesa, Spain, (S) Albacete |
| 58042 | | DB, France, (S) Alizay |
| 58044 | | DB, France, (S) Woippy, Metz |

| | | |
|---|---|---|
| 58046 | | DB, France, (S) Alizay |
| 58049 | | DB, France, (S) Alizay |
| 58050 | L53 | DB, Spain, (S) Albacete |

## Class 66

| | | | | | | | |
|---|---|---|---|---|---|---|---|
| 66010 | ECR, France | 66195 | ECR, France | 66235 | | ECR, France |
| 66022 | ECR, France | 66196 | DBC, Poland | 66236 | | ECR, France |
| 66026 | ECR, France | 66201 | ECR, France | 66237 | | DBC, Poland |
| 66028 | ECR, France | 66202 | ECR, France | 66239 | | ECR, France |
| 66029 | ECR, France | 66203 | ECR, France | 66240 | | ECR, France |
| 66032 | ECR, France | 66204 | ECR, France | 66241 | | ECR, France |
| 66033 | ECR, France | 66205 | ECR, France | 66242 | | ECR, France |
| 66036 | ECR, France | 66208 | ECR, France | 66243 | | ECR, France |
| 66038 | ECR, France | 66209 | ECR, France | 66244 | | ECR, France |
| 66042 | ECR, France | 66210 | ECR, France | 66245 | | ECR, France |
| 66045 | ECR, France | 66211 | ECR, France | 66246 | | ECR, France |
| 66049 | ECR, France | 66212 | ECR, France | 66247 | | ECR, France |
| 66052 | ECR, France | 66213 | ECR, France | 66248 | | DBC, Poland |
| 66062 | ECR, France | 66214 | ECR, France | 66249 | | ECR, France |
| 66064 | ECR, France | 66215 | ECR, France | 66411 | 66013 | FL, Poland |
| 66071 | ECR, France | 66216 | ECR, France | 66412 | 66015 | FL, Poland |
| 66072 | ECR, France | 66217 | ECR, France | 66417 | 66014 | FL, Poland |
| 66073 | ECR, France | 66218 | ECR, France | 66527 | 66016 | FL, Poland |
| 66123 | ECR, France | 66219 | ECR, France | 66530 | 66017 | FL, Poland |
| 66146 | DBC, Poland | 66220 | DBC, Poland | 66535 | 66018 | FL, Poland |
| 66153 | DBC, Poland | 66222 | ECR, France | 66582 | 66009 | FL, Poland |
| 66157 | DBC, Poland | 66223 | ECR, France | 66583 | 66010 | FL, Poland |
| 66159 | DBC, Poland | 66224 | ECR, France | 66584 | 66011 | FL, Poland |
| 66163 | DBC, Poland | 66225 | ECR, France | 66586 | 66008 | FL, Poland |
| 66166 | DBC, Poland | 66226 | ECR, France | 66595 | | FL, Poland |
| 66173 | DBC, Poland | 66227 | DBC, Poland | 66608 | 66603 | FL, Poland |
| 66178 | DBC, Poland | 66228 | ECR, France | 66609 | 66605 | FL, Poland |
| 66179 | ECR, France | 66229 | ECR, France | 66611 | 66604 | FL, Poland |
| 66180 | DBC, Poland | 66231 | ECR, France | 66612 | 66606 | FL, Poland |
| 66189 | DBC, Poland | 66232 | ECR, France | 66624 | 66602 | FL, Poland |
| 66190 | ECR, France | 66233 | ECR, France | 66625 | 66601 | FL, Poland |
| 66191 | ECR, France | 66234 | ECR, France | 66954 | | FL, Poland |
| 66193 | ECR, France | | | | | |

## Class 86

| | | | |
|---|---|---|---|
| 86213 | 91 52 00 87703-2 | Lancashire Witch | Bulmarket, Bulgaria |
| 86215 | 91 55 0450 005-8 | | FLOYD, Hungary |
| 86217 | 91 55 0450 006-6 | | FLOYD, Hungary |
| 86218 | 91 55 0450 004-1 | | FLOYD, Hungary |
| 86228 | 91 55 0450 007-4 | | FLOYD, Hungary |
| 86231 | 91 52 00 85005-4 | Lady of the Lake | Bulmarket, Bulgaria |
| 86232 | 91 55 0450 003-3 | | FLOYD, Hungary |
| 86233 | | | Bulmarket, Bulgaria (S) Ruse |
| 86234 | | | Bulmarket, Bulgaria |
| 86235 | 91 52 00 87704-0 | Novelty | Bulmarket, Bulgaria |
| 86242 | 91 55 0450 008-2 | | FLOYD, Hungary |

| 86248 | 91 55 0450 001-7 | | FLOYD, Hungary |
| 86250 | 91 55 0450 002-5 | | FLOYD, Hungary |
| 86424 | 91 55 0450 009-0 | | FLOYD, Hungary (S) Budapest |
| 86701 | 91 52 00 87701-6 | Orion | Bulmarket, Bulgaria |
| 86702 | 91 52 00 87702-4 | Cassiopeia | Bulmarket, Bulgaria |

**Class 87**

| 87003 | 91 52 00 87003-7 | | BZK, Bulgaria |
| 87004 | 91 52 00 87004-5 | Britannia | BZK, Bulgaria |
| 87006 | 91 52 00 87006-0 | | BZK, Bulgaria |
| 87007 | 91 52 00 87007-8 | | BZK, Bulgaria |
| 87008 | 87008-9 | | BZK, Bulgaria (S) Ruse |
| 87009 | 91 52 00 87009-4 | | Bulmarket, Bulgaria |
| 87010 | 91 52 00 87010-2 | | BZK, Bulgaria |
| 87012 | 91 52 00 87012-8 | | BZK, Bulgaria |
| 87013 | 91 52 00 87013-6 | | BZK, Bulgaria |
| 87014 | 87014-7 | | BZK, Bulgaria (S) Sofia |
| 87017 | 91 52 00 87017-7 | Iron Duke | Bulmarket, Bulgaria |
| 87019 | 91 52 00 87019-3 | | BZK, Bulgaria |
| 87020 | 91 52 00 87020-1 | | BZK, Bulgaria |
| 87022 | 91 52 00 87022-7 | | BZK, Bulgaria |
| 87023 | 91 52 00 87023-5 | Velocity | Bulmarket, Bulgaria |
| 87025 | 91 52 00 87025-0 | | Bulmarket, Bulgaria |
| 87026 | 91 52 00 87026-8 | | BZK, Bulgaria |
| 87028 | 91 52 00 87028-4 | | BZK, Bulgaria |
| 87029 | 91 52 00 87029-2 | | BZK, Bulgaria |
| 87033 | 91 52 00 87033-4 | | BZK, Bulgaria |
| 87034 | 91 52 00 87034-2 | | BZK, Bulgaria |

**Class 92**

| 92001 | 91 53 0 472 002-1 | Mircea Eliade | Transagent Rail, Croatia |
| 92002 | 91 53 0 472 003-9 | Lucian Blaga | Transagent Rail, Croatia |
| 92003 | | Beethoven | DB Cargo, Romania (S) |
| 92005 | 91 53 0 472-005-4 | | Transagent Rail, Croatia |
| 92012 | 91 53 0 472 001-3 | Mihai Eminescu | Transagent Rail, Croatia |
| 92022 | | Charles Dickens | DB Cargo, Bulgaria (S) Aurubis |
| 92024 | 91 53 0 472 004-7 | Marin Preda | Transagent Rail, Croatia |
| 92025 | 91 52 1 688 025-1 | Oscar Wilde | DB Cargo, Bulgaria |
| 92026 | | Britten | DB Cargo, Romania |
| 92027 | 91 52 1 688 027-7 | George Eliot | DB Cargo, Bulgaria |
| 92030 | 91 52 1 688 030-1 | Ashford | DB Cargo, Bulgaria |
| 92034 | 91 52 1 688 034-3 | Kipling | DB Cargo, Bulgaria |
| 92039 | 91 53 0 472 006-2 | Eugen Ionescu | DB Cargo, Romania |

# 2. LOCO-HAULED COACHING STOCK

# INTRODUCTION

This section contains details of all locomotive-hauled or propelled coaching stock, often referred to as carriages, which can run on Britain's national railway network.

The number of locomotive-hauled or propelled carriages in use on the national railway network is much fewer than was once the case. Those that remain fall into two distinct groups.

Firstly, there are those used by franchised and open access operators for regular timetabled services. Most of these are formed in fixed or semi-fixed formations with either locomotives or a locomotive and Driving Brake Carriage at either end which allows for push-pull operation. There are also a small number of mainly overnight trains with variable formations that use conventional locomotive haulage.

Secondly there are those used for what can best be described as excursion trains. These include a wide range of carriage types ranging from luxurious saloons to those more suited to the "bucket and spade" seaside type of excursion. These are formed into sets to suit the requirements of the day. From time to time some see limited use with franchised and open access operators to cover for stock shortages and times of exceptional demand such as major sporting events.

In addition, there remain a small number of carriages referred to as "Service Stock" which are used internally within the railway industry and are not used to convey passengers.

## FRANCHISED & OPEN ACCESS OPERATORS

For each operator regularly using locomotive-hauled carriages brief details are given here of the sphere of operation. For details of operators using HSTs see Section 2.2.

### Caledonian Sleeper

This franchise, operated by Serco, started in 2015 when the Anglo-Scottish Sleeper operation was split from the ScotRail franchise. Caledonian Sleeper operates seating and sleeping car services between London Euston and Scotland using sets of new CAF Mark 5 Sleeping Cars and seated carriages.

GBRf is contracted to supply the motive power for the Sleepers. Class 92s are used between London Euston and Edinburgh/Glasgow Central and rebuilt Class 73/9s between Edinburgh and Inverness, Aberdeen and Fort William.

### Chiltern Railways

Chiltern operates four sets of Mark 3 carriages hauled by DRS Class 68 locomotives on its Mainline services between London Marylebone and Birmingham Moor Street/Kidderminster (plus one train to Oxford). Trains operate as push-pull sets.

### Great Western Railway

The "Night Riviera" seating and sleeping car service between London Paddington and Penzance uses sets of Mark 3 carriages hauled by Class 57/6 locomotives.

### London North Eastern Railway

LNER has retained seven rakes of Mark 4 carriages and these are hauled by Class 91 locomotives in push-pull formation on a limited number of InterCity services between London King's Cross and Leeds or York. All other services on the East Coast Main Line are now in the hands of LNER's fleet of 65 "Azuma" bi-mode units. The Mark 4 sets were due to be stood down for a period from January 2021 until the summer.

### North Yorkshire Moors Railway

In addition to operating the North Yorkshire Moors Railway between Pickering and Grosmont the company operates through services to Whitby and occasionally Battersby. A fleet of Mark 1 passenger carriages and Pullman Cars are used for these services. It also operates the "North Norfolkman" services on behalf of the North Norfolk Railway between Sheringham and Cromer.

### TransPennine Express

TPE has 13 sets of new CAF Mark 5A coaches that were originally due to enter service in 2019 but due to teething problems and delays with crew training now not due to enter full service until 2021. The sets are being used on some services on the Liverpool–Scarborough route and they are also to be used on the Manchester Airport–Redcar route. They are operated using DRS Class 68s in push-pull mode.

### Transport for Wales

TfW ceased using its Mark 3 rakes during the Covid-19 lockdown in March 2020. It has taken on lease three shortened rakes of ex-LNER Mark 4s and these are due to be introduced in spring 2021 on the Cardiff–Holyhead route, in push-pull mode with Class 67s.

### West Coast Railway Company

WCRC operates two sets of Mark 1/2 carriages on its regular steam-hauled "Jacobite" trains between Fort William and Mallaig. These trains normally operate between late April and late October.

# EXCURSION TRAIN OPERATORS

Usually, three types of companies will be involved in the operation of an excursion train. There will be the promoter, the rolling stock provider and the train operator. In many cases two or more of these roles may be undertaken by the same or associated companies. Only a small number of Train Operating Companies facilitate the operation of excursion trains. This takes various forms ranging from the complete package of providing and operating the train, through offering a "hook up and haul" service, to operating the train for a third-party rolling stock custodian.

## DB Cargo UK
DBC currently operates its own luxurious train of Mark 3 carriages, called the Company Train. It also offers a hook up and haul service and regularly operates the Royal Train and the Belmond British Pullman as well as trains for Riviera Trains and their client promoters.

## Direct Rail Services
DRS has a fleet of Mark 2 carriages originally intended for use on excursion trains, that until spring 2020 were hired to ScotRail. The company also offers a hook up and haul service for Riviera Trains and its client promoters.

## GB Railfreight
GBRf initially operated excursion trains using the preserved Class 201 "Hastings" DEMU. It now also operates a small number of company excursions using hired-in carriages. The company also offers a hook up and haul service operating the Royal Scotsman luxury train, as well as trains for Riviera Trains and its client promoters.

## Locomotive Services
This vertically integrated company gained a license in 2017. From its base at Crewe excursion trains are operated across the country using its increasingly varied fleet of steam, diesel and electric locomotives and Mark 1/2/3 carriages, and from late 2020 the "Midland Pullman" HST set.

## Rail Operations Group
This company has operated a small number of excursion trains using hired in carriages. It also offers a hook up and haul service.

## Vintage Trains
This vertically integrated company gained a licence in 2018. From its base at Tyseley it operates the "Shakespeare Express" steam service between Birmingham and Stratford-upon-Avon. It also operates excursions using its fleet of steam and diesel locomotives and Mark 1/2 carriages and Pullman cars.

## West Coast Railway Company
This vertically integrated company has its own fleet of steam and diesel locomotives as well as a full range of different carriage types. It operates its own regular trains, including the luxury Northern Belle, the "Jacobite" steam service between Fort William and Mallaig, the "Dalesman" steam and diesel services over the Settle & Carlisle route and numerous excursion trains for itself and client promoters. In addition, it offers a hook up and haul service operating trains for companies such as The Princess Royal Locomotive Trust and the Scottish Railway Preservation Society.

# LAYOUT OF INFORMATION

Carriages are listed in numerical order of painted number in batches according to type.

Where a carriage has been renumbered, the former number is shown in parentheses. If a carriage has been renumbered more than once, the original number is shown first, followed by the most recent previous number.

Each carriage entry is laid out as in the following example (previous number(s) column may be omitted where not applicable):

| No. | Prev. No. | Notes | Livery | Owner | Operator | Depot/Location |
|-----|-----------|-------|--------|-------|----------|----------------|
| 82301 | (82117) | g | **CM** | AV | *CR* | AL |

**Codes:** Codes are used to denote the livery, owner, operator and depot/location of each carriage. Details of codes used can be found in Section 6 of this book.

The owner is the responsible custodian of the carriage and this may not always be the legal owner. Actual ownership can be very complicated. Some vehicles are owned by finance/leasing companies. Others are owned by subsidiary companies of a holding company or by an associate company of the responsible custodian or operator.

The operator is the organisation which facilitates the use of the carriage and may not be the actual train operating company which runs the train. If no operator is shown the carriage is considered to be not in use.

The depot is the facility primarily responsible for the carriages maintenance. Light maintenance and heavy overhauls may be carried out elsewhere.

The location is where carriages not in use are currently being kept or are stored.

# GENERAL INFORMATION

## CLASSIFICATION AND NUMBERING

Seven different numbering systems were in use on British Rail. These were the British Rail series, the four pre-nationalisation companies' series', the Pullman Car Company's series and the UIC (International Union of Railways) series. In this book BR number series carriages and former Pullman Car Company series are listed separately. There is also a separate listing of "Saloon" type carriages, that includes pre-nationalisation survivors, which are permitted to run on the national railway system, Locomotive Support Carriages and Service Stock. Please note the Mark 2 Pullman carriages were ordered after the Pullman Car Company had been nationalised and are therefore numbered in the British Rail series. The new CAF Mark 5 carriages have been allocated numbers in the British Rail series.

Also listed separately are the British Rail and Pullman Car Company number series carriages used on North Yorkshire Moors Railway and North Norfolk Railway services on very limited parts of the national railway network. This is due to their very restricted sphere of operation.

The BR number series grouped carriages of a particular type together in chronological order. Major modifications affecting type of accommodation resulted in renumbering into a more appropriate or new number series. Since privatisation such renumbering has not always taken place resulting in renumbering which has been more haphazard and greater variations within numbering groups.

With the introduction of the TOPS numbering system, coaching stock (including multiple unit vehicles) retained their original BR number unless this conflicted with a locomotive number. Carriages can be one–five digits, although no one or two-digit examples remain in use on the national network. BR generally numbered "Service Stock" in a six-digit wagon number series.

## UNITS OF MEASUREMENT

All dimensions and weights are quoted for carriages in an "as new" condition or after a major modification, such as fitting with new bogies etc. Dimensions are quoted in the order length x width. Lengths quoted are over buffers or couplers as appropriate. All widths quoted are maxima. All weights are shown as metric tonnes (t = tonnes).

# DIMENSIONS

Carriage lengths are summarised as follows:

**Mark 1:** 19.35 m or 17.37 m.
**Mark 2:** 19.66 m.
**Mark 3:** 23.00 m.
**Mark 3 HST:** 23.00 m.

**Mark 4:** 23.00 m.
**Mark 5:** 22.20 m.
**Mark 5A:** 22.20–22.37 m.

# DETAILED INFORMATION & CODES

Under each type heading, the following details are shown:

- "Mark" of carriage (see below).
- Descriptive text.
- Number of First Class seats, Standard Class seats, lavatory compartments and wheelchair spaces shown as F/S nT nW respectively. A number in brackets indicates tip-up seats (in addition to the regular seats).
- Bogie type (see below).
- Additional features.
- ETS Index.
- Weight: All weights are shown as metric tonnes.

# BOGIE TYPES

**Gresley.** LNER design of bogie first used in the "Gresley" era. Used by BR on some Mark 1 catering carriages. Now used for some saloons.

**BR Mark 1 (BR1).** Double bolster leaf spring bogie. Generally 90 mph, but Mark 1 bogies may be permitted to run at 100 mph with special maintenance. Weight: 6.1 t.

**BR Mark 2 (BR2).** Single bolster leaf-spring bogie used on certain types of non-passenger stock and suburban stock (all now withdrawn). Weight: 5.3 t.

**COMMONWEALTH (C).** Heavy, cast steel coil spring bogie. 100 mph. Weight: 6.75 t.

**B4.** Coil spring fabricated bogie. Generally 100 mph, but B4 bogies may be permitted to run at 110 mph with special maintenance. Weight: 5.2 t.

**B5.** Heavy duty version of B4. 100 mph. Weight: 5.3 t.

**B5 (SR).** A bogie originally used on Southern Region EMUs, similar in design to B5. Now also used on locomotive-hauled carriages. 100 mph.

**BT10.** A fabricated bogie designed for 125 mph. Air suspension.

**T4.** A 125 mph bogie designed by BREL (now Bombardier Transportation).

**BT41.** Fitted to Mark 4 carriages, designed by SIG in Switzerland. At present limited to 125 mph, but designed for 140 mph.

**CAF.** Fitted to CAF Mark 5 and Mark 5A carriages.

# BRAKES

Air braking is now standard on British main line trains. Carriages with other equipment are denoted:

b   Air braked, through vacuum pipe.
v   Vacuum braked.
x   Dual braked (air and vacuum).

# HEATING & VENTILATION

Electric heating and ventilation is now standard on British main-line trains. Certain carriages for use on excursion services may also have steam heating facilities, or be steam heated only. All carriages used on North Yorkshire Moors Railway and North Norfolk Railway trains have steam heating.

# NOTES ON ELECTRIC TRAIN SUPPLY

The sum of ETS indices in a train must not be more than the ETS index of the locomotive or generator van. The normal voltage on British trains is 1000 V. Suffix "X" denotes 600 amp wiring instead of 400 amp. Trains whose ETS index is higher than 66 must be formed completely of 600 amp wired stock. Class 33 and 73/1 locomotives cannot provide a suitable electric train supply for Mark 2D, Mark 2E, Mark 2F, Mark 3, Mark 3A, Mark 3B or Mark 4 carriages. Class 55 locomotives provide an ETS directly from one of their traction generators into the train line. Consequently voltage fluctuations can result in motor-alternator flashover. Thus these locomotives are not suitable for use with Mark 2D, Mark 2E, Mark 2F, Mark 3, Mark 3A, Mark 3B or Mark 4 carriages unless modified motor-alternators are fitted. Such motor alternators were fitted to Mark 2D and 2F carriages used on the East Coast Main Line, but few remain fitted.

# PUBLIC ADDRESS

It is assumed all carriages are now fitted with public address equipment, although certain stored carriages may not have this feature. In addition, it is assumed all carriages with a conductor's compartment have public address transmission facilities, as have catering carriages.

# COOKING EQUIPMENT

It is assumed that Mark 1 catering carriages have gas powered cooking equipment, whilst Mark 2, 3 and 4 catering carriages have electric powered cooking equipment unless stated otherwise.

## ADDITIONAL FEATURE CODES

(+4) Indicates tip-up seats in that carriage (in addition to the fixed seats).
d      Central Door Locking.
dg     Driver–Guard communication equipment.
f      Facelifted or fluorescent lighting.
h      "High density" seating
k      Composition brake blocks (instead of cast iron).
n      Day/night lighting.
pg     Public address transmission and driver-guard communication.
pt     Public address transmission facility.
q      Catering staff to shore telephone.
T      Toilet
TD     A universal access toilet suitable for use by person of reduced mobility.
w      Wheelchair space.

## BUILD DETAILS

**Lot Numbers**
Carriages ordered under the auspices of BR were allocated a lot (batch) number when ordered and these are quoted in class headings and sub-headings.

**Builders**
These are shown for each lot. More details and a full list of builders can be found in section 6.7.

Information on sub-contracting works which built parts of carriages eg the underframes etc is not shown.

In addition to the above, certain vintage Pullman cars were built or rebuilt at the following works:

Metropolitan Carriage & Wagon Company, Birmingham (later Alstom).
Midland Carriage & Wagon Company, Birmingham.
Pullman Car Company, Preston Park, Brighton.
Conversions have also been carried out at the Railway Technical Centre, Derby, LNWR Crewe and Blakes Fabrications, Edinburgh.

# 2.1. BRITISH RAILWAYS NUMBER SERIES COACHING STOCK

## KITCHEN FIRST

Mark 1. Spent most of its life as a Royal Train vehicle and was numbered 2907 for a time. 24/–. B5 bogies. ETS 2.

Lot No. 30633 Swindon 1961. 41 t.

| 325 | **VN** | WC | *WC* | CS | DUART |

## PULLMAN KITCHEN

Mark 2. Pressure Ventilated. Built with First Class seating but this has been replaced with a servery area. Gas cooking. 2T. B5 bogies. ETS 6.

Lot No. 30755 Derby 1966. 40 t.

| 504 | **PC** | WC | *WC* | CS | ULLSWATER |
| 506 | **PC** | WC | *WC* | CS | WINDERMERE |

## PULLMAN OPEN FIRST

Mark 2. Pressure Ventilated. 36/– 2T. B4 bogies. ETS 5.

Lot No. 30754 Derby 1966. 35 t.

**Non-standard livery:** 546 Maroon & beige.

| 546 | **O** | WC | | CS | CITY OF MANCHESTER |
| 548 | **PC** | WC | *WC* | CS | GRASMERE |
| 549 | **PC** | WC | *WC* | CS | BASSENTHWAITE |
| 550 | **PC** | WC | *WC* | CS | RYDAL WATER |
| 551 | **PC** | WC | *WC* | CS | BUTTERMERE |
| 552 | **PC** | WC | *WC* | CS | ENNERDALE WATER |
| 553 | **PC** | WC | *WC* | CS | CRUMMOCK WATER |

## PULLMAN OPEN BRAKE FIRST

Mark 2. Pressure Ventilated. 30/– 2T. B4 bogies. ETS 4.

Lot No. 30753 Derby 1966. 35 t.

| 586 | **PC** | WC | *WC* | CS | DERWENTWATER |

## BUFFET FIRST

Mark 2F. Air conditioned. Converted 1988–89/91 at BREL, Derby from Mark 2F Open Firsts. 1200/03/11/20/21 have Stones equipment, others have Temperature Ltd. 25/– 1T 1W. B4 bogies. d. ETS 6X.

**1200/03/11/20.** Lot No. 30845 Derby 1973. 33 t.
**1207/10/12/21.** Lot No. 30859 Derby 1973–74. 33 t.

| | | | | | | |
|---|---|---|---|---|---|---|
| 1200 | (3287, 6459) | **BG** | RV | *RV* | BU | |
| 1203 | (3291) | **CC** | LS | *LS* | CL | |
| 1207 | (3328, 6422) | **V** | WC | | CS | |
| 1210 | (3405, 6462) | **FS** | ER | | YA | |
| 1211 | (3305) | **PC** | LS | *LS* | CL | SNAEFELL |
| 1212 | (3427, 6453) | **BG** | RV | *RV* | BU | |
| 1220 | (3315, 6432) | **FS** | ER | | WO | |
| 1221 | (3371) | **IC** | WC | | CS | |

## KITCHEN WITH BAR

Mark 1. Built with no seats but three Pullman-style seats now fitted in bar area. B5 bogies. ETS 1.

Lot No. 30624 Cravens 1960–61. 41 t.

| | | | | | |
|---|---|---|---|---|---|
| 1566 | **VN** | WC | *WC* | CS | CAERDYDD |

## KITCHEN BUFFET UNCLASSIFIED

Mark 1. Built with 23 loose chairs. All remaining vehicles were refurbished with 23 fixed polypropylene chairs and fluorescent lighting. 1683/91 were further refurbished with 21 chairs, wheelchair space and carpets. ETS 2 (* 2X).

Now used on excursion trains with the seating area adapted to various uses including servery and food preparation areas, with some or all seating removed.

**1651–91.** Lot No. 30628 Pressed Steel 1960–61. Commonwealth bogies. 39 t.
**1730.** Lot No. 30512 BRCW 1960–61. B5 bogies. 37 t.

| | | | | | | | | | | | |
|---|---|---|---|---|---|---|---|---|---|---|---|
| 1651 | | **CC** | RV | *RV* | ZG | | 1683 | | **RB** | RV | | BU |
| 1657 | | **BG** | RV | *RV* | BU | | 1691 | | **BG** | RV | *RV* | BU |
| 1666 | x | **M** | RP | *WC* | CS | | 1730 | x | **M** | SP | *SP* | BO |
| 1671 | x* | **CH** | RV | *RV* | ZG | | | | | | | |

# BUFFET STANDARD

Mark 1. These carriages are basically an open standard with two full window spaces removed to accommodate a buffet counter, and four seats removed to allow for a stock cupboard. All remaining vehicles now have fluorescent lighting. –/44 2T. Commonwealth bogies. ETS 3.

1861 has had its toilets replaced with store cupboards.

**1813–32.** Lot No. 30520 Wolverton 1960. 38 t.
**1840.** Lot No. 30507 Wolverton 1960. 37 t.
**1859–63.** Lot No. 30670 Wolverton 1961–62. 38 t.
**1882.** Lot No. 30702 Wolverton 1962. 38 t.

| | | | | | | | | | | |
|---|---|---|---|---|---|---|---|---|---|---|
| 1813 | x | **CH** | RV | *RV* | ZG | 1860 | x | **M** | WC | *WC* | CS |
| 1832 | x | **CH** | RV | *RV* | ZG | 1861 | x | **M** | WC | *WC* | CS |
| 1840 | v | **M** | WC | *WC* | CS | 1863 | x | **CH** | LS | | CL |
| 1859 | x | **M** | SP | *SP* | BO | 1882 | x | **M** | WC | *WC* | CS |

# KITCHEN UNCLASSIFIED

Mark 1. These carriages were built as Unclassified Restaurants. They were rebuilt with buffet counters and 23 fixed polypropylene chairs, then further refurbished by fitting fluorescent lighting. Further modified for use as servery vehicle with seating removed and kitchen extended. ETS 2X.

**1953.** Lot No. 30575 Swindon 1960. B4/B5 bogies. 36.5 t.
**1961.** Lot No. 30632 Swindon 1961. Commonwealth bogies. 39 t.

| | | | | | | | | | |
|---|---|---|---|---|---|---|---|---|---|
| 1953 | | **VN** | WC | *WC* | CS | 1961 | x | **M** | WC | *WC* | CS |

# HM THE QUEEN'S SALOON

Mark 3. Converted from an Open First built 1972. Consists of a lounge, bedroom and bathroom for HM The Queen, and a combined bedroom and bathroom for the Queen's dresser. One entrance vestibule has double doors. Air conditioned. BT10 bogies. ETS 9X.

Lot No. 30886 Wolverton 1977. 36 t.

| | | | | | | |
|---|---|---|---|---|---|---|
| 2903 | (11001) | **RP** | NR | *RT* | | ZN |

# HRH THE DUKE OF EDINBURGH'S SALOON

Mark 3. Converted from an Open Standard built 1972. Consists of a combined lounge/dining room, a bedroom and a shower room for the Duke, a kitchen and a valet's bedroom and bathroom. Air conditioned. BT10 bogies. ETS 15X.

Lot No. 30887 Wolverton 1977. 36 t.

| | | | | | | |
|---|---|---|---|---|---|---|
| 2904 | (12001) | **RP** | NR | *RT* | | ZN |

# ROYAL HOUSEHOLD SLEEPING CAR

Mark 3A. Built to similar specification as Sleeping Cars 10647–729. 12 sleeping compartments for use of Royal Household with a fixed lower berth and a hinged upper berth. 2T plus shower room. Air conditioned. BT10 bogies. ETS 11X.

Lot No. 31002 Derby/Wolverton 1985. 44 t.

| 2915 | | **RP** | NR | *RT* | ZN |

# HRH THE PRINCE OF WALES'S DINING CAR

Mark 3. Converted from HST TRUK (kitchen car) built 1976. Large kitchen retained, but dining area modified for Royal use seating up to 14 at central table(s). Air conditioned. BT10 bogies. ETS 13X.

Lot No. 31059 Wolverton 1988. 43 t.

| 2916 | (40512) | **RP** | NR | *RT* | ZN |

# ROYAL KITCHEN/HOUSEHOLD DINING CAR

Mark 3. Converted from HST TRUK built 1977. Large kitchen retained and dining area slightly modified with seating for 22 Royal Household members. Air conditioned. BT10 bogies. ETS 13X.

Lot No. 31084 Wolverton 1990. 43 t.

| 2917 | (40514) | **RP** | NR | *RT* | ZN |

# ROYAL HOUSEHOLD CARS

Mark 3. Converted from HST TRUKs built 1976/77. Air conditioned. BT10 bogies. ETS 10X.

Lot Nos. 31083 (* 31085) Wolverton 1989. 41.05 t.

| 2918 | (40515) | **RP** | NR | | ZN |
| 2919 | (40518) * | **RP** | NR | | ZN |

# ROYAL HOUSEHOLD COUCHETTES

Mark 2B. Converted from Corridor Brake First built 1969. Consists of luggage accommodation, guard's compartment, workshop area, 350 kW diesel generator and staff sleeping accommodation. B5 bogies. ETS 2X (when generator not in use). ETS index ?? (when generator in use).

Lot No. 31044 Wolverton 1986. 48 t.

| 2920 | (14109, 17109) | **RP** | NR | *RT* | ZN |

Mark 2B. Converted from Corridor Brake First built 1969. Consists of luggage accommodation, kitchen, brake control equipment and staff accommodation. B5 bogies. ETS 7X.

Lot No. 31086 Wolverton 1990. 41.5 t.

2921  (14107, 17107)  **RP**  NR  *RT*  ZN

# HRH THE PRINCE OF WALES'S SLEEPING CAR

Mark 3B. Air conditioned. BT10 bogies. ETS 7X.

Lot No. 31035 Derby/Wolverton 1987.

2922  **RP**  NR  *RT*  ZN

# ROYAL SALOON

Mark 3B. Air conditioned. BT10 bogies. ETS 6X.

Lot No. 31036 Derby/Wolverton 1987.

2923  **RP**  NR  *RT*  ZN

# OPEN FIRST

Mark 1. 42/– 2T. ETS 3. Many now fitted with table lamps.

3058 was numbered DB 975313, 3068 was numbered DB 975606 and 3093 was numbered DB 977594 for a time when in departmental service for BR.

**3045.** Lot No. 30091 Doncaster 1954. B4 bogies. 33 t.
**3058–68.** Lot No. 30169 Doncaster 1955. B4 bogies. 33 t (* Commonwealth bogies 35 t).
**3093.** Lot No. 30472 BRCW 1959. B4 bogies. 33 t.
**3096–3100.** Lot No. 30576 BRCW 1959. B4 bogies. 33 t.

| | | | | | | | | | |
|---|---|---|---|---|---|---|---|---|---|
| 3045 | x **CC** | LS | *LS* | CL | | 3096 | x **M** | SP | *SP* | BO |
| 3058 | *x **M** | WC | *WC* | CS | FLORENCE | 3097 | **CH** | RV | *RV* | ZG |
| 3066 | **CC** | RV | *RV* | ZG | | 3098 | x **CH** | RV | *RV* | ZG |
| 3068 | **CC** | RV | *RV* | ZG | | 3100 | x **CC** | LS | *LS* | CL |
| 3093 | x **M** | WC | *WC* | CS | FLORENCE | | | | | |

Later design with fluorescent lighting, aluminium window frames and Commonwealth bogies.

3128/36/41/43/46/47/48 were renumbered 1058/60/63/65/68/69/70 when reclassified Restaurant Open First, then 3600/05/08/09/06/04/10 when declassified to Open Standard, but have since regained their original numbers. 3136 was numbered DB 977970 for a time when in use with Serco Railtest as a Brake Force Runner.

3105 has had its luggage racks removed and has tungsten lighting.

**3105–28.** Lot No. 30697 Swindon 1962–63. 36 t.
**3130–50.** Lot No. 30717 Swindon 1963. 36 t.

| 3105 | x | **M** | WC | *WC* | CS |
|------|---|-------|----|----|-----|
| 3106 | x | **M** | WC | *WC* | CS |
| 3107 | x | **CC** | LS |  | ZG |
| 3110 | x | **CH** | RV | *RV* | ZG |
| 3112 | x | **CH** | RV |  | ZG |
| 3113 | x | **M** | WC | *WC* | CS |
| 3115 | x | **M** | SP | *SP* | BO |
| 3117 | x | **M** | WC | *WC* | CS |
| 3119 | x | **CH** | RV | *RV* | ZG |
| 3120 |  | **CH** | RV | *RV* | ZG |
| 3121 |  | **CH** | RV | *RV* | ZG |
| 3122 | x | **CC** | LS | *LS* | CL |
| 3123 |  | **CH** | RV | *RV* | ZG |

| 3125 | x | **CC** | LS | *LS* | CL |
|------|---|-------|----|----|-----|
| 3128 | x | **M** | WC | *WC* | CS |
| 3130 | x | **M** | WC | *WC* | CS |
| 3136 | x | **M** | WC | *WC* | CS |
| 3140 | x | **CC** | LS |  | ZG |
| 3141 |  | **CH** | RV | *RV* | ZG |
| 3143 | x | **M** | WC | *WC* | CS |
| 3146 |  | **CH** | RV | *RV* | ZG |
| 3147 |  | **CH** | RV | *RV* | ZG |
| 3148 |  | **CC** | LS | *LS* | CL |
| 3149 |  | **CH** | RV | *RV* | ZG |
| 3150 |  | **M** | SP | *SP* | BO |

**Names:**

| 3105 | JULIA | 3128 | VICTORIA |
|------|-------|------|----------|
| 3106 | ALEXANDRA | 3130 | PAMELA |
| 3113 | JESSICA | 3136 | DIANA |
| 3117 | CHRISTINA | 3143 | PATRICIA |

## OPEN FIRST

Mark 2D. Air conditioned. Stones equipment. 42/– 2T. B4 bogies. ETS 5.

† Interior modified to Pullman Car standards with new seating, new panelling, tungsten lighting and table lights.

Lot No. 30821 Derby 1971–72. 34 t.

| 3174 | † | **VN** | WC | *WC* | CS | GLAMIS |
|------|---|--------|----|----|-----|--------|
| 3182 | † | **VN** | WC |  | CS | WARWICK |
| 3188 |  | **PC** | LS | *LS* | CL | CADAIR IDRIS |

## OPEN FIRST

Mark 2E. Air conditioned. Stones equipment. 42/– 2T (* 36/– 2T). B4 bogies. ETS 5.

r Refurbished with new seats.
† Interior modified to Pullman Car standards with new seating, new panelling, tungsten lighting and table lights.

Lot No. 30843 Derby 1972–73. 32.5 t. († 35.8 t).

| 3223 |  | **RV** | LS |  | CL | DIAMOND |
|------|---|--------|----|----|-----|---------|
| 3229 |  | **PC** | LS | *LS* | CL | SNOWDON |
| 3231 | * | **PC** | LS | *LS* | CL | BEN CRUACHAN |
| 3232 | dr | **BG** | WC |  | CS |  |
| 3240 |  | **RV** | LS |  | CL | SAPPHIRE |
| 3247 | † | **VN** | WC | *WC* | CS | CHATSWORTH |
| 3267 | † | **VN** | WC | *WC* | CS | BELVOIR |
| 3273 | † | **VN** | WC | *WC* | CS | ALNWICK |
| 3275 | † | **VN** | WC | *WC* | CS | HARLECH |

# OPEN FIRST

Mark 2F. Air conditioned. 3278–3314/3359–79 have Stones equipment, others have Temperature Ltd. All refurbished in the 1980s with power-operated vestibule doors, new panels and new seat trim. 42/– 2T. B4 bogies. d. ETS 5X.

r   Further refurbished with table lamps and modified seats with burgundy seat trim.

**3278–3314.** Lot No. 30845 Derby 1973. 33.5 t.
**3325–3426.** Lot No. 30859 Derby 1973–74. 33.5 t.
**3431–3438.** Lot No. 30873 Derby 1974–75. 33.5 t.

| | | | | | | | | | | | |
|---|---|---|---|---|---|---|---|---|---|---|---|
| 3278 | r | **BG** | RV | *RV* | BU | | 3356 | r | **BG** | RV | *RV* | BU |
| 3304 | r | **BG** | RV | *RV* | BU | | 3359 | r | **M** | WC | *WC* | CS |
| 3312 | | **PC** | LS | *LS* | CL | | 3360 | r | **PC** | WC | *WC* | CS |
| 3313 | r | **M** | WC | *WC* | CS | | 3362 | r | **PC** | WC | *WC* | CS |
| 3314 | r | **BG** | RV | *RV* | BU | | 3364 | r | **BG** | RV | *RV* | BU |
| 3325 | r | **V** | RV | | ZG | | 3384 | r | **PC** | LS | *LS* | CL |
| 3326 | r | **M** | WC | *WC* | CS | | 3386 | r | **BG** | RV | *RV* | BU |
| 3330 | r | **CC** | LS | *LS* | CL | | 3390 | r | **BG** | RV | *RV* | BU |
| 3333 | r | **BG** | RV | *RV* | BU | | 3392 | r | **M** | WC | *WC* | CS |
| 3340 | r | **BG** | RV | *RV* | BU | | 3395 | r | **M** | WC | *WC* | CS |
| 3344 | r | **PC** | LS | *LS* | CL | | 3397 | r | **BG** | RV | *RV* | BU |
| 3345 | r | **BG** | RV | *RV* | BU | | 3426 | r | **PC** | LS | *LS* | CL |
| 3348 | r | **PC** | LS | *LS* | CL | | 3431 | r | **M** | WC | *WC* | CS |
| 3350 | r | **M** | WC | *WC* | CS | | 3438 | r | **PC** | LS | *LS* | CL |
| 3352 | r | **M** | WC | *WC* | CS | | | | | | | |

**Names:**

| | | | | |
|---|---|---|---|---|
| 3312 | HELVELLYN | | 3384 | PEN-Y-GHENT |
| 3344 | BEN CRUACHAN | | 3426 | BEN NEVIS |
| 3348 | INGLEBOROUGH | | 3438 | BEN LOMOND |

# OPEN STANDARD

Mark 1. –/64 2T. ETS 4.

**4831–36.** Lot No. 30506 Wolverton 1959. Commonwealth bogies. 37 t.
**4854/56.** Lot No. 30525 Wolverton 1959–60. B4 bogies. 33 t.

| | | | | | | | | | | | |
|---|---|---|---|---|---|---|---|---|---|---|---|
| 4831 | x | **M** | SP | *SP* | BO | | 4854 | x | **M** | WC | *WC* | CS |
| 4832 | x | **M** | SP | *SP* | BO | | 4856 | x | **M** | SP | *SP* | BO |
| 4836 | x | **M** | SP | *SP* | BO | | | | | | | |

## OPEN STANDARD

Mark 1. Commonwealth bogies. –/64 2T. ETS 4.

**4905.** Lot No. 30646 Wolverton 1961. 36 t.
**4927–5044.** Lot No. 30690 Wolverton 1961–62. 37 t.

| | | | | | | | | | |
|---|---|---|---|---|---|---|---|---|---|
| 4905 | x | **M** | WC | *WC* | CS | 4984 | x | **M** | WC | *WC* | CS |
| 4927 | x | **CC** | RV | *RV* | ZG | 4991 | | **CH** | RV | *RV* | ZG |
| 4931 | v | **M** | WC | *WC* | CS | 4994 | x | **M** | WC | *WC* | CS |
| 4940 | x | **M** | WC | *WC* | CS | 4998 | | **CH** | RV | *RV* | ZG |
| 4946 | x | **CH** | RV | *RV* | ZG | 5009 | x | **CH** | RV | *RV* | ZG |
| 4949 | x | **CH** | RV | *RV* | ZG | 5028 | x | **M** | SP | *SP* | BO |
| 4951 | x | **M** | WC | *WC* | CS | 5032 | x | **M** | WC | *WC* | CS |
| 4954 | v | **M** | WC | *WC* | CS | 5033 | x | **M** | WC | *WC* | CS |
| 4959 | | **CH** | RV | *RV* | ZG | 5035 | x | **M** | WC | *WC* | CS |
| 4960 | x | **M** | WC | *WC* | CS | 5044 | x | **M** | WC | *WC* | CS |
| 4973 | x | **M** | WC | *WC* | CS | | | | | | |

## OPEN STANDARD

Mark 2. Pressure ventilated. –/64 2T. B4 bogies. ETS 4.

Lot No. 30751 Derby 1965–67. 32 t.

| | | | | | | | | | | |
|---|---|---|---|---|---|---|---|---|---|---|
| 5157 | v | **CH** | VT | *VT* | TM | 5200 | v | **M** | WC | *WC* | CS |
| 5171 | v | **M** | WC | *WC* | CS | 5212 | v | **CH** | VT | *VT* | TM |
| 5177 | v | **CH** | VT | *VT* | TM | 5216 | v | **M** | WC | *WC* | CS |
| 5191 | v | **CH** | VT | *VT* | TM | 5222 | v | **M** | WC | *WC* | CS |
| 5198 | v | **CH** | VT | *VT* | TM | | | | | | |

## OPEN STANDARD

Mark 2. Pressure ventilated. –/48 2T. B4 bogies. ETS 4.

Lot No. 30752 Derby 1966. 32 t.

| | | | | | | | | | | |
|---|---|---|---|---|---|---|---|---|---|---|
| 5229 | | **M** | WC | *WC* | CS | 5239 | | **M** | WC | *WC* | CS |
| 5236 | v | **M** | WC | *WC* | CS | 5249 | v | **M** | WC | *WC* | CS |
| 5237 | v | **M** | WC | *WC* | CS | | | | | | |

## OPEN STANDARD

Mark 2A. Pressure ventilated. –/64 2T (w –/62 2T). B4 bogies. ETS 4.

f   Facelifted vehicles.

**5278–92.** Lot No. 30776 Derby 1967–68. 32 t.
**5366–5419.** Lot No. 30787 Derby 1968. 32 t.

| | | | | | | | | | | |
|---|---|---|---|---|---|---|---|---|---|---|
| 5278 | | **M** | WC | *WC* | CS | 5366 | f | **CC** | LS | *LS* | CL |
| 5292 | f | **CC** | RV | | BU | 5419 | w | **M** | WC | *WC* | CS |

# OPEN STANDARD

Mark 2B. Pressure ventilated. –/62. B4 bogies. ETS 4.

Lot No. 30791 Derby 1969. 32 t.

| 5487 | **M** | WC | *WC* | CS |
|------|-------|-----|------|-----|

# OPEN STANDARD

Mark 2E. Air conditioned. Stones equipment. Refurbished with new interior panelling. –/64 2T. B4 bogies. d. ETS 5.

s  Modified design of seat headrest and centre luggage stack. –/60 2T.

**5787.** Lot No. 30837 Derby 1972. 33.5 t.
**5810.** Lot No. 30844 Derby 1972–73. 33.5 t.

| 5787 | s | **DS** | DR | *DR* | KM | | 5810 | | **DR** | DR | | CN |
|------|---|--------|-----|------|-----|--|------|--|--------|-----|--|-----|

# OPEN STANDARD

Mark 2F. Air conditioned. Temperature Ltd equipment. InterCity 70 seats. All were refurbished in the 1980s with power-operated vestibule doors, new panels and seat trim. They have subsequently undergone a second refurbishment with carpets and new seat trim. –/64 2T. B4 bogies. d. ETS 5X.

q  Fitted with two wheelchair spaces. –/60 2T 2W.
s  Fitted with centre luggage stack. –/60 2T.
t  Fitted with centre luggage stack and wheelchair space. –/58 2T 1W.
† Retention toilets.

**5910–55.** Lot No. 30846 Derby 1973. 33 t.
**5961–6158.** Lot No. 30860 Derby 1973–74. 33 t.
**6173–83.** Lot No. 30874 Derby 1974–75. 33 t.

| 5910 | q | **V** | RV | | BU | | 5991 | | **CC** | LS | *LS* | CL |
|------|-----|--------|-----|------|-----|--|------|-----|--------|-----|------|-----|
| 5912 | | **PC** | LS | *LS* | CL | | 5995 | † | **DS** | DR | *DR* | KM |
| 5919 | † pt | **DR** | DR | | CN | | 5998 | | **BG** | RV | *RV* | BU |
| 5921 | | **AR** | RV | *RV* | BU | | 6000 | t | **M** | WC | *WC* | CS |
| 5929 | | **BG** | RV | *RV* | BU | | 6001 | † | **DS** | DR | *DR* | KM |
| 5937 | | **DS** | DR | *DR* | KM | | 6006 | | **AR** | RV | | BU |
| 5945 | | **SR** | RV | | KM | | 6008 | † s | **DS** | DR | *DR* | KM |
| 5950 | | **AR** | RV | *RV* | BU | | 6012 | | **M** | WC | *WC* | CS |
| 5952 | | **BG** | RV | *RV* | BU | | 6021 | | **PC** | WC | *WC* | CS |
| 5955 | | **SR** | RV | | KM | | 6022 | s | **M** | WC | *WC* | CS |
| 5961 | pt | **BG** | RV | *RV* | BU | | 6024 | | **BG** | RV | *RV* | BU |
| 5964 | | **AR** | RV | *RV* | BU | | 6027 | q | **SR** | RV | | KM |
| 5965 | t | **SR** | RV | | BU | | 6042 | | **AR** | RV | *RV* | BU |
| 5971 | † | **DS** | DR | *DR* | KM | | 6046 | † | **DR** | DR | | CN |
| 5976 | t | **SR** | RV | | BU | | 6051 | | **BG** | RV | *RV* | BU |
| 5985 | | **AR** | RV | *RV* | BU | | 6054 | | **BG** | RV | *RV* | BU |
| 5987 | | **SR** | RV | | BU | | 6064 | † | **DS** | DR | *DR* | KM |

| 6067 | pt | **BG** | RV | *RV* | BU | | 6141 | q | **V** | RV | | BU |
|------|-----|--------|-----|------|-----|---|------|-----|--------|-----|------|-----|
| 6103 |    | **M**  | WC | *WC* | CS | | 6158 |    | **BG** | RV | *RV* | BU |
| 6115 | s  | **M**  | WC | *WC* | CS | | 6173 | †  | **DS** | DR | *DR* | KM |
| 6117 | †  | **DS** | DR | *DR* | KM | | 6176 | t  | **BG** | RV | *RV* | BU |
| 6122 | †  | **DS** | DR | *DR* | KM | | 6177 | s  | **SR** | RV | | BU |
| 6137 | s pt | **SR** | RV | | BU | | 6183 | s | **SR** | RV | | BU |

# BRAKE GENERATOR VAN

Mark 1. Renumbered 1989 from BR departmental series. Converted from Gangwayed Brake Van in 1973 to three-phase supply brake generator van for use with HST trailers. Modified 1999 for use with locomotive-hauled stock. B5 bogies. ETS index ??.

Lot No. 30400 Pressed Steel 1958.

| 6310 | (81448, 975325) | **CH** | RV | *RV* | ZG |
|------|-----------------|--------|-----|------|-----|

# GENERATOR VAN

Mark 1. Converted from Gangwayed Brake Vans in 1992. B4 (* B5) bogies. ETS index 75.

**6311**. Lot No. 30162 Pressed Steel 1958. 37.25 t.
**6312**. Lot No. 30224 Cravens 1956. 37.25 t.
**6313**. Lot No. 30484 Pressed Steel 1958. 37.25 t.

| 6311 | (80903, 92911) | | **CC** | LS | *LS* | CL |
|------|----------------|---|--------|-----|------|-----|
| 6312 | (81023, 92925) | | **M**  | WC | *WC* | CS |
| 6313 | (81553, 92167) | * | **PC** | BE | *BP* | SL |

# BUFFET STANDARD

Mark 2C. Converted from Open Standard by removal of one seating bay and replacing this with a counter with a space for a trolley, now replaced with a more substantial buffet. Adjacent toilet removed and converted to steward's washing area/store. Pressure ventilated. –/55 1T. B4 bogies. ETS 4.

Lot No. 30795 Derby 1969–70. 32.5 t.

| 6528 | (5592) | **M** | WC | *WC* | CS |
|------|--------|-------|-----|------|-----|

# SLEEPER RECEPTION CAR

Mark 2F. Converted from Open First. These vehicles consist of pantry, microwave cooking facilities, seating area for passengers (with loose chairs, staff toilet plus two bars). Later refurbished again with new "sofa" seating as well as the loose chairs. Converted at RTC, Derby (6700), Ilford (6701–05) and Derby (6706–08). Air conditioned.

6700/01/03/05–08 have Stones equipment and 6702/04 have Temperature Ltd equipment. The number of seats per coach can vary but typically is 25/– 1T (12 seats as "sofa" seating and 13 loose chairs). B4 bogies. d. ETS 5X.

6705 and 6706 have been rebuilt as private saloons. Full details awaited.

6708 also carries the branding "THE HIPPOCRENE BAR".

**6700–02/04/08.** Lot No. 30859 Derby 1973–74. 33.5 t.
**6703/05–07.** Lot No. 30845 Derby 1973. 33.5 t.

| | | | | | | |
|---|---|---|---|---|---|---|
| 6700 | (3347) | **CA** | ER | | YA | |
| 6701 | (3346) | **CA** | BR | | ZM | |
| 6702 | (3421) | **FS** | ER | | YA | |
| 6703 | (3308) | **CA** | ER | | WO | |
| 6704 | (3341) | **FS** | ER | | YA | |
| 6705 | (3310, 6430) | **CC** | LS | *LS* | CL | ARDNAMURCHAN |
| 6706 | (3283, 6421) | **CC** | LS | *LS* | CL | MOUNT MGAHINGA |
| 6707 | (3276, 6418) | **FS** | ER | | YA | |
| 6708 | (3370) | **PC** | LS | *LS* | CL | MOUNT HELICON |

# BUFFET FIRST

Mark 2D. Converted from Buffet Standard by the removal of another seating bay and fitting a more substantial buffet counter with boiler and microwave oven. Now converted to First Class with new seating and end luggage stacks. Air conditioned. Stones equipment. 30/– 1T. B4 bogies. d. ETS 5. Lot No. 30822 Derby 1971. 33 t.

| | | | | | | |
|---|---|---|---|---|---|---|
| 6723 | (5641, 6662) | **M** | WC | | CS | |
| 6724 | (5721, 6665) | **M** | WC | *WC* | CS | |

# OPEN BRAKE STANDARD WITH TROLLEY SPACE

Mark 2. This vehicle uses the same bodyshell as Mark 2 Corridor Brake Firsts and has First Class seat spacing and wider tables. Converted from Open Brake Standard by removal of one seating bay and replacing this with a counter with a space for a trolley. Adjacent toilet removed and converted to a steward's washing area/store. –/23. B4 bogies. ETS 4.

Lot No. 30757 Derby 1966. 31 t.

| | | | | | | | |
|---|---|---|---|---|---|---|---|
| 9101 | (9398) | v | **CH** | VT | *VT* | TM | |

## OPEN BRAKE STANDARD

Mark 2. These vehicles use the same bodyshell as Mark 2 Corridor Brake Firsts and have First Class seat spacing and wider tables. Pressure ventilated. –/31 1T. B4 bogies. ETS 4.

9104 was originally numbered 9401. It was renumbered when converted to Open Brake Standard with trolley space. Now returned to original layout.

Lot No. 30757 Derby 1966. 31.5 t.

| | | | | | | | | | | | | |
|---|---|---|---|---|---|---|---|---|---|---|---|---|
| 9104 | v | **M** | WC | *WC* | CS | | 9392 | v | **M** | WC | *WC* | CS |
| 9391 | | **M** | WC | *WC* | CS | | | | | | | |

## OPEN BRAKE STANDARD

Mark 2D. Air conditioned. Stones Equipment. B4 bogies. d. pg. ETS 5.

r Refurbished with new interior panelling –/31 1T.
s Refurbished with new seating –/22 1TD.

Lot No. 30824 Derby 1971. 33 t.

| | | | | | | | | | | | |
|---|---|---|---|---|---|---|---|---|---|---|---|
| 9479 | r | **PC** | LS | *LS* | CL | | 9493 | s | **M** | WC | *WC* | CS |
| 9488 | s | **SR** | DR | *DR* | KM | | | | | | | |

## OPEN BRAKE STANDARD

Mark 2E. Air conditioned. Stones Equipment. Refurbished with new interior panelling. –/32 1T (* –/30 1T 1W). B4 bogies. d. pg. ETS 5.

Lot No. 30838 Derby 1972. 33 t.

**Non-standard livery:** 9502 Pullman umber & cream.

s Modified design of seat headrest.

| | | | | | | | | | | | |
|---|---|---|---|---|---|---|---|---|---|---|---|
| 9497 | | **CA** | ER | | WO | | 9507 | s | **BG** | RV | *RV* | BU |
| 9502 | s | **0** | BE | *BP* | SL | | 9509 | s | **AV** | RV | | BU |
| 9504 | s* | **BG** | RV | *RV* | BU | | | | | | | |

## OPEN BRAKE STANDARD

Mark 2F. Air conditioned. Temperature Ltd equipment. All were refurbished in the 1980s with power-operated vestibule doors, new panels and seat trim. All now further refurbished with carpets. –/32 1T (w –/30 1T 1W). B4 bogies. d. pg. ETS 5X.

9537 has had all its seats removed for the purpose of carrying luggage.

Lot No. 30861 Derby 1974. 34 t.

| | | | | | | | | | | | |
|---|---|---|---|---|---|---|---|---|---|---|---|
| 9513 | | **IC** | ER | | WO | | 9526 | n | **BG** | RV | *RV* | BU |
| 9520 | nw | **AR** | RV | *RV* | BU | | 9527 | n | **SR** | RV | | KM |
| 9521 | | **DS** | RV | *RV* | BU | | 9537 | n | **V** | RV | | BU |
| 9525 | | **DR** | DR | | CN | | 9539 | | **SR** | RV | | KM |

# DRIVING OPEN BRAKE STANDARD

Mark 2F. Air conditioned. Temperature Ltd equipment. Push & pull (tdm system). Converted from Open Brake Standard, these vehicles originally had half cabs at the brake end. They have since been refurbished and have had their cabs widened and the cab-end gangways removed. Five vehicles (9701–03/08/14) have been converted for use in Network Rail test trains and can be found in the Service Stock section of this book. –/30(+1) 1W. B4 bogies. d. pg. Cowcatchers. ETS 5X.

Lot No. 30861 Derby 1974. Converted Glasgow 1979. Disc brakes. 34 t.

| | | | | | | | | | |
|---|---|---|---|---|---|---|---|---|---|
| 9704 | (9512) | **DS** | DR | LW | | 9709 | (9515) | **DS** | DR | LW |
| 9705 | (9519) | **DS** | DR | LW | | 9710 | (9518) | **DS** | DR | BO |
| 9707 | (9511) | **DS** | DR | LW | | | | | |

# OPEN BRAKE UNCLASSIFIED

Mark 2E. Converted from Open Standard with new seating by Railcare, Wolverton. Air conditioned. Stones equipment. Five vehicles (9801/03/06/08/10) are currently used in Network Rail test trains and can be found in the Service Stock section of this book.–/31 2T. B4 bogies. d. ETS 4X.

**9800/02.** Lot No. 30837 Derby 1972. 33.5 t.
**9804–09.** Lot No. 30844 Derby 1972–73. 33.5 t.

| | | | | | | | | | |
|---|---|---|---|---|---|---|---|---|---|
| 9800 | (5751) | **CA** | ER | WO | | 9805 | (5833) | **FS** | ER | YA |
| 9802 | (5772) | **CA** | ER | YA | | 9807 | (5851) | **FS** | ER | YA |
| 9804 | (5826) | **FS** | ER | YA | | 9809 | (5890) | **FS** | ER | YA |

# KITCHEN BUFFET FIRST

Mark 3A. Air conditioned. Converted from HST catering vehicles and Mark 3 Open Firsts. 18/– plus two seats for staff use (* 24/–, † 35 1T, ‡ 23/– 1T 1W). BT10 bogies. d. ETS 14X.

† Refurbished Great Western Railway Sleeper coaches fitted with new Transcal seating.

**Non-standard liveries:**

10211 EWS dark maroon.
10241 Livery trials.

**10211.** Lot No. 30884 Derby 1977. 39.8 t.
**10212–229.** Lot No. 30878 Derby 1975–76. 39.8 t.
**10237–259.** Lot No. 30890 Derby 1979. 39.8 t.

| | | | | | | | | | | |
|---|---|---|---|---|---|---|---|---|---|---|
| 10211 | (40510) | | **O** | DB | *DB* | TO | | 10229 | (11059) | * | **GA** | ER | | WO |
| 10212 | (11049) | | **VT** | ER | | YA | | 10237 | (10022) | * | **B** | DA | *RO* | RJ |
| 10217 | (11051) | † | **GW** | P | *GW* | PZ | | 10241 | (10009) | * | **O** | P | | IL |
| 10219 | (11047) | † | **GW** | P | *GW* | PZ | | 10249 | (10012) | ‡ | **AW** | RO | | ZA |
| 10225 | (11014) | † | **GW** | P | *GW* | PZ | | 10259 | (10025) | ‡ | **AW** | RO | | CN |

## KITCHEN BUFFET FIRST

Mark 3A. Air conditioned. Rebuilt 2011–12 and fitted with sliding plug doors. Interiors originally refurbished for Wrexham & Shropshire with Primarius seating, a new kitchen area and universal-access toilet. Retention toilets. 30/– 1TD 1W. BT10 bogies. ETS 14X.

**10271/273/274.** Lot No. 30890 Derby 1979. 41.3 t.
**10272.** Lot No. 30884 Derby 1977. 41.3 t.

| | | | | |
|---|---|---|---|---|
| 10271 (10018, 10236) | **CM** | AV | *CR* | AL |
| 10272 (40517, 10208) | **CM** | AV | *CR* | AL |
| 10273 (10021, 10230) | **CM** | AV | *CR* | AL |
| 10274 (10010, 10255) | **CM** | AV | *CR* | AL |

## KITCHEN BUFFET STANDARD

Mark 4. Air conditioned. Rebuilt from First to Standard Class with bar adjacent to seating area instead of adjacent to end of coach. Retention toilets. –/30 1T. BT41 bogies. ETS 6X.

Lot No. 31045 Metro-Cammell 1989–92. 43.2 t.

| | | | | | | | | | |
|---|---|---|---|---|---|---|---|---|---|
| 10300 | **VE** | E | *LN* | BN | 10318 | **GC** | E | | WB |
| 10301 | **GC** | E | | WB | 10319 | **VE** | E | | WS |
| 10302 | **VE** | E | | WS | 10320 | **VE** | E | | WS |
| 10303 | **VE** | E | | WS | 10321 | **GC** | E | | WB |
| 10304 | **VE** | E | | WS | 10323 | **VE** | E | | WS |
| 10305 | **VE** | E | | WS | 10324 | **VE** | E | *LN* | BN |
| 10306 | **VE** | E | *LN* | BN | 10325 | **VE** | E | *TW* | CF |
| 10307 | **VE** | E | | WS | 10326 | **VE** | E | | WS |
| 10308 | **VE** | E | | WS | 10328 | **VE** | E | *TW* | CF |
| 10309 | **VE** | E | *LN* | BN | 10329 | **VE** | E | | WS |
| 10311 | **VE** | E | *LN* | BN | 10330 | **GC** | E | | WB |
| 10312 | **VE** | E | *TW* | CF | 10331 | **VE** | E | | WS |
| 10313 | **VE** | E | *LN* | BN | 10332 | **VE** | E | | WS |
| 10315 | **VE** | E | | WS | 10333 | **VE** | E | *LN* | BN |

## BUFFET STANDARD

Mark 3A. Air conditioned. Converted from Mark 3 Open Standard at Derby 2006. –/54. d. ETS 13X.

Lot No. 30877 Derby 1975–77. 37.8 t.

| | | | | |
|---|---|---|---|---|
| 10406 (12020) | **GA** | EL | | BR |

# BUFFET STANDARD

Mark 3A. Air conditioned. Converted from Mark 3 Kitchen Buffet First 2015–16. –/54. BT10 bogies. d. ETS 13X.

**10411.** Lot No. 30884 Derby 1977. 37.8 t.
**10413/416.** Lot No. 30878 Derby 1975–76. 37.8 t.
**10417.** Lot No. 30890 Derby 1979. 37.8 t.

| 10411 | (40519, 10200) | **IC** | LS | | ZG |
|---|---|---|---|---|---|
| 10413 | (11034, 10214) | **GA** | ER | | YA |
| 10416 | (11035, 10228) | **IC** | LS | | ZG |

# SLEEPING CAR WITH PANTRY

Mark 3A. Air conditioned. Retention toilets. 12 compartments with a fixed lower berth and a hinged upper berth, plus an attendant's compartment (* 11 compartments with a fixed lower berth and a hinged upper berth + one compartment for a disabled person. 1TD). 2T. BT10 bogies. d. ETS 7X.

**Non-standard livery:** 10546 EWS dark maroon.

Lot No. 30960 Derby 1981–83. 41 t.

| 10501 | **FS** | ER | | YA | | 10584 | | **GW** | P | *GW* | PZ |
|---|---|---|---|---|---|---|---|---|---|---|---|
| 10502 | **FS** | ER | | YA | | 10589 | | **GW** | P | *GW* | PZ |
| 10504 | **FS** | LS | | KR | | 10590 | | **GW** | P | *GW* | PZ |
| 10513 | **FS** | LS | | KR | | 10594 | | **GW** | P | *GW* | PZ |
| 10519 | **FS** | LS | | CL | | 10596 | | **GW** | P | *GW* | PZ |
| 10520 | **CC** | LS | *LS* | CL | | 10598 | | **FS** | WC | | CS |
| 10532 | **GW** | P | *GW* | PZ | | 10600 | | **FS** | ER | | YA |
| 10534 | **GW** | P | *GW* | PZ | | 10601 | * | **GW** | P | *GW* | PZ |
| 10542 | **FS** | P | | LM | | 10610 | | **FS** | WC | | CS |
| 10546 | **O** | DB | *DB* | TO | | 10612 | * | **GW** | P | *GW* | PZ |
| 10551 | **FS** | P | | LA | | 10614 | | **FS** | WC | | CS |
| 10553 | **FS** | P | | LA | | 10616 | * | **GW** | P | *GW* | PZ |
| 10563 | **GW** | P | *GW* | PZ | | | | | | | |

# SLEEPING CAR

Mark 3A. Air conditioned. Retention toilets. 13 compartments with a fixed lower berth and a hinged upper berth (* 11 compartments with a fixed lower berth and a hinged upper berth + one compartment for a disabled person. 1TD). 2T. BT10 bogies. ETS 6X.

10734 was originally 2914 and used as a Royal Train staff sleeping car. It has 12 berths and a shower room and is ETS 11X.

**10648–729.** Lot No. 30961 Derby 1980–84. 43.5 t.
**10734.** Lot No. 31002 Derby/Wolverton 1985. 42.5 t.

| | | | | | | | | |
|---|---|---|---|---|---|---|---|---|
| 10648 d* | **FS** | LS | | KR | 10703 d | **FS** | WC | CS |
| 10650 d* | **FS** | LS | | KR | 10714 d* | **FS** | PO | CS |
| 10675 d | **FS** | LS | | KR | 10718 d* | **FS** | WC | CS |
| 10680 d* | **FS** | P | | LM | 10719 d* | **FS** | PO | CS |
| 10683 d | **FS** | LS | | KR | 10729 | **VN** | WC *WC* | CS |
| 10688 d | **PC** | LS | *LS* | CL | 10734 | **VN** | WC *WC* | CS |
| 10699 d* | **FS** | ER | | YA | | | | |

**Names:**

| | | | |
|---|---|---|---|
| 10729 | CREWE | 10734 | BALMORAL |

---

# OPEN FIRST

Mark 3A. Air conditioned. All refurbished with table lamps and new seat cushions and trim. 48/– 2T. BT10 bogies. d. ETS 6X.

† Reseated with Standard Class seats: –/68 2T 2W.

**Non-standard livery:** 11039 EWS dark maroon.

Lot No. 30878 Derby 1975–76. 34.3 t.

| | | | | | | | | | |
|---|---|---|---|---|---|---|---|---|---|
| 11018 | **VT** | DA *RO* | | RJ | 11039 | **0** | DB *DB* | | TO |
| 11029 † | **CM** | AV | | LM | 11048 | **VT** | DA *RO* | | RJ |
| 11031 † | **CM** | AV | | LM | | | | | |

---

# OPEN FIRST

Mark 3B. Air conditioned. InterCity 80 seats. All refurbished with table lamps and new seat cushions and trim. Retention toilets. 48/– 1T. BT10 bogies. d. ETS 6X.

† Fitted with disabled toilet and reduced seating, including three Compin Pegasus seats. 37/– 1TD 2W.

**Non-standard livery:** 11074 Original HST prototype grey & BR blue.

Lot No. 30982 Derby 1985. 36.5 t.

| | | | | | | | | | |
|---|---|---|---|---|---|---|---|---|---|
| 11068 | **IC** | LS *LS* | CL | 11090 † | **GA** | DA *RO* | | RJ |
| 11070 | **IC** | LS *LS* | CL | 11091 | **GA** | LS *LS* | | CL |
| 11074 | **0** | DA *RO* | RJ | 11092 † | **GA** | EL | | ZA |
| 11075 | **IC** | LS *LS* | CL | 11093 † | **GA** | EL | | ZA |
| 11076 | **IC** | LS *LS* | CL | 11094 † | **GA** | P | | EH |
| 11077 | **GA** | LS *LS* | CL | 11095 † | **GA** | PO | | YA |
| 11078 † | **GA** | ER | YA | 11098 † | **IC** | LS *LS* | | CL |
| 11087 † | **IC** | LS *LS* | CL | 11099 † | **GA** | EL | | ZA |
| 11088 † | **GA** | P | BU | 11101 † | **GA** | EL | | ZA |

## OPEN FIRST

Mark 4. Air conditioned. Rebuilt with new interior by Bombardier Wakefield 2003–05 (some converted from Standard Class vehicles). Retention toilets. 41/– 1T (plus 2 seats for staff use). BT41 bogies. ETS 6X.

**11201–11229.** Lot No. 31046 Metro-Cammell 1989–92. 41.3 t.
**11278–11299.** Lot No. 31049 Metro-Cammell 1989–92. 41.3 t.

| | | | | | | | | | | |
|---|---|---|---|---|---|---|---|---|---|---|
| 11201 | | **VE** | E | | WS | 11285 (12537) | **VE** | E | *LN* | BN |
| 11219 | | **VE** | E | | WS | 11286 (12482) | **VE** | E | *LN* | BN |
| 11229 | | **VE** | E | *LN* | BN | 11287 (12527) | **VE** | E | | WS |
| 11278 (12479) | **VE** | E | | | WS | 11288 (12517) | **VE** | E | *LN* | BN |
| 11279 (12521) | **VE** | E | *LN* | | BN | 11289 (12528) | **VE** | E | | WS |
| 11281 (12418) | **VE** | E | | | WS | 11295 (12475) | **VE** | E | *LN* | BN |
| 11282 (12524) | **VE** | E | | | WS | 11298 (12416) | **VE** | E | | WS |
| 11284 (12487) | **VE** | E | *LN* | | BN | 11299 (12532) | **VE** | E | | WS |

## OPEN FIRST (DISABLED)

Mark 4. Air conditioned. Rebuilt from Open First by Bombardier Wakefield 2003–05. Retention toilets. 42/– 1TD 1W. BT41 bogies. ETS 6X.

Lot No. 31046 Metro-Cammell 1989–92. 40.7 t.

| | | | | | | | | | |
|---|---|---|---|---|---|---|---|---|---|
| 11301 (11215) | **VE** | E | | WS | 11315 (11238) | **VE** | E | *LN* | BN |
| 11302 (11203) | **VE** | E | | WS | 11316 (11227) | **VE** | E | | WS |
| 11303 (11211) | **VE** | E | | WS | 11317 (11223) | **VE** | E | *LN* | BN |
| 11304 (11257) | **VE** | E | | WS | 11318 (11251) | **VE** | E | | WS |
| 11305 (11261) | **VE** | E | | WS | 11319 (11247) | **GC** | E | | WB |
| 11306 (11276) | **VE** | E | *LN* | BN | 11320 (11255) | **GC** | E | | WB |
| 11307 (11217) | **VE** | E | | WS | 11321 (11245) | **GC** | E | | WB |
| 11308 (11263) | **VE** | E | *LN* | BN | 11322 (11228) | **GC** | E | | WB |
| 11309 (11259) | **VE** | E | | WS | 11323 (11235) | **VE** | E | *TW* | CF |
| 11310 (11272) | **VE** | E | | WS | 11324 (11253) | **VE** | E | *TW* | CF |
| 11311 (11221) | **VE** | E | | WS | 11325 (11231) | **VE** | E | *TW* | CF |
| 11312 (11225) | **VE** | E | *LN* | BN | 11326 (11206) | **VE** | E | *LN* | BN |
| 11313 (11210) | **VE** | E | *LN* | BN | 11327 (11236) | **VE** | E | | WS |
| 11314 (11207) | **VE** | E | | WS | | | | | |

## OPEN FIRST

Mark 4. Air conditioned. Rebuilt from Open First by Bombardier Wakefield 2003–05. Separate area for 7 smokers, although smoking is no longer allowed. Retention toilets. 46/– 1TD 1W. BT41 bogies. ETS 6X.

Lot No. 31046 Metro-Cammell 1989–92. 42.1 t.

| | | | | | | | | | |
|---|---|---|---|---|---|---|---|---|---|
| 11401 (11214) | **VE** | E | | WS | 11405 (11204) | **VE** | E | | WS |
| 11403 (11258) | **VE** | E | | WS | 11406 (11205) | **VE** | E | *LN* | BN |
| 11404 (11202) | **VE** | E | | WS | 11407 (11256) | **VE** | E | | WS |

| | | | | | | | | | |
|---|---|---|---|---|---|---|---|---|---|
| 11408 | (11218) | **VE** | E | *LN* | BN | 11415 | (11208) | **VE** | E | *LN* | BN |

| | | | | | | | | | | | |
|---|---|---|---|---|---|---|---|---|---|---|---|
| 11408 | (11218) | **VE** | E | *LN* | BN | 11415 | (11208) | **VE** | E | *LN* | BN |
| 11409 | (11262) | **VE** | E | | WS | 11416 | (11254) | **VE** | E | | WS |
| 11411 | (11240) | **VE** | E | | WS | 11417 | (11226) | **VE** | E | *LN* | BN |
| 11412 | (11209) | **VE** | E | *LN* | BN | 11418 | (11222) | **VE** | E | | WS |
| 11413 | (11212) | **VE** | E | *LN* | BN | 11426 | (11252) | **VE** | E | *LN* | BN |
| 11414 | (11246) | **VE** | E | | WS | 11430 | (11248) | **VE** | E | | ZB |

## OPEN FIRST

CAF Mark 5A. Air conditioned. Currently entering service with TransPennine Express. Retention toilets. 30/– 1TD 2W. CAF bogies. ETS XX.

CAF Beasain 2017–18. 32.7 t.

| | | | | | | | | | |
|---|---|---|---|---|---|---|---|---|---|
| 11501 | **TP** | BN | *TP* | MA | 11508 | **TP** | BN | *TP* | MA |
| 11502 | **TP** | BN | | MA | 11509 | **TP** | BN | *TP* | MA |
| 11503 | **TP** | BN | | MA | 11510 | **TP** | BN | *TP* | MA |
| 11504 | **TP** | BN | *TP* | MA | 11511 | **TP** | BN | *TP* | MA |
| 11505 | **TP** | BN | *TP* | MA | 11512 | **TP** | BN | *TP* | MA |
| 11506 | **TP** | BN | *TP* | MA | 11513 | **TP** | BN | *TP* | MA |
| 11507 | **TP** | BN | *TP* | MA | | | | | |

## OPEN FIRST

Mark 4. Air conditioned. Converted from Kitchen Buffet Standard with new interior by Bombardier Wakefield 2005. Retention toilets. 46/– 1T. BT41 bogies. ETS 6X.

Lot No. 31046 Metro-Cammell 1989–92. 41.3 t.

| | | | | |
|---|---|---|---|---|
| 11999 | (10316) | **VE** | E | ZB |

## OPEN STANDARD

Mark 3A. Air conditioned. All refurbished with modified seat backs and new layout and further refurbished with new seat trim. –/76 2T († –/70 2T 1W, t –/72 2T, z –/70 1TD 1T 2W). BT10 bogies. d. ETS 6X.

* Further refurbished with more unidirectional seating and one toilet removed. Retention toilets. –/80 1T.
s Refurbished Sleeper day coaches fitted with new Transcal seating to a 2+2 layout and a universal access toilet. Retention toilets. –/65 1TD 1W.

12171 was converted from Open Composite 11910, formerly Open First 11010.

**Non-standard livery:** 12092 Original HST prototype grey & BR blue.

**12012–167.** Lot No. 30877 Derby 1975–77. 34.3 t.
**12171.** Lot No. 30878 Derby 1975–76. 34.3 t.

| | | | | | | | | | | |
|---|---|---|---|---|---|---|---|---|---|---|
| 12012 | * | **GA** | P | | EH | 12097 | * | **GA** | DA | *RO* | RJ |
| 12017 | t | **CM** | AV | | LM | 12098 | * | **GA** | ER | | YA |
| 12019 | * | **GA** | P | | EH | 12100 | s | **GW** | P | *GW* | PZ |
| 12021 | * | **GA** | ER | | YA | 12111 | * | **GA** | LS | | CL |
| 12026 | * | **GA** | P | | EH | 12115 | * | **GA** | P | | EH |
| 12027 | * | **GA** | P | | EH | 12116 | * | **GA** | P | | LM |
| 12032 | * | **GA** | DA | *RO* | RJ | 12119 | t | **CM** | AV | | LM |
| 12035 | * | **GA** | P | | LM | 12122 | z | **VT** | DA | *RO* | RJ |
| 12036 | † | **CM** | AV | | LM | 12125 | * | **GA** | EL | | BR |
| 12041 | * | **GA** | P | | EH | 12133 | | **VT** | DA | *RO* | RJ |
| 12043 | † | **CM** | AV | | LM | 12137 | * | **GA** | P | | LM |
| 12046 | * | **GA** | P | | LM | 12138 | | **VT** | DA | *RO* | RJ |
| 12054 | † | **CM** | AV | | LM | 12142 | s | **GW** | P | *GW* | PZ |
| 12056 | * | **GA** | P | | LM | 12146 | * | **GA** | P | | LM |
| 12061 | * | **GA** | P | | LM | 12151 | * | **GA** | P | | EH |
| 12064 | * | **GA** | DA | *RO* | RJ | 12154 | * | **GA** | EL | | BR |
| 12078 | | **VT** | DA | *RO* | RJ | 12159 | * | **GA** | P | | LM |
| 12079 | * | **GA** | P | | LM | 12161 | s | **GW** | P | *GW* | PZ |
| 12090 | * | **GA** | P | | LM | 12164 | * | **GA** | P | | LM |
| 12091 | * | **GA** | DA | *RO* | RJ | 12167 | * | **GA** | P | | LM |
| 12092 | | **0** | DA | *RO* | RJ | 12171 | * | **IC** | LS | | ZG |
| 12094 | | **CM** | AV | | LM | | | | | | |

## OPEN STANDARD

Mark 3A (†) or Mark 3B. Air conditioned. Converted from Mark 3A or 3B Open First. Fitted with Grammer seating. –/70 2T 1W. BT10 bogies. d. ETS 6X.

**12176–181/185.** Mark 3B. Lot No. 30982 Derby 1985. 38.5 t.
**12182–184.** Mark 3A. Lot No. 30878 Derby 1975–76. 38.5 t.

| | | | | |
|---|---|---|---|---|
| 12176 | (11064) | | **AW** | RO | ZA |
| 12177 | (11065) | | **AW** | RO | CN |
| 12178 | (11071) | | **AW** | RO | CN |
| 12179 | (11083) | | **AW** | RO | CN |
| 12180 | (11084) | | **AW** | RO | CN |
| 12181 | (11086) | | **AW** | RO | CN |
| 12182 | (11013) | † | **AW** | RO | CN |
| 12183 | (11027) | † | **AW** | RO | BR |
| 12184 | (11044) | † | **AW** | RO | BR |
| 12185 | (11089) | | **AW** | RO | BR |

## OPEN STANDARD (END)

Mark 4. Air conditioned. Rebuilt with new interior by Bombardier Wakefield 2003–05. Separate area for 26 smokers, although smoking is no longer allowed. Retention toilets. –/76 1T. BT41 bogies. ETS 6X.

12232 was converted from the original 12405.

**12200–231.** Lot No. 31047 Metro-Cammell 1989–91. 39.5 t.
**12232.** Lot No. 31049 Metro-Cammell 1989–92. 39.5 t.

| 12200 | **VE** | E |    | WS |
| 12201 | **VE** | E |    | WS |
| 12202 | **VE** | E |    | WS |
| 12203 | **VE** | E |    | WS |
| 12204 | **VE** | E |    | WS |
| 12205 | **VE** | E | *LN* | BN |
| 12207 | **VE** | E |    | WS |
| 12208 | **VE** | E | *LN* | BN |
| 12209 | **VE** | E |    | WS |
| 12210 | **GC** | E |    | WB |
| 12211 | **GC** | E |    | WB |
| 12212 | **VE** | E | *LN* | BN |
| 12213 | **VE** | E |    | WS |
| 12214 | **VE** | E | *LN* | BN |
| 12215 | **VE** | E |    | WS |
| 12216 | **VE** | E |    | WS |
| 12217 | **VE** | E | *TW* | CF |
| 12219 | **VE** | E | *TW* | CF |
| 12220 | **VE** | E | *LN* | BN |
| 12222 | **GC** | E |    | WB |
| 12223 | **VE** | E | *LN* | BN |
| 12224 | **GC** | E |    | WB |
| 12225 | **VE** | E | *TW* | CF |
| 12226 | **VE** | E | *LN* | BN |
| 12228 | **VE** | E | *LN* | BN |
| 12229 | **VE** | E |    | WS |
| 12230 | **VE** | E |    | WS |
| 12231 | **VE** | E |    | WS |
| 12232 | **VE** | E |    | WS |

## OPEN STANDARD (DISABLED)

Mark 4. Air conditioned. Rebuilt with new interior by Bombardier Wakefield 2003–05. Retention toilets. –/68 2W 1TD. BT41 bogies. ETS 6X.

**12300–330**. Lot No. 31048 Metro-Cammell 1989–91. 39.4 t.

| 12300 | **VE** | E |    | WS |
| 12301 | **VE** | E |    | WS |
| 12302 | **VE** | E |    | WS |
| 12303 | **VE** | E | *LN* | BN |
| 12304 | **VE** | E |    | WS |
| 12305 | **VE** | E |    | WS |
| 12307 | **VE** | E |    | WS |
| 12308 | **VE** | E |    | WS |
| 12309 | **VE** | E | *LN* | BN |
| 12310 | **GC** | E |    | WB |
| 12311 | **VE** | E | *LN* | BN |
| 12312 | **VE** | E |    | WS |
| 12313 | **VE** | E | *LN* | BN |
| 12315 | **VE** | E |    | WS |
| 12316 | **GC** | E |    | WB |
| 12317 | **VE** | E |    | WS |
| 12318 | **VE** | E |    | WS |
| 12319 | **VE** | E |    | WS |
| 12322 | **VE** | E |    | WS |
| 12323 | **GC** | E |    | WB |
| 12324 | **VE** | E |    | WS |
| 12325 | **VE** | E | *LN* | BN |
| 12326 | **GC** | E |    | WB |
| 12327 | **VE** | E |    | WS |
| 12328 | **VE** | E | *LN* | BN |
| 12329 | **VE** | E |    | WS |
| 12330 | **VE** | E | *LN* | BN |

## OPEN STANDARD

Mark 4. Air conditioned. Rebuilt with new interior by Bombardier Wakefield 2003–05. Retention toilets. –/76 1T. BT41 bogies. ETS 6X.

12405 is the second coach to carry that number. It was built from the bodyshell originally intended for 12221. The original 12405 is now 12232.

Lot No. 31049 Metro-Cammell 1989–92. 40.8 t.

| 12404 | **VE** | E | *LN* | BN | 12448 | **VE** | E | | WS |
|---|---|---|---|---|---|---|---|---|---|
| 12405 | **VE** | E | | WS | 12449 | **VE** | E | | WS |
| 12406 | **VE** | E | *LN* | BN | 12450 | **VE** | E | | WS |
| 12407 | **VE** | E | *LN* | BN | 12452 | **GC** | E | | WB |
| 12409 | **VE** | E | *LN* | BN | 12453 | **VE** | E | | WS |
| 12410 | **VE** | E | | WS | 12454 | **VE** | E | *TW* | CF |
| 12411 | **VE** | E | | WS | 12459 | **VE** | E | | WS |
| 12414 | **VE** | E | | WS | 12461 | **GC** | E | | WB |
| 12415 | **VE** | E | | WS | 12463 | **VE** | E | | ZB |
| 12417 | **VE** | E | | WS | 12465 | **VE** | E | *LN* | BN |
| 12419 | **VE** | E | | WS | 12467 | **VE** | E | | WS |
| 12420 | **VE** | E | *LN* | BN | 12468 | **VE** | E | | WS |
| 12421 | **VE** | E | | WS | 12469 | **VE** | E | *LN* | BN |
| 12422 | **VE** | E | *LN* | BN | 12472 | **VE** | E | | LM |
| 12423 | **VE** | E | | WS | 12474 | **VE** | E | *LN* | BN |
| 12424 | **VE** | E | *LN* | BN | 12477 | **GC** | E | | WB |
| 12426 | **VE** | E | *LN* | BN | 12478 | **VE** | E | | WS |
| 12427 | **VE** | E | *LN* | BN | 12480 | **VE** | E | | WS |
| 12428 | **VE** | E | | WS | 12481 | **VE** | E | *LN* | BN |
| 12429 | **VE** | E | *LN* | BN | 12483 | **VE** | E | | WS |
| 12430 | **VE** | E | *LN* | BN | 12484 | **VE** | E | | WS |
| 12431 | **VE** | E | *LN* | BN | 12485 | **VE** | E | *LN* | BN |
| 12432 | **VE** | E | *LN* | BN | 12486 | **VE** | E | | WS |
| 12433 | **VE** | E | | WS | 12488 | **VE** | E | | WS |
| 12434 | **GC** | E | | WB | 12489 | **VE** | E | | WS |
| 12436 | **VE** | E | | WS | 12513 | **VE** | E | | WS |
| 12437 | **VE** | E | | WS | 12514 | **VE** | E | | WS |
| 12439 | **VE** | E | | ZB | 12515 | **VE** | E | *LN* | BN |
| 12440 | **VE** | E | | ZB | 12518 | **VE** | E | | WS |
| 12442 | **VE** | E | *LN* | BN | 12520 | **VE** | E | | WS |
| 12443 | **VE** | E | | WS | 12522 | **VE** | E | | WS |
| 12444 | **VE** | E | *LN* | BN | 12526 | **VE** | E | | WS |
| 12446 | **VE** | E | *TW* | CF | 12533 | **VE** | E | | ZB |
| 12447 | **VE** | E | *TW* | CF | 12534 | **VE** | E | | LM |

## OPEN STANDARD

Mark 3A. Air conditioned. Rebuilt 2011–13 and fitted with sliding plug doors. Original InterCity 70 seating retained but mainly arranged around tables. Retention toilets. –/72(+6) or * –/69(+4) 1T. BT10 bogies. ETS 6X.

**12602–609/614–616/618/620**. Lot No. 30877 Derby 1975–77. 36.2 t (* 37.1 t).
**12601/613/617–619/621/623/625/627**. Lot No. 30878 Derby 1975–76. 36.2 t (* 37.1 t).

| 12602 | (12072) | | **CM** | AV | *CR* | AL |
|---|---|---|---|---|---|---|
| 12603 | (12053) | * | **CM** | AV | *CR* | AL |
| 12604 | (12131) | | **CM** | AV | *CR* | AL |
| 12605 | (11040) | * | **CM** | AV | *CR* | AL |
| 12606 | (12048) | | **CM** | AV | *CR* | AL |
| 12607 | (12038) | * | **CM** | AV | *CR* | AL |

| | | | | | |
|---|---|---|---|---|---|
| 12608 (12069) | | **CM** | AV | *CR* | AL |
| 12609 (12014) | * | **CM** | AV | *CR* | AL |
| 12610 (12117) | | **CM** | AV | *CR* | AL |
| 12613 (11042, 12173) | * | **CM** | AV | *CR* | AL |
| 12614 (12145) | | **CM** | AV | *CR* | AL |
| 12615 (12059) | * | **CM** | AV | *CR* | AL |
| 12616 (12127) | | **CM** | AV | *CR* | AL |
| 12617 (11052, 12174) | * | **CM** | AV | *CR* | AL |
| 12618 (11008, 12169) | | **CM** | AV | *CR* | AL |
| 12619 (11058, 12175) | * | **CM** | AV | *CR* | AL |
| 12620 (12124) | | **CM** | AV | *CR* | AL |
| 12621 (11046) | * | **CM** | AV | *CR* | AL |
| 12623 (11019) | * | **CM** | AV | *CR* | AL |
| 12625 (11030) | * | **CM** | AV | *CR* | AL |
| 12627 (11054) | * | **CM** | AV | *CR* | AL |

## OPEN STANDARD

CAF Mark 5A. Air conditioned. Currently entering service with TransPennine Express. Retention toilets. –/69 1T (* –/59(+6) 1T + bike spaces). CAF bogies. ETS XX.

CAF Beasain 2017–18. 31.8 t (* 31.6 t).

| | | | | | | | | | | |
|---|---|---|---|---|---|---|---|---|---|---|
| 12701 | | **TP** | BN | *TP* | MA | 12721 | * | **TP** | BN | *TP* | MA |
| 12702 | | **TP** | BN | *TP* | MA | 12722 | * | **TP** | BN | *TP* | MA |
| 12703 | * | **TP** | BN | *TP* | MA | 12723 | | **TP** | BN | *TP* | MA |
| 12704 | | **TP** | BN | | MA | 12724 | * | **TP** | BN | *TP* | MA |
| 12705 | | **TP** | BN | | MA | 12725 | | **TP** | BN | *TP* | MA |
| 12706 | * | **TP** | BN | | MA | 12726 | | **TP** | BN | *TP* | MA |
| 12707 | | **TP** | BN | | MA | 12727 | * | **TP** | BN | *TP* | MA |
| 12708 | | **TP** | BN | | MA | 12728 | | **TP** | BN | *TP* | MA |
| 12709 | * | **TP** | BN | | MA | 12729 | | **TP** | BN | *TP* | MA |
| 12710 | | **TP** | BN | *TP* | MA | 12730 | * | **TP** | BN | *TP* | MA |
| 12711 | | **TP** | BN | *TP* | MA | 12731 | | **TP** | BN | *TP* | MA |
| 12712 | * | **TP** | BN | *TP* | MA | 12732 | | **TP** | BN | *TP* | MA |
| 12713 | | **TP** | BN | *TP* | MA | 12733 | * | **TP** | BN | *TP* | MA |
| 12714 | | **TP** | BN | *TP* | MA | 12734 | | **TP** | BN | *TP* | MA |
| 12715 | * | **TP** | BN | *TP* | MA | 12735 | | **TP** | BN | *TP* | MA |
| 12716 | | **TP** | BN | *TP* | MA | 12736 | * | **TP** | BN | *TP* | MA |
| 12717 | | **TP** | BN | *TP* | MA | 12737 | | **TP** | BN | *TP* | MA |
| 12718 | * | **TP** | BN | *TP* | MA | 12738 | | **TP** | BN | *TP* | MA |
| 12719 | | **TP** | BN | *TP* | MA | 12739 | * | **TP** | BN | *TP* | MA |
| 12720 | | **TP** | BN | *TP* | MA | | | | | | |

## DRIVING OPEN BRAKE STANDARD

CAF Mark 5A. Air conditioned. Currently entering service with TransPennine Express. –/64. CAF bogies. ETS XX.

CAF Irun 2017–18. 32.9 t.

| 12801 | **TP** | BN | *TP* | MA | 12808 | **TP** | BN | *TP* | MA |
|-------|--------|----|------|----|-------|--------|----|------|----|
| 12802 | **TP** | BN |      | MA | 12809 | **TP** | BN | *TP* | MA |
| 12803 | **TP** | BN |      | MA | 12810 | **TP** | BN | *TP* | MA |
| 12804 | **TP** | BN | *TP* | MA | 12811 | **TP** | BN | *TP* | MA |
| 12805 | **TP** | BN | *TP* | MA | 12812 | **TP** | BN | *TP* | MA |
| 12806 | **TP** | BN | *TP* | MA | 12813 | **TP** | BN | *TP* | MA |
| 12807 | **TP** | BN | *TP* | MA | 12814 | **TP** | BN |      | MA |

# CORRIDOR FIRST

Mark 1. Seven compartments. 42/– 2T. B4 bogies. ETS 3.

Lot No. 30381 Swindon 1959. 33 t.
Lot No. 30667 Swindon 1962. Commonwealth bogies. 36 t.

| 13227 | x  | **CC** | LS | *LS* | CL | 13230 | xk | **M** | SP | *SP* | BO |
|-------|----|--------|----|------|----|-------|----|-------|----|------|----|
| 13229 | xk | **M**  | SP | *SP* | BO | 13306 | x  | **M** | WC | *WC* | CS |

**Name:** 13306   JOANNA

# OPEN FIRST

Mark 1 converted from Corridor First in 2013–14. 42/– 2T. Commonwealth bogies. ETS 3.

Lot No. 30667 Swindon 1962. 35 t.

| 13320 | x | **M** | WC | *WC* | CS | ANNA |
|-------|---|-------|----|------|----|------|

# CORRIDOR FIRST

Mark 2A. Seven compartments. Pressure ventilated. 42/– 2T. B4 bogies. ETS 4.

Lot No. 30774 Derby 1968. 33 t.

| 13440 | v | **M** | WC | *WC* | CS |
|-------|---|-------|----|------|----|

# SLEEPER SEATED CARRIAGE WITH BRAKE

CAF Mark 5. Air conditioned. Retention toilets. –/31 1TD 1W. CAF bogies. ETS XX.

CAF Irun 2016–18. 32.5 t.

| 15001 | **CA** | LF | *CA* | PO | 15007 | **CA** | LF | *CA* | PO |
|-------|--------|----|------|----|-------|--------|----|------|----|
| 15002 | **CA** | LF | *CA* | PO | 15008 | **CA** | LF | *CA* | PO |
| 15003 | **CA** | LF | *CA* | PO | 15009 | **CA** | LF | *CA* | PO |
| 15004 | **CA** | LF | *CA* | PO | 15010 | **CA** | LF | *CA* | PO |
| 15005 | **CA** | LF | *CA* | PO | 15011 | **CA** | LF | *CA* | PO |
| 15006 | **CA** | LF | *CA* | PO |       |        |    |      |    |

# SLEEPER LOUNGE CAR

CAF Mark 5. Air conditioned. –/30 or –/28 1W. CAF bogies. ETS XX.

CAF Beasain 2016–18. 35.5 t.

| | | | | | | | | | |
|---|---|---|---|---|---|---|---|---|---|
| 15101 | **CA** | LF | *CA* | PO | 15106 | **CA** | LF | *CA* | PO |
| 15102 | **CA** | LF | *CA* | PO | 15107 | **CA** | LF | *CA* | PO |
| 15103 | **CA** | LF | *CA* | PO | 15108 | **CA** | LF | *CA* | PO |
| 15104 | **CA** | LF | *CA* | PO | 15109 | **CA** | LF | *CA* | PO |
| 15105 | **CA** | LF | *CA* | PO | 15110 | **CA** | LF | *CA* | PO |

# SLEEPING CAR (FULLY ACCESSIBLE)

CAF Mark 5. Air conditioned. Retention toilets. Two fully accessible berths (one with double bed, one with foldable upper bed), two berths with double beds and en-suite toilets and showers, two berths with foldable upper beds. 2TD 2T, plus two showers. CAF bogies. ETS XX.

CAF Castejon/Irun 2016–18. 35.5 t.

| | | | | | | | | | |
|---|---|---|---|---|---|---|---|---|---|
| 15201 | **CA** | LF | *CA* | PO | 15208 | **CA** | LF | *CA* | PO |
| 15202 | **CA** | LF | *CA* | PO | 15209 | **CA** | LF | *CA* | PO |
| 15203 | **CA** | LF | *CA* | PO | 15210 | **CA** | LF | *CA* | PO |
| 15204 | **CA** | LF | *CA* | PO | 15211 | **CA** | LF | *CA* | PO |
| 15205 | **CA** | LF | *CA* | PO | 15212 | **CA** | LF | *CA* | PO |
| 15206 | **CA** | LF | *CA* | PO | 15213 | **CA** | LF | *CA* | PO |
| 15207 | **CA** | LF | *CA* | PO | 15214 | **CA** | LF | *CA* | PO |

# SLEEPING CAR

CAF Mark 5. Air conditioned. Retention toilets. 6 en-suite toilet/shower and 4 non en-suite compartments with a fixed lower berth and hinged upper berth. 7T. CAF bogies. ETS XX.

CAF Beasain 2016–18. 38.0 t.

| | | | | | | | | | |
|---|---|---|---|---|---|---|---|---|---|
| 15301 | **CA** | LF | *CA* | PO | 15316 | **CA** | LF | *CA* | PO |
| 15302 | **CA** | LF | *CA* | PO | 15317 | **CA** | LF | *CA* | PO |
| 15303 | **CA** | LF | *CA* | PO | 15318 | **CA** | LF | *CA* | PO |
| 15304 | **CA** | LF | *CA* | PO | 15319 | **CA** | LF | *CA* | PO |
| 15305 | **CA** | LF | *CA* | PO | 15320 | **CA** | LF | *CA* | PO |
| 15306 | **CA** | LF | *CA* | PO | 15321 | **CA** | LF | *CA* | PO |
| 15307 | **CA** | LF | *CA* | PO | 15322 | **CA** | LF | *CA* | PO |
| 15308 | **CA** | LF | *CA* | PO | 15323 | **CA** | LF | *CA* | PO |
| 15309 | **CA** | LF | *CA* | PO | 15324 | **CA** | LF | *CA* | PO |
| 15310 | **CA** | LF | *CA* | PO | 15325 | **CA** | LF | *CA* | PO |
| 15311 | **CA** | LF | *CA* | PO | 15326 | **CA** | LF | *CA* | PO |
| 15312 | **CA** | LF | *CA* | PO | 15327 | **CA** | LF | *CA* | PO |
| 15313 | **CA** | LF | *CA* | PO | 15328 | **CA** | LF | *CA* | PO |
| 15314 | **CA** | LF | *CA* | PO | 15329 | **CA** | LF | *CA* | PO |
| 15315 | **CA** | LF | *CA* | PO | 15330 | **CA** | LF | *CA* | PO |

| | | | | | | | | | |
|---|---|---|---|---|---|---|---|---|---|
| 15331 | **CA** | LF | *CA* | PO | 15336 | **CA** | LF | *CA* | PO |
| 15332 | **CA** | LF | *CA* | PO | 15337 | **CA** | LF | *CA* | PO |
| 15333 | **CA** | LF | *CA* | PO | 15338 | **CA** | LF | *CA* | PO |
| 15334 | **CA** | LF | *CA* | PO | 15339 | **CA** | LF | *CA* | PO |
| 15335 | **CA** | LF | *CA* | PO | 15340 | **CA** | LF | *CA* | PO |

## CORRIDOR BRAKE FIRST

Mark 1. Four compartments. 24/– 1T. Commonwealth bogies. ETS 2.

Lot No. 30668 Swindon 1961. 36 t.

| | | | | | | |
|---|---|---|---|---|---|---|
| 17013 | (14013) | | **CC** | LS | | ZG |
| 17018 | (14018) | v | **CH** | VT | | TM | BOTAURUS |

## CORRIDOR BRAKE FIRST

Mark 2A. Four compartments. Pressure ventilated. 24/– 1T. B4 bogies. ETS 4.

17080/090 were numbered 35516/503 for a time when declassified.

**17056.** Lot No. 30775 Derby 1967–68. 32 t.
**17080–102.** Lot No. 30786 Derby 1968. 32 t.

| | | | | | | | |
|---|---|---|---|---|---|---|---|
| 17056 | (14056) | | **PC** | LS | *LS* | CL |
| 17080 | (14080) | | **PC** | LS | | ZG |
| 17090 | (14090) | v | **CH** | VT | | TM |
| 17102 | (14102) | | **M** | WC | *WC* | CS |

## COUCHETTE/GENERATOR COACH

Mark 2B. Formerly part of Royal Train. Converted from Corridor Brake First built 1969. Consists of luggage accommodation, guard's compartment, 350 kW diesel generator and staff sleeping accommodation. Pressure ventilated. B5 bogies. ETS 5X (when generator not in use). ETS index ?? (when generator in use).

Lot No. 30888 Wolverton 1977. 46 t.

| | | | | | |
|---|---|---|---|---|---|
| 17105 | (14105, 2905) | **BG** | RV | *RV* | BU |

## CORRIDOR BRAKE FIRST

Mark 2D. Four compartments. Air conditioned. Stones equipment. 24/– 1T. B4 Bogies. ETS 5.

Lot No. 30823 Derby 1971–72. 33.5 t.

| | | | | | | | |
|---|---|---|---|---|---|---|---|
| 17159 | (14159) | d | **CC** | LS | *LS* | CL |
| 17167 | (14167) | | **VN** | WC | *WC* | CS | MOW COP |

## OPEN BRAKE UNCLASSIFIED

Mark 3B. Air conditioned. Fitted with hydraulic handbrake. Used as Sleeper day coaches. Refurbished with new Transcal seating 2018. 55/– 1T. BT10 bogies. pg. d. ETS 6X.

Lot No. 30990 Derby 1986. 35.8 t.

| 17173 | **GW** P | _GW_ | PZ | | 17175 | **GW** P | _GW_ | PZ |
| 17174 | **GW** P | _GW_ | PZ | | | | | |

## CORRIDOR STANDARD

Mark 1. –/48 2T. Eight Compartments. Commonwealth bogies. ETS 4.

Currently in use as part of the Harry Potter World exhibition at Leavesden, near Watford.

Lot No. 30685 Derby 1961–62. 36 t.

| 18756 (25756) | x | **M** | WC | | SH |

## CORRIDOR BRAKE COMPOSITE

Mark 1. There are two variants depending upon whether the Standard Class compartments have armrests. Each vehicle has two First Class and three Standard Class compartments. 12/18 2T (* 12/24 2T). Commonwealth bogies. ETS 2.

**21241–245.** Lot No. 30669 Swindon 1961–62. 36 t.
**21256.** Lot No. 30731 Derby 1963. 37 t.
**21266–272.** Lot No. 30732 Derby 1964. 37 t.

| 21241 | x | **M** | SP | _SP_ | BO | | 21266 | x* | **M** | WC | _WC_ | CS |
| 21245 | x | **M** | RV | | ZG | | 21269 | * | **CC** | RV | _RV_ | ZG |
| 21256 | x | **M** | WC | _WC_ | CS | | 21272 | x* | **CH** | RV | _RV_ | ZG |

## CORRIDOR BRAKE STANDARD

Mark 1. Four compartments. –/24 1T. ETS 2.

**35185.** Lot No. 30427 Wolverton 1959. B4 bogies. 33 t.
**35459/465.** Lot No. 30721 Wolverton 1963. Commonwealth bogies. 37 t.

| 35185 | x | **M** | SP | _SP_ | BO |
| 35459 | x | **M** | WC | _WC_ | CS |
| 35465 | x | **CC** | LS | _LS_ | CL |

# CORRIDOR BRAKE GENERATOR STANDARD

Mark 1. Four compartments. –/24 1T. Fitted with an ETS generator in the former luggage compartment. ETS 2 (when generator not in use). ETS index ?? (when generator in use).

Lot No. 30721 Wolverton 1963. Commonwealth bogies. 37 t.

35469 x **CH** RV *RV* ZG

# BRAKE/POWER KITCHEN

Mark 2C. Pressure ventilated. Converted from Corridor Brake First (declassified to Corridor Brake Standard) built 1970. Converted by West Coast Railway Company 2000–01. Consists of 60 kVA generator, guard's compartment and electric kitchen. B5 bogies. ETS ? (when generator not in use). ETS index ?? (when generator in use).

**Non-standard livery:** Brown.

Lot No. 30796 Derby 1969–70. 32.5 t.

35511 (14130, 17130) **0** LS CL

# KITCHEN CAR

Mark 1. Converted 1989/2006/2017–19 from Kitchen Buffet Unclassified. 80041/020 had buffet and seating area replaced with additional kitchen and food preparation area. 80043 had a full length kitchen fitted. Fluorescent lighting. Commonwealth or (†) B5 bogies. ETS 2X.

Lot No. 30628 Pressed Steel 1960–61. 39 t (* 36.4 t).

| 80041 (1690) | x | **M** | RV | | ZG |
|---|---|---|---|---|---|
| 80042 (1646) | | **CH** | RV | *RV* | ZG |
| 80043 (1680) | * | **PC** | LS | *LS* | CL |
| 80044 (1659) | † | **CC** | LS | *LS* | CL |

# DRIVING BRAKE VAN (110 mph)

Mark 3B. Air conditioned. T4 bogies. dg. ETS 5X. Driving Brake Vans converted for use by Network Rail can be found in the Service Stock section of this book.

**Non-standard livery:** 82146 All over silver with DB logos.

Lot No. 31042 Derby 1988. 45.2 t.

| 82107 | **GA** | EL | | BR | 82138 | **B** | DA | *RO* | RJ |
|---|---|---|---|---|---|---|---|---|---|
| 82115 | **B** | DA | *RO* | RJ | 82139 | **IC** | LS | *LS* | CL |
| 82127 | **IC** | LS | *LS* | CL | 82146 | **0** | DB | *DB* | TO |
| 82136 | **GA** | DA | *RO* | RJ | | | | | |

# DRIVING BRAKE VAN (140 mph)

Mark 4. Air conditioned. Swiss-built (SIG) bogies. dg. ETS 6X.

**Advertising livery:** 82205 Flying Scotsman (red, white & purple).

Lot No. 31043 Metro-Cammell 1988. 43.5 t.

| | | | | | | | | | | |
|---|---|---|---|---|---|---|---|---|---|---|
| 82200 | **GC** | E | | WB | | 82216 | **TW** | E | *TW* | CF |
| 82201 | **GC** | E | | WB | | 82218 | **VE** | E | | WS |
| 82202 | **VE** | E | | WS | | 82219 | **VE** | E | | WS |
| 82204 | **VE** | E | | WS | | 82220 | **VE** | E | | WS |
| 82205 | **AL** | E | *LN* | BN | | 82222 | **VE** | E | | WS |
| 82206 | **VE** | E | | WS | | 82223 | **VE** | E | *LN* | BN |
| 82207 | **VE** | E | | WS | | 82224 | **VE** | E | | WS |
| 82208 | **VE** | E | *LN* | BN | | 82225 | **VE** | E | *LN* | BN |
| 82209 | **VE** | E | | WS | | 82226 | **TW** | E | *TW* | CF |
| 82210 | **VE** | E | | WS | | 82227 | **GC** | E | | WB |
| 82211 | **VE** | E | *LN* | BN | | 82228 | **VE** | E | | WB |
| 82212 | **VE** | E | *LN* | BN | | 82229 | **TW** | E | *TW* | CF |
| 82213 | **VE** | E | *LN* | BN | | 82230 | **GC** | E | | WB |
| 82214 | **VE** | E | *LN* | BN | | 82231 | **VE** | E | | WS |
| 82215 | **VE** | E | | WS | | | | | | |

# DRIVING BRAKE VAN (110 mph)

Mark 3B. Air conditioned. T4 bogies. dg. ETS 6X.

82301–305 originally converted 2008. 82306–308 converted 2011–12. 82309 converted 2013.

g  Fitted with a diesel generator for use while stabled in terminal stations or at depots. 48.5 t.

Lot No. 31042 Derby 1988. 45.2 t.

| | | | | | | |
|---|---|---|---|---|---|---|
| 82301 | (82117) | g | **CM** | AV | *CR* | AL |
| 82302 | (82151) | g | **CM** | AV | *CR* | AL |
| 82303 | (82135) | g | **CM** | AV | *CR* | AL |
| 82304 | (82130) | g | **CM** | AV | *CR* | AL |
| 82305 | (82134) | g | **CM** | AV | *CR* | AL |
| 82306 | (82144) | | **AW** | DA | *RO* | RJ |
| 82307 | (82131) | | **AW** | RO | | BK |
| 82308 | (82108) | | **AW** | RO | | CN |
| 82309 | (82104) | g | **CM** | AV | *CR* | AL |

## GANGWAYED BRAKE VAN (100 mph)

Mark 1. Short frame (57 ft). Load 10 t. Adapted 199? for use as Brake Luggage Van. Guard's compartment retained and former baggage area adapted for secure stowage of passengers' luggage. B4 bogies. 100 mph. ETS 1X.

Lot No. 30162 Pressed Steel 1956–57. 30.5 t.

92904 (80867, 99554)          **VN**   WC   *WC*          CS

## HIGH SECURITY GENERAL UTILITY VAN

Mark 1. Short frame (57 ft). Load 14 t. Modified with new floors, three roller shutter doors per side and the end doors removed. Commonwealth bogies. ETS 0X.

Lot No. 30616 Pressed Steel 1959–60. 32 t.

94225 (86849, 93849)          **M**   WC   *WC*          CS

## GENERAL UTILITY VAN (100 mph)

Mark 1. Short frame (57 ft). Load 14 t. Screw couplers. Adapted 2013/2010 for use as a water carrier with 3000 gallon capacity. ETS 0.

**Non-standard livery:** 96100 GWR Brown.

**96100.** Lot No. 30565 Pressed Steel 1959. 30 t. B5 bogies.
**96175.** Lot No. 30403 York/Glasgow 1958–60. 32 t. Commonwealth bogies.

96100 (86734, 93734)   x   **0**   VT   *VT*          TM
96175 (86628, 93628)   x   **M**   WC   *WC*          CS

## KITCHEN CAR

Mark 1 converted from Corridor First in 2008 with staff accommodation. Commonwealth bogies. ETS 3.

Lot No. 30667 Swindon 1961. 35 t.

99316 (13321)      x      **M**   WC   *WC*          CS

## BUFFET STANDARD

Mark 1 converted from Open Standard in 2013 by the removal of two seating bays and fitting of a buffet. –/48 2T. Commonwealth bogies. ETS 4.

Lot No. 30646 Wolverton 1961. 36 t.

99318 (4912)       x      **M**   WC   *WC*          CS

## KITCHEN CAR

Mark 1 converted from Corridor Standard in 2011 with staff accommodation. Commonwealth bogies. ETS 3.

Lot No. 30685 Derby 1961–62. 34 t.

99712 (18893)      x          **M**   WC   *WC*        CS

## OPEN STANDARD

Mark 1 Corridor Standard rebuilt in 1997 as Open Standard using components from 4936. –/64 2T. Commonwealth bogies. ETS 4.

Lot No. 30685 Derby 1961–62. 36 t.

99722 (25806, 18806) x       **M**   WC   *WC*        CS

# LUL 4 TC USED AS HAULED STOCK

The Class 438 4 TC sets were unpowered units designed to work in push-pull mode with Class 430 (4 Rep) tractor units and Class 33/1, 73 and 74 locomotives. They were converted from locomotive-hauled coaching stock built 1952–57.

The vehicles listed are owned by London Underground and used on both special services on the LU Metropolitan Line and on occasional specials on the National Rail network, top-and-tailed by locomotives.

Mark 1. Trailer Brake Second side corridor with Lavatory (TBSK). Lot No. 30229. Metro-Cammell 1957. 35.5 t.

70823 (34970)   **M**   LU   *WC*   RS

Mark 1. Trailer First side corridor with Lavatory (TFK). Lot No. 30019. Swindon 1954. 33.5 t.

71163 (13097)   **M**   LU   *WC*   RS

Mark 1. Driving Trailer Second Open (DTSO).

**76297.** Lot No. 30086. Eastleigh 1955. 32.0 t.
**76324.** Lot No. 30149. Swindon 1956. 32.0 t.

76297 (3938)    **M**   LU   *WC*   RS
76324 (4009)    **M**   LU   *WC*   RS

# NNR REGISTERED CARRIAGES

These carriages are permitted to operate on the national railway network only between Sheringham and Cromer as an extension of North Norfolk Railway (NNR) "North Norfolkman" services. Only NNR coaches currently registered for use on the national railway network are listed.

## KITCHEN BUFFET STANDARD

Mark 1. Built as Unclassified Restaurant. Rebuilt with Buffet Counter and seating reduced. –/23. Commonwealth bogies. Lot No. 30632 Swindon 1960–61. 39 t.

1969   v   CC   NN   *NY*      NO

## OPEN FIRST

Mark 1. 42/–. Commonwealth bogies. Lot No. 30697 Swindon 1962–63. 36 t.

3116   v   CC   NN   *NY*      NO

## OPEN STANDARD

Mark 1. –/48 2T. BR Mark 1 bogies. Lot No. 30121 Eastleigh 1953–55. 32 t.

4372   v   CC   NN   *NY*      NO

## GANGWAYED BRAKE VAN

Mark 1. Short frame (57 ft). Now fitted with a kitchen. BR Mark 1 bogies. Lot No. 30224 Cravens 1955–56. 31.5 t.

81033 v   CC   NN   *NY*      NO

# NYMR REGISTERED CARRIAGES

These carriages are permitted to operate on the national railway network but may only be used to convey fare-paying passengers between Middlesbrough and Whitby on the Esk Valley branch as an extension of North Yorkshire Moors Railway services between Pickering and Grosmont. Only NYMR coaches currently registered for use on the national railway network are listed.

## RESTAURANT FIRST

Mark 1. 24/–. Commonwealth bogies. Lot No. 30633 Swindon 1961. 42.5 t.

| 324 | x | **PC** | NY | *NY* | NY | JOS de CRAU |
|-----|---|--------|----|------|-----|-------------|

## BUFFET STANDARD

Mark 1. –/44 2T. Commonwealth bogies.
Lot No. 30520 Wolverton 1960. 38 t.

| 1823 | v | **M** | NY | *NY* | NY |
|------|---|-------|----|------|-----|

## OPEN STANDARD

Mark 1. –/64 2T (* –/60 2W 2T, † –/60 3W 1T). BR Mark 1 bogies.
**3798/3801.** Lot No. 30079 York 1953. 33 t.
**3860/72.** Lot No. 30080 York 1954. 33 t.
**3948.** Lot No. 30086 Eastleigh 1954–55. 33 t.
**4198/4252.** Lot No. 30172 York 1956. 33 t.
**4286/90.** Lot No. 30207 BRCW 1956. 33 t.
**4455.** Lot No. 30226 BRCW 1957. 33 t.

| 3798 | v | **M** | NY | *NY* | NY | | 4198 | v | **CC** | NY | *NY* | NY |
|------|----|-------|----|------|-----|---|------|----|--------|----|------|-----|
| 3801 | v | **CC** | NY | *NY* | NY | | 4252 | v* | **CC** | NY | *NY* | NY |
| 3860 | v* | **M** | NY | *NY* | NY | | 4286 | v | **CC** | NY | *NY* | NY |
| 3872 | v† | **BG** | NY | *NY* | NY | | 4290 | v | **M** | NY | *NY* | NY |
| 3948 | v | **CC** | NY | *NY* | NY | | 4455 | v | **CC** | NY | *NY* | NY |

## OPEN STANDARD

Mark 1. –/48 2T. BR Mark 1 bogies.
**4786.** Lot No. 30376 York 1957. 33 t.
**4817.** Lot No. 30473 BRCW 1959. 33 t.

| 4786 | v | **CH** | NY | *NY* | NY | | 4817 | v | **M** | NY | *NY* | NY |
|------|---|--------|----|------|-----|---|------|---|-------|----|------|-----|

## OPEN STANDARD

Mark 1. Later vehicles built with Commonwealth bogies. –/64 2T.
Lot No. 30690 Wolverton 1961–62. Aluminium window frames. 37 t.

| 4990 | v | **M** | NY | *NY* | NY | | 5029 | v | **CH** | NY | *NY* | NY |
|------|---|-------|----|------|-----|---|------|---|--------|----|------|-----|
| 5000 | v | **M** | NY | *NY* | NY | | | | | | | |

## OPEN BRAKE STANDARD

Mark 1. –/39 1T. BR Mark 1 bogies.
Lot No. 30170 Doncaster 1956. 34 t.

9225 v **M** NY *NY* NY | 9274 v **M** NY *NY* NY

## CORRIDOR COMPOSITE

Mark 1. 24/18 1T. BR Mark 1 bogies.
**15745.** Lot No. 30179 Metro Cammell 1956. 36 t.
**16156.** Lot No. 30665 Derby 1961. 36 t.

15745 v **M** NY *NY* NY | 16156 v **CC** NY *NY* NY

## CORRIDOR BRAKE COMPOSITE

Mark 1. Two First Class and three Standard Class compartments. 12/18 2T.
BR Mark 1 bogies.
Lot No. 30185 Metro Cammell 1956. 36 t.

21100 v **CC** NY *NY* NY

## CORRIDOR BRAKE STANDARD

Mark 1. –/24 1T. BR Mark 1 bogies.
Lot No. 30233 Gloucester 1957. 35 t.

35089 v **CC** NY *NY* NY

## PULLMAN BRAKE THIRD

Built 1928 by Metropolitan Carriage & Wagon Company. –/30. Gresley
bogies. 37.5 t.

232 v **PC** NY *NY* NY CAR No. 79

## PULLMAN KITCHEN FIRST

Built by Metro-Cammell 1960–61 for East Coast Main Line services. 20/– 2T.
Commonwealth bogies. 41.2 t.

318 x **PC** NY *NY* NY ROBIN

## PULLMAN PARLOUR FIRST

Built by Metro-Cammell 1960–61 for East Coast Main Line services. 29/– 2T.
Commonwealth bogies. 38.5 t.

328 x **PC** NY *NY* NY OPAL

# 2.2. HIGH SPEED TRAIN TRAILER CARS

HSTs consist of a number of trailer cars (usually between four and nine) with a power car at each end. All trailers are classified Mark 3 and have BT10 bogies with disc brakes and central door locking. Heating is by a 415 V three-phase supply and vehicles have air conditioning. Maximum speed is 125 mph.

The trailer cars have one standard 23 m bodyshell for both First and Standard Class, thus facilitating easy conversion from one class to the other. As built all cars had facing seating around tables with Standard Class carriages having nine bays of seats per side which did not line up with the eight windows per side.

All vehicles underwent a mid-life refurbishment in the 1980s with Standard Class seating layouts revised to incorporate unidirectional seating in addition to facing. A further refurbishment programme was completed in November 2000, with each company having a different scheme as follows:

**Great Western Trains (later First Great Western).** Green seat covers and extra partitions between seat bays.

**Great North Eastern Railway.** New lighting panels and brown seat covers.

**Virgin CrossCountry.** Green seat covers. Standard Class vehicles had four seats in the centre of each carriage replaced with a luggage stack.

**Midland Mainline.** Grey seat covers, redesigned seat squabs, side carpeting and two seats in the centre of each Standard Class carriage and one in First Class carriages replaced with a luggage stack.

Since then there have been many separate, and very different, projects:

**Midland Mainline** was first to refurbish its vehicles a second time in 2003–04. This involved fitting new fluorescent and halogen ceiling lighting, although the original seats were retained, but with blue upholstery.

London St Pancras–Sheffield/Leeds and Nottingham services are now operated by **East Midlands Railway**. Previous operator East Midlands Trains embarked on another, less radical, refurbishment in 2009–10 which included retention of the original seats but with red upholstery in Standard Class and blue in First. EMR has recently replaced its sets with former LNER rakes.

**First Great Western (now Great Western Railway)** started a major rebuild of its HST sets in late 2006, with the programme completed in 2008. The new interiors featured new lighting and seating throughout. First Class seats had leather upholstery, and were made by Primarius UK. Standard Class seats were of high-back design by Grammer. A number of sets operated without a full buffet or kitchen car, instead using one of 19 TS vehicles converted to include a "mini buffet" counter for use on shorter distance services. During 2012 15 402xx or 407xx buffet vehicles were converted to Trailer Standards to make the rakes formed as 7-cars up to 8-cars.

Many of the former Great Western Railway vehicles were scrapped during 2020, but GWR is retaining 14 short 4-car sets for local and regional services. Trailers for these sets are being fitted with power doors and renumbered in the 48xxx and 49xxx series'.

Having increased its sets to 9-car sets in 2004, at the end of 2006 **GNER** embarked on a major rebuild of its HSTs. All vehicles have similar interiors to the Mark 4 "Mallard" fleet, with new Primarius seating. The refurbishment of the 13 sets was completed by **National Express East Coast** in late 2009, these trains were later operated by **Virgin Trains East Coast** and then **London North Eastern Railway**. VTEC refurbished its sets in 2015–16, with the same seats retained but with new upholstery, and leather in First Class. Some of these sets have recently been returned to service with EMR.

Open access operator **Grand Central** started operation in December 2007 with a new service from Sunderland to London King's Cross. This operator had three sets mostly using stock converted from loco-hauled Mark 3s. The seats in Standard Class have First Class spacing and in most vehicles are all facing. These sets were withdrawn in December 2017 and transferred to East Midlands Trains (now EMR). They were refurbished in 2018–19, with ex-GWR buffet cars used instead of the original Grand Central buffet cars.

**CrossCountry** reintroduced HSTs to the Cross-Country network from 2008. Five sets were refurbished at Wabtec, Doncaster principally for use on the Plymouth–Edinburgh route. Three of these sets use stock mostly converted from loco-hauled Mark 3s and two are sets ex-Midland Mainline. The interiors are similar to refurbished East Coast sets, although the seating layout is different and one toilet per carriage has been removed in favour of a luggage stack. These sets have now been fitted with sliding power doors.

**ScotRail** started operating HSTs from October 2018. The operator will have a fleet of 17 5-car and nine 4-car former GWR sets (fitted with sliding power doors) for use between Glasgow/Edinburgh and Aberdeen/Inverness, and on the Aberdeen–Inverness route. Initially some unrefurbished sets were used as cover whilst the heavily delayed programme to fit the 26 sets with sliding power doors was completed, but these have all now been withdrawn.

Crewe-based **Locomotive Services** acquired a number of former GWR and EMR HST vehicles and power cars in 2020. One rake of First Class coaches has been refurbished and was launched in autumn 2020 as the "Midland Pullman". This will be used on premium charter services.

**Operator Codes**

Operator codes are shown in the heading before each set of vehicles. The first letter is always "T" for HST carriages, denoting a Trailer vehicle. The second letter denotes the passenger accommodation in that vehicle, for example "F" for First. "GS" denotes Guards accommodation and Standard Class seating. This is followed by catering provision, with "B" for buffet, and "K" for a kitchen and buffet:

| | | | |
|---|---|---|---|
| TC | Trailer Composite | TGFB | Trailer Guard's Buffet First |
| TCK | Trailer Composite Kitchen | TSB | Trailer Buffet Standard |
| TF | Trailer First | TS | Trailer Standard |
| TFB | Trailer Buffet First | TGF | Trailer Guard's First |
| TFKB | Trailer Kitchen Buffet First | TGS | Trailer Guard's Standard |

**Power doors:** All HSTs now operated by CrossCountry, Great Western Railway and ScotRail have been fitted with power sliding doors and retention toilets. Vehicles so fitted are shown with a "p" in the Notes column.

## TRAILER BUFFET STANDARD                                    TSB

19 vehicles (40101–119) were converted at Laira 2009–10 from HST TSs for First Great Western. All other vehicles now scrapped. Grammer seating.

**40106.** Lot No. 30897 Derby 1977–79. –/70 1T. 35.5 t.

40106 (42162)     **FD**      LS          KR

## TRAILER BUFFET FIRST                                       TFB

Converted from TSB by fitting First Class seats. Renumbered from 404xx series by subtracting 200. Refurbished by First Great Western and fitted with Primarius leather seating. 23/–.

**40204–221.** Lot No. 30883 Derby 1976–77. 36.12 t.

| 40204 | **EA** A | EP | 40221 | **EA** A | EP |
| 40205 | **EA** A | EP | | | |

## TRAILER BUFFET STANDARD                                    TSB

Renumbered from 400xx series by adding 400. –/33 1W.

**40402.** Lot No. 30883 Derby 1976–77. 36.12 t.

40402     **V**      AV          WO

## TRAILER GUARD'S MINIATURE BUFFET FIRST  TGFB

Refurbished 2018–21 for ScotRail. Former Great Western Railway vehicles. Primarius leather seating. Fitted with a new corner buffet counter and kitchen. 32/– 1T.

**40601–626.** For Lot No. details see TF. 39.1 t.

| 40601 | (41032) p **SI** | A | *SR* | IS | 40614 | (41010) p **SI** | A | *SR* | IS |
| 40602 | (41038) p **SI** | A | *SR* | IS | 40615 | (41022) p **SI** | A | *SR* | IS |
| 40603 | (41006) p **SI** | A | *SR* | IS | 40616 | (41142) p **SI** | A | *SR* | IS |
| 40604 | (41024) p **SI** | A | *SR* | IS | 40617 | (41144) p **SI** | A | *SR* | IS |
| 40605 | (41094) p **SI** | A | *SR* | IS | 40618 | (41016) p **SI** | A | *SR* | IS |
| 40606 | (41104) p **SI** | A | *SR* | IS | 40619 | (41124) p **SI** | A | *SR* | IS |
| 40607 | (41136) p **SI** | A | *SR* | IS | 40620 | (41158) p **SI** | A | *SR* | IS |
| 40608 | (41122) p **SI** | A | *SR* | IS | 40621 | (41146) p **SI** | A | *SR* | IS |
| 40609 | (41020) p **SI** | A | *SR* | IS | 40622 | (41052) p **SI** | A | | ZH |
| 40610 | (41103) p **SI** | A | *SR* | IS | 40623 | (41180) p **SI** | A | *SR* | IS |
| 40611 | (41130) p **SI** | A | *SR* | IS | 40624 | (41116) p **SI** | A | *SR* | IS |
| 40612 | (41134) p **SI** | A | *SR* | IS | 40625 | (41137) p **SI** | A | *SR* | IS |
| 40613 | (41135) p **SI** | A | *SR* | IS | 40626 | (41012) p **SI** | A | *SR* | IS |

# TRAILER KITCHEN BUFFET FIRST                                    TFKB

These vehicles have larger kitchens than the 402xx and 404xx series vehicles, and are used in trains where a full meal service is required. They were renumbered from the 403xx series (in which the seats were unclassified) by adding 400 to the previous number. 17/–.

\*   Refurbished former GWR vehicles. Primarius leather seating.
m   Refurbished former LNER vehicles with Primarius leather seating.

**40700–720.** Lot No. 30921 Derby 1978–79. 38.16 t.
**40727–734.** Lot No. 30940 Derby 1979–80. 38.16 t.
**40737–753.** Lot No. 30948 Derby 1980–81. 38.16 t.
**40755.** Lot No. 30966 Derby 1982. 38.16 t.

| | | | | | | | | | |
|---|---|---|---|---|---|---|---|---|---|
| 40700 | **ST** | P | | GA | 40728 | **ST** | DA | *RO* | RJ |
| 40701 m | **VE** | P | *EM* | NL | 40734 * | **FD** | A | | EP |
| 40702 m | **VE** | P | *EM* | NL | 40739 * | **FD** | A | | ZG |
| 40704 | **VE** | A | | EP | 40740 m | **VE** | A | | NL |
| 40705 m | **VE** | A | | NL | 40741 | **ST** | P | | GA |
| 40706 m | **VE** | A | | EP | 40742 m | **VE** | A | | EP |
| 40707 * | **FD** | A | | ZG | 40748 m | **VE** | A | *EM* | NL |
| 40711 m | **VE** | A | *EM* | NL | 40749 | **ST** | P | | GA |
| 40713 * | **FD** | A | | EP | 40750 m | **VE** | A | *EM* | NL |
| 40715 * | **GW** | A | | EP | 40751 | **VE** | P | | GA |
| 40720 m | **BG** | A | | EP | 40753 | **ST** | P | | GA |
| 40727 * | **FD** | A | | ZG | 40755 * | **GW** | A | | ZG |

# TRAILER KITCHEN BUFFET FIRST                                    TFKB

These vehicles have been converted from TSBs in the 404xx series to be similar to the 407xx series vehicles. 17/–. Primarius leather seating.

40802 and 40804 were numbered 40212 and 40232 for a time when fitted with 23 First Class seats.

**40801/802/808.** Lot No. 30883 Derby 1976–77. 38.16 t.
**40804.** Lot No. 30899 Derby 1978–79. 38.16 t.

| | | | | | |
|---|---|---|---|---|---|
| 40801 | (40027, 40427) | **MP** | LS | *LS* | CL |
| 40802 | (40012, 40412) | **MP** | LS | *LS* | CL |
| 40804 | (40032, 40432) | **FD** | LS | *LS* | CL |
| 40808 | (40015, 40415) | **FD** | LS | | KR |

# TRAILER BUFFET FIRST                                            TFB

Converted from TSB by First Great Western. Refurbished with Primarius leather seating. 23/–.

**40900/902/904.** Lot No. 30883 Derby 1976–77. 36.12 t.

| | | | | |
|---|---|---|---|---|
| 40900 | (40022, 40422) | **FD** | FG | LM |
| 40902 | (40023, 40423) | **FD** | FG | LM |
| 40904 | (40001, 40401) | **GW** | FG | LM |

# TRAILER FIRST                                                    TF

As built and m 48/– 2T (m† 48/– 1T – one toilet removed for trolley space).
* Refurbished former GWR vehicles. Primarius leather seating.
m Refurbished former LNER vehicles with Primarius leather seating.
px Refurbished CrossCountry vehicles with power doors, Primarius seating and one toilet removed. 39/– 1TD 1W.
s Fitted with centre luggage stack, disabled toilet and wheelchair space. 46/– 1T 1TD 1W.
w Wheelchair space. 47/– 2T 1W.

**41026–046.** Lot No. 30881 Derby 1976–77. 33.66 t.
**41059–120.** Lot No. 30896 Derby 1977–78. 33.66 t.
**41126.** Lot No. 30938 Derby 1979–80. 33.66 t.
**41149–166.** Lot No. 30947 Derby 1980. 33.66 t.
**41167/169.** Lot No. 30963 Derby 1982. 33.66 t.
**41170.** Lot No. 30967 Derby 1982. Former prototype vehicle. 33.66 t.
**41176.** Lot No. 30897 Derby 1977. 33.66 t.
**41182/183/189.** Lot No. 30939 Derby 1979–80. 33.66 t.
**41185/187.** Lot No. 30969 Derby 1982. 33.66 t.
**41190.** Lot No. 30882 Derby 1976–77. 33.60 t.
**41193–195/201–206.** Lot No. 30878 Derby 1975–76. 34.3 t. Converted from Mark 3A Open First.
**41207–209.** Lot No. 30877 Derby 1975–77. Converted from Mark 3A Open Standard.

| | | | | | | | | | | |
|---|---|---|---|---|---|---|---|---|---|---|
| 41026 | px | **XC** | A | *XC* | LA | 41099 | m† | **VE** | A | *EM* | NL |
| 41035 | px | **XC** | A | *XC* | LA | 41100 | mw | **VE** | A | *EM* | NL |
| 41046 | s | **ST** | P | | GA | 41106 | *w | **FD** | A | | ZG |
| 41059 | *w | **MP** | LS | *LS* | CL | 41108 | *w | **MP** | LS | *LS* | CL |
| 41061 | w | **ST** | P | | GA | 41113 | s | **ST** | P | | NL |
| 41063 | | **ST** | P | | GA | 41115 | m† | **VE** | P | *EM* | NL |
| 41064 | s | **ST** | P | | GA | 41117 | | **ST** | P | | GA |
| 41066 | m† | **VE** | A | | NL | 41118 | mw | **BG** | A | | EP |
| 41067 | s | **ST** | P | | GA | 41120 | m† | **VE** | A | *EM* | NL |
| 41069 | s | **ST** | P | | GA | 41126 | *w | **FD** | SR | | DU |
| 41071 | | **ST** | P | | GA | 41149 | *w | **GW** | LS | | KR |
| 41072 | s | **ST** | P | | GA | 41150 | mw | **VE** | A | *EM* | NL |
| 41077 | | **ST** | P | | GA | 41151 | m† | **VE** | A | | NL |
| 41079 | | **ST** | P | | GA | 41152 | mw | **VE** | A | | NL |
| 41087 | m† | **VE** | A | | EP | 41160 | *w | **GW** | LS | *LS* | CL |
| 41088 | mw | **VE** | A | | EP | 41162 | *w | **MP** | LS | *LS* | CL |
| 41091 | m† | **VE** | A | | EP | 41164 | mw | **VE** | A | | GA |
| 41092 | mw | **VE** | A | | EP | 41165 | mw | **VE** | P | *EM* | NL |
| 41095 | mw | **VE** | P | *EM* | NL | 41166 | *w | **GW** | LS | *LS* | CL |
| 41097 | m† | **VE** | A | | NL | 41167 | *w | **FD** | LS | | CL |
| 41098 | mw | **VE** | A | | NL | 41169 | *w | **MP** | LS | *LS* | CL |

| | | | | | |
|---|---|---|---|---|---|
| 41170 | (41001) | m† | **BG** | A | EP |
| 41176 | (42142, 42352) | *w | **MP** | LS *LS* | CL |
| 41182 | (42278) | *w | **MP** | LS *LS* | CL |
| 41183 | (42274) | *w | **GW** | LS | ZG |

▲ Statesman Rail Pullman Car Company-liveried Mark 2F Buffet First 1211 "SNAEFELL" is seen at Oakley on the MML on 21/09/19.  **Mark Beal**

▼ WCRC maroon-liveried Mark 1 Buffet Standard 1860 is seen at Lincoln on 07/12/19.  **Robert Pritchard**

▲ BR chocolate & cream-liveried Mark 1 Open First 3149 is seen at Bletchley on 07/07/19. **Mark Beal**

▼ Royal Train-liveried Royal Household Mark 3A Sleeping Car 2915 is seen near Symington on 28/06/19. **Robin Ralston**

▲ BR blue & grey-liveried Mark 2F Open First 3345 is seen near Penzance on 13/04/19. **Robert Pritchard**

▼ WCRC maroon-liveried Mark 2A Open Standard 5419 is seen at Carluke on 02/10/19. **Robin Ralston**

▲ Chiltern Railways Mainline-liveried Mark 3A Kitchen Buffet First 10272 is seen at Dorridge on 20/06/19. **Robert Pritchard**

▼ Great Western Railway green-liveried Mark 3A Sleeping Car With Pantry 10590 is seen at London Paddington on 01/06/19. **Robert Pritchard**

▲ Northern Belle-liveried Mark 3A Sleeping Car 10729 "CREWE" is seen at Great Strickland on 19/09/20.                    **Ian Beardsley**

▼ In Greater Anglia livery with Rail Charter Services branding, Mark 3B Open First 11076 passes Ribblehead on 08/08/20.                    **Tony Christie**

▲ In the erstwhile Virgin Trains East Coast Mark 4 livery, LNER Mark 4 Open Standard (End) is seen near Retford on 06/08/20. **Ian Beardsley**

▼ TransPennine Express-liveried Mark 5A Open Standard 12730 is seen at Sheffield on 01/06/20. **Ian Beardsley**

▲ TransPennine Express-liveried Mark 5A Driving Open Brake Standard 12807 passes Ulleskelf leading the 15.34 Scarborough–Liverpool Lime Street (propelled by 68032 "Destroyer") on 19/09/20. **Andy Stoppard**

▼ BR carmine & cream-liveried Mark 2D Corridor Brake First 17159 stands at Settle on 13/08/20. **Dave Gommersall**

▲ Caledonian Sleeper-liveried Mark 5 Fully Accessible Sleeping Car 15205 is seen at Craigenhill on 27/02/20. **Robin Ralston**

▼ Northern Belle-liveried Mark 2D Corridor Brake First 17167 "MOW COP" is seen at Great Strickland on 19/09/20. **Ian Beardsley**

▲ WCRC maroon-liveried Mark 1 Corridor Brake Composite 99304 (21256) is seen at Lincoln on 07/12/19. **Robert Pritchard**

▼ In Virgin Trains East Coast livery with LNER branding, Mark 4 Driving Brake Van 82211 leads the 13.30 Edinburgh–London King's Cross through Spittal on 08/08/20. **Ian Beardsley**

▲ ScotRail InterCity-liveried HST Trailer Guard's Miniature Buffet First 40605 is seen at Inverkeithing East Junction on 16/07/20. **Robin Ralston**

▼ CrossCountry-liveried HST Trailer Guard's Standard 44021 is seen near Rotherham Masborough on 06/06/19. **Robert Pritchard**

▲ Great Western Railway-liveried HST Trailer Standard 48125 is seen near
St Germans, west of Plymouth, on 13/09/20.          **Tony Christie**

▼ Royal Scotsman Saloon 99967 "DINING CAR No. 1" is seen at Perth on
15/04/19.          **Robert Pritchard**

▲ Pullman Car Company-liveried Pullman Parlour First 213 "MINERVA" is seen at Ashford on 16/06/16.                    **Robert Pritchard**

▼ Pullman Car Company-liveried Pullman Parlour Second 351 "SAPPHIRE" is seen at Lincoln on 07/12/19.                    **Robert Pritchard**

▲ Rail Operations Group-liveried Mark 1 Barrier Vehicle 6340 is seen at Stoneycombe, near Newton Abbot, on 15/09/20. **Tony Christie**

▼ Arlington Fleet Services-liveried EMU Translator Vehicle 64707 (converted from a Class 508 driving car) is seen at Doncaster on 26/08/20. **Ian Beardsley**

▲ All over blue-liveried Mark 1 EMU Translator Vehicle 975975 is seen near Bristol Parkway on 25/05/20. **Tony Christie**

▼ Network Rail yellow-liveried Mark 1 Generator Van 6263 is seen at Whisby Nature Reserve near Lincoln on 20/08/20. **Robert Pritchard**

▲ Network Rail yellow-liveried Driving Trailer Coach 9714 is seen at Saxilby bringing up the rear of the 1Q86 10.39 March–Derby RTC (via Doncaster) test train – led by 37057 – on 04/04/20. **Robert Pritchard**

▼ Network Rail yellow-liveried Plain Line Pattern Recognition Coach 72631 (converted from a Mark 2F previously used by Gatwick Express) is seen near Saxilby on 30/05/20. **Robert Pritchard**

▲ Network Rail Inspection Saloon 975025 (converted from a Class 202 DEMU TRB) is seen near Norton Bridge being propelled by 37421 as a 5Z89 Lichfield Trent Valley–Crewe on 30/07/20. **Brad Joyce**

▼ Network Rail yellow-liveried New Measurement Train Test Coach 977993 is seen on the approaches to Sheffield on 22/06/19. **Robert Pritchard**

| 41185 | (42313) | m† | **VE** | P | *EM* | NL |
| 41187 | (42311) | *w | **FD** | LS | | KR |
| 41189 | (42298) | *w | **GW** | P | | LM |
| 41190 | (42088) | m† | **VE** | P | | NL |

The following carriages have been converted from loco-hauled Mark 3 vehicles.

| 41193 | (11060) | px | **XC** | P | *XC* | LA |
| 41194 | (11016) | px | **XC** | P | *XC* | LA |
| 41195 | (11020) | px | **XC** | P | *XC* | LA |
| 41204 | (11023) | | **EA** | A | | EP |
| 41205 | (11036) | w | **EA** | A | | EP |
| 41206 | (11055) | | **EA** | A | | EP |
| 41207 | (12033, 42403) | | **EA** | A | | EP |
| 41208 | (12112, 42406) | w | **EA** | A | | EP |
| 41209 | (12088, 42409) | | **EA** | A | | EP |

# TRAILER STANDARD                                    TS

42158 was numbered 41177 for a time when fitted with First Class seats.
42310 was numbered 41188 for a time when fitted with First Class seats.

Standard seating and m –/76 2T.
* Refurbished former Great Western Railway vehicles. Grammer seating. –/80 2T (unless h – high density).
d Former Great Western Railway vehicles with universal access toilet and 5, 6 or 7 tip-up seats. –/68 1T 1TD 2W.
h "High density" former Great Western Railway vehicles. –/84 2T.
k "High density" former Great Western Railway refurbished vehicle with disabled persons toilet and 5, 6 or 7 tip-up seats. –/72 1T 1TD 2W.
m Refurbished former LNER vehicles with Primarius seating.
pr Refurbished ScotRail vehicles with power doors and Grammer seating. –/74.
ps Refurbished ScotRail vehicles with power doors and Grammer seating. –/74 1T.
p* Refurbished ScotRail vehicles with power doors, Grammer seating and universal access toilet. –/58 1TD 2W.
px Refurbished CrossCountry vehicles with power doors and Primarius seating. –/80 1T.
p† Refurbished CrossCountry vehicles with power doors, Primarius seating and universal access toilet. –/64 1TD 2W.
u Centre luggage stack (EMR) –/74 2T.
w Centre luggage stack and wheelchair space (EMR) –72 2T 1W.
† Disabled persons toilet (LNER) –/62 1T 1TD 1W.

**42004–087.** Lot No. 30882 Derby 1976–77. 33.6 t.
**42091–250.** Lot No. 30897 Derby 1977–79. 33.6 t.
**42252–301.** Lot No. 30939 Derby 1979–80. 33.6 t.
**42307–319.** Lot No. 30969 Derby 1982. 33.6 t.
**42323–341.** Lot No. 30983 Derby 1984–85. 33.6 t.
**42342/360.** Lot No. 30949 Derby 1982. 33.47 t. Converted from TGS.
**42343/345.** Lot No. 30970 Derby 1982. 33.47 t. Converted from TGS.
**42344.** Lot No. 30964 Derby 1982. 33.47 t. Converted from TGS.

**42347/350/351/379/380/551–564**. Lot No. 30881 Derby 1976–77. 33.66 t. Converted from TF.
**42353/355–357**. Lot No. 30967 Derby 1982. Ex-prototype vehicles. 33.66 t.
**42354**. Lot No. 30897 Derby 1977. Was TF from 1983 to 1992. 33.66 t.
**42363/565–570**. Lot No. 30896 Derby 1977–78. 33.66 t. Converted from TF.
**42366–378/401–408**. Lot No. 30877 Derby 1975–77. 34.3 t. Converted from Mark 3A Open Standard.
**42384**. Lot No. 30896 Derby 1977–78. 33.66 t. Converted from TF.
**42502/506**. Lot No. 30940 Derby 1979–80. 34.8 t. Converted from TFKB.
**42503/504/511**. Lot No. 30921 Derby 1978–79. 34.8 t. Converted from TFKB.
**42571–579**. Lot No. 30938 Derby 1979–80. 33.66 t. Converted from TF.
**42580–583**. Lot No. 30947 Derby 1980. 33.66 t. Converted from TF.
**42584–586**. Lot No. 30878 Derby 1975–76. Converted from Mark 3A Open First.

| | | | | | | | | | | |
|---|---|---|---|---|---|---|---|---|---|---|
| 42004 | p* | SI | A | SR | IS | 42075 | ps | SI | A | SR | IS |
| 42007 | p* | SI | A | | ZH | 42077 | * | FD | A | | ZB |
| 42009 | *h | FD | A | | ZB | 42078 | * | FD | A | | ZB |
| 42010 | ps | SI | A | SR | IS | 42081 | *k | FD | GW | | ZB |
| 42012 | p* | SI | A | SR | IS | 42087 | *h | GW | GW | | ZB |
| 42013 | ps | SI | A | SR | IS | 42091 | m† | VE | A | EM | NL |
| 42014 | ps | SI | A | SR | IS | 42094 | *h | FD | FG | | LM |
| 42019 | ps | SI | A | SR | IS | 42095 | * | FD | FG | | LM |
| 42021 | p* | SI | A | SR | IS | 42096 | *h | FD | A | | ZB |
| 42023 | *h | FD | A | | ZB | 42097 | px | XC | A | XC | LA |
| 42024 | *k | FD | A | | EP | 42100 | u | ST | P | | GA |
| 42026 | *h | FD | A | | EP | 42104 | m | VE | A | | EP |
| 42029 | *h | FD | A | | ZB | 42106 | m | VE | A | | EP |
| 42030 | p* | SI | A | SR | IS | 42107 | pr | SI | A | SR | IS |
| 42032 | *h | FD | A | | ZB | 42109 | m | VE | P | EM | NL |
| 42033 | * | FD | A | | ZB | 42110 | m | VE | P | EM | NL |
| 42034 | pr | SI | A | SR | IS | 42116 | m† | VE | A | | NL |
| 42035 | * | FD | A | | ZB | 42118 | *h | FD | SR | | DU |
| 42036 | px | XC | A | XC | LA | 42119 | u | ST | P | | GA |
| 42037 | px | XC | A | XC | LA | 42120 | u | ST | P | | GA |
| 42038 | px | XC | A | XC | LA | 42121 | u | ST | P | | GA |
| 42045 | ps | SI | A | SR | IS | 42122 | m | VE | A | | EP |
| 42046 | ps | SI | A | SR | IS | 42124 | u | ST | P | | GA |
| 42047 | * | FD | A | | ZB | 42128 | m† | VE | A | | NL |
| 42048 | *h | FD | GW | | ZB | 42129 | ps | SI | A | SR | IS |
| 42050 | *h | FD | GW | | ZB | 42134 | m | VE | A | | EP |
| 42051 | px | XC | A | XC | LA | 42139 | u | ST | P | | GA |
| 42052 | px | XC | A | XC | LA | 42140 | u | ST | P | | GA |
| 42053 | px | XC | A | XC | LA | 42141 | u | ST | P | | GA |
| 42054 | * | FD | A | | ZB | 42143 | ps | SI | A | SR | IS |
| 42055 | p* | SI | A | SR | IS | 42144 | * | FD | A | | ZB |
| 42056 | * | FD | A | | ZB | 42145 | ps | SI | A | | ZH |
| 42066 | *k | FD | GW | | ZB | 42146 | m | VE | A | EM | NL |
| 42069 | *k | FD | SR | | DU | 42150 | m | VE | A | EM | NL |
| 42071 | *h | FD | GW | | ZB | 42151 | w | ST | P | | GA |
| 42072 | pr | SI | A | SR | IS | 42152 | u | ST | P | | GA |
| 42074 | *h | FD | GW | | ZB | 42153 | u | ST | P | | GA |

| | | | | | | | | | | |
|---|---|---|---|---|---|---|---|---|---|---|
| 42154 | m | **VE** | A | *EM* | NL | 42239 | m† | **VE** | A | *EM* | NL |
| 42155 | w | **ST** | P | | GA | 42240 | m | **VE** | A | *EM* | NL |
| 42156 | u | **ST** | P | | GA | 42241 | m | **VE** | A | | EP |
| 42157 | u | **ST** | P | | GA | 42242 | m | **BG** | A | | EP |
| 42158 | m | **VE** | A | | EP | 42243 | m | **BG** | A | | EP |
| 42159 | m† | **VE** | P | *EM* | NL | 42244 | m | **VE** | A | | EP |
| 42160 | m | **VE** | P | | NL | 42245 | pr | **SI** | A | *SR* | IS |
| 42161 | m† | **VE** | A | | EP | 42250 | ps | **SI** | A | *SR* | IS |
| 42164 | | **ST** | P | | GA | 42252 | ps | **SI** | A | *SR* | IS |
| 42165 | | **ST** | P | | GA | 42253 | p* | **SI** | A | *SR* | IS |
| 42167 | *h | **FD** | FG | | LM | 42255 | p* | **SI** | A | *SR* | IS |
| 42171 | m | **VE** | A | | EP | 42256 | ps | **SI** | A | *SR* | IS |
| 42172 | m | **VE** | A | | EP | 42257 | ps | **SI** | A | *SR* | IS |
| 42173 | *k | **FD** | GW | | ZB | 42259 | p* | **SI** | A | *SR* | IS |
| 42175 | *h | **FD** | FG | | LA | 42261 | *h | **FD** | SR | | DU |
| 42176 | *h | **GW** | P | | LM | 42265 | p* | **SI** | A | *SR* | IS |
| 42179 | m | **VE** | A | | EP | 42267 | p* | **SI** | A | *SR* | IS |
| 42180 | m | **VE** | A | | EP | 42268 | p* | **SI** | A | *SR* | IS |
| 42181 | m | **VE** | A | | EP | 42269 | ps | **SI** | A | *SR* | IS |
| 42182 | m | **VE** | A | | NL | 42275 | p* | **SI** | A | *SR* | IS |
| 42183 | p* | **SI** | A | *SR* | IS | 42276 | p* | **SI** | A | *SR* | IS |
| 42184 | ps | **SI** | A | *SR* | IS | 42277 | ps | **SI** | A | *SR* | IS |
| 42185 | * | **FD** | A | | ZB | 42279 | p* | **SI** | A | *SR* | IS |
| 42186 | m | **VE** | A | | NL | 42280 | pr | **SI** | A | *SR* | IS |
| 42188 | m† | **VE** | A | | EP | 42281 | p* | **SI** | A | *SR* | IS |
| 42189 | m† | **VE** | A | | GA | 42286 | m† | **VE** | P | | NL |
| 42190 | m | **VE** | A | | NL | 42288 | ps | **SI** | A | *SR* | IS |
| 42191 | m | **VE** | A | | NL | 42290 | px | **XC** | P | *XC* | LA |
| 42192 | m | **VE** | A | | NL | 42291 | p* | **SI** | A | *SR* | IS |
| 42193 | m | **VE** | A | | NL | 42292 | p* | **SI** | A | *SR* | IS |
| 42195 | *k | **FD** | GW | | ZB | 42293 | ps | **SI** | A | *SR* | IS |
| 42198 | m | **VE** | A | *EM* | NL | 42295 | p* | **SI** | A | *SR* | IS |
| 42199 | m | **VE** | A | *EM* | NL | 42296 | p* | **SI** | A | *SR* | IS |
| 42200 | p* | **SI** | A | *SR* | IS | 42297 | p* | **SI** | A | *SR* | IS |
| 42206 | p* | **SI** | A | *SR* | IS | 42299 | p* | **SI** | A | *SR* | IS |
| 42207 | p* | **SI** | A | *SR* | IS | 42300 | pr | **SI** | A | *SR* | IS |
| 42208 | ps | **SI** | A | *SR* | IS | 42301 | ps | **SI** | A | *SR* | IS |
| 42209 | * | **FD** | A | | ZB | 42307 | m | **VE** | P | | NL |
| 42213 | *h | **FD** | A | | ZB | 42310 | *k | **FD** | GW | | ZB |
| 42215 | m | **VE** | A | | EP | 42319 | *h | **GW** | LS | | KR |
| 42217 | *k | **FD** | GW | | ZB | 42323 | m | **VE** | A | | EP |
| 42219 | m | **VE** | A | | EP | 42325 | pr | **SI** | A | *SR* | IS |
| 42220 | w | **ST** | P | | GA | 42326 | m | **VE** | A | *EM* | NL |
| 42226 | m | **VE** | A | | EP | 42329 | w | **ST** | P | | GA |
| 42230 | u | **ST** | P | | GA | 42330 | m | **VE** | P | | NL |
| 42231 | *h | **FD** | FG | | LM | 42333 | ps | **SI** | A | *SR* | IS |
| 42234 | px | **XC** | P | *XC* | LA | 42337 | w | **ST** | P | | GA |
| 42235 | m | **VE** | A | | EP | 42340 | m | **VE** | A | | EP |
| 42237 | m | **VE** | P | *EM* | NL | 42341 | u | **ST** | P | | NL |
| 42238 | m† | **VE** | A | *EM* | NL | | | | | | |

| | | | | | | |
|---|---|---|---|---|---|---|
| 42342 | (44082) | px | **XC** | A | *XC* | LA |
| 42343 | (44095) | ps | **SI** | A | *SR* | IS |
| 42344 | (44092) | *k | **FD** | SR | | DU |
| 42345 | (44096) | p* | **SI** | A | *SR* | IS |
| 42347 | (41054) | *k | **FD** | A | | EP |
| 42350 | (41047) | ps | **SI** | A | *SR* | IS |
| 42351 | (41048) | * | **GW** | A | | ZB |
| 42353 | (42001, 41171) | *k | **FD** | GW | | ZB |
| 42354 | (42114, 41175) | m | **VE** | A | | NL |
| 42355 | (42000, 41172) | m | **VE** | A | | EP |
| 42356 | (42002, 41173) | *k | **GW** | PO | | ZG |
| 42357 | (41002, 41174) | m | **VE** | A | | EP |
| 42360 | (44084, 45084) | p* | **SI** | A | *SR* | IS |
| 42363 | (41082) | m† | **BG** | A | | EP |

42366–378 were converted from loco-hauled Mark 3 vehicles for CrossCountry.

| | | | | | | |
|---|---|---|---|---|---|---|
| 42366 | (12007) | p† | **XC** | P | *XC* | LA |
| 42367 | (12025) | px | **XC** | P | *XC* | LA |
| 42368 | (12028) | px | **XC** | P | *XC* | LA |
| 42369 | (12050) | px | **XC** | P | *XC* | LA |
| 42370 | (12086) | px | **XC** | P | *XC* | LA |
| 42371 | (12052) | p† | **XC** | P | *XC* | LA |
| 42372 | (12055) | px | **XC** | P | *XC* | LA |
| 42373 | (12071) | px | **XC** | P | *XC* | LA |
| 42374 | (12075) | p† | **XC** | P | *XC* | LA |
| 42375 | (12113) | px | **XC** | P | *XC* | LA |
| 42376 | (12085) | p† | **XC** | P | *XC* | LA |
| 42377 | (12102) | px | **XC** | P | *XC* | LA |
| 42378 | (12123) | px | **XC** | P | *XC* | LA |
| 42379 | (41036) | p† | **XC** | A | *XC* | LA |
| 42380 | (41025) | p† | **XC** | A | *XC* | LA |
| 42384 | (41078) | w | **ST** | P | | GA |

These carriages were converted from loco-hauled Mark 3 vehicles for Grand Central. They have a lower density seating layout (most seats arranged around tables). –/62 2T.

| | | | | | |
|---|---|---|---|---|---|
| 42401 | (12149) | **EA** | A | | EP |
| 42402 | (12155) | **EA** | A | | EP |
| 42404 | (12152) | **EA** | A | | EP |
| 42405 | (12136) | **EA** | A | | EP |
| 42407 | (12044) | **EA** | A | | EP |
| 42408 | (12121) | **EA** | A | | EP |

These carriages were converted from TFKB or TSB buffet cars to TS vehicles in 2011–12 at Wabtec Kilmarnock for FGW. Refurbished with Grammer seating. –/84 1T. 34.8 t.

| | | | | | |
|---|---|---|---|---|---|
| 42502 | (40331, 40731) | **FD** | WA | | ZB |
| 42503 | (40312, 40712) | **FD** | WA | | ZB |
| 42504 | (40314, 40714) | **FD** | A | | EP |
| 42506 | (40324, 40724) | **FD** | A | | EP |
| 42511 | (40309, 40709) | **FD** | A | | EP |

These carriages were converted from TF to TS vehicles in 2014 at Wabtec Kilmarnock for FGW. Refurbished with Grammer seating. –/80 1T (pr –/74). 35.5 t.

| | | | | | | |
|---|---|---|---|---|---|---|
| 42551 | (41003) | pr | **SI** | A | *SR* | IS |
| 42553 | (41009) | pr | **SI** | A | *SR* | IS |
| 42554 | (41011) | | **GW** | A | | PM |
| 42555 | (41015) | pr | **SI** | A | *SR* | IS |
| 42557 | (41019) | pr | **SI** | A | *SR* | IS |
| 42558 | (41021) | pr | **SI** | A | *SR* | IS |
| 42559 | (41023) | pr | **SI** | A | *SR* | IS |
| 42561 | (41031) | pr | **SI** | A | *SR* | IS |
| 42562 | (41037) | pr | **SI** | A | *SR* | IS |
| 42563 | (41045) | | **FD** | FG | | LM |
| 42564 | (41051) | pr | **SI** | A | | ZH |
| 42565 | (41085) | | **FD** | FG | | LM |
| 42566 | (41086) | | **FD** | FG | | PZ |
| 42567 | (41093) | pr | **SI** | A | *SR* | IS |
| 42568 | (41101) | pr | **SI** | A | *SR* | IS |
| 42569 | (41105) | | **FD** | A | | EP |
| 42570 | (41114) | | **FD** | FG | | LM |
| 42571 | (41121) | pr | **SI** | A | *SR* | IS |
| 42574 | (41129) | pr | **SI** | A | *SR* | IS |
| 42575 | (41131) | pr | **SI** | A | *SR* | IS |
| 42576 | (41133) | pr | **SI** | A | *SR* | IS |
| 42577 | (41141) | pr | **SI** | A | *SR* | IS |
| 42578 | (41143) | pr | **SI** | A | *SR* | IS |
| 42579 | (41145) | pr | **SI** | A | *SR* | IS |
| 42580 | (41155) | | **FD** | GW | | ZB |
| 42581 | (41157) | pr | **SI** | A | *SR* | IS |
| 42582 | (41163) | | **FD** | FG | | LM |
| 42583 | (41153, 42385) | | **GW** | LS | | KR |

These carriages were converted from loco-hauled carriages for Grand Central, before being converted to TS for East Midlands Railway. –/62 2T.

| | | | | | |
|---|---|---|---|---|---|
| 42584 | (11045, 41201) | **EA** | A | | EP |
| 42585 | (11017, 41202) | **EA** | A | | EP |
| 42586 | (11038, 41203) | **EA** | A | | EP |

# TRAILER GUARD'S STANDARD                                      TGS

As built and m –/65 1T.
* Refurbished Great Western Railway vehicles. Grammer seating and toilet removed for trolley store. –/67 (unless h).
† Converted to Trailer Guard's First (TGF) with Primarius seating.
p Refurbished CrossCountry vehicles with power doors and Primarius seating. –/67.
h "High density" Great Western Railway vehicles. –/71.
m Refurbished former LNER vehicles with Primarius seating.
s Fitted with centre luggage stack (EMR) –/63 1T.
t Fitted with centre luggage stack –/61 1T.

**44001–089**. Lot No. 30949 Derby 1980–82. 33.47 t.
**44093/094**. Lot No. 30964 Derby 1982. 33.47 t.
**44098/100**. Lot No. 30970 Derby 1982. 33.47 t.

| 44001 | * | **FD** | A | | EP |
|---|---|---|---|---|---|
| 44002 | *h | **FD** | GW | | ZB |
| 44005 | *h | **GW** | GW | | ZB |
| 44007 | *h | **FD** | A | | EP |
| 44010 | *h | **FD** | A | | EP |
| 44011 | * | **FD** | A | | EP |
| 44012 | p | **XC** | A | *XC* | LA |
| 44015 | * | **FD** | A | | EP |
| 44016 | *h | **FD** | GW | | ZB |
| 44017 | p | **XC** | A | *XC* | LA |
| 44018 | * | **FD** | A | | EP |
| 44020 | *h | **FD** | WA | | ZB |
| 44021 | p | **XC** | P | *XC* | LA |
| 44023 | *h | **FD** | SR | | DU |
| 44024 | *h | **FD** | WA | | ZB |
| 44029 | * | **FD** | WA | | ZB |
| 44030 | *h | **FD** | SR | | DU |
| 44031 | m | **VE** | A | | EP |
| 44032 | * | **FD** | WA | | ZB |
| 44034 | * | **FD** | A | | EP |
| 44035 | * | **FD** | WA | | ZB |
| 44038 | * | **FD** | A | | EP |
| 44039 | * | **FD** | A | | EP |
| 44040 | * | **GW** | WA | | ZB |
| 44041 | s | **ST** | P | | GA |
| 44042 | *h | **FD** | GW | | ZB |

| 44047 | s | **ST** | P | | GA |
|---|---|---|---|---|---|
| 44048 | s | **ST** | P | | GA |
| 44051 | s | **ST** | P | | NL |
| 44052 | p | **XC** | P | *XC* | LA |
| 44054 | s | **ST** | P | | GA |
| 44056 | m | **VE** | A | | EP |
| 44057 | m | **VE** | P | *EM* | NL |
| 44058 | m | **VE** | A | | EP |
| 44059 | * | **FD** | A | | EP |
| 44061 | m | **VE** | A | *EM* | NL |
| 44063 | m | **VE** | A | *EM* | NL |
| 44066 | * | **FD** | WA | | ZB |
| 44072 | p | **XC** | P | *XC* | LA |
| 44075 | m | **VE** | P | *EM* | NL |
| 44077 | m | **VE** | A | | NL |
| 44078 | † | **MP** | LS | *LS* | CL |
| 44080 | m | **VE** | A | | NL |
| 44081 | *h | **FD** | LS | *LS* | CL |
| 44085 | s | **ST** | P | | GA |
| 44086 | * | **GW** | WA | | ZB |
| 44089 | t | **V** | AV | | ZR |
| 44093 | *h | **FD** | A | | EP |
| 44094 | m | **VE** | A | *EM* | NL |
| 44098 | m | **BG** | A | | EP |
| 44100 | *h | **FD** | P | | PZ |

# TRAILER COMPOSITE KITCHEN                               TCK

Converted from Mark 3A Open Standard. Refurbished CrossCountry vehicles with Primarius seating. Small kitchen for the preparation of hot food and stowage space for two trolleys between First and Standard Class. One toilet removed. 30/8 1T.

**45001–005**. Lot No. 30877 Derby 1975–77. 34.3 t.

| 45001 | (12004) | p | **XC** | P | *XC* | LA |
|---|---|---|---|---|---|---|
| 45002 | (12106) | p | **XC** | P | *XC* | LA |
| 45003 | (12076) | p | **XC** | P | *XC* | LA |
| 45004 | (12077) | p | **XC** | P | *XC* | LA |
| 45005 | (12080) | p | **XC** | P | *XC* | LA |

## TRAILER COMPOSITE TC

Converted from TF for First Great Western 2014–15. Refurbished with Grammer seating. 24/39 1T.

**46006.** Lot No. 30896 Derby 1977–78. 35.6 t. Converted from TF.
**46010/012.** Lot No. 30938 Derby 1979–80. 35.6 t. Converted from TF.
**46014.** Lot No. 30963 Derby 1982. 35.6 t. Converted from TF.

| | | | | |
|---|---|---|---|---|
| 46006 | (41081) | **FD** | LS | ZG |
| 46010 | (41125) | **FD** | SR | DU |
| 46012 | (41147) | **FD** | LS | KR |
| 46014 | (41168) | **FD** | LS | ZG |

## TRAILER STANDARD TS

Refurbished for Great Western Railway 2017–21 and fitted with power doors and retention toilets. For use in 4-car sets on local and regional services across the South-West. Planned renumbering details for 48143–150 are provisional. –/84 1T († –/62 and 5 tip-ups 1TD 2W).

**48101–135/140–150.** For Lot No. details see TS. 36.3 t.

| | | | | | | |
|---|---|---|---|---|---|---|
| 48101 | (42093, 48111) | p | **GW** | FG | *GW* | LA |
| 48102 | (42218) | p† | **GW** | FG | *GW* | LA |
| 48103 | (42168, 48101) | p | **GW** | FG | *GW* | LA |
| 48104 | (41107, 42365) | p | **GW** | FG | *GW* | LA |
| 48105 | (42266) | p† | **GW** | FG | *GW* | LA |
| 48106 | (42258) | p | **GW** | FG | *GW* | LA |
| 48107 | (42101) | p | **GW** | FG | *GW* | LA |
| 48108 | (42174) | p† | **GW** | FG | *GW* | LA |
| 48109 | (42085) | p | **GW** | FG | *GW* | LA |
| 48110 | (42315) | p | **GW** | FG | *GW* | LA |
| 48111 | (42224) | p† | **GW** | FG | *GW* | LA |
| 48112 | (42222) | p | **GW** | FG | *GW* | LA |
| 48113 | (42177, 48102) | p | **GW** | FG | *GW* | LA |
| 48114 | (42317) | p† | **GW** | FG | *GW* | LA |
| 48115 | (42285) | p | **GW** | A | *GW* | LA |
| 48116 | (42273) | p | **GW** | A | *GW* | LA |
| 48117 | (42271) | p† | **GW** | A | *GW* | LA |
| 48118 | (42073) | p | **GW** | A | *GW* | LA |
| 48119 | (42204) | p | **GW** | A | *GW* | LA |
| 48120 | (42201) | p† | **GW** | A | *GW* | LA |
| 48121 | (42027) | p | **GW** | A | *GW* | LA |
| 48122 | (42214) | p | **GW** | A | *GW* | LA |
| 48123 | (42211) | p† | **GW** | A | *GW* | LA |
| 48124 | (42212) | p | **GW** | A | *GW* | LA |
| 48125 | (42203) | p | **GW** | A | *GW* | LA |
| 48126 | (42138) | p† | **GW** | A | *GW* | LA |
| 48127 | (42349) | p | **GW** | A | *GW* | LA |
| 48128 | (42044) | p | **GW** | A | *GW* | LA |
| 48129 | (42008) | p† | **GW** | A | *GW* | LA |

| 48130 | (42102, 48131) | p  | **GW** | FG | *GW* | LA |
| 48131 | (42042) | p  | **GW** | A | *GW* | LA |
| 48132 | (42202) | p† | **GW** | A | *GW* | LA |
| 48133 | (42003) | p  | **GW** | A | *GW* | LA |
| 48134 | (42264) | p† | **GW** | A | *GW* | LA |
| 48135 | (42251) | p† | **GW** | A | *GW* | LA |
| 48140 | (42005) | p  | **GW** | GW | *GW* | LA |
| 48141 | (42015) | p† | **GW** | GW | *GW* | LA |
| 48142 | (42016) | p  | **GW** | GW | *GW* | LA |
| 48143 | (42050) | | | | | |
| 48144 | (42066) | | | | | |
| 48145 | (42048) | | | | | |
| 48146 | (42074) | | | | | |
| 48147 | (42081) | | | | | |
| 48148 | (42071) | | | | | |
| 48149 | (42087) | | | | | |
| 48150 | (42580) | | | | | |

## TRAILER GUARD'S STANDARD                                  TGS

Refurbished for Great Western Railway 2017–21 and fitted with power doors. Planned renumbering details for 49115–117 are provisional. –/71.

**49101–117.** For Lot No. details see TGS. 35.7 t.

| 49101 | (44055) | p | **GW** | FG | *GW* | LA |
| 49102 | (44083) | p | **GW** | FG | *GW* | LA |
| 49103 | (44097) | p | **GW** | FG | *GW* | LA |
| 49104 | (44101) | p | **GW** | FG | *GW* | LA |
| 49105 | (44090) | p | **GW** | FG | *GW* | LA |
| 49106 | (44033) | p | **GW** | A | *GW* | LA |
| 49107 | (44064) | p | **GW** | A | *GW* | LA |
| 49108 | (44067) | p | **GW** | A | *GW* | LA |
| 49109 | (44003) | p | **GW** | A | *GW* | LA |
| 49110 | (44014) | p | **GW** | A | *GW* | LA |
| 49111 | (44036) | p | **GW** | A | *GW* | LA |
| 49112 | (44079) | p | **GW** | FG | *GW* | LA |
| 49113 | (44008) | p | **GW** | A | *GW* | LA |
| 49114 | (44005) | p | **GW** | GW | *GW* | LA |
| 49115 | (44016) | | | | | |
| 49116 | (44002) | | | | | |
| 49117 | (44042) | | | | | |

# 2.3. HST SET FORMATIONS

## GREAT WESTERN RAILWAY

GWR withdrew its last full length HST sets in spring 2019. The company is retaining and refurbishing 14 4-car sets for use on regional and local services in the South-West, the last of these should enter service in early 2021. At the time of writing some sets were running as 3-cars pending the arrival of the remaining vehicles.

**Number of sets:** 14.                    **Maximum number of daily diagrams:** 12.
**Formations:** 4-cars.                    **Allocation:** Laira (Plymouth).
**Other maintenance and servicing depots:** Long Rock (Penzance), St Philip's Marsh (Bristol).
**Operation:** Principally Bristol–Exeter–Plymouth–Penzance and Cardiff–Bristol–Taunton.

| Set | D | C | B | A | |
|-----|------|------|------|------|---|
| GW01 | 48103 | 48102 | 48101 | 49101 | |
| GW02 | 48106 | 48105 | 48104 | 49102 | |
| GW03 | 48109 | 48108 | 48107 | 49103 | |
| GW04 | 48112 | 48111 | 48110 | 49104 | |
| GW05 | 48115 | 48114 | 48113 | 49105 | |
| GW06 | 48118 | 48117 | 48116 | 49106 | |
| GW07 | 48121 | 48120 | 48119 | 49107 | |
| GW08 | 48124 | 48123 | 48122 | 49108 | |
| GW09 | 48127 | 48126 | 48125 | 49109 | |
| GW10 | 48130 | 48129 | 48128 | 49110 | |
| GW11 | 48133 | 48132 | 48131 | 49111 | |
| GW14 | 48142 | 48141 | 48140 | 49114 | |
| GW15 | 48145 | 48144 | 48143 | 49115 | Undergoing refurbishment |
| GW16 | 48148 | 48147 | 48146 | 49116 | Undergoing refurbishment |

**Spares:**

LA:    48134    48135    48149    48150    49112    49113    49117

# EAST MIDLANDS RAILWAY

From December 2020 East Midlands Railway reduced its HST requirement to five diagrams, mainly operating at peak times. They are mainly used on the St Pancras–Nottingham corridor during the day, with early morning and evening services to Leeds for servicing at Neville Hill. All sets are due to be withdrawn in May 2021.

The original East Midlands Trains fleet, NL01–NL12, and the three shorter 6-car ex-Grand Central sets have now been phased out in favour of former LNER sets, but this has been a very protracted process.

At the time of writing the five sets in service had been reduced to 6-cars, but the formations were fluid. Another set, NL54, is due to be returned to service, but only sets and vehicles that have been returned to service so far here are shown in the list.

**Number of serviceable sets:** 5.      **Maximum number of daily diagrams:** 5.
**Formations:** 6-cars.
**Allocation:** Neville Hill (Leeds).
**Operation:** London St Pancras–Nottingham, Sheffield/Leeds.

| NL51 | 41150 |       | 40748 | 42091 | 42150 | 42146 | 44094 |
| NL55 | 41099 |       | 40750 | 42238 | 42110 | 42199 | 44061 |
| NL56 | 41100 |       | 40711 | 42239 | 42240 | 42198 | 44063 |
| NL57 | 41115 | 41165 | 40702 | 42159 | 42109 |       | 44057 |
| NL58 | 41120 | 41095 | 40701 | 42326 | 42237 |       | 44075 |

**Spares:**

NL:   41185   42154

# CROSSCOUNTRY

CrossCountry HSTs run in 7-car formation. All fitted with power doors.

**Number of sets:** 5.      **Maximum number of daily diagrams:** 4.
**Formations:** 7-cars.      **Allocation:** Laira (Plymouth).
**Other maintenance depots:** Neville Hill (Leeds) or Edinburgh (Craigentinny).
**Operation:** Edinburgh–Leeds–Plymouth is the core route with some services extending to Dundee or Penzance.

| Set | A | B | C | D | E | F | G |
|-----|-----|-----|-----|-----|-----|-----|-----|
| XC01 | 41193 | 45001 | 42342 | 42097 | 42377 | 42380 | 44021 |
| XC02 | 41194 | 45002 | 42367 | 42037 | 42234 | 42371 | 44072 |
| XC03 | 41195 | 45003 | 42370 | 42378 | 42036 | 42376 | 44052 |
| XC04 | 41026 | 45004 | 42375 | 42369 | 42051 | 42366 | 44012 |
| XC05 | 41035 | 45005 | 42368 | 42290 | 42372 | 42379 | 44017 |

**Spares:**

LA:   42038   42052   42053   42373   42374

# SCOTRAIL

ScotRail is introducing refurbished HSTs onto its Edinburgh/Glasgow–
Aberdeen/Inverness services – branded INTER-7-CITY as they serve
Scotland's seven cities. There will ultimately be 17 5-car and nine 4-car sets
but the refurbishment programme has been running behind schedule. At
the time of writing all sets are running as 4-cars – the 5-car sets are to be
introduced during 2021.

The formations are listed here as sets had been released from Wabtec
Doncaster in 4-car formation. HA22 was written off in the Carmont accident
of August 2020 and is now stored.

**Number of sets:** 26.
**Number of diagrams as at early 2021:** 13.
**Formations:** 4-cars or 5-cars.
**Allocation:** Power cars: Haymarket (Edinburgh), Trailers: Inverness.
**Operation:** Edinburgh/Glasgow–Aberdeen, Edinburgh/Glasgow–Inverness,
Aberdeen–Inverness.

| Set | A | B | C | D | |
|-----|------|------|------|------|---|
| HA01 | 40601 | 42004 | 42561 | 42046 | |
| HA02 | 40602 | 42292 | 42562 | 42045 | |
| HA03 | 40603 | 42021 | 42557 | 42143 | |
| HA04 | 40604 | 42183 | 42559 | 42343 | |
| HA05 | 40605 | 42345 | 42034 | 42184 | |
| HA06 | 40606 | 42206 | 42581 | 42208 | |
| HA07 | 40607 | 42207 | 42574 | 42288 | |
| HA08 | 40608 | 42055 | 42571 | 42019 | |
| HA09 | 40609 | 42253 | 42107 | 42257 | |
| HA10 | 40610 | 42360 | 42551 | 42252 | |
| HA11 | 40611 | 42267 | 42325 | 42301 | |
| HA12 | 40612 | 42275 | 42576 | 42276 | |
| HA13 | 40613 | 42279 | 42280 | 42296 | |
| HA14 | 40614 | 42012 | 42245 | 42013 | |
| HA15 | 40615 | 42030 | 42579 | 42010 | |
| HA16 | 40616 | 42291 | 42577 | 42075 | |
| HA17 | 40617 | 42295 | 42558 | 42250 | |
| HA18 | 40618 | 42297 | 42555 | 42014 | |
| HA19 | 40619 | 42255 | 42568 | 42256 | |
| HA20 | 40620 | 42200 | 42575 | 42129 | |
| HA21 | 40621 | 42299 | 42300 | 42277 | |
| HA22 | 40622 | 42007 | 42564 | 42145 | Accident damage: stored |
| HA23 | 40623 | 42268 | 42567 | 42269 | |
| HA24 | 40624 | 42265 | 42553 | 42293 | |
| HA25 | 40625 | 42259 | 42578 | 42333 | |
| HA26 | 40626 | 42281 | 42072 | 42350 | |

17 extra coaches being refurbished to make sets up to 5-car rakes:
42009  42023  42029  42032  42033  42035  42047  42054  42056
42077  42078  42096  42144  42185  42209  42213  42351

# 2.4. SALOONS

Several specialist passenger carrying carriages, normally referred to as saloons are permitted to run on the national railway system. Many of these are to pre-nationalisation designs.

## WCJS FIRST CLASS SALOON

Built 1892 by LNWR, Wolverton. Originally dining saloon mounted on six-wheel bogies. Rebuilt with new underframe with four-wheel bogies in 1927. Rebuilt 1960 as observation saloon with DMU end. Gangwayed at other end. The interior has a saloon, kitchen, guards vestibule and observation lounge. 19/– 1T. Gresley bogies. 28.5 t. 75 mph. ETS x.

41      (484, 45018)   x      **M**      WC   *WC*      CS

## LNWR DINING SALOON

Built 1890 by LNWR, Wolverton. Mounted on the underframe of LMS General Utility Van 37908 in the 1980s. Contains kitchen and dining area seating 12 at tables for two. 12/–. Gresley bogies. 75 mph. 25.4 t. ETS x.

159     (5159)        x      **M**      WC   *WC*      CS

## GNR FIRST CLASS SALOON

Built 1912 by GNR, Doncaster. Contains entrance vestibule, lavatory, two separate saloons, library and luggage space. 19/– 1T. Gresley bogies. 75 mph. 29.4 t. ETS x.

**Non-standard livery:** Teak.

807     (4807)        x      **0**      WC   *WC*      CS

## LNER GENERAL MANAGERS SALOON

Built 1945 by LNER, York. Gangwayed at one end with a veranda at the other. The interior has a dining saloon seating 12, kitchen, toilet, office and nine seat lounge. 21/– 1T. B4 bogies. 75 mph. 35.7 t. ETS 3.

1999    (902260)      **M**      WC          CS          DINING CAR No. 2

# GENERAL MANAGER'S SALOON

Renumbered 1989 from London Midland Region departmental series. Formerly the LMR General Manager's saloon. Rebuilt from LMS period 1 Corridor Brake First M5033M to dia 1654 and mounted on the underframe of BR suburban Brake Standard M43232. Screw couplings have been removed. B4 bogies. 100 mph. ETS 2X.

LMS Lot No. 326 Derby 1927. 27.5 t.

6320 (5033, DM 395707) x **M** PR *PR* SK

# SUPPORT CAR

Converted 199? from Courier vehicle converted from Mark 1 Corridor Brake Standard 1986–87. Toilet retained and former compartment area replaced with train manager's office, crew locker room, linen store and dry goods store. The former luggage area has been adapted for use as an engineers' compartment and workshop. B5 bogies. 100 mph. ETS 2.

Lot No. 30721 Wolverton 1963. 35.5 t.

99545 (35466, 80207) **PC** BE *BP* SL BAGGAGE CAR No. 11

# SERVICE CAR

Converted from BR Mark 1 Corridor Brake Standard. Commonwealth bogies. 100 mph. ETS 2.

Lot No. 30721 Wolverton 1963.

99886 (35407) x **M** WC *WC* CS 86 SERVICE CAR No. 1

# ROYAL SCOTSMAN SALOONS

Built 1960 by Metro-Cammell as Pullman Kitchen Second for East Coast Main Line Services. Rebuilt 2016 as a Spa Car with two large bedrooms with bathroom/spa areas. Commonwealth bogies. xx t. ETS ?.

99337 (CAR No. 337) **M** BE *RS* HN STATE SPA CAR

Built 1960 by Metro-Cammell as Pullman Kitchen First for East Coast Main Line services. Rebuilt 2013 as dining car. Commonwealth bogies. 38.5 t. ETS ?.

99960 (321 SWIFT) **M** BE *RS* HN DINING CAR No. 2

Built 1960 by Metro-Cammell as Pullman Parlour First (§ Pullman Kitchen First) for East Coast Main Line services. Rebuilt 1990 as sleeping cars with four twin sleeping rooms (*§ three twin sleeping rooms and two single sleeping rooms at each end). Commonwealth bogies. 38.5 t. ETS ?.

| 99961 | (324 AMBER) * | M | BE | *RS* | HN | STATE CAR No. 1 |
| 99962 | (329 PEARL) | M | BE | *RS* | HN | STATE CAR No. 2 |
| 99963 | (331 TOPAZ) | M | BE | *RS* | HN | STATE CAR No. 3 |
| 99964 | (313 FINCH) § | M | BE | *RS* | HN | STATE CAR No. 4 |

Built 1960 by Metro-Cammell as Pullman Kitchen First for East Coast Main Line services. Rebuilt 1990 as observation car with open verandah seating 32. B4 bogies. 36.95 t. ETS ?.

| 99965 | (319 SNIPE) | M | BE | *RS* | HN | OBSERVATION CAR |

Built 1960 by Metro-Cammell as Pullman Kitchen First for East Coast Main Line services. Rebuilt 1993 as dining car. Commonwealth bogies. 38.5 t. ETS ?.

| 99967 | (317 RAVEN) | M | BE | *RS* | HN | DINING CAR No. 1 |

Mark 3A. Converted 1997 from a Sleeping Car at Carnforth Railway Restoration & Engineering Services. BT10 bogies. Attendant's and adjacent two sleeping compartments converted to generator room containing a 160 kW Volvo unit. In 99968 four sleeping compartments remain for staff use with another converted for use as a staff shower and toilet. The remaining five sleeping compartments have been replaced by two passenger cabins. In 99969 seven sleeping compartments remain for staff use. A further sleeping compartment, along with one toilet, have been converted to store rooms. The other two sleeping compartments have been combined to form a crew mess. 41.5 t. 99968 ETS index ?. 99969 ETS 7X (when generator not in use). ETS index ?? (when generator in use).

Lot No. 30960 Derby 1981–83.

| 99968 | (10541) | M | BE | *RS* | HN | STATE CAR No. 5 |
| 99969 | (10556) | M | BE | *RS* | HN | SERVICE CAR |

## "CLUB CAR"

Converted from BR Mark 1 Open Standard at Carnforth Railway Restoration & Engineering Services in 1994. Contains kitchen, pantry and two dining saloons. 20/– 1T. Commonwealth bogies. 100 mph. ETS 4.

Lot No. 30724 York 1963. 37 t.

| 99993 | (5067) | x | CC | LS | *LS* | CL | CLUB CAR |

## BR INSPECTION SALOON

Mark 1. Short frames. Non-gangwayed. Observation windows at each end. The interior layout consists of two saloons interspersed by a central lavatory/kitchen/guards/luggage section. 90 mph. ETS x.

BR Wagon Lot No. 3095 Swindon 1957. B4 bogies. 30.5 t.

| 999506 | | M | WC | *WC* | CS | |

# 2.5. PULLMAN CAR COMPANY SERIES

Pullman cars have never generally been numbered as such, although many have carried numbers, instead they have carried titles. However, a scheme of schedule numbers exists which generally lists cars in chronological order. In this section those numbers are shown followed by the car's title. Cars described as "kitchen" contain a kitchen in addition to passenger accommodation and have gas cooking unless otherwise stated. Cars described as "parlour" consist entirely of passenger accommodation. Cars described as "brake" contain a compartment for the use of the guard and a luggage compartment in addition to passenger accommodation.

## PULLMAN PARLOUR FIRST

Built 1927 by Midland Carriage & Wagon Company. 26/– 2T. Gresley bogies. 41 t. ETS 2.

| 213 | MINERVA | **PC** | BE | *BP* | SL |

## PULLMAN KITCHEN FIRST

Built 1928 by Metropolitan Carriage & Wagon Company. 20/– 1T. Gresley bogies. 42 t. ETS 4.

| 238 | PHYLISS | **PC** | BE | | SL |

## PULLMAN PARLOUR FIRST

Built 1928 by Metropolitan Carriage & Wagon Company. 24/– 2T. Gresley bogies. 40 t. ETS 4.

| 239 | AGATHA | **PC** | BE | | SL |
| 243 | LUCILLE | **PC** | BE | *BP* | SL |

## PULLMAN KITCHEN FIRST

Built 1925 by BRCW. Rebuilt by Midland Carriage & Wagon Company in 1928. 20/– 1T. Gresley bogies. 41 t. ETS 4.

| 245 | IBIS | **PC** | BE | *BP* | SL |

## PULLMAN PARLOUR FIRST

Built 1928 by Metropolitan Carriage & Wagon Company. 24/– 2T. Gresley bogies. ETS 4.

| 254 | ZENA | **PC** | BE | *BP* | SL |

# PULLMAN KITCHEN FIRST

Built 1928 by Metropolitan Carriage & Wagon Company. 20/– 1T. Gresley bogies. 42 t. ETS 4.

| 255 | IONE | | **PC** | BE | *BP* | SL |

# PULLMAN KITCHEN COMPOSITE

Built 1932 by Metropolitan Carriage & Wagon Company. Originally included in 6-Pul EMU. Electric cooking. 12/16 1T. EMU bogies. ETS x.

| 264 | RUTH | | **PC** | BE | | SL |

# PULLMAN KITCHEN FIRST

Built 1932 by Metropolitan Carriage & Wagon Company. Originally included in "Brighton Belle" EMUs but now used as hauled stock. Electric cooking. 20/– 1T. B5 (SR) bogies (§ EMU bogies). 44 t. ETS 2.

| 280 | AUDREY | | **PC** | BE | *BP* | SL |
| 281 | GWEN | | **PC** | BE | *BP* | SL |
| 283 | MONA | § | **PC** | BE | | SL |
| 284 | VERA | | **PC** | BE | *BP* | SL |

# PULLMAN PARLOUR THIRD

Built 1932 by Metropolitan Carriage & Wagon Company. Originally included in "Brighton Belle" EMUs. –/56 2T. EMU bogies. ETS x.

**Non-standard livery:** BR Revised Pullman (blue & white lined out in white).

| 286 | CAR No. 86 | **0** | BE | | SL |

# PULLMAN BRAKE THIRD

Built 1932 by Metropolitan Carriage & Wagon Company. Originally driving motor cars in "Brighton Belle" EMUs. Traction and control equipment removed for use as hauled stock. –/48 1T. EMU bogies. ETS x.

| 292 | CAR No. 92 | **PC** | BE | | SL |
| 293 | CAR No. 93 | **PC** | BE | | SL |

# PULLMAN PARLOUR FIRST

Built 1951 by Birmingham Railway Carriage & Wagon Company. 32/– 2T. Gresley bogies. 39 t. ETS 3.

| 301 | PERSEUS | **PC** | BE | *BP* | SL |

Built 1952 by Pullman Car Company, Preston Park using underframe and bogies from 176 RAINBOW, the body of which had been destroyed by fire. 26/– 2T. Gresley bogies. 38 t. ETS 4.

| 302 | PHOENIX | **PC** | BE | *BP* | SL |

## PULLMAN PARLOUR FIRST

Built 1951 by Birmingham Railway Carriage & Wagon Company. 32/– 2T. Gresley bogies. 39 t. ETS 3.

| 308 | CYGNUS | | **PC** | BE | *BP* | SL |
|-----|--------|---|--------|----|------|----|

## PULLMAN BAR FIRST

Built 1951 by Birmingham Railway Carriage & Wagon Company. Rebuilt 1999 by Blake Fabrications, Edinburgh with original timber-framed body replaced by a new fabricated steel body. Contains kitchen, bar, dining saloon and coupé. Electric cooking. 14/– 1T. Gresley bogies. ETS 3.

| 310 | PEGASUS | x | **PC** | LS | *LS* | CL |
|-----|---------|---|--------|----|------|----|

Also carries "THE TRIANON BAR" branding.

## PULLMAN PARLOUR FIRST

Built 1960–61 by Metro-Cammell for East Coast Main Line services. –/36 2T. Commonwealth bogies. 38.5 t. ETS x.

| 325 | AMBER | x | **PC** | WC | *WC* | CS |
|-----|---------|---|--------|----|------|----|
| 326 | EMERALD | x | **PC** | WC | *WC* | CS |

## PULLMAN KITCHEN SECOND

Built 1960–61 by Metro-Cammell for East Coast Main Line services. Commonwealth bogies. –/30 1T. 40 t. ETS x.

| 335 | CAR No. 335 | x | **PC** | VT | *VT* | TM |
|-----|-------------|---|--------|----|------|----|

## PULLMAN PARLOUR SECOND

Built 1960–61 by Metro-Cammell for East Coast Main Line services. 347 is used as an Open First. –/42 2T. Commonwealth bogies. 38.5 t. ETS x.

| 347 | CAR No. 347 | x | **M** | WC | *WC* | CS |
|-----|-------------|---|--------|----|------|----|
| 348 | TOPAZ | x | **PC** | WC | *WC* | CS |
| 349 | CAR No. 349 | x | **PC** | VT | *VT* | TM |
| 350 | TANZANITE | x | **PC** | WC | *WC* | CS |
| 351 | SAPPHIRE | x | **PC** | WC | *WC* | CS |
| 352 | AMETHYST | x | **PC** | WC | *WC* | CS |
| 353 | CAR No. 353 | x | **PC** | VT | | TM |

## PULLMAN SECOND BAR

Built 1960–61 by Metro-Cammell for East Coast Main Line services. –/24+17 bar seats. Commonwealth bogies. 38.5 t. ETS x.

| 354 | THE HADRIAN BAR | x | **PC** | WC | *WC* | CS |
|-----|-----------------|---|--------|----|------|----|

# 2.6. LOCOMOTIVE SUPPORT CARRIAGES

These carriages have been adapted from Mark 1s and Mark 2s for use as support carriages for heritage steam and diesel locomotives. Some seating is retained for the use of personnel supporting the locomotives operation with the remainder of the carriage adapted for storage, workshop, dormitory and catering purposes. These carriages can spend considerable periods of time off the national railway system when the locomotives they support are not being used on that system. No owner or operator details are included in this section. After the depot code, the locomotive(s) each carriage is usually used to support is given.

## CORRIDOR BRAKE FIRST

Mark 1. Commonwealth bogies. ETS 2.

**14007.** Lot No. 30382 Swindon 1959. 35 t.
**17025.** Lot No. 30718 Swindon 1963. Metal window frames. 36 t.

| | | | | |
|---|---|---|---|---|
| 14007 (14007, 17007) | x | **M** | NY | LNER 61264 |
| 17025 (14025) | v | **M** | CS | LMS 45690 |

## CORRIDOR BRAKE FIRST

Mark 2A. Pressure ventilated. B4 bogies. ETS 4.

**14060.** Lot No. 30775 Derby 1967–68. 32 t.
**17096.** Lot No. 30786 Derby 1968. 32 t.

| | | | | | |
|---|---|---|---|---|---|
| 14060 (14060, 17060) | v | **M** | TM | LMS 45596 | |
| 17096 (14096) | | **PC** | SL | SR 35028 | MERCATOR |

## CORRIDOR BRAKE COMPOSITE

Mark 1. ETS 2.

**21096.** Lot No. 30185 Metro-Cammell 1956. BR Mark 1 bogies. 32.5 t.
**21232.** Lot No. 30574 GRCW 1960. B4 bogies. 34 t.
**21249.** Lot No. 30669 Swindon 1961–62. Commonwealth bogies. 36 t.

| | | | | |
|---|---|---|---|---|
| 21096 | x | **M** | NY | LNER 60007 |
| 21232 | x | **M** | SK | LMS 46201 |
| 21249 | x | **M** | SL | New Build 60163 |

# CORRIDOR BRAKE STANDARD

Mark 1. Metal window frames and melamine interior panelling. ETS 2.

**35317/322.** Lot No. 30699 Wolverton 1962–63. Commonwealth bogies. 37 t.
**35451–486.** Lot No. 30721 Wolverton 1963. Commonwealth bogies. 37 t.

| | | | | |
|---|---|---|---|---|
| 35317 | x | **CC** | CL | Locomotives Services Crewe-based locomotives |
| 35322 | x | **M** | CS | WCRC Carnforth-based locomotives |
| 35451 | x | **CC** | CL | Locomotives Services Crewe-based locomotives |
| 35461 | x | **CH** | CL | GWR 5029 |
| 35463 | v | **M** | CS | WCRC Carnforth-based locomotives |
| 35468 | x | **M** | YK | National Railway Museum locomotives |
| 35470 | v | **CH** | TM | Tyseley Locomotive Works-based locos |
| 35476 | x | **M** | SK | LMS 46233 |
| 35479 | v | **M** | SH | LNER 61306 |
| 35486 | x | **M** | BQ | *Currently not in service* |

# CORRIDOR BRAKE FIRST

Mark 2C. Pressure ventilated. Renumbered when declassified. B4 bogies. ETS 4.

Lot No. 30796 Derby 1969–70. 32.5 t.

| | | | | |
|---|---|---|---|---|
| 35508 | (14128, 17128) | **M** | BQ | LMS 44871/45212/45407 |

# CORRIDOR BRAKE FIRST

Mark 2A. Pressure ventilated. Renumbered when declassified. B4 bogies. ETS 4.

Lot No. 30786 Derby 1968. 32 t.

| | | | | | |
|---|---|---|---|---|---|
| 35517 | (14088, 17088) | b | **M** | BQ | LMS 44871/45212/45407 |
| 35518 | (14097, 17097) | b | **G** | CS | SR 34067 |

# COURIER VEHICLE

Mark 1. Converted 1986–87 from Corridor Brake Standards. ETS 2.

**80204/217.** Lot No. 30699 Wolverton 1962. Commonwealth bogies. 37 t.
**80220.** Lot No. 30573 Gloucester 1960. B4 bogies. 33 t.

| | | | | |
|---|---|---|---|---|
| 80204 | (35297) | **M** | CS | WCRC Carnforth-based locomotives |
| 80217 | (35299) | **M** | CS | WCRC Carnforth-based locomotives |
| 80220 | (35276) | **M** | NY | LNER 62005 |

# 2.7. 95xxx & 99xxx RANGE NUMBER CONVERSION TABLE

The following table is presented to help readers identify carriages which may still carry numbers in the 95xxx and 99xxx number ranges of the former private owner number series, which is no longer in general use.

| 9xxxx | BR No. | 9xxxx | BR No. | 9xxxx | BR No. |
|-------|--------|-------|--------|-------|--------|
| 95402 | Pullman 326 | 99350 | Pullman 350 | 99673 | 550 |
| 99025 | Pullman 325 | 99351 | Pullman 351 | 99674 | 551 |
| 99035 | 35322 | 99352 | Pullman 352 | 99675 | 552 |
| 99040 | 21232 | 99353 | Pullman 353 | 99676 | 553 |
| 99041 | 35476 | 99354 | Pullman 354 | 99677 | 586 |
| 99052 | Saloon 41 | 99361 | Pullman 335 | 99678 | 504 |
| 99121 | 3105 | 99371 | 3128 | 99679 | 506 |
| 99122 | 3106 | 99405 | 35486 | 99680 | 17102 |
| 99125 | 3113 | 99530 | Pullman 301 | 99710 | 18767 |
| 99127 | 3117 | 99531 | Pullman 302 | 99716 * | 18808 |
| 99128 | 3130 | 99532 | Pullman 308 | 99718 | 18862 |
| 99131 | Saloon 1999 | 99534 | Pullman 245 | 99721 | 18756 |
| 99241 | 35449 | 99535 | Pullman 213 | 99723 | 35459 |
| 99302 | 13323 | 99536 | Pullman 254 | 99880 | Saloon 159 |
| 99304 | 21256 | 99537 | Pullman 280 | 99881 | Saloon 807 |
| 99311 | 1882 | 99539 | Pullman 255 | 99883 | 2108 |
| 99312 | 35463 | 99541 | Pullman 243 | 99885 | 2110 |
| 99319 | 17168 | 99543 | Pullman 284 | 99887 | 2127 |
| 99326 | 4954 | 99546 | Pullman 281 | 99953 | 35468 |
| 99327 | 5044 | 99547 | Pullman 292 | 99966 | 34525 |
| 99328 | 5033 | 99548 | Pullman 293 | 99970 | Pullman 232 |
| 99329 | 4931 | 99670 | 546 | 99972 | Pullman 318 |
| 99347 | Pullman 347 | 99671 | 548 | 99973 | 324 |
| 99348 | Pullman 348 | 99672 | 549 | 99974 | Pullman 328 |
| 99349 | Pullman 349 | | | | |

* The number 99716 has also been applied to 3416 for filming purposes.

# 2.8. SET FORMATIONS

## LNER MARK 4 SET FORMATIONS

The LNER Mark 4 sets generally run in fixed formations. Class 91 locomotives are positioned next to Coach B. Most Mark 4 sets were withdrawn in 2019–20, leaving just seven rakes still on lease to LNER.

| Set | B | C | D | E | F | H | K | L | M | DVT |
|-----|---|---|---|---|---|---|---|---|---|-----|
| BN06 | 12208 | 12406 | 12420 | 12422 | 12313 | 10309 | 11279 | 11306 | 11406 | 82208 |
| BN08 | 12205 | 12481 | 12485 | 12407 | 12328 | 10300 | 11229 | 11308 | 11408 | 82211 |
| BN12 | 12212 | 12431 | 12404 | 12426 | 12330 | 10333 | 11284 | 11312 | 11412 | 82212 |
| BN13 | 12228 | 12469 | 12430 | 12424 | 12311 | 10313 | 11285 | 11313 | 11413 | 82213 |
| BN15 | 12226 | 12442 | 12409 | 12515 | 12309 | 10306 | 11286 | 11315 | 11415 | 82214 |
| BN17 | 12223 | 12444 | 12427 | 12432 | 12303 | 10324 | 11288 | 11317 | 11417 | 82225 |
| BN26 | 12220 | 12474 | 12465 | 12429 | 12325 | 10311 | 11295 | 11326 | 11426 | 82223 |
| Spare | 12214 | | | | | | | | | 82205 |

## TfW MARK 4 SET FORMATIONS

Transport for Wales has taken three shortened four-coach Mark 4 sets to replace its Mark 3 sets. They are planned to be used on selected services on the Cardiff–Holyhead route from spring 2021, hauled by Class 67s.

| Set | | | | | DVT | |
|-----|---|---|---|---|-----|---|
| HD01 | 12225 | 12454 | 10325 | 11323 | 82226 | (ex-BN23) |
| HD02 | 12219 | 12447 | 10328 | 11324 | 82229 | (ex-BN24) |
| HD03 | 12217 | 12446 | 10312 | 11325 | 82216 | (ex-BN25) |

## TPE MARK 5A SET FORMATIONS

The entry into service of the new TransPennine Express coaches has been very protracted. They are used in fixed formations hauled by a Class 68 locomotive in push-pull mode, initially between Liverpool and Scarborough and later are planned to be introduced onto the Manchester Airport–Redcar route.

| Set | E | D | C | B | A |
|-----|---|---|---|---|---|
| TP01 | 11501 | 12701 | 12702 | 12703 | 12801 |
| TP02 | 11502 | 12704 | 12705 | 12706 | 12802 |
| TP03 | 11503 | 12707 | 12708 | 12709 | 12803 |
| TP04 | 11504 | 12710 | 12711 | 12712 | 12804 |
| TP05 | 11505 | 12713 | 12714 | 12715 | 12805 |
| TP06 | 11506 | 12716 | 12717 | 12718 | 12806 |
| TP07 | 11507 | 12719 | 12720 | 12721 | 12807 |
| TP08 | 11508 | 12722 | 12723 | 12724 | 12808 |
| TP09 | 11509 | 12725 | 12726 | 12727 | 12809 |
| TP10 | 11510 | 12728 | 12729 | 12730 | 12810 |
| TP11 | 11511 | 12731 | 12732 | 12733 | 12811 |
| TP12 | 11512 | 12734 | 12735 | 12736 | 12812 |
| TP13 | 11513 | 12737 | 12738 | 12739 | 12813 |
| Spare | | | | | 12814 |

# 2.9. SERVICE STOCK

Carriages in this section are used for internal purposes within the railway industry, ie they do not generate revenue from outside the industry. Most are numbered in the former BR departmental number series.

## BARRIER, ESCORT & TRANSLATOR VEHICLES

These vehicles are used to move multiple unit, HST and other vehicles around the national railway system.

**Barrier Vehicles.** Mark 1/2A. Renumbered from BR departmental series, or converted from various types. B4 bogies (* Commonwealth bogies).

**6330.** Mark 2A. Lot No. 30786 Derby 1968.
**6336/38/44.** Mark 1. Lot No. 30715 Gloucester 1962.
**6340.** Mark 1. Lot No. 30669 Swindon 1962.
**6346.** Mark 2A. Lot No. 30777 Derby 1967.
**6348.** Mark 1. Lot No. 30163 Pressed Steel 1957.

| 6330 | (14084, 975629) |   | **FB** | A  | *RO* | LR |
|------|-----------------|---|--------|----|------|----|
| 6336 | (81591, 92185)  |   | **FB** | A  | *GW* | LA |
| 6338 | (81581, 92180)  |   | **FB** | A  | *RO* | LR |
| 6340 | (21251, 975678) | * | **RO** | A  | *RO* | LR |
| 6344 | (81263, 92080)  |   | **RO** | A  | *RO* | LR |
| 6346 | (9422)          |   | **RO** | A  | *RO* | LR |
| 6348 | (81233, 92963)  |   | **FB** | A  | *GW* | LA |

**Mark 4 Barrier Vehicles.** Mark 2A. Converted from Corridor First. B4 bogies. Lot No. 30774 Derby 1968.

| 6352 | (13465, 19465) | **HB** | E |      | WS |
|------|----------------|--------|---|------|----|
| 6353 | (13478, 19478) | **HB** | E | *LN* | BN |

**EMU Translator Vehicles.** Mark 1. Converted 1980 from Restaurant Unclassified Opens. 6376/77 have Tightlock couplers and 6378/79 Dellner couplers. Commonwealth bogies.

Lot No. 30647 Wolverton 1959–61.

| 6376 | (1021, 975973) | **PB** | P  | *GB* | ZG *(works with 6377)* |
|------|----------------|--------|----|------|------------------------|
| 6377 | (1042, 975975) | **PB** | P  | *GB* | ZG *(works with 6376)* |
| 6378 | (1054, 975971) | **RO** | RO | *RO* | LR *(works with 6379)* |
| 6379 | (1059, 975972) | **RO** | RO | *RO* | LR *(works with 6378)* |

**Brake Force Runners.** Mark 1. Previously used as HST Barrier Vehicles. Converted from Gangwayed Brake Vans in 1994–95. B4 bogies.

**6392.** Lot No. 30715 Gloucester 1962.
**6397.** Lot No. 30716 Gloucester 1962.

| 6392 | (81588, 92183) | **PB** | CS | *CS* | ZA |
|------|----------------|--------|----|------|----|
| 6397 | (81600, 92190) | **PB** | CS | *CS* | ZA |

**HST Barrier Vehicles.** Mark 1. Converted from Gangwayed Brake Vans in 1994–95. B4 bogies.

**6393.** Lot No. 30716 Gloucester 1962.
**6394.** Lot No. 30162 Pressed Steel 1956–57.
**6398/99.** Lot No. 30400 Pressed Steel 1957–58.

| 6393 | (81609, 92196) | **PB** | P  | *GB* | ZG |
| 6394 | (80878, 92906) | **PB** | P  | *GB* | ZG |
| 6398 | (81471, 92126) | **PB** | EM | *EM* | NL |
| 6399 | (81367, 92994) | **PB** | EM | *EM* | NL |

**Escort Coaches.** Converted from Mark 2A (* Mark 2E) Open Brake Standards. 9419/28 use the same bodyshell as the Mark 2A Corridor Brake First. B4 bogies.

**9419.** Lot No.30777 Derby 1970.
**9428.** Lot No.30820 Derby 1970.
**9506/08.** Lot No.30838 Derby 1972.

| 9419 |   | **DS** | DR | *DR* | KM |
| 9428 |   | **DS** | DR | *DR* | KM |
| 9506 | * | **DS** | DR | *DR* | KM |
| 9508 | * | **DS** | DR | *DR* | KM |

**EMU Translator Vehicles.** Converted from Class 508 driving cars.

**64664.** Lot No. 30979 York 1979–80.
**64707.** Lot No. 30981 York 1979–80.

| 64664 | **AG** | A | *GB* | ZG | Liwet    | *(works with 64707)* |
| 64707 | **AG** | A | *GB* | ZG | Labezerin | *(works with 64664)* |

**EMU Translator Vehicles.** Converted from Class 489 DMLVs that had originally been Class 414/3 DMBSOs. Previously used as de-icing coaches.

Lot No. 30452 Ashford/Eastleigh 1959. Mk 4 bogies.

| 68501 | (61281) | **AG** | AF | *RO* | LR |
| 68504 | (61286) | **AG** | AF | *RO* | LR |

**Eurostar Barrier Vehicles.** Mark 1. Converted from General Utility Vans with bodies removed. Fitted with B4 bogies for use as Eurostar barrier vehicles.

**96380/381.** Lot No. 30417 Pressed Steel 1958–59.
**96383.** Lot No. 30565 Pressed Steel 1959.
**96384.** Lot No. 30616 Pressed Steel 1959–60.

| 96380 | (86386, 6380) | **B** | EU | *EU* | TI |
| 96381 | (86187, 6381) | **B** | EU | *EU* | TI |
| 96383 | (86664, 6383) | **B** | EU | *EU* | TI |
| 96384 | (86955, 6384) | **B** | EU | *EU* | TI |

**Brake Force Runners.** Converted from Motorail vans built 1998–99 by Marcroft Engineering using underframe and running gear from Motorail General Utility Vans. B5 bogies.

Lot No. 30417 Pressed Steel 1958–59.

| 96604 | (86337, 96156) | **Y** | CS | *CS* | ZA |

| | | | | | | |
|---|---|---|---|---|---|---|
| 96606 | (86324, 96213) | **Y** | CS | *CS* | ZA | |
| 96608 | (86385, 96216) | **Y** | CS | *CS* | ZA | |
| 96609 | (86327, 96217) | **Y** | CS | *CS* | ZA | |

**EMU Translator Vehicles.** Converted from various Mark 1s.

**Non-standard livery:** All over blue.

**975864**. Lot No. 30054 Eastleigh 1951–54. Commonwealth bogies.
**975867**. Lot No. 30014 York 1950–51. Commonwealth bogies.
**975875**. Lot No. 30143 Charles Roberts 1954–55. Commonwealth bogies.
**975974/978**. Lot No. 30647 Wolverton 1959–61. B4 bogies.
**977087**. Lot No. 30229 Metro–Cammell 1955–57. Commonwealth bogies.

| | | | | | | | |
|---|---|---|---|---|---|---|---|
| 975864 | (3849) | **HB** | E | | BU | | *(works with 975867)* |
| 975867 | (1006) | **HB** | E | | BU | | *(works with 975864)* |
| 975875 | (34643) | **O** | E | *RO* | LR | | *(works with 977087)* |
| 975974 | (1030) | **AG** | A | *GB* | ZG | Paschar | *(works with 975978)* |
| 975978 | (1025) | **AG** | A | *GB* | ZG | Perpetiel | *(works with 975974)* |
| 977087 | (34971) | **O** | E | *RO* | LR | | *(works with 975875)* |

# LABORATORY, TESTING & INSPECTION COACHES

These coaches are used for research, testing and inspection on the national railway system. Many are fitted with sophisticated technical equipment.

**Plain Line Pattern Recognition Coaches.** Converted from BR Mark 2F Buffet First (*) or Open Standard. B4 bogies.

**1256**. Lot No. 30845 Derby 1973.
**5981**. Lot No. 30860 Derby 1973–74.

| | | | | | | |
|---|---|---|---|---|---|---|
| 1256 | (3296) | * | **Y** | NR | *CS* | ZA |
| 5981 | | | **Y** | NR | *CS* | ZA |

**Generator Vans.** Mark 1. Converted from BR Mark 1 Gangwayed Brake Vans. B5 bogies.

**6260**. Lot No. 30400 Pressed Steel 1957–58.
**6261**. Lot No. 30323 Pressed Steel 1957.
**6262**. Lot No. 30228 Metro-Cammell 1957–58.
**6263**. Lot No. 30163 Pressed Steel 1957.
**6264**. Lot No. 30173 York 1956.

| | | | | | | |
|---|---|---|---|---|---|---|
| 6260 | (81450, 92116) | **Y** | NR | *CS* | ZA | |
| 6261 | (81284, 92988) | **Y** | NR | *CS* | ZA | |
| 6262 | (81064, 92928) | **Y** | NR | *CS* | ZA | |
| 6263 | (81231, 92961) | **Y** | NR | *CS* | ZA | |
| 6264 | (80971, 92923) | **Y** | NR | *CS* | ZA | |

**Staff Coach.** Mark 2D. Converted from BR Mark 2D Open Brake Standard. Lot No. 30824 Derby 1971. B4 bogies.

| | | | | | |
|---|---|---|---|---|---|
| 9481 | | Y | NR | *CS* | ZA |

**Test Train Brake Force Runners.** Mark 2F. Converted from BR Mark 2F Open Brake Standard. Lot No. 30861 Derby 1974. B4 bogies.

| | | | | | |
|---|---|---|---|---|---|
| 9516 | | Y | NR | *CS* | ZA *(works with 72616)* |
| 9523 | | Y | NR | *CS* | ZA |

**Driving Trailer Coaches.** Converted 2008 at Serco, Derby from Mark 2F Driving Open Brake Standards. Fitted with generator. Disc brakes. B4 bogies.

**9701–08.** Lot No. 30861 Derby 1974. Converted to Driving Open Brake Standard Glasgow 1974.
**9714.** Lot No. 30861 Derby 1974. Converted to Driving Open Brake Standard Glasgow 1986.

| | | | | | |
|---|---|---|---|---|---|
| 9701 | (9528) | Y | NR | *CS* | ZA |
| 9702 | (9510) | Y | NR | *CS* | ZA |
| 9703 | (9517) | Y | NR | *CS* | ZA |
| 9708 | (9530) | Y | NR | *CS* | ZA |
| 9714 | (9536) | Y | NR | *CS* | ZA |

**Test Train Brake Coaches.** Former Caledonian Sleeper coaches now used for staff accommodation in test trains. Fitted with toilets with retention tanks. Converted from Mark 2E Open Standard with new seating by Railcare Wolverton. B4 bogies.

**9801/03.** Lot No. 30837 Derby 1972.
**9806–10.** Lot No. 30844 Derby 1972–73.

| | | | | | |
|---|---|---|---|---|---|
| 9801 | (5760) | FB | ER | *CS* | ZA |
| 9803 | (5799) | FB | ER | *CS* | ZA |
| 9806 | (5840) | FB | ER | *CS* | ZA |
| 9808 | (5871) | FB | ER | *CS* | ZA |
| 9810 | (5892) | FB | ER | *CS* | ZA |

**Ultrasonic Test Coach.** Converted from Class 421 EMU MBSO.

**62287.** Lot No. 30808. York 1970. SR Mark 6 bogies.
**62384.** Lot No. 30816. York 1970. SR Mark 6 bogies.

| | | | | | |
|---|---|---|---|---|---|
| 62287 | | Y | NR | *CS* | ZA |
| 62384 | | Y | NR | *CS* | ZA |

**Test Train Brake Force Runners.** Converted from Mark 2F Open Standard converted to Class 488/3 EMU TSOLH. These vehicles are included in test trains to provide brake force and are not used for any other purposes. Lot No. 30860 Derby 1973–74. B4 bogies.

| | | | | | |
|---|---|---|---|---|---|
| 72612 | (6156) | Y | NR | *CS* | ZA |
| 72616 | (6007) | Y | NR | *CS* | ZA *(works with 9516)* |

**Structure Gauging Train Coach.** Converted from Mark 2F Open Standard converted to Class 488/3 EMU TSOLH. Lot No. 30860 Derby 1973–74. B4 bogies.

| | | | | | |
|---|---|---|---|---|---|
| 72630 | (6094) | Y | NR | *CS* | ZA *(works with 99666)* |

**Plain Line Pattern Recognition Coaches.** Converted from BR Mark 2F Open Standard converted to Class 488/3 EMU TSOLH. Lot No. 30860 Derby 1973–74. B4 bogies.

| | | | | | |
|---|---|---|---|---|---|
| 72631 | (6096) | Y | NR | *CS* | ZA |
| 72639 | (6070) | Y | NR | *CS* | ZA |

**Driving Trailer Coaches.** Converted from Mark 3B 110 mph Driving Brake Vans. Fitted with diesel generator. Lot No. 31042 Derby 1988. T4 bogies.

| | | | |
|---|---|---|---|
| 82111 | Y | NR | ZA |
| 82124 | Y | NR | ZA |
| 82129 | Y | NR | ZA |
| 82145 | Y | NR | ZA |

**Structure Gauging Train Coach.** Converted from BR Mark 2E Open First then converted to exhibition van. Lot No. 30843 Derby 1972–73. B4 bogies.

| | | | | | | |
|---|---|---|---|---|---|---|
| 99666 | (3250) | Y | NR | | ZA | (works with 72630) |

**Inspection Saloon.** Converted from Class 202 DEMU TRB at Stewarts Lane for use as a BR Southern Region General Manager's Saloon. Overhauled at FM Rail, Derby 2004–05 for use as a New Trains Project Saloon. Can be used in push-pull mode with suitably equipped locomotives. Eastleigh 1958. SR Mark 4 bogies.

| | | | | | | |
|---|---|---|---|---|---|---|
| 975025 | (60755) | G | NR | *CS* | ZA | CAROLINE |

**Overhead Line Equipment Test Coach ("MENTOR").** Converted from BR Mark 1 Corridor Brake Standard. Lot No. 30142 Gloucester 1954–55. Fitted with pantograph. B4 bogies.

| | | | | | |
|---|---|---|---|---|---|
| 975091 | (34615) | Y | NR | *CS* | ZA |

**New Measurement Train Conference Coach.** Converted from prototype HST TF Lot No. 30848 Derby 1972. BT10 bogies.

| | | | | | |
|---|---|---|---|---|---|
| 975814 | (11000, 41000) | Y | NR | *CS* | ZA |

**New Measurement Train Lecture Coach.** Converted from prototype HST catering vehicle. Lot No. 30849 Derby 1972–73. BT10 bogies.

| | | | | | |
|---|---|---|---|---|---|
| 975984 | (10000, 40000) | Y | NR | *CS* | ZA |

**Radio Survey Coach.** Converted from BR Mark 2E Open Standard. Lot No. 30844 Derby 1972–73. B4 bogies.

| | | | | | |
|---|---|---|---|---|---|
| 977868 | (5846) | Y | NR | *CS* | ZA |

**Staff Coach.** Converted from Royal Household couchette Lot No. 30889, which in turn had been converted from BR Mark 2B Corridor Brake First. Lot No. 30790 Derby 1969. B5 bogies.

| | | | | | |
|---|---|---|---|---|---|
| 977969 | (14112, 2906) | Y | NR | *CS* | ZA |

**Track Inspection Train Coach.** Converted from BR Mark 2E Open Standard. Lot No. 30844 Derby 1972–73. B4 bogies.

| | | | | | |
|---|---|---|---|---|---|
| 977974 | (5854) | Y | NR | *CS* | ZA |

**Electrification Measurement Coach.** Converted from BR Mark 2F Open First converted to Class 488/2 EMU TFOH. Lot No. 30859 Derby 1973–74. B4 bogies.

977983  (3407, 72503)        **Y**    NR    *CS*        ZA

**New Measurement Train Staff Coach.** Converted from HST catering vehicle. Lot No. 30884 Derby 1976–77. BT10 bogies.

977984  (40501)              **Y**    P     *CS*        ZA

**Structure Gauging Train Coaches.** Converted from Mark 2F Open Standard converted to Class 488/3 EMU TSOLH or from BR Mark 2D Open First subsequently declassified to Open Standard and then converted to exhibition van. B4 bogies.

**977985.** Lot No. 30860 Derby 1973–74.
**977986.** Lot No. 30821 Derby 1971.

977985  (6019, 72715)       **Y**    NR    *CS*        ZA *(works with 977986)*
977986  (3189, 99664)       **Y**    NR    *CS*        ZA *(works with 977985)*

**New Measurement Train Test Coach.** Converted from HST TGS. Lot No. 30949 Derby 1982. BT10 bogies.

977993  (44053)              **Y**    P     *CS*        ZA

**New Measurement Train Track Recording Coach.** Converted from HST TGS. Lot No. 30949 Derby 1982. BT10 bogies.

977994  (44087)              **Y**    P     *CS*        ZA

**New Measurement Train Coach.** Converted from HST catering vehicle. Lot No. 30921 Derby 1978–79. Fitted with generator. BT10 bogies.

977995  (40719, 40619)      **Y**    P     *CS*        ZA

**Radio Survey Coach.** Converted from Mark 2F Open Standard converted to Class 488/3 EMU TSOLH. Lot No. 30860 Derby 1973–74. B4 bogies.

977997  (72613, 6126)       **Y**    NR    *CS*        ZA

**Track Recording Coach.** Purpose built Mark 2. BR Wagon Lot No. 3830 Derby 1976. B4 bogies.

999550                       **Y**    NR    *CS*        ZA

**Ultrasonic Test Coaches.** Converted from Class 421 EMU MBSO and Class 432 EMU MSO.

**999602/605.** Lot No. 30862 York 1974. SR Mk 6 bogies.
**999606.** Lot No. 30816. York 1970. SR Mk 6 bogies.

999602  (62483)              **Y**    NR    *CS*        ZA
999605  (62482)              **Y**    NR    *CS*        ZA
999606  (62356)              **Y**    NR    *CS*        ZA

# BREAKDOWN TRAIN COACHES

These coaches are formed in trains used for the recovery of derailed railway vehicles and were converted from BR Mark 1 Corridor Brake Standard and General Utility Van. The current use of each vehicle is given.

**971001/003/004.** Lot No. 30403 York/Glasgow 1958–60. Commonwealth bogies.
**971002.** Lot No. 30417 Pressed Steel 1958–59. Commonwealth bogies.
**975087.** Lot No. 30032 Wolverton 1951–52. BR Mark 1 bogies.
**975464.** Lot No. 30386 Charles Roberts 1956–58. Commonwealth bogies.
**975471.** Lot No. 30095 Wolverton 1953–55. Commonwealth bogies.
**975477.** Lot No. 30233 GRCW 1955–57. BR Mark 1 bogies.
**975486.** Lot No. 30025 Wolverton 1950–52. Commonwealth bogies.

| | | | | | |
|---|---|---|---|---|---|
| 971001 | (86560, 94150) | Y | NR | *DB* | SP | Tool & Generator Van |
| 971002 | (86624, 94190) | Y | NR | *DB* | SP | Tool Van |
| 971003 | (86596, 94191) | Y | NR | *DB* | SP | Tool Van |
| 971004 | (86194, 94168) | Y | NR | *DB* | SP | Tool Van |
| 975087 | (34289) | Y | NR | *DB* | SP | Tool & Generator Van |
| 975464 | (35171) | Y | NR | *DB* | SP | Staff Coach |
| 975471 | (34543) | Y | NR | *DB* | SP | Staff Coach |
| 975477 | (35108) | Y | NR | *DB* | SP | Staff Coach |
| 975486 | (34100) | Y | NR | *DB* | SP | Tool & Generator Van |

# INFRASTRUCTURE MAINTENANCE COACH

**Winterisation Train Coach.** Converted from BR Mark 2E Open Standard. Lot No. 30844 Derby 1972–73. B4 bogies.

| | | | | | |
|---|---|---|---|---|---|
| 977869 | (5858) | Y | NR | *DR* | Perth CS |

# INTERNAL USER VEHICLES

These vehicles are confined to yards and depots or do not normally move.
Details are given of the internal user number (if allocated), type, former
identity, current use and location. Many no longer see regular use.

\* = Grounded body.

| | | | |
|---|---|---|---|
| 041989* | BR SPV 975423 | Stores Van | Toton Depot |
| 061202* | BR GUV 93498 | Stores Van | Laira Depot, Plymouth |
| – | BR NKA 94199 | Stores Van | EG Steels, Hamilton |
| – | BR NA 94322* | Stores Van | WCRC, Carnforth Depot |
| 083602 | BR CCT 94494 | Stores van | Three Bridges Station |
| – | BR NB 94548* | Stores van | WCRC, Carnforth Depot |
| 083637 | BR NW 99203 | Stores van | Stewarts Lane Depot |
| 083644 | BR Ferry Van 889201 | Stores van | Eastleigh Depot |
| 083664 | BR Ferry Van 889203 | Stores van | Eastleigh Depot |
| – | BR Open Standard 5636 | Instruction Coach | St Philip's Marsh Depot |
| – | BR BV 6360 | Barrier vehicle | Neville Hill Depot, Leeds |
| – | BR BV 6396 | Stores van | Longsight Depot (Manchester) |
| – | BR RFKB 10256 | Instruction Coach | Yoker Depot |
| – | BR RFKB 10260 | Instruction Coach | Yoker Depot |
| – | BR SPV 88045* | Stores Van | Thames Haven Yard |
| – | BR NL 94003 | Stores van | Burton-upon-Trent Depot |
| – | BR NK 94121 | Stores van | Toton Depot |
| – | BR NB 94438 | Stores van | Toton Depot |
| – | BR CCT 94663* | Stores van | Mossend Up Yard |
| – | BR GUV 96139 | Stores van | Longsight Depot, Manchester |
| – | BR Ferry Van 889200 | Stores van | Stewarts Lane Depot |
| – | BR Ferry Van 889202 | Stores van | Stewarts Lane Depot |
| – | SR PMV 977045* | Stores van | EMD, Longport Works |
| – | SR CCT 2516* | Stores Van | Eastleigh Depot |

**Abbreviations:**

BV = Barrier Vehicle
CCT = Covered Carriage Truck (a 4-wheeled van similar to a GUV)
GUV = General Utility Van (bogied van with side and end doors)
NAA = Propelling Control Vehicle
NB = High Security Brake Van (converted from Gangwayed Brake Van,
         gangways removed)
NK= High Security General Utility Van (end doors removed)
NKA = High Security Mail Van
NL = Newspaper Van (converted from a GUV)
NW = Bullion Van (converted from a Corridor Brake Standard)
PMV = Parcels & Miscellaneous Van (a 4-wheeled van similar to a CCT but
         without end doors)
RFKB = Kitchen Buffet First
SPV = Special Parcels Van (a 4-wheeled van converted from a Fish Van)

# 2.10. COACHING STOCK AWAITING DISPOSAL

This list shows the locations of carriages awaiting disposal. The definition of which vehicles are awaiting disposal is somewhat vague, but often these are vehicles of types not now in normal service, those not expected to see further use or that have originated from preservationists as a source of spares or possible future use or carriages which have been damaged by fire, vandalism or collision.

| | | | | | | | |
|---|---|---|---|---|---|---|---|
| 1201 | TM | 3368 | FA | 5876 | SH | 9529 | MS |
| 1252 | SH | 3379 | DE | 5888 | SH | 9531 | MS |
| 1253 | SH | 3388 | FA | 5922 | MS | 10224 | ZG |
| 1258 | CS | 3399 | FA | 5924 | MS | 10242 | LM |
| 1644 | CS | 3400 | BU | 5925 | SH | 10245 | CS |
| 1650 | CS | 3408 | CS | 5928 | TM | 10530 | ZN |
| 1652 | CS | 3416 | TM | 5943 | CS | 10578 | ZN |
| 1655 | CS | 3417 | DE | 5954 | ME | 10588 | ZN |
| 1658 | CL | 3424 | BU | 5958 | SH | 10656 | ZN |
| 1663 | CS | 4362 | BU | 5959 | MS | 11006 | BU |
| 1670 | CS | 4796 | BU | 5978 | SH | 11021 | LM |
| 1679 | RO | 4799 | BU | 6009 | SH | 11028 | ZB |
| 1696 | CL | 4849 | CS | 6029 | SH | 11033 | LM |
| 1800 | SH | 4860 | CS | 6036 | MS | 11079 | LM |
| 1883 | CL | 4932 | CS | 6041 | CS | 11097 | BU |
| 1954 | CL | 4997 | CS | 6045 | SH | 12096 | ZN |
| 2108 | CS | 5027 | BU | 6050 | CS | 12104 | LM |
| 2110 | CS | 5054 | RO | 6073 | SH | 12165 | LM |
| 2127 | CS | 5179 | TM | 6110 | ME | 13323 | CS |
| 2131 | CS | 5183 | TM | 6134 | SH | 13508 | RO |
| 2833 | CS | 5186 | TM | 6139 | ME | 17013 | ZG |
| 2909 | CS | 5194 | TM | 6151 | SH | 17168 | CS |
| 3051 | CL | 5331 | FA | 6152 | MS | 18767 | SH |
| 3060 | CL | 5386 | FA | 6154 | SH | 18808 | SH |
| 3091 | RO | 5420 | TM | 6175 | CS | 18862 | CS |
| 3241 | CS | 5453 | CS | 6179 | CS | 21268 | RO |
| 3255 | FA | 5463 | CS | 6324 | CP | 34525 | CS |
| 3277 | RO | 5478 | CS | 6351 | BU | 35333 | ZG |
| 3279 | BU | 5491 | CS | 6361 | NL | 35467 | CL |
| 3292 | BU | 5569 | CS | 6364 | CF | 68505 | ZG |
| 3295 | RO | 5631 | ME | 6365 | CF | 80212 | CS |
| 3303 | TO | 5657 | BU | 6412 | CL | 80374 | BU |
| 3309 | TM | 5710 | ZM | 6720 | FA | 80403 | CS |
| 3318 | BU | 5737 | CS | 7204 | CL | 80404 | CS |
| 3331 | BU | 5740 | CS | 7931 | BU | 80414 | SL |
| 3334 | DE | 5756 | CS | 9440 | SH | 82101 | LW |
| 3336 | DE | 5777 | BU | 9489 | CS | 82126 | LW |
| 3351 | TM | 5797 | RO | 9490 | BU | 82150 | LM |
| 3358 | BU | 5815 | SH | 9496 | DE | 92114 | ZA |

| | | | |
|---|---|---|---|
| 92159 CS | 94333 HL | 94520 BU | 96375 LM |
| 92908 CS | 94335 CL | 94522 CL | 96602 Barry |
| 93723 BY | 94336 CL | 94525 CS | 96603 CF |
| 94058 BU | 94337 WE | 94526 CS | 96605 Barry |
| 94101 CS | 94338 WE | 94527 HL | 96607 Barry |
| 94104 TO | 94344 TO | 94530 CS | 99019 CS |
| 94106 BU | 94401 CS | 94531 BU | 99884 CL |
| 94116 BU | 94406 CS | 94538 CL | 975081 BU |
| 94153 WE | 94408 CS | 94539 CS | 975280 BU |
| 94166 BU | 94410 WE | 94540 TJ | 975454 TO |
| 94170 CL | 94420 CS | 94542 CS | 975484 CS |
| 94176 BU | 94422 TO | 94545 HM | 975490 BU |
| 94177 TO | 94423 BU | 94546 HL | 975639 CS |
| 94195 BU | 94427 WE | 94547 CS | 975681 CS |
| 94196 CS | 94428 CS | 95300 CS | 975682 CS |
| 94197 BU | 94429 HM | 95410 CS | 975685 CS |
| 94207 TO | 94431 CS | 95727 WE | 975686 CS |
| 94208 TO | 94434 CL | 95754 CS | 975687 CS |
| 94214 CS | 94435 TO | 95761 WE | 975688 CS |
| 94222 CS | 94445 WE | 95763 BU | 975920 Portobello |
| 94227 HM | 94450 WE | 96110 CS | 977085 BU |
| 94229 CL | 94451 WE | 96132 CS | 977095 CS |
| 94302 HL | 94470 TO | 96135 CS | 977169 BU |
| 94303 HL | 94479 TO | 96164 CS | 977241 BU |
| 94304 MH | 94482 CS | 96165 CS | 977450 BU |
| 94306 HL | 94488 BU | 96170 CS | 977618 BY |
| 94308 CS | 94490 BU | 96178 CS | 999509 CL |
| 94310 WE | 94492 WE | 96182 CS | 083439 BU |
| 94311 WE | 94495 HL | 96191 CS | |
| 94313 WE | 94498 CS | 96192 CS | DS70220 Western |
| 94316 TO | 94501 TO | 96371 PO | Trading Estate |
| 94317 TO | 94504 HL | 96372 LM | Siding, North Acton |
| 94323 HL | 94512 CS | 96373 LM | |
| 94326 HL | 94515 ZG | 96374 YA | Pullman 315 CS |
| 94332 CS | 94517 BU | | Pullman 316 HN |

# 3. DIESEL MULTIPLE UNITS

## INTRODUCTION

This section contains details of all Diesel Multiple Units, usually referred to as DMUs, which can run on Britain's national railway network.

Since the 1980s DMUs have replaced more traditional locomotive-hauled trains on many routes. DMUs today work a wide variety of services, from long distance Intercity to inter-urban and suburban duties.

### LAYOUT OF INFORMATION

DMUs are listed in numerical order of set – using current numbers as allocated by the Rolling Stock Library. Individual "loose" vehicles are listed in numerical order after vehicles formed into fixed formations. Where sets or vehicles have been renumbered in recent years, former numbering detail is shown in parentheses. Each entry is laid out as in the following example:

| RSL Set No. | Detail | Livery | Owner | Operator | Depot | Formation | |
|---|---|---|---|---|---|---|---|
| 156 505 | w | **SR** | A | *SR* | CK | 52505 | 57505 |

**Codes:** Codes are used to denote the livery, owner, operator and depot allocation of each Diesel Multiple Unit. Details of these can be found in section 6 of this book. Where a unit or spare car is off-lease, the operator column is left blank.

**Detail Differences:** Detail differences which currently affect the areas and types of train which vehicles may work are shown, plus differences in interior layout. Where such differences occur within a class, these are shown either in the heading information or alongside the individual set or vehicle number. The following standard abbreviations are used:

e   European Railway Traffic Management System (ERTMS) signalling equipment fitted.
r   Radio Electric Token Block signalling equipment fitted.

Use of the above abbreviations indicates the equipment fitted is normally operable. Meaning of non-standard abbreviations is detailed in individual class headings.

**Set Formations:** Regular set formations are shown where these are normally maintained. Readers should note set formations might be temporarily varied from time to time to suit maintenance and/or operational requirements. Vehicles shown as "Spare" are not formed in any regular set formation.

**Names:** Only names carried with official sanction are listed. Names are shown in UPPER/lower case characters as actually shown on the name carried on the vehicle(s). Unless otherwise shown, complete units are regarded as named rather than just the individual car(s) which carry the name.

# GENERAL INFORMATION

## CLASSIFICATION AND NUMBERING

DMU Classes are listed in class number order.

First generation ("Heritage") DMUs were classified in the series 100–139.
Parry People Movers (not technically DMUs) are classified in the series 139.
Second generation DMUs are classified in the series 140–199.
Diesel Electric Multiple Units are classified in the series 200–249.
Service units are classified in the series 930–999.

First and second generation individual cars are numbered in the series 50000–59999 and 79000–79999.

Parry People Mover cars are numbered in the 39000 series.

DEMU individual cars are numbered in the series 60000–60999, except for a few former EMU vehicles which retain their EMU numbers.

For all new vehicles allocated by the Rolling Stock Library since 2014 6-digit vehicle numbers are being used. The Class 230 D-Train DEMU individual cars are numbered in the 300xxx series.

## WHEEL ARRANGEMENT

A system whereby the number of powered axles on a bogie or frame is denoted by a letter (A = 1, B = 2, C= 3 etc) and the number of unpowered axles is denoted by a number is used in this publication. The letter "o" after a letter indicates that each axle is individually powered.

## UNITS OF MEASUREMENT

Principal details and dimensions are quoted for each class in metric and/ or imperial units as considered appropriate bearing in mind common UK usage.

All dimensions and weights are quoted for vehicles in an "as new" condition with all necessary supplies (eg oil, water, sand) on board. Dimensions are quoted in the order Length – Width. All lengths quoted are over buffers or couplers as appropriate. Where two lengths are quoted, the first refers to outer vehicles in a set and the second to inner vehicles. All width dimensions quoted are maxima. All weights are shown as metric tonnes (t = tonnes).

## OPERATING CODES

These codes are used by train operating company staff to describe the various different types of vehicles and normally appear on data panels on the inner (ie non driving) ends of vehicles.

The first part of the code describes whether the car has a motor or a driving cab as follows:

DM  Driving motor     DT  Driving trailer     M  Motor       T  Trailer

The next letter is a "B" for cars with a brake compartment.
This is followed by the saloon details:

| | | | |
|---|---|---|---|
| F | First | L | denotes a vehicle with a toilet. |
| S | Standard | W | denotes a Wheelchair space. |
| C | Composite | | |

Finally vehicles with a buffet or kitchen area are suffixed RB or RMB for a miniature buffet counter.

Where two vehicles of the same type are formed within the same unit, the above codes may be suffixed by (A) and (B) to differentiate between the vehicles.

A composite is a vehicle containing both First and Standard Class accommodation, whilst a brake vehicle is a vehicle containing separate specific accommodation for the conductor.

Where vehicles have been declassified, the correct operating code which describes the actual vehicle layout is quoted in this publication.

# BUILD DETAILS

## Lot Numbers
Vehicles ordered under the auspices of BR were allocated a Lot (batch) number when ordered and these are quoted in class headings and sub-headings. Vehicles ordered since 1995 have no Lot Numbers, but the manufacturer and location that they were built is given.

## Builders
These are shown for each lot. More details and a full list of builders can be found in section 6.7.

Information on sub-contracting works which built parts of carriages eg the underframes etc is not shown.

# ACCOMMODATION

The information given in class headings and sub-headings is in the form F/S nT (or TD) nW. For example 12/54 1T 1W denotes 12 First Class and 54 Standard Class seats, one toilet and one space for a wheelchair. A number in brackets (ie (+2)) denotes tip-up seats (in addition to the fixed seats). Tip-up seats in vestibules do not count. The seating layout of open saloons is shown as 2+1, 2+2 or 3+2 as the case may be. Where units have First Class accommodation as well as Standard Class and the layout is different for each class then these are shown separately prefixed by "1:" and "2:".

TD denotes a universal access toilet suitable for use by people with disabilities. By law all trains should have been fitted with such facilities by the start of 2020, but a number of trains were not made compliant in time and have been given time-limited dispensations for continued operation.

# 3.1. DIESEL MECHANICAL & DIESEL HYDRAULIC UNITS

## 3.1.1. FIRST GENERATION UNIT

### CLASS 121                    PRESSED STEEL SUBURBAN

First generation unit. Used by Chiltern Railways until 2017, and then sold to Locomotives Services for use as a route learning vehicle.
**Construction:** Steel.
**Engines:** Two Leyland 1595 of 112 kW (150 hp) at 1800 rpm.
**Transmission:** Mechanical. Cardan shaft and freewheel to a four-speed epicyclic gearbox and final drive.
**Bogies:** DD10.
**Brakes:** Vacuum.
**Couplers:** Screw.
**Dimensions:** 20.45 x 2.82 m.
**Gangways:** Non gangwayed single cars with cabs at each end.
**Wheel arrangement:** 1-A + A-1.
**Doors:** Manually-operated slam.
**Maximum Speed:** 70 mph.
**Seating Layout:** 3+2 facing.
**Multiple Working:** "Blue Square" coupling code. First Generation vehicles cannot be coupled to Second Generation units.

Fitted with central door locking.

Formerly in departmental use as 977828.

**DMBS.** Lot No. 30518 1960. –/65. 38.0 t.

121 034        **G**    LS    *LS*      CL      55034

## 3.1.2. PARRY PEOPLE MOVERS

## CLASS 139                                          PPM-60

Gas/flywheel hybrid drive Railcars used on the Stourbridge Junction–
Stourbridge Town branch.
**Body construction:** Stainless steel framework.
**Chassis construction:** Welded mild steel box section.
**Primary Drive:** Ford MVH420 2.3 litre 64 kW (86 hp) LPG fuel engine driving
through Newage marine gearbox, Tandler bevel box and 4 "V" belt driver
to flywheel.
**Flywheel Energy Store:** 500 kg, 1 m diameter, normal operational speed
range 1000–1500 rpm.
**Final transmission:** 4 "V" belt driver from flywheel to Tandler bevel box,
Linde hydrostatic transmission and spiral bevel gearbox at No. 2 end axle.
**Braking:** Normal service braking by regeneration to flywheel (1 m/s/s);
emergency/parking braking by sprung-on, air-off disc brakes (3 m/s/s).
**Maximum Speed:** 45 mph.              **Dimensions:** 8.7 x 2.4 m.
**Doors:** Deans powered doors, double-leaf folding (one per side).
**Seating Layout:** 1+1 unidirectional/facing.
**Multiple Working:** Not applicable.

**39001–002. DMS.** Main Road Sheet Metal, Leyland 2007–08. –/17(+4) 1W.
12.5 t.

| | | | | |
|---|---|---|---|---|
| 139 001 | **WM** P | *WM* | SJ | 39001 |
| 139 002 | **WM** P | *WM* | SJ | 39002 |

## 3.1.3. SECOND GENERATION UNITS

All units in this section have air brakes and are equipped with public
address, with transmission equipment on driving vehicles and flexible
diaphragm gangways. Except where otherwise stated, transmission is
Voith 211r hydraulic with a cardan shaft to a Gmeinder GM190 final drive.

## CLASS 142          PACER          BREL DERBY/LEYLAND

DMS–DMSL. The remaining Class 142s were withdrawn from passenger
service at the end of 2020 although Northern plans to use some of its
remaining units for crew training duties during 2021.

**Construction:** Steel underframe, rivetted steel body and roof. Built from
Leyland National bus parts on Leyland Bus four-wheeled underframes.
**Engines:** One Cummins LT10-R of 165 kW (225 hp) at 1950 rpm.
**Couplers:** BSI at outer ends, bar within unit.
**Dimensions:** 15.55 x 2.80 m.
**Gangways:** Within unit only.            **Wheel Arrangement:** 1-A + A-1.
**Doors:** Twin-leaf inward pivoting.      **Maximum Speed:** 75 mph.
**Seating Layout:** 3+2 mainly unidirectional bus/bench style unless stated.
**Multiple Working:** Within class and with Classes 143, 144, 150, 153, 155,
156, 158 and 159.

c Units refurbished for Arriva Trains Wales. Fitted with 2+2 individual Chapman seating.
s Fitted with 2+2 individual high-back seating.
t Former First North Western facelifted units – DMS fitted with a luggage/bicycle rack and wheelchair space.
u Merseytravel units – Fitted with 3+2 individual low-back seating.

**55543–588. DMS.** Lot No. 31003 1985–86. –/62 (c –/46(+6) 2W, s –/56, t –/53 or 55 1W, u –/52 or 54 1W). 24.5 t.
**55593–638. DMSL.** Lot No. 31004 1985–86. –/59 1T (c –/44(+6) 1T 2W, s –/50 1T, u –/60 1T). 25.0 t.
**55706–745. DMS.** Lot No. 31013 1986–87. –/62 (c –/46(+6) 2W, s –/56, t –/53 or 55 1W, u –/52 or 54 1W). 24.5 t.
**55752–791. DMSL.** Lot No. 31014 1986–87. –/59 1T (c –/44(+6) 1T 2W, s –/50 1T, u –/60 1T). 25.0 t.

| | | | | | | |
|---|---|---|---|---|---|---|
| 142 002 | c | AV | A | LE | 55543 | 55593 |
| 142 003 | | NO | AF | ZG | 55544 | 55594 |
| 142 004 | t | NO | A | HT | 55545 | 55595 |
| 142 006 | c | AV | A | LE | 55547 | 55597 |
| 142 007 | t | NO | AF | ZG | 55548 | 55598 |
| 142 010 | c | AV | A | CF | 55551 | 55601 |
| 142 014 | t | NO | AF | ZG | 55555 | 55605 |
| 142 018 | s | NO | A | HT | 55559 | 55609 |
| 142 023 | t | NO | A | HT | 55564 | 55614 |
| 142 032 | t | NO | AF | ZG | 55573 | 55623 |
| 142 047 | u | NO | A | GA | 55588 | 55638 |
| 142 056 | u | NO | AF | ZG | 55706 | 55752 |
| 142 058 | u | NO | A | HT | 55708 | 55754 |
| 142 065 | s | NO | A | HT | 55715 | 55761 |
| 142 068 | t | NO | A | HT | 55718 | 55764 |
| 142 069 | c | AV | A | LE | 55719 | 55765 |
| 142 070 | t | NO | A | HT | 55720 | 55766 |
| 142 071 | s | NO | A | HT | 55721 | 55767 |
| 142 072 | c | AV | A | CF | 55722 | 55768 |
| 142 073 | c | AV | A | LE | 55723 | 55769 |
| 142 074 | c | AV | A | LE | 55724 | 55770 |
| 142 075 | c | AV | A | LE | 55725 | 55771 |
| 142 076 | c | AV | A | CF | 55726 | 55772 |
| 142 077 | c | AV | A | LE | 55727 | 55773 |
| 142 078 | s | NO | A | HT | 55728 | 55774 |
| 142 080 | c | AV | A | LE | 55730 | 55776 |
| 142 081 | c | AV | A | LE | 55731 | 55777 |
| 142 082 | c | AV | A | LE | 55732 | 55778 |
| 142 083 | c | AV | A | LE | 55733 | 55779 |
| 142 085 | c | AV | A | LE | 55735 | 55781 |
| 142 086 | s | NO | A | CF | 55736 | 55782 |
| 142 087 | s | NO | A | HT | 55737 | 55783 |
| 142 089 | s | NO | AF | ZG | 55739 | 55785 |
| 142 090 | s | NO | A | HT | 55740 | 55786 |
| 142 094 | s | NO | A | HT | 55744 | 55790 |
| 142 095 | s | NO | A | HT | 55745 | 55791 |

# CLASS 143      PACER      ALEXANDER/BARCLAY

DMS–DMSL. Similar design to Class 142, but bodies built by W Alexander with Barclay underframes. The TfW Class 143s are due to be withdrawn by the end of May 2021.

**Construction:** Steel underframe, aluminium alloy body and roof. Alexander bus bodywork on four-wheeled underframes.
**Engines:** One Cummins LT10-R of 165 kW (225 hp) at 1950 rpm.
**Couplers:** BSI at outer ends, bar within unit.
**Dimensions:** 15.45 x 2.80 m.
**Gangways:** Within unit only.            **Wheel Arrangement:** 1-A + A-1.
**Doors:** Twin-leaf inward pivoting.      **Maximum Speed:** 75 mph.
**Seating Layout:** 2+2 high-back Chapman seating, mainly unidirectional.
**Multiple Working:** Within class and with Classes 142, 144, 150, 153, 155, 156, 158 and 159.
**DMS.** Lot No. 31005 Andrew Barclay 1985–86. –/48(+6) 2W. 24.0 t.
**DMSL.** Lot No. 31006 Andrew Barclay 1985–86. –/44(+6) 1T 2W. 24.5 t.

| 143 601 | **AV** | TW | *TW* |    | CF | 55642 | 55667 |
|---------|--------|-----|------|----|-----|-------|-------|
| 143 602 | **AW** | P   | *TW* |    | CF | 55651 | 55668 |
| 143 603 | **GW** | P   |      |    | PM | 55658 | 55669 |
| 143 604 | **AW** | P   | *TW* |    | CF | 55645 | 55670 |
| 143 605 | **AW** | P   | *TW* |    | CF | 55646 | 55671 |
| 143 606 | **AW** | P   | *TW* |    | CF | 55647 | 55672 |
| 143 607 | **AW** | P   | *TW* |    | CF | 55648 | 55673 |
| 143 608 | **AW** | P   | *TW* |    | CF | 55649 | 55674 |
| 143 609 | **AV** | TW  | *TW* |    | CF | 55650 | 55675 |
| 143 610 | **AV** | TW  | *TW* |    | CF | 55643 | 55676 |
| 143 611 | **GW** | P   |      |    | LE | 55652 | 55677 |
| 143 614 | **AV** | TW  | *TW* |    | CF | 55655 | 55680 |
| 143 616 | **AW** | P   | *TW* |    | CF | 55657 | 55682 |
| 143 617 | **GW** | GW  |      |    | PM | 55644 | 55683 |
| 143 618 | **GW** | GW  |      |    | PM | 55659 | 55684 |
| 143 619 | **GW** | GW  |      |    | PM | 55660 | 55685 |
| 143 620 | **GW** | P   |      |    | LE | 55661 | 55686 |
| 143 621 | **GW** | P   |      |    | LE | 55662 | 55687 |
| 143 622 | **AW** | P   | *TW* |    | CF | 55663 | 55688 |
| 143 623 | **AW** | P   | *TW* |    | CF | 55664 | 55689 |
| 143 624 | **AW** | P   | *TW* |    | CF | 55665 | 55690 |
| 143 625 | **AW** | P   | *TW* |    | CF | 55666 | 55691 |

# CLASS 144      PACER      ALEXANDER/BREL DERBY

DMS–DMSL or DMS–MS–DMSL. As Class 143, but underframes built by BREL. Class 144s finished in service with Northern in April 2020. Three have been sold to Vintage Trains and the remaining units are waiting transfer to their new homes.

**Construction:** Steel underframe, aluminium alloy body and roof. Alexander bus bodywork on four-wheeled underframes.

**Engines:** One Cummins LT10-R of 165 kW (225 hp) at 1950 rpm.
**Couplers:** BSI at outer ends, bar within unit.
**Dimensions:** 15.45/15.43 x 2.80 m.
**Gangways:** Within unit only.          **Wheel Arrangement:** 1-A + A-1.
**Doors:** Twin-leaf inward pivoting.      **Maximum Speed:** 75 mph.
**Seating Layout:** 2+2 high-back Richmond seating, mainly unidirectional.
**Multiple Working:** Within class and with Classes 142, 143, 150, 153, 155, 156, 158 and 159.

**Non-standard livery:** 144 012 144evolution (blue & purple).

**DMS.** Lot No. 31015 BREL Derby 1986–87. –/45(+3) 1W 24.0 t.
**MS.** Lot No. 31037 BREL Derby 1987. –/58. 23.5 t.
**DMSL.** Lot No. 31016 BREL Derby 1986–87. –/41(+3) 1T. 24.5 t.

† Prototype demonstrator unit, refurbished as a trial, with new Fainsa seating and a universal access toilet. Details are as follows:
**DMS 55812:** Lot No. 31015 BREL Derby 1986–87. –/43(+3). 27.2 t
**DMSL 55835:** Lot No. 31016 BREL Derby 1986–87. –/35 1TD 2W. 28.0 t.

| | | | | | | |
|---|---|---|---|---|---|---|
| 144 001 | **NO** | P | | WS | 55801 | | 55824 |
| 144 002 | **NO** | P | | WS | 55802 | | 55825 |
| 144 005 | **NO** | P | | WS | 55805 | | 55828 |
| 144 012 | † | **O** | P | DR | 55812 | | 55835 |
| 144 014 | **NO** | VT | | TM | 55814 | 55850 | 55837 |
| 144 015 | **NO** | P | | DR | 55815 | 55851 | 55838 |
| 144 019 | **NO** | VT | | TM | 55819 | 55855 | 55842 |
| 144 021 | **NO** | P | | DR | 55821 | 55857 | 55844 |
| 144 023 | **NO** | VT | | TM | 55823 | 55859 | 55846 |
| Spare | **NO** | P | | WS | 55808 | | |

**Name:** 144 001 THE PENISTONE LINE PARTNERSHIP

# CLASS 150/0          SPRINTER          BREL YORK

DMSL–MS–DMS. Prototype Sprinter. Fitted with a universal access toilet.

**Construction:** Steel.
**Engines:** One Cummins NT855R5 of 213 kW (285 hp) at 2100 rpm.
**Bogies:** BX8P (powered), BX8T (non-powered).
**Couplers:** BSI at outer end of driving vehicles, bar non-driving ends.
**Dimensions:** 19.93/19.92 x 2.73 m.
**Gangways:** Within unit only.          **Wheel Arrangement:** 2-B + 2-B + B-2.
**Doors:** Twin-leaf sliding.              **Maximum Speed:** 75 mph.
**Seating Layout:** 3+2 (mainly unidirectional).
**Multiple Working:** Within class and with Classes 142, 143, 144, 153, 155, 156, 158, 159, 170 and 172.

**DMSL.** Lot No. 30984 1984. –/72 1TD 2W. 35.4 t.
**MS.** Lot No. 30986 1984. –/92. 35.0 t.
**DMS.** Lot No. 30985 1984. –/69(+6). 34.7 t.

| | | | | | | | |
|---|---|---|---|---|---|---|---|
| 150 001 | **NR** | A | *NO* | NH | 55200 | 55400 | 55300 |
| 150 002 | **NR** | A | *NO* | NH | 55201 | 55401 | 55301 |

# CLASS 150/1    SPRINTER    BREL YORK

DMSL–DMS. All fitted with a universal access toilet.

**Construction:** Steel.
**Engines:** One Cummins NT855R5 of 213 kW (285 hp) at 2100 rpm.
**Bogies:** BP38 (powered), BT38 (non-powered).
**Couplers:** BSI.
**Dimensions:** 19.74 x 2.82 m.
**Gangways:** Within unit only.        **Wheel Arrangement:** 2-B + B-2.
**Doors:** Twin-leaf sliding.          **Maximum Speed:** 75 mph.
**Seating Layout:** 3+2 facing as built but units operated by Centro were
reseated with mainly unidirectional seating.
**Multiple Working:** Within class and with Classes 142, 143, 144, 153, 155,
156, 158, 159, 170 and 172.

† Refurbished Northern units with original Ashbourne seating.
* Refurbished Northern units. Chapman seating.

**DMSL.** Lot No. 31011 1985–86. * –/55(+3) 1TD 2W, † –/56(+3) or –/57(+3)
1TD 2W. 38.3 t.
**DMS.** Lot No. 31012 1985–86. * –/65, † –/70(+6) or –/71(+6)). 38.1 t.

| | | | | | | | |
|---|---|---|---|---|---|---|---|
| 150 101 | † | **NR** | A | *NO* | NH | 52101 | 57101 |
| 150 102 | † | **NR** | A | *NO* | NH | 52102 | 57102 |
| 150 103 | † | **NR** | A | *NO* | NH | 52103 | 57103 |
| 150 104 | † | **NR** | A | *NO* | NH | 52104 | 57104 |
| 150 105 | † | **NR** | A | *NO* | NH | 52105 | 57105 |
| 150 106 | † | **NR** | A | *NO* | NH | 52106 | 57106 |
| 150 107 | † | **NR** | A | *NO* | NH | 52107 | 57107 |
| 150 108 | † | **NR** | A | *NO* | NH | 52108 | 57108 |
| 150 109 | † | **NR** | A | *NO* | NH | 52109 | 57109 |
| 150 110 | † | **NR** | A | *NO* | NH | 52110 | 57110 |
| 150 111 | † | **NR** | A | *NO* | NH | 52111 | 57111 |
| 150 112 | † | **NR** | A | *NO* | NH | 52112 | 57112 |
| 150 113 | † | **NR** | A | *NO* | NH | 52113 | 57113 |
| 150 114 | † | **NR** | A | *NO* | NH | 52114 | 57114 |
| 150 115 | † | **NR** | A | *NO* | NH | 52115 | 57115 |
| 150 116 | † | **NR** | A | *NO* | NH | 52116 | 57116 |
| 150 117 | † | **NR** | A | *NO* | NH | 52117 | 57117 |
| 150 118 | † | **NR** | A | *NO* | NH | 52118 | 57118 |
| 150 119 | † | **NR** | A | *NO* | NH | 52119 | 57119 |
| 150 120 | † | **NR** | A | *NO* | NH | 52120 | 57120 |
| 150 121 | † | **NR** | A | *NO* | NH | 52121 | 57121 |
| 150 122 | † | **NR** | A | *NO* | NH | 52122 | 57122 |
| 150 123 | † | **NR** | A | *NO* | NH | 52123 | 57123 |
| 150 124 | † | **NR** | A | *NO* | NH | 52124 | 57124 |
| 150 125 | † | **NR** | A | *NO* | NH | 52125 | 57125 |
| 150 126 | † | **NR** | A | *NO* | NH | 52126 | 57126 |
| 150 127 | † | **NR** | A | *NO* | NH | 52127 | 57127 |
| 150 128 | † | **NR** | A | *NO* | NH | 52128 | 57128 |
| 150 129 | † | **NR** | A | *NO* | NH | 52129 | 57129 |

| 150 130 | † | **NR** | A | *NO* | NH | 52130 | 57130 |
| 150 131 | † | **NR** | A | *NO* | NH | 52131 | 57131 |
| 150 132 | † | **NR** | A | *NO* | NH | 52132 | 57132 |
| 150 133 | * | **NR** | A | *NO* | NH | 52133 | 57133 |
| 150 134 | * | **NR** | A | *NO* | NH | 52134 | 57134 |
| 150 135 | * | **NR** | A | *NO* | NH | 52135 | 57135 |
| 150 136 | * | **NR** | A | *NO* | NH | 52136 | 57136 |
| 150 137 | * | **NR** | A | *NO* | NH | 52137 | 57137 |
| 150 138 | * | **NR** | A | *NO* | NH | 52138 | 57138 |
| 150 139 | * | **NR** | A | *NO* | NH | 52139 | 57139 |
| 150 140 | * | **NR** | A | *NO* | NH | 52140 | 57140 |
| 150 141 | * | **NR** | A | *NO* | NH | 52141 | 57141 |
| 150 142 | * | **NR** | A | *NO* | NH | 52142 | 57142 |
| 150 143 | * | **NR** | A | *NO* | NH | 52143 | 57143 |
| 150 144 | * | **NR** | A | *NO* | NH | 52144 | 57144 |
| 150 145 | * | **NR** | A | *NO* | NH | 52145 | 57145 |
| 150 146 | * | **NR** | A | *NO* | NH | 52146 | 57146 |
| 150 147 | * | **NR** | A | *NO* | NH | 52147 | 57147 |
| 150 148 | * | **NR** | A | *NO* | NH | 52148 | 57148 |
| 150 149 | * | **NR** | A | *NO* | NH | 52149 | 57149 |
| 150 150 | * | **NR** | A | *NO* | NH | 52150 | 57150 |

## CLASS 150/2     SPRINTER                    BREL YORK

DMSL–DMS.

**Construction:** Steel.
**Engines:** One Cummins NT855R5 of 213 kW (285 hp) at 2100 rpm.
**Bogies:** BP38 (powered), BT38 (non-powered).
**Couplers:** BSI.
**Dimensions:** 19.74 x 2.82 m.
**Gangways:** Throughout.                   **Wheel Arrangement:** 2-B + B-2.
**Doors:** Twin-leaf sliding.               **Maximum Speed:** 75 mph.
**Seating Layout:** 3+2 mainly unidirectional seating as built, but most units have now been refurbished with new 2+2 seating.
**Multiple Working:** Within class and with Classes 142, 143, 144, 153, 155, 156, 158, 159, 170 and 172.

c  Former First North Western units with 3+2 Chapman seating.
q  Refurbished Great Western Railway units with a universal access toilet. Original Ashbourne seating. Full details awaited.
t  Refurbished Transport for Wales units with 2+2 Chapman seating and a universal access toilet.
*  Refurbished Great Western Railway units with 2+2 Chapman seating and a universal access toilet.
† Refurbished Northern units with a universal access toilet. 3+2 Chapman seating.
§  Refurbished Northern units with a universal access toilet. Original Ashbourne seating.

150 209 is formed DMS–DMS (two toiletless vehicles).

**DMSL.** Lot No. 31017 1986–87. * –/50(+4) 1TD 2W, † –/58(+3) 1TD 2W, § –/58 1TD 2W, c –/62 1TD, t –/50 1TD 2W. 37.5 t (* 35.8 t, † and § 38.1 t).
**DMS.** Lot No. 31018 1986–87. * –/58(+10), † –/70(+6), § –/72(+3), c –/70, t –/58(+6). 36.5 t.

| | | | | | | |
|---|---|---|---|---|---|---|
| 150 201 | † | **NR** | A | *NO* | NL | 52201 | 57201 |
| 150 202 | q | **GW** | A | *GW* | EX | 52202 | 57202 |
| 150 203 | † | **NR** | A | *NO* | NL | 52203 | 57203 |
| 150 204 | † | **NR** | A | *NO* | NL | 52204 | 57204 |
| 150 205 | † | **NR** | A | *NO* | NL | 52205 | 57205 |
| 150 206 | † | **NR** | A | *NO* | NL | 52206 | 57206 |
| 150 207 | c | **GW** | A | *GW* | EX | 52207 | 57207 |
| 150 208 | t | **AW** | P | *TW* | CF | 52208 | 57208 |
| 150 209 | | **NR** | A | *NO* | NH | 57209 | 57212 |
| 150 210 | † | **NR** | A | *NO* | NL | 52210 | 57210 |
| 150 211 | † | **NR** | A | *NO* | NL | 52211 | 57211 |
| 150 213 | t | **AW** | P | *TW* | CF | 52213 | 57213 |
| 150 214 | § | **NR** | A | *NO* | NL | 52214 | 57214 |
| 150 215 | † | **NR** | A | *NO* | NL | 52215 | 57215 |
| 150 216 | q | **GW** | A | *GW* | EX | 52216 | 57216 |
| 150 217 | t | **AW** | P | *TW* | CF | 52217 | 57217 |
| 150 218 | † | **NR** | A | *NO* | NL | 52218 | 57218 |
| 150 219 | * | **FB** | P | *GW* | EX | 52219 | 57219 |
| 150 220 | † | **NR** | A | *NO* | NH | 52220 | 57220 |
| 150 221 | * | **GW** | P | *GW* | EX | 52221 | 57221 |
| 150 222 | † | **NR** | A | *NO* | NL | 52222 | 57222 |
| 150 223 | † | **NR** | A | *NO* | NH | 52223 | 57223 |
| 150 224 | † | **NR** | A | *NO* | NH | 52224 | 57224 |
| 150 225 | † | **NR** | A | *NO* | NH | 52225 | 57225 |
| 150 226 | † | **NR** | A | *NO* | NH | 52226 | 57226 |
| 150 227 | t | **AW** | P | *TW* | CF | 52227 | 57227 |
| 150 228 | § | **NR** | P | *NO* | NL | 52228 | 57228 |
| 150 229 | t | **AW** | P | *TW* | CF | 52229 | 57229 |
| 150 230 | t | **AW** | P | *TW* | CF | 52230 | 57230 |
| 150 231 | t | **AW** | P | *TW* | CF | 52231 | 57231 |
| 150 232 | * | **GW** | P | *GW* | EX | 52232 | 57232 |
| 150 233 | * | **GW** | P | *GW* | EX | 52233 | 57233 |
| 150 234 | * | **GW** | P | *GW* | EX | 52234 | 57234 |
| 150 235 | t | **AW** | P | *TW* | CF | 52235 | 57235 |
| 150 236 | t | **AW** | P | *TW* | CF | 52236 | 57236 |
| 150 237 | t | **AW** | P | *TW* | CF | 52237 | 57237 |
| 150 238 | * | **FB** | P | *GW* | EX | 52238 | 57238 |
| 150 239 | * | **GW** | P | *GW* | EX | 52239 | 57239 |
| 150 240 | t | **AW** | P | *TW* | CF | 52240 | 57240 |
| 150 241 | t | **AW** | P | *TW* | CF | 52241 | 57241 |
| 150 242 | t | **AW** | P | *TW* | CF | 52242 | 57242 |
| 150 243 | * | **GW** | P | *GW* | EX | 52243 | 57243 |
| 150 244 | * | **GW** | P | *GW* | EX | 52244 | 57244 |
| 150 245 | t | **AW** | P | *TW* | CF | 52245 | 57245 |
| 150 246 | * | **GW** | P | *GW* | EX | 52246 | 57246 |
| 150 247 | * | **GW** | P | *GW* | EX | 52247 | 57247 |

| | | | | | | |
|---|---|---|---|---|---|---|
| 150 248 | * | **GW** | P | *GW* | EX | 52248 | 57248 |
| 150 249 | * | **GW** | P | *GW* | EX | 52249 | 57249 |
| 150 250 | t | **AW** | P | *TW* | CF | 52250 | 57250 |
| 150 251 | t | **AW** | P | *TW* | CF | 52251 | 57251 |
| 150 252 | t | **AW** | P | *TW* | CF | 52252 | 57252 |
| 150 253 | t | **AW** | P | *TW* | CF | 52253 | 57253 |
| 150 254 | t | **AW** | P | *TW* | CF | 52254 | 57254 |
| 150 255 | t | **AW** | P | *TW* | CF | 52255 | 57255 |
| 150 256 | t | **AW** | P | *TW* | CF | 52256 | 57256 |
| 150 257 | t | **AW** | P | *TW* | CF | 52257 | 57257 |
| 150 258 | t | **AW** | P | *TW* | CF | 52258 | 57258 |
| 150 259 | t | **AW** | P | *TW* | CF | 52259 | 57259 |
| 150 260 | t | **AW** | P | *TW* | CF | 52260 | 57260 |
| 150 261 | * | **GW** | P | *GW* | EX | 52261 | 57261 |
| 150 262 | t | **AW** | P | *TW* | CF | 52262 | 57262 |
| 150 263 | * | **GW** | P | *GW* | EX | 52263 | 57263 |
| 150 264 | t | **AW** | P | *TW* | CF | 52264 | 57264 |
| 150 265 | * | **GW** | P | *GW* | EX | 52265 | 57265 |
| 150 266 | * | **GW** | P | *GW* | EX | 52266 | 57266 |
| 150 267 | t | **AW** | P | *TW* | CF | 52267 | 57267 |
| 150 268 | § | **NR** | P | *NO* | NL | 52268 | 57268 |
| 150 269 | § | **NR** | P | *NO* | NL | 52269 | 57269 |
| 150 270 | § | **NR** | P | *NO* | NL | 52270 | 57270 |
| 150 271 | § | **NR** | P | *NO* | NL | 52271 | 57271 |
| 150 272 | § | **NR** | P | *NO* | NL | 52272 | 57272 |
| 150 273 | § | **NR** | P | *NO* | NL | 52273 | 57273 |
| 150 274 | § | **NR** | P | *NO* | NL | 52274 | 57274 |
| 150 275 | § | **NR** | P | *NO* | NL | 52275 | 57275 |
| 150 276 | § | **NR** | P | *NO* | NL | 52276 | 57276 |
| 150 277 | § | **NR** | P | *NO* | NL | 52277 | 57277 |
| 150 278 | t | **AW** | P | *TW* | CF | 52278 | 57278 |
| 150 279 | t | **AW** | P | *TW* | CF | 52279 | 57279 |
| 150 280 | t | **AW** | P | *TW* | CF | 52280 | 57280 |
| 150 281 | t | **AW** | P | *TW* | CF | 52281 | 57281 |
| 150 282 | t | **AW** | P | *TW* | CF | 52282 | 57282 |
| 150 283 | t | **AW** | P | *TW* | CF | 52283 | 57283 |
| 150 284 | t | **AW** | P | *TW* | CF | 52284 | 57284 |
| 150 285 | t | **AW** | P | *TW* | CF | 52285 | 57285 |

**Names:**

| | |
|---|---|
| 150 214 | The Bentham Line A Dementia-Friendly Railway |
| 150 275 | The Yorkshire Regiment Yorkshire Warrior |

## CLASS 153     SUPER SPRINTER     LEYLAND BUS

DMSL. Converted by Hunslet-Barclay, Kilmarnock from Class 155 2-car units.

**Construction:** Steel underframe, rivetted steel body and roof. Built from Leyland National bus parts on Leyland Bus bogied underframes.
**Engine:** One Cummins NT855R5 of 213 kW (285 hp) at 2100 rpm.
**Bogies:** One P3-10 (powered) and one BT38 (non-powered).

**Couplers**: BSI.
**Dimensions**: 23.21 x 2.70 m.
**Gangways**: Throughout.                  **Wheel Arrangement**: 2-B.
**Doors**: Single-leaf sliding plug.       **Maximum Speed**: 75 mph.
**Seating Layout**: 2+2 facing/unidirectional.
**Multiple Working**: Within class and with Classes 142, 143, 144, 150, 155, 156, 158, 159, 170 and 172.

Cars numbered in the 573xx series were renumbered by adding 50 to their original number so that the last two digits correspond with the set number.
c  Chapman seating.
d  Richmond seating.
†  Refurbished Transport for Wales units with a new universal access toilet.

§ 153305/370/373/377/380 are being converted to bicycle carrying vehicles for use with ScotRail on the West Highland Line from 2021.

**Non-standard livery**: 153377 ScotRail active travel (**SR** livery with various graphics).

**52301–52335. DMSL**. Lot No. 31026 1987–88. Converted under Lot No. 31115 1991–92. –/72(+3) 1T 1W. (s –/72 1T 1W, t –/72(+2) 1T 1W), † –/56(+5) 1TD 2W). 41.2 t.
**57301–57335. DMSL**. Lot No. 31027 1987–88. Converted under Lot No. 31115 1991–92. –/72(+3) 1T 1W (s –/72 1T 1W, † –/56(+5) 1TD 2W). 41.2 t.

| 153 301 | d | **NO** | A | *NO* | NH | 52301 | |
| 153 302 | c | **EM** | A | | EP | 52302 | |
| 153 303 | †c | **TW** | A | *TW* | CF | 52303 | |
| 153 304 | ds | **NO** | A | *NO* | NH | 52304 | |
| 153 305 | d | **U** | A | | ZM | 52305 | |
| 153 307 | d | **NO** | A | *NO* | NH | 52307 | |
| 153 308 | c | **EM** | A | *EM* | NM | 52308 | |
| 153 311 | c | **EM** | P | | BU | 52311 | |
| 153 312 | † | **TW** | A | *TW* | CF | 52312 | |
| 153 315 | ds | **NO** | A | *NO* | NH | 52315 | |
| 153 316 | c | **NO** | P | *NO* | NH | 52316 | John "Longitude" Harrison Inventor of the Marine Chronometer |
| 153 317 | ds | **NO** | A | *NO* | NH | 52317 | |
| 153 319 | c | **EM** | A | *EM* | NM | 52319 | |
| 153 320 | †c | **TW** | P | *TW* | CF | 52320 | |
| 153 323 | †c | **TW** | P | *TW* | CF | 52323 | |
| 153 324 | c | **NO** | P | *NO* | NH | 52324 | |
| 153 325 | †c | **TW** | P | *TW* | CF | 52325 | |
| 153 327 | †c | **TW** | A | *TW* | CF | 52327 | |
| 153 328 | ds | **NO** | A | *NO* | NH | 52328 | |
| 153 329 | †c | **TW** | P | *TW* | CF | 52329 | |
| 153 330 | cs | **NO** | P | *NO* | NH | 52330 | |
| 153 331 | d | **NO** | A | *NO* | NH | 52331 | |
| 153 332 | c | **NO** | P | *NO* | NH | 52332 | |
| 153 333 | †c | **TW** | P | *TW* | CF | 52333 | |
| 153 334 | ct | **LM** | P | | BU | 52334 | |
| 153 351 | d | **NO** | A | *NO* | NH | 57351 | |

| 153 352 | ds | **NO** | A | *NO* | NH | 57352 | |
| 153 353 | †c | **TW** | A | *TW* | CF | 57353 | |
| 153 354 | c | **LM** | P | | BU | 57354 | |
| 153 355 | c | **EM** | A | *EM* | NM | 57355 | |
| 153 356 | c | **LM** | P | | BU | 57356 | |
| 153 357 | c | **EM** | A | *EM* | NM | 57357 | |
| 153 358 | c | **NO** | P | *NO* | NH | 57358 | |
| 153 359 | c | **NO** | P | *NO* | NH | 57359 | |
| 153 360 | c | **NO** | P | *NO* | NH | 57360 | |
| 153 361 | †c | **TW** | P | *TW* | CF | 57361 | |
| 153 362 | †c | **TW** | A | *TW* | CF | 57362 | |
| 153 363 | cs | **NO** | P | *NO* | NH | 57363 | |
| 153 364 | c | **LM** | P | | BU | 57364 | |
| 153 365 | c | **LM** | P | | BU | 57365 | |
| 153 366 | c | **LM** | P | | BU | 57366 | |
| 153 367 | †c | **TW** | P | *TW* | CF | 57367 | |
| 153 369 | †c | **TW** | P | *TW* | CF | 57369 | |
| 153 370 | d | **GW** | A | | ZM | 57370 | |
| 153 371 | c | **LM** | P | | TS | 57371 | |
| 153 373 | d | **GW** | A | | ZM | 57373 | |
| 153 374 | c | **EM** | A | | CF | 57374 | |
| 153 375 | c | **LM** | P | | TS | 57375 | |
| 153 376 | c | **EM** | P | *EM* | NM | 57376 | X24-EXPEDITIOUS |
| 153 377 | § | **0** | A | *SR* | CK | 57377 | |
| 153 378 | d | **NO** | A | *NO* | NH | 57378 | |
| 153 379 | c | **EM** | P | *EM* | NM | 57379 | |
| 153 380 | d | **GW** | A | | ZM | 57380 | |
| 153 381 | c | **EM** | P | | BU | 57381 | |
| 153 383 | c | **EM** | P | | BU | 57383 | Ecclesbourne Valley Railway 150 Years |
| 153 384 | c | **EM** | P | *EM* | NM | 57384 | |
| 153 385 | c | **EM** | P | | BU | 57385 | |

**Class 153/9.** Transport for Wales units that are not PRM compliant. Renumbered into the 1539xx series as they must operate with a PRM compliant unit. Toilets locked out of use.

| 153 906 | (153 306) | c | **GA** | P | *TW* | CF | 52306 |
| 153 909 | (153 309) | c | **GA** | P | *TW* | CF | 52309 |
| 153 910 | (153 310) | c | **EM** | P | *TW* | CF | 52310 |
| 153 913 | (153 313) | cs | **EM** | P | *TW* | CF | 52313 |
| 153 914 | (153 314) | c | **GA** | P | *TW* | CF | 52314 |
| 153 918 | (153 318) | d | **EM** | A | *TW* | CF | 52318 |
| 153 921 | (153 321) | ct | **EM** | P | *TW* | CF | 52321 |
| 153 922 | (153 322) | c | **GA** | P | *TW* | CF | 52322 |
| 153 926 | (153 326) | c | **EM** | P | *TW* | CF | 52326 |
| 153 935 | (153 335) | c | **GA** | P | *TW* | CF | 52335 |
| 153 968 | (153 368) | d | **EM** | A | *TW* | CF | 57368 |
| 153 972 | (153 372) | d | **EM** | A | *TW* | CF | 57372 |
| 153 982 | (153 382) | d | **EM** | A | *TW* | CF | 57382 |

# CLASS 155   SUPER SPRINTER          LEYLAND BUS

DMSL–DMS. Fitted with a universal access toilet.

**Construction:** Steel underframe, rivetted steel body and roof. Built from Leyland National bus parts on Leyland Bus bogied underframes.
**Engines:** One Cummins NT855R5 of 213 kW (285 hp) at 2100 rpm.
**Bogies:** One P3-10 (powered) and one BT38 (non-powered).
**Couplers:** BSI.
**Dimensions:** 23.21 x 2.70 m.

| | | |
|---|---|---|
| **Gangways:** Throughout. | **Wheel Arrangement:** 2-B + B-2. |
| **Doors:** Single-leaf sliding plug. | **Maximum Speed:** 75 mph. |

**Seating Layout:** 2+2 facing/unidirectional Chapman seating.
**Multiple Working:** Within class and with Classes 142, 143, 144, 150, 153, 156, 158, 159, 170 and 172.

**DMSL.** Lot No. 31057 1988. –/64 1TD 2W. 39.0 t.
**DMS.** Lot No. 31058 1988. –/76. 40.4 t.

| 155 341 | **NR** | P | *NO* | NL | 52341 | 57341 |
|---------|--------|---|------|----|-------|-------|
| 155 342 | **NR** | P | *NO* | NL | 52342 | 57342 |
| 155 343 | **NR** | P | *NO* | NL | 52343 | 57343 |
| 155 344 | **NR** | P | *NO* | NL | 52344 | 57344 |
| 155 345 | **NR** | P | *NO* | NL | 52345 | 57345 |
| 155 346 | **NR** | P | *NO* | NL | 52346 | 57346 |
| 155 347 | **NR** | P | *NO* | NL | 52347 | 57347 |

# CLASS 156   SUPER SPRINTER   METRO-CAMMELL

DMSL–DMS.

**Construction:** Steel.
**Engines:** One Cummins NT855R5 of 213 kW (285 hp) at 2100 rpm.
**Bogies:** One P3-10 (powered) and one BT38 (non-powered).
**Couplers:** BSI.
**Dimensions:** 23.03 x 2.73 m.

| | | |
|---|---|---|
| **Gangways:** Throughout. | **Wheel Arrangement:** 2-B + B-2. |
| **Doors:** Single-leaf sliding. | **Maximum Speed:** 75 mph. |

**Seating Layout:** 2+2 facing/unidirectional.
**Multiple Working:** Within class and with Classes 142, 143, 144, 150, 153, 155, 158, 159, 170 and 172.

† East Midlands Railway (former Greater Anglia) units fitted with a universal access toilet. Chapman seating.
\* Angel-owned Northern units fitted with a universal access toilet. Richmond seating.
§ Porterbrook-owned Northern units fitted with a universal access toilet. Chapman seating.
b Refurbished as a demonstrator unit by Brodies, Kilmarnock with a universal access toilet. Full details awaited.
m East Midlands Railway units fitted with a universal access toilet. Chapman seating.

n Northern units refurbished with new Fainsa seating and universal access toilet.
w ScotRail units refurbished with new Fainsa seating and universal access toilet.

**Non-standard livery:** 156413 and 156414 All over blue with yellow doors.

**Northern promotional vinyls:** 156480 Royal Air Force (light blue & white)

**DMSL.** Lot No. 31028 1988–89. † –/62 1TD 2W, * –/64(+2) 1TD 2W, § –/62(+2) 1TD 2W, m –/62 (+2) 1TD 2W, u –/68, w –/66(+3) 1TD 2W. 38.6 t.
**DMS.** Lot No. 31029 1987–89. † –/74, * –/72(+4), u –/72, w –/76. 36.1 t.

| | | | | | | |
|---|---|---|---|---|---|---|
| 156 401 | m | **EM** | P | *EM* | DY | 52401 57401 |
| 156 403 | m | **EM** | P | *EM* | DY | 52403 57403 |
| 156 404 | m | **EM** | P | *EM* | DY | 52404 57404 |
| 156 405 | m | **EI** | P | *EM* | DY | 52405 57405 |
| 156 406 | m | **EI** | P | *EM* | DY | 52406 57406 |
| 156 408 | m | **EM** | P | *EM* | DY | 52408 57408 |
| 156 410 | m | **EM** | P | *EM* | DY | 52410 57410 |
| 156 411 | m | **EM** | P | *EM* | DY | 52411 57411 |
| 156 413 | m | **0** | P | *EM* | DY | 52413 57413 |
| 156 414 | m | **0** | P | *EM* | DY | 52414 57414 |
| 156 415 | m | **EM** | P | *EM* | DY | 52415 57415 |
| 156 420 | § | **NR** | P | *NO* | NH | 52420 57420 |
| 156 421 | § | **NR** | P | *NO* | HT | 52421 57421 |
| 156 423 | § | **NR** | P | *NO* | NH | 52423 57423 |
| 156 424 | § | **NR** | P | *NO* | NH | 52424 57424 |
| 156 425 | § | **NR** | P | *NO* | NH | 52425 57425 |
| 156 426 | § | **NR** | P | *NO* | NH | 52426 57426 |
| 156 427 | § | **NR** | P | *NO* | NH | 52427 57427 |
| 156 428 | § | **NR** | P | *NO* | NH | 52428 57428 |
| 156 429 | § | **NR** | P | *NO* | NH | 52429 57429 |
| 156 430 | w | **SR** | A | *SR* | CK | 52430 57430 |
| 156 431 | w | **SR** | A | *SR* | CK | 52431 57431 |
| 156 432 | w | **SR** | A | *SR* | CK | 52432 57432 |
| 156 433 | w | **SR** | A | *SR* | CK | 52433 57433 |
| 156 434 | w | **SR** | A | *SR* | CK | 52434 57434 |
| 156 435 | w | **SR** | A | *SR* | CK | 52435 57435 |
| 156 436 | w | **SR** | A | *SR* | CK | 52436 57436 |
| 156 437 | w | **SR** | A | *SR* | CK | 52437 57437 |
| 156 438 | * | **NR** | A | *NO* | HT | 52438 57438 |
| 156 439 | w | **SR** | A | *SR* | CK | 52439 57439 |
| 156 440 | § | **NR** | P | *NO* | HT | 52440 57440 |
| 156 441 | § | **NR** | P | *NO* | NH | 52441 57441 |
| 156 442 | w | **SR** | A | *SR* | CK | 52442 57442 |
| 156 443 | * | **NR** | A | *NO* | HT | 52443 57443 |
| 156 444 | * | **NR** | A | *NO* | HT | 52444 57444 |
| 156 445 | rw | **SR** | A | *SR* | CK | 52445 57445 |
| 156 446 | rw | **SR** | A | *SR* | CK | 52446 57446 |
| 156 447 | n | **NR** | A | *NO* | HT | 52447 57447 |
| 156 448 | * | **NR** | A | *NO* | HT | 52448 57448 |
| 156 449 | n | **NR** | A | *NO* | HT | 52449 57449 |

| | | | | | | | |
|---|---|---|---|---|---|---|---|
| 156 450 | rw | **SR** | A | *SR* | CK | 52450 | 57450 |
| 156 451 | * | **NR** | A | *NO* | HT | 52451 | 57451 |
| 156 452 | § | **NR** | P | *NO* | NH | 52452 | 57452 |
| 156 453 | rw | **SR** | A | *SR* | CK | 52453 | 57453 |
| 156 454 | * | **NR** | A | *NO* | HT | 52454 | 57454 |
| 156 455 | § | **NR** | P | *NO* | NH | 52455 | 57455 |
| 156 456 | rw | **SR** | A | *SR* | CK | 52456 | 57456 |
| 156 457 | rw | **SR** | A | *SR* | CK | 52457 | 57457 |
| 156 458 | rw | **SR** | A | *SR* | CK | 52458 | 57458 |
| 156 459 | § | **NR** | P | *NO* | NH | 52459 | 57459 |
| 156 460 | § | **NR** | P | *NO* | NH | 52460 | 57460 |
| 156 461 | § | **NR** | P | *NO* | NH | 52461 | 57461 |
| 156 462 | w | **SR** | A | *SR* | CK | 52462 | 57462 |
| 156 463 | * | **NR** | A | *NO* | HT | 52463 | 57463 |
| 156 464 | § | **NR** | P | *NO* | NH | 52464 | 57464 |
| 156 465 | n | **NR** | A | *NO* | HT | 52465 | 57465 |
| 156 466 | § | **NR** | P | *NO* | NH | 52466 | 57466 |
| 156 467 | w | **SR** | A | *SR* | CK | 52467 | 57467 |
| 156 468 | * | **NR** | A | *NO* | HT | 52468 | 57468 |
| 156 469 | * | **NR** | A | *NO* | HT | 52469 | 57469 |
| 156 470 | m | **EM** | A | *EM* | DY | 52470 | 57470 |
| 156 471 | * | **NR** | A | *NO* | HT | 52471 | 57471 |
| 156 472 | * | **NR** | A | *NO* | HT | 52472 | 57472 |
| 156 473 | m | **EM** | A | *EM* | DY | 52473 | 57473 |
| 156 474 | rw | **SR** | A | *SR* | CK | 52474 | 57474 |
| 156 475 | * | **NR** | A | *NO* | HT | 52475 | 57475 |
| 156 476 | rw | **SR** | A | *SR* | CK | 52476 | 57476 |
| 156 477 | rw | **SR** | A | *SR* | CK | 52477 | 57477 |
| 156 478 | rb | **SR** | BR | *SR* | CK | 52478 | 57478 |
| 156 479 | * | **NR** | A | *NO* | HT | 52479 | 57479 |
| 156 480 | * | **NR** | A | *NO* | HT | 52480 | 57480 |
| 156 481 | * | **NR** | A | *NO* | HT | 52481 | 57481 |
| 156 482 | * | **NR** | A | *NO* | HT | 52482 | 57482 |
| 156 483 | * | **NR** | A | *NO* | HT | 52483 | 57483 |
| 156 484 | * | **NR** | A | *NO* | HT | 52484 | 57484 |
| 156 485 | n | **NR** | A | *NO* | HT | 52485 | 57485 |
| 156 486 | * | **NR** | A | *NO* | HT | 52486 | 57486 |
| 156 487 | * | **NR** | A | *NO* | HT | 52487 | 57487 |
| 156 488 | * | **NR** | A | *NO* | HT | 52488 | 57488 |
| 156 489 | * | **NR** | A | *NO* | HT | 52489 | 57489 |
| 156 490 | * | **NR** | A | *NO* | HT | 52490 | 57490 |
| 156 491 | * | **NR** | A | *NO* | HT | 52491 | 57491 |
| 156 492 | rw | **SR** | A | *SR* | CK | 52492 | 57492 |
| 156 493 | rw | **SR** | A | *SR* | CK | 52493 | 57493 |
| 156 494 | w | **SR** | A | *SR* | CK | 52494 | 57494 |
| 156 495 | w | **SR** | A | *SR* | CK | 52495 | 57495 |
| 156 496 | n | **NR** | A | *NO* | HT | 52496 | 57496 |
| 156 497 | m | **EM** | A | *EM* | DY | 52497 | 57497 |
| 156 498 | m | **EM** | A | *EM* | DY | 52498 | 57498 |
| 156 499 | rt | **SR** | A | *SR* | CK | 52499 | 57499 |
| 156 500 | rw | **SR** | A | *SR* | CK | 52500 | 57500 |

| | | | | | | | |
|---|---|---|---|---|---|---|---|
| 156 501 | w | **SR** | A | *SR* | CK | 52501 | 57501 |
| 156 502 | w | **SR** | A | *SR* | CK | 52502 | 57502 |
| 156 503 | w | **SR** | A | *SR* | CK | 52503 | 57503 |
| 156 504 | w | **SR** | A | *SR* | CK | 52504 | 57504 |
| 156 505 | w | **SR** | A | *SR* | CK | 52505 | 57505 |
| 156 506 | w | **SR** | A | *SR* | CK | 52506 | 57506 |
| 156 507 | w | **SR** | A | *SR* | CK | 52507 | 57507 |
| 156 508 | w | **SR** | A | *SR* | CK | 52508 | 57508 |
| 156 509 | w | **SR** | A | *SR* | CK | 52509 | 57509 |
| 156 510 | w | **SR** | A | *SR* | CK | 52510 | 57510 |
| 156 511 | w | **SR** | A | *SR* | CK | 52511 | 57511 |
| 156 512 | w | **SR** | A | *SR* | CK | 52512 | 57512 |
| 156 513 | w | **SR** | A | *SR* | CK | 52513 | 57513 |
| 156 514 | w | **SR** | A | *SR* | CK | 52514 | 57514 |

**Names:**

| | |
|---|---|
| 156 469 | The Royal Northumberland Fusiliers (The Fighting Fifth) |
| 156 480 | Spirit of The Royal Air Force |
| 156 483 | William George 'Billy' Hardy 14/01/1903 – 10/03/1950 |

**Class 156/9.** Former Greater Anglia units now operated by East Midlands Railway and renumbered in the 156/9 series.

| | | | | | | | | |
|---|---|---|---|---|---|---|---|---|
| 156 902 | (156 402) | † | **EI** | P | *EM* | DY | 52402 | 57402 |
| 156 907 | (156 407) | † | **EI** | P | *EM* | DY | 52407 | 57407 |
| 156 909 | (156 409) | † | **EI** | P | *EM* | DY | 52409 | 57409 |
| 156 912 | (156 412) | † | **EI** | P | *EM* | DY | 52412 | 57412 |
| 156 916 | (156 416) | † | **EI** | P | *EM* | DY | 52416 | 57416 |
| 156 917 | (156 417) | † | **EI** | P | *EM* | DY | 52417 | 57417 |
| 156 918 | (156 418) | † | **EI** | P | *EM* | DY | 52418 | 57418 |
| 156 919 | (156 419) | † | **EI** | P | *EM* | DY | 52419 | 57419 |
| 156 922 | (156 422) | † | **EI** | P | *EM* | DY | 52422 | 57422 |

# CLASS 158/0                                                    BREL

DMSL(B)–DMSL(A) or DMCL–DMSL or DMSL–MSL–DMSL.

**Construction:** Welded aluminium.
**Engines:** 158 701–813/158 880–890/158 950–959: One Cummins NTA855R1 of 260 kW (350 hp) at 2100 rpm.
158 815–862: One Perkins 2006-TWH of 260 kW (350 hp) at 2100 rpm.
158 863–872: One Cummins NTA855R3 of 300 kW (400 hp) at 1900 rpm.
**Bogies:** One BREL P4 (powered) and one BREL T4 (non-powered) per car.
**Couplers:** BSI.                           **Dimensions:** 22.57 x 2.70 m.
**Gangways:** Throughout.                     **Wheel Arrangement:** 2-B + B-2.
**Doors:** Twin-leaf swing plug.              **Maximum Speed:** 90 mph.
**Seating Layout:** 2+2 facing/unidirectional.
**Multiple Working:** Within class and with Classes 142, 143, 144, 150, 153, 155, 156, 159, 170 and 172.

ScotRail 158s 158 701–736/738–741 are "fitted" for RETB. When a unit arrives at Inverness the cab display unit is clipped on and plugged in.

Transport for Wales units have ETCS plugged in at Shrewsbury for working the Cambrian Lines.

* Refurbished ScotRail units fitted with Grammer seating, additional luggage racks and cycle stowage areas.
  ScotRail units 158 726–736/738–741 are fitted with Richmond seating.
† Refurbished East Midlands Railway units fitted with Grammer seating.
§ Northern refurbished 3-car units (original seating).
n Fully refurbished Northern units with new Fainsa seating.
p Refurbished ScotRail units with Richmond seating.
s Refurbished Transport for Wales units with Grammer seating.
v Northern units with modifications for operation beyond 2020 (original seating).
z Refurbished Great Western Railway units. Units 158 745–749/751/762/767 (some formed into 3-car sets) have Richmond seating.

**DMSL(B).** Lot No. 31051 BREL Derby 1989–92. † 68(+3) 1TD 2W, § –/64(+3) 1TD 2W, cv –/62 1TD 2W, n –/66 1TD 2W, p –/60(+4) 1TD 2W, s –/64(+4) 1TD 2W, v –/64 1TD 2W, w –/66 1TD 2W, z –/62 1TD 2W. 38.5 t.
**MSL.** Lot No. 31050 BREL Derby 1991. –/68 1T. 38.5 t.
**DMSL(A).** Lot No. 31052 BREL Derby 1989–92. († –/74, v –/68 1T, n –/72 1T, * & p –/64(+2) 1T, z –/68) plus cycle stowage area. 38.5 t.

The above details refer to the "as built" condition. The following DMSL(B) have now been converted to DMCL as follows:
**52701–736/738–741 (ScotRail).** 15/53 1TD 1W (* refurbished sets –/60(+6) 1TD 1W plus cycle stowage area).

| | | | | | | | |
|---|---|---|---|---|---|---|---|
| 158 701 | * | **SR** | P | *SR* | IS | 52701 | 57701 |
| 158 702 | * | **SR** | P | *SR* | IS | 52702 | 57702 |
| 158 703 | * | **SR** | P | *SR* | IS | 52703 | 57703 |
| 158 704 | * | **SR** | P | *SR* | IS | 52704 | 57704 |
| 158 705 | * | **SR** | P | *SR* | IS | 52705 | 57705 |
| 158 706 | * | **SR** | P | *SR* | IS | 52706 | 57706 |
| 158 707 | * | **SR** | P | *SR* | IS | 52707 | 57707 |
| 158 708 | * | **SR** | P | *SR* | IS | 52708 | 57708 |
| 158 709 | * | **SR** | P | *SR* | IS | 52709 | 57709 |
| 158 710 | * | **SR** | P | *SR* | IS | 52710 | 57710 |
| 158 711 | * | **SR** | P | *SR* | IS | 52711 | 57711 |
| 158 712 | * | **SR** | P | *SR* | IS | 52712 | 57712 |
| 158 713 | * | **SR** | P | *SR* | IS | 52713 | 57713 |
| 158 714 | * | **SR** | P | *SR* | IS | 52714 | 57714 |
| 158 715 | * | **SR** | P | *SR* | IS | 52715 | 57715 |
| 158 716 | * | **SR** | P | *SR* | IS | 52716 | 57716 |
| 158 717 | * | **SR** | P | *SR* | IS | 52717 | 57717 |
| 158 718 | * | **SR** | P | *SR* | IS | 52718 | 57718 |
| 158 719 | * | **SR** | P | *SR* | IS | 52719 | 57719 |
| 158 720 | * | **SR** | P | *SR* | IS | 52720 | 57720 |
| 158 721 | * | **SR** | P | *SR* | IS | 52721 | 57721 |
| 158 722 | * | **SR** | P | *SR* | IS | 52722 | 57722 |
| 158 723 | * | **SR** | P | *SR* | IS | 52723 | 57723 |
| 158 724 | * | **SR** | P | *SR* | IS | 52724 | 57724 |
| 158 725 | * | **SR** | P | *SR* | IS | 52725 | 57725 |

| | | | | | | | |
|---|---|---|---|---|---|---|---|
| 158 726 | p | **SR** | P | *SR* | CK | 52726 | 57726 |
| 158 727 | p | **SR** | P | *SR* | CK | 52727 | 57727 |
| 158 728 | p | **SR** | P | *SR* | CK | 52728 | 57728 |
| 158 729 | p | **SR** | P | *SR* | CK | 52729 | 57729 |
| 158 730 | p | **SR** | P | *SR* | CK | 52730 | 57730 |
| 158 731 | p | **SR** | P | *SR* | CK | 52731 | 57731 |
| 158 732 | p | **SR** | P | *SR* | CK | 52732 | 57732 |
| 158 733 | p | **SR** | P | *SR* | CK | 52733 | 57733 |
| 158 734 | p | **SR** | P | *SR* | CK | 52734 | 57734 |
| 158 735 | p | **SR** | P | *SR* | CK | 52735 | 57735 |
| 158 736 | p | **SR** | P | *SR* | CK | 52736 | 57736 |
| 158 738 | p | **SR** | P | *SR* | CK | 52738 | 57738 |
| 158 739 | p | **SR** | P | *SR* | CK | 52739 | 57739 |
| 158 740 | p | **SR** | P | *SR* | CK | 52740 | 57740 |
| 158 741 | p | **SR** | P | *SR* | CK | 52741 | 57741 |
| 158 745 | z | **GW** | P | *GW* | EX | 52745 | 57745 |
| 158 747 | z | **GW** | P | *GW* | EX | 52747 | 57747 |
| 158 749 | z | **GW** | P | *GW* | EX | 52749 | 57749 |
| 158 750 | z | **GW** | P | *GW* | EX | 52750 | 57750 |
| 158 752 | § | **NR** | P | *NO* | NL | 52752 | 58716 | 57752 |
| 158 753 | § | **NR** | P | *NO* | NL | 52753 | 58710 | 57753 |
| 158 754 | § | **NR** | P | *NO* | NL | 52754 | 58708 | 57754 |
| 158 755 | § | **NR** | P | *NO* | NL | 52755 | 58702 | 57755 |
| 158 756 | § | **NR** | P | *NO* | NL | 52756 | 58712 | 57756 |
| 158 757 | § | **NR** | P | *NO* | NL | 52757 | 58706 | 57757 |
| 158 758 | § | **NR** | P | *NO* | NL | 52758 | 58714 | 57758 |
| 158 759 | § | **NR** | P | *NO* | NL | 52759 | 58713 | 57759 |
| 158 760 | z | **GW** | P | *GW* | EX | 52760 | 57760 |
| 158 762 | z | **GW** | P | *GW* | EX | 52762 | 57762 |
| 158 763 | z | **GW** | P | *GW* | EX | 52763 | 57763 |
| 158 765 | z | **GW** | P | *GW* | EX | 52765 | 57765 |
| 158 766 | z | **GW** | P | *GW* | EX | 52766 | 57766 |
| 158 767 | z | **GW** | P | *GW* | EX | 52767 | 57767 |
| 158 769 | z | **GW** | P | *GW* | EX | 52769 | 57769 |
| 158 770 | † | **ST** | P | *EM* | NM | 52770 | 57770 |
| 158 773 | † | **EI** | P | *EM* | NM | 52773 | 57773 |
| 158 774 | † | **EI** | P | *EM* | NM | 52774 | 57774 |
| 158 777 | † | **ST** | P | *EM* | NM | 52777 | 57777 |
| 158 780 | † | **ST** | A | *EM* | NM | 52780 | 57780 |
| 158 782 | n | **NR** | A | *NO* | NL | 52782 | 57782 |
| 158 783 | † | **ST** | A | *EM* | NM | 52783 | 57783 |
| 158 784 | n | **NR** | A | *NO* | NL | 52784 | 57784 |
| 158 785 | † | **ST** | A | *EM* | NM | 52785 | 57785 |
| 158 786 | n | **NR** | A | *NO* | NL | 52786 | 57786 |
| 158 787 | n | **NR** | A | *NO* | NL | 52787 | 57787 |
| 158 788 | † | **ST** | A | *EM* | NM | 52788 | 57788 |
| 158 789 | n | **NR** | A | *NO* | NL | 52789 | 57789 |
| 158 790 | n | **NR** | A | *NO* | NL | 52790 | 57790 |
| 158 791 | n | **NR** | A | *NO* | NL | 52791 | 57791 |
| 158 792 | n | **NR** | A | *NO* | HT | 52792 | 57792 |
| 158 793 | n | **NR** | A | *NO* | NL | 52793 | 57793 |

| | | | | | | | | |
|---|---|---|---|---|---|---|---|---|
| 158 794 | n | **NR** | A | *NO* | NL | 52794 | 57794 | |
| 158 795 | n | **NR** | A | *NO* | NL | 52795 | 57795 | |
| 158 796 | n | **NR** | A | *NO* | NL | 52796 | 57796 | |
| 158 797 | n | **NR** | A | *NO* | NL | 52797 | 57797 | |
| 158 798 | z | **GW** | P | *GW* | PM | 52798 | 58715 | 57798 |
| 158 799 | † | **ST** | P | *EM* | NM | 52799 | 57799 | |
| 158 806 | † | **ST** | P | *EM* | NM | 52806 | 57806 | |
| 158 810 | † | **ST** | P | *EM* | NM | 52810 | 57810 | |
| 158 812 | † | **ST** | P | *EM* | NM | 52812 | 57812 | |
| 158 813 | † | **ST** | P | *EM* | NM | 52813 | 57813 | |
| 158 815 | n | **NR** | A | *NO* | HT | 52815 | 57815 | |
| 158 816 | n | **NR** | A | *NO* | HT | 52816 | 57816 | |
| 158 817 | n | **NR** | A | *NO* | HT | 52817 | 57817 | |
| 158 818 | es | **TW** | A | *TW* | MN | 52818 | 57818 | |
| 158 819 | es | **TW** | A | *TW* | MN | 52819 | 57819 | |
| 158 820 | es | **TW** | A | *TW* | MN | 52820 | 57820 | |
| 158 821 | es | **TW** | A | *TW* | MN | 52821 | 57821 | |
| 158 822 | es | **TW** | A | *TW* | MN | 52822 | 57822 | |
| 158 823 | es | **TW** | A | *TW* | MN | 52823 | 57823 | |
| 158 824 | es | **TW** | A | *TW* | MN | 52824 | 57824 | |
| 158 825 | es | **TW** | A | *TW* | MN | 52825 | 57825 | |
| 158 826 | es | **TW** | A | *TW* | MN | 52826 | 57826 | |
| 158 827 | es | **TW** | A | *TW* | MN | 52827 | 57827 | |
| 158 828 | es | **TW** | A | *TW* | MN | 52828 | 57828 | |
| 158 829 | es | **TW** | A | *TW* | MN | 52829 | 57829 | |
| 158 830 | es | **TW** | A | *TW* | MN | 52830 | 57830 | |
| 158 831 | es | **TW** | A | *TW* | MN | 52831 | 57831 | |
| 158 832 | es | **TW** | A | *TW* | MN | 52832 | 57832 | |
| 158 833 | es | **TW** | A | *TW* | MN | 52833 | 57833 | |
| 158 834 | es | **TW** | A | *TW* | MN | 52834 | 57834 | |
| 158 835 | es | **TW** | A | *TW* | MN | 52835 | 57835 | |
| 158 836 | es | **TW** | A | *TW* | MN | 52836 | 57836 | |
| 158 837 | es | **TW** | A | *TW* | MN | 52837 | 57837 | |
| 158 838 | es | **TW** | A | *TW* | MN | 52838 | 57838 | |
| 158 839 | es | **TW** | A | *TW* | MN | 52839 | 57839 | |
| 158 840 | es | **TW** | A | *TW* | MN | 52840 | 57840 | |
| 158 841 | es | **TW** | A | *TW* | MN | 52841 | 57841 | |
| 158 842 | n | **NR** | A | *NO* | HT | 52842 | 57842 | |
| 158 843 | n | **NR** | A | *NO* | HT | 52843 | 57843 | |
| 158 844 | n | **NR** | A | *NO* | HT | 52844 | 57844 | |
| 158 845 | n | **NR** | A | *NO* | HT | 52845 | 57845 | |
| 158 846 | † | **ST** | A | *EM* | NM | 52846 | 57846 | |
| 158 847 | † | **ST** | A | *EM* | NM | 52847 | 57847 | |
| 158 848 | n | **NR** | A | *NO* | HT | 52848 | 57848 | |
| 158 849 | n | **NR** | A | *NO* | HT | 52849 | 57849 | |
| 158 850 | n | **NR** | A | *NO* | HT | 52850 | 57850 | |
| 158 851 | n | **NR** | A | *NO* | HT | 52851 | 57851 | |
| 158 852 | † | **ST** | A | *EM* | NM | 52852 | 57852 | |
| 158 853 | n | **NR** | A | *NO* | HT | 52853 | 57853 | |
| 158 854 | † | **ST** | A | *EM* | NM | 52854 | 57854 | |
| 158 855 | n | **NR** | A | *NO* | HT | 52855 | 57855 | |

| 158 856 | † | **ST** | A | *EM* | NM | 52856 | 57856 |
| 158 857 | † | **ST** | A | *EM* | NM | 52857 | 57857 |
| 158 858 | † | **ST** | A | *EM* | NM | 52858 | 57858 |
| 158 859 | n | **NR** | A | *NO* | HT | 52859 | 57859 |
| 158 860 | n | **NR** | A | *NO* | HT | 52860 | 57860 |
| 158 861 | v | **NO** | A | *NO* | HT | 52861 | 57861 |
| 158 862 | † | **ST** | A | *EM* | NM | 52862 | 57862 |
| 158 863 | † | **ST** | A | *EM* | NM | 52863 | 57863 |
| 158 864 | † | **ST** | A | *EM* | NM | 52864 | 57864 |
| 158 865 | † | **ST** | A | *EM* | NM | 52865 | 57865 |
| 158 866 | † | **ST** | A | *EM* | NM | 52866 | 57866 |
| 158 867 | n | **NR** | A | *NO* | NL | 52867 | 57867 |
| 158 868 | n | **NR** | A | *NO* | NL | 52868 | 57868 |
| 158 869 | n | **NR** | A | *NO* | NL | 52869 | 57869 |
| 158 870 | n | **NR** | A | *NO* | NL | 52870 | 57870 |
| 158 871 | n | **NR** | A | *NO* | NL | 52871 | 57871 |
| 158 872 | n | **NR** | A | *NO* | NL | 52872 | 57872 |

**Names:**

| 158 847 | Lincoln Castle Explorer |
| 158 854 | The Station Volunteer |
| 158 861 | Magna Carta 800 Lincoln 2015 |
| 158 864 | ELR 50 VISIT LINCOLNSHIRE in 2020 |

**Class 158/8. Refurbished South Western Railway and East Midlands Railway units.** Converted from former TransPennine Express units at Wabtec, Doncaster in 2007. 2+1 seating in First Class.

158 885 has been fitted with new ZF transmission as a trial.

Details as Class 158/0 except:

**DMCL.** Lot No. 31051 BREL Derby 1989–92. 13/40(+2) 1TD 1W. 38.5 t.
**DMSL.** Lot No. 31052 BREL Derby 1989–92. –/70 1T. 38.5 t.

| 158 880 | (158 737) | **ST** | P | *SW* | SA | 52737 | 57737 |
| 158 881 | (158 742) | **ST** | P | *SW* | SA | 52742 | 57742 |
| 158 882 | (158 743) | **ST** | P | *SW* | SA | 52743 | 57743 |
| 158 883 | (158 744) | **ST** | P | *SW* | SA | 52744 | 57744 |
| 158 884 | (158 772) | **ST** | P | *SW* | SA | 52772 | 57772 |
| 158 885 | (158 775) | **ST** | P | *SW* | SA | 52775 | 57775 |
| 158 886 | (158 779) | **ST** | P | *SW* | SA | 52779 | 57779 |
| 158 887 | (158 781) | **SW** | P | *SW* | SA | 52781 | 57781 |
| 158 888 | (158 802) | **SW** | P | *SW* | SA | 52802 | 57802 |
| 158 889 | (158 808) | **ST** | P | *EM* | NM | 52808 | 57808 |
| 158 890 | (158 814) | **SW** | P | *SW* | SA | 52814 | 57814 |

# CLASS 158/9                                          BREL

DMSL–DMS. Units leased by West Yorkshire PTE but managed by Eversholt Rail. Refurbished with new Fainsa seating. Details as Class 158/0 except for seating and toilets.

**DMSL.** Lot No. 31051 BREL Derby 1990–92. –/66 1TD 2W. 38.5 t.
**DMS.** Lot No. 31052 BREL Derby 1990–92. –/72 and parcels area. 38.5 t.

| 158 901 | **NR** | E | *NO* | NL | 52901 | 57901 |
| 158 902 | **NR** | E | *NO* | NL | 52902 | 57902 |
| 158 903 | **NR** | E | *NO* | NL | 52903 | 57903 |
| 158 904 | **NR** | E | *NO* | NL | 52904 | 57904 |
| 158 905 | **NR** | E | *NO* | NL | 52905 | 57905 |
| 158 906 | **NR** | E | *NO* | NL | 52906 | 57906 |
| 158 907 | **NR** | E | *NO* | NL | 52907 | 57907 |
| 158 908 | **NR** | E | *NO* | NL | 52908 | 57908 |
| 158 909 | **NR** | E | *NO* | NL | 52909 | 57909 |
| 158 910 | **NR** | E | *NO* | NL | 52910 | 57910 |

## CLASS 158/0 BREL

DMSL(A)–DMSL(B)–DMSL(A). Units reformed as 3-car hybrid sets for Great Western Railway. For vehicle details see above. Formations can be flexible depending on when unit exams become due.

| 158 950 | **GW** | P | *GW* | PM | 57751 | 52761 | 57761 |
| 158 951 | **GW** | P | *GW* | PM | 52751 | 52764 | 57764 |
| 158 956 | **GW** | P | *GW* | PM | 52748 | 52768 | 57768 |
| 158 957 | **GW** | P | *GW* | PM | 57748 | 52771 | 57771 |
| 158 958 | **GW** | P | *GW* | PM | 57746 | 52776 | 57776 |
| 158 959 | **GW** | P | *GW* | PM | 52746 | 52778 | 57778 |

## CLASS 159/0 BREL

DMCL–MSL–DMSL. Built as Class 158. Converted before entering passenger service to Class 159 by Rosyth Dockyard.

**Construction:** Welded aluminium.
**Engines:** One Cummins NTA855R3 of 300 kW (400 hp) at 1900 rpm.
**Bogies:** One BREL P4 (powered) and one BREL T4 (non-powered) per car.
**Couplers:** BSI. **Dimensions:** 22.16 x 2.70 m.
**Gangways:** Throughout. **Wheel Arrangement:** 2-B + B-2 + B-2.
**Doors:** Twin-leaf swing plug. **Maximum Speed:** 90 mph.
**Seating Layout:** 1: 2+1 facing, 2: 2+2 facing/unidirectional.
**Multiple Working:** Within class and with Classes 142, 143, 144, 150, 153, 155, 156, 158 and 170.

**DMCL.** Lot No. 31051 BREL Derby 1992–93. 23/28 1TD 1W. 38.5 t.
**MSL.** Lot No. 31050 BREL Derby 1992–93. –/70(+6) 1T. 38.5 t.
**DMSL.** Lot No. 31052 BREL Derby 1992–93. –/72 1T. 38.5 t.

| 159 001 | **SW** | P | *SW* | SA | 52873 | 58718 | 57873 |
| 159 002 | **SW** | P | *SW* | SA | 52874 | 58719 | 57874 |
| 159 003 | **SW** | P | *SW* | SA | 52875 | 58720 | 57875 |
| 159 004 | **SW** | P | *SW* | SA | 52876 | 58721 | 57876 |
| 159 005 | **SW** | P | *SW* | SA | 52877 | 58722 | 57877 |
| 159 006 | **SW** | P | *SW* | SA | 52878 | 58723 | 57878 |

| 159 007 | **SW** | P | *SW* | SA | 52879 | 58724 | 57879 |
| 159 008 | **SW** | P | *SW* | SA | 52880 | 58725 | 57880 |
| 159 009 | **SW** | P | *SW* | SA | 52881 | 58726 | 57881 |
| 159 010 | **SW** | P | *SW* | SA | 52882 | 58727 | 57882 |
| 159 011 | **SW** | P | *SW* | SA | 52883 | 58728 | 57883 |
| 159 012 | **SW** | P | *SW* | SA | 52884 | 58729 | 57884 |
| 159 013 | **SW** | P | *SW* | SA | 52885 | 58730 | 57885 |
| 159 014 | **SW** | P | *SW* | SA | 52886 | 58731 | 57886 |
| 159 015 | **SW** | P | *SW* | SA | 52887 | 58732 | 57887 |
| 159 016 | **SW** | P | *SW* | SA | 52888 | 58733 | 57888 |
| 159 017 | **SW** | P | *SW* | SA | 52889 | 58734 | 57889 |
| 159 018 | **SW** | P | *SW* | SA | 52890 | 58735 | 57890 |
| 159 019 | **SW** | P | *SW* | SA | 52891 | 58736 | 57891 |
| 159 020 | **SW** | P | *SW* | SA | 52892 | 58737 | 57892 |
| 159 021 | **SW** | P | *SW* | SA | 52893 | 58738 | 57893 |
| 159 022 | **SW** | P | *SW* | SA | 52894 | 58739 | 57894 |

## CLASS 159/1                                            BREL

DMCL–MSL–DMSL. Units converted from Class 158s at Wabtec, Doncaster in 2006–07 for South West Trains.

Details as Class 158/0 except:
**Seating Layout:** 1: 2+1 facing, 2: 2+2 facing/unidirectional.

**DMCL.** Lot No. 31051 BREL Derby 1989–92. 24/24(+2) 1TD 2W. 38.5 t.
**MSL.** Lot No. 31050 BREL Derby 1989–92. –/70 1T. 38.5 t.
**DMSL.** Lot No. 31052 BREL Derby 1989–92. –/72 1T. 38.5 t.

| 159 101 | (158 800) | **ST** | P | *SW* | SA | 52800 | 58717 | 57800 |
| 159 102 | (158 803) | **ST** | P | *SW* | SA | 52803 | 58703 | 57803 |
| 159 103 | (158 804) | **ST** | P | *SW* | SA | 52804 | 58704 | 57804 |
| 159 104 | (158 805) | **ST** | P | *SW* | SA | 52805 | 58705 | 57805 |
| 159 105 | (158 807) | **ST** | P | *SW* | SA | 52807 | 58707 | 57807 |
| 159 106 | (158 809) | **ST** | P | *SW* | SA | 52809 | 58709 | 57809 |
| 159 107 | (158 811) | **ST** | P | *SW* | SA | 52811 | 58711 | 57811 |
| 159 108 | (158 801) | **ST** | P | *SW* | SA | 52801 | 58701 | 57801 |

## CLASS 165/0      NETWORK TURBO               BREL

DMSL–DMS and DMSL–MS–DMS. Chiltern Railways units. Refurbished 2003–05 with First Class seats removed and air conditioning fitted.

**Construction:** Welded aluminium.
**Engines:** One Perkins 2006-TWH of 260 kW (350 hp) at 2100 rpm.
**Bogies:** BREL P3-17 (powered), BREL T3-17 (non-powered).
**Couplers:** BSI.
**Dimensions:** 23.50/23.25 x 2.81 m.
**Gangways:** Within unit only.          **Wheel Arrangement:** 2-B (+ B-2) + B-2.
**Doors:** Twin-leaf swing plug.          **Maximum Speed:** 75 mph.
**Seating Layout:** 2+2/3+2 facing/unidirectional.
**Multiple Working:** Within class and with Classes 166, 168, 170 and 172.

Fitted with tripcocks for working over London Underground tracks between Harrow-on-the-Hill and Amersham.

**58801–822/58873–878. DMSL.** Lot No. 31087 BREL York 1990. –/77(+7) 1TD 2W. 42.1 t.
**58823–833. DMSL.** Lot No. 31089 BREL York 1991–92. –/77(+7) 1TD 2W. 40.1 t.
**MS.** Lot No. 31090 BREL York 1991–92. –/106. 37.0 t.
**DMS.** Lot No. 31088 BREL York 1991–92. –/94. 41.5 t.

| | | | | | | | |
|---|---|---|---|---|---|---|---|
| 165 001 | **CR** | A | *CR* | AL | 58801 | | 58834 |
| 165 002 | **CR** | A | *CR* | AL | 58802 | | 58835 |
| 165 003 | **CR** | A | *CR* | AL | 58803 | | 58836 |
| 165 004 | **CR** | A | *CR* | AL | 58804 | | 58837 |
| 165 005 | **CR** | A | *CR* | AL | 58805 | | 58838 |
| 165 006 | **CR** | A | *CR* | AL | 58806 | | 58839 |
| 165 007 | **CR** | A | *CR* | AL | 58807 | | 58840 |
| 165 008 | **CR** | A | *CR* | AL | 58808 | | 58841 |
| 165 009 | **CR** | A | *CR* | AL | 58809 | | 58842 |
| 165 010 | **CR** | A | *CR* | AL | 58810 | | 58843 |
| 165 011 | **CR** | A | *CR* | AL | 58811 | | 58844 |
| 165 012 | **CR** | A | *CR* | AL | 58812 | | 58845 |
| 165 013 | **CR** | A | *CR* | AL | 58813 | | 58846 |
| 165 014 | **CR** | A | *CR* | AL | 58814 | | 58847 |
| 165 015 | **CR** | A | *CR* | AL | 58815 | | 58848 |
| 165 016 | **CR** | A | *CR* | AL | 58816 | | 58849 |
| 165 017 | **CR** | A | *CR* | AL | 58817 | | 58850 |
| 165 018 | **CR** | A | *CR* | AL | 58818 | | 58851 |
| 165 019 | **CR** | A | *CR* | AL | 58819 | | 58852 |
| 165 020 | **CR** | A | *CR* | AL | 58820 | | 58853 |
| 165 021 | **CR** | A | *CR* | AL | 58821 | | 58854 |
| 165 022 | **CR** | A | *CR* | AL | 58822 | | 58855 |
| 165 023 | **CR** | A | *CR* | AL | 58873 | | 58867 |
| 165 024 | **CR** | A | *CR* | AL | 58874 | | 58868 |
| 165 025 | **CR** | A | *CR* | AL | 58875 | | 58869 |
| 165 026 | **CR** | A | *CR* | AL | 58876 | | 58870 |
| 165 027 | **CR** | A | *CR* | AL | 58877 | | 58871 |
| 165 028 | **CR** | A | *CR* | AL | 58878 | | 58872 |
| 165 029 | **CR** | A | *CR* | AL | 58823 | 55404 | 58856 |
| 165 030 | **CR** | A | *CR* | AL | 58824 | 55405 | 58857 |
| 165 031 | **CR** | A | *CR* | AL | 58825 | 55406 | 58858 |
| 165 032 | **CR** | A | *CR* | AL | 58826 | 55407 | 58859 |
| 165 033 | **CR** | A | *CR* | AL | 58827 | 55408 | 58860 |
| 165 034 | **CR** | A | *CR* | AL | 58828 | 55409 | 58861 |
| 165 035 | **CR** | A | *CR* | AL | 58829 | 55410 | 58862 |
| 165 036 | **CR** | A | *CR* | AL | 58830 | 55411 | 58863 |
| 165 037 | **CR** | A | *CR* | AL | 58831 | 55412 | 58864 |
| 165 038 | **CR** | A | *CR* | AL | 58832 | 55413 | 58865 |
| 165 039 | **CR** | A | *CR* | AL | 58833 | 55414 | 58866 |

# CLASS 165/1    NETWORK TURBO     BREL

Great Western Railway units. DMSL–MS–DMS or DMSL–DMS. In 2015 GWR removed First Class from all its Class 165s, it was later reinstated on the 3-car units. Air cooling equipment fitted.

**Construction:** Welded aluminium.
**Engines:** One Perkins 2006-TWH of 260 kW (350 hp) at 2100 rpm.
**Bogies:** BREL P3-17 (powered), BREL T3-17 (non-powered).
**Couplers:** BSI.
**Dimensions:** 23.50/23.25 x 2.81 m.
**Gangways:** Within unit only.     **Wheel Arrangement:** 2-B (+ B-2) + B-2.
**Doors:** Twin-leaf swing plug.     **Maximum Speed:** 90 mph.
**Seating Layout:** 3+2/2+2 facing/unidirectional.
**Multiple Working:** Within class and with Classes 166, 168, 170 and 172.

**58953–969. DMSL.** Lot No. 31098 BREL York 1992. 16/51 1TD 2W. 40.8 t.
**58879–898. DMSL.** Lot No. 31096 BREL York 1992. –/73 1TD 2W. 40.8 t.
**MS.** Lot No. 31099 BREL 1992. –/106. 38.1 t.
**DMS.** Lot No. 31097 BREL 1992. –/84. 37.0 t.

| | | | | | | |
|---|---|---|---|---|---|---|
| 165 101 | **GW** | A | *GW* | RG | 58953 | 55415 | 58916 |
| 165 102 | **GW** | A | *GW* | RG | 58954 | 55416 | 58917 |
| 165 103 | **GW** | A | *GW* | RG | 58955 | 55417 | 58918 |
| 165 104 | **GW** | A | *GW* | RG | 58956 | 55418 | 58919 |
| 165 105 | **GW** | A | *GW* | RG | 58957 | 55419 | 58920 |
| 165 106 | **GW** | A | *GW* | RG | 58958 | 55420 | 58921 |
| 165 107 | **GW** | A | *GW* | RG | 58959 | 55421 | 58922 |
| 165 108 | **GW** | A | *GW* | RG | 58960 | 55422 | 58923 |
| 165 109 | **GW** | A | *GW* | RG | 58961 | 55423 | 58924 |
| 165 110 | **GW** | A | *GW* | RG | 58962 | 55424 | 58925 |
| 165 111 | **GW** | A | *GW* | RG | 58963 | 55425 | 58926 |
| 165 112 | **GW** | A | *GW* | RG | 58964 | 55426 | 58927 |
| 165 113 | **GW** | A | *GW* | RG | 58965 | 55427 | 58928 |
| 165 114 | **GW** | A | *GW* | RG | 58966 | 55428 | 58929 |
| 165 116 | **GW** | A | *GW* | RG | 58968 | 55430 | 58931 |
| 165 117 | **GW** | A | *GW* | RG | 58969 | 55431 | 58932 |
| 165 118 | **GW** | A | *GW* | RG | 58879 | | 58933 |
| 165 119 | **GW** | A | *GW* | RG | 58880 | | 58934 |
| 165 120 | **GW** | A | *GW* | RG | 58881 | | 58935 |
| 165 121 | **GW** | A | *GW* | RG | 58882 | | 58936 |
| 165 122 | **GW** | A | *GW* | RG | 58883 | | 58937 |
| 165 123 | **GW** | A | *GW* | RG | 58884 | | 58938 |
| 165 124 | **GW** | A | *GW* | RG | 58885 | | 58939 |
| 165 125 | **GW** | A | *GW* | RG | 58886 | | 58940 |
| 165 126 | **GW** | A | *GW* | RG | 58887 | | 58941 |
| 165 127 | **GW** | A | *GW* | RG | 58888 | | 58942 |
| 165 128 | **GW** | A | *GW* | PM | 58889 | | 58943 |
| 165 129 | **GW** | A | *GW* | PM | 58890 | | 58944 |
| 165 130 | **GW** | A | *GW* | PM | 58891 | | 58945 |
| 165 131 | **GW** | A | *GW* | PM | 58892 | | 58946 |
| 165 132 | **GW** | A | *GW* | PM | 58893 | | 58947 |

| 165 133 | **GW** | A | *GW* | PM | 58894 | 58948 |
| 165 134 | **GW** | A | *GW* | PM | 58895 | 58949 |
| 165 135 | **GW** | A | *GW* | PM | 58896 | 58950 |
| 165 136 | **GW** | A | *GW* | PM | 58897 | 58951 |
| 165 137 | **GW** | A | *GW* | PM | 58898 | 58952 |

## CLASS 166      NETWORK EXPRESS TURBO      ABB

DMCL–MS–DMSL. Great Western Railway units, built for Paddington–Oxford/Newbury services. Air conditioned and with additional luggage space compared to the Class 165s. The DMSL vehicles have had their 16 First Class seats declassified.

**Construction:** Welded aluminium.
**Engines:** One Perkins 2006-TWH of 260 kW (350 hp) at 2100 rpm.
**Bogies:** BREL P3-17 (powered), BREL T3-17 (non-powered).
**Couplers:** BSI.
**Dimensions:** 23.50 x 2.81 m.
**Gangways:** Within unit only.        **Wheel Arrangement:** 2-B + B-2 + B-2.
**Doors:** Twin-leaf swing plug.        **Maximum Speed:** 90 mph.
**Seating Layout:** 1: 2+2 facing, 2: 2+2/3+2 facing/unidirectional.
**Multiple Working:** Within class and with Classes 165, 168, 170 and 172.

**DMCL.** Lot No. 31116 ABB York 1992–93. 16/53 1TD 2W. 41.2 t.
**MS.** Lot No. 31117 ABB York 1992–93. –/91. 39.9 t.
**DMSL.** Lot No. 31116 ABB York 1992–93. –/84 1T. 39.6 t.

| 166 201 | **FB** | A | *GW* | PM | 58101 | 58601 | 58122 |
| 166 202 | **FB** | A | *GW* | PM | 58102 | 58602 | 58123 |
| 166 203 | **FB** | A | *GW* | PM | 58103 | 58603 | 58124 |
| 166 204 | **GW** | A | *GW* | PM | 58104 | 58604 | 58125 |
| 166 205 | **GW** | A | *GW* | PM | 58105 | 58605 | 58126 |
| 166 206 | **GW** | A | *GW* | PM | 58106 | 58606 | 58127 |
| 166 207 | **FB** | A | *GW* | PM | 58107 | 58607 | 58128 |
| 166 208 | **GW** | A | *GW* | PM | 58108 | 58608 | 58129 |
| 166 209 | **FB** | A | *GW* | PM | 58109 | 58609 | 58130 |
| 166 210 | **GW** | A | *GW* | PM | 58110 | 58610 | 58131 |
| 166 211 | **FB** | A | *GW* | PM | 58111 | 58611 | 58132 |
| 166 212 | **GW** | A | *GW* | PM | 58112 | 58612 | 58133 |
| 166 213 | **GW** | A | *GW* | PM | 58113 | 58613 | 58134 |
| 166 214 | **GW** | A | *GW* | PM | 58114 | 58614 | 58135 |
| 166 215 | **FB** | A | *GW* | PM | 58115 | 58615 | 58136 |
| 166 216 | **GW** | A | *GW* | PM | 58116 | 58616 | 58137 |
| 166 217 | **GW** | A | *GW* | PM | 58117 | 58617 | 58138 |
| 166 218 | **GW** | A | *GW* | PM | 58118 | 58618 | 58139 |
| 166 219 | **GW** | A | *GW* | PM | 58119 | 58619 | 58140 |
| 166 220 | **GW** | A | *GW* | PM | 58120 | 58620 | 58141 |
| 166 221 | **FB** | A | *GW* | PM | 58121 | 58621 | 58142 |

**Names:**

| 166 204 | Norman Topsom MBE |
| 166 220 | Roger Watkins THE GWR MASTER TRAIN PLANNER |
| 166 221 | Reading Train Care Depot/READING TRAIN CARE DEPOT *(alt sides)* |

# CLASS 168   CLUBMAN   ADTRANZ/BOMBARDIER

Air conditioned.

**Construction:** Welded aluminium bodies with bolt-on steel ends.
**Engines:** One MTU 6R183TD13H of 315 kW (422 hp) at 1900 rpm.
**Transmission:** Hydraulic. Voith T211rzze to ZF final drive.
**Bogies:** One Adtranz P3–23 and one BREL T3–23 per car.
**Couplers:** BSI at outer ends, bar within unit.
**Dimensions:** Class 168/0: 24.10/23.61 x 2.69 m. Others: 23.62/23.61 x 2.69 m.
**Gangways:** Within unit only.   **Wheel Arrangement:** 2-B (+ B-2 + B-2) + B-2.
**Doors:** Twin-leaf swing plug.   **Maximum Speed:** 100 mph.
**Seating Layout:** 2+2 facing/unidirectional.
**Multiple Working:** Within class and with Classes 165 and 166.

Fitted with tripcocks for working over London Underground tracks between Harrow-on-the-Hill and Amersham.

**Class 168/0.** Original Design. DMSL(A)–MS–MSL–DMSL(B) or DMSL(A)–MSL–MS–DMSL(B).

58451–455 were numbered 58656–660 for a time when used in 168 106–110.

**58151–155. DMSL(A).** Adtranz Derby 1997–98. –/57 1TD 1W. 44.0 t.
**58651–655. MSL.** Adtranz Derby 1998. –/73 1T. 41.0 t.
**58451–455. MS.** Adtranz Derby 1998. –/77. 41.0 t.
**58251–255. DMSL(B).** Adtranz Derby 1998. –/68 1T. 43.6 t.

| | | | | | | | |
|---|---|---|---|---|---|---|---|
| 168 001 | **CL** | P | *CR* | AL | 58151 | 58651 | 58451 | 58251 |
| 168 002 | **CL** | P | *CR* | AL | 58152 | 58652 | 58452 | 58252 |
| 168 003 | **CL** | P | *CR* | AL | 58153 | 58653 | 58453 | 58253 |
| 168 004 | **CL** | P | *CR* | AL | 58154 | 58654 | 58454 | 58254 |
| 168 005 | **CL** | P | *CR* | AL | 58155 | 58655 | 58455 | 58255 |

**Class 168/1.** These units are effectively Class 170s. DMSL(A)–MSL–MS–DMSL(B) or DMSL(A)–MS–DMSL(B).

58461–463 have been renumbered from 58661–663.

**58156–163. DMSL(A).** Adtranz Derby 2000. –/57 1TD 2W. 45.2 t.
**58456–460. MS.** Bombardier Derby 2002. –/76. 41.8 t.
**58756–757. MSL.** Bombardier Derby 2002. –/73 1T. 42.9 t.
**58461–463. MS.** Adtranz Derby 2000. –/76. 42.4 t.
**58256–263. DMSL(B).** Adtranz Derby 2000. –/69 1T. 45.2 t.

| | | | | | | | |
|---|---|---|---|---|---|---|---|
| 168 106 | **CL** | P | *CR* | AL | 58156 | 58756 | 58456 | 58256 |
| 168 107 | **CL** | P | *CR* | AL | 58157 | 58757 | 58457 | 58257 |
| 168 108 | **CL** | P | *CR* | AL | 58158 | | 58458 | 58258 |
| 168 109 | **CL** | P | *CR* | AL | 58159 | | 58459 | 58259 |
| 168 110 | **CL** | P | *CR* | AL | 58160 | | 58460 | 58260 |
| 168 111 | **CL** | E | *CR* | AL | 58161 | | 58461 | 58261 |
| 168 112 | **CL** | E | *CR* | AL | 58162 | | 58462 | 58262 |
| 168 113 | **CL** | E | *CR* | AL | 58163 | | 58463 | 58263 |

**Class 168/2.** These units are effectively Class 170s. DMSL(A)–(MS)–MS–DMSL(B).

**58164–169. DMSL(A).** Bombardier Derby 2003–04. –/57 1TD 2W. 45.4 t.
**58365–367. MS.** Bombardier Derby 2006. –/76. 43.3 t.
**58464/468/469. MS.** Bombardier Derby 2003–04. –/76. 44.0 t.
**58465–467. MS.** Bombardier Derby 2006. –/76. 43.3 t.
**58264–269. DMSL(B).** Bombardier Derby 2003–04. –/69 1T. 45.5 t.

| 168 214 | **CL** | P | *CR* | AL | 58164 |       | 58464 | 58264 |
| 168 215 | **CL** | P | *CR* | AL | 58165 | 58365 | 58465 | 58265 |
| 168 216 | **CL** | P | *CR* | AL | 58166 | 58366 | 58466 | 58266 |
| 168 217 | **CL** | P | *CR* | AL | 58167 | 58367 | 58467 | 58267 |
| 168 218 | **CL** | P | *CR* | AL | 58168 |       | 58468 | 58268 |
| 168 219 | **CL** | P | *CR* | AL | 58169 |       | 58469 | 58269 |

**Class 168/3.** Former South West Trains/TransPennine Express Class 170s taken on by Chiltern Railways in 2015–16 and renumbered in the 168 3xx series. 170 309 was originally numbered 170 399. DMSL(A)–DMSL(B).

**50301–308/399. DMCL.** Adtranz Derby 2000–01. –/59 1TD 2W. 45.8 t.
**79301–308/399. DMSL.** Adtranz Derby 2000–01. –/69 1T. 45.8 t.

| 168 321 | (170 301) | **CL** | P | *CR* | AL | 50301 | 79301 |
| 168 322 | (170 302) | **CL** | P | *CR* | AL | 50302 | 79302 |
| 168 323 | (170 303) | **CL** | P | *CR* | AL | 50303 | 79303 |
| 168 324 | (170 304) | **CL** | P | *CR* | AL | 50304 | 79304 |
| 168 325 | (170 305) | **CL** | P | *CR* | AL | 50305 | 79305 |
| 168 326 | (170 306) | **CL** | P | *CR* | AL | 50306 | 79306 |
| 168 327 | (170 307) | **CL** | P | *CR* | AL | 50307 | 79307 |
| 168 328 | (170 308) | **CL** | P | *CR* | AL | 50308 | 79308 |
| 168 329 | (170 309) | **CL** | P | *CR* | AL | 50399 | 79399 |

# CLASS 170   TURBOSTAR ADTRANZ/BOMBARDIER

Various formations. Air conditioned.

**Construction:** Welded aluminium bodies with bolt-on steel ends.
**Engines:** One MTU 6R183TD13H of 315 kW (422 hp) at 1900 rpm.
**Transmission:** Hydraulic. Voith T211rzze to ZF final drive.
**Bogies:** One Adtranz P3–23 and one BREL T3–23 per car.
**Couplers:** BSI at outer ends, bar within later build units.
**Dimensions:** 23.62/23.61 x 2.69 m.
**Gangways:** Within unit only.          **Wheel Arrangement:** 2-B (+ B-2) + B-2.
**Doors:** Twin-leaf sliding plug.        **Maximum Speed:** 100 mph.
**Seating Layout:** 1: 2+1 facing/unidirectional. 2: 2+2 unidirectional/facing.
**Multiple Working:** Within class and with Classes 150, 153, 155, 156, 158, 159 and 172.

**Class 170/1. CrossCountry (former Midland Mainline) units.** Lazareni seating. DMSL–MS–DMCL/DMSL–DMCL.

**DMSL.** Adtranz Derby 1998–99. –/59 1TD 2W. 45.0 t.
**MS.** Adtranz Derby 2001. –/80. 43.0 t.
**DMCL.** Adtranz Derby 1998–99. 9/52 1T. 44.8 t

| 170 101 | **XC** | P | *XC* | TS | 50101 | 55101 | 79101 |
|---------|--------|---|------|-----|-------|-------|-------|
| 170 102 | **XC** | P | *XC* | TS | 50102 | 55102 | 79102 |
| 170 103 | **XC** | P | *XC* | TS | 50103 | 55103 | 79103 |
| 170 104 | **XC** | P | *XC* | TS | 50104 | 55104 | 79104 |
| 170 105 | **XC** | P | *XC* | TS | 50105 | 55105 | 79105 |
| 170 106 | **XC** | P | *XC* | TS | 50106 | 55106 | 79106 |
| 170 107 | **XC** | P | *XC* | TS | 50107 | 55107 | 79107 |
| 170 108 | **XC** | P | *XC* | TS | 50108 | 55108 | 79108 |
| 170 109 | **XC** | P | *XC* | TS | 50109 | 55109 | 79109 |
| 170 110 | **XC** | P | *XC* | TS | 50110 | 55110 | 79110 |
| 170 111 | **XC** | P | *XC* | TS | 50111 |       | 79111 |
| 170 112 | **XC** | P | *XC* | TS | 50112 |       | 79112 |
| 170 113 | **XC** | P | *XC* | TS | 50113 |       | 79113 |
| 170 114 | **XC** | P | *XC* | TS | 50114 |       | 79114 |
| 170 115 | **XC** | P | *XC* | TS | 50115 |       | 79115 |
| 170 116 | **XC** | P | *XC* | TS | 50116 |       | 79116 |
| 170 117 | **XC** | P | *XC* | TS | 50117 |       | 79117 |

**Class 170/2. Transport for Wales 3-car units.** Previously operated by Greater Anglia. Chapman seating. DMCL–MSL–DMSL.

**DMCL.** Adtranz Derby 1999. 7/39 1TD 2W. 44.3 t.
**MSL.** Adtranz Derby 1999. –/74 1T. 42.8 t.
**DMSL.** Adtranz Derby 1999. –/66 1T. 44.8 t.

| 170 201 | **GA** | P | *TW* | CF | 50201 | 56201 | 79201 |
|---------|--------|---|------|-----|-------|-------|-------|
| 170 202 | **GA** | P | *TW* | CF | 50202 | 56202 | 79202 |
| 170 203 | **GA** | P | *TW* | CF | 50203 | 56203 | 79203 |
| 170 204 | **GA** | P | *TW* | CF | 50204 | 56204 | 79204 |
| 170 205 | **GA** | P | *TW* | CF | 50205 | 56205 | 79205 |
| 170 206 | **GA** | P | *TW* | CF | 50206 | 56206 | 79206 |
| 170 207 | **GA** | P | *TW* | CF | 50207 | 56207 | 79207 |
| 170 208 | **GA** | P | *TW* | CF | 50208 | 56208 | 79208 |

**Class 170/2. Transport for Wales 2-car units.** Previously operated by Greater Anglia. Chapman seating. DMSL–DMCL.

**DMSL.** Bombardier Derby 2002. –/57 1TD 2W. 45.7 t.
**DMCL.** Bombardier Derby 2002. 9/53 1T. 45.7 t.

| 170 270 | **GA** | P | *TW* | CF | 50270 | 79270 |
|---------|--------|---|------|-----|-------|-------|
| 170 271 | **GA** | P | *TW* | CF | 50271 | 79271 |
| 170 272 | **GA** | P | *TW* | CF | 50272 | 79272 |
| 170 273 | **GA** | P | *TW* | CF | 50273 | 79273 |

**Class 170/3. Units built for Hull Trains, now used by ScotRail.** Chapman seating. DMSL–MSL–DMSL.

**DMSL(A).** Bombardier Derby 2004. –/55 1TD 2W. 46.5 t.
**MSL.** Bombardier Derby 2004. –/71 1T. 44.7 t.
**DMSL(B).** Bombardier Derby 2004. –/67 1T. 47.0 t.

| 170 393 | **SR** | P | *SR* | HA | 50393 | 56393 | 79393 |
|---------|--------|---|------|-----|-------|-------|-------|
| 170 394 | **SR** | P | *SR* | HA | 50394 | 56394 | 79394 |
| 170 395 | **SR** | P | *SR* | HA | 50395 | 56395 | 79395 |
| 170 396 | **SR** | P | *SR* | HA | 50396 | 56396 | 79396 |

**Class 170/3. CrossCountry units.** Lazareni seating. DMSL–MS–DMCL.

**DMSL.** Bombardier Derby 2002. –/59 1TD 2W. 45.4 t.
**MS.** Bombardier Derby 2002. –/80. 43.0 t.
**DMCL.** Bombardier Derby 2002. 9/52 1T. 45.8 t.

| | | | | | | | | |
|---|---|---|---|---|---|---|---|---|
| 170 397 | **XC** | P | *XC* | TS | 50397 | 56397 | 79397 | |
| 170 398 | **XC** | P | *XC* | TS | 50398 | 56398 | 79398 | |

**Class 170/4. ScotRail and East Midlands Railway units.** Chapman seating. DMCL–MS–DMCL.

**Advertising livery:** 170 407 BTP text number 61016 (blue).

**DMCL(A).** Adtranz Derby 1999–2001. 9/43 1TD 2W. 45.2 t.
**MS.** Adtranz Derby 1999–2001. –/76. 42.5 t.
**DMCL(B).** Adtranz Derby 1999–2001. 9/49 1T. 45.2 t.

| | | | | | | | | |
|---|---|---|---|---|---|---|---|---|
| 170 401 | **SR** | P | *SR* | HA | 50401 | 56401 | 79401 | |
| 170 402 | **SR** | P | *SR* | HA | 50402 | 56402 | 79402 | |
| 170 403 | **SR** | P | *SR* | HA | 50403 | 56403 | 79403 | |
| 170 404 | **SR** | P | *SR* | HA | 50404 | 56404 | 79404 | |
| 170 405 | **SR** | P | *SR* | HA | 50405 | 56405 | 79405 | |
| 170 406 | **SR** | P | *SR* | HA | 50406 | 56406 | 79406 | |
| 170 407 | **AL** | P | *SR* | HA | 50407 | 56407 | 79407 | |
| 170 408 | **SR** | P | *SR* | HA | 50408 | 56408 | 79408 | |
| 170 409 | **SR** | P | *SR* | HA | 50409 | 56409 | 79409 | |
| 170 410 | **SR** | P | *SR* | HA | 50410 | 56410 | 79410 | |
| 170 411 | **SR** | P | *SR* | HA | 50411 | 56411 | 79411 | |
| 170 412 | **SR** | P | *SR* | HA | 50412 | 56412 | 79412 | |
| 170 413 | **SR** | P | *SR* | HA | 50413 | 56413 | 79413 | |
| 170 414 | **SR** | P | *SR* | HA | 50414 | 56414 | 79414 | |
| 170 415 | **SR** | P | *SR* | HA | 50415 | 56415 | 79415 | |
| 170 416 | **ER** | E | *EM* | DY | 50416 | 56416 | 79416 | |
| 170 417 | **ER** | E | *EM* | DY | 50417 | 56417 | 79417 | The Key Worker |
| 170 418 | **ER** | E | *EM* | DY | 50418 | 56418 | 79418 | |
| 170 419 | **ER** | E | *EM* | DY | 50419 | 56419 | 79419 | |
| 170 420 | **ER** | E | *EM* | DY | 50420 | 56420 | 79420 | |

**Class 170/4. ScotRail units.** Chapman seating. DMCL–MS–DMCL.

**DMCL.** Bombardier Derby 2003–05. 9/43 1TD 2W. 46.8 t.
**MS.** Bombardier Derby 2003–05. –/76. 43.7 t.
**DMCL.** Bombardier Derby 2003–05. 9/49 1T. 46.5 t.

| | | | | | | | |
|---|---|---|---|---|---|---|---|
| 170 425 | **SR** | P | *SR* | HA | 50425 | 56425 | 79425 |
| 170 426 | **SR** | P | *SR* | HA | 50426 | 56426 | 79426 |
| 170 427 | **SR** | P | *SR* | HA | 50427 | 56427 | 79427 |
| 170 428 | **SR** | P | *SR* | HA | 50428 | 56428 | 79428 |
| 170 429 | **SR** | P | *SR* | HA | 50429 | 56429 | 79429 |
| 170 430 | **SR** | P | *SR* | HA | 50430 | 56430 | 79430 |
| 170 431 | **SR** | P | *SR* | HA | 50431 | 56431 | 79431 |
| 170 432 | **SR** | P | *SR* | HA | 50432 | 56432 | 79432 |
| 170 433 | **SR** | P | *SR* | HA | 50433 | 56433 | 79433 |
| 170 434 | **SR** | P | *SR* | HA | 50434 | 56434 | 79434 |

**Class 170/4. ScotRail and Northern units.** Originally built as Standard Class only. 170 450–457 were retro-fitted with First Class but those used by Northern are now Standard Class only. Chapman seating. DMSL–MS–DMSL or † DMCL–MS–DMCL.

**DMSL/DMCL.** Bombardier Derby 2004–05. –/55 1TD 2W († 9/47 1TD 2W). 46.3 t.
**MS.** Bombardier Derby 2004–05. –/76. 43.4 t.
**DMSL/DMCL.** Bombardier Derby 2004–05. –/67 1T († 9/49 1T 1W). 46.4 t.

| | | | | | | | |
|---|---|---|---|---|---|---|---|
| 170 450 | † | **SR** | P | *SR* | HA | 50450 | 56450 | 79450 |
| 170 451 | † | **SR** | P | *SR* | HA | 50451 | 56451 | 79451 |
| 170 452 | † | **SR** | P | *SR* | HA | 50452 | 56452 | 79452 |
| 170 453 | † | **NR** | P | *NO* | NL | 50453 | 56453 | 79453 |
| 170 454 | † | **NR** | P | *NO* | NL | 50454 | 56454 | 79454 |
| 170 455 | † | **NR** | P | *NO* | NL | 50455 | 56455 | 79455 |
| 170 456 | † | **NR** | P | *NO* | NL | 50456 | 56456 | 79456 |
| 170 457 | † | **NR** | P | *NO* | NL | 50457 | 56457 | 79457 |
| 170 458 | | **NR** | P | *NO* | NL | 50458 | 56458 | 79458 |
| 170 459 | | **NR** | P | *NO* | NL | 50459 | 56459 | 79459 |
| 170 460 | | **NR** | P | *NO* | NL | 50460 | 56460 | 79460 |
| 170 461 | | **NR** | P | *NO* | NL | 50461 | 56461 | 79461 |

**Class 170/4. ScotRail and Northern units.** Standard Class only units. Chapman seating. DMSL–MS–DMSL.

**50470–471. DMSL(A).** Adtranz Derby 2001. –/55 1TD 2W. 45.1 t.
**50472–478. DMSL(A).** Bombardier Derby 2004–05. –/57 1TD 2W. 45.8 t.
**56470–471. MS.** Adtranz Derby 2001. –/76. 42.4 t.
**56472–478. MS.** Bombardier Derby 2004–05. –/76. 43.0 t.
**79470–471. DMSL(B).** Adtranz Derby 2001. –/67 1T. 45.1 t.
**79472–478. DMSL(B).** Bombardier Derby 2004–05. –/67 1T. 45.8 t.

| | | | | | | | |
|---|---|---|---|---|---|---|---|
| 170 470 | **SR** | P | *SR* | HA | 50470 | 56470 | 79470 |
| 170 471 | **SR** | P | *SR* | HA | 50471 | 56471 | 79471 |
| 170 472 | **NR** | P | *NO* | NL | 50472 | 56472 | 79472 |
| 170 473 | **NR** | P | *NO* | NL | 50473 | 56473 | 79473 |
| 170 474 | **NR** | P | *NO* | NL | 50474 | 56474 | 79474 |
| 170 475 | **NR** | P | *NO* | NL | 50475 | 56475 | 79475 |
| 170 476 | **NR** | P | *NO* | NL | 50476 | 56476 | 79476 |
| 170 477 | **NR** | P | *NO* | NL | 50477 | 56477 | 79477 |
| 170 478 | **NR** | P | *NO* | NL | 50478 | 56478 | 79478 |

**Class 170/5. West Midlands Trains 2-car units.** Lazareni seating. DMSL–DMSL.

170 530–535 were reduced from 3-car units to 2-car units in 2020 prior to their transfer to East Midlands Railway in 2021.

**DMSL(A).** Adtranz Derby 1999–2000. –/55 1TD 2W. 45.8 t.
**DMSL(B).** Adtranz Derby 1999–2000. –/67 1T. 45.9 t.

| | | | | | | |
|---|---|---|---|---|---|---|
| 170 501 | **WI** | P | *WM* | TS | 50501 | 79501 |
| 170 502 | **WI** | P | *WM* | TS | 50502 | 79502 |
| 170 503 | **WI** | P | *WM* | TS | 50503 | 79503 |
| 170 504 | **WI** | P | *WM* | TS | 50504 | 79504 |
| 170 505 | **WI** | P | *WM* | TS | 50505 | 79505 |

| 170 506 | **WI** | P | *WM* | TS | 50506 | 79506 |
| 170 507 | **WI** | P | *WM* | TS | 50507 | 79507 |
| 170 508 | **WI** | P | *WM* | TS | 50508 | 79508 |
| 170 509 | **WI** | P | *WM* | TS | 50509 | 79509 |
| 170 510 | **WI** | P | *WM* | TS | 50510 | 79510 |
| 170 511 | **WI** | P | *WM* | TS | 50511 | 79511 |
| 170 512 | **WI** | P | *WM* | TS | 50512 | 79512 |
| 170 513 | **WI** | P | *WM* | TS | 50513 | 79513 |
| 170 514 | **WI** | P | *WM* | TS | 50514 | 79514 |
| 170 515 | **WI** | P | *WM* | TS | 50515 | 79515 |
| 170 516 | **WI** | P | *WM* | TS | 50516 | 79516 |
| 170 517 | **WI** | P | *WM* | TS | 50517 | 79517 |

| 170 530 | (170 630) | **WI** | P | *WM* | TS | 50630 | 79630 |
| 170 531 | (170 631) | **WI** | P | *WM* | TS | 50631 | 79631 |
| 170 532 | (170 632) | **WI** | P | *WM* | TS | 50632 | 79632 |
| 170 533 | (170 633) | **WI** | P | *WM* | TS | 50633 | 79633 |
| 170 534 | (170 634) | **WI** | P | *WM* | TS | 50634 | 79634 |
| 170 535 | (170 635) | **WI** | P | *WM* | TS | 50635 | 79635 |

**Class 170/6. CrossCountry 3-car units.** Lazareni seating. DMSL–MS–DMCL.

170 618–623 were augmented from 2-car to 3-car in late 2020/early 2021 using centre cars from 170 630–635, having been built as 2-car units 170 518–523.

**DMSL.** Adtranz Derby 2000. –/59 1TD 2W. 45.8 t.
**MS.** Adtranz Derby 2000. –/80. 42.4 t.
**DMCL.** Adtranz Derby 2000. 9/52 1T. 45.9 t.

| 170 618 | (170 518) | **XC** | P | *XC* | TS | 50518 | 56630 | 79518 |
| 170 619 | (170 519) | **XC** | P | *XC* | TS | 50519 | 56631 | 79519 |
| 170 620 | (170 520) | **XC** | P | *XC* | TS | 50520 | 56632 | 79520 |
| 170 621 | (170 521) | **XC** | P | *XC* | TS | 50521 | 56633 | 79521 |
| 170 622 | (170 522) | **XC** | P | *XC* | TS | 50522 | 56634 | 79522 |
| 170 623 | (170 523) | **XC** | P | *XC* | TS | 50523 | 56635 | 79523 |

| 170 636 | **XC** | P | *XC* | TS | 50636 | 56636 | 79636 |
| 170 637 | **XC** | P | *XC* | TS | 50637 | 56637 | 79637 |
| 170 638 | **XC** | P | *XC* | TS | 50638 | 56638 | 79638 |
| 170 639 | **XC** | P | *XC* | TS | 50639 | 56639 | 79639 |

# CLASS 171          TURBOSTAR          BOMBARDIER

DMCL–DMSL or DMCL–MS–MS–DMCL. Southern units. Air conditioned. Chapman seating.

**Construction:** Welded aluminium bodies with bolt-on steel ends.
**Engines:** One MTU 6R183TD13H of 315 kW (422 hp) at 1900 rpm.
**Transmission:** Hydraulic. Voith T211rzze to ZF final drive.
**Bogies:** One Adtranz P3–23 and one BREL T3–23 per car.
**Couplers:** Dellner 12 at outer ends, bar within unit (Class 171/8).

▲ West Midlands Railway-liveried Parry People Mover 139 001 arrives at Stourbridge Junction with the 10.30 from Stourbridge Town on 18/06/19. **John Binch**

▼ In Arriva Trains livery with TfW vinyls, 142 069 and 143 623 stand at Cardiff Central after arrival with the 11.42 from Bridgend on 27/05/19. **Brian Garvin**

▲ Great Western Railway-liveried 143 611 and 150 261 run alongside the River Exe at Powderham with the 18.24 Paignton–Exeter St Davids on 23/06/20. **Tony Christie**

▼ Northern-liveried 150 223 calls at Saxilby with the 10.54 Sheffield–Lincoln on 20/04/20. **Robert Pritchard**

▲ Still in London Midland livery, West Midlands Railway Class 153s 153 364 and 153 371 climb the Lickey Incline with a service from Hereford to Birmingham New Street on 21/05/19. **Tony Christie**

▼ Northern-liveried 155 341 and 155 347 head south from Colton Junction with the 10.50 York–Hull on 28/10/19. **Paul Biggs**

▲ In the East Midlands Railway interim livery, 156 405 approaches Saxilby with the 13.01 Doncaster–Lincoln on 27/03/20. **Robert Pritchard**

▼ Transport for Wales-liveried 158 833 passes Wistanstow with the 10.31 Manchester Piccadilly–Milford Haven on 24/07/20. **Paul Biggs**

▲ South Western Railway-liveried 159 013 and 159 004 approach Axminster with the 09.25 Exeter St Davids–London Waterloo on 18/09/20. **Tony Christie**

▼ Great Western Railway-liveried 166 208 stands at Cardiff Central with the 15.30 to Portsmouth Harbour on 07/09/19. **Robert Pritchard**

▲ Chiltern Railways-liveried 168 005 is seen at King's Sutton with the 16.15 London Marylebone–Kidderminster on 13/09/19. **Paul Biggs**

▼ ScotRail-liveried 170 410 passes Dalmeny with the 11.02 Aberdeen–Edinburgh on 12/10/19. **Robert Pritchard**

▲ East Midlands Railway-liveried 170 416 passes Burton Joyce with the 5Z04 11.24 Nottingham–Newark Castle crew training trip on 02/06/20. **Alan Wass**

▼ Southern-liveried 171 402 and 171 801 are seen between Forest Hill and Sydenham with the 17.07 London Bridge–Uckfield on 11/07/18. **Robert Pritchard**

▲ West Midlands Railway-liveried 172 344 arrives at Birmingham Snow Hill with the 18.42 Worcester Foregate Street–Whitlocks End on 20/06/19.
**Robert Pritchard**

▼ Transport for Wales-liveried 175 010 passes Wistanstow with the 09.31 Manchester Piccadilly–Carmarthen on 21/07/20. **Paul Biggs**

▲ Grand Central-liveried 180 104 passes Doncaster with the 12.30 Sunderland–London King's Cross on 18/11/19. **Robert Pritchard**

▼ TransPennine Express-liveried 185 131 passes Rotherham Masborough with the 06.53 Manchester Airport–Cleethorpes on 20/09/19. **Robert Pritchard**

▲ Northern-liveried 195 024 arrives at Saxilby with the 06.35 Sheffield–Lincoln on 02/06/20. **Robert Pritchard**

▼ Brand new West Midlands Railway-liveried 196 101 passes Malvern Link with the 5Z37 14.35 Tyseley–Hereford test run on 23/07/20. **Raymond Coates**

▲ Preserved "Hastings" DEMU 1001 passes Foxton with 1Z30 06.36 Hastings–King's Lynn tour on 21/04/18. **Nigel Gibbs**

▼ CrossCountry-liveried 220 007 and 220 003 leave Sheffield with the 15.39 Newcastle–Bristol Temple Meads on 08/09/20. **Robert Pritchard**

▲ CrossCountry-liveried 221 129 is seen near Burnmouth with the 08.20 Aberdeen–Penzance on 17/09/19. **Robin Ralston**

▼ Transport for Wales-liveried Vivarail-built 230 006 leaves Norton Junction with a 15.41 Moreton-in-Marsh–Kidderminster test run on 20/05/20. These units will operate the Wrexham–Bidston line. **Dave Gommersall**

▲ In East Midlands Railway interim livery, 222 008 approaches Sheffield with the 08.31 from London St Pancras on 09/09/20. **Robert Pritchard**

▼ Network Rail Plasser & Theurer 09-3X-Dynamic Tamper DR 73115 and USP 5000-RT Regulator DR 77905 pass Overton on the ECML with the 08.10 Tyne Yard–York Yard South on 04/09/20. **Ian Beardsley**

▲ Colas Rail Plasser & Theurer 08-16/4x4C100-RT Tamper DR 73925 "Europa" is seen at Crewe on 10/04/19. **Cliff Beeton**

▼ VolkerRail Matisa B 66 UC Tamper DR 75503 "Gill Cowling" passes Saxilby with 6Q69 11.12 Doncaster DCE Sidings–Huntingdon Down Sidings on 14/09/20.
**Robert Pritchard**

▲ VolkerRail Matisa R 24 S Regulator DR 77801 passes Saxilby with the 12.32 Scunthorpe Frodingham–Worksop on 17/04/20. **Robert Pritchard**

▼ Network Rail Loram C44 Rail Grinding Train DR 79501–DR 79507 is seen at Worthing on 27/03/19 after arrival from Paddock Wood. **John Vaughan**

▲ Track Assessment Unit 950 001, built to Class 150/1 design, passes East Midlands Parkway with 2Z02 11.00 Derby RTC–Reading on 29/05/20. **Paul Biggs**

▼ Network Rail Independent Drift Snowplough ADB 965234 is seen on the rear of the 10.53 Derby RTC–York with 37259, 37218 and ADB 965236 (leading) on 20/08/19. **Tony Christie**

**Dimensions:** 23.62/23.61 x 2.69 m.
**Gangways:** Within unit only. **Wheel Arrangement:** 2-B (+ B-2 + B-2) + B-2.
**Doors:** Twin-leaf swing plug. **Maximum Speed:** 100 mph.
**Seating Layout:** 1: 2+1 facing/unidirectional. 2: 2+2 facing/unidirectional.
**Multiple Working:** Within class and with EMU Classes 375 and 377 in an emergency.

**Class 171/2. 2-car units rebuilt from ScotRail Class 170s.** DMCL–DMSL.

Originally built as 3-car units 170 421/423, but renumbered as Class 171 when fitted with Dellner couplers.

**DMCL.** Adtranz Derby 1999–2001. 9/43 1TD 2W. 45.2 t.
**DMSL.** Adtranz Derby 1999–2001. 9/49 1T. 45.2 t.

| | | | | | | |
|---|---|---|---|---|---|---|
| 171 201 | **SN** | E | *SN* | SU | 50421 | 79421 |
| 171 202 | **SN** | E | *SN* | SU | 50423 | 79423 |

**Class 171/4. 4-car units rebuilt from ScotRail Class 170s.** DMCL(A)–MS–MS–DMCL(B).

Reformed and renumbered Class 171s in 2016 using vehicles from ScotRail 3-car Class 170s 170 421–424.

**DMCL(A).** Adtranz Derby 1999–2001. 9/43 1TD 2W. 45.2 t.
**MS.** Adtranz Derby 1999–2001. –/76. 42.5 t.
**DMCL(B).** Adtranz Derby 1999–2001. 9/49 1T. 45.2 t.

| | | | | | | | | |
|---|---|---|---|---|---|---|---|---|
| 171 401 | **SN** | E | *SN* | SU | 50422 | 56421 | 56422 | 79422 |
| 171 402 | **SN** | E | *SN* | SU | 50424 | 56423 | 56424 | 79424 |

**Class 171/7. 2-car units.** DMCL–DMSL.

171 721–726 were built as Class 170s (170 721–726), but renumbered as Class 171 when fitted with Dellner couplers.

171 730 was formerly South West Trains unit 170 392, before transferring to Southern in 2007.

**50721–726. DMCL.** Bombardier Derby 2003. 9/43 1TD 2W. 47.6 t.
**50727–729. DMCL.** Bombardier Derby 2005. 9/43 1TD 2W. 46.3 t.
**50392. DMCL.** Bombardier Derby 2003. 9/43 1TD 2W. 46.6 t.
**79721–726. DMSL.** Bombardier Derby 2003. –/64 1T. 47.8 t.
**79727–729. DMSL.** Bombardier Derby 2005. –/64 1T. 46.2 t.
**79392. DMSL.** Bombardier Derby 2003. –/64 1T. 46.5 t.

| | | | | | | |
|---|---|---|---|---|---|---|
| 171 721 | **SN** | P | *SN* | SU | 50721 | 79721 |
| 171 722 | **SN** | P | *SN* | SU | 50722 | 79722 |
| 171 723 | **SN** | P | *SN* | SU | 50723 | 79723 |
| 171 724 | **SN** | P | *SN* | SU | 50724 | 79724 |
| 171 725 | **SN** | P | *SN* | SU | 50725 | 79725 |
| 171 726 | **SN** | P | *SN* | SU | 50726 | 79726 |
| 171 727 | **SN** | P | *SN* | SU | 50727 | 79727 |
| 171 728 | **SN** | P | *SN* | SU | 50728 | 79728 |
| 171 729 | **SN** | P | *SN* | SU | 50729 | 79729 |
| 171 730 | **SN** | P | *SN* | SU | 50392 | 79392 |

**Class 171/8. 4-car units.** DMCL(A)–MS–MS–DMCL(B).

**DMCL(A).** Bombardier Derby 2004. 9/43 1TD 2W. 46.5 t.
**MS.** Bombardier Derby 2004. –/74. 43.7 t.
**DMCL(B).** Bombardier Derby 2004. 9/50 1T. 46.5 t.

| | | | | | | | | |
|---|---|---|---|---|---|---|---|---|
| 171 801 | **SN** | P | *SN* | SU | 50801 | 54801 | 56801 | 79801 |
| 171 802 | **SN** | P | *SN* | SU | 50802 | 54802 | 56802 | 79802 |
| 171 803 | **SN** | P | *SN* | SU | 50803 | 54803 | 56803 | 79803 |
| 171 804 | **SN** | P | *SN* | SU | 50804 | 54804 | 56804 | 79804 |
| 171 805 | **SN** | P | *SN* | SU | 50805 | 54805 | 56805 | 79805 |
| 171 806 | **SN** | P | *SN* | SU | 50806 | 54806 | 56806 | 79806 |

# CLASS 172          TURBOSTAR          BOMBARDIER

New generation Chiltern Railways and West Midlands Trains Turbostars. Air conditioned.

**Construction:** Welded aluminium bodies with bolt-on steel ends.
**Engines:** One MTU 6H1800R83 of 360 kW (483 hp) at 1800 rpm.
**Transmission:** Mechanical. Supplied by ZF, Germany.
**Bogies:** B5006 type "lightweight" bogies.
**Couplers:** BSI at outer ends, bar within unit.
**Dimensions:** 23.62/23.00 x 2.69 m.
**Gangways:** 172/0 & 172/1: Within unit only. 172/2: Throughout.
**Wheel Arrangement:** 2-B (+ B-2) + B-2.
**Doors:** Twin-leaf sliding plug.
**Maximum Speed:** 100 mph.
**Seating Layout:** 2+2 facing/unidirectional.
**Multiple Working:** Within class and with Classes 150, 153, 155, 156, 158, 159, 165, 166 and 170.

**Class 172/0. West Midlands Trains units.** Formerly operated by London Overground. DMSL–DMS.

**59311–318. DMSL.** Bombardier Derby 2009–10. –/57(+4) 1TD 2W. 41.6 t.
**59411–418. DMS.** Bombardier Derby 2009–10. –/64(+12). 41.5 t.

| | | | | | | |
|---|---|---|---|---|---|---|
| 172 001 | **WM** | A | *WM* | TS | 59311 | 59411 |
| 172 002 | **WM** | A | *WM* | TS | 59312 | 59412 |
| 172 003 | **WM** | A | *WM* | TS | 59313 | 59413 |
| 172 004 | **WM** | A | *WM* | TS | 59314 | 59414 |
| 172 005 | **WM** | A | *WM* | TS | 59315 | 59415 |
| 172 006 | **WM** | A | *WM* | TS | 59316 | 59416 |
| 172 007 | **WM** | A | *WM* | TS | 59317 | 59417 |
| 172 008 | **WM** | A | *WM* | TS | 59318 | 59418 |

**Class 172/1. Chiltern Railways units.** DMSL–DMS.

**59111–114. DMSL.** Bombardier Derby 2009–10. –/60(+5) 1TD 2W. 42.4 t.
**59211–214. DMS.** Bombardier Derby 2009–10. –/80. 41.8 t.

| | | | | | | |
|---|---|---|---|---|---|---|
| 172 101 | **CR** | A | *CR* | AL | 59111 | 59211 |
| 172 102 | **CR** | A | *CR* | AL | 59112 | 59212 |
| 172 103 | **CR** | A | *CR* | AL | 59113 | 59213 |
| 172 104 | **CR** | A | *CR* | AL | 59114 | 59214 |

**Class 172/2. West Midlands Trains 2-car units**. DMSL–DMS. Used on local services via Birmingham Snow Hill.

**50211–222. DMSL**. Bombardier Derby 2010–11. –/52(+11) 1TD 2W. 42.5 t.
**79211–222. DMS**. Bombardier Derby 2010–11. –/68(+8). 41.9 t.

| | | | | | | |
|---|---|---|---|---|---|---|
| 172 211 | **WM** | P | *WM* | TS | 50211 | 79211 |
| 172 212 | **WM** | P | *WM* | TS | 50212 | 79212 |
| 172 213 | **WM** | P | *WM* | TS | 50213 | 79213 |
| 172 214 | **WM** | P | *WM* | TS | 50214 | 79214 |
| 172 215 | **WM** | P | *WM* | TS | 50215 | 79215 |
| 172 216 | **WM** | P | *WM* | TS | 50216 | 79216 |
| 172 217 | **WM** | P | *WM* | TS | 50217 | 79217 |
| 172 218 | **WM** | P | *WM* | TS | 50218 | 79218 |
| 172 219 | **WM** | P | *WM* | TS | 50219 | 79219 |
| 172 220 | **WM** | P | *WM* | TS | 50220 | 79220 |
| 172 221 | **WM** | P | *WM* | TS | 50221 | 79221 |
| 172 222 | **WM** | P | *WM* | TS | 50222 | 79222 |

**Class 172/3. West Midlands Trains 3-car units**. DMSL–MS–DMS. Used on local services via Birmingham Snow Hill.

At the time of writing 172 333/338 are running with misformed formations, as shown.

**50331–345. DMSL**. Bombardier Derby 2010–11. –/52(+11) 1TD 2W. 42.5 t.
**56331–345. MS**. Bombardier Derby 2010–11. –/72(+8). 38.8 t.
**79331–345. DMS**. Bombardier Derby 2010–11. –/68(+8). 41.9 t.

| | | | | | | | |
|---|---|---|---|---|---|---|---|
| 172 331 | **WM** | P | *WM* | TS | 50331 | 56331 | 79331 |
| 172 332 | **WM** | P | *WM* | TS | 50332 | 56332 | 79332 |
| 172 333 | **WM** | P | *WM* | TS | 50338 | 56333 | 79333 |
| 172 334 | **WM** | P | *WM* | TS | 50334 | 56334 | 79334 |
| 172 335 | **WM** | P | *WM* | TS | 50335 | 56335 | 79335 |
| 172 336 | **WM** | P | *WM* | TS | 50336 | 56336 | 79336 |
| 172 337 | **WM** | P | *WM* | TS | 50337 | 56337 | 79337 |
| 172 338 | **WM** | P | *WM* | TS | 50333 | 56338 | 79338 |
| 172 339 | **WM** | P | *WM* | TS | 50339 | 56339 | 79339 |
| 172 340 | **WM** | P | *WM* | TS | 50340 | 56340 | 79340 |
| 172 341 | **WM** | P | *WM* | TS | 50341 | 56341 | 79341 |
| 172 342 | **WM** | P | *WM* | TS | 50342 | 56342 | 79342 |
| 172 343 | **WM** | P | *WM* | TS | 50343 | 56343 | 79343 |
| 172 344 | **WM** | P | *WM* | TS | 50344 | 56344 | 79344 |
| 172 345 | **WM** | P | *WM* | TS | 50345 | 56345 | 79345 |

# CLASS 175          CORADIA 1000          ALSTOM

Air conditioned.

**Construction:** Steel.
**Engines:** One Cummins N14 of 335 kW (450 hp).
**Transmission:** Hydraulic. Voith T211rzze to ZF Voith final drive.
**Bogies:** ACR (Alstom FBO) – LTB-MBS1, TB-MB1, MBS1-LTB.
**Couplers:** Scharfenberg outer ends and bar within unit (Class 175/1).
**Dimensions:** 23.70 x 2.73 m.
**Gangways:** Within unit only.           **Wheel Arrangement:** 2-B (+ B-2) + B-2.
**Doors:** Single-leaf swing plug.        **Maximum Speed:** 100 mph.
**Seating Layout:** 2+2 facing/unidirectional.
**Multiple Working:** Within class and with Class 180.

At the time of writing sets 175 004/005/006/101/109/115 are running with misformed formations, as shown.

**Class 175/0.** DMSL–DMSL. 2-car units.

**DMSL(A).** Alstom Birmingham 1999–2000. –/54 1TD 2W. 48.8 t.
**DMSL(B).** Alstom Birmingham 1999–2000. –/64 1T. 50.7 t.

| 175 001 | **TW** | A | *TW* | CH | 50701 | 79701 |
|---------|--------|---|------|-----|-------|-------|
| 175 002 | **TW** | A | *TW* | CH | 50702 | 79702 |
| 175 003 | **TW** | A | *TW* | CH | 50703 | 79703 |
| 175 004 | **TW** | A | *TW* | CH | 50759 | 79759 |
| 175 005 | **TW** | A | *TW* | CH | 50705 | 79751 |
| 175 006 | **TW** | A | *TW* | CH | 50706 | 79765 |
| 175 007 | **TW** | A | *TW* | CH | 50707 | 79707 |
| 175 008 | **TW** | A | *TW* | CH | 50708 | 79708 |
| 175 009 | **TW** | A | *TW* | CH | 50709 | 79709 |
| 175 010 | **TW** | A | *TW* | CH | 50710 | 79710 |
| 175 011 | **TW** | A | *TW* | CH | 50711 | 79711 |

**Class 175/1.** DMSL–MSL–DMSL. 3-car units.

**DMSL(A).** Alstom Birmingham 1999–2001. –/54 1TD 2W. 50.7 t.
**MSL.** Alstom Birmingham 1999–2001. –/68 1T. 47.5 t.
**DMSL(B).** Alstom Birmingham 1999–2001. –/64 1T. 49.5 t.

| 175 101 | **TW** | A | *TW* | CH | 50751 | 56751 | 79704 |
|---------|--------|---|------|-----|-------|-------|-------|
| 175 102 | **TW** | A | *TW* | CH | 50752 | 56752 | 79752 |
| 175 103 | **TW** | A | *TW* | CH | 50753 | 56753 | 79753 |
| 175 104 | **TW** | A | *TW* | CH | 50754 | 56754 | 79754 |
| 175 105 | **AV** | A | *TW* | CH | 50755 | 56755 | 79755 |
| 175 106 | **AV** | A | *TW* | CH | 50756 | 56756 | 79756 |
| 175 107 | **TW** | A | *TW* | CH | 50757 | 56757 | 79757 |
| 175 108 | **AV** | A | *TW* | CH | 50758 | 56758 | 79758 |
| 175 109 | **AV** | A | *TW* | CH | 50704 | 56759 | 79705 |
| 175 110 | **AV** | A | *TW* | CH | 50760 | 56760 | 79760 |
| 175 111 | **AV** | A | *TW* | CH | 50761 | 56761 | 79761 |
| 175 112 | **AV** | A | *TW* | CH | 50762 | 56762 | 79762 |

| 175 113 | **TW** | A | *TW* | CH | 50763 | 56763 | 79763 |
| 175 114 | **AV** | A | *TW* | CH | 50764 | 56764 | 79764 |
| 175 115 | **AV** | A | *TW* | CH | 50765 | 56765 | 79706 |
| 175 116 | **TW** | A | *TW* | CH | 50766 | 56766 | 79766 |

## CLASS 180              CORADIA 1000              ALSTOM

Air conditioned.

**Construction:** Steel.
**Engines:** One Cummins QSK19 of 560 kW (750 hp) at 2100 rpm.
**Transmission:** Hydraulic. Voith T312br to Voith final drive.
**Bogies:** ACR (Alstom FBO): LTB1-MBS2, TB1-MB2, TB1-MB2, TB2-MB2, MBS2-LTB1.
**Couplers:** Scharfenberg outer ends, bar within unit.
**Dimensions:** 23.71/23.03 x 2.73 m.
**Gangways:** Within unit only.
**Wheel Arrangement:** 2-B + B-2 + B-2 + B-2 + B-2.
**Doors:** Single-leaf swing plug.       **Maximum Speed:** 125 mph.
**Seating Layout:** 1: 2+1 facing/unidirectional, 2: 2+2 facing/unidirectional.
**Multiple Working:** Within class and with Class 175.

**DMSL(A).** Alstom Birmingham 2000–01. –/46 2W 1TD. 51.7 t.
**MFL.** Alstom Birmingham 2000–01. 42/– 1T 1W + catering point. 49.6 t.
**MSL.** Alstom Birmingham 2000–01. –/68 1T. 49.5 t.
**MSLRB.** Alstom Birmingham 2000–01. –/56 1T. 50.3 t.
**DMSL(B).** Alstom Birmingham 2000–01. –/56 1T. 51.4 t.

| 180 101 | **GC** | A | *GC* | HT | 50901 | 54901 | 55901 | 56901 | 59901 |
| 180 102 | **GC** | A | *GC* | HT | 50902 | 54902 | 55902 | 56902 | 59902 |
| 180 103 | **GC** | A | *GC* | HT | 50903 | 54903 | 55903 | 56903 | 59903 |
| 180 104 | **GC** | A | *GC* | HT | 50904 | 54904 | 55904 | 56904 | 59904 |
| 180 105 | **GC** | A | *GC* | HT | 50905 | 54905 | 55905 | 56905 | 59905 |
| 180 106 | **GC** | A | *GC* | HT | 50906 | 54906 | 55906 | 56906 | 59906 |
| 180 107 | **GC** | A | *GC* | HT | 50907 | 54907 | 55907 | 56907 | 59907 |
| 180 108 | **GC** | A | *GC* | HT | 50908 | 54908 | 55908 | 56908 | 59908 |
| 180 109 | **EI** | A | *EM* | DY | 50909 | 54909 | 55909 | 56909 | 59909 |
| 180 110 | **EI** | A | *EM* | DY | 50910 | 54910 | 55910 | 56910 | 59910 |
| 180 111 | **EI** | A | *EM* | DY | 50911 | 54911 | 55911 | 56911 | 59911 |
| 180 112 | **GC** | A | *GC* | HT | 50912 | 54912 | 55912 | 56912 | 59912 |
| 180 113 | **EI** | A | *EM* | DY | 50913 | 54913 | 55913 | 56913 | 59913 |
| 180 114 | **GC** | A | *GC* | HT | 50914 | 54914 | 55914 | 56914 | 59914 |

**Names (carried on DMSL(A):**

| 180 105 | THE YORKSHIRE ARTIST ASHLEY JACKSON |
| 180 107 | HART OF THE NORTH |
| 180 108 | WILLIAM SHAKESPEARE |
| 180 112 | JAMES HERRIOT |
| 180 114 | KIRKGATE CALLING |

# CLASS 185          DESIRO UK          SIEMENS

Air conditioned. Grammer seating in Standard Class and Fainsa in First Class.

**Construction:** Aluminium.
**Engines:** One Cummins QSK19 of 560 kW (750 hp) at 2100 rpm.
**Transmission:** Voith.                    **Bogies:** Siemens.
**Couplers:** Dellner 12.                    **Dimensions:** 23.76/23.75 x 2.66 m.
**Gangways:** Within unit only.             **Wheel Arrangement:** 2-B + 2-B + B-2.
**Doors:** Double-leaf sliding plug.        **Maximum Speed:** 100 mph.
**Seating Layout:** 1: 2+1 facing/unidirectional, 2: 2+2 facing/unidirectional.
**Multiple Working:** Within class only.

**DMCL.** Siemens Krefeld 2005–06. 15/18(+8) 2W 1TD + catering point. 55.4 t.
**MSL.** Siemens Krefeld 2005–06. –/72 1T. 52.7 t.
**DMS.** Siemens Krefeld 2005–06. –/64(+4). 54.9 t.

| | | | | | | | |
|---|---|---|---|---|---|---|---|
| 185 101 | **TP** | E | *TP* | AK | 51101 | 53101 | 54101 |
| 185 102 | **TP** | E | *TP* | AK | 51102 | 53102 | 54102 |
| 185 103 | **TP** | E | *TP* | AK | 51103 | 53103 | 54103 |
| 185 104 | **TP** | E | *TP* | AK | 51104 | 53104 | 54104 |
| 185 105 | **TP** | E | *TP* | AK | 51105 | 53105 | 54105 |
| 185 106 | **TP** | E | *TP* | AK | 51106 | 53106 | 54106 |
| 185 107 | **TP** | E | *TP* | AK | 51107 | 53107 | 54107 |
| 185 108 | **TP** | E | *TP* | AK | 51108 | 53108 | 54108 |
| 185 109 | **TP** | E | *TP* | AK | 51109 | 53109 | 54109 |
| 185 110 | **TP** | E | *TP* | AK | 51110 | 53110 | 54110 |
| 185 111 | **TP** | E | *TP* | AK | 51111 | 53111 | 54111 |
| 185 112 | **TP** | E | *TP* | AK | 51112 | 53112 | 54112 |
| 185 113 | **TP** | E | *TP* | AK | 51113 | 53113 | 54113 |
| 185 114 | **TP** | E | *TP* | AK | 51114 | 53114 | 54114 |
| 185 115 | **TP** | E | *TP* | AK | 51115 | 53115 | 54115 |
| 185 116 | **TP** | E | *TP* | AK | 51116 | 53116 | 54116 |
| 185 117 | **TP** | E | *TP* | AK | 51117 | 53117 | 54117 |
| 185 118 | **TP** | E | *TP* | AK | 51118 | 53118 | 54118 |
| 185 119 | **TP** | E | *TP* | AK | 51119 | 53119 | 54119 |
| 185 120 | **TP** | E | *TP* | AK | 51120 | 53120 | 54120 |
| 185 121 | **TP** | E | *TP* | AK | 51121 | 53121 | 54121 |
| 185 122 | **TP** | E | *TP* | AK | 51122 | 53122 | 54122 |
| 185 123 | **TP** | E | *TP* | AK | 51123 | 53123 | 54123 |
| 185 124 | **TP** | E | *TP* | AK | 51124 | 53124 | 54124 |
| 185 125 | **TP** | E | *TP* | AK | 51125 | 53125 | 54125 |
| 185 126 | **TP** | E | *TP* | AK | 51126 | 53126 | 54126 |
| 185 127 | **TP** | E | *TP* | AK | 51127 | 53127 | 54127 |
| 185 128 | **TP** | E | *TP* | AK | 51128 | 53128 | 54128 |
| 185 129 | **TP** | E | *TP* | AK | 51129 | 53129 | 54129 |
| 185 130 | **TP** | E | *TP* | AK | 51130 | 53130 | 54130 |
| 185 131 | **TP** | E | *TP* | AK | 51131 | 53131 | 54131 |
| 185 132 | **TP** | E | *TP* | AK | 51132 | 53132 | 54132 |
| 185 133 | **TP** | E | *TP* | AK | 51133 | 53133 | 54133 |
| 185 134 | **TP** | E | *TP* | AK | 51134 | 53134 | 54134 |
| 185 135 | **TP** | E | *TP* | AK | 51135 | 53135 | 54135 |

| 185 136 | **TP** | E | *TP* | AK | 51136 | 53136 | 54136 |
| 185 137 | **TP** | E | *TP* | AK | 51137 | 53137 | 54137 |
| 185 138 | **TP** | E | *TP* | AK | 51138 | 53138 | 54138 |
| 185 139 | **TP** | E | *TP* | AK | 51139 | 53139 | 54139 |
| 185 140 | **TP** | E | *TP* | AK | 51140 | 53140 | 54140 |
| 185 141 | **TP** | E | *TP* | AK | 51141 | 53141 | 54141 |
| 185 142 | **TP** | E | *TP* | AK | 51142 | 53142 | 54142 |
| 185 143 | **TP** | E | *TP* | AK | 51143 | 53143 | 54143 |
| 185 144 | **TP** | E | *TP* | AK | 51144 | 53144 | 54144 |
| 185 145 | **TP** | E | *TP* | AK | 51145 | 53145 | 54145 |
| 185 146 | **TP** | E | *TP* | AK | 51146 | 53146 | 54146 |
| 185 147 | **TP** | E | *TP* | AK | 51147 | 53147 | 54147 |
| 185 148 | **TP** | E | *TP* | AK | 51148 | 53148 | 54148 |
| 185 149 | **TP** | E | *TP* | AK | 51149 | 53149 | 54149 |
| 185 150 | **TP** | E | *TP* | AK | 51150 | 53150 | 54150 |
| 185 151 | **TP** | E | *TP* | AK | 51151 | 53151 | 54151 |

## CLASS 195                          CIVITY                          CAF

DMS–DMS or DMS–MS–DMS. New Northern units. Air conditioned.

**Construction:** Aluminium.
**Engines:** One Rolls-Royce MTU 6H 1800 R85L of 390 kW (523 hp) per car.
**Transmission:** Mechanical, supplied by ZF, Germany.
**Bogies:** CAF.
**Couplers:** Dellner.                          **Dimensions:** 24.03/23.35 x 2.71 m.
**Gangways:** Within unit only.                 **Wheel Arrangement:**
**Doors:** Sliding plug.                        **Maximum Speed:** 100 mph.
**Seating Layout:** 2+2 facing/unidirectional.
**Multiple Working:** Within class only.

**Class 195/0.** DMS–DMS. 2-car units.

**DMS(A).** CAF Zaragoza/Irun/Newport 2017–20. –/45(+8) 1TD 2W. 43.9 t.
**DMS(B).** CAF Zaragoza/Irun/Newport 2017–20. –/63(+7). 43.2 t.

| 195 001 | **NR** | E | *NO* | NH | 101001 | 103001 |
| 195 002 | **NR** | E | *NO* | NH | 101002 | 103002 |
| 195 003 | **NR** | E | *NO* | NH | 101003 | 103003 |
| 195 004 | **NR** | E | *NO* | NH | 101004 | 103004 |
| 195 005 | **NR** | E | *NO* | NH | 101005 | 103005 |
| 195 006 | **NR** | E | *NO* | NH | 101006 | 103006 |
| 195 007 | **NR** | E | *NO* | NH | 101007 | 103007 |
| 195 008 | **NR** | E | *NO* | NH | 101008 | 103008 |
| 195 009 | **NR** | E | *NO* | NH | 101009 | 103009 |
| 195 010 | **NR** | E | *NO* | NH | 101010 | 103010 |
| 195 011 | **NR** | E | *NO* | NH | 101011 | 103011 |
| 195 012 | **NR** | E | *NO* | NH | 101012 | 103012 |
| 195 013 | **NR** | E | *NO* | NH | 101013 | 103013 |
| 195 014 | **NR** | E | *NO* | NH | 101014 | 103014 |
| 195 015 | **NR** | E | *NO* | NH | 101015 | 103015 |
| 195 016 | **NR** | E | *NO* | NH | 101016 | 103016 |

| 195 017 | **NR** | E | *NO* | NH | 101017 | 103017 |
| 195 018 | **NR** | E | *NO* | NH | 101018 | 103018 |
| 195 019 | **NR** | E | *NO* | NH | 101019 | 103019 |
| 195 020 | **NR** | E | *NO* | NH | 101020 | 103020 |
| 195 021 | **NR** | E | *NO* | NH | 101021 | 103021 |
| 195 022 | **NR** | E | *NO* | NH | 101022 | 103022 |
| 195 023 | **NR** | E | *NO* | NH | 101023 | 103023 |
| 195 024 | **NR** | E | *NO* | NH | 101024 | 103024 |
| 195 025 | **NR** | E | *NO* | NH | 101025 | 103025 |

**Class 195/1.** DMS–MS–DMS. 3-car units.

**DMS(A).** CAF Zaragoza/Irun/Newport 2017–20. –/45(+8) 1TD 2W. 43.9 t.
**MS.** CAF Zaragoza/Irun/Newport 2017–20. –/76(+4).
**DMS(B).** CAF Zaragoza/Irun/Newport 2017–20. –/63(+7). 43.2 t.

| 195 101 | **NR** | E | *NO* | NH | 101101 | 102101 | 103101 | |
| 195 102 | **NR** | E | *NO* | NH | 101102 | 102102 | 103102 | |
| 195 103 | **NR** | E | *NO* | NH | 101103 | 102103 | 103103 | |
| 195 104 | **NR** | E | *NO* | NH | 101104 | 102104 | 103104 | Deva Victrix |
| 195 105 | **NR** | E | *NO* | NH | 101105 | 102105 | 103105 | |
| 195 106 | **NR** | E | *NO* | NH | 101106 | 102106 | 103106 | |
| 195 107 | **NR** | E | *NO* | NH | 101107 | 102107 | 103107 | |
| 195 108 | **NR** | E | *NO* | NH | 101108 | 102108 | 103108 | |
| 195 109 | **NR** | E | *NO* | NH | 101109 | 102109 | 103109 | |
| 195 110 | **NR** | E | *NO* | NH | 101110 | 102110 | 103110 | |
| 195 111 | **NR** | E | *NO* | NH | 101111 | 102111 | 103111 | Key Worker |
| 195 112 | **NR** | E | *NO* | NH | 101112 | 102112 | 103112 | |
| 195 113 | **NR** | E | *NO* | NH | 101113 | 102113 | 103113 | |
| 195 114 | **NR** | E | *NO* | NH | 101114 | 102114 | 103114 | |
| 195 115 | **NR** | E | *NO* | NH | 101115 | 102115 | 103115 | |
| 195 116 | **NR** | E | *NO* | NH | 101116 | 102116 | 103116 | Proud to be Northern |
| 195 117 | **NR** | E | *NO* | NH | 101117 | 102117 | 103117 | |
| 195 118 | **NR** | E | *NO* | NH | 101118 | 102118 | 103118 | |
| 195 119 | **NR** | E | *NO* | NH | 101119 | 102119 | 103119 | |
| 195 120 | **NR** | E | *NO* | NH | 101120 | 102120 | 103120 | |
| 195 121 | **NR** | E | *NO* | NH | 101121 | 102121 | 103121 | |
| 195 122 | **NR** | E | *NO* | NH | 101122 | 102122 | 103122 | |
| 195 123 | **NR** | E | *NO* | NH | 101123 | 102123 | 103123 | |
| 195 124 | **NR** | E | *NO* | NH | 101124 | 102124 | 103124 | |
| 195 125 | **NR** | E | *NO* | NH | 101125 | 102125 | 103125 | |
| 195 126 | **NR** | E | *NO* | NH | 101126 | 102126 | 103126 | |
| 195 127 | **NR** | E | *NO* | NH | 101127 | 102127 | 103127 | |
| 195 128 | **NR** | E | *NO* | NH | 101128 | 102128 | 103128 | Calder Champion |
| 195 129 | **NR** | E | *NO* | NH | 101129 | 102129 | 103129 | |
| 195 130 | **NR** | E | *NO* | NH | 101130 | 102130 | 103130 | |
| 195 131 | **NR** | E | *NO* | NH | 101131 | 102131 | 103131 | |
| 195 132 | **NR** | E | *NO* | NH | 101132 | 102132 | 103132 | |
| 195 133 | **NR** | E | *NO* | NH | 101133 | 102133 | 103133 | |

# CLASS 196            CIVITY                          CAF

DMS–DMS or DMS–MS–MS–DMS. New units currently being delivered to West Midlands Trains for local services around Birmingham. Air conditioned. Full details awaited. Due to enter service in 2021.

**Construction:** Aluminium.
**Engines:** One Rolls-Royce MTU 6H 1800 R85L of 390 kW (523 hp) per car.
**Transmission:** Mechanical, supplied by ZF, Germany.
**Bogies:** CAF.
**Couplers:** Dellner.                    **Dimensions:**
**Gangways:** Throughout.                 **Wheel Arrangement:**
**Doors:** Sliding plug.                  **Maximum Speed:** 100 mph.
**Seating Layout:** 2+2 facing/unidirectional.
**Multiple Working:** Within class only.

**Class 196/0.** DMS–DMS. 2-car units.

**DMS(A).** CAF Zaragoza/Beasain/Newport 2019–21.
**DMS(B).** CAF Zaragoza/Beasain/Newport 2019–21.

| | | | |
|---|---|---|---|
| 196 001 | **WM** CO | 121001 | 124001 |
| 196 002 | **WM** CO | 121002 | 124002 |
| 196 003 | **WM** CO | 121003 | 124003 |
| 196 004 | **WM** CO | 121004 | 124004 |
| 196 005 | **WM** CO | 121005 | 124005 |
| 196 006 | **WM** CO | 121006 | 124006 |
| 196 007 | **WM** CO | 121007 | 124007 |
| 196 008 | **WM** CO | 121008 | 124008 |
| 196 009 | **WM** CO | 121009 | 124009 |
| 196 010 | **WM** CO | 121010 | 124010 |
| 196 011 | **WM** CO | 121011 | 124011 |
| 196 012 | **WM** CO | 121012 | 124012 |

**Class 196/1.** DMS–MS–MS–DMS. 4-car units.

**DMS(A).** CAF Zaragoza/Irun/Newport 2019–21.
**MS(A).** CAF Zaragoza/Irun/Newport 2019–21.
**MS(B).** CAF Zaragoza/Irun/Newport 2019–21.
**DMS(B).** CAF Zaragoza/Irun/Newport 2019–21.

| | | | | | |
|---|---|---|---|---|---|
| 196 101 | **WM** CO | 121101 | 122101 | 123101 | 124101 |
| 196 102 | **WM** CO | 121102 | 122102 | 123102 | 124102 |
| 196 103 | **WM** CO | 121103 | 122103 | 123103 | 124103 |
| 196 104 | **WM** CO | 121104 | 122104 | 123104 | 124104 |
| 196 105 | **WM** CO | 121105 | 122105 | 123105 | 124105 |
| 196 106 | **WM** CO | 121106 | 122106 | 123106 | 124106 |
| 196 107 | **WM** CO | 121107 | 122107 | 123107 | 124107 |
| 196 108 | **WM** CO | 121108 | 122108 | 123108 | 124108 |
| 196 109 | **WM** CO | 121109 | 122109 | 123109 | 124109 |
| 196 110 | **WM** CO | 121110 | 122110 | 123110 | 124110 |
| 196 111 | **WM** CO | 121111 | 122111 | 123111 | 124111 |
| 196 112 | **WM** CO | 121112 | 122112 | 123112 | 124112 |
| 196 113 | **WM** CO | 121113 | 122113 | 123113 | 124113 |
| 196 114 | **WM** CO | 121114 | 122114 | 123114 | 124114 |

# CLASS 197                  CIVITY                              CAF

DMS–DMS or DMS–MS–DMS. New units currently under construction for Transport for Wales. Air conditioned. Full details awaited. Due to enter service 2022–24. 21 2-car units will be fitted with ETCS signalling equipment for operating the Cambrian Lines.

**Construction:** Aluminium.
**Engines:** One Rolls-Royce MTU 6H 1800 R85L of 390 kW (523 hp) per car.
**Transmission:** Mechanical, supplied by ZF, Germany.
**Bogies:** CAF.

| | |
|---|---|
| **Couplers:** Dellner. | **Dimensions:** |
| **Gangways:** Throughout. | **Wheel Arrangement:** |
| **Doors:** Sliding plug. | **Maximum Speed:** 100 mph. |

**Seating Layout:** 2+2 facing/unidirectional.
**Multiple Working:** Within class only.

**Class 197/0.** DMS–DMS. 2-car units.

**DMS(A).** CAF Beasain/Newport 2020–23.
**DMS(B).** CAF Beasain/Newport 2020–23.

| | | |
|---|---|---|
| 197 001 | 131001 | 133001 |
| 197 002 | 131002 | 133002 |
| 197 003 | 131003 | 133003 |
| 197 004 | 131004 | 133004 |
| 197 005 | 131005 | 133005 |
| 197 006 | 131006 | 133006 |
| 197 007 | 131007 | 133007 |
| 197 008 | 131008 | 133008 |
| 197 009 | 131009 | 133009 |
| 197 010 | 131010 | 133010 |
| 197 011 | 131011 | 133011 |
| 197 012 | 131012 | 133012 |
| 197 013 | 131013 | 133013 |
| 197 014 | 131014 | 133014 |
| 197 015 | 131015 | 133015 |
| 197 016 | 131016 | 133016 |
| 197 017 | 131017 | 133017 |
| 197 018 | 131018 | 133018 |
| 197 019 | 131019 | 133019 |
| 197 020 | 131020 | 133020 |
| 197 021 | 131021 | 133021 |
| 197 022 | 131022 | 133022 |
| 197 023 | 131023 | 133023 |
| 197 024 | 131024 | 133024 |
| 197 025 | 131025 | 133025 |
| 197 026 | 131026 | 133026 |
| 197 027 | 131027 | 133027 |
| 197 028 | 131028 | 133028 |
| 197 029 | 131029 | 133029 |
| 197 030 | 131030 | 133030 |
| 197 031 | 131031 | 133031 |

| | | | |
|---|---|---|---|
| 197 032 | 131032 | 133032 | |
| 197 033 | 131033 | 133033 | |
| 197 034 | 131034 | 133034 | |
| 197 035 | 131035 | 133035 | |
| 197 036 | 131036 | 133036 | |
| 197 037 | 131037 | 133037 | |
| 197 038 | 131038 | 133038 | |
| 197 039 | 131039 | 133039 | |
| 197 040 | 131040 | 133040 | |
| 197 041 | 131041 | 133041 | |
| 197 042 | 131042 | 133042 | |
| 197 043 | 131043 | 133043 | |
| 197 044 | 131044 | 133044 | |
| 197 045 | 131045 | 133045 | |
| 197 046 | 131046 | 133046 | |
| 197 047 | 131047 | 133047 | |
| 197 048 | 131048 | 133048 | |
| 197 049 | 131049 | 133049 | |
| 197 050 | 131050 | 133050 | |
| 197 051 | 131051 | 133051 | |

**Class 197/1**. DMS–MS–DMS. 3-car units.

**DMS(A)**. CAF Beasain/Newport 2020–23.
**MS**. CAF Beasain/Newport 2020–23.
**DMS(B)**. CAF Beasain/Newport 2020–23.

| | | | |
|---|---|---|---|
| 197 101 | 131101 | 132101 | 133101 |
| 197 102 | 131102 | 132102 | 133102 |
| 197 103 | 131103 | 132103 | 133103 |
| 197 104 | 131104 | 132104 | 133104 |
| 197 105 | 131105 | 132105 | 133105 |
| 197 106 | 131106 | 132106 | 133106 |
| 197 107 | 131107 | 132107 | 133107 |
| 197 108 | 131108 | 132108 | 133108 |
| 197 109 | 131109 | 132109 | 133109 |
| 197 110 | 131110 | 132110 | 133110 |
| 197 111 | 131111 | 132111 | 133111 |
| 197 112 | 131112 | 132112 | 133112 |
| 197 113 | 131113 | 132113 | 133113 |
| 197 114 | 131114 | 132114 | 133114 |
| 197 115 | 131115 | 132115 | 133115 |
| 197 116 | 131116 | 132116 | 133116 |
| 197 117 | 131117 | 132117 | 133117 |
| 197 118 | 131118 | 132118 | 133118 |
| 197 119 | 131119 | 132119 | 133119 |
| 197 120 | 131120 | 132120 | 133120 |
| 197 121 | 131121 | 132121 | 133121 |
| 197 122 | 131122 | 132122 | 133122 |
| 197 123 | 131123 | 132123 | 133123 |
| 197 124 | 131124 | 132124 | 133124 |
| 197 125 | 131125 | 132125 | 133125 |
| 197 126 | 131126 | 132126 | 133126 |

# 3.2. DIESEL ELECTRIC UNITS

## CLASS 201/202    PRESERVED "HASTINGS" UNIT    BR

DMBS–TSL–TSL–TSRB–TSL–DMBS.

Preserved unit made up from two Class 201 short-frame cars and three Class 202 long-frame cars. The "Hastings" units were made with narrow body-profiles for use on the section between Tonbridge and Battle which had tunnels of restricted loading gauge. These tunnels were converted to single track operation in the 1980s thus allowing standard loading gauge stock to be used. The set also contains a Class 411 EMU trailer (not Hastings line gauge) and a Class 422 EMU buffet car.

**Construction:** Steel.
**Engine:** One English Electric 4SRKT Mk. 2 of 450 kW (600 hp) at 850 rpm.
**Main Generator:** English Electric EE824.
**Traction Motors:** Two English Electric EE507 mounted on the inner bogie.
**Bogies:** SR Mk 4. (Former EMU TSL vehicles have Commonwealth bogies).
**Couplers:** Drophead buckeye.
**Dimensions:** 18.40 x 2.50 m (60000), 20.35 x 2.50 m (60116/118/529), 18.36 x 2.50 m (60501), 20.35 x 2.82 (69337), 20.30 x 2.82 (70262).
**Gangways:** Within unit only.          **Doors:** Manually operated slam.
**Wheel arrangement:** 2-Bo + 2-2 + 2-2 + 2-2- + 2-2- + Bo-2.
**Brakes:** Electro-pneumatic and automatic air.
**Maximum Speed:** 75 mph.          **Seating Layout:** 2+2 facing.
**Multiple Working:** Other ex-BR Southern Region DEMU vehicles.
**60000. DMBS.** Lot No. 30329 Eastleigh 1957. –/22. 55.0 t.
**60116. DMBS.** Lot No. 30395 Eastleigh 1957. –/31. 56.0 t.
**60118. DMBS.** Lot No. 30395 Eastleigh 1957. –/30. 56.0 t.
**60501. TSL.** Lot No. 30331 Eastleigh 1957. –/52 2T. 29.5 t.
**60529. TSL.** Lot No. 30397 Eastleigh 1957. –/60 2T. 30.5 t.
**69337. TSRB (ex-Class 422 EMU).** Lot No. 30805 York 1970. –/40. 35.0 t.
**70262. TSL (ex-Class 411/5 EMU).** Lot No. 30455 Eastleigh 1958. –/64 2T. 31.5 t.

| | | | | | | | | | |
|---|---|---|---|---|---|---|---|---|---|
| 201 001 | **G** | HD | *HD* | SE | 60116 | 60529 | 70262 | 69337 | 60501 | 60118 |
| Spare | **G** | HD | *HD* | SE | 60000 | | | | |

**Names:**

| | | | | |
|---|---|---|---|---|
| 60000 | Hastings | | 60118 | Tunbridge Wells |
| 60116 | Mountfield | | | |

## CLASS 220          VOYAGER          BOMBARDIER

DMS–MS–MS–DMF.

**Construction:** Steel.
**Engine:** Cummins QSK19 of 520 kW (700 hp) at 1800 rpm.
**Transmission:** Two Alstom Onix 800 three-phase traction motors of 275 kW.
**Braking:** Rheostatic and electro-pneumatic.

**Bogies:** Bombardier B5005.
**Couplers:** Dellner 12 at outer ends, bar within unit.
**Dimensions:** 23.85/23.00 (602xx) x 2.73 m.
**Gangways:** Within unit only.
**Wheel Arrangement:** 1A-A1 + 1A-A1 + 1A-A1 + 1A-A1.
**Doors:** Single-leaf swing plug.
**Maximum Speed:** 125 m.p.h.
**Seating Layout:** 1: 2+1 facing/unidirectional, 2: 2+2 mainly unidirectional.
**Multiple Working:** Within class and with Classes 221 and 222 (in an emergency). Also can be controlled from Class 57/3 locomotives.

**DMS.** Bombardier Bruges/Wakefield 2000–01. –/42 1TD 1W. 51.1 t.
**MS(A).** Bombardier Bruges/Wakefield 2000–01. –/66. 45.9 t.
**MS(B).** Bombardier Bruges/Wakefield 2000–01. –/66 1TD. 46.7 t.
**DMF.** Bombardier Bruges/Wakefield 2000–01. 26/– 1TD 1W. 50.9 t.

| 220 001 | **XC** | BN | *XC* | CZ | 60301 | 60701 | 60201 | 60401 |
|---------|--------|----|------|----|-------|-------|-------|-------|
| 220 002 | **XC** | BN | *XC* | CZ | 60302 | 60702 | 60202 | 60402 |
| 220 003 | **XC** | BN | *XC* | CZ | 60303 | 60703 | 60203 | 60403 |
| 220 004 | **XC** | BN | *XC* | CZ | 60304 | 60704 | 60204 | 60404 |
| 220 005 | **XC** | BN | *XC* | CZ | 60305 | 60705 | 60205 | 60405 |
| 220 006 | **XC** | BN | *XC* | CZ | 60306 | 60706 | 60206 | 60406 |
| 220 007 | **XC** | BN | *XC* | CZ | 60307 | 60707 | 60207 | 60407 |
| 220 008 | **XC** | BN | *XC* | CZ | 60308 | 60708 | 60208 | 60408 |
| 220 009 | **XC** | BN | *XC* | CZ | 60309 | 60709 | 60209 | 60409 |
| 220 010 | **XC** | BN | *XC* | CZ | 60310 | 60710 | 60210 | 60410 |
| 220 011 | **XC** | BN | *XC* | CZ | 60311 | 60711 | 60211 | 60411 |
| 220 012 | **XC** | BN | *XC* | CZ | 60312 | 60712 | 60212 | 60412 |
| 220 013 | **XC** | BN | *XC* | CZ | 60313 | 60713 | 60213 | 60413 |
| 220 014 | **XC** | BN | *XC* | CZ | 60314 | 60714 | 60214 | 60414 |
| 220 015 | **XC** | BN | *XC* | CZ | 60315 | 60715 | 60215 | 60415 |
| 220 016 | **XC** | BN | *XC* | CZ | 60316 | 60716 | 60216 | 60416 |
| 220 017 | **XC** | BN | *XC* | CZ | 60317 | 60717 | 60217 | 60417 |
| 220 018 | **XC** | BN | *XC* | CZ | 60318 | 60718 | 60218 | 60418 |
| 220 019 | **XC** | BN | *XC* | CZ | 60319 | 60719 | 60219 | 60419 |
| 220 020 | **XC** | BN | *XC* | CZ | 60320 | 60720 | 60220 | 60420 |
| 220 021 | **XC** | BN | *XC* | CZ | 60321 | 60721 | 60221 | 60421 |
| 220 022 | **XC** | BN | *XC* | CZ | 60322 | 60722 | 60222 | 60422 |
| 220 023 | **XC** | BN | *XC* | CZ | 60323 | 60723 | 60223 | 60423 |
| 220 024 | **XC** | BN | *XC* | CZ | 60324 | 60724 | 60224 | 60424 |
| 220 025 | **XC** | BN | *XC* | CZ | 60325 | 60725 | 60225 | 60425 |
| 220 026 | **XC** | BN | *XC* | CZ | 60326 | 60726 | 60226 | 60426 |
| 220 027 | **XC** | BN | *XC* | CZ | 60327 | 60727 | 60227 | 60427 |
| 220 028 | **XC** | BN | *XC* | CZ | 60328 | 60728 | 60228 | 60428 |
| 220 029 | **XC** | BN | *XC* | CZ | 60329 | 60729 | 60229 | 60429 |
| 220 030 | **XC** | BN | *XC* | CZ | 60330 | 60730 | 60230 | 60430 |
| 220 031 | **XC** | BN | *XC* | CZ | 60331 | 60731 | 60231 | 60431 |
| 220 032 | **XC** | BN | *XC* | CZ | 60332 | 60732 | 60232 | 60432 |
| 220 033 | **XC** | BN | *XC* | CZ | 60333 | 60733 | 60233 | 60433 |
| 220 034 | **XC** | BN | *XC* | CZ | 60334 | 60734 | 60234 | 60434 |

# CLASS 221     SUPER VOYAGER     BOMBARDIER

* DMS–MS–MS–MSRMB–DMF (Avanti West Coast units) or DMS–MS–(MS)–MS–DMF (CrossCountry units). Built as tilting units but tilt now isolated on CrossCountry sets.

**Construction:** Steel.
**Engine:** Cummins QSK19 of 520 kW (700 hp) at 1800 rpm.
**Transmission:** Two Alstom Onix 800 three-phase traction motors of 275 kW.
**Braking:** Rheostatic and electro-pneumatic.
**Bogies:** Bombardier HVP.
**Couplers:** Dellner 12 at outer ends, bar within unit.
**Dimensions:** 23.67 x 2.73 m.
**Gangways:** Within unit only.
**Wheel Arrangement:** 1A-A1 + 1A-A1 + 1A-A1 (+ 1A-A1) + 1A-A1.
**Doors:** Single-leaf swing plug.
**Maximum Speed:** 125 mph.
**Seating Layout:** 1: 2+1 facing/unidirectional, 2: 2+2 mainly unidirectional.
**Multiple Working:** Within class and with Classes 220 and 222 (in an emergency). Also can be controlled from Class 57/3 locomotives.

* Avanti West Coast units. MSRMB moved adjacent to the DMF. The seating in this vehicle (2+2 facing) can be used by First or Standard Class passengers depending on demand.

**Advertising livery:** 221 115 Dark grey Bombardier branding on end vehicles.

**DMS.** Bombardier Bruges/Wakefield 2001–02. –/42 1TD 1W. 58.5 t (* 58.9 t.)
**60751–794 MS (* MSRMB).** Bombardier Bruges/Wakefield 2001–02. –/66 (* –/52). 54.1 t (* 55.9 t.)
**60951–994. MS.** Bombardier Bruges/Wakefield 2001–02. –/66 1TD (* –/68 1TD). 54.8 t (* 54.3 t.)
**60851–890. MS.** Bombardier Bruges/Wakefield 2001–02. –/62 1TD (* –/68 1TD). 54.4 t (* 55.0 t.)
**DMF.** Bombardier Bruges/Wakefield 2001–02. 26/– 1TD 1W. 58.9 t (* 59.1 t.)

| 221 101 | * | VW | BN | AW | CZ | 60351 | 60951 | 60851 | 60751 | 60451 |
|---|---|---|---|---|---|---|---|---|---|---|
| 221 102 | * | VT | BN | AW | CZ | 60352 | 60952 | 60852 | 60752 | 60452 |
| 221 103 | * | VT | BN | AW | CZ | 60353 | 60953 | 60853 | 60753 | 60453 |
| 221 104 | * | VT | BN | AW | CZ | 60354 | 60954 | 60854 | 60754 | 60454 |
| 221 105 | * | VT | BN | AW | CZ | 60355 | 60955 | 60855 | 60755 | 60455 |
| 221 106 | * | VT | BN | AW | CZ | 60356 | 60956 | 60856 | 60756 | 60456 |
| 221 107 | * | VT | BN | AW | CZ | 60357 | 60957 | 60857 | 60757 | 60457 |
| 221 108 | * | VT | BN | AW | CZ | 60358 | 60958 | 60858 | 60758 | 60458 |
| 221 109 | * | VT | BN | AW | CZ | 60359 | 60959 | 60859 | 60759 | 60459 |
| 221 110 | * | VT | BN | AW | CZ | 60360 | 60960 | 60860 | 60760 | 60460 |
| 221 111 | * | VT | BN | AW | CZ | 60361 | 60961 | 60861 | 60761 | 60461 |
| 221 112 | * | VT | BN | AW | CZ | 60362 | 60962 | 60862 | 60762 | 60462 |
| 221 113 | * | VT | BN | AW | CZ | 60363 | 60963 | 60863 | 60763 | 60463 |
| 221 114 | * | VT | BN | AW | CZ | 60364 | 60964 | 60864 | 60764 | 60464 |
| 221 115 | * | AL | BN | AW | CZ | 60365 | 60965 | 60865 | 60765 | 60465 |
| 221 116 | * | VT | BN | AW | CZ | 60366 | 60966 | 60866 | 60766 | 60466 |
| 221 117 | * | VT | BN | AW | CZ | 60367 | 60967 | 60867 | 60767 | 60467 |

| | | | | | | | | | |
|---|---|---|---|---|---|---|---|---|---|
| 221 118 | * | **VT** | BN | *AW* | CZ | 60368 | 60968 | 60868 | 60768 | 60468 |
| 221 119 | | **XC** | BN | *XC* | CZ | 60369 | 60769 | 60969 | 60869 | 60469 |
| 221 120 | | **XC** | BN | *XC* | CZ | 60370 | 60770 | 60970 | 60870 | 60470 |
| 221 121 | | **XC** | BN | *XC* | CZ | 60371 | 60771 | 60971 | 60871 | 60471 |
| 221 122 | | **XC** | BN | *XC* | CZ | 60372 | 60772 | 60972 | 60872 | 60472 |
| 221 123 | | **XC** | BN | *XC* | CZ | 60373 | 60773 | 60973 | 60873 | 60473 |
| 221 124 | | **XC** | BN | *XC* | CZ | 60374 | 60774 | 60974 | 60874 | 60474 |
| 221 125 | | **XC** | BN | *XC* | CZ | 60375 | 60775 | 60975 | 60875 | 60475 |
| 221 126 | | **XC** | BN | *XC* | CZ | 60376 | 60776 | 60976 | 60876 | 60476 |
| 221 127 | | **XC** | BN | *XC* | CZ | 60377 | 60777 | 60977 | 60877 | 60477 |
| 221 128 | | **XC** | BN | *XC* | CZ | 60378 | 60778 | 60978 | 60878 | 60478 |
| 221 129 | | **XC** | BN | *XC* | CZ | 60379 | 60779 | 60979 | 60879 | 60479 |
| 221 130 | | **XC** | BN | *XC* | CZ | 60380 | 60780 | 60980 | 60880 | 60480 |
| 221 131 | | **XC** | BN | *XC* | CZ | 60381 | 60781 | 60981 | 60881 | 60481 |
| 221 132 | | **XC** | BN | *XC* | CZ | 60382 | 60782 | 60982 | 60882 | 60482 |
| 221 133 | | **XC** | BN | *XC* | CZ | 60383 | 60783 | 60983 | 60883 | 60483 |
| 221 134 | | **XC** | BN | *XC* | CZ | 60384 | 60784 | 60984 | 60884 | 60484 |
| 221 135 | | **XC** | BN | *XC* | CZ | 60385 | 60785 | 60985 | 60885 | 60485 |
| 221 136 | | **XC** | BN | *XC* | CZ | 60386 | 60786 | | 60886 | 60486 |
| 221 137 | | **XC** | BN | *XC* | CZ | 60387 | 60787 | 60987 | 60887 | 60487 |
| 221 138 | | **XC** | BN | *XC* | CZ | 60388 | 60788 | 60988 | 60888 | 60488 |
| 221 139 | | **XC** | BN | *XC* | CZ | 60389 | 60789 | 60989 | 60889 | 60489 |
| 221 140 | | **XC** | BN | *XC* | CZ | 60390 | 60790 | | 60890 | 60490 |
| 221 141 | | **XC** | BN | *XC* | CZ | 60391 | 60791 | 60991 | | 60491 |
| 221 142 | * | **VT** | BN | *AW* | CZ | 60392 | 60992 | 60986 | 60792 | 60492 |
| 221 143 | * | **VT** | BN | *AW* | CZ | 60393 | 60993 | 60994 | 60793 | 60493 |
| 221 144 | | **XC** | BN | *XC* | CZ | 60394 | 60794 | 60990 | | 60494 |

**Names (carried on MS No. 609xx):**

| | |
|---|---|
| 221 101 | 101 SQUADRON |
| 221 114 | ROYAL AIR FORCE CENTENARY 1918–2018 |

---

# CLASS 222          MERIDIAN          BOMBARDIER

**Construction:** Steel.
**Engine:** Cummins QSK19 of 560 kW (750 hp) at 1800 rpm.
**Transmission:** Two Alstom Onix 800 three-phase traction motors of 275 kW.
**Braking:** Rheostatic and electro-pneumatic.
**Bogies:** Bombardier B5005.          **Dimensions:** 23.85/23.00 x 2.73 m.
**Couplers:** Dellner at outer ends, bar within unit.
**Gangways:** Within unit only.          **Wheel Arrangement:** All cars 1A-A1.
**Doors:** Single-leaf swing plug.          **Maximum Speed:** 125 mph.
**Seating Layout:** 1: 2+1, 2: 2+2 facing/unidirectional.
**Multiple Working:** Within class and with Classes 220 and 221 (in an emergency).

**222 001–006.** 7-car units. DMF–MF–MF–MSRMB–MS–MS–DMS.

The 7-car units were built as 9-car units, before being reduced to 8-car sets and then later to 7-car sets to strengthen all 4-car units to 5-cars. 222 007 was built as a 9-car unit but later reduced to a 5-car unit.

**DMRF.** Bombardier Bruges 2004–05. 22/– 1TD 1W. 52.8 t.
**MF.** Bombardier Bruges 2004–05. 42/– 1T. 46.8 t.
**MSRMB.** Bombardier Bruges 2004–05. –/62. 48.0 t.
**MS.** Bombardier Bruges 2004–05. –/68 1T. 47.0 t.
**DMS.** Bombardier Bruges 2004–05. –/38 1TD 1W. 49.4 t.

| | | | | | | | | |
|---|---|---|---|---|---|---|---|---|
| 222 001 | **ST** | E | *EM* | DY | 60241 | 60445 | 60341 | 60621 |
| | | | | | 60561 | 60551 | 60161 | |
| 222 002 | **EI** | E | *EM* | DY | 60242 | 60346 | 60342 | 60622 |
| | | | | | 60562 | 60544 | 60162 | |
| 222 003 | **ST** | E | *EM* | DY | 60243 | 60446 | 60343 | 60623 |
| | | | | | 60563 | 60553 | 60163 | |
| 222 004 | **EI** | E | *EM* | DY | 60244 | 60345 | 60344 | 60624 |
| | | | | | 60564 | 60554 | 60164 | |
| 222 005 | **ST** | E | *EM* | DY | 60245 | 60347 | 60443 | 60625 |
| | | | | | 60555 | 60565 | 60165 | |
| 222 006 | **EI** | E | *EM* | DY | 60246 | 60447 | 60441 | 60626 |
| | | | | | 60566 | 60556 | 60166 | |

**Names (carried on MSRMB or DMS (222 003)):**

222 001  THE ENTREPRENEUR EXPRESS
222 002  THE CUTLERS' COMPANY
222 003  TORNADO
222 004  CHILDREN'S HOSPITAL SHEFFIELD
222 006  THE CARBON CUTTER

**222 007–023.** 5-car units. DMF–MC–MSRMB–MS–DMS.

**DMRF.** Bombardier Bruges 2003–04. 22/– 1TD 1W. 52.8 t.
**MC.** Bombardier Bruges 2003–04. 28/22 1T. 48.6 t.
**MSRMB.** Bombardier Bruges 2003–04. –/62. 49.6 t.
**MS.** Bombardier Bruges 2004–05. –/68 1T. 47.0 t.
**DMS.** Bombardier Bruges 2003–04. –/40 1TD 1W. 51.0 t.

| | | | | | | | | | |
|---|---|---|---|---|---|---|---|---|---|
| 222 007 | **ST** | E | *EM* | DY | 60247 | 60442 | 60627 | 60567 | 60167 |
| 222 008 | **EI** | E | *EM* | DY | 60248 | 60918 | 60628 | 60545 | 60168 |
| 222 009 | **EI** | E | *EM* | DY | 60249 | 60919 | 60629 | 60557 | 60169 |
| 222 010 | **EI** | E | *EM* | DY | 60250 | 60920 | 60630 | 60546 | 60170 |
| 222 011 | **EI** | E | *EM* | DY | 60251 | 60921 | 60631 | 60531 | 60171 |
| 222 012 | **EI** | E | *EM* | DY | 60252 | 60922 | 60632 | 60532 | 60172 |
| 222 013 | **EI** | E | *EM* | DY | 60253 | 60923 | 60633 | 60533 | 60173 |
| 222 014 | **EI** | E | *EM* | DY | 60254 | 60924 | 60634 | 60534 | 60174 |
| 222 015 | **ST** | E | *EM* | DY | 60255 | 60925 | 60635 | 60535 | 60175 |
| 222 016 | **ST** | E | *EM* | DY | 60256 | 60926 | 60636 | 60536 | 60176 |
| 222 017 | **ST** | E | *EM* | DY | 60257 | 60927 | 60637 | 60537 | 60177 |
| 222 018 | **EI** | E | *EM* | DY | 60258 | 60928 | 60638 | 60444 | 60178 |
| 222 019 | **ST** | E | *EM* | DY | 60259 | 60929 | 60639 | 60547 | 60179 |
| 222 020 | **ST** | E | *EM* | DY | 60260 | 60930 | 60640 | 60543 | 60180 |
| 222 021 | **ST** | E | *EM* | DY | 60261 | 60931 | 60641 | 60552 | 60181 |
| 222 022 | **EI** | E | *EM* | DY | 60262 | 60932 | 60642 | 60542 | 60182 |
| 222 023 | **ST** | E | *EM* | DY | 60263 | 60933 | 60643 | 60541 | 60183 |

**Names (carried on MSRMB or DMS):**

222 008  Derby Etches Park
222 015  175 YEARS OF DERBY'S RAILWAYS 1839–2014
222 017  LIONS CLUB INTERNATIONAL CENTENARY 1917–2017
222 022  INVEST IN NOTTINGHAM

**222 101–104. 4-car former Hull Trains units.** DMF–MC–MSRMB–DMS.

**DMRF.** Bombardier Bruges 2005. 22/– 1TD 1W. 52.8 t.
**MC.** Bombardier Bruges 2005. 11/46 1T. 47.1 t.
**MSRMB.** Bombardier Bruges 2005. –/62. 48.0 t.
**DMS.** Bombardier Bruges 2005.  –/40 1TD 1W. 49.4 t.

| | | | | | | | | |
|---|---|---|---|---|---|---|---|---|
| 222 101 | **EI** | E | *EM* | DY | 60271 | 60571 | 60681 | 60191 |
| 222 102 | **ST** | E | *EM* | DY | 60272 | 60572 | 60682 | 60192 |
| 222 103 | **ST** | E | *EM* | DY | 60273 | 60573 | 60683 | 60193 |
| 222 104 | **ER** | E | *EM* | DY | 60274 | 60574 | 60684 | 60194 |

# CLASS 230  D-TRAIN  METRO-CAMMELL/VIVARAIL

The Class 230 D-Train is a DEMU or diesel-battery unit rebuilt from former London Underground D78 Stock by Vivarail at Long Marston. The D-Train uses the bodyshells, bogies and electric traction motors of D78 Stock. Instead of being powered by electricity the motors are instead powered by new underfloor-mounted diesel engines: two per driving car. Modern IGBT electronic controls replace the previous mechanical camshaft controllers, incorporating automotive stop-start technology and dynamic braking.

230 001 was a prototype unit and was followed by 230 002, a prototype diesel-battery hybrid. West Midlands Trains ordered three diesel sets (numbered 230 003–005) for use on the Bedford–Bletchley Marston Vale Line from spring 2019. This was followed by an order by Transport for Wales for five 3-car diesel-battery hybrid sets (numbered 230 006–010) which are due to enter service in 2021 on the Wrexham–Bidston line.

Vivarail acquired more than 200 redundant D78 Stock vehicles that are stored at Long Marston and it is hoped that orders for further conversions will be forthcoming. South Western Railway has ordered five straight electric sets for the Isle of Wight (see Class 484).

**Construction:** Aluminium.
**Engine:** 2 x Ford Duratorq 3.2 litre engines of 150 kW (200 hp). 230 002 and 230 006–010 have 60 x 24V batteries.
**Traction motors:** TSA TMW 32-43-4 AC motors of 135 kW.
**Control System:** IGBT Inverter.        **Braking:** Rheostatic & Dynamic.
**Bogies:** Bombardier FLEXX1000 flexible-frame.
**Dimensions:** 18.37/18.12 x 2.85 m.
**Couplers:** LUL automatic wedgelock. **Gangways:** Within unit only.
**Wheel Arrangement:** Bo-Bo + 2-2 + Bo-Bo.
**Doors:** Sliding.        **Maximum Speed:** 60 mph.
**Seating Layout:** Longitudinal or 2+2 facing.
**Multiple Working:** Within class.

Rebuilt from former London Underground D78 Stock 2016–20. Original D78 numbers are shown alongside the new running numbers.

**Class 230/0. Prototype diesel or diesel-battery units.**
230 001 and potentially 230 002 as a 2-car are to be exported to the USA.

**DMS(A).** Metro-Cammell Birmingham 1979–83. 28.0 t (* 27.0 t).
**TS.** Metro-Cammell Birmingham 1979–83. 20.0 t.
**DMS(B).** Metro-Cammell Birmingham 1979–83. 28.0 t (* 23.0 t).

| 230 001 | **VI** | VI | | LM | 300001 (7058) | 300201 (17058) | 300101 (7511) |
| 230 002 * | **VI** | VI | | LM | 300002 (7122) | 300202 (17091) | 300102 (7067) |

**Class 230/0. West Midlands Trains diesel units.**

**DMS(A).** Metro-Cammell Birmingham 1979–83. –/58(+2). 33.3 t.
**DMS(B).** Metro-Cammell Birmingham 1979–83. –/40(+7) 1TD 2W. 32.3 t.

| 230 003 | **LN** | VI | *WM* | BY | 300003 (7069) | | 300103 (7127) |
| 230 004 | **LN** | VI | *WM* | BY | 300004 (7100) | | 300104 (7500) |
| 230 005 | **LN** | VI | *WM* | BY | 300005 (7066) | | 300105 (7128) |

**Class 230/0. Transport for Wales diesel-battery units.** Full details awaited.

**DMS(A).** Metro-Cammell Birmingham 1979–83.
**TS.** Metro-Cammell Birmingham 1979–83.
**DMS(B).** Metro-Cammell Birmingham 1979–83.

| 230 006 | **TW** | TW | | BD | 300006 (7098) | 300206 (17066) | 300106 (7510) |
| 230 007 | **TW** | TW | | BD | 300007 (7103) | 300207 (17063) | 300107 (7529) |
| 230 008 | **TW** | TW | | BD | 300008 (7120) | 300208 (17050) | 300108 (7065) |
| 230 009 | **TW** | TW | | BD | 300009 (7055) | 300209 (17084) | 300109 (7523) |
| 230 010 | **TW** | TW | | | 300010 (7090) | 300210 (17071) | 300110 (7017) |

---

# CLASS 231      FLIRT DMU      STADLER

DMS–TS–PP–TS–DMS. New articulated FLIRT DMUs for Transport for Wales featuring a centre power pack housing diesel engines (with no passenger accommodation in this vehicle) similar to the Greater Anglia Class 755. Air conditioned. Full details awaited. Due to enter service 2022 on the Cheltenham–Maesteg and Cardiff–Ebbw Vale lines.

**Construction:** Aluminium.
**Engines:** Four Deutz V8 of 480 kW (645 hp).
**Bogies:** Stadler/Jacobs.
**Couplers:** Dellner 10.      **Dimensions:**
**Gangways:** Within unit.      **Wheel Arrangement:** Bo-2-2-2-2-Bo.
**Doors:** Sliding plug.      **Maximum Speed:** 90 mph.
**Seating Layout:** 2+2 unidirectional/facing.
**Multiple Working:** Within class only.

**DMS(A).** Stadler Bussnang 2021–22.
**TS(A).** Stadler Bussnang 2021–22.
**PP.** Stadler Bussnang 2021–22.
**TS(B).** Stadler Bussnang 2021–22.
**DMS(B).** Stadler Bussnang 2021–22.

| | | | | | |
|---|---|---|---|---|---|
| 231 001 | 381001 | 381201 | 381401 | 381301 | 381101 |
| 231 002 | 381002 | 381202 | 381402 | 381302 | 381102 |
| 231 003 | 381003 | 381203 | 381403 | 381303 | 381103 |
| 231 004 | 381004 | 381204 | 381404 | 381304 | 381104 |
| 231 005 | 381005 | 381205 | 381405 | 381305 | 381105 |
| 231 006 | 381006 | 381206 | 381406 | 381306 | 381106 |
| 231 007 | 381007 | 381207 | 381407 | 381307 | 381107 |
| 231 008 | 381008 | 381208 | 381408 | 381308 | 381108 |
| 231 009 | 381009 | 381209 | 381409 | 381309 | 381109 |
| 231 010 | 381010 | 381210 | 381410 | 381310 | 381110 |
| 231 011 | 381011 | 381211 | 381411 | 381311 | 381111 |

# 3.3. DMU VEHICLES IN INDUSTRIAL SERVICE

This list comprises DMU vehicles that have been withdrawn from active service but continue to be used in industrial service (such as for use in emergency training).

| | | | |
|---|---|---|---|
| 142 033 | 55574 | 55624 | South Wales Police RFC Ground, Waterton Cross, Bridgend |
| 142 043 | 55584 | 55634 | Sussex Police Training Centre, Kingstanding, near Crowborough |
| 144 009 | 55809 | 55832 | East Lancashire Railway (reserved for Greater Manchester Fire & Rescue Service) |

# 4. ELECTRIC MULTIPLE UNITS

# INTRODUCTION

This section contains details of all Electric Multiple Units, usually referred to as EMUs, which can run on Britain's national railway network.

The number of EMUs in operation has been steadily increasing in recent years as both more lines have been opened or have been electrified and as the number of passengers travelling on the network has increased. EMUs work a wide variety of services, from long distance Intercity (such as the Class 390 Pendolinos) to inter-urban and suburban duties.

## LAYOUT OF INFORMATION

25 kV AC 50 Hz overhead EMUs and dual voltage EMUs are listed in numerical order of set numbers. Individual "loose" vehicles are listed in numerical order after vehicles formed into fixed formations.

750 V DC third rail EMUs are listed in numerical order of class number, then in numerical order of set number. Some of these use the former Southern Region four-digit set numbers. These are derived from theoretical six digit set numbers which are the four-digit set number prefixed by the first two numbers of the class.

Where sets or vehicles have been renumbered in recent years, former numbering detail is shown alongside current detail. Each entry is laid out as in the following example:

| Set No. | Detail | Livery | Owner | Operator | Allocation | Formation |
|---------|--------|--------|-------|----------|------------|-----------|
| 5912 | * | **SS** | P | *SW* | WD | 77835 62837 67400 77836 |

**Codes:** Codes are used to denote the livery, owner, operator and depot allocation of each Electric Multiple Unit. Details of these can be found in section 6 of this book. Where a unit or spare car is off-lease, the operator column is left blank.

**Detail Differences:** Detail differences which currently affect the areas and types of train which vehicles may work are shown, plus differences in interior layout. Where such differences occur within a class, these are shown either in the heading information or alongside the individual set or vehicle number.

**Set Formations:** Regular set formations are shown where these are normally maintained. Readers should note set formations might be temporarily varied from time to time to suit maintenance and/or operational requirements. Vehicles shown as "Spare" are not formed in any regular set formation.

**Names:** Only names carried with official sanction are listed. Names are shown in UPPER/lower case characters as actually shown on the name carried on the vehicle(s). Unless otherwise shown, complete units are regarded as named rather than just the individual car(s) which carry the name.

# GENERAL INFORMATION

## CLASSIFICATION AND NUMBERING

25 kV AC 50 Hz overhead and "Versatile" EMUs are classified in the series 300–399. 750 V DC third rail EMUs are classified in the series 400–599. More recently dual-voltage units have been numbered in the 700+ series and Hitachi IEP design units in the 800+ series. Most of the Class 8xx units are bi-mode units which can operate under both diesel or electric power.

Until 2014 EMU individual cars were numbered in the series 61000–78999, except for vehicles used on the Isle of Wight – which are numbered in a separate series, and the Class 378s, 380s and 395s, which took up the 38xxx and 39xxx series'.

For all new vehicles allocated by the Rolling Stock Library since 2014 6-digit vehicle numbers have been used.

Any vehicle constructed or converted to replace another vehicle following accident damage and carrying the same number as the original vehicle is denoted by the suffix[II] in this publication

## WHEEL ARRANGEMENT

A system whereby the number of powered axles on a bogie or frame is denoted by a letter (A = 1, B = 2, C= 3 etc) and the number of unpowered axles is denoted by a number is used in this publication. The letter "o" after a letter indicates that each axle is individually powered.

## UNITS OF MEASUREMENT

Principal details and dimensions are quoted for each class in metric and/or imperial units as considered appropriate bearing in mind common UK usage.

All dimensions and weights are quoted for vehicles in an "as new" condition with all necessary supplies (eg oil, water, sand) on board. Dimensions are quoted in the order Length – Width. All lengths quoted are over buffers or couplers as appropriate. Where two lengths are quoted, the first refers to outer vehicles in a set and the second to inner vehicles. All width dimensions quoted are maxima. All weights are shown as metric tonnes (t = tonnes).

Bogie Types are quoted in the format motored/non-motored (eg BP20/BT13 denotes BP20 motored bogies and BT non-motored bogies).

Unless noted to the contrary, all vehicles listed have bar couplers at non-driving ends.

Unless stated, traction motors power details refer to each motored car per unit.

Vehicles ordered under the auspices of BR were allocated a Lot (batch) number when ordered and these are quoted in class headings and sub-headings. Vehicles ordered since 1995 have no Lot Numbers, but the manufacturer and location that they were built is given.

# OPERATING CODES

These codes are used by train operating company staff to describe the various different types of vehicles and normally appear on data panels on the inner (ie non driving) ends of vehicles.

A "B" prefix indicates a battery vehicle.

A "P" prefix indicates a trailer vehicle on which is mounted the pantograph, instead of the default case where the pantograph is mounted on a motor vehicle.

The first part of the code describes whether or not the car has a motor or a driving cab as follows:

DM  Driving motor      DT Driving trailer     M  Motor       T  Trailer

The next letter is a "B" for cars with a brake compartment.
This is followed by the saloon details:

F    First                           S    Standard                  C  Composite

The next letter denotes the style of accommodation, which is "O" for Open for all EMU vehicles still in service.

Finally, vehicles with a buffet or kitchen area are suffixed RB or RMB for a miniature buffet counter.

Where two vehicles of the same type are formed within the same unit, the above codes may be suffixed by (A) and (B) to differentiate between vehicles.

A composite is a vehicle containing both First and Standard Class accommodation, whilst a brake vehicle is a vehicle containing separate specific accommodation for the conductor.

# ACCOMMODATION

The information given in class headings and sub-headings is in the form F/S nT (or TD) nW. For example 12/54 1T 1W denotes 12 First Class and 54 Standard Class seats, one toilet and one space for a wheelchair. A number in brackets (ie (+2)) denotes tip-up seats (in addition to the fixed seats). Tip-up seats in vestibules do not count. The seating layout of open saloons is shown as 2+1, 2+2 or 3+2 as the case may be. Where units have First Class accommodation as well as Standard Class and the layout is different for each class then these are shown separately prefixed by "1:" and "2:".

TD denotes a universal access toilet suitable for use by people with disabilities. By law all trains should have been fitted with such facilities by the start of 2020, but a number of trains were not made compliant in time and have been given time-limited dispensations for continued operation.

# 4.1. 25 kV AC 50 Hz OVERHEAD & DUAL VOLTAGE UNITS

Except where otherwise stated, all units in this section operate on 25 kV AC 50 Hz overhead only.

## CLASS 313                                                          BREL YORK

Inner suburban units.

**Formation:** DMS–TS–BDMS.
**Systems:** 25 kV AC overhead/750 V DC third rail (pantographs removed on 313/2).
**Construction:** Steel underframe, aluminium alloy body and roof.
**Traction Motors:** Four GEC G310AZ of 82.125 kW.
**Wheel Arrangement:** Bo-Bo + 2-2 + Bo-Bo.
**Braking:** Disc & rheostatic.          **Dimensions:** 20.33/20.18 x 2.82 m.
**Bogies:** BX1.                         **Couplers:** Tightlock.
**Gangways:** Within unit + end doors.  **Control System:** Camshaft.
**Doors:** Sliding.                      **Maximum Speed:** 75 mph.
**Seating Layout:** 2+2 high back facing.
**Multiple Working:** Within class.

**Class 313/1. Network Rail test unit.** Used for ETCS signalling testing. Details as 313/2 below, although this unit has been heavily modified from its original condition and now includes a toilet.

313 121    **Y**    BN   *GB*    ZG    62549  71233  62613

**Class 313/2. Southern units.** Refurbished for Brighton Coastway services. 750 V DC only (pantographs removed).

**DMS.** Lot No. 30879 1976–77. –/64. 37.0 t.
**TS.** Lot No. 30880 1976–77. –/64(+2). 31.0 t.
**BDMS.** Lot No. 30885 1976–77. –/64. 37.0 t.

| | | | | | | | |
|---|---|---|---|---|---|---|---|
| 313 201 | (313 101) | **BG** | BN | *SN* | BI | 62529 | 71213 | 62593 |
| 313 202 | (313 102) | **SN** | BN | *SN* | BI | 62530 | 71214 | 62594 |
| 313 203 | (313 103) | **SN** | BN | *SN* | BI | 62531 | 71215 | 62595 |
| 313 204 | (313 104) | **SN** | BN | *SN* | BI | 62532 | 71216 | 62596 |
| 313 205 | (313 105) | **SN** | BN | *SN* | BI | 62533 | 71217 | 62597 |
| 313 206 | (313 106) | **SN** | BN | *SN* | BI | 62534 | 71218 | 62598 |
| 313 207 | (313 107) | **SN** | BN | *SN* | BI | 62535 | 71219 | 62599 |
| 313 208 | (313 108) | **SN** | BN | *SN* | BI | 62536 | 71220 | 62600 |
| 313 209 | (313 109) | **SN** | BN | *SN* | BI | 62537 | 71221 | 62601 |
| 313 210 | (313 110) | **SN** | BN | *SN* | BI | 62538 | 71222 | 62602 |
| 313 211 | (313 111) | **SN** | BN | *SN* | BI | 62539 | 71223 | 62603 |
| 313 212 | (313 112) | **SN** | BN | *SN* | BI | 62540 | 71224 | 62604 |
| 313 213 | (313 113) | **SN** | BN | *SN* | BI | 62541 | 71225 | 62605 |
| 313 214 | (313 114) | **SN** | BN | *SN* | BI | 62542 | 71226 | 62606 |
| 313 215 | (313 115) | **SN** | BN | *SN* | BI | 62543 | 71227 | 62607 |
| 313 216 | (313 116) | **SN** | BN | *SN* | BI | 62544 | 71228 | 62608 |
| 313 217 | (313 117) | **SN** | BN | *SN* | BI | 62545 | 71229 | 62609 |

| 313 219 | (313 119) | **SN** | BN | *SN* | BI | 62547 | 71231 | 62611 |
| 313 220 | (313 120) | **SN** | BN | *SN* | BI | 62548 | 71232 | 62612 |

## CLASS 314                                    BREL YORK

Inner suburban units. All units removed from service by the end of 2019:
314 209 has been retained for conversion to a testbed hydrogen unit.

**Formation:** DMS–PTS–DMS.
**Construction:** Steel underframe, aluminium alloy body and roof.
**Traction Motors:** Four GEC G310AZ (* Brush TM61-53) of 82.125 kW.
**Wheel Arrangement:** Bo-Bo + 2-2 + Bo-Bo.
**Braking:** Disc & rheostatic.          **Dimensions:** 20.33/20.18 x 2.82 m.
**Bogies:** BX1.                          **Couplers:** Tightlock.
**Gangways:** Within unit + end doors.  **Control System:** Thyristor.
**Doors:** Sliding.                       **Maximum Speed:** 70 mph.
**Seating Layout:** 3+2 low-back facing.
**Multiple Working:** Within class and with Class 315.

**DMS.** Lot No. 30912 1979. –/68. 34.5 t.
**PTS.** Lot No. 30913 1979. –/76. 33.0 t.
**DMS.** Lot No. 30912 1979. –/68. 34.5 t.

| 314 209 | **SR** | SR | | BO | 64599 | 71458 | 64600 |

## CLASS 315                                    BREL YORK

Inner suburban units. The remaining units of this class are due to be
withdrawn during 2021.

**Formation:** DMS–TS–PTS–DMS.
**Construction:** Steel underframe, aluminium alloy body and roof.
**Traction Motors:** Four Brush TM61-53 (* GEC G310AZ) of 82.125 kW.
**Wheel Arrangement:** Bo-Bo + 2-2 + 2-2 + Bo-Bo.
**Braking:** Disc & rheostatic.          **Dimensions:** 20.18 x 2.82 m.
**Bogies:** BX1.                          **Couplers:** Tightlock.
**Gangways:** Within unit + end doors.  **Control System:** Thyristor.
**Doors:** Sliding.                       **Maximum Speed:** 75 mph.
**Seating Layout:** 3+2 low-back facing.
**Multiple Working:** Within class and with Class 314 and 317.

**DMS.** Lot No. 30902 1980–81. –/74. 38.2 t.
**TS.** Lot No. 30904 1980–81. –/86. 27.4 t.
**PTS.** Lot No. 30903 1980–81. –/75(+7) 2W. 33.8 t.
**DMS.** Lot No. 30902 1980–81. –/74. 38.2 t.

| 315 809 | **LO** | E | | ZN | 64477 | 71289 | 71397 | 64478 |
| 315 818 | **TF** | E | *XR* | IL | 64495 | 71298 | 71406 | 64496 |
| 315 819 | **TF** | E | *XR* | IL | 64497 | 71299 | 71407 | 64498 |
| 315 820 | **TF** | E | *XR* | IL | 64499 | 71300 | 71408 | 64500 |
| 315 826 | **TF** | E | *XR* | IL | 64511 | 71306 | 71414 | 64512 |
| 315 834 | **TF** | E | *XR* | IL | 64527 | 71314 | 71422 | 64528 |
| 315 837 | **TF** | E | *XR* | IL | 64533 | 71317 | 71425 | 64534 |

| | | | | | | | | |
|---|---|---|---|---|---|---|---|---|
| 315838 | | **TF** | E | *XR* | IL | 64535 | 71318 | 71426 | 64536 |
| 315839 | | **TF** | E | *XR* | IL | 64537 | 71319 | 71427 | 64538 |
| 315844 | * | **TF** | E | *XR* | IL | 64547 | 71324 | 71432 | 64548 |
| 315847 | * | **TF** | E | *XR* | IL | 64553 | 71327 | 71435 | 64554 |
| 315848 | * | **TF** | E | *XR* | IL | 64540 | 71328 | 71436 | 64556 |
| 315851 | * | **TF** | E | *XR* | IL | 64561 | 71331 | 71439 | 64562 |
| 315853 | * | **TF** | E | *XR* | IL | 64565 | 71333 | 71441 | 64566 |
| 315854 | * | **TF** | E | *XR* | IL | 64567 | 71334 | 71442 | 64568 |
| 315856 | * | **TF** | E | *XR* | IL | 64571 | 71336 | 71444 | 64572 |
| 315857 | * | **TF** | E | *XR* | IL | 64573 | 71337 | 71445 | 64574 |

# CLASS 317                                    BREL YORK/DERBY

Outer suburban units.

**Formation:** Various, see sub-class headings.
**Construction:** Steel.
**Traction Motors:** Four GEC G315BZ of 247.5 kW (except 317 722, see below).
**Wheel Arrangement:** 2-2 + Bo-Bo + 2-2 + 2-2.
**Braking:** Disc.                          **Dimensions:** 19.83/20.18 x 2.82 m.
**Bogies:** BP20 (MS), BT13 (others).       **Couplers:** Tightlock.
**Gangways:** Throughout                     **Control System:** Thyristor.
**Doors:** Sliding.                          **Maximum Speed:** 100 mph.
**Seating Layout:** Various, see sub-class headings.
**Multiple Working:** Within class & with Classes 315, 318, 319, 320, 321, 322 and 323.

**Class 317/1.** Pressure ventilated.

**Formation:** DTS–MS–TC–DTS.
**Seating Layout:** 1: 2+2 facing, 2: 3+2 facing.

* Fitted with a universal access toilet. Full details awaited.

**DTS(A).** Lot No. 30955 York 1981–82. –/74. 29.5 t.
**MS.** Lot No. 30958 York 1981–82. –/79. 49.0 t.
**TC.** Lot No. 30957 Derby 1981–82. 22/46 2T. 29.0 t.
**DTS(B).** Lot No. 30956 York 1981–82. –/71. 29.5 t.

| | | | | | | | | |
|---|---|---|---|---|---|---|---|---|
| 317337 | * | **TL** | A | *GA* | IL | 77036 | 62671 | 71613 | 77084 |
| 317338 | * | **TL** | A | *GA* | IL | 77037 | 62698 | 71614 | 77085 |
| 317339 | * | **TL** | A | *GA* | IL | 77038 | 62699 | 71615 | 77086 |
| 317340 | * | **TL** | A | *GA* | IL | 77039 | 62700 | 71616 | 77087 |
| 317341 | * | **TL** | A | *GA* | IL | 77040 | 62701 | 71617 | 77088 |
| 317342 | * | **TL** | A | *GA* | IL | 77041 | 62702 | 71618 | 77089 |
| 317343 | * | **TL** | A | *GA* | IL | 77042 | 62703 | 71619 | 77090 |
| 317344 | * | **GA** | A | *GA* | IL | 77029 | 62690 | 71620 | 77091 |
| 317345 | | **GA** | A | *GA* | IL | 77044 | 62705 | 71621 | 77092 |
| 317346 | | **GA** | A | *GA* | IL | 77045 | 62706 | 71622 | 77093 |
| 317347 | * | **GA** | A | *GA* | IL | 77046 | 62707 | 71623 | 77094 |
| 317348 | * | **TL** | A | *GA* | IL | 77047 | 62708 | 71624 | 77095 |

**Names (carried on TC):**

317345  Driver John Webb          |   317348  Richard A Jenner

**Class 317/5.** Pressure ventilated. Units renumbered from Class 317/1 in 2005 for West Anglia Metro services. Refurbished with new upholstery and Passenger Information Systems. Details as Class 317/1.

The original DTS 77048 was written off after the Cricklewood accident of 1983. A replacement vehicle was built at Wolverton in 1987 and given the same number.

| | | | | | | | | |
|---|---|---|---|---|---|---|---|---|
| 317501 | * | **GA** | A | *GA* | IL | 77024 | 62661 | 71577 | 77048<sup>II</sup> |
| 317502 | * | **GA** | A | *GA* | IL | 77001 | 62662 | 71578 | 77049 |
| 317504 | * | **GA** | A | *GA* | IL | 77003 | 62664 | 71580 | 77051 |
| 317505 | | **GA** | A | | EP | 77004 | 62665 | 71581 | 77052 |
| 317506 | * | **GA** | A | *GA* | IL | 77005 | 62666 | 71582 | 77053 |
| 317507 | * | **GA** | A | *GA* | IL | 77006 | 62667 | 71583 | 77054 |
| 317508 | * | **GA** | A | *GA* | IL | 77010 | 62697 | 71587 | 77058 |
| 317509 | | **GA** | A | | Harwich | 77011 | 62672 | 71588 | 77059 |
| 317510 | * | **GA** | A | *GA* | IL | 77012 | 62673 | 71589 | 77060 |
| 317511 | * | **GA** | A | *GA* | IL | 77014 | 62675 | 71591 | 77062 |
| 317512 | * | **GA** | A | *GA* | IL | 77015 | 62676 | 71592 | 77050 |
| 317513 | * | **GA** | A | *GA* | IL | 77016 | 62679 | 71593 | 77064 |
| 317515 | * | **GA** | A | *GA* | IL | 77019 | 62680 | 71596 | 77067 |

**Name (carried on TC):** 317507 University of Cambridge 800 Years 1209–2009

**Class 317/6.** Convection heating. Units converted from Class 317/2 by Railcare, Wolverton 1998–99 with Chapman seating.

**Formation:** DTS–MS–TS–DTC.
**Seating Layout:** 2+2 facing.

**77200–219. DTS.** Lot No. 30994 York 1985–86. –/64. 29.5 t.
**77280–283. DTS.** Lot No. 31007 York 1987. –/64. 29.5 t.
**62846–865. MS.** Lot No. 30996 York 1985–86. –/71. 49.0 t.
**62886–889. MS.** Lot No. 31009 York 1987. –/71. 49.0 t.
**71734–753. TS.** Lot No. 30997 York 1985–86. –/60(+3) 2T. 29.0 t.
**71762–765. TS.** Lot No. 31010 York 1987. –/60(+3) 2T. 29.0 t.
**77220–239. DTC.** Lot No. 30995 York 1985–86. 24/36. 29.5 t.
**77284–287. DTC.** Lot No. 31008 York 1987. 24/36. 29.5 t.

| | | | | | | | | |
|---|---|---|---|---|---|---|---|
| 317649 | **GA** | A | | Harwich | 77200 | 62846 | 71734 | 77220 |
| 317650 | **GA** | A | *GA* | IL | 77201 | 62847 | 71735 | 77221 |
| 317651 | **GA** | A | | Harwich | 77202 | 62848 | 71736 | 77222 |
| 317652 | **GA** | A | *GA* | IL | 77203 | 62849 | 71739 | 77223 |
| 317654 | **GA** | A | | Harwich | 77205 | 62851 | 71737 | 77225 |
| 317657 | **NC** | A | | EP | 77208 | 62854 | 71741 | 77228 |
| 317658 | **GA** | A | *GA* | IL | 77209 | 62855 | 71743 | 77229 |
| 317659 | **GA** | A | | EP | 77210 | 62856 | 71744 | 77230 |
| 317660 | **GA** | A | | EP | 77211 | 62857 | 71745 | 77231 |
| 317662 | **GA** | A | | EP | 77213 | 62858 | 71747 | 77233 |
| 317663 | **GA** | A | | EP | 77214 | 62860 | 71748 | 77234 |
| 317665 | **GA** | A | | EP | 77216 | 62862 | 71750 | 77236 |
| 317667 | **GA** | A | | EP | 77218 | 62864 | 71751 | 77238 |
| 317668 | **GA** | A | | EP | 77219 | 62865 | 71753 | 77239 |
| 317669 | **NC** | A | | EP | 77280 | 62886 | 71762 | 77284 |

| 317670 | **GA** | A |    | EP | 77281 | 62887 | 71763 | 77285 |
| 317671 | **NC** | A |    | EP | 77282 | 62888 | 71764 | 77286 |
| 317672 | **GA** | A |    | EP | 77283 | 62889 | 71765 | 77287 |

**Name (carried on DTC):** 317654   Richard Wells

**Class 317/7.** Units converted from Class 317/1 by Railcare, Wolverton 2000 for Stansted Express services between London Liverpool Street and Stansted. Air conditioning. Fitted with luggage stacks. Most operated by London Overground until 2020 but now being returned to service with Greater Anglia.

† 317722 received new Bombardier MJA 280-8 AC traction motors as part of an Angel trial. Two vehicles (77021 and 62682, now in **GA** livery) also received an interior refurbishment with new Fainsa seating whilst the other two vehicles were left in their Stansted Express condition (still in **NX** livery).

**Formation:** DTS–MS–TS–DTC.
**Seating Layout:** 1: 2+1 facing, 2: 2+2 facing.

**DTS.** Lot No. 30955 York 1981–82. –/52 + catering point. 31.4 t.
**MS.** Lot No. 30958 York 1981–82. –/62 (* –/64). 51.3 t.
**TS.** Lot No. 30957 Derby 1981–82. –/42(+5) 1TD 1T 1W. 30.2 t.
**DTC.** Lot No. 30956 York 1981–82. 22/16 + catering point. 31.6 t.

| 317708 |   | **LO** | A |    | IL | 77007 | 62668 | 71584 | 77055 |
| 317709 |   | **LO** | A | *GA* | IL | 77008 | 62669 | 71585 | 77056 |
| 317710 |   | **LO** | A | *GA* | IL | 77009 | 62670 | 71586 | 77057 |
| 317714 |   | **LO** | A |    | WB | 77013 | 62674 | 71590 | 77061 |
| 317719 |   | **LO** | A | *GA* | IL | 77018 | 62679 | 71595 | 77066 |
| 317722 | † | **GA/NX** | A |    | EP | 77021 | 62682 | 71598 | 77069 |
| 317723 |   | **LO** | A | *GA* | IL | 77022 | 62683 | 71599 | 77070 |
| 317729 |   | **LO** | A |    | WB | 77028 | 62689 | 71605 | 77076 |
| 317732 |   | **LO** | A |    | IL | 77031 | 62692 | 71608 | 77079 |

**Class 317/8.** Pressure Ventilated. Units refurbished and renumbered from Class 317/1 in 2005–06 at Wabtec, Doncaster for use on Stansted Express services. Displaced from Stansted services in 2011.

* Fitted with a universal access toilet. Full details awaited.

**Formation:** DTS–MS–TC–DTS.
**Seating Layout:** 1: 2+2 facing, 2: 3+2 facing.

**DTS(A).** Lot No. 30955 York 1981–82. –/66. 29.5 t.
**MS.** Lot No. 30958 York 1981–82. –/71. 49.0 t.
**TC.** Lot No. 30957 Derby 1981–82. 20/42 2T († –/62 2T). 29.0 t.
**DTS(B).** Lot No. 30956 York 1981–82. –/66. 29.5 t.

| 317881 | * | **GA** | A | *GA* | IL | 77020 | 62681 | 71597 | 77068 |
| 317882 | * | **GA** | A | *GA* | IL | 77023 | 62684 | 71600 | 77071 |
| 317883 | * | **GA** | A | *GA* | IL | 77000 | 62685 | 71601 | 77072 |
| 317884 | * | **GA** | A | *GA* | IL | 77025 | 62686 | 71602 | 77073 |
| 317885 | * | **GA** | A | *GA* | IL | 77026 | 62687 | 71603 | 77074 |
| 317886 | * | **GA** | A | *GA* | IL | 77027 | 62688 | 71604 | 77075 |

| | | | | | | | | |
|---|---|---|---|---|---|---|---|---|
| 317887 | † | **LO** | A | EP | 77043 | 62704 | 71606 | 77077 |
| 317888 | † | **LO** | A | EP | 77030 | 62691 | 71607 | 77078 |
| 317889 | † | **LO** | A | EP | 77032 | 62693 | 71609 | 77080 |
| 317890 | † | **LO** | A | EP | 77033 | 62694 | 71610 | 77081 |
| 317891 | † | **LO** | A | EP | 77034 | 62695 | 71611 | 77082 |
| 317892 | † | **LO** | A | EP | 77035 | 62696 | 71612 | 77083 | Ilford Depot |

# CLASS 318                                          BREL YORK

Outer suburban units.

**Formation**: DTS–MS–DTS.
**Construction**: Steel.
**Traction Motors**: Four Brush TM 2141 of 268 kW.
**Wheel Arrangement**: 2-2 + Bo-Bo + 2-2.
**Braking**: Disc.                        **Dimensions**: 19.83/19.92 x 2.82 m.
**Bogies**: BP20 (MS), BT13 (others).    **Couplers**: Tightlock.
**Gangways**: Within unit.               **Control System**: Thyristor.
**Doors**: Sliding.                      **Maximum Speed**: 90 mph.
**Seating Layout**: 3+2 facing.
**Multiple Working**: Within class & with Classes 317, 319, 320, 321, 322 and 323.

**77240–259. DTS.** Lot No. 30999 1985–86. –/55 1TD 2W. 32.0 t.
**77288. DTS.** Lot No. 31020 1987. –/55 1TD 2W. 32.0 t.
**62866–885. MS.** Lot No. 30998 1985–86. –/79. 53.0 t.
**62890. MS.** Lot No. 31019 1987. –/79. 53.0 t.
**77260–279. DTS.** Lot No. 31000 1985–86. –/69(+2). 31.6 t.
**77289. DTS.** Lot No. 31021 1987. –/69(+2). 31.6 t.

| | | | | | | | |
|---|---|---|---|---|---|---|---|
| 318250 | **SR** | E | *SR* | GW | 77240 | 62866 | 77260 |
| 318251 | **SR** | E | *SR* | GW | 77241 | 62867 | 77261 |
| 318252 | **SR** | E | *SR* | GW | 77242 | 62868 | 77262 |
| 318253 | **SR** | E | *SR* | GW | 77243 | 62869 | 77263 |
| 318254 | **SR** | E | *SR* | GW | 77244 | 62870 | 77264 |
| 318255 | **SR** | E | *SR* | GW | 77245 | 62871 | 77265 |
| 318256 | **SR** | E | *SR* | GW | 77246 | 62872 | 77266 |
| 318257 | **SR** | E | *SR* | GW | 77247 | 62873 | 77267 |
| 318258 | **SR** | E | *SR* | GW | 77248 | 62874 | 77268 |
| 318259 | **SR** | E | *SR* | GW | 77249 | 62875 | 77269 |
| 318260 | **SR** | E | *SR* | GW | 77250 | 62876 | 77270 |
| 318261 | **SR** | E | *SR* | GW | 77251 | 62877 | 77271 |
| 318262 | **SR** | E | *SR* | GW | 77252 | 62878 | 77272 |
| 318263 | **SR** | E | *SR* | GW | 77253 | 62879 | 77273 |
| 318264 | **SR** | E | *SR* | GW | 77254 | 62880 | 77274 |
| 318265 | **SR** | E | *SR* | GW | 77255 | 62881 | 77275 |
| 318266 | **SR** | E | *SR* | GW | 77256 | 62882 | 77276 |
| 318267 | **SR** | E | *SR* | GW | 77257 | 62883 | 77277 |
| 318268 | **SR** | E | *SR* | GW | 77258 | 62884 | 77278 |
| 318269 | **SR** | E | *SR* | GW | 77259 | 62885 | 77279 |
| 318270 | **SR** | E | *SR* | GW | 77288 | 62890 | 77289 |

# CLASS 319                                                    BREL YORK

Express and outer suburban units. Units shown * or † have a universal access toilet. Some units are being rebuilt as bi-modes (see Class 769 and Class 799).

**Formation:** Various, see sub-class headings.
**Systems:** 25 kV AC overhead/750 V DC third rail.
**Construction:** Steel.
**Traction Motors:** Four GEC G315BZ of 268 kW.
**Wheel Arrangement:** 2-2 + Bo-Bo + 2-2 + 2-2.
**Braking:** Disc.                               **Dimensions:** 20.17/20.16 x 2.82 m.
**Bogies:** P7-4 (MS), T3-7 (others).           **Couplers:** Tightlock.
**Gangways:** Within unit + end doors.          **Control System:** GTO chopper.
**Doors:** Sliding.                             **Maximum Speed:** 100 mph.
**Seating Layout:** Various, see sub-class headings.
**Multiple Working:** Within class & with Classes 317, 318, 320, 321, 322 and 323.

**Class 319/0.** DTS–MS–TS–DTS.

**Seating Layout:** 3+2 facing.

**DTS(A).** Lot No. 31022 (odd nos.) 1987–88. –/82 (* –/79). 28.2 t (* 30.7 t).
**MS.** Lot No. 31023 1987–88. –/82 (* –/81). 49.2 t (* 50.9 t).
**TS.** Lot No. 31024 1987–88. –/77 2T (* –/63 1TD 2W, † –/64 1TD 2W). 31.0 t (*† 32.5 t).
**DTS(B).** Lot No. 31025 (even nos.) 1987–88. –/78 (* –/79). 28.1 t (* 30.0 t).

| | | | | | | | | |
|---|---|---|---|---|---|---|---|---|
| 319005 | * | TL | P | WM | NN | 77299 | 62895 | 71776 | 77298 |
| 319009 | | TL | P | | ZG | 77307 | 62899 | 71780 | 77306 |
| 319010 | | TL | P | | ZG | 77309 | 62900 | 71781 | 77308 |
| 319011 | | TL | P | | ZG | 77311 | 62901 | 71782 | 77310 |
| 319012 | * | TL | P | WM | NN | 77313 | 62902 | 71783 | 77312 |
| 319013 | † | LM | P | WM | NN | 77315 | 62903 | 71784 | 77314 |

**Name (carried on TS):**  319011   John Ruskin College

**Class 319/2.** DTS–MS–TS–DTC. Units converted from Class 319/0.

**Seating Layout:** 1: 2+1 facing, 2: 2+2/3+2 facing.

**DTS.** Lot No. 31022 (odd nos.) 1987–88. –/64. 30.0 t.
**MS.** Lot No. 31023 1987–88. –/73. 51.0 t.
**TS.** Lot No. 31024 1987–88. –/52 1TD 1T. 31.0 t.
**DTC.** Lot No. 31025 (even nos.) 1987–88. 18/36. 30.0 t.

| | | | | | | | | |
|---|---|---|---|---|---|---|---|---|
| 319214 | * | TL | P | WM | NN | 77317 | 62904 | 71785 | 77316 |
| 319215 | * | TL | P | WM | NN | 77319 | 62905 | 71786 | 77318 |
| 319216 | * | LM | P | WM | NN | 77321 | 62906 | 71787 | 77320 |
| 319217 | * | TL | P | WM | NN | 77323 | 62907 | 71788 | 77322 |
| 319218 | * | TL | P | WM | NN | 77325 | 62908 | 71789 | 77324 |
| 319219 | * | TL | P | WM | NN | 77327 | 62909 | 71790 | 77326 |
| 319220 | * | TL | P | WM | NN | 77329 | 62910 | 71791 | 77328 |

**Class 319/3.** DTS–MS–TS–DTS. Converted from Class 319/1.

Refurbished with a new universal access toilet except 319 373, which has been converted for carrying parcels and roller-cages for Orion.

**Seating Layout:** 3+2 facing.

**Non-standard livery:** 319 373 Orion dark blue.

**DTS(A).** Lot No. 31063 1990. –/79. 29.0 t.
**MS.** Lot No. 31064 1990. –/81. 50.6 t.
**TS.** Lot No. 31065 1990. –/64 1TD 2W. 31.0 t.
**DTS(B).** Lot No. 31066 1990. –/79. 29.7 t.

| | | | | | | | | |
|---|---|---|---|---|---|---|---|---|
| 319 361 | * | **NR** | P | *NO* | AN | 77459 | 63043 | 71929 | 77458 |
| 319 362 | * | **NR** | P | | LM | 77461 | 63044 | 71930 | 77460 |
| 319 363 | * | **NR** | P | | LM | 77463 | 63045 | 71931 | 77462 |
| 319 364 | * | **NR** | P | | NN | 77465 | 63046 | 71932 | 77464 |
| 319 365 | * | **NR** | P | | LM | 77467 | 63047 | 71933 | 77466 |
| 319 366 | * | **NR** | P | *NO* | AN | 77469 | 63048 | 71934 | 77468 |
| 319 367 | * | **NR** | P | *NO* | AN | 77471 | 63049 | 71935 | 77470 |
| 319 368 | * | **NR** | P | *NO* | AN | 77473 | 63050 | 71936 | 77472 |
| 319 369 | * | **NR** | P | *NO* | AN | 77475 | 63051 | 71937 | 77474 |
| 319 370 | * | **NR** | P | *NO* | AN | 77477 | 63052 | 71938 | 77476 |
| 319 371 | * | **NR** | P | | LM | 77479 | 63053 | 71939 | 77478 |
| 319 372 | * | **TL** | P | *NO* | AN | 77481 | 63054 | 71940 | 77480 |
| 319 373 | | **0** | P | | ZG | 77483 | 63055 | 71941 | 77482 |
| 319 374 | * | **NR** | P | | LM | 77485 | 63056 | 71942 | 77484 |
| 319 375 | * | **NR** | P | *NO* | AN | 77487 | 63057 | 71943 | 77486 |
| 319 376 | * | **NR** | P | | LM | 77489 | 63058 | 71944 | 77488 |
| 319 377 | * | **NR** | P | | ZG | 77491 | 63059 | 71945 | 77490 |
| 319 378 | * | **NR** | P | *NO* | AN | 77493 | 63060 | 71946 | 77492 |
| 319 379 | * | **NR** | P | *NO* | AN | 77495 | 63061 | 71947 | 77494 |
| 319 380 | * | **NR** | P | | ZG | 77497 | 63062 | 71948 | 77496 |
| 319 381 | * | **NR** | P | *NO* | AN | 77973 | 63093 | 71979 | 77974 |
| 319 382 | * | **NR** | P | | ZN | 77975 | 63094 | 71980 | 77976 |
| 319 383 | * | **NR** | P | *NO* | AN | 77977 | 63095 | 71981 | 77978 |
| 319 384 | * | **NR** | P | *NO* | AN | 77979 | 63096 | 71982 | 77980 |
| 319 385 | * | **NR** | P | *NO* | AN | 77981 | 63097 | 71983 | 77982 |
| 319 386 | * | **NR** | P | *NO* | AN | 77983 | 63098 | 71984 | 77984 |

**Class 319/4.** DTC–MS–TS–DTS. Converted from Class 319/0. Refurbished with carpets. DTS(A) converted to composite.

Eight units (319 424/431/434/442/448/450/456/458) have been converted to Class 769 bi-mode units for Northern (see Class 769).

319 421/426/445/452 have been converted to Class 769 bi-mode units for Transport for Wales (see Class 769).

319 422/423/425/427/428/430/432/435–440/443/444/446/447/449/459 have been or are being to Class 769 tri-mode units for Great Western Railway.

**Non-standard livery:** 319 454 Porterbrook Innovation Hub (blue).

**Seating Layout:** 1: 2+1 facing 2: 2+2/3+2 facing.

**77331–381. DTC.** Lot No. 31022 (odd nos.) 1987–88. 12/51 (* 12/50). 30.0t (* 31.0t).
**77441–457. DTC.** Lot No. 31038 (odd nos.) 1988. 12/51 (* 12/50). 30.0t (* 31.0t).
**62911–936. MS.** Lot No. 31023 1987–88. –/74 (* –/75). 49.2t (* 52.4t).
**62961–974. MS.** Lot No. 31039 1988. –/74 (* –/75). 49.2t (* 52.4t).
**71792–817. TS.** Lot No. 31024 1987–88. –/67 2T (* –/58 1TD 2W). 31.0t (* 33.7t).
**71866–879. TS.** Lot No. 31040 1988. –67 2T (* –/58 1TD 2W). 31.0t (* 33.7t).
**77330–380. DTS.** Lot No. 31025 (even nos.) 1987–88. –/71 1W (* –/73). 28.1t (* 30.7t).
**77430–456. DTS.** Lot No. 31041 1988. –/71 1W (* –/73). 28.1t (* 30.7t).

| | | | | | | | | | |
|---|---|---|---|---|---|---|---|---|---|
| 319422 | * | GW | P | | ZN | 77333 | 62912 | 71793 | 77332 |
| 319423 | * | GW | P | | ZN | 77335 | 62913 | 71794 | 77334 |
| 319425 | * | GW | P | | LB | 77339 | 62915 | 71796 | 77338 |
| 319427 | * | GW | P | | ZN | 77343 | 62917 | 71798 | 77342 |
| 319428 | * | GW | P | | LB | 77345 | 62918 | 71799 | 77344 |
| 319429 | * | LM | P | WM | NN | 77347 | 62919 | 71800 | 77346 |
| 319432 | * | TL | P | | LB | 77353 | 62922 | 71803 | 77352 |
| 319433 | * | LM | P | WM | NN | 77355 | 62923 | 71804 | 77354 |
| 319435 | * | TL | P | | ZN | 77359 | 62925 | 71806 | 77358 |
| 319437 | * | TL | P | | LB | 77363 | 62927 | 71808 | 77362 |
| 319438 | * | TL | P | | LB | 77365 | 62928 | 71809 | 77364 |
| 319439 | * | TL | P | | ZN | 77367 | 62929 | 71810 | 77366 |
| 319440 | * | TL | P | | ZN | 77369 | 62930 | 71811 | 77368 |
| 319441 | * | LM | P | WM | NN | 77371 | 62931 | 71812 | 77370 |
| 319444 | * | TL | P | | ZA | 77377 | 62934 | 71815 | 77376 |
| 319447 | * | TL | P | | ZN | 77431 | 62961 | 71866 | 77430 |
| 319449 | * | TL | P | | ZN | 77435 | 62963 | 71868 | 77434 |
| 319451 | | FU | P | | LM | 77439 | 62965 | 71870 | 77438 |
| 319453 | | FU | P | | LM | 77443 | 62967 | 71872 | 77442 |
| 319454 | | O | P | | LM | 77445 | 62968 | 71873 | 77444 |
| 319455 | | FU | P | | LM | 77447 | 62969 | 71874 | 77446 |
| 319457 | * | LM | P | WM | NN | 77451 | 62971 | 71876 | 77450 |
| 319459 | * | TL | P | | LB | 77455 | 62973 | 71878 | 77454 |
| 319460 | * | LM | P | WM | NN | 77457 | 62974 | 71879 | 77456 |

**Name (carried on TS):** 319444　　City of St Albans

## CLASS 320　　　　　　　　　　　　　　　　BREL YORK

Suburban units. In 2016–19 ScotRail received 320401/403/404/411–418/420 (ex-Class 321s) which were refurbished and reformed as 3-cars.

**Formation:** DTS–MS–DTS.
**Construction:** Steel
**Traction Motors:** Four Brush TM2141B of 268 kW.
**Wheel Arrangement:** 2-2 + Bo-Bo + 2-2.
**Braking:** Disc.　　　　　　　　　　**Dimensions:** 19.95 x 2.82 m.
**Bogies:** P7-4 (MS), T3-7 (others).　　**Couplers:** Tightlock.
**Gangways:** Within unit.　　　　　　**Control System:** Thyristor.
**Doors:** Sliding.　　　　　　　　　　**Maximum Speed:** 90 mph.
**Seating Layout:** 3+2 facing.
**Multiple Working:** Within class & with Classes 317, 318, 319, 321, 322 and 323.

**Class 320/3.** Original build.

**DTS(A).** Lot No. 31060 1990. –/51(+4) 1TD 2W. 31.7 t.
**MS.** Lot No. 31062 1990. –/78. 52.6 t.
**DTS(B).** Lot No. 31061 1990. –/73(+2). 31.6 t.

| | | | | | | | |
|---|---|---|---|---|---|---|---|
| 320 301 | **SR** | E | *SR* | GW | 77899 | 63021 | 77921 |
| 320 302 | **SR** | E | *SR* | GW | 77900 | 63022 | 77922 |
| 320 303 | **SR** | E | *SR* | GW | 77901 | 63023 | 77923 |
| 320 304 | **SR** | E | *SR* | GW | 77902 | 63024 | 77924 |
| 320 305 | **SR** | E | *SR* | GW | 77903 | 63025 | 77925 |
| 320 306 | **SR** | E | *SR* | GW | 77904 | 63026 | 77926 |
| 320 307 | **SR** | E | *SR* | GW | 77905 | 63027 | 77927 |
| 320 308 | **SR** | E | *SR* | GW | 77906 | 63028 | 77928 |
| 320 309 | **SR** | E | *SR* | GW | 77907 | 63029 | 77929 |
| 320 310 | **SR** | E | *SR* | GW | 77908 | 63030 | 77930 |
| 320 311 | **SR** | E | *SR* | GW | 77909 | 63031 | 77931 |
| 320 312 | **SR** | E | *SR* | GW | 77910 | 63032 | 77932 |
| 320 313 | **SR** | E | *SR* | GW | 77911 | 63033 | 77933 |
| 320 314 | **SR** | E | *SR* | GW | 77912 | 63034 | 77934 |
| 320 315 | **SR** | E | *SR* | GW | 77913 | 63035 | 77935 |
| 320 316 | **SR** | E | *SR* | GW | 77914 | 63036 | 77936 |
| 320 317 | **SR** | E | *SR* | GW | 77915 | 63037 | 77937 |
| 320 318 | **SR** | E | *SR* | GW | 77916 | 63038 | 77938 |
| 320 319 | **SR** | E | *SR* | GW | 77917 | 63039 | 77939 |
| 320 320 | **SR** | E | *SR* | GW | 77918 | 63040 | 77940 |
| 320 321 | **SR** | E | *SR* | GW | 77919 | 63041 | 77941 |
| 320 322 | **SR** | E | *SR* | GW | 77920 | 63042 | 77942 |

**Class 320/4.** Former London Midland Class 321s reduced to 3-car formation and refurbished as Class 320/4s by Wabtec Doncaster/Kilmarnock 2015–19.

The original vehicles 71966 and 77960 from 321418 (now 320418) and 78114 and 63082 from 321420 (now 320420) were written off after the Watford Junction accident in 1996. The undamaged vehicles were formed together as 321418 whilst four new vehicles were built in 1997, taking the same numbers as the scrapped vehicles, and these became the second 321420.

**DTS(A).** Lot No. 31060 1990. –/54(+4) 1TD 2W. 32.0 t.
**MS.** Lot No. 31062 1990. –/79. 52.2 t.
**DTS(B).** Lot No. 31061 1990. –/74(+2). 32.0 t.

| | | | | | | | |
|---|---|---|---|---|---|---|---|
| 320 401 | (321 401) | **SR** | E | *SR* | GW | 78095 | 63063 | 77943 |
| 320 403 | (321 403) | **SR** | E | *SR* | GW | 78097 | 63065 | 77945 |
| 320 404 | (321 404) | **SR** | E | *SR* | GW | 78098 | 63066 | 77946 |
| 320 411 | (321 411) | **SR** | E | *SR* | GW | 78105 | 63073 | 77953 |
| 320 412 | (321 412) | **SR** | E | *SR* | GW | 78106 | 63074 | 77954 |
| 320 413 | (321 413) | **SR** | E | *SR* | GW | 78107 | 63075 | 77955 |
| 320 414 | (321 414) | **SR** | E | *SR* | GW | 78108 | 63076 | 77956 |
| 320 415 | (321 415) | **SR** | E | *SR* | GW | 78109 | 63077 | 77957 |
| 320 416 | (321 416) | **SR** | E | *SR* | GW | 78110 | 63078 | 77958 |
| 320 417 | (321 417) | **SR** | E | *SR* | GW | 78111 | 63079 | 77959 |
| 320 418 | (321 418) | **SR** | E | *SR* | GW | 78112 | 63080 | 77962 |
| 320 420 | (321 420) | **SR** | E | *SR* | GW | 78114ᴵᴵ | 63082ᴵᴵ | 77960ᴵᴵ |

# CLASS 321                                          BREL YORK

Outer suburban units.

**Formation:** DTC (DTS on Class 321/9)–MS–TS–DTS.
**Construction:** Steel.
**Traction Motors:** Four Brush TM2141C of 268 kW (* Four TSA010163 AC motors of 300 kW).
**Wheel Arrangement:** 2-2 + Bo-Bo + 2-2 + 2-2.
**Braking:** Disc (* and regenerative).    **Dimensions:** 19.95 x 2.82 m.
**Bogies:** P7-4 (MS), T3-7 (others).    **Couplers:** Tightlock.
**Gangways:** Within unit.
**Control System:** Thyristor (* IGBT Inverter).
**Doors:** Sliding.                         **Maximum Speed:** 100 mph.
**Seating Layout:** 1: 2+2 facing, 2: 3+2 facing.
**Multiple Working:** Within class & with Classes 317, 318, 319, 320, 322 and 323.
**Class 321/3.**

* "Renatus" rebuilt units with completely new interiors, air conditioning and Quantum seating, still arranged to a 3+2 layout in Standard Class. Fitted with new TSA AC traction motors.

**DTC.** Lot No. 31053 1988–90. 16/57 (321 347–366 16/56) (* 16/31(+4) 1TD 2W. 29.7 t (* 34.1 t).
**MS.** Lot No. 31054 1988–90. –/82 (* –/80). 51.5 t (* 53.8 t).
**TS.** Lot No. 31055 1988–90. –/75 2T (* –/78 1T). 29.1 t (* 31.7 t).
**DTS.** Lot No. 31056 1988–90. –/78 (* –/76). 29.7 t (* 32.8 t.)

| | | | | | | | | |
|---|---|---|---|---|---|---|---|---|
| 321301 | * | GR | E | GA | IL | 78049 | 62975 | 71880 | 77853 |
| 321302 | * | GR | E | GA | IL | 78050 | 62976 | 71881 | 77854 |
| 321303 | * | GR | E | GA | IL | 78051 | 62977 | 71882 | 77855 |
| 321304 | * | GR | E | GA | IL | 78052 | 62978 | 71883 | 77856 |
| 321305 | * | GR | E | GA | IL | 78053 | 62979 | 71884 | 77857 |
| 321306 | * | GR | E | GA | IL | 78054 | 62980 | 71885 | 77858 |
| 321307 | * | GR | E | GA | IL | 78055 | 62981 | 71886 | 77859 |
| 321308 | * | GR | E | GA | IL | 78056 | 62982 | 71887 | 77860 |
| 321309 | * | GR | E | GA | IL | 78057 | 62983 | 71888 | 77861 |
| 321310 | * | GR | E | GA | IL | 78058 | 62984 | 71889 | 77862 |
| 321311 | * | GR | E | GA | IL | 78059 | 62985 | 71890 | 77863 |
| 321312 | * | GR | E | GA | IL | 78060 | 62986 | 71891 | 77864 |
| 321313 | * | GR | E | GA | IL | 78061 | 62987 | 71892 | 77865 |
| 321314 | * | GR | E | GA | IL | 78062 | 62988 | 71893 | 77866 |
| 321315 | * | GR | E | GA | IL | 78063 | 62989 | 71894 | 77867 |
| 321316 | * | GR | E | GA | IL | 78064 | 62990 | 71895 | 77868 |
| 321317 | * | GR | E | GA | IL | 78065 | 62991 | 71896 | 77869 |
| 321318 | * | GR | E | GA | IL | 78066 | 62992 | 71897 | 77870 |
| 321319 | * | GR | E | GA | IL | 78067 | 62993 | 71898 | 77871 |
| 321320 | * | GR | E | GA | IL | 78068 | 62994 | 71899 | 77872 |
| 321321 | * | GR | E | GA | IL | 78069 | 62995 | 71900 | 77873 |
| 321322 | * | GR | E | GA | IL | 78070 | 62996 | 71901 | 77874 |
| 321323 | * | GR | E | GA | IL | 78071 | 62997 | 71902 | 77875 |
| 321324 | * | GR | E | GA | IL | 78072 | 62998 | 71903 | 77876 |

| 321 325 | * | GR | E | GA | IL | 78073 | 62999 | 71904 | 77877 |
| 321 326 | * | GR | E | GA | IL | 78074 | 63000 | 71905 | 77878 |
| 321 327 | * | GR | E | GA | IL | 78075 | 63001 | 71906 | 77879 |
| 321 328 | * | GR | E | GA | IL | 78076 | 63002 | 71907 | 77880 |
| 321 329 | * | GR | E | GA | IL | 78077 | 63003 | 71908 | 77881 |
| 321 330 | * | GR | E | GA | IL | 78078 | 63004 | 71909 | 77882 |
| 321 331 | | NC | E | GA | IL | 78079 | 63005 | 71910 | 77883 |
| 321 332 | | NC | E | GA | IL | 78080 | 63006 | 71911 | 77884 |
| 321 333 | | NC | E | GA | IL | 78081 | 63007 | 71912 | 77885 |
| 321 334 | | NC | E | GA | IL | 78082 | 63008 | 71913 | 77886 |
| 321 335 | | NC | E | GA | IL | 78083 | 63009 | 71914 | 77887 |
| 321 336 | | NC | E | GA | IL | 78084 | 63010 | 71915 | 77888 |
| 321 337 | | NC | E | GA | IL | 78085 | 63011 | 71916 | 77889 |
| 321 338 | | NC | E | GA | IL | 78086 | 63012 | 71917 | 77890 |
| 321 339 | | NC | E | GA | IL | 78087 | 63013 | 71918 | 77891 |
| 321 340 | | NC | E | GA | IL | 78088 | 63014 | 71919 | 77892 |
| 321 341 | | NC | E | GA | IL | 78089 | 63015 | 71920 | 77893 |
| 321 342 | | NC | E | GA | IL | 78090 | 63016 | 71921 | 77894 |
| 321 343 | | NC | E | GA | IL | 78091 | 63017 | 71922 | 77895 |
| 321 344 | | NC | E | GA | IL | 78092 | 63018 | 71923 | 77896 |
| 321 345 | | NC | E | GA | IL | 78093 | 63019 | 71924 | 77897 |
| 321 346 | | NC | E | GA | IL | 78094 | 63020 | 71925 | 77898 |
| 321 347 | | NC | E | GA | IL | 78131 | 63105 | 71991 | 78280 |
| 321 348 | | NC | E | GA | IL | 78132 | 63106 | 71992 | 78281 |
| 321 349 | | NC | E | GA | IL | 78133 | 63107 | 71993 | 78282 |
| 321 350 | | NC | E | GA | IL | 78134 | 63108 | 71994 | 78283 |
| 321 351 | | NC | E | GA | IL | 78135 | 63109 | 71995 | 78284 |
| 321 352 | | NC | E | GA | IL | 78136 | 63110 | 71996 | 78285 |
| 321 353 | | NC | E | GA | IL | 78137 | 63111 | 71997 | 78286 |
| 321 354 | | NC | E | GA | IL | 78138 | 63112 | 71998 | 78287 |
| 321 355 | | NC | E | GA | IL | 78139 | 63113 | 71999 | 78288 |
| 321 356 | | NC | E | GA | IL | 78140 | 63114 | 72000 | 78289 |
| 321 357 | | NC | E | GA | IL | 78141 | 63115 | 72001 | 78290 |
| 321 358 | | NC | E | GA | IL | 78142 | 63116 | 72002 | 78291 |
| 321 359 | | GA | E | GA | IL | 78143 | 63117 | 72003 | 78292 |
| 321 360 | | NC | E | GA | IL | 78144 | 63118 | 72004 | 78293 |
| 321 361 | | GA | E | GA | IL | 78145 | 63119 | 72005 | 78294 |
| 321 362 | | GA | E | GA | IL | 78146 | 63120 | 72006 | 78295 |
| 321 363 | | GA | E | GA | IL | 78147 | 63121 | 72007 | 78296 |
| 321 364 | | GA | E | GA | IL | 78148 | 63122 | 72008 | 78297 |
| 321 365 | | GA | E | GA | IL | 78149 | 63123 | 72009 | 78298 |
| 321 366 | | GA | E | GA | IL | 78150 | 63124 | 72010 | 78299 |

**Names (carried on TS):**

321 334 Amsterdam
321 336 GEOFFREY FREEMAN ALLEN
321 342 R. Barnes
321 343 RSA RAILWAY STUDY ASSOCIATION
321 351 London Southend Airport
321 361 Phoenix

**Class 321/4.**

The DTCs of 321 421–437 have had 12 First Class seats declassified.

Units 321 401/403/404/411–418/420 have been refurbished as Class 320/4 3-car units for ScotRail (their TS vehicles are stored or have been scrapped).

† Now-stored 321 448 received an interior refurbishment as an Eversholt demonstrator unit. Fitted with two different types of interior using seats supplied by Quantum it acted as the pilot unit for the "Renatus" work on the Class 321/3s. It is also fitted with the new TSA AC traction motors.

Units 321 437 and 321 448 and to be converted to prototype 3-car Class 600 Hydogen Multiple Units by Alstom.

**Non-standard livery:** 321 448 Eversholt demonstrator (silver with blue doors and multi-coloured stripes).

**DTC.** Lot No. 31067 1989–90. 28/40 (321 421–437 16/52, 321 438–447 16/56). 29.8 t. († 16/30(+4) 1TD 2W 33.9 t).
**MS.** Lot No. 31068 1989–90. –/79 (321 438–447 –/82). 51.6 t († –/82. 54.0 t).
**TS.** Lot No. 31069 1989–90. –/74 2T (321 438–447 –/75 2T). 29.2 t († –/62 1T. 31.7 t).
**DTS.** Lot No. 31070 1989–90. –/78. 29.8 t. († –/58. 33.2 t).

| | | | | | | | | |
|---|---|---|---|---|---|---|---|---|
| 321 402 | **FB** | E | *GA* | IL | 78096 | 63064 | 71950 | 77944 |
| 321 405 | **FB** | E | *GA* | IL | 78099 | 63067 | 71953 | 77947 |
| 321 406 | **FB** | E | *GA* | IL | 78100 | 63068 | 71954 | 77948 |
| 321 407 | **FB** | E | *GA* | IL | 78101 | 63069 | 71955 | 77949 |
| 321 408 | **FB** | E | *GA* | IL | 78102 | 63070 | 71956 | 77950 |
| 321 409 | **FB** | E | *GA* | IL | 78103 | 63071 | 71957 | 77951 |
| 321 410 | **FB** | E | *GA* | IL | 78104 | 63072 | 71958 | 77952 |
| 321 419 | **FB** | E | *GA* | IL | 78113 | 63081 | 71967 | 77961 |
| 321 421 | **NC** | E | *GA* | IL | 78115 | 63083 | 71969 | 77963 |
| 321 422 | **NC** | E | *GA* | IL | 78116 | 63084 | 71970 | 77964 |
| 321 423 | **NC** | E | *GA* | IL | 78117 | 63085 | 71971 | 77965 |
| 321 424 | **NX** | E | *GA* | IL | 78118 | 63086 | 71972 | 77966 |
| 321 425 | **NC** | E | *GA* | IL | 78119 | 63087 | 71973 | 77967 |
| 321 426 | **NX** | E | *GA* | IL | 78120 | 63088 | 71974 | 77968 |
| 321 427 | **NX** | E | *GA* | IL | 78121 | 63089 | 71975 | 77969 |
| 321 428 | **NX** | E | *GA* | IL | 78122 | 63090 | 71976 | 77970 |
| 321 429 | **NX** | E | *GA* | IL | 78123 | 63091 | 71977 | 77971 |
| 321 430 | **NX** | E | *GA* | IL | 78124 | 63092 | 71978 | 77972 |
| 321 431 | **NX** | E | *GA* | IL | 78151 | 63125 | 72011 | 78300 |
| 321 432 | **NC** | E | *GA* | IL | 78152 | 63126 | 72012 | 78301 |
| 321 433 | **NC** | E | *GA* | IL | 78153 | 63127 | 72013 | 78302 |
| 321 434 | **NC** | E | *GA* | IL | 78154 | 63128 | 72014 | 78303 |
| 321 435 | **NC** | E | *GA* | IL | 78155 | 63129 | 72015 | 78304 |
| 321 436 | **NC** | E | *GA* | IL | 78156 | 63130 | 72016 | 78305 |
| 321 437 | **NC** | E | | Widnes | 78157 | 63131 | | 78306 |
| 321 438 | **GA** | E | *GA* | IL | 78158 | 63132 | 72018 | 78307 |
| 321 439 | **GA** | E | *GA* | IL | 78159 | 63133 | 72019 | 78308 |
| 321 440 | **GA** | E | *GA* | IL | 78160 | 63134 | 72020 | 78309 |
| 321 441 | **GA** | E | *GA* | IL | 78161 | 63135 | 72021 | 78310 |
| 321 442 | **GA** | E | *GA* | IL | 78162 | 63136 | 72022 | 78311 |

| 321443 | **GA** | E | *GA* | IL | 78125 | 63099 | 71985 | 78274 |
| 321444 | **NC** | E | *GA* | IL | 78126 | 63100 | 71986 | 78275 |
| 321445 | **NC** | E | *GA* | IL | 78127 | 63101 | 71987 | 78276 |
| 321446 | **NC** | E | *GA* | IL | 78128 | 63102 | 71988 | 78277 |
| 321447 | **GA** | E | *GA* | IL | 78129 | 63103 | 71989 | 78278 |
| 321448 † | **O** | E | | Lackenby | 78130 | | 71990 | 78279 |
| Spare | **LM** | E | | ZB (S) | 71959 | | | |

**Names (carried on TS):**

321409 Dame Alice Owen's School 400 Years of Learning
321428 The Essex Commuter
321442 Crouch Valley 1889–2014
321444 Essex Lifeboats
321446 George Mullings

**Class 321/9.** DTS(A)–MS–TS–DTS(B).

**DTS(A).** Lot No. 31108 1991. –/45(+6) 1TD 2W. 31.7 t.
**MS.** Lot No. 31109 1991. –/79. 52.1 t.
**TS.** Lot No. 31110 1991. –/78. 30.6 t.
**DTS(B).** Lot No. 31111 1991. –/79. 30.6 t.

| 321901 | **NB** | E | *GA* | IL | 77990 | 63153 | 72128 | 77993 |
| 321902 | **NB** | E | *GA* | IL | 77991 | 63154 | 72129 | 77994 |
| 321903 | **NB** | E | *GA* | IL | 77992 | 63155 | 72130 | 77995 |

# CLASS 322                                          BREL YORK

Units built for use on Stansted Airport services, used for a number of years with ScotRail before transfer to Northern and in 2020 to Greater Anglia.

**Formation:** DTS–MS–TS–DTS.
**Construction:** Steel.
**Traction Motors:** Four Brush TM2141C of 268 kW.
**Wheel Arrangement:** 2-2 + Bo-Bo + 2-2 + 2-2.
**Braking:** Disc. **Dimensions:** 19.95/19.92 x 2.82 m.
**Bogies:** P7-4 (MS), T3-7 (others). **Couplers:** Tightlock.
**Gangways:** Within unit. **Control System:** Thyristor.
**Doors:** Sliding. **Maximum Speed:** 100 mph.
**Seating Layout:** 3+2 facing.
**Multiple Working:** Within class & with Classes 317, 318, 319, 320, 321 and 323.

**DTS(A).** Lot No. 31094 1990. –/54(+4) 1TD 2W. 31.7 t.
**MS.** Lot No. 31092 1990. –/83. 52.1 t.
**TS.** Lot No. 31093 1990. –/80 1T. 30.6 t.
**DTS(B).** Lot No. 31091 1990. –/79. 30.6 t.

| 322481 | **NB** | E | *GA* | IL | 78163 | 63137 | 72023 | 77985 |
| 322482 | **NB** | E | *GA* | IL | 78164 | 63138 | 72024 | 77986 |
| 322483 | **NB** | E | *GA* | IL | 78165 | 63139 | 72025 | 77987 |
| 322484 | **NB** | E | *GA* | IL | 78166 | 63140 | 72026 | 77988 |
| 322485 | **NB** | E | *GA* | IL | 78167 | 63141 | 72027 | 77989 |

# CLASS 323  HUNSLET TRANSPORTATION PROJECTS

Suburban units.

**Formation:** DMS–PTS–DMS.
**Construction:** Welded aluminium alloy.
**Traction Motors:** Four Holec DMKT 52/24 asynchronous of 146 kW.
**Wheel Arrangement:** Bo-Bo + 2-2 + Bo-Bo.
**Braking:** Disc & regenerative.          **Dimensions:** 23.37/23.44 x 2.80 m.
**Bogies:** SRP BP62 (DMS), BT52 (PTS). **Couplers:** Tightlock.
**Gangways:** Within unit.                **Control System:** IGBT Inverter.
**Doors:** Sliding plug.                   **Maximum Speed:** 90 mph.
**Seating Layout:** 3+2 facing/unidirectional.
**Multiple Working:** Within class & with Classes 317, 318, 319, 320, 321 and 322.

DMS(B) vehicles 65003 and 65005 in 323203/205 and 65019 and 65021 in 323219/221 switched between units following accident damage and were not returned to their original sets, instead swapping numbers.

**DMS(A).** Lot No. 31112 Hunslet 1992–93. –/97. 41.0 t.
**TS.** Lot No. 31113 Hunslet 1992–93. –/81(+3) 1TD 2W. 39.4t.
**DMS(B).** Lot No. 31114 Hunslet 1992–93. –/97. 41.0 t.

| | | | | | | | |
|---|---|---|---|---|---|---|---|
| 323201 | **WI** | P | *WM* | SO | 64001 | 72201 | 65001 |
| 323202 | **WI** | P | *WM* | SO | 64002 | 72202 | 65002 |
| 323203 | **WI** | P | *WM* | SO | 64003 | 72203 | 65003 |
| 323204 | **WI** | P | *WM* | SO | 64004 | 72204 | 65004 |
| 323205 | **WI** | P | *WM* | SO | 64005 | 72205 | 65005 |
| 323206 | **WI** | P | *WM* | SO | 64006 | 72206 | 65006 |
| 323207 | **WI** | P | *WM* | SO | 64007 | 72207 | 65007 |
| 323208 | **WI** | P | *WM* | SO | 64008 | 72208 | 65008 |
| 323209 | **WI** | P | *WM* | SO | 64009 | 72209 | 65009 |
| 323210 | **WI** | P | *WM* | SO | 64010 | 72210 | 65010 |
| 323211 | **WI** | P | *WM* | SO | 64011 | 72211 | 65011 |
| 323212 | **WI** | P | *WM* | SO | 64012 | 72212 | 65012 |
| 323213 | **WI** | P | *WM* | SO | 64013 | 72213 | 65013 |
| 323214 | **WI** | P | *WM* | SO | 64014 | 72214 | 65014 |
| 323215 | **WI** | P | *WM* | SO | 64015 | 72215 | 65015 |
| 323216 | **WI** | P | *WM* | SO | 64016 | 72216 | 65016 |
| 323217 | **WI** | P | *WM* | SO | 64017 | 72217 | 65017 |
| 323218 | **WI** | P | *WM* | SO | 64018 | 72218 | 65018 |
| 323219 | **WI** | P | *WM* | SO | 64019 | 72219 | 65019 |
| 323220 | **WI** | P | *WM* | SO | 64020 | 72220 | 65020 |
| 323221 | **WI** | P | *WM* | SO | 64021 | 72221 | 65021 |
| 323222 | **WI** | P | *WM* | SO | 64022 | 72222 | 65022 |
| 323223 | **NR** | P | *NO* | AN | 64023 | 72223 | 65023 |
| 323224 | **NR** | P | *NO* | AN | 64024 | 72224 | 65024 |
| 323225 | **NR** | P | *NO* | AN | 64025 | 72225 | 65025 |
| 323226 | **NR** | P | *NO* | AN | 64026 | 72226 | 65026 |
| 323227 | **NR** | P | *NO* | AN | 64027 | 72227 | 65027 |
| 323228 | **NR** | P | *NO* | AN | 64028 | 72228 | 65028 |
| 323229 | **NR** | P | *NO* | AN | 64029 | 72229 | 65029 |

| 323 230 | **NR** | P | *NO* | AN | 64030 | 72230 | 65030 |
| 323 231 | **NR** | P | *NO* | AN | 64031 | 72231 | 65031 |
| 323 232 | **NR** | P | *NO* | AN | 64032 | 72232 | 65032 |
| 323 233 | **NR** | P | *NO* | AN | 64033 | 72233 | 65033 |
| 323 234 | **NR** | P | *NO* | AN | 64034 | 72234 | 65034 |
| 323 235 | **NR** | P | *NO* | AN | 64035 | 72235 | 65035 |
| 323 236 | **NR** | P | *NO* | AN | 64036 | 72236 | 65036 |
| 323 237 | **NR** | P | *NO* | AN | 64037 | 72237 | 65037 |
| 323 238 | **NR** | P | *NO* | AN | 64038 | 72238 | 65038 |
| 323 239 | **NR** | P | *NO* | AN | 64039 | 72239 | 65039 |
| 323 240 | **WI** | P | *WM* | SO | 64040 | 72340 | 65040 |
| 323 241 | **WI** | P | *WM* | SO | 64041 | 72341 | 65041 |
| 323 242 | **WI** | P | *WM* | SO | 64042 | 72342 | 65042 |
| 323 243 | **WI** | P | *WM* | SO | 64043 | 72343 | 65043 |

**Name (carried on TS):**

323 241   Dave Pomroy 323 Fleet Engineer 40 Years Service

# CLASS 325                                                     ABB DERBY

Postal units based on Class 319s. Compatible with diesel or electric locomotive haulage. Built for dual voltage use, but 750 V DC third rail shoe gear has been removed as it is not required on current duties.

**Formation:** DTPMV–MPMV–TPMV–DTPMV.
**System:** 25 kV AC overhead.
**Construction:** Steel.
**Traction Motors:** Four GEC G315BZ of 268 kW.
**Wheel Arrangement:** 2-2 + Bo-Bo + 2-2 + 2-2.
**Braking:** Disc.                           **Dimensions:** 19.33 x 2.82 m.
**Bogies:** P7-4 (MPMV), T3-7 (others).      **Couplers:** Drop-head buckeye.
**Gangways:** None.                          **Control System:** GTO Chopper.
**Doors:** Roller shutter.                   **Maximum Speed:** 100 mph.
**Multiple Working:** Within class.

**DTPMV.** Lot No. 31144 1995. 29.1 t.
**MPMV.** Lot No. 31145 1995. 49.5 t.
**TPMV.** Lot No. 31146 1995. 30.7 t.

| 325 001 | **RM** | RM | *DB* | CE | 68300 | 68340 | 68360 | 68301 |
| 325 002 | **RM** | RM | *DB* | CE | 68302 | 68341 | 68361 | 68303 |
| 325 003 | **RM** | RM | *DB* | CE | 68304 | 68342 | 68362 | 68305 |
| 325 004 | **RM** | RM | *DB* | CE | 68306 | 68343 | 68363 | 68307 |
| 325 005 | **RM** | RM | *DB* | CE | 68308 | 68344 | 68364 | 68309 |
| 325 006 | **RM** | RM | *DB* | CE | 68310 | 68345 | 68365 | 68311 |
| 325 007 | **RM** | RM | *DB* | CE | 68312 | 68346 | 68366 | 68313 |
| 325 008 | **RM** | RM | *DB* | CE | 68314 | 68347 | 68367 | 68315 |
| 325 009 | **RM** | RM | *DB* | CE | 68316 | 68349 | 68368 | 68317 |
| 325 011 | **RM** | RM | *DB* | CE | 68320 | 68350 | 68370 | 68321 |
| 325 012 | **RM** | RM | *DB* | CE | 68322 | 68351 | 68371 | 68323 |
| 325 013 | **RM** | RM | *DB* | CE | 68324 | 68352 | 68372 | 68325 |
| 325 014 | **RM** | RM | *DB* | CE | 68326 | 68353 | 68373 | 68327 |

| 325015 | **RM** | RM | *DB* | CE | 68328 | 68354 | 68374 | 68329 |
| 325016 | **RM** | RM | *DB* | CE | 68330 | 68355 | 68375 | 68331 |

**Name (carried on one side of each DTPMV):**

325008    Peter Howarth CBE

# CLASS 331               CIVITY               CAF

New Northern outer suburban units.

**Formation:** DMS–PTS–DMS or DMS–PTS–TS–DMS.
**Construction:** Aluminium.
**Traction Motors:** Four TSA asynchronous of 220 kW.
**Wheel Arrangement:** Bo-Bo + 2-2 + Bo-Bo or Bo-Bo + 2-2 + 2-2 + Bo-Bo.
**Braking:** Disc & regenerative.       **Dimensions:** 24.03/23.35 x 2.55 m.
**Bogies:** CAF.                        **Couplers:** Dellner.
**Gangways:** Within unit.              **Control System:** IGBT Inverter.
**Doors:** Sliding plug.                **Maximum Speed:** 100 mph.
**Heating & ventilation:** Air conditioning.
**Seating:** 2+2 facing/unidirectional.  **Multiple Working:** Within class.

**Class 331/0.** DMS–PTS–DMS. 3-car units. Used in North-West England.

**DMS.** CAF Zaragoza/Newport 2017–20. –/45(+8) 1TD 2W. 40.8 t.
**PTS.** CAF Zaragoza/Newport 2017–20. –/76(+4). 34.9 t.
**DMS.** CAF Zaragoza/Newport 2017–20. –/63(+7). 39.8 t.

| 331001 | **NR** | E | *NO* | AN | 463001 | 464001 | 466001 |
| 331002 | **NR** | E | *NO* | AN | 463002 | 464002 | 466002 |
| 331003 | **NR** | E | *NO* | AN | 463003 | 464003 | 466003 |
| 331004 | **NR** | E | *NO* | AN | 463004 | 464004 | 466004 |
| 331005 | **NR** | E | *NO* | AN | 463005 | 464005 | 466005 |
| 331006 | **NR** | E | *NO* | AN | 463006 | 464006 | 466006 |
| 331007 | **NR** | E | *NO* | AN | 463007 | 464007 | 466007 |
| 331008 | **NR** | E | *NO* | AN | 463008 | 464008 | 466008 |
| 331009 | **NR** | E | *NO* | AN | 463009 | 464009 | 466009 |
| 331010 | **NR** | E | *NO* | AN | 463010 | 464010 | 466010 |
| 331011 | **NR** | E | *NO* | AN | 463011 | 464011 | 466011 |
| 331012 | **NR** | E | *NO* | AN | 463012 | 464012 | 466012 |
| 331013 | **NR** | E | *NO* | AN | 463013 | 464013 | 466013 |
| 331014 | **NR** | E | *NO* | AN | 463014 | 464014 | 466014 |
| 331015 | **NR** | E | *NO* | AN | 463015 | 464015 | 466015 |
| 331016 | **NR** | E | *NO* | AN | 463016 | 464016 | 466016 |
| 331017 | **NR** | E | *NO* | AN | 463017 | 464017 | 466017 |
| 331018 | **NR** | E | *NO* | AN | 463018 | 464018 | 466018 |
| 331019 | **NR** | E | *NO* | AN | 463019 | 464019 | 466019 |
| 331020 | **NR** | E | *NO* | AN | 463020 | 464020 | 466020 |
| 331021 | **NR** | E | *NO* | AN | 463021 | 464021 | 466021 |
| 331022 | **NR** | E | *NO* | AN | 463022 | 464022 | 466022 |
| 331023 | **NR** | E | *NO* | AN | 463023 | 464023 | 466023 |
| 331024 | **NR** | E | *NO* | AN | 463024 | 464024 | 466024 |
| 331025 | **NR** | E | *NO* | AN | 463025 | 464025 | 466025 |

| 331 026 | **NR** | E | *NO* | AN | 463026 | 464026 | 466026 |
| 331 027 | **NR** | E | *NO* | AN | 463027 | 464027 | 466027 |
| 331 028 | **NR** | E | *NO* | AN | 463028 | 464028 | 466028 |
| 331 029 | **NR** | E | *NO* | AN | 463029 | 464029 | 466029 |
| 331 030 | **NR** | E | *NO* | AN | 463030 | 464030 | 466030 |
| 331 031 | **NR** | E | *NO* | AN | 463031 | 464031 | 466031 |

**Class 331/1.** DMS–PTS–TS–DMS. 4-car units. Used in West Yorkshire.

**DMS.** CAF Zaragoza/Newport 2017–19. –/45(+8) 1TD 2W. 40.8 t.
**PTS.** CAF Zaragoza/Newport 2017–19. –/76(+4). 34.9 t.
**TS.** CAF Zaragoza/Newport 2017–19. –/76(+4). 30.1 t.
**DMS.** CAF Zaragoza/Newport 2017–19. –/63(+7). 39.8 t.

| 331 101 | **NR** | E | *NO* | NL | 463101 | 464101 | 465101 | 466101 |
| 331 102 | **NR** | E | *NO* | NL | 463102 | 464102 | 465102 | 466102 |
| 331 103 | **NR** | E | *NO* | NL | 463103 | 464103 | 465103 | 466103 |
| 331 104 | **NR** | E | *NO* | NL | 463104 | 464104 | 465104 | 466104 |
| 331 105 | **NR** | E | *NO* | NL | 463105 | 464105 | 465105 | 466105 |
| 331 106 | **NR** | E | *NO* | NL | 463106 | 464106 | 465106 | 466106 |
| 331 107 | **NR** | E | *NO* | NL | 463107 | 464107 | 465107 | 466107 |
| 331 108 | **NR** | E | *NO* | NL | 463108 | 464108 | 465108 | 466108 |
| 331 109 | **NR** | E | *NO* | NL | 463109 | 464109 | 465109 | 466109 |
| 331 110 | **NR** | E | *NO* | NL | 463110 | 464110 | 465110 | 466110 |
| 331 111 | **NR** | E | *NO* | NL | 463111 | 464111 | 465111 | 466111 |
| 331 112 | **NR** | E | *NO* | NL | 463112 | 464112 | 465112 | 466112 |

**Names (carried on driving cars):**

| 331 106 | Proud to be Northern | | 331 110 | Proud to be Northern |

# CLASS 332    HEATHROW EXPRESS CAF/SIEMENS

These dedicated Heathrow Express units were all withdrawn by the end of 2020 (replaced by Class 387s) and are currently awaiting disposal.

**Formation:** DMS–TS–PTS–(TS)–DMF.
**Construction:** Steel.
**Traction Motors:** Two Siemens monomotors asynchronous of 350 kW.
**Wheel Arrangement:** B-B + 2-2 + 2-2 (+ 2-2) + B-B.
**Braking:** Disc. **Dimensions:** 23.74/23.35/23.14 x 2.75 m.
**Bogies:** CAF. **Couplers:** Scharfenberg 10L.
**Gangways:** Within unit. **Control System:** IGBT Inverter.
**Doors:** Sliding plug. **Maximum Speed:** 100 mph.
**Heating & ventilation:** Air conditioning.
**Seating:** 1: 1+1 facing/unidirectional, 2: 2+2 mainly unidirectional.
**Multiple Working:** Within class.

**Advertising livery:** Tata Communications (various colours).

**DMS**. CAF 1997–98. –/43(+8). 49.9 t.
**72400–412. TS**. CAF 1997–98. –/64(+11). 38.4 t.
**PTS**. CAF 1997–98. –/39(+11) 1TD 2W. 47.6 t.
**72415–418. TS**. CAF 2002. –/56 35.8 t.
**DMF**. CAF 1997–98. 20/–. 49.5 t.

| | | | | | | | | |
|---|---|---|---|---|---|---|---|---|
| 332001 | **AL** | HE | OH | 78400 | 72412 | 63400 | | 78401 |
| 332004 | **AL** | HE | OH | 78406 | 72405 | 63403 | | 78407 |
| 332006 | **AL** | HE | OH | 78410 | 72410 | 63405 | 72415 | 78411 |
| 332008 | **AL** | HE | OH | 78414 | 72413 | 63407 | 72418 | 78415 |
| 332009 | **AL** | HE | OH | 78416 | 72400 | 63408 | 72416 | 78417 |
| 332011 | **AL** | HE | OH | 78420 | 72403 | 63410 | | 78421 |
| 332013 | **AL** | HE | OH | 78424 | 72408 | 63412 | | 78425 |

# CLASS 333 {CAF/SIEMENS}

West Yorkshire area suburban units.

**Formation:** DMS–PTS–TS–DMS.
**Construction:** Steel.
**Traction Motors:** Two Siemens monomotors asynchronous of 350 kW.
**Wheel Arrangement:** B-B + 2-2 + 2-2 + B-B.
**Braking:** Disc. **Dimensions:** 23.74/23.35 x 2.75 m.
**Bogies:** CAF. **Couplers:** Dellner 10L.
**Gangways:** Within unit. **Control System:** IGBT Inverter.
**Doors:** Sliding plug. **Maximum Speed:** 100 mph.
**Heating & ventilation:** Air conditioning. **Multiple Working:** Within class.
**Seating Layout:** 3+2 facing/unidirectional.

333001–008 were made up to 4-car units from 3-car units in 2002.

333009–016 were made up to 4-car units from 3-car units in 2003.

**DMS(A)**. (odd Nos.) CAF Zaragoza 2001. –/90. 50.0 t.
**PTS**. CAF Zaragoza 2001. –/73(+7) 1TD 2W. 46.0 t.
**TS**. CAF Zaragoza 2002–03. –/100. 38.5 t.
**DMS(B)**. (even Nos.) CAF Zaragoza 2001. –/90. 50.0 t.

| | | | | | | | |
|---|---|---|---|---|---|---|---|
| 333001 | **NR** | A | *NO* | NL | 78451 | 74461 | 74477 | 78452 |
| 333002 | **NR** | A | *NO* | NL | 78453 | 74462 | 74478 | 78454 |
| 333003 | **NR** | A | *NO* | NL | 78455 | 74463 | 74479 | 78456 |
| 333004 | **NR** | A | *NO* | NL | 78457 | 74464 | 74480 | 78458 |
| 333005 | **NR** | A | *NO* | NL | 78459 | 74465 | 74481 | 78460 |
| 333006 | **NR** | A | *NO* | NL | 78461 | 74466 | 74482 | 78462 |
| 333007 | **NR** | A | *NO* | NL | 78463 | 74467 | 74483 | 78464 |
| 333008 | **NR** | A | *NO* | NL | 78465 | 74468 | 74484 | 78466 |
| 333009 | **NR** | A | *NO* | NL | 78467 | 74469 | 74485 | 78468 |
| 333010 | **NR** | A | *NO* | NL | 78469 | 74470 | 74486 | 78470 |
| 333011 | **NR** | A | *NO* | NL | 78471 | 74471 | 74487 | 78472 |
| 333012 | **NR** | A | *NO* | NL | 78473 | 74472 | 74488 | 78474 |
| 333013 | **NR** | A | *NO* | NL | 78475 | 74473 | 74489 | 78476 |
| 333014 | **NR** | A | *NO* | NL | 78477 | 74474 | 74490 | 78478 |
| 333015 | **NR** | A | *NO* | NL | 78479 | 74475 | 74491 | 78480 |
| 333016 | **NR** | A | *NO* | NL | 78481 | 74476 | 74492 | 78482 |

# CLASS 334    JUNIPER    ALSTOM BIRMINGHAM

Outer suburban units.

**Formation:** DMS–PTS–DMS.
**Construction:** Steel.
**Traction Motors:** Two Alstom ONIX 800 asynchronous of 270 kW.
**Wheel Arrangement:** 2-Bo + 2-2 + Bo-2.
**Braking:** Disc.                              **Dimensions:** 21.01/19.94 x 2.80 m.
**Bogies:** Alstom LTB3/TBP3.                   **Couplers:** Dellner.
**Gangways:** Within unit.                      **Control System:** IGBT Inverter.
**Doors:** Sliding plug.                        **Maximum Speed:** 90 mph.
**Heating & ventilation:** Air conditioning.
**Seating Layout:** 2+2 facing/unidirectional (3+2 in PTS).
**Multiple Working:** Within class.

**DMS(A).** Alstom Birmingham 1999–2001. –/64. 42.6 t.
**PTS.** Alstom Birmingham 1999–2001. –/55 1TD 1W. 39.4 t.
**DMS(B).** Alstom Birmingham 1999–2001. –/59(+3). 42.6 t.

| | | | | | | | |
|---|---|---|---|---|---|---|---|
| 334001 | **SR** | E | *SR* | GW | 64101 | 74301 | 65101 |
| 334002 | **SR** | E | *SR* | GW | 64102 | 74302 | 65102 |
| 334003 | **SR** | E | *SR* | GW | 64103 | 74303 | 65103 |
| 334004 | **SR** | E | *SR* | GW | 64104 | 74304 | 65104 |
| 334005 | **SR** | E | *SR* | GW | 64105 | 74305 | 65105 |
| 334006 | **SR** | E | *SR* | GW | 64106 | 74306 | 65106 |
| 334007 | **SR** | E | *SR* | GW | 64107 | 74307 | 65107 |
| 334008 | **SR** | E | *SR* | GW | 64108 | 74308 | 65108 |
| 334009 | **SR** | E | *SR* | GW | 64109 | 74309 | 65109 |
| 334010 | **SR** | E | *SR* | GW | 64110 | 74310 | 65110 |
| 334011 | **SR** | E | *SR* | GW | 64111 | 74311 | 65111 |
| 334012 | **SR** | E | *SR* | GW | 64112 | 74312 | 65112 |
| 334013 | **SR** | E | *SR* | GW | 64113 | 74313 | 65113 |
| 334014 | **SR** | E | *SR* | GW | 64114 | 74314 | 65114 |
| 334015 | **SR** | E | *SR* | GW | 64115 | 74315 | 65115 |
| 334016 | **SR** | E | *SR* | GW | 64116 | 74316 | 65116 |
| 334017 | **SR** | E | *SR* | GW | 64117 | 74317 | 65117 |
| 334018 | **SR** | E | *SR* | GW | 64118 | 74318 | 65118 |
| 334019 | **SR** | E | *SR* | GW | 64119 | 74319 | 65119 |
| 334020 | **SR** | E | *SR* | GW | 64120 | 74320 | 65120 |
| 334021 | **SR** | E | *SR* | GW | 64121 | 74321 | 65121 |
| 334022 | **SR** | E | *SR* | GW | 64122 | 74322 | 65122 |
| 334023 | **SR** | E | *SR* | GW | 64123 | 74323 | 65123 |
| 334024 | **SR** | E | *SR* | GW | 64124 | 74324 | 65124 |
| 334025 | **SR** | E | *SR* | GW | 64125 | 74325 | 65125 |
| 334026 | **SR** | E | *SR* | GW | 64126 | 74326 | 65126 |
| 334027 | **SR** | E | *SR* | GW | 64127 | 74327 | 65127 |
| 334028 | **SR** | E | *SR* | GW | 64128 | 74328 | 65128 |
| 334029 | **SR** | E | *SR* | GW | 64129 | 74329 | 65129 |
| 334030 | **SR** | E | *SR* | GW | 64130 | 74330 | 65130 |
| 334031 | **SR** | E | *SR* | GW | 64131 | 74331 | 65131 |
| 334032 | **SR** | E | *SR* | GW | 64132 | 74332 | 65132 |

| 334033 | **SR** | E | *SR* | GW | 64133 | 74333 | 65133 |
| 334034 | **SR** | E | *SR* | GW | 64134 | 74334 | 65134 |
| 334035 | **SR** | E | *SR* | GW | 64135 | 74335 | 65135 |
| 334036 | **SR** | E | *SR* | GW | 64136 | 74336 | 65136 |
| 334037 | **SR** | E | *SR* | GW | 64137 | 74337 | 65137 |
| 334038 | **SR** | E | *SR* | GW | 64138 | 74338 | 65138 |
| 334039 | **SR** | E | *SR* | GW | 64139 | 74339 | 65139 |
| 334040 | **SR** | E | *SR* | GW | 64140 | 74340 | 65140 |

# CLASS 345        AVENTRA        BOMBARDIER DERBY

These 9-car units are being delivered for London's Crossrail/Elizabeth Line. Some units are in service as 7-car units, mainly on services between Liverpool Street, ahead of the heavily delayed opening of the full Elizabeth Line, now not expected until 2022. 9-car units are in service on trains from Paddington to Heathrow Airport and Reading.

The design is marketed as "Aventra" by Bombardier and is a development of the successful Electrostar design.

**Formation:** DMS–PMS–MS–MS*–TS–MS*–MS–PMS–DMS.
* Initially these MS vehicles are missing from some units. For units in traffic that are missing these vehicles, the missing vehicles are shown in *italics*.
**System:** 25 kV AC overhead.
**Construction:** Aluminium.
**Traction Motors:** Two Bombardier asynchronous of 265 kW.
**Wheel Arrangement:** 2-Bo + Bo-2 + Bo-Bo (+ Bo-2) + 2-2 (+ 2-Bo) + Bo-Bo + 2-Bo + Bo-2.
**Braking:** Disc & regenerative.          **Dimensions:** 23.62/22.50 m x 2.78 m.
**Bogies:** FLEXX B5000 inside-frame.    **Couplers:** Dellner.
**Gangways:** Within unit.                **Control System:** IGBT Inverter.
**Doors:** Sliding plug (three per vehicle). **Maximum Speed:** 90 mph.
**Heating & ventilation:** Air conditioning.
**Seating Layout:** Mostly longitudinal, with some 2+2 facing.
**Multiple Working:** Within class.

**DMS(A).** Bombardier Derby 2015–19. –/46. 39.0 t.
**PMS(A).** Bombardier Derby 2015–19. –/46(+6). 37.1 t.
**MS(A).** Bombardier Derby 2015–19. –/46(+6). 36.5 t.
**MS(B).** Bombardier Derby 2015–19. –/49(+3). 31.4 t.
**TS.** Bombardier Derby 2015–19. –/38(+12). 29.7 t.
**MS(C).** Bombardier Derby 2015–19. –/49(+3). 31.4 t.
**MS(D).** Bombardier Derby 2015–19. –/46(+6). 37.2 t.
**PMS(B).** Bombardier Derby 2015–19. –/46(+6). 37.1 t.
**DMS(B).** Bombardier Derby 2015–19. –/46. 39.0 t.

| 345001 | **XR** | RF | | | 340101 | 340201 | 340301 | 340401 | 340501 |
| | | | | | 340601 | 340701 | 340801 | 340901 | |
| 345002 | **XR** | RF | | | 340102 | 340202 | 340302 | 340402 | 340502 |
| | | | | | 340602 | 340702 | 340802 | 340902 | |
| 345003 | **XR** | RF | *XR* | OC | 340103 | 340203 | 340303 | *340403* | 340503 |
| | | | | | *340603* | 340703 | 340803 | 340903 | |

| | | | | | | | | | |
|---|---|---|---|---|---|---|---|---|---|
| 345004 | **XR** | RF | *XR* | OC | 340104 | 340204 | 340304 | 340404 | 340504 |
| | | | | | 340604 | 340704 | 340804 | 340904 | |
| 345005 | **XR** | RF | *XR* | OC | 340105 | 340205 | 340305 | *340405* | 340505 |
| | | | | | *340605* | 340705 | 340805 | 340905 | |
| 345006 | **XR** | RF | *XR* | OC | 340106 | 340206 | 340306 | *340406* | 340506 |
| | | | | | *340606* | 340706 | 340806 | 340906 | |
| 345007 | **XR** | RF | *XR* | OC | 340107 | 340207 | 340307 | *340407* | 340507 |
| | | | | | *340607* | 340707 | 340807 | 340907 | |
| 345008 | **XR** | RF | *XR* | OC | 340108 | 340208 | 340308 | *340408* | 340508 |
| | | | | | *340608* | 340708 | 340808 | 340908 | |
| 345009 | **XR** | RF | *XR* | OC | 340109 | 340209 | 340309 | 340409 | 340509 |
| | | | | | *340609* | 340709 | 340809 | 340909 | |
| 345010 | **XR** | RF | *XR* | OC | 340110 | 340210 | 340310 | *340410* | 340510 |
| | | | | | *340610* | 340710 | 340810 | 340910 | |
| 345011 | **XR** | RF | *XR* | OC | 340111 | 340211 | 340311 | *340411* | 340511 |
| | | | | | *340611* | 340711 | 340811 | 340911 | |
| 345012 | **XR** | RF | *XR* | OC | 340112 | 340212 | 340312 | *340412* | 340512 |
| | | | | | *340612* | 340712 | 340812 | 340912 | |
| 345013 | **XR** | RF | *XR* | OC | 340113 | 340213 | 340313 | *340413* | 340513 |
| | | | | | *340613* | 340713 | 340813 | 340913 | |
| 345014 | **XR** | RF | *XR* | OC | 340114 | 340214 | 340314 | *340414* | 340514 |
| | | | | | *340614* | 340714 | 340814 | 340914 | |
| 345015 | **XR** | RF | *XR* | OC | 340115 | 340215 | 340315 | *340415* | 340515 |
| | | | | | *340615* | 340715 | 340815 | 340915 | |
| 345016 | **XR** | RF | *XR* | OC | 340116 | 340216 | 340316 | *340416* | 340516 |
| | | | | | *340616* | 340716 | 340816 | 340916 | |
| 345017 | **XR** | RF | *XR* | OC | 340117 | 340217 | 340317 | *340417* | 340517 |
| | | | | | *340617* | 340717 | 340817 | 340917 | |
| 345018 | **XR** | RF | | | 340118 | 340218 | 340318 | 340418 | 340518 |
| | | | | | 340618 | 340718 | 340818 | 340918 | |
| 345019 | **XR** | RF | | | 340119 | 340219 | 340319 | 340419 | 340519 |
| | | | | | 340619 | 340719 | 340819 | 340919 | |
| 345020 | **XR** | RF | *XR* | OC | 340120 | 340220 | 340320 | *340420* | 340520 |
| | | | | | *340620* | 340720 | 340820 | 340920 | |
| 345021 | **XR** | RF | *XR* | OC | 340121 | 340221 | 340321 | 340421 | 340521 |
| | | | | | 340621 | 340721 | 340821 | 340921 | |
| 345022 | **XR** | RF | *XR* | OC | 340122 | 340222 | 340322 | *340422* | 340522 |
| | | | | | *340622* | 340722 | 340822 | 340922 | |
| 345023 | **XR** | RF | *XR* | OC | 340123 | 340223 | 340323 | 340423 | 340523 |
| | | | | | 340623 | 340723 | 340823 | 340923 | |
| 345024 | **XR** | RF | | | 340124 | 340224 | 340324 | 340424 | 340524 |
| | | | | | 340624 | 340724 | 340824 | 340924 | |
| 345025 | **XR** | RF | | | 340125 | 340225 | 340325 | 340425 | 340525 |
| | | | | | 340625 | 340725 | 340825 | 340925 | |
| 345026 | **XR** | RF | | | 340126 | 340226 | 340326 | 340426 | 340526 |
| | | | | | 340626 | 340726 | 340826 | 340926 | |
| 345027 | **XR** | RF | *XR* | OC | 340127 | 340227 | 340327 | 340427 | 340527 |
| | | | | | 340627 | 340727 | 340827 | 340927 | |
| 345028 | **XR** | RF | *XR* | OC | 340128 | 340228 | 340328 | 340428 | 340528 |
| | | | | | 340628 | 340728 | 340828 | 340928 | |

| 345 029 | **XR** | RF | *XR* | OC | 340129 | 340229 | 340329 | *340429* | 340529 |
|---------|--------|----|------|-----|--------|--------|--------|----------|--------|
|         |        |    |      |     | *340629* | 340729 | 340829 | 340929 |        |
| 345 030 | **XR** | RF | *XR* | OC | 340130 | 340230 | 340330 | 340430 | 340530 |
|         |        |    |      |     | 340630 | 340730 | 340830 | 340930 |        |
| 345 031 | **XR** | RF |      |     | 340131 | 340231 | 340331 | 340431 | 340531 |
|         |        |    |      |     | 340631 | 340731 | 340831 | 340931 |        |
| 345 032 | **XR** | RF |      |     | 340132 | 340232 | 340332 | 340432 | 340532 |
|         |        |    |      |     | 340632 | 340732 | 340832 | 340932 |        |
| 345 033 | **XR** | RF |      |     | 340133 | 340233 | 340333 | 340433 | 340533 |
|         |        |    |      |     | 340633 | 340733 | 340833 | 340933 |        |
| 345 034 | **XR** | RF | *XR* | OC | 340134 | 340234 | 340334 | 340434 | 340534 |
|         |        |    |      |     | 340634 | 340734 | 340834 | 340934 |        |
| 345 035 | **XR** | RF | *XR* | OC | 340135 | 340235 | 340335 | 340435 | 340535 |
|         |        |    |      |     | 340635 | 340735 | 340835 | 340935 |        |
| 345 036 | **XR** | RF |      |     | 340136 | 340236 | 340336 | 340436 | 340536 |
|         |        |    |      |     | 340636 | 340736 | 340836 | 340936 |        |
| 345 037 | **XR** | RF | *XR* | OC | 340137 | 340237 | 340337 | 340437 | 340537 |
|         |        |    |      |     | 340637 | 340737 | 340837 | 340937 |        |
| 345 038 | **XR** | RF | *XR* | OC | 340138 | 340238 | 340338 | *340438* | 340538 |
|         |        |    |      |     | *340638* | 340738 | 340838 | 340938 |        |
| 345 039 | **XR** | RF | *XR* | OC | 340139 | 340239 | 340339 | *340439* | 340539 |
|         |        |    |      |     | *340639* | 340739 | 340839 | 340939 |        |
| 345 040 | **XR** | RF | *XR* | OC | 340140 | 340240 | 340340 | *340440* | 340540 |
|         |        |    |      |     | *340640* | 340740 | 340840 | 340940 |        |
| 345 041 | **XR** | RF |      |     | 340141 | 340241 | 340341 | 340441 | 340541 |
|         |        |    |      |     | 340641 | 340741 | 340841 | 340941 |        |
| 345 042 | **XR** | RF | *XR* | OC | 340142 | 340242 | 340342 | *340442* | 340542 |
|         |        |    |      |     | *340642* | 340742 | 340842 | 340942 |        |
| 345 043 | **XR** | RF | *XR* | OC | 340143 | 340243 | 340343 | 340443 | 340543 |
|         |        |    |      |     | 340643 | 340743 | 340843 | 340943 |        |
| 345 044 | **XR** | RF | *XR* | OC | 340144 | 340244 | 340344 | *340444* | 340544 |
|         |        |    |      |     | *340644* | 340744 | 340844 | 340944 |        |
| 345 045 | **XR** | RF |      |     | 340145 | 340245 | 340345 | 340445 | 340545 |
|         |        |    |      |     | 340645 | 340745 | 340845 | 340945 |        |
| 345 046 | **XR** | RF |      |     | 340146 | 340246 | 340346 | 340446 | 340546 |
|         |        |    |      |     | 340646 | 340746 | 340846 | 340946 |        |
| 345 047 | **XR** | RF | *XR* | OC | 340147 | 340247 | 340347 | 340447 | 340547 |
|         |        |    |      |     | 340647 | 340747 | 340847 | 340947 |        |
| 345 048 | **XR** | RF |      |     | 340148 | 340248 | 340348 | 340448 | 340548 |
|         |        |    |      |     | 340648 | 340748 | 340848 | 340948 |        |
| 345 049 | **XR** | RF | *XR* | OC | 340149 | 340249 | 340349 | *340449* | 340549 |
|         |        |    |      |     | *340649* | 340749 | 340849 | 340949 |        |
| 345 050 | **XR** | RF |      |     | 340150 | 340250 | 340350 | 340450 | 340550 |
|         |        |    |      |     | 340650 | 340750 | 340850 | 340950 |        |
| 345 051 | **XR** | RF | *XR* | OC | 340151 | 340251 | 340351 | *340451* | 340551 |
|         |        |    |      |     | *340651* | 340751 | 340851 | 340951 |        |
| 345 052 | **XR** | RF | *XR* | OC | 340152 | 340252 | 340352 | *340452* | 340552 |
|         |        |    |      |     | *340652* | 340752 | 340852 | 340952 |        |
| 345 053 | **XR** | RF | *XR* | OC | 340153 | 340253 | 340353 | 340453 | 340553 |
|         |        |    |      |     | 340653 | 340753 | 340853 | 340953 |        |

| 345 054 | **XR** | RF | *XR* | OC | 340154 | 340254 | 340354 | 340454 | 340554 |
|---------|--------|----|------|----|--------|--------|--------|--------|--------|
|         |        |    |      |    | 340654 | 340754 | 340854 | 340954 |        |
| 345 055 | **XR** | RF | *XR* | OC | 340155 | 340255 | 340355 | 340455 | 340555 |
|         |        |    |      |    | 340655 | 340755 | 340855 | 340955 |        |
| 345 056 | **XR** | RF | *XR* | OC | 340156 | 340256 | 340356 | *340456* | 340556 |
|         |        |    |      |    | *340656* | 340756 | 340856 | 340956 |        |
| 345 057 | **XR** | RF | *XR* | OC | 340157 | 340257 | 340357 | *340457* | 340557 |
|         |        |    |      |    | *340657* | 340757 | 340857 | 340957 |        |
| 345 058 | **XR** | RF | *XR* | OC | 340158 | 340258 | 340358 | 340458 | 340558 |
|         |        |    |      |    | 340658 | 340758 | 340858 | 340958 |        |
| 345 059 | **XR** | RF | *XR* | OC | 340159 | 340259 | 340359 | 340459 | 340559 |
|         |        |    |      |    | 340659 | 340759 | 340859 | 340959 |        |
| 345 060 | **XR** | RF | *XR* | OC | 340160 | 340260 | 340360 | 340460 | 340560 |
|         |        |    |      |    | 340660 | 340760 | 340860 | 340960 |        |
| 345 061 | **XR** | RF | *XR* | OC | 340161 | 340261 | 340361 | 340461 | 340561 |
|         |        |    |      |    | 340661 | 340761 | 340861 | 340961 |        |
| 345 062 | **XR** | RF | *XR* | OC | 340162 | 340262 | 340362 | 340462 | 340562 |
|         |        |    |      |    | 340662 | 340762 | 340862 | 340962 |        |
| 345 063 | **XR** | RF | *XR* | OC | 340163 | 340263 | 340363 | *340463* | 340563 |
|         |        |    |      |    | *340663* | 340763 | 340863 | 340963 |        |
| 345 064 | **XR** | RF | *XR* | OC | 340164 | 340264 | 340364 | *340464* | 340564 |
|         |        |    |      |    | *340664* | 340764 | 340864 | 340964 |        |
| 345 065 | **XR** | RF | *XR* | OC | 340165 | 340265 | 340365 | 340465 | 340565 |
|         |        |    |      |    | 340665 | 340765 | 340865 | 340965 |        |
| 345 066 | **XR** | RF | *XR* | OC | 340166 | 340266 | 340366 | 340466 | 340566 |
|         |        |    |      |    | 340666 | 340766 | 340866 | 340966 |        |
| 345 067 | **XR** | RF |      |    | 340167 | 340267 | 340367 | 340467 | 340567 |
|         |        |    |      |    | 340667 | 340767 | 340867 | 340967 |        |
| 345 068 | **XR** | RF | *XR* | OC | 340168 | 340268 | 340368 | 340468 | 340568 |
|         |        |    |      |    | 340668 | 340768 | 340868 | 340968 |        |
| 345 069 | **XR** | RF |      |    | 340169 | 340269 | 340369 | 340469 | 340569 |
|         |        |    |      |    | 340669 | 340769 | 340869 | 340969 |        |
| 345 070 | **XR** | RF | *XR* | OC | 340170 | 340270 | 340370 | 340470 | 340570 |
|         |        |    |      |    | 340670 | 340770 | 340870 | 340970 |        |

# CLASS 350             DESIRO UK                    SIEMENS

Outer suburban and long distance units.

**Formation:** DMC–TC–PTS–DMC.
**Systems:** 25 kV AC overhead (350/1s built with 750 V DC, but equipment currently decommissioned).
**Construction:** Welded aluminium.
**Traction Motors:** 4 Siemens 1TB2016-0GB02 asynchronous of 250 kW.
**Wheel Arrangement:** Bo-Bo + 2-2 + 2-2 + Bo-Bo.
**Braking:** Disc & regenerative.          **Dimensions:** 20.34 x 2.79 m.
**Bogies:** SGP SF5000.                     **Couplers:** Dellner 12.
**Gangways:** Throughout.                   **Control System:** IGBT Inverter.
**Doors:** Sliding plug.                     **Maximum Speed:** 110 mph.
**Heating & ventilation:** Air conditioning.
**Seating Layout:** Various, see sub-class headings.

**Multiple Working:** Within class.

**Class 350/1.** Original-build units owned by Angel Trains. Formerly part of an aborted South West Trains 5-car Class 450/2 order. 2+2 seating.

**Seating Layout:** 1: 2+2 facing, 2: 2+2 facing/unidirectional.

**Advertising livery:** 350 110 Project 110 (silver centre cars).

**DMS(A).** Siemens Krefeld 2004–05. –/60. 48.7 t.
**TC.** Siemens Krefeld/Prague 2004–05. 24/32 1T. 36.2 t.
**PTS.** Siemens Krefeld/Prague 2004–05. –/50(+9) 1TD 2W. 45.2 t.
**DMS(B).** Siemens Krefeld 2004–05. –/60. 49.2 t.

| | | | | | | | | |
|---|---|---|---|---|---|---|---|---|
| 350 101 | **LN** | A | *WM* | NN | 63761 | 66811 | 66861 | 63711 |
| 350 102 | **LN** | A | *WM* | NN | 63762 | 66812 | 66862 | 63712 |
| 350 103 | **LN** | A | *WM* | NN | 63765 | 66813 | 66863 | 63713 |
| 350 104 | **LN** | A | *WM* | NN | 63764 | 66814 | 66864 | 63714 |
| 350 105 | **LM** | A | *WM* | NN | 63763 | 66815 | 66868 | 63715 |
| 350 106 | **LN** | A | *WM* | NN | 63766 | 66816 | 66866 | 63716 |
| 350 107 | **LM** | A | *WM* | NN | 63767 | 66817 | 66867 | 63717 |
| 350 108 | **LN** | A | *WM* | NN | 63768 | 66818 | 66865 | 63718 |
| 350 109 | **LM** | A | *WM* | NN | 63769 | 66819 | 66869 | 63719 |
| 350 110 | **AL** | A | *WM* | NN | 63770 | 66820 | 66870 | 63720 |
| 350 111 | **LN** | A | *WM* | NN | 63771 | 66821 | 66871 | 63721 |
| 350 112 | **LM** | A | *WM* | NN | 63772 | 66822 | 66872 | 63722 |
| 350 113 | **LM** | A | *WM* | NN | 63773 | 66823 | 66873 | 63723 |
| 350 114 | **LM** | A | *WM* | NN | 63774 | 66824 | 66874 | 63724 |
| 350 115 | **LN** | A | *WM* | NN | 63775 | 66825 | 66875 | 63725 |
| 350 116 | **LM** | A | *WM* | NN | 63776 | 66826 | 66876 | 63726 |
| 350 117 | **LM** | A | *WM* | NN | 63777 | 66827 | 66877 | 63727 |
| 350 118 | **LM** | A | *WM* | NN | 63778 | 66828 | 66878 | 63728 |
| 350 119 | **LM** | A | *WM* | NN | 63779 | 66829 | 66879 | 63729 |
| 350 120 | **LM** | A | *WM* | NN | 63780 | 66830 | 66880 | 63730 |
| 350 121 | **LN** | A | *WM* | NN | 63781 | 66831 | 66881 | 63731 |
| 350 122 | **LN** | A | *WM* | NN | 63782 | 66832 | 66882 | 63732 |
| 350 123 | **LN** | A | *WM* | NN | 63783 | 66833 | 66883 | 63733 |
| 350 124 | **LM** | A | *WM* | NN | 63784 | 66834 | 66884 | 63734 |
| 350 125 | **LN** | A | *WM* | NN | 63785 | 66835 | 66885 | 63735 |
| 350 126 | **LM** | A | *WM* | NN | 63786 | 66836 | 66886 | 63736 |
| 350 127 | **LM** | A | *WM* | NN | 63787 | 66837 | 66887 | 63737 |
| 350 128 | **LM** | A | *WM* | NN | 63788 | 66838 | 66888 | 63738 |
| 350 129 | **LN** | A | *WM* | NN | 63789 | 66839 | 66889 | 63739 |
| 350 130 | **LN** | A | *WM* | NN | 63790 | 66840 | 66890 | 63740 |

**Class 350/2.** Owned by Porterbrook Leasing.

**Seating Layout:** 1: 2+2 facing, 2: 3+2 facing/unidirectional.

At the time of writing sets 350 233/246/264 are running with misformed formations, as shown.

**DMS(A).** Siemens Krefeld 2008–09. –/70. 43.7 t.
**TC.** Siemens Krefeld 2008–09. 24/42 1T. 35.3 t.
**PTS.** Siemens Prague 2008–09. –/61(+9) 1TD 2W. 42.9 t.
**DMS(B).** Siemens Krefeld 2008–09. –/70. 44.2 t.

| 350 231 | LI | P | *WM* | NN | 61431 | 65231 | 67531 | 61531 |
|---|---|---|---|---|---|---|---|---|
| 350 232 | LI | P | *WM* | NN | 61432 | 65232 | 67532 | 61532 |
| 350 233 | LM | P | *WM* | NN | 61433 | 65233 | 67533 | 61546 |
| 350 234 | LI | P | *WM* | NN | 61434 | 65234 | 67534 | 61534 |
| 350 235 | LM | P | *WM* | NN | 61435 | 65235 | 67535 | 61535 |
| 350 236 | LM | P | *WM* | NN | 61436 | 65236 | 67536 | 61536 |
| 350 237 | LM | P | *WM* | NN | 61437 | 65237 | 67537 | 61537 |
| 350 238 | LM | P | *WM* | NN | 61438 | 65238 | 67538 | 61538 |
| 350 239 | LI | P | *WM* | NN | 61439 | 65239 | 67539 | 61539 |
| 350 240 | LI | P | *WM* | NN | 61440 | 65240 | 67540 | 61540 |
| 350 241 | LM | P | *WM* | NN | 61441 | 65241 | 67541 | 61541 |
| 350 242 | LM | P | *WM* | NN | 61442 | 65242 | 67542 | 61542 |
| 350 243 | LM | P | *WM* | NN | 61443 | 65243 | 67543 | 61543 |
| 350 244 | LI | P | *WM* | NN | 61444 | 65244 | 67544 | 61544 |
| 350 245 | LI | P | *WM* | NN | 61445 | 65245 | 67545 | 61545 |
| 350 246 | LM | P | *WM* | NN | 61446 | 65246 | 67546 | 61564 |
| 350 247 | LM | P | *WM* | NN | 61447 | 65247 | 67547 | 61547 |
| 350 248 | LM | P | *WM* | NN | 61448 | 65248 | 67548 | 61548 |
| 350 249 | LM | P | *WM* | NN | 61449 | 65249 | 67549 | 61549 |
| 350 250 | LM | P | *WM* | NN | 61450 | 65250 | 67550 | 61550 |
| 350 251 | LM | P | *WM* | NN | 61451 | 65251 | 67551 | 61551 |
| 350 252 | LI | P | *WM* | NN | 61452 | 65252 | 67552 | 61552 |
| 350 253 | LI | P | *WM* | NN | 61453 | 65253 | 67553 | 61553 |
| 350 254 | LI | P | *WM* | NN | 61454 | 65254 | 67554 | 61554 |
| 350 255 | LM | P | *WM* | NN | 61455 | 65255 | 67555 | 61555 |
| 350 256 | LM | P | *WM* | NN | 61456 | 65256 | 67556 | 61556 |
| 350 257 | LI | P | *WM* | NN | 61457 | 65257 | 67557 | 61557 |
| 350 258 | LI | P | *WM* | NN | 61458 | 65258 | 67558 | 61558 |
| 350 259 | LI | P | *WM* | NN | 61459 | 65259 | 67559 | 61559 |
| 350 260 | LM | P | *WM* | NN | 61460 | 65260 | 67560 | 61560 |
| 350 261 | LM | P | *WM* | NN | 61461 | 65261 | 67561 | 61561 |
| 350 262 | LI | P | *WM* | NN | 61462 | 65262 | 67562 | 61562 |
| 350 263 | LI | P | *WM* | NN | 61463 | 65263 | 67563 | 61563 |
| 350 264 | LM | P | *WM* | NN | 61464 | 65264 | 67564 | 61533 |
| 350 265 | LM | P | *WM* | NN | 61465 | 65265 | 67565 | 61565 |
| 350 266 | LM | P | *WM* | NN | 61466 | 65266 | 67566 | 61566 |
| 350 267 | LI | P | *WM* | NN | 61467 | 65267 | 67567 | 61567 |

**Class 350/3.** Owned by Angel Trains.

**Seating Layout:** 1: 2+2 facing, 2: 2+2 facing/unidirectional.

**DMS(A).** Siemens Krefeld 2014. –/60. 44.2 t.
**TC.** Siemens Krefeld 2014. 24/36 1T. 36.3 t.
**PTS.** Siemens Krefeld 2014. –/50(+9) 1TD 2W. 44.0 t.
**DMS(B).** Siemens Krefeld 2014. –/60. 45.0 t.

| 350 368 | LN | A | *WM* | NN | 60141 | 60511 | 60651 | 60151 |
|---|---|---|---|---|---|---|---|---|
| 350 369 | LN | A | *WM* | NN | 60142 | 60512 | 60652 | 60152 |
| 350 370 | LN | A | *WM* | NN | 60143 | 60513 | 60653 | 60153 |
| 350 371 | LN | A | *WM* | NN | 60144 | 60514 | 60654 | 60154 |
| 350 372 | LN | A | *WM* | NN | 60145 | 60515 | 60655 | 60155 |
| 350 373 | LN | A | *WM* | NN | 60146 | 60516 | 60656 | 60156 |

| 350374 | **LN** | A | *WM* | NN | 60147 | 60517 | 60657 | 60157 |
| 350375 | **LN** | A | *WM* | NN | 60148 | 60518 | 60658 | 60158 |
| 350376 | **LN** | A | *WM* | NN | 60149 | 60519 | 60659 | 60159 |
| 350377 | **LN** | A | *WM* | NN | 60150 | 60520 | 60660 | 60160 |

**Names (carried on one side of PTS):**

350375   Vic Hall | 350377   Graham Taylor OBE

**Class 350/4.** Owned by Angel Trains. Previously operated by TransPennine Express before transfer to West Midlands Trains in 2019–20.

**Seating Layout:** 1: 2+1 facing, 2: 2+2 facing/unidirectional.

**DMS(A).** Siemens Krefeld 2013–14. –/56. 44.2 t.
**TC.** Siemens Krefeld 2013–14. 19/24 1T. 36.2 t.
**PTS.** Siemens Krefeld 2013–14. –/42 1TD 1T. 44.6 t.
**DMS(B).** Siemens Krefeld 2013–14. –/56. 45.0 t.

| 350401 | **LN** | A | *WM* | NN | 60691 | 60901 | 60941 | 60671 |
| 350402 | **LN** | A | *WM* | NN | 60692 | 60902 | 60942 | 60672 |
| 350403 | **LN** | A | *WM* | NN | 60693 | 60903 | 60943 | 60673 |
| 350404 | **LN** | A | *WM* | NN | 60694 | 60904 | 60944 | 60674 |
| 350405 | **LN** | A | *WM* | NN | 60695 | 60905 | 60945 | 60675 |
| 350406 | **LN** | A | *WM* | NN | 60696 | 60906 | 60946 | 60676 |
| 350407 | **LN** | A | *WM* | NN | 60697 | 60907 | 60947 | 60677 |
| 350408 | **LN** | A | *WM* | NN | 60698 | 60908 | 60948 | 60678 |
| 350409 | **LN** | A | *WM* | NN | 60699 | 60909 | 60949 | 60679 |
| 350410 | **LN** | A | *WM* | NN | 60700 | 60910 | 60950 | 60680 |

# CLASS 357 ELECTROSTAR
## ADTRANZ/BOMBARDIER DERBY

Provision for 750 V DC supply if required.

**Formation:** DMS–MS–PTS–DMS.
**Construction:** Welded aluminium alloy underframe, sides and roof with steel ends. All sections bolted together.
**Traction Motors:** Two Adtranz asynchronous of 250 kW.
**Wheel Arrangement:** 2-Bo + 2-Bo + 2-2 + Bo-2.
**Braking:** Disc & regenerative.        **Dimensions:** 20.40/19.99 x 2.80 m.
**Bogies:** Adtranz P3-25/T3-25.          **Couplers:** Tightlock.
**Gangways:** Within unit.                **Control System:** IGBT Inverter.
**Doors:** Sliding plug.                  **Maximum Speed:** 100 mph.
**Heating & ventilation:** Air conditioning.
**Seating Layout:** 3+2 facing/unidirectional.
**Multiple Working:** Within class.

**Class 357/0.** Owned by Porterbrook Leasing.

**DMS(A).** Adtranz Derby 1999–2001. –/71. 40.7 t.
**MS.** Adtranz Derby 1999–2001. –/78. 36.7 t.
**PTS.** Adtranz Derby 1999–2001. –/58(+4) 1TD 2W. 39.5 t.
**DMS(B).** Adtranz Derby 1999–2001. –/71. 40.7 t.

| 357 001 | **C2** | P | *C2* | EM | 67651 | 74151 | 74051 | 67751 |
| 357 002 | **C2** | P | *C2* | EM | 67652 | 74152 | 74052 | 67752 |
| 357 003 | **C2** | P | *C2* | EM | 67653 | 74153 | 74053 | 67753 |
| 357 004 | **C2** | P | *C2* | EM | 67654 | 74154 | 74054 | 67754 |
| 357 005 | **C2** | P | *C2* | EM | 67655 | 74155 | 74055 | 67755 |
| 357 006 | **C2** | P | *C2* | EM | 67656 | 74156 | 74056 | 67756 |
| 357 007 | **C2** | P | *C2* | EM | 67657 | 74157 | 74057 | 67757 |
| 357 008 | **C2** | P | *C2* | EM | 67658 | 74158 | 74058 | 67758 |
| 357 009 | **C2** | P | *C2* | EM | 67659 | 74159 | 74059 | 67759 |
| 357 010 | **C2** | P | *C2* | EM | 67660 | 74160 | 74060 | 67760 |
| 357 011 | **C2** | P | *C2* | EM | 67661 | 74161 | 74061 | 67761 |
| 357 012 | **C2** | P | *C2* | EM | 67662 | 74162 | 74062 | 67762 |
| 357 013 | **C2** | P | *C2* | EM | 67663 | 74163 | 74063 | 67763 |
| 357 014 | **C2** | P | *C2* | EM | 67664 | 74164 | 74064 | 67764 |
| 357 015 | **C2** | P | *C2* | EM | 67665 | 74165 | 74065 | 67765 |
| 357 016 | **C2** | P | *C2* | EM | 67666 | 74166 | 74066 | 67766 |
| 357 017 | **C2** | P | *C2* | EM | 67667 | 74167 | 74067 | 67767 |
| 357 018 | **C2** | P | *C2* | EM | 67668 | 74168 | 74068 | 67768 |
| 357 019 | **C2** | P | *C2* | EM | 67669 | 74169 | 74069 | 67769 |
| 357 020 | **C2** | P | *C2* | EM | 67670 | 74170 | 74070 | 67770 |
| 357 021 | **C2** | P | *C2* | EM | 67671 | 74171 | 74071 | 67771 |
| 357 022 | **C2** | P | *C2* | EM | 67672 | 74172 | 74072 | 67772 |
| 357 023 | **C2** | P | *C2* | EM | 67673 | 74173 | 74073 | 67773 |
| 357 024 | **C2** | P | *C2* | EM | 67674 | 74174 | 74074 | 67774 |
| 357 025 | **C2** | P | *C2* | EM | 67675 | 74175 | 74075 | 67775 |
| 357 026 | **C2** | P | *C2* | EM | 67676 | 74176 | 74076 | 67776 |
| 357 027 | **C2** | P | *C2* | EM | 67677 | 74177 | 74077 | 67777 |
| 357 028 | **C2** | P | *C2* | EM | 67678 | 74178 | 74078 | 67778 |
| 357 029 | **C2** | P | *C2* | EM | 67679 | 74179 | 74079 | 67779 |
| 357 030 | **C2** | P | *C2* | EM | 67680 | 74180 | 74080 | 67780 |
| 357 031 | **C2** | P | *C2* | EM | 67681 | 74181 | 74081 | 67781 |
| 357 032 | **C2** | P | *C2* | EM | 67682 | 74182 | 74082 | 67782 |
| 357 033 | **C2** | P | *C2* | EM | 67683 | 74183 | 74083 | 67783 |
| 357 034 | **C2** | P | *C2* | EM | 67684 | 74184 | 74084 | 67784 |
| 357 035 | **C2** | P | *C2* | EM | 67685 | 74185 | 74085 | 67785 |
| 357 036 | **C2** | P | *C2* | EM | 67686 | 74186 | 74086 | 67786 |
| 357 037 | **C2** | P | *C2* | EM | 67687 | 74187 | 74087 | 67787 |
| 357 038 | **C2** | P | *C2* | EM | 67688 | 74188 | 74088 | 67788 |
| 357 039 | **C2** | P | *C2* | EM | 67689 | 74189 | 74089 | 67789 |
| 357 040 | **C2** | P | *C2* | EM | 67690 | 74190 | 74090 | 67790 |
| 357 041 | **C2** | P | *C2* | EM | 67691 | 74191 | 74091 | 67791 |
| 357 042 | **C2** | P | *C2* | EM | 67692 | 74192 | 74092 | 67792 |
| 357 043 | **C2** | P | *C2* | EM | 67693 | 74193 | 74093 | 67793 |
| 357 044 | **C2** | P | *C2* | EM | 67694 | 74194 | 74094 | 67794 |
| 357 045 | **C2** | P | *C2* | EM | 67695 | 74195 | 74095 | 67795 |
| 357 046 | **C2** | P | *C2* | EM | 67696 | 74196 | 74096 | 67796 |

**Names (carried on DMS(A) and DMS(B) (one plate on each)):**

357 001  BARRY FLAXMAN
357 002  ARTHUR LEWIS STRIDE 1841–1922
357 003  SOUTHEND city.on.sea

357004  TONY AMOS
357005  SOUTHEND: 2017 Alternative City of Culture
357006  DIAMOND JUBILEE 1952–2012
357007  Sir Andrew Foster
357011  JOHN LOWING
357018  Remembering our Fallen 88 1914–1918
357028  London, Tilbury & Southend Railway 1854–2004
357029  THOMAS WHITELEGG 1840–1922
357030  ROBERT HARBEN WHITELEGG 1871–1957

**Class 357/2.** Owned by Angel Trains.

**DMS(A).** Bombardier Derby 2001–02. –/71. 40.7 t.
**MS.** Bombardier Derby 2001–02. –/78. 36.7 t.
**PTS.** Bombardier Derby 2001–02. –/58(+4) 1TD 2W. 39.5 t.
**DMS(B).** Bombardier Derby 2001–02. –/71. 40.7 t.

| | | | | | | | | |
|---|---|---|---|---|---|---|---|---|
| 357201 | **C2** | A | *C2* | EM | 68601 | 74701 | 74601 | 68701 |
| 357202 | **C2** | A | *C2* | EM | 68602 | 74702 | 74602 | 68702 |
| 357203 | **C2** | A | *C2* | EM | 68603 | 74703 | 74603 | 68703 |
| 357204 | **C2** | A | *C2* | EM | 68604 | 74704 | 74604 | 68704 |
| 357205 | **C2** | A | *C2* | EM | 68605 | 74705 | 74605 | 68705 |
| 357206 | **C2** | A | *C2* | EM | 68606 | 74706 | 74606 | 68706 |
| 357207 | **C2** | A | *C2* | EM | 68607 | 74707 | 74607 | 68707 |
| 357208 | **C2** | A | *C2* | EM | 68608 | 74708 | 74608 | 68708 |
| 357209 | **C2** | A | *C2* | EM | 68609 | 74709 | 74609 | 68709 |
| 357210 | **C2** | A | *C2* | EM | 68610 | 74710 | 74610 | 68710 |
| 357211 | **C2** | A | *C2* | EM | 68611 | 74711 | 74611 | 68711 |

**Names (carried on DMS(A) and DMS(B) (one plate on each)):**

| | | | |
|---|---|---|---|
| 357201 | KEN BIRD | 357206 | MARTIN AUNGIER |
| 357202 | KENNY MITCHELL | 357207 | JOHN PAGE |
| 357203 | HENRY PUMFRETT | 357208 | DAVE DAVIS |
| 357204 | DEREK FOWERS | 357209 | JAMES SNELLING |
| 357205 | JOHN D'SILVA | | |

**Class 357/3.** Owned by Angel Trains. In 2015–16 17 Class 357/2s (357 212–228) were reconfigured as "high density" units 357 312–328 with fewer seats and more standing room for shorter distance workings.

**Seating Layout:** 2+2 facing/unidirectional.

**DMS(A).** Bombardier Derby 2001–02. –/56. 40.7 t.
**MS.** Bombardier Derby 2001–02. –/60. 36.7 t.
**PTS.** Bombardier Derby 2001–02. –/50 1TD 2W. 39.5 t.
**DMS(B).** Bombardier Derby 2001–02. –/56. 40.7 t.

| | | | | | | | | | |
|---|---|---|---|---|---|---|---|---|---|
| 357312 | (357212) | **C2** | A | *C2* | EM | 68612 | 74712 | 74612 | 68712 |
| 357313 | (357213) | **C2** | A | *C2* | EM | 68613 | 74713 | 74613 | 68713 |
| 357314 | (357214) | **C2** | A | *C2* | EM | 68614 | 74714 | 74614 | 68714 |
| 357315 | (357215) | **C2** | A | *C2* | EM | 68615 | 74715 | 74615 | 68715 |
| 357316 | (357216) | **C2** | A | *C2* | EM | 68616 | 74716 | 74616 | 68716 |
| 357317 | (357217) | **C2** | A | *C2* | EM | 68617 | 74717 | 74617 | 68717 |
| 357318 | (357218) | **C2** | A | *C2* | EM | 68618 | 74718 | 74618 | 68718 |

| 357 319 | (357 219) | **C2** | A | *C2* | EM | 68619 | 74719 | 74619 | 68719 |
| 357 320 | (357 220) | **C2** | A | *C2* | EM | 68620 | 74720 | 74620 | 68720 |
| 357 321 | (357 221) | **C2** | A | *C2* | EM | 68621 | 74721 | 74621 | 68721 |
| 357 322 | (357 222) | **C2** | A | *C2* | EM | 68622 | 74722 | 74622 | 68722 |
| 357 323 | (357 223) | **C2** | A | *C2* | EM | 68623 | 74723 | 74623 | 68723 |
| 357 324 | (357 224) | **C2** | A | *C2* | EM | 68624 | 74724 | 74624 | 68724 |
| 357 325 | (357 225) | **C2** | A | *C2* | EM | 68625 | 74725 | 74625 | 68725 |
| 357 326 | (357 226) | **C2** | A | *C2* | EM | 68626 | 74726 | 74626 | 68726 |
| 357 327 | (357 227) | **C2** | A | *C2* | EM | 68627 | 74727 | 74627 | 68727 |
| 357 328 | (357 228) | **C2** | A | *C2* | EM | 68628 | 74728 | 74628 | 68728 |

**Names (carried on DMS(A) and DMS(B) (one plate on each)):**

357 313 UPMINSTER I.E.C.C.
357 317 ALLAN BURNELL
357 327 SOUTHEND UNITED

## CLASS 360/0     DESIRO UK                    SIEMENS

Outer suburban/express units. Transferring to East Midlands Railway for use on the London St Pancras–Corby route from May 2021.

**Formation:** DMC–PTS–TS–DMC.
**Construction:** Welded aluminium.
**Traction Motors:** Four Siemens 1TB2016-0GB02 asynchronous of 250 kW.
**Wheel Arrangement:** Bo-Bo + 2-2 + 2-2 + Bo-Bo.
**Braking:** Disc & regenerative.     **Dimensions:** 20.34 x 2.80 m.
**Bogies:** SGP SF5000.               **Couplers:** Dellner 12.
**Gangways:** Within unit.            **Control System:** IGBT Inverter.
**Doors:** Sliding plug.              **Maximum Speed:** 100 mph.
**Heating & ventilation:** Air conditioning.
**Seating Layout:** 1: 2+2 facing, 2: 3+2 facing/unidirectional.
**Multiple Working:** Within class.

**DMC(A).** Siemens Krefeld 2002–03. 8/59. 45.0 t.
**PTS.** Siemens Vienna 2002–03. –/60(+9) 1TD 2W. 43.6 t.
**TS.** Siemens Vienna 2002–03. –/78. 34.3 t.
**DMC(B).** Siemens Krefeld 2002–03. 8/59. 44.1 t.

| 360 101 | **FB** | A | *EM* | BF | 65551 | 72551 | 74551 | 68551 |
| 360 102 | **FB** | A | *EM* | BF | 65552 | 72552 | 74552 | 68552 |
| 360 103 | **FB** | A | *EM* | BF | 65553 | 72553 | 74553 | 68553 |
| 360 104 | **FB** | A | *EM* | BF | 65554 | 72554 | 74554 | 68554 |
| 360 105 | **FB** | A | *EM* | BF | 65555 | 72555 | 74555 | 68555 |
| 360 106 | **FB** | A | *EM* | BF | 65556 | 72556 | 74556 | 68556 |
| 360 107 | **FB** | A | *EM* | BF | 65557 | 72557 | 74557 | 68557 |
| 360 108 | **FB** | A | *EM* | BF | 65558 | 72558 | 74558 | 68558 |
| 360 109 | **FB** | A | *EM* | BF | 65559 | 72559 | 74559 | 68559 |
| 360 110 | **FB** | A | *GA* | IL | 65560 | 72560 | 74560 | 68560 |
| 360 111 | **FB** | A | *GA* | IL | 65561 | 72561 | 74561 | 68561 |
| 360 112 | **FB** | A | *GA* | IL | 65562 | 72562 | 74562 | 68562 |
| 360 113 | **FB** | A | *EM* | BF | 65563 | 72563 | 74563 | 68563 |
| 360 114 | **FB** | A | *GA* | IL | 65564 | 72564 | 74564 | 68564 |

| 360 115 | **FB** | A | *GA* | IL | 65565 | 72565 | 74565 | 68565 |
| 360 116 | **FB** | A | *EM* | BF | 65566 | 72566 | 74566 | 68566 |
| 360 117 | **FB** | A | *EM* | BF | 65567 | 72567 | 74567 | 68567 |
| 360 118 | **FB** | A | *EM* | BF | 65568 | 72568 | 74568 | 68568 |
| 360 119 | **FB** | A | *GA* | IL | 65569 | 72569 | 74569 | 68569 |
| 360 120 | **FB** | A | *EM* | BF | 65570 | 72570 | 74570 | 68570 |
| 360 121 | **FB** | A | *EM* | BF | 65571 | 72571 | 74571 | 68571 |

## CLASS 360/2　　DESIRO UK　　SIEMENS

4-car Class 350 testbed units rebuilt for use by Heathrow Express on "Heathrow Connect" stopping services. The Class 360/2s were stored in 2020, their duties having been taken over by Class 345s.

Original 4-car sets 360 201–204 were made up to 5-cars during 2007 using additional TSs. A fifth unit (360 205) was delivered in late 2005 as a 5-car.

**Formation:** DMS–PTS–TS–TS–DMS.
**Construction:** Welded aluminium.
**Traction Motors:** Four Siemens 1TB2016-0GB02 asynchronous of 250 kW.
**Wheel Arrangement:** Bo-Bo + 2-2 + 2-2 + 2-2 + Bo-Bo.

| | |
|---|---|
| **Braking:** Disc & regenerative. | **Dimensions:** 20.34 x 2.80 m. |
| **Bogies:** SGP SF5000. | **Couplers:** Dellner 12. |
| **Gangways:** Within unit. | **Control System:** IGBT Inverter. |
| **Doors:** Sliding plug. | **Maximum Speed:** 100 mph. |

**Heating & ventilation:** Air conditioning.
**Seating Layout:** 3+2 (* 2+2) facing/unidirectional.
**Multiple Working:** Within class.

**DMS(A).** Siemens Krefeld 2002–06. –/63 (* –/54). 44.8 t.
**PTS.** Siemens Krefeld 2002–06. –/57(+9) 1TD 2W (* –/48(+9) 2W). 44.2 t.
**TS(A).** Siemens Krefeld 2005–06. –/74 (* –/62). 35.3 t.
**TS(B).** Siemens Krefeld 2002–06. –/74 (* –/62). 34.1 t.
**DMS(B).** Siemens Krefeld 2002–06. –/63 (* –/54). 44.4 t.

| 360 201 | | **HC** | HE | OH | 78431 | 63421 | 72431 | 72421 | 78441 |
| 360 202 | | **HC** | HE | OH | 78432 | 63422 | 72432 | 72422 | 78442 |
| 360 203 | | **HC** | HE | OH | 78433 | 63423 | 72433 | 72423 | 78443 |
| 360 204 | | **HC** | HE | OH | 78434 | 63424 | 72434 | 72424 | 78444 |
| 360 205 | * | **HE** | HE | OH | 78435 | 63425 | 72435 | 72425 | 78445 |

## CLASS 365　　NETWORKER EXPRESS　　ABB YORK

Outer suburban units.

**Formation:** DMC–TS–PTS–DMC.
**Systems:** 25 kV AC overhead but with 750 V DC third rail capability (units 365 501–516 were formerly used on DC lines in the South-East).
**Construction:** Welded aluminium alloy.
**Traction Motors:** Four GEC-Alsthom G354CX asynchronous of 157 kW.
**Wheel Arrangement:** Bo-Bo + 2-2 + 2-2 + Bo-Bo.

| | |
|---|---|
| **Braking:** Disc & rheostatic. | **Dimensions:** 20.89/20.06 x 2.81 m. |
| **Bogies:** ABB P3-16/T3-16. | **Couplers:** Tightlock. |
| **Gangways:** Within unit. | **Control System:** GTO Inverter. |

**Doors:** Sliding plug.                    **Maximum Speed:** 100 mph.
**Seating Layout:** 1: 2+2 facing, 2: 2+2 facing.
**Multiple Working:** Within class only.

**DMC(A).** Lot No. 31133 1994–95. 12/56. 41.7 t.
**TS.** Lot No. 31134 1994–95. –/58 1TD 2W 32.9 t.
**PTS.** Lot No. 31135 1994–95. –/70 1T. 35.2 t.
**DMC(B).** Lot No. 31136 1994–95. 12/56. 41.7 t.

| | | | | | | | | |
|---|---|---|---|---|---|---|---|---|
| 365501 | TL | TF |    | CY | 65894 | 72241 | 72240 | 65935 |
| 365502 | TL | TF | GN | HE | 65895 | 72243 | 72242 | 65936 |
| 365503 | TL | TF |    | CY | 65896 | 72245 | 72244 | 65937 |
| 365504 | TL | TF | GN | HE | 65897 | 72247 | 72246 | 65938 |
| 365505 | TL | TF |    | CY | 65898 | 72249 | 72248 | 65939 |
| 365506 | TL | TF | GN | HE | 65899 | 72251 | 72250 | 65940 |
| 365507 | TL | TF |    | CY | 65900 | 72253 | 72252 | 65941 |
| 365508 | TL | TF | GN | HE | 65901 | 72255 | 72254 | 65942 |
| 365509 | TL | TF |    | CY | 65902 | 72257 | 72256 | 65943 |
| 365510 | TL | TF | GN | HE | 65903 | 72259 | 72258 | 65944 |
| 365511 | TL | TF | GN | HE | 65904 | 72261 | 72260 | 65945 |
| 365512 | TL | TF | GN | HE | 65905 | 72263 | 72262 | 65946 |
| 365513 | TL | TF |    | CY | 65906 | 72265 | 72264 | 65947 |
| 365514 | TL | TF | GN | HE | 65907 | 72267 | 72266 | 65948 |
| 365515 | TL | TF |    | CY | 65908 | 72269 | 72268 | 65949 |
| 365516 | TL | TF | GN | HE | 65909 | 72271 | 72270 | 65950 |
| 365517 | TL | TF |    | CY | 65910 | 72273 | 72272 | 65951 |
| 365518 | TL | TF | GN | HE | 65911 | 72275 | 72274 | 65952 |
| 365519 | TL | TF |    | CY | 65912 | 72277 | 72276 | 65953 |
| 365520 | TL | TF | GN | HE | 65913 | 72279 | 72278 | 65954 |
| 365521 | TL | TF |    | CY | 65914 | 72281 | 72280 | 65955 |
| 365522 | TL | TF | GN | HE | 65915 | 72283 | 72282 | 65956 |
| 365523 | TL | TF |    | CY | 65916 | 72285 | 72284 | 65957 |
| 365524 | TL | TF | GN | HE | 65917 | 72287 | 72286 | 65958 |
| 365525 | TL | TF |    | MA | 65918 | 72289 | 72288 | 65959 |
| 365527 | TL | TF |    | CY | 65920 | 72293 | 72292 | 65961 |
| 365528 | TL | TF | GN | HE | 65921 | 72295 | 72294 | 65962 |
| 365529 | TL | TF |    | CY | 65922 | 72297 | 72296 | 65963 |
| 365530 | TL | TF | GN | HE | 65923 | 72299 | 72298 | 65964 |
| 365531 | TL | TF |    | CY | 65924 | 72301 | 72300 | 65965 |
| 365532 | TL | TF | GN | HE | 65925 | 72303 | 72302 | 65966 |
| 365533 | TL | TF |    | CY | 65926 | 72305 | 72304 | 65967 |
| 365534 | TL | TF | GN | HE | 65927 | 72307 | 72306 | 65968 |
| 365535 | TL | TF |    | CY | 65928 | 72309 | 72308 | 65969 |
| 365536 | TL | TF | GN | HE | 65929 | 72311 | 72310 | 65970 |
| 365537 | TL | TF |    | CY | 65930 | 72313 | 72312 | 65971 |
| 365538 | TL | TF | GN | HE | 65931 | 72315 | 72314 | 65972 |
| 365539 | TL | TF | GN | HE | 65932 | 72317 | 72316 | 65973 |
| 365540 | TL | TF | GN | HE | 65933 | 72319 | 72318 | 65974 |
| 365541 | TL | TF |    | CY | 65934 | 72321 | 72320 | 65975 |

**Name (carried on each DMC):**

365537      Daniel Edwards (1974–2010) Cambridge Driver

# CLASS 375 ELECTROSTAR
## ADTRANZ/BOMBARDIER DERBY

Express and outer suburban units.

**Formation:** Various, see sub-class headings.
**Systems:** 25 kV AC overhead/750 V DC third rail (some third rail only with provision for retro-fitting of AC equipment).
**Construction:** Welded aluminium alloy underframe, sides and roof with steel ends. All sections bolted together.
**Traction Motors:** Two Adtranz asynchronous of 250 kW.
**Wheel Arrangement:** 2-Bo (+ 2-Bo) + 2-2 + Bo-2.
**Braking:** Disc & regenerative.     **Dimensions:** 20.40/19.99 x 2.80 m.
**Bogies:** Adtranz P3-25/T3-25.     **Couplers:** Dellner 12.
**Gangways:** Throughout.     **Control System:** IGBT Inverter.
**Doors:** Sliding plug.     **Maximum Speed:** 100 mph.
**Heating & ventilation:** Air conditioning.
**Seating Layout:** 1: 2+2 facing/unidirectional. 2: 2+2 facing/unidirectional (except 375/9 – 3+2 facing/unidirectional).
**Multiple Working:** Within class and with Classes 376, 377, 378 and 379.

**Class 375/3.** Express units. 750 V DC only. DMS–TS–DMC.

**DMS.** Bombardier Derby 2001–02. –/60. 43.8 t.
**TS.** Bombardier Derby 2001–02. –/56 1TD 2W. 35.5 t.
**DMC.** Bombardier Derby 2001–02. 12/48. 43.8 t.

| | | | | | | | |
|---|---|---|---|---|---|---|---|
| 375301 | **SB** | E | *SE* | RM | 67921 | 74351 | 67931 |
| 375302 | **SB** | E | *SE* | RM | 67922 | 74352 | 67932 |
| 375303 | **SB** | E | *SE* | RM | 67923 | 74353 | 67933 |
| 375304 | **SB** | E | *SE* | RM | 67924 | 74354 | 67934 |
| 375305 | **SB** | E | *SE* | RM | 67925 | 74355 | 67935 |
| 375306 | **SB** | E | *SE* | RM | 67926 | 74356 | 67936 |
| 375307 | **SB** | E | *SE* | RM | 67927 | 74357 | 67937 |
| 375308 | **SB** | E | *SE* | RM | 67928 | 74358 | 67938 |
| 375309 | **SB** | E | *SE* | RM | 67929 | 74359 | 67939 |
| 375310 | **SB** | E | *SE* | RM | 67930 | 74360 | 67940 |

**Class 375/6.** Express units. 25 kV AC/750 V DC. DMS–MC–PTS–DMS.

**DMS(A).** Adtranz Derby 1999–2001. –/60. 46.2 t.
**MC.** Adtranz Derby 1999–2001. 16/50 1T. 40.5 t.
**PTS.** Adtranz Derby 1999–2001. –/56 1TD 2W. 40.7 t.
**DMS(B).** Adtranz Derby 1999–2001. –/60. 46.2 t.

| | | | | | | | | |
|---|---|---|---|---|---|---|---|---|
| 375601 | **SB** | E | *SE* | RM | 67801 | 74251 | 74201 | 67851 |
| 375602 | **SB** | E | *SE* | RM | 67802 | 74252 | 74202 | 67852 |
| 375603 | **SB** | E | *SE* | RM | 67803 | 74253 | 74203 | 67853 |
| 375604 | **SB** | E | *SE* | RM | 67804 | 74254 | 74204 | 67854 |
| 375605 | **SB** | E | *SE* | RM | 67805 | 74255 | 74205 | 67855 |
| 375606 | **SB** | E | *SE* | RM | 67806 | 74256 | 74206 | 67856 |
| 375607 | **SB** | E | *SE* | RM | 67807 | 74257 | 74207 | 67857 |
| 375608 | **SB** | E | *SE* | RM | 67808 | 74258 | 74208 | 67858 |

| 375609 | SB | E | SE | RM | 67809 | 74259 | 74209 | 67859 |
| 375610 | SB | E | SE | RM | 67810 | 74260 | 74210 | 67860 |
| 375611 | SB | E | SE | RM | 67811 | 74261 | 74211 | 67861 |
| 375612 | SB | E | SE | RM | 67812 | 74262 | 74212 | 67862 |
| 375613 | SB | E | SE | RM | 67813 | 74263 | 74213 | 67863 |
| 375614 | SB | E | SE | RM | 67814 | 74264 | 74214 | 67864 |
| 375615 | SB | E | SE | RM | 67815 | 74265 | 74215 | 67865 |
| 375616 | SB | E | SE | RM | 67816 | 74266 | 74216 | 67866 |
| 375617 | SB | E | SE | RM | 67817 | 74267 | 74217 | 67867 |
| 375618 | SB | E | SE | RM | 67818 | 74268 | 74218 | 67868 |
| 375619 | SB | E | SE | RM | 67819 | 74269 | 74219 | 67869 |
| 375620 | SB | E | SE | RM | 67820 | 74270 | 74220 | 67870 |
| 375621 | SB | E | SE | RM | 67821 | 74271 | 74221 | 67871 |
| 375622 | SB | E | SE | RM | 67822 | 74272 | 74222 | 67872 |
| 375623 | SB | E | SE | RM | 67823 | 74273 | 74223 | 67873 |
| 375624 | SB | E | SE | RM | 67824 | 74274 | 74224 | 67874 |
| 375625 | SB | E | SE | RM | 67825 | 74275 | 74225 | 67875 |
| 375626 | SB | E | SE | RM | 67826 | 74276 | 74226 | 67876 |
| 375627 | SB | E | SE | RM | 67827 | 74277 | 74227 | 67877 |
| 375628 | SB | E | SE | RM | 67828 | 74278 | 74228 | 67878 |
| 375629 | SB | E | SE | RM | 67829 | 74279 | 74229 | 67879 |
| 375630 | SB | E | SE | RM | 67830 | 74280 | 74230 | 67880 |

**Names (carried on one side of each MC or TS):**

375619 Driver John Neve | 375623 Hospice in the Weald

**Class 375/7.** Express units. 750 V DC only. DMS–MC–TS–DMS.

**DMS(A).** Bombardier Derby 2001–02. –/60. 43.8 t.
**MC.** Bombardier Derby 2001–02. 16/50 1T. 36.4 t.
**TS.** Bombardier Derby 2001–02. –/56 1TD 2W. 34.1 t.
**DMS(B).** Bombardier Derby 2001–02. –/60. 43.8 t.

| 375701 | SB | E | SE | RM | 67831 | 74281 | 74231 | 67881 |
| 375702 | SB | E | SE | RM | 67832 | 74282 | 74232 | 67882 |
| 375703 | SB | E | SE | RM | 67833 | 74283 | 74233 | 67883 |
| 375704 | SB | E | SE | RM | 67834 | 74284 | 74234 | 67884 |
| 375705 | SB | E | SE | RM | 67835 | 74285 | 74235 | 67885 |
| 375706 | SB | E | SE | RM | 67836 | 74286 | 74236 | 67886 |
| 375707 | SB | E | SE | RM | 67837 | 74287 | 74237 | 67887 |
| 375708 | SB | E | SE | RM | 67838 | 74288 | 74238 | 67888 |
| 375709 | SB | E | SE | RM | 67839 | 74289 | 74239 | 67889 |
| 375710 | SB | E | SE | RM | 67840 | 74290 | 74240 | 67890 |
| 375711 | SB | E | SE | RM | 67841 | 74291 | 74241 | 67891 |
| 375712 | SB | E | SE | RM | 67842 | 74292 | 74242 | 67892 |
| 375713 | SB | E | SE | RM | 67843 | 74293 | 74243 | 67893 |
| 375714 | SB | E | SE | RM | 67844 | 74294 | 74244 | 67894 |
| 375715 | SB | E | SE | RM | 67845 | 74295 | 74245 | 67895 |

**Names (carried on one side of each MC or TS):**

375701 Kent Air Ambulance Explorer | 375714  Rochester Cathedral
375710 Rochester Castle |

**Class 375/8.** Express units. 750 V DC only. DMS–MC–TS–DMS.

375 801–820 are fitted with de-icing equipment. TS weighs 36.5 t.

**DMS(A).** Bombardier Derby 2004. –/60. 43.3 t.
**MC.** Bombardier Derby 2004. 16/50 1T. 39.8 t.
**TS.** Bombardier Derby 2004. –/52 1TD 2W. 35.9 t.
**DMS(B).** Bombardier Derby 2004. –/64. 43.3 t.

| | | | | | | | | |
|---|---|---|---|---|---|---|---|---|
| 375801 | **SB** | E | *SE* | RM | 73301 | 79001 | 78201 | 73701 |
| 375802 | **SB** | E | *SE* | RM | 73302 | 79002 | 78202 | 73702 |
| 375803 | **SB** | E | *SE* | RM | 73303 | 79003 | 78203 | 73703 |
| 375804 | **SB** | E | *SE* | RM | 73304 | 79004 | 78204 | 73704 |
| 375805 | **SB** | E | *SE* | RM | 73305 | 79005 | 78205 | 73705 |
| 375806 | **SB** | E | *SE* | RM | 73306 | 79006 | 78206 | 73706 |
| 375807 | **SB** | E | *SE* | RM | 73307 | 79007 | 78207 | 73707 |
| 375808 | **SB** | E | *SE* | RM | 73308 | 79008 | 78208 | 73708 |
| 375809 | **SB** | E | *SE* | RM | 73309 | 79009 | 78209 | 73709 |
| 375810 | **SB** | E | *SE* | RM | 73310 | 79010 | 78210 | 73710 |
| 375811 | **SB** | E | *SE* | RM | 73311 | 79011 | 78211 | 73711 |
| 375812 | **SB** | E | *SE* | RM | 73312 | 79012 | 78212 | 73712 |
| 375813 | **SB** | E | *SE* | RM | 73313 | 79013 | 78213 | 73713 |
| 375814 | **SB** | E | *SE* | RM | 73314 | 79014 | 78214 | 73714 |
| 375815 | **SB** | E | *SE* | RM | 73315 | 79015 | 78215 | 73715 |
| 375816 | **SB** | E | *SE* | RM | 73316 | 79016 | 78216 | 73716 |
| 375817 | **SB** | E | *SE* | RM | 73317 | 79017 | 78217 | 73717 |
| 375818 | **SB** | E | *SE* | RM | 73318 | 79018 | 78218 | 73718 |
| 375819 | **SB** | E | *SE* | RM | 73319 | 79019 | 78219 | 73719 |
| 375820 | **SB** | E | *SE* | RM | 73320 | 79020 | 78220 | 73720 |
| 375821 | **SB** | E | *SE* | RM | 73321 | 79021 | 78221 | 73721 |
| 375822 | **SB** | E | *SE* | RM | 73322 | 79022 | 78222 | 73722 |
| 375823 | **SB** | E | *SE* | RM | 73323 | 79023 | 78223 | 73723 |
| 375824 | **SB** | E | *SE* | RM | 73324 | 79024 | 78224 | 73724 |
| 375825 | **SB** | E | *SE* | RM | 73325 | 79025 | 78225 | 73725 |
| 375826 | **SB** | E | *SE* | RM | 73326 | 79026 | 78226 | 73726 |
| 375827 | **SB** | E | *SE* | RM | 73327 | 79027 | 78227 | 73727 |
| 375828 | **SB** | E | *SE* | RM | 73328 | 79028 | 78228 | 73728 |
| 375829 | **SB** | E | *SE* | RM | 73329 | 79029 | 78229 | 73729 |
| 375830 | **SB** | E | *SE* | RM | 73330 | 79030 | 78230 | 73730 |

**Name** (carried on one side of each MS or TS):

375823   Ashford Proudly Served by Rail for 175 years

**Class 375/9.** Outer suburban units. 750 V DC only. DMC–MS–TS–DMC.

**DMC(A).** Bombardier Derby 2003–04. 12/59. 43.4 t.
**MS.** Bombardier Derby 2003–04. –/73 1T. 39.3 t.
**TS.** Bombardier Derby 2003–04. –/62 1TD 2W. 35.6 t.
**DMC(B).** Bombardier Derby 2003–04. 12/59. 43.4 t.

| | | | | | | | | |
|---|---|---|---|---|---|---|---|---|
| 375901 | **SB** | E | *SE* | RM | 73331 | 79031 | 79061 | 73731 |
| 375902 | **SB** | E | *SE* | RM | 73332 | 79032 | 79062 | 73732 |
| 375903 | **SB** | E | *SE* | RM | 73333 | 79033 | 79063 | 73733 |
| 375904 | **SB** | E | *SE* | RM | 73334 | 79034 | 79064 | 73734 |

| 375 905 | **SB** | E | *SE* | RM | 73335 | 79035 | 79065 | 73735 |
| 375 906 | **SB** | E | *SE* | RM | 73336 | 79036 | 79066 | 73736 |
| 375 907 | **SB** | E | *SE* | RM | 73337 | 79037 | 79067 | 73737 |
| 375 908 | **SB** | E | *SE* | RM | 73338 | 79038 | 79068 | 73738 |
| 375 909 | **SB** | E | *SE* | RM | 73339 | 79039 | 79069 | 73739 |
| 375 910 | **SB** | E | *SE* | RM | 73340 | 79040 | 79070 | 73740 |
| 375 911 | **SB** | E | *SE* | RM | 73341 | 79041 | 79071 | 73741 |
| 375 912 | **SB** | E | *SE* | RM | 73342 | 79042 | 79072 | 73742 |
| 375 913 | **SB** | E | *SE* | RM | 73343 | 79043 | 79073 | 73743 |
| 375 914 | **SB** | E | *SE* | RM | 73344 | 79044 | 79074 | 73744 |
| 375 915 | **SB** | E | *SE* | RM | 73345 | 79045 | 79075 | 73745 |
| 375 916 | **SB** | E | *SE* | RM | 73346 | 79046 | 79076 | 73746 |
| 375 917 | **SB** | E | *SE* | RM | 73347 | 79047 | 79077 | 73747 |
| 375 918 | **SB** | E | *SE* | RM | 73348 | 79048 | 79078 | 73748 |
| 375 919 | **SB** | E | *SE* | RM | 73349 | 79049 | 79079 | 73749 |
| 375 920 | **SB** | E | *SE* | RM | 73350 | 79050 | 79080 | 73750 |
| 375 921 | **SB** | E | *SE* | RM | 73351 | 79051 | 79081 | 73751 |
| 375 922 | **SB** | E | *SE* | RM | 73352 | 79052 | 79082 | 73752 |
| 375 923 | **SB** | E | *SE* | RM | 73353 | 79053 | 79083 | 73753 |
| 375 924 | **SB** | E | *SE* | RM | 73354 | 79054 | 79084 | 73754 |
| 375 925 | **SB** | E | *SE* | RM | 73355 | 79055 | 79085 | 73755 |
| 375 926 | **SB** | E | *SE* | RM | 73356 | 79056 | 79086 | 73756 |
| 375 927 | **SB** | E | *SE* | RM | 73357 | 79057 | 79087 | 73757 |

# CLASS 376   ELECTROSTAR   BOMBARDIER DERBY

Inner suburban units.

**Formation:** DMS–MS–TS–MS–DMS.
**System:** 750 V DC third rail.
**Construction:** Welded aluminium alloy underframe, sides and roof with steel ends. All sections bolted together.
**Traction Motors:** Two Bombardier asynchronous of 200 kW.
**Wheel Arrangement:** 2-Bo + 2-Bo + 2-2 + Bo-2 + Bo-2.
**Braking:** Disc & regenerative.      **Dimensions:** 20.40/19.99 x 2.80 m.
**Bogies:** Bombardier P3-25/T3-25.   **Couplers:** Dellner 12.
**Gangways:** Within unit.             **Control System:** IGBT Inverter.
**Doors:** Sliding.                    **Maximum Speed:** 75 mph.
**Heating & ventilation:** Pressure heating and ventilation.
**Seating Layout:** 2+2 low density facing.
**Multiple Working:** Within class and with Classes 375, 377, 378 and 379.

**DMS(A).** Bombardier Derby 2004–05. –/36(+6) 1W. 42.1 t.
**MS.** Bombardier Derby 2004–05. –/48. 36.2 t.
**TS.** Bombardier Derby 2004–05. –/48. 36.3 t.
**DMS(B).** Bombardier Derby 2004–05. –/36(+6) 1W. 42.1 t.

| 376 001 | **CN** | E | *SE* | SG | 61101 63301 64301 63501 61601 |
| 376 002 | **CN** | E | *SE* | SG | 61102 63302 64302 63502 61602 |
| 376 003 | **CN** | E | *SE* | SG | 61103 63303 64303 63503 61603 |
| 376 004 | **CN** | E | *SE* | SG | 61104 63304 64304 63504 61604 |
| 376 005 | **CN** | E | *SE* | SG | 61105 63305 64305 63505 61605 |

| | | | | | | | | | |
|---|---|---|---|---|---|---|---|---|---|
| 376006 | **CN** | E | *SE* | SG | 61106 | 63306 | 64306 | 63506 | 61606 |
| 376007 | **CN** | E | *SE* | SG | 61107 | 63307 | 64307 | 63507 | 61607 |
| 376008 | **CN** | E | *SE* | SG | 61108 | 63308 | 64308 | 63508 | 61608 |
| 376009 | **CN** | E | *SE* | SG | 61109 | 63309 | 64309 | 63509 | 61609 |
| 376010 | **CN** | E | *SE* | SG | 61110 | 63310 | 64310 | 63510 | 61610 |
| 376011 | **CN** | E | *SE* | SG | 61111 | 63311 | 64311 | 63511 | 61611 |
| 376012 | **CN** | E | *SE* | SG | 61112 | 63312 | 64312 | 63512 | 61612 |
| 376013 | **CN** | E | *SE* | SG | 61113 | 63313 | 64313 | 63513 | 61613 |
| 376014 | **CN** | E | *SE* | SG | 61114 | 63314 | 64314 | 63514 | 61614 |
| 376015 | **CN** | E | *SE* | SG | 61115 | 63315 | 64315 | 63515 | 61615 |
| 376016 | **CN** | E | *SE* | SG | 61116 | 63316 | 64316 | 63516 | 61616 |
| 376017 | **CN** | E | *SE* | SG | 61117 | 63317 | 64317 | 63517 | 61617 |
| 376018 | **CN** | E | *SE* | SG | 61118 | 63318 | 64318 | 63518 | 61618 |
| 376019 | **CN** | E | *SE* | SG | 61119 | 63319 | 64319 | 63519 | 61619 |
| 376020 | **CN** | E | *SE* | SG | 61120 | 63320 | 64320 | 63520 | 61620 |
| 376021 | **CN** | E | *SE* | SG | 61121 | 63321 | 64321 | 63521 | 61621 |
| 376022 | **CN** | E | *SE* | SG | 61122 | 63322 | 64322 | 63522 | 61622 |
| 376023 | **CN** | E | *SE* | SG | 61123 | 63323 | 64323 | 63523 | 61623 |
| 376024 | **CN** | E | *SE* | SG | 61124 | 63324 | 64324 | 63524 | 61624 |
| 376025 | **CN** | E | *SE* | SG | 61125 | 63325 | 64325 | 63525 | 61625 |
| 376026 | **CN** | E | *SE* | SG | 61126 | 63326 | 64326 | 63526 | 61626 |
| 376027 | **CN** | E | *SE* | SG | 61127 | 63327 | 64327 | 63527 | 61627 |
| 376028 | **CN** | E | *SE* | SG | 61128 | 63328 | 64328 | 63528 | 61628 |
| 376029 | **CN** | E | *SE* | SG | 61129 | 63329 | 64329 | 63529 | 61629 |
| 376030 | **CN** | E | *SE* | SG | 61130 | 63330 | 64330 | 63530 | 61630 |
| 376031 | **CN** | E | *SE* | SG | 61131 | 63331 | 64331 | 63531 | 61631 |
| 376032 | **CN** | E | *SE* | SG | 61132 | 63332 | 64332 | 63532 | 61632 |
| 376033 | **CN** | E | *SE* | SG | 61133 | 63333 | 64333 | 63533 | 61633 |
| 376034 | **CN** | E | *SE* | SG | 61134 | 63334 | 64334 | 63534 | 61634 |
| 376035 | **CN** | E | *SE* | SG | 61135 | 63335 | 64335 | 63535 | 61635 |
| 376036 | **CN** | E | *SE* | SG | 61136 | 63336 | 64336 | 63536 | 61636 |

**Name (carried on TSO):** 376001   Alan Doggett

# CLASS 377    ELECTROSTAR    BOMBARDIER DERBY

Express and outer suburban units.

**Formation:** Various, see sub-class headings.
**Systems:** 25 kV AC overhead/750 V DC third rail or third rail only with provision for retro-fitting of AC equipment.
**Construction:** Welded aluminium alloy underframe, sides and roof with steel ends. All sections bolted together.
**Traction Motors:** Two Bombardier asynchronous of 250 kW.
**Wheel Arrangement:** 2-Bo + 2-2 + Bo-2 or 2-Bo + 2-Bo + 2-2 + Bo-2 or 2-Bo + 2-Bo + 2-2 + Bo-2 + Bo-2.

| | |
|---|---|
| **Braking:** Disc & regenerative. | **Dimensions:** 20.39/20.00 x 2.80 m. |
| **Bogies:** Bombardier P3-25/T3-25. | **Couplers:** Dellner 12. |
| **Gangways:** Throughout. | **Control System:** IGBT Inverter. |
| **Doors:** Sliding plug. | **Maximum Speed:** 100 mph. |
| **Heating & ventilation:** Air conditioning. | |

**Seating Layout:** Various, see sub-class headings.
**Multiple Working:** Within class and with Classes 375, 376, 378, 379 and 387.

**Class 377/1.** 750 V DC only. DMC–MS–TS–DMC.
**Seating layout:** 1: 2+2 facing/unidirectional, 2: 2+2 facing/unidirectional (377 101–119), 3+2/2+2 facing/unidirectional (377 120–139), 3+2 (middle cars and 2+2 (end cars) facing/unidirectional (377 140–164).

**DMC(A).** Bombardier Derby 2002–03. 12/48 (s 12/56). 44.8 t.
**MS.** Bombardier Derby 2002–03. –/62 (s –/70, t –/69). 1T. 39.0 t.
**TS.** Bombardier Derby 2002–03. –/52 (s –/60, t –/57). 1TD 2W. 35.4 t.
**DMC(B).** Bombardier Derby 2002–03. 12/48 (s 12/56). 43.4 t.

| | | | | | | | | |
|---|---|---|---|---|---|---|---|---|
| 377 101 | | **SN** | P | *SN* | SU | 78501 | 77101 | 78901 | 78701 |
| 377 102 | | **SN** | P | *SN* | SU | 78502 | 77102 | 78902 | 78702 |
| 377 103 | | **SN** | P | *SN* | SU | 78503 | 77103 | 78903 | 78703 |
| 377 104 | | **SN** | P | *SN* | SU | 78504 | 77104 | 78904 | 78704 |
| 377 105 | | **SN** | P | *SN* | SU | 78505 | 77105 | 78905 | 78705 |
| 377 106 | | **SN** | P | *SN* | SU | 78506 | 77106 | 78906 | 78706 |
| 377 107 | | **SN** | P | *SN* | SU | 78507 | 77107 | 78907 | 78707 |
| 377 108 | | **SN** | P | *SN* | SU | 78508 | 77108 | 78908 | 78708 |
| 377 109 | | **SN** | P | *SN* | SU | 78509 | 77109 | 78909 | 78709 |
| 377 110 | | **SN** | P | *SN* | SU | 78510 | 77110 | 78910 | 78710 |
| 377 111 | | **SN** | P | *SN* | SU | 78511 | 77111 | 78911 | 78711 |
| 377 112 | | **SN** | P | *SN* | SU | 78512 | 77112 | 78912 | 78712 |
| 377 113 | | **SN** | P | *SN* | SU | 78513 | 77113 | 78913 | 78713 |
| 377 114 | | **SN** | P | *SN* | SU | 78514 | 77114 | 78914 | 78714 |
| 377 115 | | **SN** | P | *SN* | SU | 78515 | 77115 | 78915 | 78715 |
| 377 116 | | **SN** | P | *SN* | SU | 78516 | 77116 | 78916 | 78716 |
| 377 117 | | **SN** | P | *SN* | SU | 78517 | 77117 | 78917 | 78717 |
| 377 118 | | **SN** | P | *SN* | SU | 78518 | 77118 | 78918 | 78718 |
| 377 119 | | **SN** | P | *SN* | SU | 78519 | 77119 | 78919 | 78719 |
| 377 120 | s | **SN** | P | *SN* | SU | 78520 | 77120 | 78920 | 78720 |
| 377 121 | s | **SN** | P | *SN* | SU | 78521 | 77121 | 78921 | 78721 |
| 377 122 | s | **SN** | P | *SN* | SU | 78522 | 77122 | 78922 | 78722 |
| 377 123 | s | **SN** | P | *SN* | SU | 78523 | 77123 | 78923 | 78723 |
| 377 124 | s | **SN** | P | *SN* | SU | 78524 | 77124 | 78924 | 78724 |
| 377 125 | s | **SN** | P | *SN* | SU | 78525 | 77125 | 78925 | 78725 |
| 377 126 | s | **SN** | P | *SN* | SU | 78526 | 77126 | 78926 | 78726 |
| 377 127 | s | **SN** | P | *SN* | SU | 78527 | 77127 | 78927 | 78727 |
| 377 128 | s | **SN** | P | *SN* | SU | 78528 | 77128 | 78928 | 78728 |
| 377 129 | s | **SN** | P | *SN* | SU | 78529 | 77129 | 78929 | 78729 |
| 377 130 | s | **SN** | P | *SN* | SU | 78530 | 77130 | 78930 | 78730 |
| 377 131 | s | **SN** | P | *SN* | SU | 78531 | 77131 | 78931 | 78731 |
| 377 132 | s | **SN** | P | *SN* | SU | 78532 | 77132 | 78932 | 78732 |
| 377 133 | s | **SN** | P | *SN* | SU | 78533 | 77133 | 78933 | 78733 |
| 377 134 | s | **SN** | P | *SN* | SU | 78534 | 77134 | 78934 | 78734 |
| 377 135 | s | **SN** | P | *SN* | SU | 78535 | 77135 | 78935 | 78735 |
| 377 136 | s | **SN** | P | *SN* | SU | 78536 | 77136 | 78936 | 78736 |
| 377 137 | s | **SN** | P | *SN* | SU | 78537 | 77137 | 78937 | 78737 |
| 377 138 | s | **SN** | P | *SN* | SU | 78538 | 77138 | 78938 | 78738 |
| 377 139 | s | **SN** | P | *SN* | SU | 78539 | 77139 | 78939 | 78739 |

| | | | | | | | | |
|---|---|---|---|---|---|---|---|---|
| 377 140 | t | **SN** | P | *SN* | SU | 78540 | 77140 | 78940 | 78740 |
| 377 141 | t | **SN** | P | *SN* | SU | 78541 | 77141 | 78941 | 78741 |
| 377 142 | t | **SN** | P | *SN* | SU | 78542 | 77142 | 78942 | 78742 |
| 377 143 | t | **SN** | P | *SN* | SU | 78543 | 77143 | 78943 | 78743 |
| 377 144 | t | **SN** | P | *SN* | SU | 78544 | 77144 | 78944 | 78744 |
| 377 145 | t | **SN** | P | *SN* | SU | 78545 | 77145 | 78945 | 78745 |
| 377 146 | t | **SN** | P | *SN* | SU | 78546 | 77146 | 78946 | 78746 |
| 377 147 | t | **SN** | P | *SN* | SU | 78547 | 77147 | 78947 | 78747 |
| 377 148 | t | **SN** | P | *SN* | SU | 78548 | 77148 | 78948 | 78748 |
| 377 149 | t | **SN** | P | *SN* | SU | 78549 | 77149 | 78949 | 78749 |
| 377 150 | t | **SN** | P | *SN* | SU | 78550 | 77150 | 78950 | 78750 |
| 377 151 | t | **SN** | P | *SN* | SU | 78551 | 77151 | 78951 | 78751 |
| 377 152 | t | **SN** | P | *SN* | SU | 78552 | 77152 | 78952 | 78752 |
| 377 153 | t | **SN** | P | *SN* | SU | 78553 | 77153 | 78953 | 78753 |
| 377 154 | t | **SN** | P | *SN* | SU | 78554 | 77154 | 78954 | 78754 |
| 377 155 | t | **SN** | P | *SN* | SU | 78555 | 77155 | 78955 | 78755 |
| 377 156 | t | **SN** | P | *SN* | SU | 78556 | 77156 | 78956 | 78756 |
| 377 157 | t | **SN** | P | *SN* | SU | 78557 | 77157 | 78957 | 78757 |
| 377 158 | t | **SN** | P | *SN* | SU | 78558 | 77158 | 78958 | 78758 |
| 377 159 | t | **SN** | P | *SN* | SU | 78559 | 77159 | 78959 | 78759 |
| 377 160 | t | **SN** | P | *SN* | SU | 78560 | 77160 | 78960 | 78760 |
| 377 161 | t | **SN** | P | *SN* | SU | 78561 | 77161 | 78961 | 78761 |
| 377 162 | t | **SN** | P | *SN* | SU | 78562 | 77162 | 78962 | 78762 |
| 377 163 | t | **SN** | P | *SE* | RM | 78563 | 77163 | 78963 | 78763 |
| 377 164 | t | **SN** | P | *SE* | RM | 78564 | 77164 | 78964 | 78764 |

**Class 377/2.** 25 kV AC/750 V DC. DMC–MS–PTS–DMC. Dual-voltage units.
**Seating layout:** 1: 2+2 facing/unidirectional, 2: 2+2 and 3+2 facing/unidirectional (3+2 seating in middle cars only).

**DMC(A).** Bombardier Derby 2003–04. 12/48. 44.2 t.
**MS.** Bombardier Derby 2003–04. –/69 1T. 39.8 t.
**PTS.** Bombardier Derby 2003–04. –/57 1TD 2W. 40.1 t.
**DMC(B).** Bombardier Derby 2003–04. 12/48. 44.2 t.

| | | | | | | | | |
|---|---|---|---|---|---|---|---|---|
| 377 201 | | **SN** | P | *SN* | SU | 78571 | 77171 | 78971 | 78771 |
| 377 202 | | **SN** | P | *SN* | SU | 78572 | 77172 | 78972 | 78772 |
| 377 203 | | **SN** | P | *SN* | SU | 78573 | 77173 | 78973 | 78773 |
| 377 204 | | **SN** | P | *SN* | SU | 78574 | 77174 | 78974 | 78774 |
| 377 205 | | **SN** | P | *SN* | SU | 78575 | 77175 | 78975 | 78775 |
| 377 206 | | **SN** | P | *SN* | SU | 78576 | 77176 | 78976 | 78776 |
| 377 207 | | **SN** | P | *SN* | SU | 78577 | 77177 | 78977 | 78777 |
| 377 208 | | **SN** | P | *SN* | SU | 78578 | 77178 | 78978 | 78778 |
| 377 209 | | **SN** | P | *SN* | SU | 78579 | 77179 | 78979 | 78779 |
| 377 210 | | **SN** | P | *SN* | SU | 78580 | 77180 | 78980 | 78780 |
| 377 211 | | **SN** | P | *SN* | SU | 78581 | 77181 | 78981 | 78781 |
| 377 212 | | **SN** | P | *SN* | SU | 78582 | 77182 | 78982 | 78782 |
| 377 213 | | **SN** | P | *SN* | SU | 78583 | 77183 | 78983 | 78783 |
| 377 214 | | **SN** | P | *SN* | SU | 78584 | 77184 | 78984 | 78784 |
| 377 215 | | **SN** | P | *SN* | SU | 78585 | 77185 | 78985 | 78785 |

**Class 377/3.** 750 V DC only. DMC–TS–DMC.
**Seating Layout:** 1: 2+2 facing/unidirectional, 2: 2+2 facing/unidirectional.

Units built as Class 375, but renumbered in the Class 377/3 range when fitted with Dellner couplers.

377 342 was formerly 377 442. It had been reformed as a 3-car unit owing to fire damage to MS vehicle 78842 in 2016.

**DMC(A).** Bombardier Derby 2001–02. 12/48. 43.5 t.
**TS.** Bombardier Derby 2001–02. –/56 1TD 2W. 35.4 t.
**DMC(B).** Bombardier Derby 2001–02. 12/48. 43.5 t.

| | | | | | | | |
|---|---|---|---|---|---|---|---|
| 377 301 | (375 311) | **SN** | P | *SN* | SU | 68201 74801 68401 |
| 377 302 | (375 312) | **SN** | P | *SN* | SU | 68202 74802 68402 |
| 377 303 | (375 313) | **SN** | P | *SN* | SU | 68203 74803 68403 |
| 377 304 | (375 314) | **SN** | P | *SN* | SU | 68204 74804 68404 |
| 377 305 | (375 315) | **SN** | P | *SN* | SU | 68205 74805 68405 |
| 377 306 | (375 316) | **SN** | P | *SN* | SU | 68206 74806 68406 |
| 377 307 | (375 317) | **SN** | P | *SN* | SU | 68207 74807 68407 |
| 377 308 | (375 318) | **SN** | P | *SN* | SU | 68208 74808 68408 |
| 377 309 | (375 319) | **SN** | P | *SN* | SU | 68209 74809 68409 |
| 377 310 | (375 320) | **SN** | P | *SN* | SU | 68210 74810 68410 |
| 377 311 | (375 321) | **SN** | P | *SN* | SU | 68211 74811 68411 |
| 377 312 | (375 322) | **SN** | P | *SN* | SU | 68212 74812 68412 |
| 377 313 | (375 323) | **SN** | P | *SN* | SU | 68213 74813 68413 |
| 377 314 | (375 324) | **SN** | P | *SN* | SU | 68214 74814 68414 |
| 377 315 | (375 325) | **SN** | P | *SN* | SU | 68215 74815 68415 |
| 377 316 | (375 326) | **SN** | P | *SN* | SU | 68216 74816 68416 |
| 377 317 | (375 327) | **SN** | P | *SN* | SU | 68217 74817 68417 |
| 377 318 | (375 328) | **SN** | P | *SN* | SU | 68218 74818 68418 |
| 377 319 | (375 329) | **SN** | P | *SN* | SU | 68219 74819 68419 |
| 377 320 | (375 330) | **SN** | P | *SN* | SU | 68220 74820 68420 |
| 377 321 | (375 331) | **SN** | P | *SN* | SU | 68221 74821 68421 |
| 377 322 | (375 332) | **SN** | P | *SN* | SU | 68222 74822 68422 |
| 377 323 | (375 333) | **SN** | P | *SN* | SU | 68223 74823 68423 |
| 377 324 | (375 334) | **SN** | P | *SN* | SU | 68224 74824 68424 |
| 377 325 | (375 335) | **SN** | P | *SN* | SU | 68225 74825 68425 |
| 377 326 | (375 336) | **SN** | P | *SN* | SU | 68226 74826 68426 |
| 377 327 | (375 337) | **SN** | P | *SN* | SU | 68227 74827 68427 |
| 377 328 | (375 338) | **SN** | P | *SN* | SU | 68228 74828 68428 |
| | | | | | | | |
| 377 342 | (377 442) | **SN** | P | *SN* | SU | 73442 78642 73842 |

**Class 377/4.** 750 V DC only. DMC–MS–TS–DMC.
**Seating Layout:** 1: 2+2 facing/two seats longitudinal, 2: 2+2 and 3+2 facing/unidirectional (3+2 seating in middle cars only).

**DMC(A).** Bombardier Derby 2004–05. 10/48. 43.1 t.
**MS.** Bombardier Derby 2004–05. –/69 1T. 39.3 t.
**TS.** Bombardier Derby 2004–05. –/56 1TD 2W. 35.3 t.
**DMC(B).** Bombardier Derby 2004–05. 10/48. 43.2 t.

| | | | | | | |
|---|---|---|---|---|---|---|
| 377 401 | **SN** | P | *SN* | SU | 73401 78801 78601 73801 |
| 377 402 | **SN** | P | *SN* | SU | 73402 78802 78602 73802 |

| | | | | | | | | |
|---|---|---|---|---|---|---|---|---|
| 377 403 | **SN** | P | *SN* | SU | 73403 | 78803 | 78603 | 73803 |
| 377 404 | **SN** | P | *SN* | SU | 73404 | 78804 | 78604 | 73804 |
| 377 405 | **SN** | P | *SN* | SU | 73405 | 78805 | 78605 | 73805 |
| 377 406 | **SN** | P | *SN* | SU | 73406 | 78806 | 78606 | 73806 |
| 377 407 | **SN** | P | *SN* | SU | 73407 | 78807 | 78607 | 73807 |
| 377 408 | **SN** | P | *SN* | SU | 73408 | 78808 | 78608 | 73808 |
| 377 409 | **SN** | P | *SN* | SU | 73409 | 78809 | 78609 | 73809 |
| 377 410 | **SN** | P | *SN* | SU | 73410 | 78810 | 78610 | 73810 |
| 377 411 | **SN** | P | *SN* | SU | 73411 | 78811 | 78611 | 73811 |
| 377 412 | **SN** | P | *SN* | SU | 73412 | 78812 | 78612 | 73812 |
| 377 413 | **SN** | P | *SN* | SU | 73413 | 78813 | 78613 | 73813 |
| 377 414 | **SN** | P | *SN* | SU | 73414 | 78814 | 78614 | 73814 |
| 377 415 | **SN** | P | *SN* | SU | 73415 | 78815 | 78615 | 73815 |
| 377 416 | **SN** | P | *SN* | SU | 73416 | 78816 | 78616 | 73816 |
| 377 417 | **SN** | P | *SN* | SU | 73417 | 78817 | 78617 | 73817 |
| 377 418 | **SN** | P | *SN* | SU | 73418 | 78818 | 78618 | 73818 |
| 377 419 | **SN** | P | *SN* | SU | 73419 | 78819 | 78619 | 73819 |
| 377 420 | **SN** | P | *SN* | SU | 73420 | 78820 | 78620 | 73820 |
| 377 421 | **SN** | P | *SN* | SU | 73421 | 78821 | 78621 | 73821 |
| 377 422 | **SN** | P | *SN* | SU | 73422 | 78822 | 78622 | 73822 |
| 377 423 | **SN** | P | *SN* | SU | 73423 | 78823 | 78623 | 73823 |
| 377 424 | **SN** | P | *SN* | SU | 73424 | 78824 | 78624 | 73824 |
| 377 425 | **SN** | P | *SN* | SU | 73425 | 78825 | 78625 | 73825 |
| 377 426 | **SN** | P | *SN* | SU | 73426 | 78826 | 78626 | 73826 |
| 377 427 | **SN** | P | *SN* | SU | 73427 | 78827 | 78627 | 73827 |
| 377 428 | **SN** | P | *SN* | SU | 73428 | 78828 | 78628 | 73828 |
| 377 429 | **SN** | P | *SN* | SU | 73429 | 78829 | 78629 | 73829 |
| 377 430 | **SN** | P | *SN* | SU | 73430 | 78830 | 78630 | 73830 |
| 377 431 | **SN** | P | *SN* | SU | 73431 | 78831 | 78631 | 73831 |
| 377 432 | **SN** | P | *SN* | SU | 73432 | 78832 | 78632 | 73832 |
| 377 433 | **SN** | P | *SN* | SU | 73433 | 78833 | 78633 | 73833 |
| 377 434 | **SN** | P | *SN* | SU | 73434 | 78834 | 78634 | 73834 |
| 377 435 | **SN** | P | *SN* | SU | 73435 | 78835 | 78635 | 73835 |
| 377 436 | **SN** | P | *SN* | SU | 73436 | 78836 | 78636 | 73836 |
| 377 437 | **SN** | P | *SN* | SU | 73437 | 78837 | 78637 | 73837 |
| 377 438 | **SN** | P | *SN* | SU | 73438 | 78838 | 78638 | 73838 |
| 377 439 | **SN** | P | *SN* | SU | 73439 | 78839 | 78639 | 73839 |
| 377 440 | **SN** | P | *SN* | SU | 73440 | 78840 | 78640 | 73840 |
| 377 441 | **SN** | P | *SN* | SU | 73441 | 78841 | 78641 | 73841 |
| 377 443 | **SN** | P | *SN* | SU | 73443 | 78843 | 78643 | 73843 |
| 377 444 | **SN** | P | *SN* | SU | 73444 | 78844 | 78644 | 73844 |
| 377 445 | **SN** | P | *SN* | SU | 73445 | 78845 | 78645 | 73845 |
| 377 446 | **SN** | P | *SN* | SU | 73446 | 78846 | 78646 | 73846 |
| 377 447 | **SN** | P | *SN* | SU | 73447 | 78847 | 78647 | 73847 |
| 377 448 | **SN** | P | *SN* | SU | 73448 | 78848 | 78648 | 73848 |
| 377 449 | **SN** | P | *SN* | SU | 73449 | 78849 | 78649 | 73849 |
| 377 450 | **SN** | P | *SN* | SU | 73450 | 78850 | 78650 | 73850 |
| 377 451 | **SN** | P | *SN* | SU | 73451 | 78851 | 78651 | 73851 |
| 377 452 | **SN** | P | *SN* | SU | 73452 | 78852 | 78652 | 73852 |
| 377 453 | **SN** | P | *SN* | SU | 73453 | 78853 | 78653 | 73853 |
| 377 454 | **SN** | P | *SN* | SU | 73454 | 78854 | 78654 | 73854 |

| 377455 | **SN** | P | *SN* | SU | 73455 | 78855 | 78655 | 73855 |
|--------|--------|---|------|----|-------|-------|-------|-------|
| 377456 | **SN** | P | *SN* | SU | 73456 | 78856 | 78656 | 73856 |
| 377457 | **SN** | P | *SN* | SU | 73457 | 78857 | 78657 | 73857 |
| 377458 | **SN** | P | *SN* | SU | 73458 | 78858 | 78658 | 73858 |
| 377459 | **SN** | P | *SN* | SU | 73459 | 78859 | 78659 | 73859 |
| 377460 | **SN** | P | *SN* | SU | 73460 | 78860 | 78660 | 73860 |
| 377461 | **SN** | P | *SN* | SU | 73461 | 78861 | 78661 | 73861 |
| 377462 | **SN** | P | *SN* | SU | 73462 | 78862 | 78662 | 73862 |
| 377463 | **SN** | P | *SN* | SU | 73463 | 78863 | 78663 | 73863 |
| 377464 | **SN** | P | *SN* | SU | 73464 | 78864 | 78664 | 73864 |
| 377465 | **SN** | P | *SN* | SU | 73465 | 78865 | 78665 | 73865 |
| 377466 | **SN** | P | *SN* | SU | 73466 | 78866 | 78666 | 73866 |
| 377467 | **SN** | P | *SN* | SU | 73467 | 78867 | 78667 | 73867 |
| 377468 | **SN** | P | *SN* | SU | 73468 | 78868 | 78668 | 73868 |
| 377469 | **SN** | P | *SN* | SU | 73469 | 78869 | 78669 | 73869 |
| 377470 | **SN** | P | *SN* | SU | 73470 | 78870 | 78670 | 73870 |
| 377471 | **SN** | P | *SN* | SU | 73471 | 78871 | 78671 | 73871 |
| 377472 | **SN** | P | *SN* | SU | 73472 | 78872 | 78672 | 73872 |
| 377473 | **SN** | P | *SN* | SU | 73473 | 78873 | 78673 | 73873 |
| 377474 | **SN** | P | *SN* | SU | 73474 | 78874 | 78674 | 73874 |
| 377475 | **SN** | P | *SN* | SU | 73475 | 78875 | 78675 | 73875 |
| Spare | **SN** | P | | ZN | | 78842 | | |

**Class 377/5.** 25kV AC/750V DC. DMC–MS–PTS–DMS. Dual-voltage units. Details as Class 377/2 unless stated.

**DMC.** Bombardier Derby 2008–09. 10/48. 43.1t.
**MS.** Bombardier Derby 2008–09. –/69 1T. 40.3t.
**PTS.** Bombardier Derby 2008–09. –/56 1TD 2W. 40.6 t.
**DMS.** Bombardier Derby 2008–09. –/58. 44.9t.

| 377501 | **FB** | P | *SE* | RM | 73501 | 75901 | 74901 | 73601 |
|--------|--------|---|------|----|-------|-------|-------|-------|
| 377502 | **FB** | P | *SE* | RM | 73502 | 75902 | 74902 | 73602 |
| 377503 | **FB** | P | *SE* | RM | 73503 | 75903 | 74903 | 73603 |
| 377504 | **FB** | P | *SE* | RM | 73504 | 75904 | 74904 | 73604 |
| 377505 | **FB** | P | *SE* | RM | 73505 | 75905 | 74905 | 73605 |
| 377506 | **FB** | P | *SE* | RM | 73506 | 75906 | 74906 | 73606 |
| 377507 | **FB** | P | *SE* | RM | 73507 | 75907 | 74907 | 73607 |
| 377508 | **FB** | P | *SE* | RM | 73508 | 75908 | 74908 | 73608 |
| 377509 | **FB** | P | *SE* | RM | 73509 | 75909 | 74909 | 73609 |
| 377510 | **FB** | P | *SE* | RM | 73510 | 75910 | 74910 | 73610 |
| 377511 | **FB** | P | *SE* | RM | 73511 | 75911 | 74911 | 73611 |
| 377512 | **FB** | P | *SE* | RM | 73512 | 75912 | 74912 | 73612 |
| 377513 | **FB** | P | *SE* | RM | 73513 | 75913 | 74913 | 73613 |
| 377514 | **FB** | P | *SE* | RM | 73514 | 75914 | 74914 | 73614 |
| 377515 | **FB** | P | *SE* | RM | 73515 | 75915 | 74915 | 73615 |
| 377516 | **FB** | P | *SE* | RM | 73516 | 75916 | 74916 | 73616 |
| 377517 | **FB** | P | *SE* | RM | 73517 | 75917 | 74917 | 73617 |
| 377518 | **FB** | P | *SE* | RM | 73518 | 75918 | 74918 | 73618 |
| 377519 | **FB** | P | *SE* | RM | 73519 | 75919 | 74919 | 73619 |
| 377520 | **FB** | P | *SE* | RM | 73520 | 75920 | 74920 | 73620 |
| 377521 | **FB** | P | *SE* | RM | 73521 | 75921 | 74921 | 73621 |

| 377522 | **FB** | P | *SE* | RM | 73522 | 75922 | 74922 | 73622 |
| 377523 | **FB** | P | *SE* | RM | 73523 | 75923 | 74923 | 73623 |

**Class 377/6.** 750V DC. DMS–MS–TS–MS–DMS. 5-car suburban units fitted with Fainsa seating. Technically the same as the 377/5s but using the slightly modified Class 379-style bodyshell.

**Seating Layout:** 2+2 facing/unidirectional.

**DMS.** Bombardier Derby 2012–13. 24/36. 44.7 t.
**MS.** Bombardier Derby 2012–13. –/64 1T. 38.8 t.
**TS.** Bombardier Derby 2012–13. –/46(+2) 1TD 2W. 37.8 t.
**MS.** Bombardier Derby 2012–13. –/66. 38.3 t.
**DMS.** Bombardier Derby 2012–13. –/62. 44.7 t.

| 377601 | **SN** | P | *SN* | SU | 70101 | 70201 | 70301 | 70401 | 70501 |
| 377602 | **SN** | P | *SN* | SU | 70102 | 70202 | 70302 | 70402 | 70502 |
| 377603 | **SN** | P | *SN* | SU | 70103 | 70203 | 70303 | 70403 | 70503 |
| 377604 | **SN** | P | *SN* | SU | 70104 | 70204 | 70304 | 70404 | 70504 |
| 377605 | **SN** | P | *SN* | SU | 70105 | 70205 | 70305 | 70405 | 70505 |
| 377606 | **SN** | P | *SN* | SU | 70106 | 70206 | 70306 | 70406 | 70506 |
| 377607 | **SN** | P | *SN* | SU | 70107 | 70207 | 70307 | 70407 | 70507 |
| 377608 | **SN** | P | *SN* | SU | 70108 | 70208 | 70308 | 70408 | 70508 |
| 377609 | **SN** | P | *SN* | SU | 70109 | 70209 | 70309 | 70409 | 70509 |
| 377610 | **SN** | P | *SN* | SU | 70110 | 70210 | 70310 | 70410 | 70510 |
| 377611 | **SN** | P | *SN* | SU | 70111 | 70211 | 70311 | 70411 | 70511 |
| 377612 | **SN** | P | *SN* | SU | 70112 | 70212 | 70312 | 70412 | 70512 |
| 377613 | **SN** | P | *SN* | SU | 70113 | 70213 | 70313 | 70413 | 70513 |
| 377614 | **SN** | P | *SN* | SU | 70114 | 70214 | 70314 | 70414 | 70514 |
| 377615 | **SN** | P | *SN* | SU | 70115 | 70215 | 70315 | 70415 | 70515 |
| 377616 | **SN** | P | *SN* | SU | 70116 | 70216 | 70316 | 70416 | 70516 |
| 377617 | **SN** | P | *SN* | SU | 70117 | 70217 | 70317 | 70417 | 70517 |
| 377618 | **SN** | P | *SN* | SU | 70118 | 70218 | 70318 | 70418 | 70518 |
| 377619 | **SN** | P | *SN* | SU | 70119 | 70219 | 70319 | 70419 | 70519 |
| 377620 | **SN** | P | *SN* | SU | 70120 | 70220 | 70320 | 70420 | 70520 |
| 377621 | **SN** | P | *SN* | SU | 70121 | 70221 | 70321 | 70421 | 70521 |
| 377622 | **SN** | P | *SN* | SU | 70122 | 70222 | 70322 | 70422 | 70522 |
| 377623 | **SN** | P | *SN* | SU | 70123 | 70223 | 70323 | 70423 | 70523 |
| 377624 | **SN** | P | *SN* | SU | 70124 | 70224 | 70324 | 70424 | 70524 |
| 377625 | **SN** | P | *SN* | SU | 70125 | 70225 | 70325 | 70425 | 70525 |
| 377626 | **SN** | P | *SN* | SU | 70126 | 70226 | 70326 | 70426 | 70526 |

**Class 377/7.** 25kV AC/750V DC. DMS–MS–TS–MS–DMS. Dual-voltage units, used on both the South Croydon–Milton Keynes cross-London services and on suburban services alongside the Class 377/6s.

**DMS.** Bombardier Derby 2013–14. 24/36. 45.6 t.
**MS.** Bombardier Derby 2013–14. –/64 1T. 41.0 t.
**PTS.** Bombardier Derby 2013–14. –/46(+2) 1TD 2W. 40.9 t.
**MS.** Bombardier Derby 2013–14. –/66. 39.6 t.
**DMS.** Bombardier Derby 2013–14. –/62. 45.2 t.

| 377701 | **SN** | P | *SN* | SU | 65201 | 70601 | 65601 | 70701 | 65401 |
| 377702 | **SN** | P | *SN* | SU | 65202 | 70602 | 65602 | 70702 | 65402 |

| 377703 | **SN** | P | *SN* | SU | 65203 70603 65603 70703 65403 |
| 377704 | **SN** | P | *SN* | SU | 65204 70604 65604 70704 65404 |
| 377705 | **SN** | P | *SN* | SU | 65205 70605 65605 70705 65405 |
| 377706 | **SN** | P | *SN* | SU | 65206 70606 65606 70706 65406 |
| 377707 | **SN** | P | *SN* | SU | 65207 70607 65607 70707 65407 |
| 377708 | **SN** | P | *SN* | SU | 65208 70608 65608 70708 65408 |

# CLASS 378   CAPITALSTAR   BOMBARDIER DERBY

These suburban Electrostars are designated "Capitalstars" by TfL.

**Formation:** DMS–MS–TS–MS–DMS or DMS–MS–PTS–MS–DMS.
**System:** Class 378/1 750 V DC third rail only. Class 378/2 25 kV AC overhead and 750 V DC third rail.
**Construction:** Welded aluminium alloy underframe, sides and roof with steel ends. All sections bolted together.
**Traction Motors:** Three Bombardier asynchronous of 200 kW.
**Wheel Arrangement:** 1A-Bo + 1A-Bo + 2-2 + Bo-1A + Bo-1A.
**Braking:** Disc & regenerative.    **Dimensions:** 20.46/20.14 x 2.80 m.
**Bogies:** Bombardier P3-25/T3-25.    **Couplers:** Dellner 12.
**Gangways:** Within unit + end doors. **Control System:** IGBT Inverter.
**Doors:** Sliding.                    **Maximum Speed:** 75 mph.
**Heating & ventilation:** Air conditioning.
**Seating Layout:** Longitudinal ("tube style") low density.
**Multiple Working:** Within class and with Classes 375, 376, 377 and 379.

57 extra MSs (in the 384xx number series) were delivered 2014–15 to make all units up to 5-cars.

**Class 378/1.** 750 V DC. DMS–MS–TS–MS–DMS. Third rail only units used on the East London Line. Provision for retro-fitting as dual voltage.

378 150–154 are fitted with de-icing equipment.

**DMS(A).** Bombardier Derby 2009–10. –/36. 43.1 t.
**MS(A).** Bombardier Derby 2009–10. –/40. 39.3 t.
**TS.** Bombardier Derby 2009–10. –/34(+6) 2W. 34.3 t.
**MS(B).** Bombardier Derby 2014–15. –/40. 40.2 t.
**DMS(B).** Bombardier Derby 2009–10. –/36. 42.7 t.

| 378135 | **LD** | QW | *LO* | NG | 38035 38235 38335 38435 38135 |
| 378136 | **LD** | QW | *LO* | NG | 38036 38236 38336 38436 38136 |
| 378137 | **LO** | QW | *LO* | NG | 38037 38237 38337 38437 38137 |
| 378138 | **LO** | QW | *LO* | NG | 38038 38238 38338 38438 38138 |
| 378139 | **LO** | QW | *LO* | NG | 38039 38239 38339 38439 38139 |
| 378140 | **LO** | QW | *LO* | NG | 38040 38240 38340 38440 38140 |
| 378141 | **LO** | QW | *LO* | NG | 38041 38241 38341 38441 38141 |
| 378142 | **LO** | QW | *LO* | NG | 38042 38242 38342 38442 38142 |
| 378143 | **LO** | QW | *LO* | NG | 38043 38243 38343 38443 38143 |
| 378144 | **LO** | QW | *LO* | NG | 38044 38244 38344 38444 38144 |
| 378145 | **LO** | QW | *LO* | NG | 38045 38245 38345 38445 38145 |
| 378146 | **LO** | QW | *LO* | NG | 38046 38246 38346 38446 38146 |
| 378147 | **LD** | QW | *LO* | NG | 38047 38247 38347 38447 38147 |
| 378148 | **LO** | QW | *LO* | NG | 38048 38248 38348 38448 38148 |

| 378149 | **LO** | QW | *LO* | NG | 38049 38249 38349 38449 38149 |
| 378150 | **LD** | QW | *LO* | NG | 38050 38250 38350 38450 38150 |
| 378151 | **LO** | QW | *LO* | NG | 38051 38251 38351 38451 38151 |
| 378152 | **LO** | QW | *LO* | NG | 38052 38252 38352 38452 38152 |
| 378153 | **LO** | QW | *LO* | NG | 38053 38253 38353 38453 38153 |
| 378154 | **LO** | QW | *LO* | NG | 38054 38254 38354 38454 38154 |

**Name (carried on DMS(A)):** 378135   Daks Hamilton

**Class 378/2.** 25 kV AC/750 V DC. DMS–MS–PTS–MS–DMS or DMS–MS–PTS–DMS. Dual-voltage units mainly used on North London Railway services. 378201–224 were built as 3-car units 378001–024 and extended to 4-car units in 2010.

Fitted with tripcocks for operation on the tracks shared with London Underground between Queens Park and Harrow & Wealdstone.

378216–220 are fitted with de-icing equipment.

**DMS(A).** Bombardier Derby 2008–11. –/36. 43.4 t.
**MS(A).** Bombardier Derby 2008–11. –/40. 39.6 t.
**PTS.** Bombardier Derby 2008–11. –/34(+6) 2W. 39.2 t.
**MS(B).** Bombardier Derby 2014–15. –/40. 40.4 t.
**DMS(B).** Bombardier Derby 2008–11. –/36. 43.1 t.

| 378201 | **LO** | QW | *LO* | NG | 38001 38201 38301 38401 38101 |
| 378202 | **LO** | QW | *LO* | NG | 38002 38202 38302 38402 38102 |
| 378203 | **LO** | QW | *LO* | NG | 38003 38203 38303 38403 38103 |
| 378204 | **LD** | QW | *LO* | NG | 38004 38204 38304 38404 38104 |
| 378205 | **LO** | QW | *LO* | NG | 38005 38205 38305 38405 38105 |
| 378206 | **LD** | QW | *LO* | NG | 38006 38206 38306 38406 38106 |
| 378207 | **LO** | QW | *LO* | NG | 38007 38207 38307 38407 38107 |
| 378208 | **LO** | QW | *LO* | NG | 38008 38208 38308 38408 38108 |
| 378209 | **LO** | QW | *LO* | NG | 38009 38209 38309 38409 38109 |
| 378210 | **LO** | QW | *LO* | NG | 38010 38210 38310 38410 38110 |
| 378211 | **LD** | QW | *LO* | NG | 38011 38211 38311 38411 38111 |
| 378212 | **LO** | QW | *LO* | NG | 38012 38212 38312 38412 38112 |
| 378213 | **LO** | QW | *LO* | NG | 38013 38213 38313 38413 38113 |
| 378214 | **LO** | QW | *LO* | NG | 38014 38214 38314 38414 38114 |
| 378215 | **LO** | QW | *LO* | NG | 38015 38215 38315 38415 38115 |
| 378216 | **LO** | QW | *LO* | NG | 38016 38216 38316 38416 38116 |
| 378217 | **LO** | QW | *LO* | NG | 38017 38217 38317 38417 38117 |
| 378218 | **LO** | QW | *LO* | NG | 38018 38218 38318 38418 38118 |
| 378219 | **LO** | QW | *LO* | NG | 38019 38219 38319 38419 38119 |
| 378220 | **LO** | QW | *LO* | NG | 38020 38220 38320 38420 38120 |
| 378221 | **LO** | QW | *LO* | NG | 38021 38221 38321 38421 38121 |
| 378222 | **LO** | QW | *LO* | NG | 38022 38222 38322 38422 38122 |
| 378223 | **LO** | QW | *LO* | NG | 38023 38223 38323 38423 38123 |
| 378224 | **LO** | QW | *LO* | NG | 38024 38224 38324 38424 38124 |
| 378225 | **LO** | QW | *LO* | NG | 38025 38225 38325 38425 38125 |
| 378226 | **LO** | QW | *LO* | NG | 38026 38226 38326 38426 38126 |
| 378227 | **LO** | QW | *LO* | NG | 38027 38227 38327 38427 38127 |
| 378228 | **LO** | QW | *LO* | NG | 38028 38228 38328 38428 38128 |
| 378229 | **LO** | QW | *LO* | NG | 38029 38229 38329 38429 38129 |

| 378230 | **LO** | QW | *LO* | NG | 38030 | 38230 | 38330 | 38430 | 38130 |
| 378231 | **LO** | QW | *LO* | NG | 38031 | 38231 | 38331 | 38431 | 38131 |
| 378232 | **LD** | QW | *LO* | NG | 38032 | 38232 | 38332 | 38432 | 38132 |
| 378233 | **LO** | QW | *LO* | NG | 38033 | 38233 | 38333 | 38433 | 38133 |
| 378234 | **LO** | QW | *LO* | NG | 38034 | 38234 | 38334 | 38434 | 38134 |
| 378255 | **LO** | QW | *LO* | NG | 38055 | 38255 | 38355 | 38455 | 38155 |
| 378256 | **LO** | QW | *LO* | NG | 38056 | 38256 | 38356 | 38456 | 38156 |
| 378257 | **LO** | QW | *LO* | NG | 38057 | 38257 | 38357 | 38457 | 38157 |

**Names (carried on DMS(A)):**

| 378204 | Professor Sir Peter Hall | | 378233 | Ian Brown CBE |
| 378232 | Jeff Langston | | | |

# CLASS 379 ELECTROSTAR BOMBARDIER DERBY

Express Electrostars built for Liverpool Street–Stansted Airport and Liverpool Street–Cambridge services.

**Formation:** DMS–MS–PTS–DMC.
**System:** 25 kV AC overhead.
**Construction:** Welded aluminium alloy underframe, sides and roof with steel ends. All sections bolted together.
**Traction Motors:** Two Bombardier asynchronous of 200 kW.
**Wheel Arrangement:** 2-Bo + 2-Bo + 2-2 + Bo-2.
**Braking:** Disc & regenerative.      **Dimensions:** 20.00 x 2.80 m.
**Bogies:** Bombardier P3-25/T3-25.      **Couplers:** Dellner 12.
**Gangways:** Throughout.      **Control System:** IGBT Inverter.
**Doors:** Sliding plug.      **Maximum Speed:** 100 mph.
**Heating & ventilation:** Air conditioning.
**Seating Layout:** 1: 2+1 facing. 2: 2+2 facing/unidirectional.
**Multiple Working:** Within class and with Classes 375, 376, 377 and 378.

**DMS.** Bombardier Derby 2010–11. –/60. 42.1 t.
**MS.** Bombardier Derby 2010–11. –/62 1T. 38.6 t.
**PTS.** Bombardier Derby 2010–11. –/43(+2) 1TD 2W. 40.9 t.
**DMC.** Bombardier Derby 2010–11. 20/24. 42.3 t.

| 379001 | **NC** | AK | *GA* | IL | 61201 | 61701 | 61901 | 62101 |
| 379002 | **NC** | AK | *GA* | IL | 61202 | 61702 | 61902 | 62102 |
| 379003 | **NC** | AK | *GA* | IL | 61203 | 61703 | 61903 | 62103 |
| 379004 | **NC** | AK | *GA* | IL | 61204 | 61704 | 61904 | 62104 |
| 379005 | **NC** | AK | *GA* | IL | 61205 | 61705 | 61905 | 62105 |
| 379006 | **NC** | AK | *GA* | IL | 61206 | 61706 | 61906 | 62106 |
| 379007 | **NC** | AK | *GA* | IL | 61207 | 61707 | 61907 | 62107 |
| 379008 | **NC** | AK | *GA* | IL | 61208 | 61708 | 61908 | 62108 |
| 379009 | **NC** | AK | *GA* | IL | 61209 | 61709 | 61909 | 62109 |
| 379010 | **NC** | AK | *GA* | IL | 61210 | 61710 | 61910 | 62110 |
| 379011 | **NC** | AK | *GA* | IL | 61211 | 61711 | 61911 | 62111 |
| 379012 | **NC** | AK | *GA* | IL | 61212 | 61712 | 61912 | 62112 |
| 379013 | **NC** | AK | *GA* | IL | 61213 | 61713 | 61913 | 62113 |
| 379014 | **NC** | AK | *GA* | IL | 61214 | 61714 | 61914 | 62114 |

| | | | | | | | | |
|---|---|---|---|---|---|---|---|---|
| 379015 | **NC** | AK | *GA* | IL | 61215 | 61715 | 61915 | 62115 |
| 379016 | **NC** | AK | *GA* | IL | 61216 | 61716 | 61916 | 62116 |
| 379017 | **NC** | AK | *GA* | IL | 61217 | 61717 | 61917 | 62117 |
| 379018 | **NC** | AK | *GA* | IL | 61218 | 61718 | 61918 | 62118 |
| 379019 | **NC** | AK | *GA* | IL | 61219 | 61719 | 61919 | 62119 |
| 379020 | **NC** | AK | *GA* | IL | 61220 | 61720 | 61920 | 62120 |
| 379021 | **NC** | AK | *GA* | IL | 61221 | 61721 | 61921 | 62121 |
| 379022 | **NC** | AK | *GA* | IL | 61222 | 61722 | 61922 | 62122 |
| 379023 | **NC** | AK | *GA* | IL | 61223 | 61723 | 61923 | 62123 |
| 379024 | **NC** | AK | *GA* | IL | 61224 | 61724 | 61924 | 62124 |
| 379025 | **NC** | AK | *GA* | IL | 61225 | 61725 | 61925 | 62125 |
| 379026 | **NC** | AK | *GA* | IL | 61226 | 61726 | 61926 | 62126 |
| 379027 | **NC** | AK | *GA* | IL | 61227 | 61727 | 61927 | 62127 |
| 379028 | **NC** | AK | *GA* | IL | 61228 | 61728 | 61928 | 62128 |
| 379029 | **NC** | AK | *GA* | IL | 61229 | 61729 | 61929 | 62129 |
| 379030 | **NC** | AK | *GA* | IL | 61230 | 61730 | 61930 | 62130 |

**Names (carried on end cars):**

| | | | |
|---|---|---|---|
| 379005 | Stansted Express | 379015 | City of Cambridge |
| 379011 | Ely Cathedral | 379025 | Go Discover |
| 379012 | The West Anglian | | |

# CLASS 380   DESIRO UK   SIEMENS

ScotRail units mainly used on Strathclyde area services.

**Formation:** DMS–PTS–DMS or DMS–PTS–TS–DMS.
**System:** 25 kV AC overhead.
**Construction:** Welded aluminium with steel ends.
**Traction Motors:** Four Siemens ITB2016-0GB02 asynchronous of 250 kW.
**Wheel Arrangement:** Bo-Bo + 2-2 (+2-2) + Bo-Bo

| | |
|---|---|
| **Braking:** Disc & regenerative. | **Dimensions:** 23.78/23.57 x 2.80 m. |
| **Bogies:** SGP SF5000. | **Couplers:** Voith. |
| **Gangways:** Throughout. | **Control System:** IGBT Inverter. |
| **Doors:** Sliding plug. | **Maximum Speed:** 100 mph. |
| **Heating & ventilation:** Air conditioning. | **Seating Layout:** 2+2 facing/unidirectional. |
| **Multiple Working:** Within class. | |

**DMS(A).** Siemens Krefeld 2009–10. –/70. 45.0 t.
**PTS.** Siemens Krefeld 2009–10. –/57(+12) 1TD 2W. 42.7 t.
**TS.** Siemens Krefeld 2009–10. –/74 1T. 34.8 t.
**DMS(B).** Siemens Krefeld 2009–10. –/64(+5). 44.9 t.

**Class 380/0.** 3-car units. **Formation:** DMS–PTS–DMS.

| | | | | | | | |
|---|---|---|---|---|---|---|---|
| 380001 | **SR** | E | *SR* | GW | 38501 | 38601 | 38701 |
| 380002 | **SR** | E | *SR* | GW | 38502 | 38602 | 38702 |
| 380003 | **SR** | E | *SR* | GW | 38503 | 38603 | 38703 |
| 380004 | **SR** | E | *SR* | GW | 38504 | 38604 | 38704 |
| 380005 | **SR** | E | *SR* | GW | 38505 | 38605 | 38705 |
| 380006 | **SR** | E | *SR* | GW | 38506 | 38606 | 38706 |
| 380007 | **SR** | E | *SR* | GW | 38507 | 38607 | 38707 |

| 380008 | **SR** | E | *SR* | GW | 38508 | 38608 | | 38708 |
| 380009 | **SR** | E | *SR* | GW | 38509 | 38609 | | 38709 |
| 380010 | **SR** | E | *SR* | GW | 38510 | 38610 | | 38710 |
| 380011 | **SR** | E | *SR* | GW | 38511 | 38611 | | 38711 |
| 380012 | **SR** | E | *SR* | GW | 38512 | 38612 | | 38712 |
| 380013 | **SR** | E | *SR* | GW | 38513 | 38613 | | 38713 |
| 380014 | **SR** | E | *SR* | GW | 38514 | 38614 | | 38714 |
| 380015 | **SR** | E | *SR* | GW | 38515 | 38615 | | 38715 |
| 380016 | **SR** | E | *SR* | GW | 38516 | 38616 | | 38716 |
| 380017 | **SR** | E | *SR* | GW | 38517 | 38617 | | 38717 |
| 380018 | **SR** | E | *SR* | GW | 38518 | 38618 | | 38718 |
| 380019 | **SR** | E | *SR* | GW | 38519 | 38619 | | 38719 |
| 380020 | **SR** | E | *SR* | GW | 38520 | 38620 | | 38720 |
| 380021 | **SR** | E | *SR* | GW | 38521 | 38621 | | 38721 |
| 380022 | **SR** | E | *SR* | GW | 38522 | 38622 | | 38722 |

**Class 380/1.** 4-car units. **Formation:** DMS–PTS–TS–DMS.

| 380101 | **SR** | E | *SR* | GW | 38551 | 38651 | 38851 | 38751 |
| 380102 | **SR** | E | *SR* | GW | 38552 | 38652 | 38852 | 38752 |
| 380103 | **SR** | E | *SR* | GW | 38553 | 38653 | 38853 | 38753 |
| 380104 | **SR** | E | *SR* | GW | 38554 | 38654 | 38854 | 38754 |
| 380105 | **SR** | E | *SR* | GW | 38555 | 38655 | 38855 | 38755 |
| 380106 | **SR** | E | *SR* | GW | 38556 | 38656 | 38856 | 38756 |
| 380107 | **SR** | E | *SR* | GW | 38557 | 38657 | 38857 | 38757 |
| 380108 | **SR** | E | *SR* | GW | 38558 | 38658 | 38858 | 38758 |
| 380109 | **SR** | E | *SR* | GW | 38559 | 38659 | 38859 | 38759 |
| 380110 | **SR** | E | *SR* | GW | 38560 | 38660 | 38860 | 38760 |
| 380111 | **SR** | E | *SR* | GW | 38561 | 38661 | 38861 | 38761 |
| 380112 | **SR** | E | *SR* | GW | 38562 | 38662 | 38862 | 38762 |
| 380113 | **SR** | E | *SR* | GW | 38563 | 38663 | 38863 | 38763 |
| 380114 | **SR** | E | *SR* | GW | 38564 | 38664 | 38864 | 38764 |
| 380115 | **SR** | E | *SR* | GW | 38565 | 38665 | 38865 | 38765 |
| 380116 | **SR** | E | *SR* | GW | 38566 | 38666 | 38866 | 38766 |

# CLASS 385                    AT200                    HITACHI

New 3- and 4-car ScotRail units, financed by Caledonian Rail Leasing.

**Formation:** DMS–PTS–DMS or DMC–PTS–TS–DMS.
**System:** 25 kV AC overhead.
**Construction:** Aluminium.
**Traction Motors:** Four Hitachi asynchronous of 250 kW.
**Wheel Arrangement:** Bo-Bo + 2-2 + Bo-2 or Bo-Bo + 2-2 + 2-2 + Bo-Bo.
**Braking:** Disc & regenerative.
**Dimensions:** 23.18/22.08 x 2.74 m.      **Couplers:** Dellner.
**Bogies:** Hitachi.                        **Control System:** IGBT Inverter.
**Gangways:** Throughout.                   **Maximum Speed:** 100 mph.
**Doors:** Sliding plug.                    **Multiple Working:** Within class only.
**Heating & ventilation:** Air conditioning.
**Seating Layout:** 1: 2+1 facing. 2: 2+2 facing/unidirectional.

**Class 385/0.** 3-car units. Standard Class only. **Formation:** DMS–PTS–DMS.

**DMS(A):** Hitachi Newton Aycliffe/Kasado 2016–18. –/48(+9) 1TD 2W. 44.6 t.
**PTS:** Hitachi Newton Aycliffe/Kasado 2016–18. –/80. 38.4 t.
**DMS(B):** Hitachi Newton Aycliffe/Kasado 2016–18. –62(+5) 1T. 42.0 t.

| | | | | | | | |
|---|---|---|---|---|---|---|---|
| 385001 | **SR** | CL | *SR* | EC | 441001 | 442001 | 444001 |
| 385002 | **SR** | CL | *SR* | EC | 441002 | 442002 | 444002 |
| 385003 | **SR** | CL | *SR* | EC | 441003 | 442003 | 444003 |
| 385004 | **SR** | CL | *SR* | EC | 441004 | 442004 | 444004 |
| 385005 | **SR** | CL | *SR* | EC | 441005 | 442005 | 444005 |
| 385006 | **SR** | CL | *SR* | EC | 441006 | 442006 | 444006 |
| 385007 | **SR** | CL | *SR* | EC | 441007 | 442007 | 444007 |
| 385008 | **SR** | CL | *SR* | EC | 441008 | 442008 | 444008 |
| 385009 | **SR** | CL | *SR* | EC | 441009 | 442009 | 444009 |
| 385010 | **SR** | CL | *SR* | EC | 441010 | 442010 | 444010 |
| 385011 | **SR** | CL | *SR* | EC | 441011 | 442011 | 444011 |
| 385012 | **SR** | CL | *SR* | EC | 441012 | 442012 | 444012 |
| 385013 | **SR** | CL | *SR* | EC | 441013 | 442013 | 444013 |
| 385014 | **SR** | CL | *SR* | EC | 441014 | 442014 | 444014 |
| 385015 | **SR** | CL | *SR* | EC | 441015 | 442015 | 444015 |
| 385016 | **SR** | CL | *SR* | EC | 441016 | 442016 | 444016 |
| 385017 | **SR** | CL | *SR* | EC | 441017 | 442017 | 444017 |
| 385018 | **SR** | CL | *SR* | EC | 441018 | 442018 | 444018 |
| 385019 | **SR** | CL | *SR* | EC | 441019 | 442019 | 444019 |
| 385020 | **SR** | CL | *SR* | EC | 441020 | 442020 | 444020 |
| 385021 | **SR** | CL | *SR* | EC | 441021 | 442021 | 444021 |
| 385022 | **SR** | CL | *SR* | EC | 441022 | 442022 | 444022 |
| 385023 | **SR** | CL | *SR* | EC | 441023 | 442023 | 444023 |
| 385024 | **SR** | CL | *SR* | EC | 441024 | 442024 | 444024 |
| 385025 | **SR** | CL | *SR* | EC | 441025 | 442025 | 444025 |
| 385026 | **SR** | CL | *SR* | EC | 441026 | 442026 | 444026 |
| 385027 | **SR** | CL | *SR* | EC | 441027 | 442027 | 444027 |
| 385028 | **SR** | CL | *SR* | EC | 441028 | 442028 | 444028 |
| 385029 | **SR** | CL | *SR* | EC | 441029 | 442029 | 444029 |
| 385030 | **SR** | CL | *SR* | EC | 441030 | 442030 | 444030 |
| 385031 | **SR** | CL | *SR* | EC | 441031 | 442031 | 444031 |
| 385032 | **SR** | CL | *SR* | EC | 441032 | 442032 | 444032 |
| 385033 | **SR** | CL | *SR* | EC | 441033 | 442033 | 444033 |
| 385034 | **SR** | CL | *SR* | EC | 441034 | 442034 | 444034 |
| 385035 | **SR** | CL | *SR* | EC | 441035 | 442035 | 444035 |
| 385036 | **SR** | CL | *SR* | EC | 441036 | 442036 | 444036 |
| 385037 | **SR** | CL | *SR* | EC | 441037 | 442037 | 444037 |
| 385038 | **SR** | CL | *SR* | EC | 441038 | 442038 | 444038 |
| 385039 | **SR** | CL | *SR* | EC | 441039 | 442039 | 444039 |
| 385040 | **SR** | CL | *SR* | EC | 441040 | 442040 | 444040 |
| 385041 | **SR** | CL | *SR* | EC | 441041 | 442041 | 444041 |
| 385042 | **SR** | CL | *SR* | EC | 441042 | 442042 | 444042 |
| 385043 | **SR** | CL | *SR* | EC | 441043 | 442043 | 444043 |
| 385044 | **SR** | CL | *SR* | EC | 441044 | 442044 | 444044 |
| 385045 | **SR** | CL | *SR* | EC | 441045 | 442045 | 444045 |
| 385046 | **SR** | CL | *SR* | EC | 441046 | 442046 | 444046 |

**Class 385/1.** 4-car units. Standard Class and First Class seating.
**Formation:** DMC–PTS–TS–DMS.

**DMC:** Hitachi Newton Aycliffe/Kasado 2016–18. 20/15(+9) 1TD 2W. 44.7 t.
**PTS:** Hitachi Newton Aycliffe/Kasado 2016–18. –/80. 38.4 t.
**TS:** Hitachi Newton Aycliffe/Kasado 2016–18. –/80. 31.5 t.
**DMS:** Hitachi Newton Aycliffe/Kasado 2016–18. –62(+5) 1T. 44.5 t.

| | | | | | | | |
|---|---|---|---|---|---|---|---|
| 385 101 | **SR** | CL | *SR* | EC | 441101 | 442101 | 443101 | 444101 |
| 385 102 | **SR** | CL | *SR* | EC | 441102 | 442102 | 443102 | 444102 |
| 385 103 | **SR** | CL | *SR* | EC | 441103 | 442103 | 443103 | 444103 |
| 385 104 | **SR** | CL | *SR* | EC | 441104 | 442104 | 443104 | 444104 |
| 385 105 | **SR** | CL | *SR* | EC | 441105 | 442105 | 443105 | 444105 |
| 385 106 | **SR** | CL | *SR* | EC | 441106 | 442106 | 443106 | 444106 |
| 385 107 | **SR** | CL | *SR* | EC | 441107 | 442107 | 443107 | 444107 |
| 385 108 | **SR** | CL | *SR* | EC | 441108 | 442108 | 443108 | 444108 |
| 385 109 | **SR** | CL | *SR* | EC | 441109 | 442109 | 443109 | 444109 |
| 385 110 | **SR** | CL | *SR* | EC | 441110 | 442110 | 443110 | 444110 |
| 385 111 | **SR** | CL | *SR* | EC | 441111 | 442111 | 443111 | 444111 |
| 385 112 | **SR** | CL | *SR* | EC | 441112 | 442112 | 443112 | 444112 |
| 385 113 | **SR** | CL | *SR* | EC | 441113 | 442113 | 443113 | 444113 |
| 385 114 | **SR** | CL | *SR* | EC | 441114 | 442114 | 443114 | 444114 |
| 385 115 | **SR** | CL | *SR* | EC | 441115 | 442115 | 443115 | 444115 |
| 385 116 | **SR** | CL | *SR* | EC | 441116 | 442116 | 443116 | 444116 |
| 385 117 | **SR** | CL | *SR* | EC | 441117 | 442117 | 443117 | 444117 |
| 385 118 | **SR** | CL | *SR* | EC | 441118 | 442118 | 443118 | 444118 |
| 385 119 | **SR** | CL | *SR* | EC | 441119 | 442119 | 443119 | 444119 |
| 385 120 | **SR** | CL | *SR* | EC | 441120 | 442120 | 443120 | 444120 |
| 385 121 | **SR** | CL | *SR* | EC | 441121 | 442121 | 443121 | 444121 |
| 385 122 | **SR** | CL | *SR* | EC | 441122 | 442122 | 443122 | 444122 |
| 385 123 | **SR** | CL | *SR* | EC | 441123 | 442123 | 443123 | 444123 |
| 385 124 | **SR** | CL | *SR* | EC | 441124 | 442124 | 443124 | 444124 |

# CLASS 387    ELECTROSTAR    BOMBARDIER DERBY

The first 29 110 mph Class 387/1s were delivered in 2014–15 for Thameslink. In 2016–17 these transferred to Great Northern for services from King's Cross to Cambridge/King's Lynn and Peterborough.

A further 27 Class 387/2 units were delivered to Southern for Gatwick Express services in 2016.

Great Western Railway took 45 Class 387/1s for services between London Paddington and Reading, Didcot Parkway and Newbury and these now reach Swindon for stabling. 387 130–141 have been fitted with ETCS and are dedicated to the Heathrow Express service.

Part of a speculative order by Porterbrook Leasing, c2c has six Class 387/3s on lease for five years from late 2016.

**Formation:** DMC–MS–PTS–DMS.
**System:** 25 kV AC overhead and 750 V DC third rail.

**Construction:** Welded aluminium alloy underframe, sides and roof with steel ends. All sections bolted together.
**Traction Motors:** Two Bombardier asynchronous of 250 kW.
**Wheel Arrangement:** 2-Bo + 2-Bo + 2-2 + Bo-2.
**Braking:** Disc & regenerative. **Dimensions:** 20.39/20.00 x 2.80 m.
**Bogies:** Bombardier P3-25/T3-25. **Couplers:** Dellner 12.
**Gangways:** Throughout. **Control System:** IGBT Inverter.
**Doors:** Sliding plug. **Maximum Speed:** 110 mph.
**Heating & ventilation:** Air conditioning.
**Seating Layout:** 2+2 facing/unidirectional.
**Multiple Working:** Within class and with Class 377.

**Class 387/1.** Units built for Thameslink, but now used by Great Northern.

**DMC.** Bombardier Derby 2014–15. 22/34. 46.0 t.
**MS.** Bombardier Derby 2014–15. –/62 1T. 41.3 t.
**PTS.** Bombardier Derby 2014–15. –/45(+2) 1TD 2W. 41.6 t.
**DMS.** Bombardier Derby 2014–15. –/60. 45.9 t.

| | | | | | | | | |
|---|---|---|---|---|---|---|---|---|
| 387 101 | **TG** | P | *GN* | HE | 421101 | 422101 | 423101 | 424101 |
| 387 102 | **TG** | P | *GN* | HE | 421102 | 422102 | 423102 | 424102 |
| 387 103 | **TG** | P | *GN* | HE | 421103 | 422103 | 423103 | 424103 |
| 387 104 | **TG** | P | *GN* | HE | 421104 | 422104 | 423104 | 424104 |
| 387 105 | **TG** | P | *GN* | HE | 421105 | 422105 | 423105 | 424105 |
| 387 106 | **TG** | P | *GN* | HE | 421106 | 422106 | 423106 | 424106 |
| 387 107 | **TG** | P | *GN* | HE | 421107 | 422107 | 423107 | 424107 |
| 387 108 | **TG** | P | *GN* | HE | 421108 | 422108 | 423108 | 424108 |
| 387 109 | **TG** | P | *GN* | HE | 421109 | 422109 | 423109 | 424109 |
| 387 110 | **TG** | P | *GN* | HE | 421110 | 422110 | 423110 | 424110 |
| 387 111 | **TG** | P | *GN* | HE | 421111 | 422111 | 423111 | 424111 |
| 387 112 | **TG** | P | *GN* | HE | 421112 | 422112 | 423112 | 424112 |
| 387 113 | **TG** | P | *GN* | HE | 421113 | 422113 | 423113 | 424113 |
| 387 114 | **TG** | P | *GN* | HE | 421114 | 422114 | 423114 | 424114 |
| 387 115 | **TG** | P | *GN* | HE | 421115 | 422115 | 423115 | 424115 |
| 387 116 | **TG** | P | *GN* | HE | 421116 | 422116 | 423116 | 424116 |
| 387 117 | **TG** | P | *GN* | HE | 421117 | 422117 | 423117 | 424117 |
| 387 118 | **TG** | P | *GN* | HE | 421118 | 422118 | 423118 | 424118 |
| 387 119 | **TG** | P | *GN* | HE | 421119 | 422119 | 423119 | 424119 |
| 387 120 | **TG** | P | *GN* | HE | 421120 | 422120 | 423120 | 424120 |
| 387 121 | **TG** | P | *GN* | HE | 421121 | 422121 | 423121 | 424121 |
| 387 122 | **TG** | P | *GN* | HE | 421122 | 422122 | 423122 | 424122 |
| 387 123 | **TG** | P | *GN* | HE | 421123 | 422123 | 423123 | 424123 |
| 387 124 | **TG** | P | *GN* | HE | 421124 | 422124 | 423124 | 424124 |
| 387 125 | **TG** | P | *GN* | HE | 421125 | 422125 | 423125 | 424125 |
| 387 126 | **TG** | P | *GN* | HE | 421126 | 422126 | 423126 | 424126 |
| 387 127 | **TG** | P | *GN* | HE | 421127 | 422127 | 423127 | 424127 |
| 387 128 | **TG** | P | *GN* | HE | 421128 | 422128 | 423128 | 424128 |
| 387 129 | **TG** | P | *GN* | HE | 421129 | 422129 | 423129 | 424129 |

**Name (carried on DMC):** 387 124   Paul McCann

**Class 387/1.** Heathrow Express and Great Western Railway units.

\* Fitted with First Class and a modified seating layout for use on Heathrow Express services. Full details awaited.

**DMS(A).** Bombardier Derby 2016–17. –/56. 46.0 t.
**MS.** Bombardier Derby 2016–17. –/62 1T. 41.3 t.
**PTS.** Bombardier Derby 2016–17. –/45(+2) 1TD 2W. 41.6 t.
**DMS(B).** Bombardier Derby 2016–17. –/60. 45.9 t.

| | | | | | | | | |
|---|---|---|---|---|---|---|---|---|
| 387 130 | \* | **HX** | P | *HE* | RG | 421130 | 422130 | 423130 | 424130 |
| 387 131 | \* | **HX** | P | *HE* | RG | 421131 | 422131 | 423131 | 424131 |
| 387 132 | \* | **HX** | P | *HE* | RG | 421132 | 422132 | 423132 | 424132 |
| 387 133 | \* | **HX** | P | *HE* | RG | 421133 | 422133 | 423133 | 424133 |
| 387 134 | \* | **HX** | P | *HE* | RG | 421134 | 422134 | 423134 | 424134 |
| 387 135 | \* | **HX** | P | *HE* | RG | 421135 | 422135 | 423135 | 424135 |
| 387 136 | \* | **HX** | P | *HE* | RG | 421136 | 422136 | 423136 | 424136 |
| 387 137 | \* | **HX** | P | *HE* | RG | 421137 | 422137 | 423137 | 424137 |
| 387 138 | \* | **HX** | P | *HE* | RG | 421138 | 422138 | 423138 | 424138 |
| 387 139 | \* | **HX** | P | *HE* | RG | 421139 | 422139 | 423139 | 424139 |
| 387 140 | \* | **HX** | P | *HE* | RG | 421140 | 422140 | 423140 | 424140 |
| 387 141 | \* | **HX** | P | *HE* | RG | 421141 | 422141 | 423141 | 424141 |
| 387 142 | | **GW** | P | *GW* | RG | 421142 | 422142 | 423142 | 424142 |
| 387 143 | | **GW** | P | *GW* | RG | 421143 | 422143 | 423143 | 424143 |
| 387 144 | | **GW** | P | *GW* | RG | 421144 | 422144 | 423144 | 424144 |
| 387 145 | | **GW** | P | *GW* | RG | 421145 | 422145 | 423145 | 424145 |
| 387 146 | | **GW** | P | *GW* | RG | 421146 | 422146 | 423146 | 424146 |
| 387 147 | | **GW** | P | *GW* | RG | 421147 | 422147 | 423147 | 424147 |
| 387 148 | | **GW** | P | *GW* | RG | 421148 | 422148 | 423148 | 424148 |
| 387 149 | | **GW** | P | *GW* | RG | 421149 | 422149 | 423149 | 424149 |
| 387 150 | | **GW** | P | *GW* | RG | 421150 | 422150 | 423150 | 424150 |
| 387 151 | | **GW** | P | *GW* | RG | 421151 | 422151 | 423151 | 424151 |
| 387 152 | | **GW** | P | *GW* | RG | 421152 | 422152 | 423152 | 424152 |
| 387 153 | | **GW** | P | *GW* | RG | 421153 | 422153 | 423153 | 424153 |
| 387 154 | | **GW** | P | *GW* | RG | 421154 | 422154 | 423154 | 424154 |
| 387 155 | | **GW** | P | *GW* | RG | 421155 | 422155 | 423155 | 424155 |
| 387 156 | | **GW** | P | *GW* | RG | 421156 | 422156 | 423156 | 424156 |
| 387 157 | | **GW** | P | *GW* | RG | 421157 | 422157 | 423157 | 424157 |
| 387 158 | | **GW** | P | *GW* | RG | 421158 | 422158 | 423158 | 424158 |
| 387 159 | | **GW** | P | *GW* | RG | 421159 | 422159 | 423159 | 424159 |
| 387 160 | | **GW** | P | *GW* | RG | 421160 | 422160 | 423160 | 424160 |
| 387 161 | | **GW** | P | *GW* | RG | 421161 | 422161 | 423161 | 424161 |
| 387 162 | | **GW** | P | *GW* | RG | 421162 | 422162 | 423162 | 424162 |
| 387 163 | | **GW** | P | *GW* | RG | 421163 | 422163 | 423163 | 424163 |
| 387 164 | | **GW** | P | *GW* | RG | 421164 | 422164 | 423164 | 424164 |
| 387 165 | | **GW** | P | *GW* | RG | 421165 | 422165 | 423165 | 424165 |
| 387 166 | | **GW** | P | *GW* | RG | 421166 | 422166 | 423166 | 424166 |
| 387 167 | | **GW** | P | *GW* | RG | 421167 | 422167 | 423167 | 424167 |
| 387 168 | | **GW** | P | *GW* | RG | 421168 | 422168 | 423168 | 424168 |
| 387 169 | | **GW** | P | *GW* | RG | 421169 | 422169 | 423169 | 424169 |
| 387 170 | | **GW** | P | *GW* | RG | 421170 | 422170 | 423170 | 424170 |
| 387 171 | | **GW** | P | *GW* | RG | 421171 | 422171 | 423171 | 424171 |

| 387 172 | **GW** | P | *GW* | RG | 421172 | 422172 | 423172 | 424172 |
| 387 173 | **GW** | P | *GW* | RG | 421173 | 422173 | 423173 | 424173 |
| 387 174 | **GW** | P | *GW* | RG | 421174 | 422174 | 423174 | 424174 |

**Class 387/2.** Southern units built for use Gatwick Express-branded services on the London Victoria–Gatwick Airport–Brighton route, but also used on other Southern routes.

**DMC.** Bombardier Derby 2015–16. 22/34. 46.0 t.
**MS.** Bombardier Derby 2015–16. –/60 1T. 41.3 t.
**PTS.** Bombardier Derby 2015–16. –/45(+2) 1TD 2W. 41.6 t.
**DMS.** Bombardier Derby 2015–16. –/60. 45.9 t.

| 387 201 | **GX** | P | *SN* | SL | 421201 | 422201 | 423201 | 424201 |
| 387 202 | **GX** | P | *SN* | SL | 421202 | 422202 | 423202 | 424202 |
| 387 203 | **GX** | P | *SN* | SL | 421203 | 422203 | 423203 | 424203 |
| 387 204 | **GX** | P | *SN* | SL | 421204 | 422204 | 423204 | 424204 |
| 387 205 | **GX** | P | *SN* | SL | 421205 | 422205 | 423205 | 424205 |
| 387 206 | **GX** | P | *SN* | SL | 421206 | 422206 | 423206 | 424206 |
| 387 207 | **GX** | P | *SN* | SL | 421207 | 422207 | 423207 | 424207 |
| 387 208 | **GX** | P | *SN* | SL | 421208 | 422208 | 423208 | 424208 |
| 387 209 | **GX** | P | *SN* | SL | 421209 | 422209 | 423209 | 424209 |
| 387 210 | **GX** | P | *SN* | SL | 421210 | 422210 | 423210 | 424210 |
| 387 211 | **GX** | P | *SN* | SL | 421211 | 422211 | 423211 | 424211 |
| 387 212 | **GX** | P | *SN* | SL | 421212 | 422212 | 423212 | 424212 |
| 387 213 | **GX** | P | *SN* | SL | 421213 | 422213 | 423213 | 424213 |
| 387 214 | **GX** | P | *SN* | SL | 421214 | 422214 | 423214 | 424214 |
| 387 215 | **GX** | P | *SN* | SL | 421215 | 422215 | 423215 | 424215 |
| 387 216 | **GX** | P | *SN* | SL | 421216 | 422216 | 423216 | 424216 |
| 387 217 | **GX** | P | *SN* | SL | 421217 | 422217 | 423217 | 424217 |
| 387 218 | **GX** | P | *SN* | SL | 421218 | 422218 | 423218 | 424218 |
| 387 219 | **GX** | P | *SN* | SL | 421219 | 422219 | 423219 | 424219 |
| 387 220 | **GX** | P | *SN* | SL | 421220 | 422220 | 423220 | 424220 |
| 387 221 | **GX** | P | *SN* | SL | 421221 | 422221 | 423221 | 424221 |
| 387 222 | **GX** | P | *SN* | SL | 421222 | 422222 | 423222 | 424222 |
| 387 223 | **GX** | P | *SN* | SL | 421223 | 422223 | 423223 | 424223 |
| 387 224 | **GX** | P | *SN* | SL | 421224 | 422224 | 423224 | 424224 |
| 387 225 | **GX** | P | *SN* | SL | 421225 | 422225 | 423225 | 424225 |
| 387 226 | **GX** | P | *SN* | SL | 421226 | 422226 | 423226 | 424226 |
| 387 227 | **GX** | P | *SN* | SL | 421227 | 422227 | 423227 | 424227 |

**Class 387/3.** c2c units. Originally ordered speculatively by Porterbrook Leasing.

**DMS(A).** Bombardier Derby 2016. –/56. 46.0 t.
**MS.** Bombardier Derby 2016. –/62 1T. 41.3 t.
**PTS.** Bombardier Derby 2016. –/45(+2) 1TD 2W. 41.6 t.
**DMS(B).** Bombardier Derby 2016. –/60. 45.9 t.

| 387 301 | **C2** | P | *C2* | EM | 421301 | 422301 | 423301 | 424301 |
| 387 302 | **C2** | P | *C2* | EM | 421302 | 422302 | 423302 | 424302 |
| 387 303 | **C2** | P | *C2* | EM | 421303 | 422303 | 423303 | 424303 |
| 387 304 | **C2** | P | *C2* | EM | 421304 | 422304 | 423304 | 424304 |
| 387 305 | **C2** | P | *C2* | EM | 421305 | 422305 | 423305 | 424305 |
| 387 306 | **C2** | P | *C2* | EM | 421306 | 422306 | 423306 | 424306 |

# CLASS 390          PENDOLINO          ALSTOM

Tilting units used on the West Coast Main Line.

**Formation:** As listed below.                    **Construction:** Welded aluminium alloy.
**Traction Motors:** Two Alstom ONIX 800 of 425 kW.
**Wheel Arrangement:** 1A-A1 + 1A-A1 + 2-2 + 1A-A1 (+ 2-2 + 1A-A1) + 2-2 +
1A-A1 + 2-2 + 1A-A1 + 1A-A1.                    **Braking:** Disc, rheostatic & regenerative.
**Dimensions:** 24.80/23.90 x 2.73 m.          **Couplers:** Dellner 12.
**Bogies:** Fiat-SIG.                           **Control System:** IGBT Inverter.
**Gangways:** Within unit.                      **Maximum Speed:** 125 mph.
**Doors:** Sliding plug.                        **Heating & ventilation:** Air conditioning.
**Seating Layout:** 1: 2+1 facing/unidirectional, 2: 2+2 facing/unidirectional.
**Multiple Working:** Within class. Can also be controlled from Class 57/3 locos.

Units up to 390034 were delivered as 8-car sets, without the TS (688xx).
During 2004–05 these units were increased to 9-cars.

62 extra vehicles were built 2010–12 to lengthen 31 sets to 11-cars. On
renumbering units were renumbered by adding 100 to the set number. Four new
complete 11-car units were also delivered. All these extra vehicles were built
at Savigliano, Italy (all original Pendolino vehicles were built at Birmingham).

The 9-car units had their MF(B) converted to an MS in 2015 to give them a
better balance of Standard to First Class seating.

390033 was written off in the Lambrigg accident of February 2007.
**Advertising livery:** 390 119 PRIDE (various colours).

Apart from 390 155/156, units in **AT** livery only carry this on their end cars.

**DMRBF:** Alstom Birmingham/Savigliano 2001–05/2010–12. 18/–. 56.3 t.
**MF(A):** Alstom Birmingham/Savigliano 2001–05/2010–12. 37/–(+2) 1TD 1W. 52.3 t.
**PTF:** Alstom Birmingham/Savigliano 2001–05/2010–12. 44/– 1T. 51.2 t.
**MF(B: 11-car):** Alstom Birmingham/Savigliano 2001–05/2010–12. 46/– 1T. 52.3 t.
**MS(C: 9-car):** Alstom Birmingham/Savigliano 2001–05/2010–12. –/76 1T. 52.3 t.
**(TS:** Alstom Savigliano 2010–12. –/74 1T. 49.2 t.)
**(MS:** Alstom Savigliano 2010–12. –/76 1T. 52.2 t.)
**TS:** Alstom Birmingham/Savigliano 2001–05/2010–12. –/76 1T. 45.5 t.
**MS(A):** Alstom Birmingham/Savigliano 2001–05/2010–12. –/62(+4) 1TD 1W. 52.0 t.
**PTSRMB:** Alstom Birmingham/Savigliano 2001–05/2010–12. –/48. 53.2 t.
**MS(B):** Alstom Birmingham/Savigliano 2001–05/2010–12. –/62(+2) 1TD 1W. 52.5 t.
**DMS:** Alstom Birmingham/Savigliano 2001–05/2010–12. –/46 1T. 54.5 t.

**Class 390/0.** Original build 9-car units.

**Formation:** DMRF–MF–PTF–MS–TS–MS–PTSRMB–MS–DMS.

| 390 001 | **AT** | A | *AW* MA | 69101 | 69401 | 69501 | 69601 | 68801 |
|---------|--------|---|---------|-------|-------|-------|-------|-------|
|         |        |   |         | 69701 | 69801 | 69901 | 69201 |       |
| 390 002 | **AT** | A | *AW* MA | 69102 | 69402 | 69502 | 69602 | 68802 |
|         |        |   |         | 69702 | 69802 | 69902 | 69202 |       |
| 390 005 | **VW** | A | *AW* MA | 69105 | 69405 | 69505 | 69605 | 68805 |
|         |        |   |         | 69705 | 69805 | 69905 | 69205 |       |
| 390 006 | **AT** | A | *AW* MA | 69106 | 69406 | 69506 | 69606 | 68806 |
|         |        |   |         | 69706 | 69806 | 69906 | 69206 |       |

| 390 008 | **AT** | A | *AW* MA | 69108 69408 69508 69608 68808 |
| | | | | 69708 69808 69908 69208 |
| 390 009 | **AT** | A | *AW* MA | 69109 69409 69509 69609 68809 |
| | | | | 69709 69809 69909 69209 |
| 390 010 | **VW** | A | *AW* MA | 69110 69410 69510 69610 68810 |
| | | | | 69710 69810 69910 69210 |
| 390 011 | **AT** | A | *AW* MA | 69111 69411 69511 69611 68811 |
| | | | | 69711 69811 69911 69211 |
| 390 013 | **AT** | A | *AW* MA | 69113 69413 69513 69613 68813 |
| | | | | 69713 69813 69913 69213 |
| 390 016 | **AT** | A | *AW* MA | 69116 69416 69516 69616 68816 |
| | | | | 69716 69816 69916 69216 |
| 390 020 | **VW** | A | *AW* MA | 69120 69420 69520 69620 68820 |
| | | | | 69720 69820 69920 69220 |
| 390 039 | **AT** | A | *AW* MA | 69139 69439 69539 69639 68839 |
| | | | | 69739 69839 69939 69239 |
| 390 040 | **AT** | A | *AW* MA | 69140 69440 69540 69640 68840 |
| | | | | 69740 69840 69940 69240 |
| 390 042 | **AT** | A | *AW* MA | 69142 69442 69542 69642 68842 |
| | | | | 69742 69842 69942 69242 |
| 390 043 | **AT** | A | *AW* MA | 69143 69443 69543 69643 68843 |
| | | | | 69743 69843 69943 69243 |
| 390 044 | **AT** | A | *AW* MA | 69144 69444 69544 69644 68844 |
| | | | | 69744 69844 69944 69244 |
| 390 045 | **AT** | A | *AW* MA | 69145 69445 69545 69645 68845 |
| | | | | 69745 69845 69945 69245 |
| 390 046 | **AT** | A | *AW* MA | 69146 69446 69546 69646 68846 |
| | | | | 69746 69846 69946 69246 |
| 390 047 | **AT** | A | *AW* MA | 69147 69447 69547 69647 68847 |
| | | | | 69747 69847 69947 69247 |
| 390 049 | **AT** | A | *AW* MA | 69149 69449 69549 69649 68849 |
| | | | | 69749 69849 69949 69249 |
| 390 050 | **AT** | A | *AW* MA | 69150 69450 69550 69650 68850 |
| | | | | 69750 69850 69950 69250 |

**Class 390/1.** Original build 9-car units later extended to 11-cars, except 390 154–157 which were built new (in Italy) as 11-cars.
**Formation:** DMRF–MF–PTF–MF–TS–MS–TS–MS–PTSRMB–MS–DMS.

| 390 103 | **AT** | A | *AW* MA | 69103 69403 69503 69603 65303 68903 |
| | | | | 68803 69703 69803 69903 69203 |
| 390 104 | **AT** | A | *AW* MA | 69104 69404 69504 69604 65304 68904 |
| | | | | 68804 69704 69804 69904 69204 |
| 390 107 | **AT** | A | *AW* MA | 69107 69407 69507 69607 65307 68907 |
| | | | | 68807 69707 69807 69907 69207 |
| 390 112 | **AT** | A | *AW* MA | 69112 69412 69512 69612 65312 68912 |
| | | | | 68812 69712 69812 69912 69212 |
| 390 114 | **AT** | A | *AW* MA | 69114 69414 69514 69614 65314 68914 |
| | | | | 68814 69714 69814 69914 69214 |
| 390 115 | **AT** | A | *AW* MA | 69115 69415 69515 69615 65315 68915 |
| | | | | 68815 69715 69815 69915 69215 |

| 390 117 | **AT** | A | *AW* MA | 69117 69417 69517 69617 65317 68917 |
| | | | | 68817 69717 69817 69917 69217 |
| 390 118 | **AT** | A | *AW* MA | 69118 69418 69518 69618 65318 68918 |
| | | | | 68818 69718 69818 69918 69218 |
| 390 119 | **AT** | A | *AW* MA | 69119 69419 69519 69619 65319 68919 |
| | | | | 68819 69719 69819 69919 69219 |
| 390 121 | **AT** | A | *AW* MA | 69121 69421 69521 69621 65321 68921 |
| | | | | 68821 69721 69821 69921 69221 |
| 390 122 | **AT** | A | *VW* MA | 69122 69422 69522 69622 65322 68922 |
| | | | | 68822 69722 69822 69922 69222 |
| 390 123 | **AT** | A | *AW* MA | 69123 69423 69523 69623 65323 68923 |
| | | | | 68823 69723 69823 69923 69223 |
| 390 124 | **AT** | A | *AW* MA | 69124 69424 69524 69624 65324 68924 |
| | | | | 68824 69724 69824 69924 69224 |
| 390 125 | **AT** | A | *AW* MA | 69125 69425 69525 69625 65325 68925 |
| | | | | 68825 69725 69825 69925 69225 |
| 390 126 | **AT** | A | *AW* MA | 69126 69426 69526 69626 65326 68926 |
| | | | | 68826 69726 69826 69926 69226 |
| 390 127 | **AT** | A | *AW* MA | 69127 69427 69527 69627 65327 68927 |
| | | | | 68827 69727 69827 69927 69227 |
| 390 128 | **AT** | A | *AW* MA | 69128 69428 69528 69628 65328 68928 |
| | | | | 68828 69728 69828 69928 69228 |
| 390 129 | **AT** | A | *AW* MA | 69129 69429 69529 69629 65329 68929 |
| | | | | 68829 69729 69829 69929 69229 |
| 390 130 | **AT** | A | *AW* MA | 69130 69430 69530 69630 65330 68930 |
| | | | | 68830 69730 69830 69930 69230 |
| 390 131 | **VW** | A | *AW* MA | 69131 69431 69531 69631 65331 68931 |
| | | | | 68831 69731 69831 69931 69231 |
| 390 132 | **AT** | A | *AW* MA | 69132 69432 69532 69632 65332 68932 |
| | | | | 68832 69732 69832 69932 69232 |
| 390 134 | **AT** | A | *AW* MA | 69134 69434 69534 69634 65334 68934 |
| | | | | 68834 69734 69834 69934 69234 |
| 390 135 | **AT** | A | *AW* MA | 69135 69435 69535 69635 65335 68935 |
| | | | | 68835 69735 69835 69935 69235 |
| 390 136 | **AT** | A | *AW* MA | 69136 69436 69536 69636 65336 68936 |
| | | | | 68836 69736 69836 69936 69236 |
| 390 137 | **AT** | A | *VW* MA | 69137 69437 69537 69637 65337 68937 |
| | | | | 68837 69737 69837 69937 69237 |
| 390 138 | **AT** | A | *AW* MA | 69138 69438 69538 69638 65338 68938 |
| | | | | 68838 69738 69838 69938 69238 |
| 390 141 | **AT** | A | *AW* MA | 69141 69441 69541 69641 65341 68941 |
| | | | | 68841 69741 69841 69941 69241 |
| 390 148 | **AT** | A | *AW* MA | 69148 69448 69548 69648 65348 68948 |
| | | | | 68848 69748 69848 69948 69248 |
| 390 151 | **AT** | A | *VW* MA | 69151 69451 69551 69651 65351 68951 |
| | | | | 68851 69751 69851 69951 69251 |
| 390 152 | **AT** | A | *VW* MA | 69152 69452 69552 69652 65352 68952 |
| | | | | 68852 69752 69852 69952 69252 |
| 390 153 | **AT** | A | *AW* MA | 69153 69453 69553 69653 65353 68953 |
| | | | | 68853 69753 69853 69953 69253 |

| | | | | | | | | | | |
|---|---|---|---|---|---|---|---|---|---|---|
| 390154 | **AT** | A | *AW* MA | 69154 | 69454 | 69554 | 69654 | 65354 | 68954 | |
| | | | | 68854 | 69754 | 69854 | 69954 | 69254 | | |
| 390155 | **AT** | A | *AW* MA | 69155 | 69455 | 69555 | 69655 | 65355 | 68955 | |
| | | | | 68855 | 69755 | 69855 | 69955 | 69255 | | |
| 390156 | **AT** | A | *AW* MA | 69156 | 69456 | 69556 | 69656 | 65356 | 68956 | |
| | | | | 68856 | 69756 | 69856 | 69956 | 69256 | | |
| 390157 | **AT** | A | *AW* MA | 69157 | 69457 | 69557 | 69657 | 65357 | 68957 | |
| | | | | 68857 | 69757 | 69857 | 69957 | 69257 | | |

**Names (carried on MF No. 696xx):**

| | | | |
|---|---|---|---|
| 390001 | Bee Together | 390122 | Penny the Pendolino |
| 390002 | Stephen Sutton | 390125 | Virgin Stagecoach |
| 390005 | City of Wolverhampton | 390128 | City of Preston |
| 390006 | Rethink Mental Illness | 390129 | City of Stoke-on-Trent |
| 390008 | CHARLES RENNIE MACKINTOSH | 390130 | City of Edinburgh |
| 390009 | Treaty of Union | 390131 | City of Liverpool |
| 390010 | Cumbrian Spirit | 390132 | City of Birmingham |
| 390011 | City of Lichfield | 390134 | City of Carlisle |
| 390013 | Blackpool Belle | 390135 | City of Lancaster |
| 390039 | Lady Godiva | 390136 | City of Coventry |
| 390047 | CLIC Sargent | 390138 | City of London |
| 390104 | Alstom Pendolino | 390148 | Flying Scouseman |
| 390114 | City of Manchester | 390151 | Unknown Soldier |
| 390115 | Crewe – All Change | 390154 | Matthew Flinders |
| 390117 | Blue Peter | 390156 | Pride and Prosperity |
| 390119 | PROGRESS | 390157 | Chad Varah |

# CLASS 395          JAVELIN          HITACHI JAPAN

6-car dual-voltage units used on Southeastern High Speed trains from London St Pancras.

**Formation:** PDTS–MS–MS–MS–MS–PDTS.
**Systems:** 25 kV AC overhead/750 V DC third rail.
**Construction:** Aluminium.
**Traction Motors:** Four Hitachi asynchronous of 210 kW.
**Wheel Arrangement:** 2-2 + Bo-Bo + Bo-Bo + Bo-Bo + Bo-Bo + 2-2.
**Braking:** Disc, rheostatic & regenerative.

| | |
|---|---|
| **Dimensions:** 20.88/20.0 x 2.81 m. | **Couplers:** Scharfenberg. |
| **Bogies:** Hitachi. | **Control System:** IGBT Inverter. |
| **Gangways:** Within unit. | **Maximum Speed:** 140 mph. |
| **Doors:** Single-leaf sliding. | **Multiple Working:** Within class only. |

**Heating & ventilation:** Air conditioning.
**Seating Layout:** 2+2 facing/unidirectional (mainly unidirectional).

**PDTS(A):** Hitachi Kasado, Japan 2006–09. –/28(+12) 1TD 2W. 46.7 t.
**MS:** Hitachi Kasado, Japan 2006–09. –/66. 45.0t–45.7 t.
**PDTS(B):** Hitachi Kasado, Japan 2006–09. –/48 1T. 46.7 t.

| | | | | | | | | | | |
|---|---|---|---|---|---|---|---|---|---|---|
| 395001 | **SB** | E | *SE* AD | 39011 | 39012 | 39013 | 39014 | 39015 | 39016 | |
| 395002 | **SB** | E | *SE* AD | 39021 | 39022 | 39023 | 39024 | 39025 | 39026 | |
| 395003 | **SB** | E | *SE* AD | 39031 | 39032 | 39033 | 39034 | 39035 | 39036 | |

| 395 004 | **SB** | E | *SE* | AD | 39041 | 39042 | 39043 | 39044 | 39045 | 39046 |
| 395 005 | **SB** | E | *SE* | AD | 39051 | 39052 | 39053 | 39054 | 39055 | 39056 |
| 395 006 | **SB** | E | *SE* | AD | 39061 | 39062 | 39063 | 39064 | 39065 | 39066 |
| 395 007 | **SB** | E | *SE* | AD | 39071 | 39072 | 39073 | 39074 | 39075 | 39076 |
| 395 008 | **SB** | E | *SE* | AD | 39081 | 39082 | 39083 | 39084 | 39085 | 39086 |
| 395 009 | **SB** | E | *SE* | AD | 39091 | 39092 | 39093 | 39094 | 39095 | 39096 |
| 395 010 | **SB** | E | *SE* | AD | 39101 | 39102 | 39103 | 39104 | 39105 | 39106 |
| 395 011 | **SB** | E | *SE* | AD | 39111 | 39112 | 39113 | 39114 | 39115 | 39116 |
| 395 012 | **SB** | E | *SE* | AD | 39121 | 39122 | 39123 | 39124 | 39125 | 39126 |
| 395 013 | **SB** | E | *SE* | AD | 39131 | 39132 | 39133 | 39134 | 39135 | 39136 |
| 395 014 | **SB** | E | *SE* | AD | 39141 | 39142 | 39143 | 39144 | 39145 | 39146 |
| 395 015 | **SB** | E | *SE* | AD | 39151 | 39152 | 39153 | 39154 | 39155 | 39156 |
| 395 016 | **SB** | E | *SE* | AD | 39161 | 39162 | 39163 | 39164 | 39165 | 39166 |
| 395 017 | **SB** | E | *SE* | AD | 39171 | 39172 | 39173 | 39174 | 39175 | 39176 |
| 395 018 | **SB** | E | *SE* | AD | 39181 | 39182 | 39183 | 39184 | 39185 | 39186 |
| 395 019 | **SB** | E | *SE* | AD | 39191 | 39192 | 39193 | 39194 | 39195 | 39196 |
| 395 020 | **SB** | E | *SE* | AD | 39201 | 39202 | 39203 | 39204 | 39205 | 39206 |
| 395 021 | **SB** | E | *SE* | AD | 39211 | 39212 | 39213 | 39214 | 39215 | 39216 |
| 395 022 | **SB** | E | *SE* | AD | 39221 | 39222 | 39223 | 39224 | 39225 | 39226 |
| 395 023 | **SB** | E | *SE* | AD | 39231 | 39232 | 39233 | 39234 | 39235 | 39236 |
| 395 024 | **SB** | E | *SE* | AD | 39241 | 39242 | 39243 | 39244 | 39245 | 39246 |
| 395 025 | **SB** | E | *SE* | AD | 39251 | 39252 | 39253 | 39254 | 39255 | 39256 |
| 395 026 | **SB** | E | *SE* | AD | 39261 | 39262 | 39263 | 39264 | 39265 | 39266 |
| 395 027 | **SB** | E | *SE* | AD | 39271 | 39272 | 39273 | 39274 | 39275 | 39276 |
| 395 028 | **SB** | E | *SE* | AD | 39281 | 39282 | 39283 | 39284 | 39285 | 39286 |
| 395 029 | **SB** | E | *SE* | AD | 39291 | 39292 | 39293 | 39294 | 39295 | 39296 |

**Names (carried on end cars):**

| | |
|---|---|
| 395 001 Dame Kelly Holmes | 395 018 THE VICTORY Javelin |
| 395 002 Sebastian Coe | 395 019 Jessica Ennis |
| 395 003 Sir Steve Redgrave | 395 020 Jason Kenny |
| 395 004 Sir Chris Hoy | 395 021 Ed Clancy MBE |
| 395 005 Dame Tanni Grey-Thompson | 395 022 Alistair Brownlee |
| 395 006 Daley Thompson | 395 023 Ellie Simmonds |
| 395 007 Steve Backley | 395 024 Jonnie Peacock |
| 395 008 Ben Ainslie | 395 025 Victoria Pendleton |
| 395 009 Rebecca Adlington | 395 026 Marc Woods |
| 395 010 Duncan Goodhew | 395 027 Hannah Cockcroft |
| 395 011 Katherine Grainger | 395 028 Laura Trott |
| 395 013 HORNBY Visitor Centre Margate, Kent | 395 029 David Weir |
| 395 014 Dina Asher-Smith | |

# CLASS 397              CIVITY              CAF

New TransPennine Express units mainly used on the West Coast Main Line
Manchester Airport–Edinburgh/Glasgow services.

**Formation:** DMF–PTS–MS–PTS–DMS.
**Construction:** Aluminium.
**Traction Motors:** Four TSA of 220 kW.
**Wheel Arrangement:**

**Braking:** Disc and regenerative.
**Bogies:** CAF.
**Gangways:** Within unit.
**Doors:** Sliding plug.
**Heating & ventilation:** Air conditioning.
**Seating:** 1: 2+1 facing/unidirectional; 2: 2+2 facing/unidirectional.
**Multiple Working:** Within class.

**Dimensions:** 24.03/23.35 x 2.71 m.
**Couplers:** Dellner.
**Control System:** IGBT Inverter.
**Maximum Speed:** 125 mph.

**DMF.** CAF Beasain 2017–19. 24/– 1TD 2W. 41.4 t.
**PTS(A).** CAF Beasain 2017–19. –/76. 34.5 t.
**MS.** CAF Beasain 2017–19. –/68 2T. 36.6 t.
**PTS(B).** CAF Beasain 2017–19. –/76. 34.9 t.
**DMS.** CAF Beasain 2017–19. –/44(+8) 1T. 39.2 t.

| | | | | | | | | | |
|---|---|---|---|---|---|---|---|---|---|
| 397 001 | **TP** | E | *TP* | MA | 471001 | 472001 | 473001 | 474001 | 475001 |
| 397 002 | **TP** | E | *TP* | MA | 471002 | 472002 | 473002 | 474002 | 475002 |
| 397 003 | **TP** | E | *TP* | MA | 471003 | 472003 | 473003 | 474003 | 475003 |
| 397 004 | **TP** | E | *TP* | MA | 471004 | 472004 | 473004 | 474004 | 475004 |
| 397 005 | **TP** | E | *TP* | MA | 471005 | 472005 | 473005 | 474005 | 475005 |
| 397 006 | **TP** | E | *TP* | MA | 471006 | 472006 | 473006 | 474006 | 475006 |
| 397 007 | **TP** | E | *TP* | MA | 471007 | 472007 | 473007 | 474007 | 475007 |
| 397 008 | **TP** | E | *TP* | MA | 471008 | 472008 | 473008 | 474008 | 475008 |
| 397 009 | **TP** | E | *TP* | MA | 471009 | 472009 | 473009 | 474009 | 475009 |
| 397 010 | **TP** | E | *TP* | MA | 471010 | 472010 | 473010 | 474010 | 475010 |
| 397 011 | **TP** | E | *TP* | MA | 471011 | 472011 | 473011 | 474011 | 475011 |
| 397 012 | **TP** | E | *TP* | MA | 471012 | 472012 | 473012 | 474012 | 475012 |

# CLASS 398      CITYLINK      STADLER

New 3-car Citylink bi-mode electric/battery metro tram-train units under construction for Transport for Wales for use on the Cardiff Valley Lines (Aberdare, Merthyr Tydfil, Treherbert and Cardiff City Line). They will also be capable as operating on-street as tramway vehicles on a new line from Cardiff Bay to a new station at Flourish.

Full details awaited and numbering of individual vehicle numbers is to be confirmed.

**Formation:** DMS–TS–DMS.
**Systems:** 25 kV AC overhead/battery.
**Construction:** Steel.
**Traction Motors:** 4 x 140 kW (per unit).
**Wheel Arrangement:** Bo-2-2-Bo.
**Braking:** Disc, regenerative & emergency track.
**Dimensions:** 40.00 x 2.65 m (full set).
**Bogies:**
**Gangways:** Within unit.
**Doors:** Sliding plug.
**Seating Layout:** 2+2 unidirectional/facing.
**Couplers:**
**Control System:** IGBT Inverter.
**Maximum Speed:** 62 mph.
**Multiple Working:** Within class only.

**DMS(A):** Stadler, Valencia 2020–22.
**TS:** Stadler, Valencia 2020–22.
**DMS(B):** Stadler, Valencia 2020–22.

398 001
398 002
398 003
398 004
398 005
398 006
398 007
398 008
398 009
398 010
398 011
398 012
398 013
398 014
398 015
398 016
398 017
398 018
398 019
398 020
398 021
398 022
398 023
398 024
398 025
398 026
398 027
398 028
398 029
398 030
398 031
398 032
398 033
398 034
398 035
398 036

# CLASS 399    CITYLINK    VOSSLOH/STADLER

The Class 399s are tram-trains used on the pilot Sheffield–Rotherham Parkgate tram-train service, operated by Stagecoach Supertram. Dual-voltage 750 V DC/25 kV AC (although currently only operating on 750 V DC). For operation on Network Rail lines EMU running numbers 399 201–207 are carried (as well as vehicle numbers in the 999xxx series), in addition to the Stagecoach Supertram fleet numbers 201–207.

The 399s entered service on the Supertram network in autumn 2017 and on the national railway network as tram-trains from October 2018.

Following two accidents in autumn 2018 units 399 202 and 399 204 are operating in mixed formations, as shown.

At the time of writing units 399 201–204 have tram-train wheel profiles for operating on the National Rail network to Rotherham Parkgate. 399 205–207 can only operate on the tramway network, but could be modified to operate to Rotherham if required, 399 206 having been modified to operate to Rotherham in 2018–20 to cover for the accident damaged 399 204.

**Formation:** DMS–MS–DMS.
**Systems:** 750 V DC/25 kV AC overhead.
**Construction:** Steel.
**Traction Motors:** Six VEM of 145 kW (per unit).
**Wheel Arrangement:** Bo-2-Bo-Bo.
**Braking:** Disc, regenerative & emergency track.
**Dimensions:** 37.20 x 2.65 m (full set). **Couplers:** Albert (emergency use).
**Bogies:** Vossloh.                              **Control System:** IGBT Inverter.
**Gangways:** Within unit.                      **Maximum Speed:** 60 mph.
**Doors:** Sliding plug.                          **Multiple Working:** Within class only.
**Seating Layout:** 2+2 facing/unidirectional.
**Weight:** 64 t.

**DMS(A):** Vossloh, Valencia 2014–15. –/22(+4) 1W.
**MS:** Vossloh, Valencia 2014–15. –/44.
**DMS(B):** Vossloh, Valencia 2014–15. –/22(+4) 1W.

| 399 201 | **SD** | SY | *SY* | NU | 999001 | 999101 | 999201 |
|---------|--------|----|------|----|--------|--------|--------|
| 399 202 | **SD** | SY | *SY* | NU | 999002 | 999102 | 999204 |
| 399 203 | **SD** | SY | *SY* | NU | 999003 | 999103 | 999203 |
| 399 204 | **SD** | SY | *SY* | NU | 999004 | 999104 | 999202 |
| 399 205 | **SD** | SY | *SY* | NU | 999005 | 999105 | 999205 |
| 399 206 | **SD** | SY | *SY* | NU | 999006 | 999106 | 999206 |
| 399 207 | **SD** | SY | *SY* | NU | 999007 | 999107 | 999207 |

**Name (carried on cars 999002 and 999204):**

399 202   Theo – The Children's Hospital Charity

# 4.2. 750 V DC THIRD RAIL EMUs

These classes use the third rail system at 750 V DC (unless stated). Outer couplers are buckeyes on units built before 1982 with bar couplers within the units. Newer units generally have Dellner outer couplers.

## CLASS 442          WESSEX EXPRESS          BREL DERBY

Units built for Waterloo–Bournemouth–Weymouth services. Previously operated by South West Trains and latterly by Southern until 2017. The 18 remaining fully intact units have received an interior refurbishment and are being returned to service with South Western Railway, mainly for use on the Portsmouth route. These are also being retractioned with AC motors.

**Formation:** DTC–TS–MBS–TS–DTS.
**Construction:** Steel.
**Traction Motors:** Four EE546 of 300 kW recovered from Class 432s († Four TSA AC motors).
**Wheel Arrangement:** 2-2 + 2-2 + Bo-Bo + 2-2 + 2-2.
**Braking:** Disc.                           **Dimensions:** 23.15/23.00 x 2.74 m.
**Bogies:** Two BREL P7 motor bogies (MBS). T3 bogies (trailer cars).
**Couplers:** Buckeye.
**Control System:** 1986-type. († IGBT Inverter).
**Gangways:** Throughout.               **Maximum Speed:** 100 mph.
**Doors:** Sliding plug.                **Heating & Ventilation:** Air conditioning.
**Seating Layout (rebuilt):** 1: 2+2 unidirectional/facing; 2: 2+2 unidirectional/facing.
**Multiple Working:** Within class and Class 33/1 & 73 locos in an emergency.

**DTC.** Lot No. 31030 Derby 1988–89. 32/44. 38.5 t.
**TS.** Lot No. 31032 Derby 1988–89. –/76 2T. 37.5 t.
**MBS.** Lot No. 31034 Derby 1988–89. –/66. 55.0 t.
**TS(W).** Lot No. 31033 Derby 1988–89. –/64(+3) 1TD 1T 2W. 37.8 t.
**DTS.** Lot No. 31031 Derby 1988–89. –/80. 37.3 t.

| | | | | | | | | | |
|---|---|---|---|---|---|---|---|---|---|
| 442 402 | | **SW** | A | | BM | 77383 | 71819 | 62938 | 71843 | 77407 |
| 442 403 | † | **SW** | A | *SW* | BM | 77384 | 71820 | 62941 | 71844 | 77408 |
| 442 404 | † | **SW** | A | | BM | 77385 | 71821 | 62939 | 71845 | 77409 |
| 442 406 | | **SW** | A | *SW* | BM | 77389 | 71823 | 62942 | 71847 | 77411 |
| 442 408 | † | **SW** | A | *SW* | BM | 77387 | 71825 | 62945 | 71849 | 77413 |
| 442 409 | | **SW** | A | | BM | 77390 | 71826 | 62946 | 71850 | 77414 |
| 442 410 | | **SW** | A | *SW* | BM | 77391 | 71827 | 62948 | 71851 | 77415 |
| 442 411 | † | **SW** | A | | BM | 77392 | 71828 | 62940 | 71858 | 77422 |
| 442 413 | † | **SW** | A | *SW* | BM | 77394 | 71830 | 62949 | 71854 | 77418 |
| 442 414 | † | **SW** | A | *SW* | BM | 77395 | 71831 | 62950 | 71855 | 77419 |
| 442 415 | † | **SW** | A | | BM | 77396 | 71832 | 62951 | 71856 | 77420 |
| 442 416 | † | **SW** | A | | BM | 77397 | 71833 | 62952 | 71857 | 77421 |
| 442 417 | | **SW** | A | *SW* | BM | 77398 | 71834 | 62953 | 71852 | 77416 |
| 442 418 | † | **SW** | A | | BM | 77399 | 71835 | 62954 | 71859 | 77423 |
| 442 419 | † | **SW** | A | | BM | 77400 | 71836 | 62955 | 71860 | 77424 |
| 442 420 | | **SW** | A | *SW* | BM | 77401 | 71837 | 62956 | 71861 | 77425 |
| 442 422 | † | **SW** | A | | BM | 77403 | 71839 | 62958 | 71863 | 77427 |

| 442 423 | **SW** | A | *SW* | BM | 77404 71840 62959 71864 77428 |
|---------|--------|---|------|----|-------------------------------|
| Spare | **GV** | A | | ZG | 77382 (ex-442 401) |
| Spare | **GV** | A | | ZG | 77386 71822 71846 77410 (ex-442 405) |
| Spare | **GV** | A | | ZG | 77388 71824 71848 77412 (ex-442 407) |
| Spare | **GV** | A | | ZG | 77393 71829 71853 77417 (ex-442 412) |
| Spare | **GV** | A | | ZG | 77405 71841 71865 77429 (ex-442 424) |

# CLASS 444    DESIRO UK    SIEMENS

Express units.

**Formation:** DMS–TS–TS–TS–DMC.
**Construction:** Aluminium.
**Traction Motors:** Four Siemens 1TB2016-0GB02 asynchronous of 250 kW.
**Wheel Arrangement:** Bo-Bo + 2-2 + 2-2 + 2-2 + Bo-Bo.
**Braking:** Disc, rheostatic & regenerative. **Dimensions:** 23.57 x 2.69 m.
**Bogies:** SGP SF5000. **Couplers:** Dellner 12.
**Gangways:** Throughout. **Control System:** IGBT Inverter.
**Doors:** Single-leaf sliding plug. **Maximum Speed:** 100 mph.
**Heating & Ventilation:** Air conditioning.
**Seating Layout:** 1: 2+2 facing/unidirectional, 2: 2+2 facing/unidirectional.
**Multiple Working:** Within class and with Class 450.

**DMS.** Siemens Vienna/Krefeld 2003–04. –/76. 51.0 t.
**TS 67101–145.** Siemens Vienna/Krefeld 2003–04. –/76 1T. 40.3 t.
**TS 67151–195.** Siemens Vienna/Krefeld 2003–04. –/76 1T. 36.8 t.
**TS.** Siemens Vienna/Krefeld 2003–04. –59 1TD 1T 2W. 42.1 t.
**DMC.** Siemens Vienna/Krefeld 2003–04. 32/40. 51.3 t.

| 444 001 | **ST** | A | *SW* | NT | 63801 67101 67151 67201 63851 |
|---------|--------|---|------|----|-------------------------------|
| 444 002 | **SW** | A | *SW* | NT | 63802 67102 67152 67202 63852 |
| 444 003 | **SW** | A | *SW* | NT | 63803 67103 67153 67203 63853 |
| 444 004 | **ST** | A | *SW* | NT | 63804 67104 67154 67204 63854 |
| 444 005 | **ST** | A | *SW* | NT | 63805 67105 67155 67205 63855 |
| 444 006 | **SW** | A | *SW* | NT | 63806 67106 67156 67206 63856 |
| 444 007 | **SW** | A | *SW* | NT | 63807 67107 67157 67207 63857 |
| 444 008 | **ST** | A | *SW* | NT | 63808 67108 67158 67208 63858 |
| 444 009 | **ST** | A | *SW* | NT | 63809 67109 67159 67209 63859 |
| 444 010 | **ST** | A | *SW* | NT | 63810 67110 67160 67210 63860 |
| 444 011 | **SW** | A | *SW* | NT | 63811 67111 67161 67211 63861 |
| 444 012 | **SW** | A | *SW* | NT | 63812 67112 67162 67212 63862 |
| 444 013 | **ST** | A | *SW* | NT | 63813 67113 67163 67213 63863 |
| 444 014 | **SW** | A | *SW* | NT | 63814 67114 67164 67214 63864 |
| 444 015 | **SW** | A | *SW* | NT | 63815 67115 67165 67215 63865 |
| 444 016 | **ST** | A | *SW* | NT | 63816 67116 67166 67216 63866 |
| 444 017 | **SW** | A | *SW* | NT | 63817 67117 67167 67217 63867 |
| 444 018 | **SW** | A | *SW* | NT | 63818 67118 67168 67218 63868 |
| 444 019 | **SW** | A | *SW* | NT | 63819 67119 67169 67219 63869 |
| 444 020 | **ST** | A | *SW* | NT | 63820 67120 67170 67220 63870 |
| 444 021 | **SW** | A | *SW* | NT | 63821 67121 67171 67221 63871 |
| 444 022 | **ST** | A | *SW* | NT | 63822 67122 67172 67222 63872 |

| | | | | | | | | | |
|---|---|---|---|---|---|---|---|---|---|
| 444 023 | **SW** | A | *SW* | NT | 63823 | 67123 | 67173 | 67223 | 63873 |
| 444 024 | **SW** | A | *SW* | NT | 63824 | 67124 | 67174 | 67224 | 63874 |
| 444 025 | **ST** | A | *SW* | NT | 63825 | 67125 | 67175 | 67225 | 63875 |
| 444 026 | **ST** | A | *SW* | NT | 63826 | 67126 | 67176 | 67226 | 63876 |
| 444 027 | **ST** | A | *SW* | NT | 63827 | 67127 | 67177 | 67227 | 63877 |
| 444 028 | **ST** | A | *SW* | NT | 63828 | 67128 | 67178 | 67228 | 63878 |
| 444 029 | **SW** | A | *SW* | NT | 63829 | 67129 | 67179 | 67229 | 63879 |
| 444 030 | **SW** | A | *SW* | NT | 63830 | 67130 | 67180 | 67230 | 63880 |
| 444 031 | **ST** | A | *SW* | NT | 63831 | 67131 | 67181 | 67231 | 63881 |
| 444 032 | **SW** | A | *SW* | NT | 63832 | 67132 | 67182 | 67232 | 63882 |
| 444 033 | **ST** | A | *SW* | NT | 63833 | 67133 | 67183 | 67233 | 63883 |
| 444 034 | **ST** | A | *SW* | NT | 63834 | 67134 | 67184 | 67234 | 63884 |
| 444 035 | **ST** | A | *SW* | NT | 63835 | 67135 | 67185 | 67235 | 63885 |
| 444 036 | **ST** | A | *SW* | NT | 63836 | 67136 | 67186 | 67236 | 63886 |
| 444 037 | **SW** | A | *SW* | NT | 63837 | 67137 | 67187 | 67237 | 63887 |
| 444 038 | **SW** | A | *SW* | NT | 63838 | 67138 | 67188 | 67238 | 63888 |
| 444 039 | **ST** | A | *SW* | NT | 63839 | 67139 | 67189 | 67239 | 63889 |
| 444 040 | **SW** | A | *SW* | NT | 63840 | 67140 | 67190 | 67240 | 63890 |
| 444 041 | **ST** | A | *SW* | NT | 63841 | 67141 | 67191 | 67241 | 63891 |
| 444 042 | **SW** | A | *SW* | NT | 63842 | 67142 | 67192 | 67242 | 63892 |
| 444 043 | **ST** | A | *SW* | NT | 63843 | 67143 | 67193 | 67243 | 63893 |
| 444 044 | **ST** | A | *SW* | NT | 63844 | 67144 | 67194 | 67244 | 63894 |
| 444 045 | **ST** | A | *SW* | NT | 63845 | 67145 | 67195 | 67245 | 63895 |

**Names (carried on TSRMB):**

| | | | |
|---|---|---|---|
| 444 001 | NAOMI HOUSE | 444 038 | SOUTH WESTERN RAILWAY |
| 444 012 | DESTINATION WEYMOUTH | 444 040 | THE D-DAY STORY PORTSMOUTH |
| 444 018 | THE FAB 444 | | |

# CLASS 450          DESIRO UK          SIEMENS

Outer suburban units.

**Formation:** DMC–TS–TS–DMC.
**Construction:** Aluminium.
**Traction Motors:** Four Siemens 1TB2016-0GB02 asynchronous of 250 kW.
**Wheel Arrangement:** Bo-Bo + 2-2 + 2-2 + Bo-Bo.
**Braking:** Disc, rheostatic & regenerative. **Dimensions:** 20.34 x 2.79 m.
**Bogies:** SGP SF5000.                      **Couplers:** Dellner 12.
**Gangways:** Throughout.                     **Control System:** IGBT Inverter.
**Doors:** Sliding plug.                      **Maximum Speed:** 100 mph.
**Heating & Ventilation:** Air conditioning.
**Seating Layout:** 1: 2+2 facing/unidirectional, 2: 3+2 facing/unidirectional.
**Multiple Working:** Within class and with Class 444.

**Class 450/0. Standard units.**

450043–070 were numbered 450543–570 between 2007/08 and 2019. Some seats were removed to create more standing room. They were renumbered back into the 450/0 series in 2019 at the same time as the whole class was refurbished.

**DMC(A).** Siemens Krefeld/Vienna 2002–06. 8/62. 48.0 t.
**TS(A).** Siemens Krefeld/Vienna 2002–06. –/69(+4) 1T. 35.8 t.
**TS(B).** Siemens Krefeld/Vienna 2002–06. –/61(+9) 1TD 2W. 39.8 t.
**DMC(B).** Siemens Krefeld/Vienna 2002–06. 8/62. 48.6 t.

| | | | | | | | | |
|---|---|---|---|---|---|---|---|---|
| 450001 | **SD** | A | *SW* | NT | 63201 | 64201 | 68101 | 63601 |
| 450002 | **SD** | A | *SW* | NT | 63202 | 64202 | 68102 | 63602 |
| 450003 | **SD** | A | *SW* | NT | 63203 | 64203 | 68103 | 63603 |
| 450004 | **SD** | A | *SW* | NT | 63204 | 64204 | 68104 | 63604 |
| 450005 | **SD** | A | *SW* | NT | 63205 | 64205 | 68105 | 63605 |
| 450006 | **SW** | A | *SW* | NT | 63206 | 64206 | 68106 | 63606 |
| 450007 | **SD** | A | *SW* | NT | 63207 | 64207 | 68107 | 63607 |
| 450008 | **SD** | A | *SW* | NT | 63208 | 64208 | 68108 | 63608 |
| 450009 | **SD** | A | *SW* | NT | 63209 | 64209 | 68109 | 63609 |
| 450010 | **SD** | A | *SW* | NT | 63210 | 64210 | 68110 | 63610 |
| 450011 | **SD** | A | *SW* | NT | 63211 | 64211 | 68111 | 63611 |
| 450012 | **SD** | A | *SW* | NT | 63212 | 64212 | 68112 | 63612 |
| 450013 | **SD** | A | *SW* | NT | 63213 | 64213 | 68113 | 63613 |
| 450014 | **SD** | A | *SW* | NT | 63214 | 64214 | 68114 | 63614 |
| 450015 | **SD** | A | *SW* | NT | 63215 | 64215 | 68115 | 63615 |
| 450016 | **SD** | A | *SW* | NT | 63216 | 64216 | 68116 | 63616 |
| 450017 | **SD** | A | *SW* | NT | 63217 | 64217 | 68117 | 63617 |
| 450018 | **SD** | A | *SW* | NT | 63218 | 64218 | 68118 | 63618 |
| 450019 | **SD** | A | *SW* | NT | 63219 | 64219 | 68119 | 63619 |
| 450020 | **SW** | A | *SW* | NT | 63220 | 64220 | 68120 | 63620 |
| 450021 | **SW** | A | *SW* | NT | 63221 | 64221 | 68121 | 63621 |
| 450022 | **SD** | A | *SW* | NT | 63222 | 64222 | 68122 | 63622 |
| 450023 | **SD** | A | *SW* | NT | 63223 | 64223 | 68123 | 63623 |
| 450024 | **SD** | A | *SW* | NT | 63224 | 64224 | 68124 | 63624 |
| 450025 | **SD** | A | *SW* | NT | 63225 | 64225 | 68125 | 63625 |
| 450026 | **SD** | A | *SW* | NT | 63226 | 64226 | 68126 | 63626 |
| 450027 | **SD** | A | *SW* | NT | 63227 | 64227 | 68127 | 63627 |
| 450028 | **SD** | A | *SW* | NT | 63228 | 64228 | 68128 | 63628 |
| 450029 | **SD** | A | *SW* | NT | 63229 | 64229 | 68129 | 63629 |
| 450030 | **SD** | A | *SW* | NT | 63230 | 64230 | 68130 | 63630 |
| 450031 | **SD** | A | *SW* | NT | 63231 | 64231 | 68131 | 63631 |
| 450032 | **SD** | A | *SW* | NT | 63232 | 64232 | 68132 | 63632 |
| 450033 | **SD** | A | *SW* | NT | 63233 | 64233 | 68133 | 63633 |
| 450034 | **SD** | A | *SW* | NT | 63234 | 64234 | 68134 | 63634 |
| 450035 | **SD** | A | *SW* | NT | 63235 | 64235 | 68135 | 63635 |
| 450036 | **SW** | A | *SW* | NT | 63236 | 64236 | 68136 | 63636 |
| 450037 | **SD** | A | *SW* | NT | 63237 | 64237 | 68137 | 63637 |
| 450038 | **SD** | A | *SW* | NT | 63238 | 64238 | 68138 | 63638 |
| 450039 | **SW** | A | *SW* | NT | 63239 | 64239 | 68139 | 63639 |
| 450040 | **SD** | A | *SW* | NT | 63240 | 64240 | 68140 | 63640 |
| 450041 | **SD** | A | *SW* | NT | 63241 | 64241 | 68141 | 63641 |
| 450042 | **SD** | A | *SW* | NT | 63242 | 64242 | 68142 | 63642 |
| 450043 | **SW** | A | *SW* | NT | 63243 | 64243 | 68143 | 63643 |
| 450044 | **SD** | A | *SW* | NT | 63244 | 64244 | 68144 | 63644 |
| 450045 | **SD** | A | *SW* | NT | 63245 | 64245 | 68145 | 63645 |
| 450046 | **SD** | A | *SW* | NT | 63246 | 64246 | 68146 | 63646 |

| 450047 | **SD** | A | *SW* | NT | 63247 | 64247 | 68147 | 63647 |
|--------|--------|---|------|----|-------|-------|-------|-------|
| 450048 | **SW** | A | *SW* | NT | 63248 | 64248 | 68148 | 63648 |
| 450049 | **SD** | A | *SW* | NT | 63249 | 64249 | 68149 | 63649 |
| 450050 | **SD** | A | *SW* | NT | 63250 | 64250 | 68150 | 63650 |
| 450051 | **SD** | A | *SW* | NT | 63251 | 64251 | 68151 | 63651 |
| 450052 | **SD** | A | *SW* | NT | 63252 | 64252 | 68152 | 63652 |
| 450053 | **SD** | A | *SW* | NT | 63253 | 64253 | 68153 | 63653 |
| 450054 | **SD** | A | *SW* | NT | 63254 | 64254 | 68154 | 63654 |
| 450055 | **SD** | A | *SW* | NT | 63255 | 64255 | 68155 | 63655 |
| 450056 | **SW** | A | *SW* | NT | 63256 | 64256 | 68156 | 63656 |
| 450057 | **SD** | A | *SW* | NT | 63257 | 64257 | 68157 | 63657 |
| 450058 | **SD** | A | *SW* | NT | 63258 | 64258 | 68158 | 63658 |
| 450059 | **SD** | A | *SW* | NT | 63259 | 64259 | 68159 | 63659 |
| 450060 | **SD** | A | *SW* | NT | 63260 | 64260 | 68160 | 63660 |
| 450061 | **SD** | A | *SW* | NT | 63261 | 64261 | 68161 | 63661 |
| 450062 | **SD** | A | *SW* | NT | 63262 | 64262 | 68162 | 63662 |
| 450063 | **SD** | A | *SW* | NT | 63263 | 64263 | 68163 | 63663 |
| 450064 | **SD** | A | *SW* | NT | 63264 | 64264 | 68164 | 63664 |
| 450065 | **SD** | A | *SW* | NT | 63265 | 64265 | 68165 | 63665 |
| 450066 | **SD** | A | *SW* | NT | 63266 | 64266 | 68166 | 63666 |
| 450067 | **SD** | A | *SW* | NT | 63267 | 64267 | 68167 | 63667 |
| 450068 | **SD** | A | *SW* | NT | 63268 | 64268 | 68168 | 63668 |
| 450069 | **SD** | A | *SW* | NT | 63269 | 64269 | 68169 | 63669 |
| 450070 | **SD** | A | *SW* | NT | 63270 | 64270 | 68170 | 63670 |
| 450071 | **SD** | A | *SW* | NT | 63271 | 64271 | 68171 | 63671 |
| 450072 | **SD** | A | *SW* | NT | 63272 | 64272 | 68172 | 63672 |
| 450073 | **SD** | A | *SW* | NT | 63273 | 64273 | 68173 | 63673 |
| 450074 | **SD** | A | *SW* | NT | 63274 | 64274 | 68174 | 63674 |
| 450075 | **SD** | A | *SW* | NT | 63275 | 64275 | 68175 | 63675 |
| 450076 | **SD** | A | *SW* | NT | 63276 | 64276 | 68176 | 63676 |
| 450077 | **SD** | A | *SW* | NT | 63277 | 64277 | 68177 | 63677 |
| 450078 | **SD** | A | *SW* | NT | 63278 | 64278 | 68178 | 63678 |
| 450079 | **SD** | A | *SW* | NT | 63279 | 64279 | 68179 | 63679 |
| 450080 | **SD** | A | *SW* | NT | 63280 | 64280 | 68180 | 63680 |
| 450081 | **SD** | A | *SW* | NT | 63281 | 64281 | 68181 | 63681 |
| 450082 | **SD** | A | *SW* | NT | 63282 | 64282 | 68182 | 63682 |
| 450083 | **SD** | A | *SW* | NT | 63283 | 64283 | 68183 | 63683 |
| 450084 | **SD** | A | *SW* | NT | 63284 | 64284 | 68184 | 63684 |
| 450085 | **SD** | A | *SW* | NT | 63285 | 64285 | 68185 | 63685 |
| 450086 | **SD** | A | *SW* | NT | 63286 | 64286 | 68186 | 63686 |
| 450087 | **SD** | A | *SW* | NT | 63287 | 64287 | 68187 | 63687 |
| 450088 | **SD** | A | *SW* | NT | 63288 | 64288 | 68188 | 63688 |
| 450089 | **SD** | A | *SW* | NT | 63289 | 64289 | 68189 | 63689 |
| 450090 | **SD** | A | *SW* | NT | 63290 | 64290 | 68190 | 63690 |
| 450091 | **SD** | A | *SW* | NT | 63291 | 64291 | 68191 | 63691 |
| 450092 | **SD** | A | *SW* | NT | 63292 | 64292 | 68192 | 63692 |
| 450093 | **SD** | A | *SW* | NT | 63293 | 64293 | 68193 | 63693 |
| 450094 | **SD** | A | *SW* | NT | 63294 | 64294 | 68194 | 63694 |
| 450095 | **SD** | A | *SW* | NT | 63295 | 64295 | 68195 | 63695 |
| 450096 | **SD** | A | *SW* | NT | 63296 | 64296 | 68196 | 63696 |
| 450097 | **SD** | A | *SW* | NT | 63297 | 64297 | 68197 | 63697 |

| 450098 | **SD** | A | *SW* | NT | 63298 | 64298 | 68198 | 63698 |
| 450099 | **SD** | A | *SW* | NT | 63299 | 64299 | 68199 | 63699 |
| 450100 | **SD** | A | *SW* | NT | 63300 | 64300 | 68200 | 63700 |
| 450101 | **SW** | A | *SW* | NT | 63701 | 66851 | 66801 | 63751 |
| 450102 | **SD** | A | *SW* | NT | 63702 | 66852 | 66802 | 63752 |
| 450103 | **SD** | A | *SW* | NT | 63703 | 66853 | 66803 | 63753 |
| 450104 | **SD** | A | *SW* | NT | 63704 | 66854 | 66804 | 63754 |
| 450105 | **SD** | A | *SW* | NT | 63705 | 66855 | 66805 | 63755 |
| 450106 | **SD** | A | *SW* | NT | 63706 | 66856 | 66806 | 63756 |
| 450107 | **SW** | A | *SW* | NT | 63707 | 66857 | 66807 | 63757 |
| 450108 | **SD** | A | *SW* | NT | 63708 | 66858 | 66808 | 63758 |
| 450109 | **SD** | A | *SW* | NT | 63709 | 66859 | 66809 | 63759 |
| 450110 | **SD** | A | *SW* | NT | 63710 | 66860 | 66810 | 63760 |
| 450111 | **SW** | A | *SW* | NT | 63901 | 66921 | 66901 | 63921 |
| 450112 | **SD** | A | *SW* | NT | 63902 | 66922 | 66902 | 63922 |
| 450113 | **SW** | A | *SW* | NT | 63903 | 66923 | 66903 | 63923 |
| 450114 | **SD** | A | *SW* | NT | 63904 | 66924 | 66904 | 63924 |
| 450115 | **SD** | A | *SW* | NT | 63905 | 66925 | 66905 | 63925 |
| 450116 | **SD** | A | *SW* | NT | 63906 | 66926 | 66906 | 63926 |
| 450117 | **SD** | A | *SW* | NT | 63907 | 66927 | 66907 | 63927 |
| 450118 | **SD** | A | *SW* | NT | 63908 | 66928 | 66908 | 63928 |
| 450119 | **SW** | A | *SW* | NT | 63909 | 66929 | 66909 | 63929 |
| 450120 | **SD** | A | *SW* | NT | 63910 | 66930 | 66910 | 63930 |
| 450121 | **SD** | A | *SW* | NT | 63911 | 66931 | 66911 | 63931 |
| 450122 | **SD** | A | *SW* | NT | 63912 | 66932 | 66912 | 63932 |
| 450123 | **SD** | A | *SW* | NT | 63913 | 66933 | 66913 | 63933 |
| 450124 | **SD** | A | *SW* | NT | 63914 | 66934 | 66914 | 63934 |
| 450125 | **SD** | A | *SW* | NT | 63915 | 66935 | 66915 | 63935 |
| 450126 | **SD** | A | *SW* | NT | 63916 | 66936 | 66916 | 63936 |
| 450127 | **SW** | A | *SW* | NT | 63917 | 66937 | 66917 | 63937 |

**Names (carried on DMSO(B)):**

| 450015 | DESIRO | 450114 | FAIRBRIDGE investing in the future |
| 450042 | TRELOAR COLLEGE | 450127 | DAVE GUNSON |

# CLASS 455                                                          BREL YORK

Inner suburban units. During 2016–17 the South Western Railway fleet was fitted with new AC traction motors by Vossloh Kiepe.

**Formation:** DTS–MS–TS–DTS.
**Construction:** Steel. Class 455/7 TS have a steel underframe and an aluminium alloy body and roof.
**Traction Motors:** Four GEC507-20J of 185 kW, some recovered from Class 405s (* Four TSA010163 AC motors of 240 kW).
**Wheel Arrangement:** 2-2 + Bo-Bo + 2-2 + 2-2.
**Braking:** Disc (* and regenerative).     **Dimensions:** 19.92/19.83 x 2.82 m.
**Bogies:** P7 (motor) and T3 (455/8 & 455/9) BX1 (455/7) trailer.
**Gangways:** Within unit + end doors (sealed on Southern units).
**Couplers:** Tightlock.                    **Maximum Speed:** 75 mph.
**Control System:** 1982-type, camshaft (* IGBT Inverter).

**Doors:** Sliding.                    **Heating & Ventilation:** Various.
**Seating Layout:** All units refurbished. SWR units: 2+2 high-back unidirectional/
facing seating. Southern units: 3+2 high back mainly facing seating.
**Multiple Working:** Within class and with Class 456.

**Class 455/7. South Western Railway units.** Second series with TSs
originally in Class 508s. Pressure heating & ventilation.

**DTS.** Lot No. 30976 1984–85. –/50(+4) 1W. 30.8t.
**MS.** Lot No. 30975 1984–85. –/68. 45.7t.
**TS.** Lot No. 30944 1979–80. –/68. 26.1t.

| | | | | | | | | |
|---|---|---|---|---|---|---|---|---|
| 5701 | * | **SS** | P | *SW* | WD | 77727 | 62783 | 71545 | 77728 |
| 5702 | * | **SS** | P | *SW* | WD | 77729 | 62784 | 71547 | 77730 |
| 5703 | * | **SS** | P | *SW* | WD | 77731 | 62785 | 71540 | 77732 |
| 5704 | * | **SS** | P | *SW* | WD | 77733 | 62786 | 71548 | 77734 |
| 5705 | * | **SS** | P | *SW* | WD | 77735 | 62787 | 71565 | 77736 |
| 5706 | * | **SS** | P | *SW* | WD | 77737 | 62788 | 71534 | 77738 |
| 5707 | * | **SS** | P | *SW* | WD | 77739 | 62789 | 71536 | 77740 |
| 5708 | * | **SS** | P | *SW* | WD | 77741 | 62790 | 71560 | 77742 |
| 5709 | * | **SS** | P | *SW* | WD | 77743 | 62791 | 71532 | 77744 |
| 5710 | * | **SS** | P | *SW* | WD | 77745 | 62792 | 71566 | 77746 |
| 5711 | * | **SS** | P | *SW* | WD | 77747 | 62793 | 71542 | 77748 |
| 5712 | * | **SS** | P | *SW* | WD | 77749 | 62794 | 71546 | 77750 |
| 5713 | * | **SS** | P | *SW* | WD | 77751 | 62795 | 71567 | 77752 |
| 5714 | * | **SS** | P | *SW* | WD | 77753 | 62796 | 71539 | 77754 |
| 5715 | * | **SS** | P | *SW* | WD | 77755 | 62797 | 71535 | 77756 |
| 5716 | * | **SS** | P | *SW* | WD | 77757 | 62798 | 71564 | 77758 |
| 5717 | * | **SS** | P | *SW* | WD | 77759 | 62799 | 71528 | 77760 |
| 5718 | * | **SS** | P | *SW* | WD | 77761 | 62800 | 71557 | 77762 |
| 5719 | * | **SS** | P | *SW* | WD | 77763 | 62801 | 71558 | 77764 |
| 5720 | * | **SS** | P | *SW* | WD | 77765 | 62802 | 71568 | 77766 |
| 5721 | * | **SS** | P | *SW* | WD | 77767 | 62803 | 71553 | 77768 |
| 5722 | * | **SS** | P | *SW* | WD | 77769 | 62804 | 71533 | 77770 |
| 5723 | * | **SS** | P | *SW* | WD | 77771 | 62805 | 71526 | 77772 |
| 5724 | * | **SS** | P | *SW* | WD | 77773 | 62806 | 71561 | 77774 |
| 5725 | * | **SS** | P | *SW* | WD | 77775 | 62807 | 71541 | 77776 |
| 5726 | * | **SS** | P | *SW* | WD | 77777 | 62808 | 71556 | 77778 |
| 5727 | * | **SS** | P | *SW* | WD | 77779 | 62809 | 71562 | 77780 |
| 5728 | * | **SS** | P | *SW* | WD | 77781 | 62810 | 71527 | 77782 |
| 5729 | * | **SS** | P | *SW* | WD | 77783 | 62811 | 71550 | 77784 |
| 5730 | * | **SS** | P | *SW* | WD | 77785 | 62812 | 71551 | 77786 |
| 5731 | * | **SS** | P | *SW* | WD | 77787 | 62813 | 71555 | 77788 |
| 5732 | * | **SS** | P | *SW* | WD | 77789 | 62814 | 71552 | 77790 |
| 5733 | * | **SS** | P | *SW* | WD | 77791 | 62815 | 71549 | 77792 |
| 5734 | * | **SS** | P | *SW* | WD | 77793 | 62816 | 71531 | 77794 |
| 5735 | * | **SS** | P | *SW* | WD | 77795 | 62817 | 71563 | 77796 |
| 5736 | * | **SS** | P | *SW* | WD | 77797 | 62818 | 71554 | 77798 |
| 5737 | * | **SS** | P | *SW* | WD | 77799 | 62819 | 71544 | 77800 |
| 5738 | * | **SS** | P | *SW* | WD | 77801 | 62820 | 71529 | 77802 |
| 5739 | * | **SS** | P | *SW* | WD | 77803 | 62821 | 71537 | 77804 |
| 5740 | * | **SS** | P | *SW* | WD | 77805 | 62822 | 71530 | 77806 |

| 5741 | * | **SS** | P | *SW* | WD | 77807 | 62823 | 71559 | 77808 |
| 5742 | * | **SS** | P | *SW* | WD | 77809 | 62824 | 71543 | 77810 |
| 5750 | * | **SS** | P | *SW* | WD | 77811 | 62825 | 71538 | 77812 |

**Class 455/8. Southern units.** First series. Pressure heating & ventilation. Fitted with in-cab air conditioning systems meaning that the end door has been sealed.

**DTS.** Lot No. 30972 York 1982–84. –/74. 33.6 t.
**MS.** Lot No. 30973 York 1982–84. –/84. 45.6 t.
**TS.** Lot No. 30974 York 1982–84. –/75(+3) 2W. 34.0 t.

| 455801 | **SN** | E | *SN* | SL | 77627 | 62709 | 71657 | 77580 |
| 455802 | **SN** | E | *SN* | SL | 77581 | 62710 | 71664 | 77582 |
| 455803 | **SN** | E | *SN* | SL | 77583 | 62711 | 71639 | 77584 |
| 455804 | **SN** | E | *SN* | SL | 77585 | 62712 | 71640 | 77586 |
| 455805 | **SN** | E | *SN* | SL | 77587 | 62713 | 71641 | 77588 |
| 455806 | **SN** | E | *SN* | SL | 77589 | 62714 | 71642 | 77590 |
| 455807 | **SN** | E | *SN* | SL | 77591 | 62715 | 71643 | 77592 |
| 455808 | **SN** | E | *SN* | SL | 77637 | 62716 | 71644 | 77594 |
| 455809 | **SN** | E | *SN* | SL | 77623 | 62717 | 71648 | 77602 |
| 455810 | **SN** | E | *SN* | SL | 77597 | 62718 | 71646 | 77598 |
| 455811 | **SN** | E | *SN* | SL | 77599 | 62719 | 71647 | 77600 |
| 455812 | **SN** | E | *SN* | SL | 77595 | 62720 | 71645 | 77626 |
| 455813 | **SN** | E | *SN* | SL | 77603 | 62721 | 71649 | 77604 |
| 455814 | **SN** | E | *SN* | SL | 77605 | 62722 | 71650 | 77606 |
| 455815 | **SN** | E | *SN* | SL | 77607 | 62723 | 71651 | 77608 |
| 455816 | **SN** | E | *SN* | SL | 77609 | 62724 | 71652 | 77633 |
| 455817 | **SN** | E | *SN* | SL | 77611 | 62725 | 71653 | 77612 |
| 455818 | **SN** | E | *SN* | SL | 77613 | 62726 | 71654 | 77632 |
| 455819 | **SN** | E | *SN* | SL | 77615 | 62727 | 71637 | 77616 |
| 455820 | **SN** | E | *SN* | SL | 77617 | 62728 | 71656 | 77618 |
| 455821 | **SN** | E | *SN* | SL | 77619 | 62729 | 71655 | 77620 |
| 455822 | **SN** | E | *SN* | SL | 77621 | 62730 | 71658 | 77622 |
| 455823 | **SN** | E | *SN* | SL | 77601 | 62731 | 71659 | 77596 |
| 455824 | **SN** | E | *SN* | SL | 77593 | 62732 | 71660 | 77624 |
| 455825 | **SN** | E | *SN* | SL | 77579 | 62733 | 71661 | 77628 |
| 455826 | **SN** | E | *SN* | SL | 77630 | 62734 | 71662 | 77629 |
| 455827 | **SN** | E | *SN* | SL | 77610 | 62735 | 71663 | 77614 |
| 455828 | **SN** | E | *SN* | SL | 77631 | 62736 | 71638 | 77634 |
| 455829 | **SN** | E | *SN* | SL | 77635 | 62737 | 71665 | 77636 |
| 455830 | **SN** | E | *SN* | SL | 77625 | 62743 | 71666 | 77638 |
| 455831 | **SN** | E | *SN* | SL | 77639 | 62739 | 71667 | 77640 |
| 455832 | **SN** | E | *SN* | SL | 77641 | 62740 | 71668 | 77642 |
| 455833 | **SN** | E | *SN* | SL | 77643 | 62741 | 71669 | 77644 |
| 455834 | **SN** | E | *SN* | SL | 77645 | 62742 | 71670 | 77646 |
| 455835 | **SN** | E | *SN* | SL | 77647 | 62738 | 71671 | 77648 |
| 455836 | **SN** | E | *SN* | SL | 77649 | 62744 | 71672 | 77650 |
| 455837 | **SN** | E | *SN* | SL | 77651 | 62745 | 71673 | 77652 |
| 455838 | **SN** | E | *SN* | SL | 77653 | 62746 | 71674 | 77654 |
| 455839 | **SN** | E | *SN* | SL | 77655 | 62747 | 71675 | 77656 |
| 455840 | **SN** | E | *SN* | SL | 77657 | 62748 | 71676 | 77658 |

| 455841 | **SN** | E | *SN* | SL | 77659 | 62749 | 71677 | 77660 |
| 455842 | **SN** | E | *SN* | SL | 77661 | 62750 | 71678 | 77662 |
| 455843 | **SN** | E | *SN* | SL | 77663 | 62751 | 71679 | 77664 |
| 455844 | **SN** | E | *SN* | SL | 77665 | 62752 | 71680 | 77666 |
| 455845 | **SN** | E | *SN* | SL | 77667 | 62753 | 71681 | 77668 |
| 455846 | **SN** | E | *SN* | SL | 77669 | 62754 | 71682 | 77670 |

**Class 455/8. South Western Railway units.** First series. Pressure heating & ventilation.

**DTS.** Lot No. 30972 York 1982–84. –50(+4) 1W. 29.5 t.
**MS.** Lot No. 30973 York 1982–84. –/68. 45.6 t.
**TS.** Lot No. 30974 York 1982–84. –/68. 27.1 t.

| 5847 | * | **SS** | P | *SW* | WD | 77671 | 62755 | 71683 | 77672 |
| 5848 | * | **SS** | P | *SW* | WD | 77673 | 62756 | 71684 | 77674 |
| 5849 | * | **SS** | P | *SW* | WD | 77675 | 62757 | 71685 | 77676 |
| 5850 | * | **SS** | P | *SW* | WD | 77677 | 62758 | 71686 | 77678 |
| 5851 | * | **SS** | P | *SW* | WD | 77679 | 62759 | 71687 | 77680 |
| 5852 | * | **SS** | P | *SW* | WD | 77681 | 62760 | 71688 | 77682 |
| 5853 | * | **SS** | P | *SW* | WD | 77683 | 62761 | 71689 | 77684 |
| 5854 | * | **SS** | P | *SW* | WD | 77685 | 62762 | 71690 | 77686 |
| 5855 | * | **SS** | P | *SW* | WD | 77687 | 62763 | 71691 | 77688 |
| 5856 | * | **SS** | P | *SW* | WD | 77689 | 62764 | 71692 | 77690 |
| 5857 | * | **SS** | P | *SW* | WD | 77691 | 62765 | 71693 | 77692 |
| 5858 | * | **SS** | P | *SW* | WD | 77693 | 62766 | 71694 | 77694 |
| 5859 | * | **SS** | P | *SW* | WD | 77695 | 62767 | 71695 | 77696 |
| 5860 | * | **SS** | P | *SW* | WD | 77697 | 62768 | 71696 | 77698 |
| 5861 | * | **SS** | P | *SW* | WD | 77699 | 62769 | 71697 | 77700 |
| 5862 | * | **SS** | P | *SW* | WD | 77701 | 62770 | 71698 | 77702 |
| 5863 | * | **SS** | P | *SW* | WD | 77703 | 62771 | 71699 | 77704 |
| 5864 | * | **SS** | P | *SW* | WD | 77705 | 62772 | 71700 | 77706 |
| 5865 | * | **SS** | P | *SW* | WD | 77707 | 62773 | 71701 | 77708 |
| 5866 | * | **SS** | P | *SW* | WD | 77709 | 62774 | 71702 | 77710 |
| 5867 | * | **SS** | P | *SW* | WD | 77711 | 62775 | 71703 | 77712 |
| 5868 | * | **SS** | P | *SW* | WD | 77713 | 62776 | 71704 | 77714 |
| 5869 | * | **SS** | P | *SW* | WD | 77715 | 62777 | 71705 | 77716 |
| 5870 | * | **SS** | P | *SW* | WD | 77717 | 62778 | 71706 | 77718 |
| 5871 | * | **SS** | P | *SW* | WD | 77719 | 62779 | 71707 | 77720 |
| 5872 | * | **SS** | P | *SW* | WD | 77721 | 62780 | 71708 | 77722 |
| 5873 | * | **SS** | P | *SW* | WD | 77723 | 62781 | 71709 | 77724 |
| 5874 | * | **SS** | P | *SW* | WD | 77725 | 62782 | 71710 | 77726 |

**Class 455/9. South Western Railway units.** Third series. Convection heating.
**Dimensions:** 19.96/20.18 x 2.82 m.

67301 and 67400 were converted from Class 210 DEMU vehicles to replace accident damaged cars.

**DTS.** Lot No. 30991 York 1985. –/50(+4) 1W. 30.7 t.
**MS.** Lot No. 30992 York 1985. –/68. 46.3 t.
**MS 67301.** Lot No. 30932 Derby 1981. –/68.        t.
**TS.** Lot No. 30993 York 1985. –/68. 28.3 t.
**TS 67400.** Lot No. 30932 Derby 1981. –/68. 26.5 t.

| 5901 | * | **SS** | P | *SW* | WD | 77813 | 62826 | 71714 | 77814 |
| 5902 | * | **SS** | P | *SW* | WD | 77815 | 62827 | 71715 | 77816 |
| 5903 | * | **SS** | P | *SW* | WD | 77817 | 62828 | 71716 | 77818 |
| 5904 | * | **SS** | P | *SW* | WD | 77819 | 62829 | 71717 | 77820 |
| 5905 | * | **SS** | P | *SW* | WD | 77821 | 62830 | 71725 | 77822 |
| 5906 | * | **SS** | P | *SW* | WD | 77823 | 62831 | 71719 | 77824 |
| 5907 | * | **SS** | P | *SW* | WD | 77825 | 62832 | 71720 | 77826 |
| 5908 | * | **SS** | P | *SW* | WD | 77827 | 62833 | 71721 | 77828 |
| 5909 | * | **SS** | P | *SW* | WD | 77829 | 62834 | 71722 | 77830 |
| 5910 | * | **SS** | P | *SW* | WD | 77831 | 62835 | 71723 | 77832 |
| 5911 | * | **SS** | P | *SW* | WD | 77833 | 62836 | 71724 | 77834 |
| 5912 | * | **SS** | P | *SW* | WD | 77835 | 62837 | 67400 | 77836 |
| 5913 | * | **SS** | P | *SW* | WD | 77837 | 67301 | 71726 | 77838 |
| 5914 | * | **SS** | P | *SW* | WD | 77839 | 62839 | 71727 | 77840 |
| 5915 | * | **SS** | P | *SW* | WD | 77841 | 62840 | 71728 | 77842 |
| 5916 | * | **SS** | P | *SW* | WD | 77843 | 62841 | 71729 | 77844 |
| 5917 | * | **SS** | P | *SW* | WD | 77845 | 62842 | 71730 | 77846 |
| 5918 | * | **SS** | P | *SW* | WD | 77847 | 62843 | 71732 | 77848 |
| 5919 | * | **SS** | P | *SW* | WD | 77849 | 62844 | 71718 | 77850 |
| 5920 | * | **SS** | P | *SW* | WD | 77851 | 62845 | 71733 | 77852 |

# CLASS 456                                              BREL YORK

Inner suburban units previously operated by Southern, but now operated by South Western Railway.

**Formation:** DMS–DTS.
**Construction:** Steel underframe, aluminium alloy body & roof.
**Traction Motors:** Two GEC507-21J of 185 kW, some recovered from Class 405s.
**Wheel Arrangement:** 2-Bo + 2-2.      **Dimensions:** 20.61 x 2.82 m.
**Braking:** Disc.                      **Couplers:** Tightlock.
**Bogies:** P7 (motor) and T3 (trailer).  **Control System:** GTO Chopper.
**Gangways:** Within unit.               **Maximum Speed:** 75 mph.
**Doors:** Sliding.
**Seating Layout:** 2+2 facing/unidirectional.
**Heating & Ventilation:** Convection heating.
**Multiple Working:** Within class and with Class 455.

**DMS.** Lot No. 31073 1990–91. –/59. 43.3 t.
**DTS.** Lot No. 31074 1990–91. –/54(+5). 32.3 t.

| 456 001 | **SS** | P | *SW* | WD | 64735 | 78250 |
| 456 002 | **SS** | P | *SW* | WD | 64736 | 78251 |
| 456 003 | **SS** | P | *SW* | WD | 64737 | 78252 |
| 456 004 | **SS** | P | *SW* | WD | 64738 | 78253 |
| 456 005 | **SS** | P | *SW* | WD | 64739 | 78254 |
| 456 006 | **SS** | P | *SW* | WD | 64740 | 78255 |
| 456 007 | **SS** | P | *SW* | WD | 64741 | 78256 |
| 456 008 | **SS** | P | *SW* | WD | 64742 | 78257 |
| 456 009 | **SS** | P | *SW* | WD | 64743 | 78258 |
| 456 010 | **SS** | P | *SW* | WD | 64744 | 78259 |
| 456 011 | **SS** | P | *SW* | WD | 64745 | 78260 |

| 456012 | **SS** | P | *SW* | WD | 64746 | 78261 |
| 456013 | **SS** | P | *SW* | WD | 64747 | 78262 |
| 456014 | **SS** | P | *SW* | WD | 64748 | 78263 |
| 456015 | **SS** | P | *SW* | WD | 64749 | 78264 |
| 456016 | **SS** | P | *SW* | WD | 64750 | 78265 |
| 456017 | **SS** | P | *SW* | WD | 64751 | 78266 |
| 456018 | **SS** | P | *SW* | WD | 64752 | 78267 |
| 456019 | **SS** | P | *SW* | WD | 64753 | 78268 |
| 456020 | **SS** | P | *SW* | WD | 64754 | 78269 |
| 456021 | **SS** | P | *SW* | WD | 64755 | 78270 |
| 456022 | **SS** | P | *SW* | WD | 64756 | 78271 |
| 456023 | **SS** | P | *SW* | WD | 64757 | 78272 |
| 456024 | **SS** | P | *SW* | WD | 64758 | 78273 |

# CLASS 458      JUNIPER      ALSTOM BIRMINGHAM

Outer suburban units. Between 2013 and 2016 the fleet of 30 4-car Class 458 units and the former Gatwick Express fleet of eight 8-car Class 460 units was combined to form a fleet of 36 5-car Standard Class only Class 458/5s. The work was carried out at Wabtec Doncaster and Brush Loughborough. Former Class 460 driving cars 67901/903/907/908 were not included in this programme and were scrapped.

After lengthening each unit was renumbered into the 458 5xx series. All individual vehicles retained their original numbers.

**Formation:** DMC–TS*–TS–MS–DMC (* ex-Class 460 in 458 501–530).
**Construction:** Steel.                    **Dimensions:** 21.16 or 21.06 x 2.80 m.
**Traction Motors:** Two Alstom ONIX 800 asynchronous of 270 kW.
**Wheel Arrangement:** 2-Bo + 2-2 + 2-2 + Bo-2 + Bo-2.
**Braking:** Disc & regenerative.       **Control System:** IGBT Inverter.
**Bogies:** ACR.                              **Doors:** Sliding plug.
**Gangways:** Throughout.
**Couplers:** Voith 136.
**Maximum Speed:** 75 mph.
**Heating & Ventilation:** Air conditioning. **Multiple Working:** Within class.
**Seating Layout:** 2+2 facing/unidirectional.

**DMC(A).** Alstom 1998–2000. –/60. 45.7 t.
**TS.** Alstom 1998–99. 458 501–530 –/56; 458 531–536 –/52 1T. 34.4 t.
**TS.** Alstom 1998–2000. –/42 1TD 2W. 34.1 t.
**MS.** Alstom 1998–2000. 458 501–530 –56 1T; 458 531–536 –/56. 40.1 t.
**DMC(B).** Alstom 1998–2000. –/60. 44.9 t.

| 458501 | **SD** | P | *SW* | WD | 67601 74431 74001 74101 67701 |
| 458502 | **SD** | P | *SW* | WD | 67602 74421 74002 74102 67702 |
| 458503 | **SD** | P | *SW* | WD | 67603 74441 74003 74103 67703 |
| 458504 | **SD** | P | *SW* | WD | 67604 74451 74004 74104 67704 |
| 458505 | **SD** | P | *SW* | WD | 67605 74425 74005 74105 67705 |
| 458506 | **SD** | P | *SW* | WD | 67606 74436 74006 74106 67706 |
| 458507 | **SD** | P | *SW* | WD | 67607 74428 74007 74107 67707 |
| 458508 | **SD** | P | *SW* | WD | 67608 74433 74008 74108 67708 |

| 458509 | **SD** | P | *SW* | WD | 67609 74452 74009 74109 67709 |
| 458510 | **SD** | P | *SW* | WD | 67610 74405 74010 74110 67710 |
| 458511 | **SD** | P | *SW* | WD | 67611 74435 74011 74111 67711 |
| 458512 | **SD** | P | *SW* | WD | 67612 74427 74012 74112 67712 |
| 458513 | **SD** | P | *SW* | WD | 67613 74437 74013 74113 67713 |
| 458514 | **SD** | P | *SW* | WD | 67614 74407 74014 74114 67714 |
| 458515 | **SD** | P | *SW* | WD | 67615 74404 74015 74115 67715 |
| 458516 | **SD** | P | *SW* | WD | 67616 74406 74016 74116 67716 |
| 458517 | **SD** | P | *SW* | WD | 67617 74426 74017 74117 67717 |
| 458518 | **SD** | P | *SW* | WD | 67618 74432 74018 74118 67718 |
| 458519 | **SD** | P | *SW* | WD | 67619 74403 74019 74119 67719 |
| 458520 | **SD** | P | *SW* | WD | 67620 74401 74020 74120 67720 |
| 458521 | **SD** | P | *SW* | WD | 67621 74438 74021 74121 67721 |
| 458522 | **SD** | P | *SW* | WD | 67622 74424 74022 74122 67722 |
| 458523 | **SD** | P | *SW* | WD | 67623 74434 74023 74123 67723 |
| 458524 | **SD** | P | *SW* | WD | 67624 74402 74024 74124 67724 |
| 458525 | **SD** | P | *SW* | WD | 67625 74422 74025 74125 67725 |
| 458526 | **SD** | P | *SW* | WD | 67626 74442 74026 74126 67726 |
| 458527 | **SD** | P | *SW* | WD | 67627 74412 74027 74127 67727 |
| 458528 | **SD** | P | *SW* | WD | 67628 74408 74028 74128 67728 |
| 458529 | **SD** | P | *SW* | WD | 67629 74423 74029 74129 67729 |
| 458530 | **SD** | P | *SW* | WD | 67630 74411 74030 74130 67730 |

The following units were converted entirely from Class 460s.

| 458531 | **SD** | P | *SW* | WD | 67913 74418 74458 74458 67912 |
| 458532 | **SD** | P | *SW* | WD | 67904 74417 74447 74457 67905 |
| 458533 | **SD** | P | *SW* | WD | 67917 74413 74443 74453 67916 |
| 458534 | **SD** | P | *SW* | WD | 67914 74414 74444 74454 67918 |
| 458535 | **SD** | P | *SW* | WD | 67915 74415 74445 74455 67911 |
| 458536 | **SD** | P | *SW* | WD | 67906 74416 74448 74456 67902 |

# CLASS 465                                              NETWORKER

Inner and outer suburban units.

**Formation:** DMS–TS–TS–DMS.
**Construction:** Welded aluminium alloy.
**Traction Motors:** Four Hitachi asynchronous of 280 kW (Classes 465/0 and 465/1) or Four GEC-Alsthom G352BY of 280 kW (Classes 465/2 and 465/9).
**Wheel Arrangement:** Bo-Bo + 2-2 + 2-2 + Bo-Bo.
**Braking:** Disc & rheostatic and regenerative (Classes 465/0 and 465/1 only).
**Bogies:** BREL P3/T3 (465/0 and 465/1), SRP BP62/BT52 (465/2 and 465/9).
**Dimensions:** 20.89/20.06 x 2.81 m.
**Control System:** IGBT Inverter (465/0 and 465/1) or 1992-type GTO Inverter.
**Gangways:** Within unit.                    **Couplers:** Tightlock.
**Doors:** Sliding plug.                        **Maximum Speed:** 75 mph.
**Seating Layout:** 3+2 facing/unidirectional.
**Multiple Working:** Within class and with Class 466.

**64759–808. DMS(A).** Lot No. 31100 BREL York 1991–93. –/86. 39.2t.
**64809–858. DMS(B).** Lot No. 31100 BREL York 1991–93. –/86. 39.2t.
**65734–749. DMS(A).** Lot No. 31103 Metro-Cammell 1991–93. –/86. 39.2t.
**65784–799. DMS(B).** Lot No. 31103 Metro-Cammell 1991–93. –/86. 39.2t.
**65800–846. DMS(A).** Lot No. 31130 ABB York 1993–94. –/86. 39.2t.
**65847–893. DMS(B).** Lot No. 31130 ABB York 1993–94. –/86. 39.2t.
**72028–126 (even nos.) TS.** Lot No. 31102 BREL York 1991–93. –/90. 27.2t.
**72029–127 (odd nos.) TS.** Lot No. 31101 BREL York 1991–93. –/65(+7) 1TD 2W. 29.6 t.
**72787–817 (odd nos.) TS.** Lot No. 31104 Metro-Cammell 1991–92. –/65(+7) 1TD 2W. 29.6 t.
**72788–818 (even nos.) TS.** Lot No. 31105 Metro-Cammell 1991–92. –/90. 29.4t.
**72900–992 (even nos.) TS.** Lot No. 31102 ABB York 1993–94. –/90. 27.2t.
**72901–993 (odd nos.) TS.** Lot No. 31101 ABB York 1993–94. –/65(+7) 1TD 2W. 29.6 t.

**Class 465/0.** Built by BREL/ABB.

| | | | | | | | | |
|---|---|---|---|---|---|---|---|---|
| 465 001 | **SE** | E | *SE* | SG | 64759 | 72028 | 72029 | 64809 |
| 465 002 | **SE** | E | *SE* | SG | 64760 | 72030 | 72031 | 64810 |
| 465 003 | **SE** | E | *SE* | SG | 64761 | 72032 | 72033 | 64811 |
| 465 004 | **SE** | E | *SE* | SG | 64762 | 72034 | 72035 | 64812 |
| 465 005 | **SE** | E | *SE* | SG | 64763 | 72036 | 72037 | 64813 |
| 465 006 | **SE** | E | *SE* | SG | 64764 | 72038 | 72039 | 64814 |
| 465 007 | **SE** | E | *SE* | SG | 64765 | 72040 | 72041 | 64815 |
| 465 008 | **SE** | E | *SE* | SG | 64766 | 72042 | 72043 | 64816 |
| 465 009 | **SE** | E | *SE* | SG | 64767 | 72044 | 72045 | 64817 |
| 465 010 | **SE** | E | *SE* | SG | 64768 | 72046 | 72047 | 64818 |
| 465 011 | **SE** | E | *SE* | SG | 64769 | 72048 | 72049 | 64819 |
| 465 012 | **SE** | E | *SE* | SG | 64770 | 72050 | 72051 | 64820 |
| 465 013 | **SE** | E | *SE* | SG | 64771 | 72052 | 72053 | 64821 |
| 465 014 | **SE** | E | *SE* | SG | 64772 | 72054 | 72055 | 64822 |
| 465 015 | **SE** | E | *SE* | SG | 64773 | 72056 | 72057 | 64823 |
| 465 016 | **SE** | E | *SE* | SG | 64774 | 72058 | 72059 | 64824 |
| 465 017 | **SE** | E | *SE* | SG | 64775 | 72060 | 72061 | 64825 |
| 465 018 | **SE** | E | *SE* | SG | 64776 | 72062 | 72063 | 64826 |
| 465 019 | **SE** | E | *SE* | SG | 64777 | 72064 | 72065 | 64827 |
| 465 020 | **SE** | E | *SE* | SG | 64778 | 72066 | 72067 | 64828 |
| 465 021 | **SE** | E | *SE* | SG | 64779 | 72068 | 72069 | 64829 |
| 465 022 | **SE** | E | *SE* | SG | 64780 | 72070 | 72071 | 64830 |
| 465 023 | **SE** | E | *SE* | SG | 64781 | 72072 | 72073 | 64831 |
| 465 024 | **SE** | E | *SE* | SG | 64782 | 72074 | 72075 | 64832 |
| 465 025 | **SE** | E | *SE* | SG | 64783 | 72076 | 72077 | 64833 |
| 465 026 | **SE** | E | *SE* | SG | 64784 | 72078 | 72079 | 64834 |
| 465 027 | **SE** | E | *SE* | SG | 64785 | 72080 | 72081 | 64835 |
| 465 028 | **SE** | E | *SE* | SG | 64786 | 72082 | 72083 | 64836 |
| 465 029 | **SE** | E | *SE* | SG | 64787 | 72084 | 72085 | 64837 |
| 465 030 | **SE** | E | *SE* | SG | 64788 | 72086 | 72087 | 64838 |
| 465 031 | **SE** | E | *SE* | SG | 64789 | 72088 | 72089 | 64839 |
| 465 032 | **SE** | E | *SE* | SG | 64790 | 72090 | 72091 | 64840 |
| 465 033 | **SE** | E | *SE* | SG | 64791 | 72092 | 72093 | 64841 |
| 465 034 | **SE** | E | *SE* | SG | 64792 | 72094 | 72095 | 64842 |

▲ Network Rail yellow-liveried 313 121 is used for ETCS signalling testing. On 31/07/20 it arrives into Littlehampton with 5Z14, the 11.14 test run from Eastleigh Works. **Robert Armstrong**

▼ Greater Anglia-liveried 317 505 arrives at St Margarets with the 12.39 Hertford East–London Liverpool Street on 09/02/19. **Robert Pritchard**

▲ ScotRail-liveried 320 412 and 318 262 call at Carntyne with the 10.37 Balloch–Airdrie on 17/09/20. **Robin Ralston**

▼ In West Midlands Railway interim livery, 323 243 pauses at Alvechurch with a Cross City service for Redditch on 21/05/19. **Tony Christie**

▲ Northern-liveried 331 008 is seen stabled at Liverpool Lime Street on 05/10/19. **Robert Pritchard**

▼ In Tata Communications advertising livery, Heathrow Express 332 007 passes Southall with the 11.27 Heathrow T5–Paddington on 20/05/18. **Jamie Squibbs**

▲ ScotRail-liveried 334 022+334 021 are seen at Hillend, between Blackridge and Caldercruix, with the 19.22 Edinburgh–Helensburgh Central on 16/07/19. **Robin Ralston**

▼ Elizabeth Line 9-car unit 345 027 leaves Ealing Broadway with a service from Hayes & Harlington to London Paddington on 13/10/19. **Robert Pritchard**

▲ Still in the original Connex livery, 376 031+376 024 arrive at St Johns with the 17.32 Hayes–London Cannon Street on 05/08/18. **Robert Pritchard**

▼ Southern-liveried 377 210+377 207 approach South Kenton with the 13.23 Watford Junction–Clapham Junction on 09/12/18. **Robert Pritchard**

▲ New London Overground-liveried 378 206 is seen at Clapham Junction with the 10.30 to Stratford on 10/09/20. **Jamie Squibbs**

▼ ScotRail-liveried 385 030+385 024 are seen near Drem with the 15.12 Dunbar–Edinburgh on 11/10/19. **Robin Ralston**

▲ Gatwick Express-liveried 387 211/208/206 leave Gatwick Airport with the 09.54 to London Victoria on 07/09/18. **Robert Pritchard**

▼ With its end cars in the new Avanti West Coast livery, 390 104 passes Cartland with the 12.37 Glasgow Central–London Euston on 18/09/20. **Ian Lothian**

▲ Southeastern blue-liveried 395 017 is seen on HS1 near Lenham with the 13.25 London St Pancras–Ramsgate–St Pancras on 15/09/20. **Jamie Squibbs**

▼ South Western Railway-liveried 444 017 and SWT-liveried 444 002 pass Hook with the 07.10 Weymouth–London Waterloo on 10/09/20. **Tony Christie**

▲ In the old South West Trains red livery, Class 455s 5848+5735 approach Guildford with the 15.09 London Waterloo–Guildford on 04/09/19. **Robin Ralston**

▼ In the SWT blue livery, 458 523+458 533 pass through the leafy west London suburbs near Mortlake with the 10.42 Reading–London Waterloo on 11/08/18.
**Robert Pritchard**

▲ Southeastern suburban-liveried 466 042 brings up the rear of the 11.52 Dover Priory–London Victoria (led by 465 919) on departure from Dover on 16/04/19.
**Robert Pritchard**

▼ Merseyrail-liveried 507 033 and 507 015 are seen near Wallasey Grove Road with the 19.08 New Brighton–Liverpool Central on 19/07/20. **Jamie Squibbs**

▲ Thameslink-liveried 700 055 passes Stoats Nest Jn, Coulsdon with the 16.05 Cricklewood–Three Bridges depot empty stock on 04/08/18.    **Robert Pritchard**

▼ South Western Railway has a large fleet of Class 701 Aventras on order from Bombardier. On 20/08/20 10-car set 701 005 passes Winchfield with the 5Q30 Eastleigh–London Waterloo test run.    **Chris Wilson**

▲ London Overground 710/1s work services out of Liverpool Street. On 05/08/20 710 123+710 129 arrive at Bethnal Green with the 10.00 Liverpool Street–Enfield Town. **Joel Coulson**

▼ Great Northern Moorgate line unit 717 010 exits Potters Bar Tunnels with the 08.58 Welwyn Garden City–Moorgate on 18/05/20. **Jamie Squibbs**

▲ New Greater Anglia Aventras 720 536+720 517 descend Belstead Bank towards Ipswich with the 5Q36 09.50 Ilford–Ipswich test run on 24/06/20. **Keith Partlow**

▼ The first Class 730 Aventra for West Midlands Railway, 730 001, is seen on test at Velim in the Czech Republic on 09/08/20. **Vladimír Fišar**

▲ Greater Anglia 3-car Class 755 bi-mode unit 755 336 leaves Ipswich empty stock to Marks Tey to take up the Marks Yet–Sudbury branch diagram on 04/03/20. **Robert Pritchard**

▼ Transport for Wales-liveried 769 008, a rebuilt Class 319 with diesel engines fitted, approaches Cardiff Queen Street with a 5Z72 14.27 Rhymney–Cardiff Canton driver training run on 06/08/20. **Martin Turner**

▲ New Merseyrail unit 777 003 is seen at the official launch of the class at Kirkdale depot on 28/01/20. **Robert Pritchard**

▼ LNER Azuma 801 206 passes Spittal, south of Berwick-upon-Tweed, with the 14.00 Edinburgh–London King's Cross on 08/08/20. **Ian Beardsley**

▲ TransPennine Express-liveried bi-mode unit 802 210 is operating in diesel mode as it passes Spittal with the 14.16 Newcastle–Edinburgh on 08/08/20.
**Ian Beardsley**

▼ Siemens e320 Eurostar 4002/01 passes Rainham on HS1 with the 14.52 Brussels–London St Pancras on 22/10/17. **Robert Pritchard**

| 465035 | **SE** | E | *SE* | SG | 64793 | 72096 | 72097 | 64843 |
| 465036 | **SE** | E | *SE* | SG | 64794 | 72098 | 72099 | 64844 |
| 465037 | **SE** | E | *SE* | SG | 64795 | 72100 | 72101 | 64845 |
| 465038 | **SE** | E | *SE* | SG | 64796 | 72102 | 72103 | 64846 |
| 465039 | **SE** | E | *SE* | SG | 64797 | 72104 | 72105 | 64847 |
| 465040 | **SE** | E | *SE* | SG | 64798 | 72106 | 72107 | 64848 |
| 465041 | **SE** | E | *SE* | SG | 64799 | 72108 | 72109 | 64849 |
| 465042 | **SE** | E | *SE* | SG | 64800 | 72110 | 72111 | 64850 |
| 465043 | **SE** | E | *SE* | SG | 64801 | 72112 | 72113 | 64851 |
| 465044 | **SE** | E | *SE* | SG | 64802 | 72114 | 72115 | 64852 |
| 465045 | **SE** | E | *SE* | SG | 64803 | 72116 | 72117 | 64853 |
| 465046 | **SE** | E | *SE* | SG | 64804 | 72118 | 72119 | 64854 |
| 465047 | **SE** | E | *SE* | SG | 64805 | 72120 | 72121 | 64855 |
| 465048 | **SE** | E | *SE* | SG | 64806 | 72122 | 72123 | 64856 |
| 465049 | **SE** | E | *SE* | SG | 64807 | 72124 | 72125 | 64857 |
| 465050 | **SE** | E | *SE* | SG | 64808 | 72126 | 72127 | 64858 |

**Class 465/1.** Built by BREL/ABB. Similar to Class 465/0 but with detail differences.

| 465151 | **SE** | E | *SE* | SG | 65800 | 72900 | 72901 | 65847 |
| 465152 | **SE** | E | *SE* | SG | 65801 | 72902 | 72903 | 65848 |
| 465153 | **SE** | E | *SE* | SG | 65802 | 72904 | 72905 | 65849 |
| 465154 | **SE** | E | *SE* | SG | 65803 | 72906 | 72907 | 65850 |
| 465155 | **SE** | E | *SE* | SG | 65804 | 72908 | 72909 | 65851 |
| 465156 | **SE** | E | *SE* | SG | 65805 | 72910 | 72911 | 65852 |
| 465157 | **SE** | E | *SE* | SG | 65806 | 72912 | 72913 | 65853 |
| 465158 | **SE** | E | *SE* | SG | 65807 | 72914 | 72915 | 65854 |
| 465159 | **SE** | E | *SE* | SG | 65808 | 72916 | 72917 | 65855 |
| 465160 | **SE** | E | *SE* | SG | 65809 | 72918 | 72919 | 65856 |
| 465161 | **SE** | E | *SE* | SG | 65810 | 72920 | 72921 | 65857 |
| 465162 | **SE** | E | *SE* | SG | 65811 | 72922 | 72923 | 65858 |
| 465163 | **SE** | E | *SE* | SG | 65812 | 72924 | 72925 | 65859 |
| 465164 | **SE** | E | *SE* | SG | 65813 | 72926 | 72927 | 65860 |
| 465165 | **SE** | E | *SE* | SG | 65814 | 72928 | 72929 | 65861 |
| 465166 | **SE** | E | *SE* | SG | 65815 | 72930 | 72931 | 65862 |
| 465167 | **SE** | E | *SE* | SG | 65816 | 72932 | 72933 | 65863 |
| 465168 | **SE** | E | *SE* | SG | 65817 | 72934 | 72935 | 65864 |
| 465169 | **SE** | E | *SE* | SG | 65818 | 72936 | 72937 | 65865 |
| 465170 | **SE** | E | *SE* | SG | 65819 | 72938 | 72939 | 65866 |
| 465171 | **SE** | E | *SE* | SG | 65820 | 72940 | 72941 | 65867 |
| 465172 | **SE** | E | *SE* | SG | 65821 | 72942 | 72943 | 65868 |
| 465173 | **SE** | E | *SE* | SG | 65822 | 72944 | 72945 | 65869 |
| 465174 | **SE** | E | *SE* | SG | 65823 | 72946 | 72947 | 65870 |
| 465175 | **SE** | E | *SE* | SG | 65824 | 72948 | 72949 | 65871 |
| 465176 | **SE** | E | *SE* | SG | 65825 | 72950 | 72951 | 65872 |
| 465177 | **SE** | E | *SE* | SG | 65826 | 72952 | 72953 | 65873 |
| 465178 | **SE** | E | *SE* | SG | 65827 | 72954 | 72955 | 65874 |
| 465179 | **SE** | E | *SE* | SG | 65828 | 72956 | 72957 | 65875 |
| 465180 | **SE** | E | *SE* | SG | 65829 | 72958 | 72959 | 65876 |
| 465181 | **SE** | E | *SE* | SG | 65830 | 72960 | 72961 | 65877 |
| 465182 | **SE** | E | *SE* | SG | 65831 | 72962 | 72963 | 65878 |

| 465 183 | **SE** | E | *SE* | SG | 65832 | 72964 | 72965 | 65879 |
| 465 184 | **SE** | E | *SE* | SG | 65833 | 72966 | 72967 | 65880 |
| 465 185 | **SE** | E | *SE* | SG | 65834 | 72968 | 72969 | 65881 |
| 465 186 | **SE** | E | *SE* | SG | 65835 | 72970 | 72971 | 65882 |
| 465 187 | **SE** | E | *SE* | SG | 65836 | 72972 | 72973 | 65883 |
| 465 188 | **SE** | E | *SE* | SG | 65837 | 72974 | 72975 | 65884 |
| 465 189 | **SE** | E | *SE* | SG | 65838 | 72976 | 72977 | 65885 |
| 465 190 | **SE** | E | *SE* | SG | 65839 | 72978 | 72979 | 65886 |
| 465 191 | **SE** | E | *SE* | SG | 65840 | 72980 | 72981 | 65887 |
| 465 192 | **SE** | E | *SE* | SG | 65841 | 72982 | 72983 | 65888 |
| 465 193 | **SE** | E | *SE* | SG | 65842 | 72984 | 72985 | 65889 |
| 465 194 | **SE** | E | *SE* | SG | 65843 | 72986 | 72987 | 65890 |
| 465 195 | **SE** | E | *SE* | SG | 65844 | 72988 | 72989 | 65891 |
| 465 196 | **SE** | E | *SE* | SG | 65845 | 72990 | 72991 | 65892 |
| 465 197 | **SE** | E | *SE* | SG | 65846 | 72992 | 72993 | 65893 |

**Class 465/2.** Built by Metro-Cammell. **Dimensions:** 20.80/20.15 x 2.81 m.

| 465 235 | **SE** | A | *SE* | SG | 65734 | 72787 | 72788 | 65784 |
| 465 236 | **SE** | A | *SE* | SG | 65735 | 72789 | 72790 | 65785 |
| 465 237 | **SE** | A | *SE* | SG | 65736 | 72791 | 72792 | 65786 |
| 465 238 | **SE** | A | *SE* | SG | 65737 | 72793 | 72794 | 65787 |
| 465 239 | **SE** | A | *SE* | SG | 65738 | 72795 | 72796 | 65788 |
| 465 240 | **SE** | A | *SE* | SG | 65739 | 72797 | 72798 | 65789 |
| 465 241 | **SE** | A | *SE* | SG | 65740 | 72799 | 72800 | 65790 |
| 465 242 | **SE** | A | *SE* | SG | 65741 | 72801 | 72802 | 65791 |
| 465 243 | **SE** | A | *SE* | SG | 65742 | 72803 | 72804 | 65792 |
| 465 244 | **SE** | A | *SE* | SG | 65743 | 72805 | 72806 | 65793 |
| 465 245 | **SE** | A | *SE* | SG | 65744 | 72807 | 72808 | 65794 |
| 465 246 | **SE** | A | *SE* | SG | 65745 | 72809 | 72810 | 65795 |
| 465 247 | **SE** | A | *SE* | SG | 65746 | 72811 | 72812 | 65796 |
| 465 248 | **SE** | A | *SE* | SG | 65747 | 72813 | 72814 | 65797 |
| 465 249 | **SE** | A | *SE* | SG | 65748 | 72815 | 72816 | 65798 |
| 465 250 | **SE** | A | *SE* | SG | 65749 | 72817 | 72818 | 65799 |

**Class 465/9.** Built by Metro-Cammell. Refurbished 2005 for longer distance services, with the addition of First Class. Details as Class 465/0 unless stated.

**Formation:** DMC–TS–TS–DMC.
**Seating Layout:** 1: 2+2 facing/unidirectional, 2: 3+2 facing/unidirectional.

**65700–733. DMC(A).** Lot No. 31103 Metro-Cammell 1991–93. 12/68. 39.2t.
**72719–785 (odd nos.) TS(A).** Lot No. 31104 Metro-Cammell 1991–92. –/65(+7) 1TD 2W. 30.3t.
**72720–786 (even nos.) TS(B).** Lot No. 31105 Metro-Cammell 1991–92. –/90. 29.5t.
**65750–783. DMC(B).** Lot No. 31103 Metro-Cammell 1991–93. 12/68. 39.2t.

| 465 901 | (465 201) | **SE** | A | *SE* | SG | 65700 72719 72720 65750 |
| 465 902 | (465 202) | **SE** | A | *SE* | SG | 65701 72721 72722 65751 |
| 465 903 | (465 203) | **SE** | A | *SE* | SG | 65702 72723 72724 65752 |
| 465 904 | (465 204) | **SE** | A | *SE* | SG | 65703 72725 72726 65753 |
| 465 905 | (465 205) | **SE** | A | *SE* | SG | 65704 72727 72728 65754 |
| 465 906 | (465 206) | **SE** | A | *SE* | SG | 65705 72729 72730 65755 |
| 465 907 | (465 207) | **SE** | A | *SE* | SG | 65706 72731 72732 65756 |

| | | | | | | | | |
|---|---|---|---|---|---|---|---|---|
| 465908 | (465208) | **SE** | A | *SE* | SG | 65707 | 72733 72734 | 65757 |
| 465909 | (465209) | **SE** | A | *SE* | SG | 65708 | 72735 72736 | 65758 |
| 465910 | (465210) | **SE** | A | *SE* | SG | 65709 | 72737 72738 | 65759 |
| 465911 | (465211) | **SE** | A | *SE* | SG | 65710 | 72739 72740 | 65760 |
| 465912 | (465212) | **SE** | A | *SE* | SG | 65711 | 72741 72742 | 65761 |
| 465913 | (465213) | **SE** | A | *SE* | SG | 65712 | 72743 72744 | 65762 |
| 465914 | (465214) | **SE** | A | *SE* | SG | 65713 | 72745 72746 | 65763 |
| 465915 | (465215) | **SE** | A | *SE* | SG | 65714 | 72747 72748 | 65764 |
| 465916 | (465216) | **SE** | A | *SE* | SG | 65715 | 72749 72750 | 65765 |
| 465917 | (465217) | **SE** | A | *SE* | SG | 65716 | 72751 72752 | 65766 |
| 465918 | (465218) | **SE** | A | *SE* | SG | 65717 | 72753 72754 | 65767 |
| 465919 | (465219) | **SE** | A | *SE* | SG | 65718 | 72755 72756 | 65768 |
| 465920 | (465220) | **SE** | A | *SE* | SG | 65719 | 72757 72758 | 65769 |
| 465921 | (465221) | **SE** | A | *SE* | SG | 65720 | 72759 72760 | 65770 |
| 465922 | (465222) | **SE** | A | *SE* | SG | 65721 | 72761 72762 | 65771 |
| 465923 | (465223) | **SE** | A | *SE* | SG | 65722 | 72763 72764 | 65772 |
| 465924 | (465224) | **SE** | A | *SE* | SG | 65723 | 72765 72766 | 65773 |
| 465925 | (465225) | **SE** | A | *SE* | SG | 65724 | 72767 72768 | 65774 |
| 465926 | (465226) | **SE** | A | *SE* | SG | 65725 | 72769 72770 | 65775 |
| 465927 | (465227) | **SE** | A | *SE* | SG | 65726 | 72771 72772 | 65776 |
| 465928 | (465228) | **SE** | A | *SE* | SG | 65727 | 72773 72774 | 65777 |
| 465929 | (465229) | **SE** | A | *SE* | SG | 65728 | 72775 72776 | 65778 |
| 465930 | (465230) | **SE** | A | *SE* | SG | 65729 | 72777 72778 | 65779 |
| 465931 | (465231) | **SE** | A | *SE* | SG | 65730 | 72779 72780 | 65780 |
| 465932 | (465232) | **SE** | A | *SE* | SG | 65731 | 72781 72782 | 65781 |
| 465933 | (465233) | **SE** | A | *SE* | SG | 65732 | 72783 72784 | 65782 |
| 465934 | (465234) | **SE** | A | *SE* | SG | 65733 | 72785 72786 | 65783 |

## CLASS 466      NETWORKER      GEC-ALSTHOM

Inner and outer suburban units.

**Formation:** DMS–DTS.
**Construction:** Welded aluminium alloy.
**Traction Motors:** Two GEC-Alsthom G352AY asynchronous of 280 kW.
**Wheel Arrangement:** Bo-Bo + 2-2.    **Couplers:** Tightlock.
**Braking:** Disc, rheostatic & regen.    **Control System:** 1992-type GTO Inverter.
**Dimensions:** 20.80 x 2.80 m.    **Maximum Speed:** 75 mph.
**Bogies:** BREL P3/T3.    **Doors:** Sliding plug.
**Gangways:** Within unit.
**Seating Layout:** 3+2 facing/unidirectional.
**Multiple Working:** Within class and with Class 465.

**DMS.** Lot No. 31128 Birmingham 1993–94. –/86. 40.6t.
**DTS.** Lot No. 31129 Birmingham 1993–94. –/82 1T. 31.4t.

| | | | | | | |
|---|---|---|---|---|---|---|
| 466001 | **SE** | A | *SE* | SG | 64860 | 78312 |
| 466002 | **SE** | A | *SE* | SG | 64861 | 78313 |
| 466003 | **SE** | A | *SE* | SG | 64862 | 78314 |
| 466004 | **SE** | A | *SE* | SG | 64863 | 78315 |
| 466005 | **SE** | A | *SE* | SG | 64864 | 78316 |
| 466006 | **SE** | A | *SE* | SG | 64865 | 78317 |

| | | | | | | |
|---|---|---|---|---|---|---|
| 466 007 | **SE** | A | *SE* | SG | 64866 | 78318 |
| 466 008 | **SE** | A | *SE* | SG | 64867 | 78319 |
| 466 009 | **SE** | A | *SE* | SG | 64868 | 78320 |
| 466 010 | **SE** | A | *SE* | SG | 64869 | 78321 |
| 466 011 | **SE** | A | *SE* | SG | 64870 | 78322 |
| 466 012 | **SE** | A | *SE* | SG | 64871 | 78323 |
| 466 013 | **SE** | A | *SE* | SG | 64872 | 78324 |
| 466 014 | **SE** | A | *SE* | SG | 64873 | 78325 |
| 466 015 | **SE** | A | *SE* | SG | 64874 | 78326 |
| 466 016 | **SE** | A | *SE* | SG | 64875 | 78327 |
| 466 017 | **SE** | A | *SE* | SG | 64876 | 78328 |
| 466 018 | **SE** | A | *SE* | SG | 64877 | 78329 |
| 466 019 | **SE** | A | *SE* | SG | 64878 | 78330 |
| 466 020 | **SE** | A | *SE* | SG | 64879 | 78331 |
| 466 021 | **SE** | A | *SE* | SG | 64880 | 78332 |
| 466 022 | **SE** | A | *SE* | SG | 64881 | 78333 |
| 466 023 | **SE** | A | *SE* | SG | 64882 | 78334 |
| 466 024 | **SE** | A | *SE* | SG | 64883 | 78335 |
| 466 025 | **SE** | A | *SE* | SG | 64884 | 78336 |
| 466 026 | **SE** | A | *SE* | SG | 64885 | 78337 |
| 466 027 | **SE** | A | *SE* | SG | 64886 | 78338 |
| 466 028 | **SE** | A | *SE* | SG | 64887 | 78339 |
| 466 029 | **SE** | A | *SE* | SG | 64888 | 78340 |
| 466 030 | **SE** | A | *SE* | SG | 64889 | 78341 |
| 466 031 | **SE** | A | *SE* | SG | 64890 | 78342 |
| 466 032 | **SE** | A | *SE* | SG | 64891 | 78343 |
| 466 033 | **SE** | A | *SE* | SG | 64892 | 78344 |
| 466 034 | **SE** | A | *SE* | SG | 64893 | 78345 |
| 466 035 | **SE** | A | *SE* | SG | 64894 | 78346 |
| 466 036 | **SE** | A | *SE* | SG | 64895 | 78347 |
| 466 037 | **SE** | A | *SE* | SG | 64896 | 78348 |
| 466 038 | **SE** | A | *SE* | SG | 64897 | 78349 |
| 466 039 | **SE** | A | *SE* | SG | 64898 | 78350 |
| 466 040 | **SE** | A | *SE* | SG | 64899 | 78351 |
| 466 041 | **SE** | A | *SE* | SG | 64900 | 78352 |
| 466 042 | **SE** | A | *SE* | SG | 64901 | 78353 |
| 466 043 | **SE** | A | *SE* | SG | 64902 | 78354 |

# CLASS 483                                                    METRO-CAMMELL

Built 1938 onwards for LTE. Converted 1989–90 for the Isle of Wight Line.
The remaining units were withdrawn from service at the start of 2021.

**Formation:** DMS–DMS.
**Construction:** Steel.
**Traction Motors:** Two Crompton Parkinson/GEC/BTH LT100 of 125 kW.
**Braking:** Tread.
**Bogies:** LT design.
**Gangways:** None. End doors.
**Control System:** Pneumatic Camshaft Motor (PCM).

**System:** 660 V DC third rail.
**Wheel arrangement:** A1-1A + A1-1A.
**Dimensions:** 16.15 x 2.69 m.
**Couplers:** Wedgelock.

**Doors:** Sliding.　　　　　　　　　**Maximum Speed:** 45 mph.
**Seating Layout:** Longitudinal or 2+2 facing/unidirectional.
**Multiple Working:** Within class.

The last three numbers of the unit number only are carried.

Former London Underground numbers are shown in parentheses.

**DMS(A).** Lot No. 31071. –/40. 27.4 t.
**DMS(B).** Lot No. 31072. –/42. 27.4 t.

| | | | | | | | | |
|---|---|---|---|---|---|---|---|---|
| 483 002 | **LT** | SW | RY | 122 | (10221) | 225 | (11142) | RAPTOR |
| 483 004 | **LT** | SW | RY | 124 | (10205) | 224 | (11205) | |
| 483 006 | **LT** | SW | RY | 126 | (10297) | 226 | (11297) | |
| 483 007 | **LT** | SW | RY | 127 | (10291) | 227 | (11291) | |
| 483 008 | **LT** | SW | RY | 128 | (10255) | 228 | (11255) | |
| 483 009 | **LT** | SW | RY | 129 | (10229) | 229 | (11229) | |

# CLASS 484  D-TRAIN  METRO-CAMMELL/VIVARAIL

South Western Railway has five 2-car D-Trains on order for the Isle of Wight Line and these are due to enter service in spring 2021. Similar to the converted Class 230 DMUs or diesel-battery units, the Class 484s are straight third-rail EMUs, rebuilt from former London Underground D78 stock. Full details awaited.

**Formation:** DMS–DMS.　　　　　　　**System:** 660 V DC third rail.
**Construction:** Aluminium.　　　　　　**Wheel Arrangement:**
**Traction motors:** TSA AC motors.　　 **Couplers:**
**Braking:** Rheostatic & Dynamic.　　　**Dimensions:** 18.37 x 2.85 m.
**Bogies:** Bombardier FLEXX1000 flexible-frame.
**Gangways:** Within unit only.
**Control System:** IGBT Inverter.
**Doors:** Sliding.　　　　　　　　　　**Maximum Speed:** 60 mph.
**Seating Layout:** Longitudinal or 2+2 facing.
**Multiple Working:** Within class.

**DMS(A).** Metro-Cammell Birmingham 1979–83.
**DMS(B).** Metro-Cammell Birmingham 1979–83.

| | | | | | | | |
|---|---|---|---|---|---|---|---|
| 484 001 | **SW** | LF | RY | 131 | (7086) | 231 | (7011) |
| 484 002 | **SW** | LF | | 132 | (7068) | 232 | (7002) |
| 484 003 | **SW** | LF | | 133 | (7051) | 233 | (7083) |
| 484 004 | **SW** | LF | | 134 | (7074) | 234 | (7111) |
| 484 005 | **SW** | LF | | 135 | (7124) | 235 | (7093) |

# CLASS 507                                          **BREL YORK**

**Formation:** BDMS–TS–DMS.
**Construction:** Steel underframe, aluminium alloy body and roof.
**Traction Motors:** Four GEC G310AZ of 82.125 kW.
**Wheel Arrangement:** Bo-Bo + 2-2 + Bo-Bo.
**Braking:** Disc & rheostatic.          **Dimensions:** 20.18 x 2.82 m.
**Bogies:** BX1.                          **Couplers:** Tightlock.
**Gangways:** Within unit + end doors.   **Control System:** Camshaft.
**Doors:** Sliding.                       **Maximum Speed:** 75 mph.
**Seating Layout:** All refurbished with 2+2 high-back facing seating.
**Multiple Working:** Within class and with Class 508.

Fitted with tripcocks for operating on the Merseyrail Wirral Lines.

**Advertising livery:** 507 002 Liverpool Hope University (white).

**BDMS.** Lot No. 30906 1978–80. –/56(+3) 1W. 37.0 t.
**TS.** Lot No. 30907 1978–80. –/74. 25.5 t.
**DMS.** Lot No. 30908 1978–80. –/56(+3) 1W. 35.5 t.

| | | | | | | |
|---|---|---|---|---|---|---|
| 507 001 | **MY** | A | *ME* | BD | 64367 | 71342 | 64405 |
| 507 002 | **AL** | A | *ME* | BD | 64368 | 71343 | 64406 |
| 507 003 | **MY** | A | *ME* | BD | 64369 | 71344 | 64407 |
| 507 004 | **MY** | A | *ME* | BD | 64388 | 71345 | 64408 |
| 507 005 | **MY** | A | *ME* | BD | 64371 | 71346 | 64409 |
| 507 006 | **MY** | A | *ME* | BD | 64372 | 71347 | 64410 |
| 507 007 | **MY** | A | *ME* | BD | 64373 | 71348 | 64411 |
| 507 008 | **MY** | A | *ME* | BD | 64374 | 71349 | 64412 |
| 507 009 | **MY** | A | *ME* | BD | 64375 | 71350 | 64413 |
| 507 010 | **MY** | A | *ME* | BD | 64376 | 71351 | 64414 |
| 507 011 | **MY** | A | *ME* | BD | 64377 | 71352 | 64415 |
| 507 012 | **MY** | A | *ME* | BD | 64378 | 71353 | 64416 |
| 507 013 | **MY** | A | *ME* | BD | 64379 | 71354 | 64417 |
| 507 014 | **MY** | A | *ME* | BD | 64380 | 71355 | 64418 |
| 507 015 | **MY** | A | *ME* | BD | 64381 | 71356 | 64419 |
| 507 016 | **MY** | A | *ME* | BD | 64382 | 71357 | 64420 |
| 507 017 | **MY** | A | *ME* | BD | 64383 | 71358 | 64421 |
| 507 018 | **MY** | A | *ME* | BD | 64384 | 71359 | 64422 |
| 507 019 | **MY** | A | *ME* | BD | 64385 | 71360 | 64423 |
| 507 020 | **MY** | A | *ME* | BD | 64386 | 71361 | 64424 |
| 507 021 | **MY** | A | *ME* | BD | 64387 | 71362 | 64425 |
| 507 023 | **MY** | A | *ME* | BD | 64389 | 71364 | 64427 |
| 507 024 | **MY** | A | *ME* | BD | 64390 | 71365 | 64428 |
| 507 025 | **MY** | A | *ME* | BD | 64391 | 71366 | 64429 |
| 507 026 | **MY** | A | *ME* | BD | 64392 | 71367 | 64430 |
| 507 027 | **MY** | A | *ME* | BD | 64393 | 71368 | 64431 |
| 507 028 | **MY** | A | *ME* | BD | 64394 | 71369 | 64432 |
| 507 029 | **MY** | A | *ME* | BD | 64395 | 71370 | 64433 |
| 507 030 | **MY** | A | *ME* | BD | 64396 | 71371 | 64434 |
| 507 031 | **MY** | A | *ME* | BD | 64397 | 71372 | 64435 |
| 507 032 | **MY** | A | *ME* | BD | 64398 | 71373 | 64436 |
| 507 033 | **MY** | A | *ME* | BD | 64399 | 71374 | 64437 |

**Names:**

507 004   Bob Paisley
507 008   Harold Wilson
507 009   Dixie Dean
507 016   Merseyrail – celebrating the first ten years (2003–2013)
507 020   John Peel
507 021   Red Rum
507 023   Operations Inspector Stuart Mason
507 026   Councillor George Howard
507 033   Councillor Jack Spriggs

# CLASS 508                                                    BREL YORK

**Formation:** DMS–TS–BDMS.
**Construction:** Steel underframe, aluminium alloy body and roof.
**Traction Motors:** Four GEC G310AZ of 82.125 kW.
**Wheel Arrangement:** Bo-Bo + 2-2 + Bo-Bo.
**Braking:** Disc & rheostatic.          **Dimensions:** 20.18 x 2.82 m.
**Bogies:** BX1.                         **Couplers:** Tightlock.
**Gangways:** Within unit + end doors. **Control System:** Camshaft.
**Doors:** Sliding.                      **Maximum Speed:** 75 mph.
**Seating Layout:** All refurbished with 2+2 high-back facing seating.
**Multiple Working:** Within class and with Class 507.

Fitted with tripcocks for operating on the Merseyrail Wirral Lines.

**Advertising livery:** 508 111 Beatles Story (blue).

**DMS.** Lot No. 30979 1979–80. –/56(+3) 1W. 36.0 t.
**TS.** Lot No. 30980 1979–80. –/74. 26.5 t.
**BDMS.** Lot No. 30981 1979–80. –/56(+3) 1W. 36.5 t.

| 508 103 | **MY** | A | *ME* | BD | 64651 | 71485 | 64694 |
| 508 104 | **MY** | A | *ME* | BD | 64652 | 71486 | 64695 |
| 508 108 | **MY** | A | *ME* | BD | 64656 | 71490 | 64699 |
| 508 111 | **AL** | A | *ME* | BD | 64659 | 71493 | 64702 |
| 508 112 | **MY** | A | *ME* | BD | 64660 | 71494 | 64703 |
| 508 114 | **MY** | A | *ME* | BD | 64662 | 71496 | 64705 |
| 508 115 | **MY** | A | *ME* | BD | 64663 | 71497 | 64706 |
| 508 117 | **MY** | A | *ME* | BD | 64665 | 71499 | 64708 |
| 508 120 | **MY** | A | *ME* | BD | 64668 | 71502 | 64711 |
| 508 122 | **MY** | A | *ME* | BD | 64670 | 71504 | 64713 |
| 508 123 | **MY** | A | *ME* | BD | 64671 | 71505 | 64714 |
| 508 124 | **MY** | A | *ME* | BD | 64672 | 71506 | 64715 |
| 508 125 | **MY** | A | *ME* | BD | 64673 | 71507 | 64716 |
| 508 126 | **MY** | A | *ME* | BD | 64674 | 71508 | 64717 |
| 508 127 | **MY** | A | *ME* | BD | 64675 | 71509 | 64718 |
| 508 128 | **MY** | A | *ME* | BD | 64676 | 71510 | 64719 |
| 508 130 | **MY** | A | *ME* | BD | 64678 | 71512 | 64721 |
| 508 131 | **MY** | A | *ME* | BD | 64679 | 71513 | 64722 |
| 508 136 | **MY** | A | *ME* | BD | 64684 | 71518 | 64727 |
| 508 137 | **MY** | A | *ME* | BD | 64685 | 71519 | 64728 |

| 508 138 | **MY** | A | *ME* | BD | 64686 | 71520 | 64729 |
| 508 139 | **MY** | A | *ME* | BD | 64687 | 71521 | 64730 |
| 508 140 | **MY** | A | *ME* | BD | 64688 | 71522 | 64731 |
| 508 141 | **MY** | A | *ME* | BD | 64689 | 71523 | 64732 |
| 508 143 | **MY** | A | *ME* | BD | 64691 | 71525 | 64734 |

**Names:**

| 508 111 | The Beatles | 508 136 | Wilfred Owen MC |
| 508 123 | William Roscoe | | |

# 4.3. DUAL VOLTAGE OR 25 kV AC OVERHEAD UNITS

The Class 7xx series is being used for some new-build EMUs built from 2014 onwards as freight wagons take up many of the remaining potential Class 3xx series'.

| **CLASS 700** | **DESIRO CITY** | **SIEMENS** |

The Class 700s are the large new fleet of EMUs for Govia Thameslink, entering service between 2016 and 2018. The units are financed by Cross London Trains (a consortium of Siemens Project Ventures, Innisfree Ltd and 3i Infrastructure Ltd).

**Formation (8-car):** DMC–PTS–MS–TS–TS–MS–PTS–DMC or
**(12-car):** DMC–PTS–MS–MS–TS–TS–TS–TS–MS–MS–PTS–DMC.
**Systems:** 25 kV AC overhead/750 V DC third rail.
**Construction:** Aluminium.
**Traction Motors:** Four Siemens asynchronous of 200 kW.
**Wheel Arrangement (8-car):** Bo-Bo + 2-2 + Bo-Bo + 2-2 + 2-2 + Bo-Bo + 2-2 + Bo-Bo. **(12-car):** Bo-Bo + 2-2 + Bo-Bo + Bo-Bo + 2-2 + 2-2 + 2-2 + 2-2 + Bo-Bo + Bo-Bo + 2-2 + Bo-Bo.
**Braking:** Disc, tread & regenerative. **Dimensions:** 20.52/20.16 m x 2.80 m.
**Bogies:** Siemens SF7000 inside-frame. **Couplers:** Dellner 12.
**Gangways:** Within unit.                **Control System:** IGBT Inverter.
**Doors:** Sliding plug.                   **Maximum Speed:** 100 mph.
**Heating & ventilation:** Air conditioning.
**Seating Layout:** 2+2 facing/unidirectional.
**Multiple Working:** Within class and with Classes 707 and 717.

**Class 700/0.** 8-car units.

**DMC(A).** Siemens Krefeld 2014–18. 26/16(+3). 38.5 t.
**PTS.** Siemens Krefeld 2014–18. –/54 1T. 33.1 t.
**MS.** Siemens Krefeld 2014–18. –/64. 36.2 t.
**TS.** Siemens Krefeld 2014–18. –/56(+3). 28.7 t.
**TS(W).** Siemens Krefeld 2014–18. –/40(+8) 1TD 2W. 29.1 t.
**MS.** Siemens Krefeld 2014–18. –/64. 36.2 t.
**PTS.** Siemens Krefeld 2014–18. –/54 1T. 33.2 t.
**DMC(B).** Siemens Krefeld 2014–18. 26/16(+3). 38.5 t.

| 700001 | **TL** CT *TL* TB | 401001 | 402001 | 403001 | 406001 |
| | | 407001 | 410001 | 411001 | 412001 |
| 700002 | **TL** CT *TL* TB | 401002 | 402002 | 403002 | 406002 |
| | | 407002 | 410002 | 411002 | 412002 |
| 700003 | **TL** CT *TL* TB | 401003 | 402003 | 403003 | 406003 |
| | | 407003 | 410003 | 411003 | 412003 |
| 700004 | **TL** CT *TL* TB | 401004 | 402004 | 403004 | 406004 |
| | | 407004 | 410004 | 411004 | 412004 |
| 700005 | **TL** CT *TL* TB | 401005 | 402005 | 403005 | 406005 |
| | | 407005 | 410005 | 411005 | 412005 |
| 700006 | **TL** CT *TL* TB | 401006 | 402006 | 403006 | 406006 |
| | | 407006 | 410006 | 411006 | 412006 |
| 700007 | **TL** CT *TL* TB | 401007 | 402007 | 403007 | 406007 |
| | | 407007 | 410007 | 411007 | 412007 |
| 700008 | **TL** CT *TL* TB | 401008 | 402008 | 403008 | 406008 |
| | | 407008 | 410008 | 411008 | 412008 |
| 700009 | **TL** CT *TL* TB | 401009 | 402009 | 403009 | 406009 |
| | | 407009 | 410009 | 411009 | 412009 |
| 700010 | **TL** CT *TL* TB | 401010 | 402010 | 403010 | 406010 |
| | | 407010 | 410010 | 411010 | 412010 |
| 700011 | **TL** CT *TL* TB | 401011 | 402011 | 403011 | 406011 |
| | | 407011 | 410011 | 411011 | 412011 |
| 700012 | **TL** CT *TL* TB | 401012 | 402012 | 403012 | 406012 |
| | | 407012 | 410012 | 411012 | 412012 |
| 700013 | **TL** CT *TL* TB | 401013 | 402013 | 403013 | 406013 |
| | | 407013 | 410013 | 411013 | 412013 |
| 700014 | **TL** CT *TL* TB | 401014 | 402014 | 403014 | 406014 |
| | | 407014 | 410014 | 411014 | 412014 |
| 700015 | **TL** CT *TL* TB | 401015 | 402015 | 403015 | 406015 |
| | | 407015 | 410015 | 411015 | 412015 |
| 700016 | **TL** CT *TL* TB | 401016 | 402016 | 403016 | 406016 |
| | | 407016 | 410016 | 411016 | 412016 |
| 700017 | **TL** CT *TL* TB | 401017 | 402017 | 403017 | 406017 |
| | | 407017 | 410017 | 411017 | 412017 |
| 700018 | **TL** CT *TL* TB | 401018 | 402018 | 403018 | 406018 |
| | | 407018 | 410018 | 411018 | 412018 |
| 700019 | **TL** CT *TL* TB | 401019 | 402019 | 403019 | 406019 |
| | | 407019 | 410019 | 411019 | 412019 |
| 700020 | **TL** CT *TL* TB | 401020 | 402020 | 403020 | 406020 |
| | | 407020 | 410020 | 411020 | 412020 |
| 700021 | **TL** CT *TL* TB | 401021 | 402021 | 403021 | 406021 |
| | | 407021 | 410021 | 411021 | 412021 |
| 700022 | **TL** CT *TL* TB | 401022 | 402022 | 403022 | 406022 |
| | | 407022 | 410022 | 411022 | 412022 |
| 700023 | **TL** CT *TL* TB | 401023 | 402023 | 403023 | 406023 |
| | | 407023 | 410023 | 411023 | 412023 |
| 700024 | **TL** CT *TL* TB | 401024 | 402024 | 403024 | 406024 |
| | | 407024 | 410024 | 411024 | 412024 |
| 700025 | **TL** CT *TL* TB | 401025 | 402025 | 403025 | 406025 |
| | | 407025 | 410025 | 411025 | 412025 |

| | | | | | | | | |
|---|---|---|---|---|---|---|---|---|
| 700 026 | **TL** | CT | *TL* | TB | 401026 | 402026 | 403026 | 406026 |
| | | | | | 407026 | 410026 | 411026 | 412026 |
| 700 027 | **TL** | CT | *TL* | TB | 401027 | 402027 | 403027 | 406027 |
| | | | | | 407027 | 410027 | 411027 | 412027 |
| 700 028 | **TL** | CT | *TL* | TB | 401028 | 402028 | 403028 | 406028 |
| | | | | | 407028 | 410028 | 411028 | 412028 |
| 700 029 | **TL** | CT | *TL* | TB | 401029 | 402029 | 403029 | 406029 |
| | | | | | 407029 | 410029 | 411029 | 412029 |
| 700 030 | **TL** | CT | *TL* | TB | 401030 | 402030 | 403030 | 406030 |
| | | | | | 407030 | 410030 | 411030 | 412030 |
| 700 031 | **TL** | CT | *TL* | TB | 401031 | 402031 | 403031 | 406031 |
| | | | | | 407031 | 410031 | 411031 | 412031 |
| 700 032 | **TL** | CT | *TL* | TB | 401032 | 402032 | 403032 | 406032 |
| | | | | | 407032 | 410032 | 411032 | 412032 |
| 700 033 | **TL** | CT | *TL* | TB | 401033 | 402033 | 403033 | 406033 |
| | | | | | 407033 | 410033 | 411033 | 412033 |
| 700 034 | **TL** | CT | *TL* | TB | 401034 | 402034 | 403034 | 406034 |
| | | | | | 407034 | 410034 | 411034 | 412034 |
| 700 035 | **TL** | CT | *TL* | TB | 401035 | 402035 | 403035 | 406035 |
| | | | | | 407035 | 410035 | 411035 | 412035 |
| 700 036 | **TL** | CT | *TL* | TB | 401036 | 402036 | 403036 | 406036 |
| | | | | | 407036 | 410036 | 411036 | 412036 |
| 700 037 | **TL** | CT | *TL* | TB | 401037 | 402037 | 403037 | 406037 |
| | | | | | 407037 | 410037 | 411037 | 412037 |
| 700 038 | **TL** | CT | *TL* | TB | 401038 | 402038 | 403038 | 406038 |
| | | | | | 407038 | 410038 | 411038 | 412038 |
| 700 039 | **TL** | CT | *TL* | TB | 401039 | 402039 | 403039 | 406039 |
| | | | | | 407039 | 410039 | 411039 | 412039 |
| 700 040 | **TL** | CT | *TL* | TB | 401040 | 402040 | 403040 | 406040 |
| | | | | | 407040 | 410040 | 411040 | 412040 |
| 700 041 | **TL** | CT | *TL* | TB | 401041 | 402041 | 403041 | 406041 |
| | | | | | 407041 | 410041 | 411041 | 412041 |
| 700 042 | **TL** | CT | *TL* | TB | 401042 | 402042 | 403042 | 406042 |
| | | | | | 407042 | 410042 | 411042 | 412042 |
| 700 043 | **TL** | CT | *TL* | TB | 401043 | 402043 | 403043 | 406043 |
| | | | | | 407043 | 410043 | 411043 | 412043 |
| 700 044 | **TL** | CT | *TL* | TB | 401044 | 402044 | 403044 | 406044 |
| | | | | | 407044 | 410044 | 411044 | 412044 |
| 700 045 | **TL** | CT | *TL* | TB | 401045 | 402045 | 403045 | 406045 |
| | | | | | 407045 | 410045 | 411045 | 412045 |
| 700 046 | **TL** | CT | *TL* | TB | 401046 | 402046 | 403046 | 406046 |
| | | | | | 407046 | 410046 | 411046 | 412046 |
| 700 047 | **TL** | CT | *TL* | TB | 401047 | 402047 | 403047 | 406047 |
| | | | | | 407047 | 410047 | 411047 | 412047 |
| 700 048 | **TL** | CT | *TL* | TB | 401048 | 402048 | 403048 | 406048 |
| | | | | | 407048 | 410048 | 411048 | 412048 |
| 700 049 | **TL** | CT | *TL* | TB | 401049 | 402049 | 403049 | 406049 |
| | | | | | 407049 | 410049 | 411049 | 412049 |
| 700 050 | **TL** | CT | *TL* | TB | 401050 | 402050 | 403050 | 406050 |
| | | | | | 407050 | 410050 | 411050 | 412050 |

| 700 051 | **TL** CT *TL* | TB | 401051 | 402051 | 403051 | 406051 |
| | | | 407051 | 410051 | 411051 | 412051 |
| 700 052 | **TL** CT *TL* | TB | 401052 | 402052 | 403052 | 406052 |
| | | | 407052 | 410052 | 411052 | 412052 |
| 700 053 | **TL** CT *TL* | TB | 401053 | 402053 | 403053 | 406053 |
| | | | 407053 | 410053 | 411053 | 412053 |
| 700 054 | **TL** CT *TL* | TB | 401054 | 402054 | 403054 | 406054 |
| | | | 407054 | 410054 | 411054 | 412054 |
| 700 055 | **TL** CT *TL* | TB | 401055 | 402055 | 403055 | 406055 |
| | | | 407055 | 410055 | 411055 | 412055 |
| 700 056 | **TL** CT *TL* | TB | 401056 | 402056 | 403056 | 406056 |
| | | | 407056 | 410056 | 411056 | 412056 |
| 700 057 | **TL** CT *TL* | TB | 401057 | 402057 | 403057 | 406057 |
| | | | 407057 | 410057 | 411057 | 412057 |
| 700 058 | **TL** CT *TL* | TB | 401058 | 402058 | 403058 | 406058 |
| | | | 407058 | 410058 | 411058 | 412058 |
| 700 059 | **TL** CT *TL* | TB | 401059 | 402059 | 403059 | 406059 |
| | | | 407059 | 410059 | 411059 | 412059 |
| 700 060 | **TL** CT *TL* | TB | 401060 | 402060 | 403060 | 406060 |
| | | | 407060 | 410060 | 411060 | 412060 |

**Class 700/1.** 12-car units.

**DMC(A).** Siemens Krefeld 2013–18. 26/20. 38.2 t.
**PTS.** Siemens Krefeld 2013–18. –/54 1T. 34.4 t.
**MS.** Siemens Krefeld 2013–18. –/60(+3). 36.0 t.
**MS.** Siemens Krefeld 2013–18. –/56 1T. 35.8 t.
**TS.** Siemens Krefeld 2013–18. –/64. 26.8 t.
**TS.** Siemens Krefeld 2013–18. –/56(+3). 28.3 t.
**TS(W).** Siemens Krefeld 2013–18. –/38(+9) 1TD 2W. 28.7 t.
**TS.** Siemens Krefeld 2013–18. –/64. 27.9 t.
**MS.** Siemens Krefeld 2013–18. –/56 1T. 35.6 t.
**MS.** Siemens Krefeld 2013–18. –/60(+3). 35.3 t.
**PTS.** Siemens Krefeld 2013–18. –/54 1T. 34.4 t.
**DMC(B).** Siemens Krefeld 2013–18. 26/20. 38.2 t.

| 700 101 | **TL** CT *TL* | TB | 401101 402101 403101 404101 405101 406101 |
| | | | 407101 408101 409101 410101 411101 412101 |
| 700 102 | **TL** CT *TL* | TB | 401102 402102 403102 404102 405102 406102 |
| | | | 407102 408102 409102 410102 411102 412102 |
| 700 103 | **TL** CT *TL* | TB | 401103 402103 403103 404103 405103 406103 |
| | | | 407103 408103 409103 410103 411103 412103 |
| 700 104 | **TL** CT *TL* | TB | 401104 402104 403104 404104 405104 406104 |
| | | | 407104 408104 409104 410104 411104 412104 |
| 700 105 | **TL** CT *TL* | TB | 401105 402105 403105 404105 405105 406105 |
| | | | 407105 408105 409105 410105 411105 412105 |
| 700 106 | **TL** CT *TL* | TB | 401106 402106 403106 404106 405106 406106 |
| | | | 407106 408106 409106 410106 411106 412106 |
| 700 107 | **TL** CT *TL* | TB | 401107 402107 403107 404107 405107 406107 |
| | | | 407107 408107 409107 410107 411107 412107 |
| 700 108 | **TL** CT *TL* | TB | 401108 402108 403108 404108 405108 406108 |
| | | | 407108 408108 409108 410108 411108 412108 |

| | | | | | | | | | | |
|---|---|---|---|---|---|---|---|---|---|---|
| 700 109 | **TL** CT *TL* | TB | 401109 | 402109 | 403109 | 404109 | 405109 | 406109 | | |
| | | | 407109 | 408109 | 409109 | 410109 | 411109 | 412109 | | |
| 700 110 | **TL** CT *TL* | TB | 401110 | 402110 | 403110 | 404110 | 405110 | 406110 | | |
| | | | 407110 | 408110 | 409110 | 410110 | 411110 | 412110 | | |
| 700 111 | **TL** CT *TL* | TB | 401111 | 402111 | 403111 | 404111 | 405111 | 406111 | | |
| | | | 407111 | 408111 | 409111 | 410111 | 411111 | 412111 | | |
| 700 112 | **TL** CT *TL* | TB | 401112 | 402112 | 403112 | 404112 | 405112 | 406112 | | |
| | | | 407112 | 408112 | 409112 | 410112 | 411112 | 412112 | | |
| 700 113 | **TL** CT *TL* | TB | 401113 | 402113 | 403113 | 404113 | 405113 | 406113 | | |
| | | | 407113 | 408113 | 409113 | 410113 | 411113 | 412113 | | |
| 700 114 | **TL** CT *TL* | TB | 401114 | 402114 | 403114 | 404114 | 405114 | 406114 | | |
| | | | 407114 | 408114 | 409114 | 410114 | 411114 | 412114 | | |
| 700 115 | **TL** CT *TL* | TB | 401115 | 402115 | 403115 | 404115 | 405115 | 406115 | | |
| | | | 407115 | 408115 | 409115 | 410115 | 411115 | 412115 | | |
| 700 116 | **TL** CT *TL* | TB | 401116 | 402116 | 403116 | 404116 | 405116 | 406116 | | |
| | | | 407116 | 408116 | 409116 | 410116 | 411116 | 412116 | | |
| 700 117 | **TL** CT *TL* | TB | 401117 | 402117 | 403117 | 404117 | 405117 | 406117 | | |
| | | | 407117 | 408117 | 409117 | 410117 | 411117 | 412117 | | |
| 700 118 | **TL** CT *TL* | TB | 401118 | 402118 | 403118 | 404118 | 405118 | 406118 | | |
| | | | 407118 | 408118 | 409118 | 410118 | 411118 | 412118 | | |
| 700 119 | **TL** CT *TL* | TB | 401119 | 402119 | 403119 | 404119 | 405119 | 406119 | | |
| | | | 407119 | 408119 | 409119 | 410119 | 411119 | 412119 | | |
| 700 120 | **TL** CT *TL* | TB | 401120 | 402120 | 403120 | 404120 | 405120 | 406120 | | |
| | | | 407120 | 408120 | 409120 | 410120 | 411120 | 412120 | | |
| 700 121 | **TL** CT *TL* | TB | 401121 | 402121 | 403121 | 404121 | 405121 | 406121 | | |
| | | | 407121 | 408121 | 409121 | 410121 | 411121 | 412121 | | |
| 700 122 | **TL** CT *TL* | TB | 401122 | 402122 | 403122 | 404122 | 405122 | 406122 | | |
| | | | 407122 | 408122 | 409122 | 410122 | 411122 | 412122 | | |
| 700 123 | **TL** CT *TL* | TB | 401123 | 402123 | 403123 | 404123 | 405123 | 406123 | | |
| | | | 407123 | 408123 | 409123 | 410123 | 411123 | 412123 | | |
| 700 124 | **TL** CT *TL* | TB | 401124 | 402124 | 403124 | 404124 | 405124 | 406124 | | |
| | | | 407124 | 408124 | 409124 | 410124 | 411124 | 412124 | | |
| 700 125 | **TL** CT *TL* | TB | 401125 | 402125 | 403125 | 404125 | 405125 | 406125 | | |
| | | | 407125 | 408125 | 409125 | 410125 | 411125 | 412125 | | |
| 700 126 | **TL** CT *TL* | TB | 401126 | 402126 | 403126 | 404126 | 405126 | 406126 | | |
| | | | 407126 | 408126 | 409126 | 410126 | 411126 | 412126 | | |
| 700 127 | **TL** CT *TL* | TB | 401127 | 402127 | 403127 | 404127 | 405127 | 406127 | | |
| | | | 407127 | 408127 | 409127 | 410127 | 411127 | 412127 | | |
| 700 128 | **TL** CT *TL* | TB | 401128 | 402128 | 403128 | 404128 | 405128 | 406128 | | |
| | | | 407128 | 408128 | 409128 | 410128 | 411128 | 412128 | | |
| 700 129 | **TL** CT *TL* | TB | 401129 | 402129 | 403129 | 404129 | 405129 | 406129 | | |
| | | | 407129 | 408129 | 409129 | 410129 | 411129 | 412129 | | |
| 700 130 | **TL** CT *TL* | TB | 401130 | 402130 | 403130 | 404130 | 405130 | 406130 | | |
| | | | 407130 | 408130 | 409130 | 410130 | 411130 | 412130 | | |
| 700 131 | **TL** CT *TL* | TB | 401131 | 402131 | 403131 | 404131 | 405131 | 406131 | | |
| | | | 407131 | 408131 | 409131 | 410131 | 411131 | 412131 | | |
| 700 132 | **TL** CT *TL* | TB | 401132 | 402132 | 403132 | 404132 | 405132 | 406132 | | |
| | | | 407132 | 408132 | 409132 | 410132 | 411132 | 412132 | | |
| 700 133 | **TL** CT *TL* | TB | 401133 | 402133 | 403133 | 404133 | 405133 | 406133 | | |
| | | | 407133 | 408133 | 409133 | 410133 | 411133 | 412133 | | |

| | | | | | | | | | | |
|---|---|---|---|---|---|---|---|---|---|---|
| 700 134 | **TL** CT *TL* | TB | 401134 | 402134 | 403134 | 404134 | 405134 | 406134 | | |
| | | | 407134 | 408134 | 409134 | 410134 | 411134 | 412134 | | |
| 700 135 | **TL** CT *TL* | TB | 401135 | 402135 | 403135 | 404135 | 405135 | 406135 | | |
| | | | 407135 | 408135 | 409135 | 410135 | 411135 | 412135 | | |
| 700 136 | **TL** CT *TL* | TB | 401136 | 402136 | 403136 | 404136 | 405136 | 406136 | | |
| | | | 407136 | 408136 | 409136 | 410136 | 411136 | 412136 | | |
| 700 137 | **TL** CT *TL* | TB | 401137 | 402137 | 403137 | 404137 | 405137 | 406137 | | |
| | | | 407137 | 408137 | 409137 | 410137 | 411137 | 412137 | | |
| 700 138 | **TL** CT *TL* | TB | 401138 | 402138 | 403138 | 404138 | 405138 | 406138 | | |
| | | | 407138 | 408138 | 409138 | 410138 | 411138 | 412138 | | |
| 700 139 | **TL** CT *TL* | TB | 401139 | 402139 | 403139 | 404139 | 405139 | 406139 | | |
| | | | 407139 | 408139 | 409139 | 410139 | 411139 | 412139 | | |
| 700 140 | **TL** CT *TL* | TB | 401140 | 402140 | 403140 | 404140 | 405140 | 406140 | | |
| | | | 407140 | 408140 | 409140 | 410140 | 411140 | 412140 | | |
| 700 141 | **TL** CT *TL* | TB | 401141 | 402141 | 403141 | 404141 | 405141 | 406141 | | |
| | | | 407141 | 408141 | 409141 | 410141 | 411141 | 412141 | | |
| 700 142 | **TL** CT *TL* | TB | 401142 | 402142 | 403142 | 404142 | 405142 | 406142 | | |
| | | | 407142 | 408142 | 409142 | 410142 | 411142 | 412142 | | |
| 700 143 | **TL** CT *TL* | TB | 401143 | 402143 | 403143 | 404143 | 405143 | 406143 | | |
| | | | 407143 | 408143 | 409143 | 410143 | 411143 | 412143 | | |
| 700 144 | **TL** CT *TL* | TB | 401144 | 402144 | 403144 | 404144 | 405144 | 406144 | | |
| | | | 407144 | 408144 | 409144 | 410144 | 411144 | 412144 | | |
| 700 145 | **TL** CT *TL* | TB | 401145 | 402145 | 403145 | 404145 | 405145 | 406145 | | |
| | | | 407145 | 408145 | 409145 | 410145 | 411145 | 412145 | | |
| 700 146 | **TL** CT *TL* | TB | 401146 | 402146 | 403146 | 404146 | 405146 | 406146 | | |
| | | | 407146 | 408146 | 409146 | 410146 | 411146 | 412146 | | |
| 700 147 | **TL** CT *TL* | TB | 401147 | 402147 | 403147 | 404147 | 405147 | 406147 | | |
| | | | 407147 | 408147 | 409147 | 410147 | 411147 | 412147 | | |
| 700 148 | **TL** CT *TL* | TB | 401148 | 402148 | 403148 | 404148 | 405148 | 406148 | | |
| | | | 407148 | 408148 | 409148 | 410148 | 411148 | 412148 | | |
| 700 149 | **TL** CT *TL* | TB | 401149 | 402149 | 403149 | 404149 | 405149 | 406149 | | |
| | | | 407149 | 408149 | 409149 | 410149 | 411149 | 412149 | | |
| 700 150 | **TL** CT *TL* | TB | 401150 | 402150 | 403150 | 404150 | 405150 | 406150 | | |
| | | | 407150 | 408150 | 409150 | 410150 | 411150 | 412150 | | |
| 700 151 | **TL** CT *TL* | TB | 401151 | 402151 | 403151 | 404151 | 405151 | 406151 | | |
| | | | 407151 | 408151 | 409151 | 410151 | 411151 | 412151 | | |
| 700 152 | **TL** CT *TL* | TB | 401152 | 402152 | 403152 | 404152 | 405152 | 406152 | | |
| | | | 407152 | 408152 | 409152 | 410152 | 411152 | 412152 | | |
| 700 153 | **TL** CT *TL* | TB | 401153 | 402153 | 403153 | 404153 | 405153 | 406153 | | |
| | | | 407153 | 408153 | 409153 | 410153 | 411153 | 412153 | | |
| 700 154 | **TL** CT *TL* | TB | 401154 | 402154 | 403154 | 404154 | 405154 | 406154 | | |
| | | | 407154 | 408154 | 409154 | 410154 | 411154 | 412154 | | |
| 700 155 | **TL** CT *TL* | TB | 401155 | 402155 | 403155 | 404155 | 405155 | 406155 | | |
| | | | 407155 | 408155 | 409155 | 410155 | 411155 | 412155 | | |

# CLASS 701        AVENTRA    BOMBARDIER DERBY

South Western Railway has 60 10-car and 30 5-car Aventra EMUs on order from Bombardier, financed by Rock Rail. The first units have been delivered for testing and they are due to enter service in 2021–22. The units have been branded "Arterio" by SWR and will be used mainly on inner and outer suburban duties, replacing Classes 455, 456, 458 and 707.

**Formation (10-car):** DMS–MS–TS–MS–MS–MS–MS–TS–MS–DMS or
**(5-car):** DMS–MS–TS–MS–DMS.
**Systems:** 750 V DC third rail.
**Construction:** Aluminium.
**Traction Motors:** Two Bombardier asynchronous of 250 kW.
**Wheel Arrangement (10-car):** 2-Bo + Bo-2 + 2-2 + 2-Bo + Bo-2 + 2-Bo + Bo-2 + 2-2 + 2-Bo + Bo-2 or (5-car): 2-Bo + Bo-2 + 2-2 + 2-Bo + Bo-2.
**Braking:** Disc, rheostatic & regenerative.
**Dimensions:** 20.88/19.90 m x 2.78 m.
**Bogies:** FLEXX B5000 inside-frame.  **Couplers:** Dellner 12.
**Gangways:** Within unit.            **Control System:** IGBT Inverter.
**Doors:** Sliding plug.              **Maximum Speed:** 100 mph.
**Heating & ventilation:** Air conditioning.
**Seating Layout:** 2+2 unidirectional/facing.
**Multiple Working:** Within class.

**Class 701/0.** 10-car units.

**DMS(A).** Bombardier Derby 2020–21. –/56.      t.
**MS.** Bombardier Derby 2020–21. –/60.      t.
**TS.** Bombardier Derby 2020–21. –/34(+10) 1TD 2W.      t.
**MS.** Bombardier Derby 2020–21. –/60.      t.
**MS.** Bombardier Derby 2020–21. –/60.      t.
**MS.** Bombardier Derby 2020–21. –/60.      t.
**MS.** Bombardier Derby 2020–21. –/60.      t.
**TS.** Bombardier Derby 2020–21. –/34(+10) 1TD 2W.      t.
**MS.** Bombardier Derby 2020–21. –/60.      t.
**DMS(B).** Bombardier Derby 2020–21. –/56.      t.

| | | | | | | | |
|---|---|---|---|---|---|---|---|
| 701001 | **SW** | RR | 480001 | 481001 | 482001 | 483001 | 484001 |
| | | | 485001 | 486001 | 487001 | 488001 | 489001 |
| 701002 | **SW** | RR | 480002 | 481002 | 482002 | 483002 | 484002 |
| | | | 485002 | 486002 | 487002 | 488002 | 489002 |
| 701003 | **SW** | RR | 480003 | 481003 | 482003 | 483003 | 484003 |
| | | | 485003 | 486003 | 487003 | 488003 | 489003 |
| 701004 | **SW** | RR | 480004 | 481004 | 482004 | 483004 | 484004 |
| | | | 485004 | 486004 | 487004 | 488004 | 489004 |
| 701005 | **SW** | RR | 480005 | 481005 | 482005 | 483005 | 484005 |
| | | | 485005 | 486005 | 487005 | 488005 | 489005 |
| 701006 | **SW** | RR | 480006 | 481006 | 482006 | 483006 | 484006 |
| | | | 485006 | 486006 | 487006 | 488006 | 489006 |
| 701007 | **SW** | RR | 480007 | 481007 | 482007 | 483007 | 484007 |
| | | | 485007 | 486007 | 487007 | 488007 | 489007 |

| | | | | | | | |
|---|---|---|---|---|---|---|---|
| 701 008 | **SW** RR | 480008 | 481008 | 482008 | 483008 | 484008 |
| | | 485008 | 486008 | 487008 | 488008 | 489008 |
| 701 009 | **SW** RR | 480009 | 481009 | 482009 | 483009 | 484009 |
| | | 485009 | 486009 | 487009 | 488009 | 489009 |
| 701 010 | **SW** RR | 480010 | 481010 | 482010 | 483010 | 484010 |
| | | 485010 | 486010 | 487010 | 488010 | 489010 |
| 701 011 | **SW** RR | 480011 | 481011 | 482011 | 483011 | 484011 |
| | | 485011 | 486011 | 487011 | 488011 | 489011 |
| 701 012 | **SW** RR | 480012 | 481012 | 482012 | 483012 | 484012 |
| | | 485012 | 486012 | 487012 | 488012 | 489012 |
| 701 013 | **SW** RR | 480013 | 481013 | 482013 | 483013 | 484013 |
| | | 485013 | 486013 | 487013 | 488013 | 489013 |
| 701 014 | **SW** RR | 480014 | 481014 | 482014 | 483014 | 484014 |
| | | 485014 | 486014 | 487014 | 488014 | 489014 |
| 701 015 | **SW** RR | 480015 | 481015 | 482015 | 483015 | 484015 |
| | | 485015 | 486015 | 487015 | 488015 | 489015 |
| 701 016 | **SW** RR | 480016 | 481016 | 482016 | 483016 | 484016 |
| | | 485016 | 486016 | 487016 | 488016 | 489016 |
| 701 017 | **SW** RR | 480017 | 481017 | 482017 | 483017 | 484017 |
| | | 485017 | 486017 | 487017 | 488017 | 489017 |
| 701 018 | **SW** RR | 480018 | 481018 | 482018 | 483018 | 484018 |
| | | 485018 | 486018 | 487018 | 488018 | 489018 |
| 701 019 | **SW** RR | 480019 | 481019 | 482019 | 483019 | 484019 |
| | | 485019 | 486019 | 487019 | 488019 | 489019 |
| 701 020 | **SW** RR | 480020 | 481020 | 482020 | 483020 | 484020 |
| | | 485020 | 486020 | 487020 | 488020 | 489020 |
| 701 021 | **SW** RR | 480021 | 481021 | 482021 | 483021 | 484021 |
| | | 485021 | 486021 | 487021 | 488021 | 489021 |
| 701 022 | **SW** RR | 480022 | 481022 | 482022 | 483022 | 484022 |
| | | 485022 | 486022 | 487022 | 488022 | 489022 |
| 701 023 | **SW** RR | 480023 | 481023 | 482023 | 483023 | 484023 |
| | | 485023 | 486023 | 487023 | 488023 | 489023 |
| 701 024 | **SW** RR | 480024 | 481024 | 482024 | 483024 | 484024 |
| | | 485024 | 486024 | 487024 | 488024 | 489024 |
| 701 025 | **SW** RR | 480025 | 481025 | 482025 | 483025 | 484025 |
| | | 485025 | 486025 | 487025 | 488025 | 489025 |
| 701 026 | **SW** RR | 480026 | 481026 | 482026 | 483026 | 484026 |
| | | 485026 | 486026 | 487026 | 488026 | 489026 |
| 701 027 | **SW** RR | 480027 | 481027 | 482027 | 483027 | 484027 |
| | | 485027 | 486027 | 487027 | 488027 | 489027 |
| 701 028 | **SW** RR | 480028 | 481028 | 482028 | 483028 | 484028 |
| | | 485028 | 486028 | 487028 | 488028 | 489028 |
| 701 029 | **SW** RR | 480029 | 481029 | 482029 | 483029 | 484029 |
| | | 485029 | 486029 | 487029 | 488029 | 489029 |
| 701 030 | **SW** RR | 480030 | 481030 | 482030 | 483030 | 484030 |
| | | 485030 | 486030 | 487030 | 488030 | 489030 |
| 701 031 | **SW** RR | 480031 | 481031 | 482031 | 483031 | 484031 |
| | | 485031 | 486031 | 487031 | 488031 | 489031 |
| 701 032 | **SW** RR | 480032 | 481032 | 482032 | 483032 | 484032 |
| | | 485032 | 486032 | 487032 | 488032 | 489032 |

| | | | | | | | |
|---|---|---|---|---|---|---|---|
| 701033 | **SW** RR | 480033 | 481033 | 482033 | 483033 | 484033 |
| | | 485033 | 486033 | 487033 | 488033 | 489033 |
| 701034 | **SW** RR | 480034 | 481034 | 482034 | 483034 | 484034 |
| | | 485034 | 486034 | 487034 | 488034 | 489034 |
| 701035 | **SW** RR | 480035 | 481035 | 482035 | 483035 | 484035 |
| | | 485035 | 486035 | 487035 | 488035 | 489035 |
| 701036 | **SW** RR | 480036 | 481036 | 482036 | 483036 | 484036 |
| | | 485036 | 486036 | 487036 | 488036 | 489036 |
| 701037 | **SW** RR | 480037 | 481037 | 482037 | 483037 | 484037 |
| | | 485037 | 486037 | 487037 | 488037 | 489037 |
| 701038 | **SW** RR | 480038 | 481038 | 482038 | 483038 | 484038 |
| | | 485038 | 486038 | 487038 | 488038 | 489038 |
| 701039 | **SW** RR | 480039 | 481039 | 482039 | 483039 | 484039 |
| | | 485039 | 486039 | 487039 | 488039 | 489039 |
| 701040 | **SW** RR | 480040 | 481040 | 482040 | 483040 | 484040 |
| | | 485040 | 486040 | 487040 | 488040 | 489040 |
| 701041 | **SW** RR | 480041 | 481041 | 482041 | 483041 | 484041 |
| | | 485041 | 486041 | 487041 | 488041 | 489041 |
| 701042 | **SW** RR | 480042 | 481042 | 482042 | 483042 | 484042 |
| | | 485042 | 486042 | 487042 | 488042 | 489042 |
| 701043 | **SW** RR | 480043 | 481043 | 482043 | 483043 | 484043 |
| | | 485043 | 486043 | 487043 | 488043 | 489043 |
| 701044 | **SW** RR | 480044 | 481044 | 482044 | 483044 | 484044 |
| | | 485044 | 486044 | 487044 | 488044 | 489044 |
| 701045 | **SW** RR | 480045 | 481045 | 482045 | 483045 | 484045 |
| | | 485045 | 486045 | 487045 | 488045 | 489045 |
| 701046 | **SW** RR | 480046 | 481046 | 482046 | 483046 | 484046 |
| | | 485046 | 486046 | 487046 | 488046 | 489046 |
| 701047 | **SW** RR | 480047 | 481047 | 482047 | 483047 | 484047 |
| | | 485047 | 486047 | 487047 | 488047 | 489047 |
| 701048 | **SW** RR | 480048 | 481048 | 482048 | 483048 | 484048 |
| | | 485048 | 486048 | 487048 | 488048 | 489048 |
| 701049 | **SW** RR | 480049 | 481049 | 482049 | 483049 | 484049 |
| | | 485049 | 486049 | 487049 | 488049 | 489049 |
| 701050 | **SW** RR | 480050 | 481050 | 482050 | 483050 | 484050 |
| | | 485050 | 486050 | 487050 | 488050 | 489050 |
| 701051 | **SW** RR | 480051 | 481051 | 482051 | 483051 | 484051 |
| | | 485051 | 486051 | 487051 | 488051 | 489051 |
| 701052 | **SW** RR | 480052 | 481052 | 482052 | 483052 | 484052 |
| | | 485052 | 486052 | 487052 | 488052 | 489052 |
| 701053 | **SW** RR | 480053 | 481053 | 482053 | 483053 | 484053 |
| | | 485053 | 486053 | 487053 | 488053 | 489053 |
| 701054 | **SW** RR | 480054 | 481054 | 482054 | 483054 | 484054 |
| | | 485054 | 486054 | 487054 | 488054 | 489054 |
| 701055 | **SW** RR | 480055 | 481055 | 482055 | 483055 | 484055 |
| | | 485055 | 486055 | 487055 | 488055 | 489055 |
| 701056 | **SW** RR | 480056 | 481056 | 482056 | 483056 | 484056 |
| | | 485056 | 486056 | 487056 | 488056 | 489056 |
| 701057 | **SW** RR | 480057 | 481057 | 482057 | 483057 | 484057 |
| | | 485057 | 486057 | 487057 | 488057 | 489057 |

| 701058 | **SW** RR | 480058 | 481058 | 482058 | 483058 | 484058 |
| | | 485058 | 486058 | 487058 | 488058 | 489058 |
| 701059 | **SW** RR | 480059 | 481059 | 482059 | 483059 | 484059 |
| | | 485059 | 486059 | 487059 | 488059 | 489059 |
| 701060 | **SW** RR | 480060 | 481060 | 482060 | 483060 | 484060 |
| | | 485060 | 486060 | 487060 | 488060 | 489060 |

**Class 701/5.** 5-car units.

**DMS(A).** Bombardier Derby 2020–21. –/56.          t.
**MS.** Bombardier Derby 2020–21. –/60.          t.
**TS.** Bombardier Derby 2020–21. –/34(+10) 1TD 2W.          t.
**MS.** Bombardier Derby 2020–21. –/60.          t.
**DMS(B).** Bombardier Derby 2020–21. –/56.          t.

| 701501 | **SW** RR | 480101 | 481101 | 482101 | 483101 | 484101 |
| 701502 | **SW** RR | 480102 | 481102 | 482102 | 483102 | 484102 |
| 701503 | **SW** RR | 480103 | 481103 | 482103 | 483103 | 484103 |
| 701504 | **SW** RR | 480104 | 481104 | 482104 | 483104 | 484104 |
| 701505 | **SW** RR | 480105 | 481105 | 482105 | 483105 | 484105 |
| 701506 | **SW** RR | 480106 | 481106 | 482106 | 483106 | 484106 |
| 701507 | **SW** RR | 480107 | 481107 | 482107 | 483107 | 484107 |
| 701508 | **SW** RR | 480108 | 481108 | 482108 | 483108 | 484108 |
| 701509 | **SW** RR | 480109 | 481109 | 482109 | 483109 | 484109 |
| 701510 | **SW** RR | 480110 | 481110 | 482110 | 483110 | 484110 |
| 701511 | **SW** RR | 480111 | 481111 | 482111 | 483111 | 484111 |
| 701512 | **SW** RR | 480112 | 481112 | 482112 | 483112 | 484112 |
| 701513 | **SW** RR | 480113 | 481113 | 482113 | 483113 | 484113 |
| 701514 | **SW** RR | 480114 | 481114 | 482114 | 483114 | 484114 |
| 701515 | **SW** RR | 480115 | 481115 | 482115 | 483115 | 484115 |
| 701516 | **SW** RR | 480116 | 481116 | 482116 | 483116 | 484116 |
| 701517 | **SW** RR | 480117 | 481117 | 482117 | 483117 | 484117 |
| 701518 | **SW** RR | 480118 | 481118 | 482118 | 483118 | 484118 |
| 701519 | **SW** RR | 480119 | 481119 | 482119 | 483119 | 484119 |
| 701520 | **SW** RR | 480120 | 481120 | 482120 | 483120 | 484120 |
| 701521 | **SW** RR | 480121 | 481121 | 482121 | 483121 | 484121 |
| 701522 | **SW** RR | 480122 | 481122 | 482122 | 483122 | 484122 |
| 701523 | **SW** RR | 480123 | 481123 | 482123 | 483123 | 484123 |
| 701524 | **SW** RR | 480124 | 481124 | 482124 | 483124 | 484124 |
| 701525 | **SW** RR | 480125 | 481125 | 482125 | 483125 | 484125 |
| 701526 | **SW** RR | 480126 | 481126 | 482126 | 483126 | 484126 |
| 701527 | **SW** RR | 480127 | 481127 | 482127 | 483127 | 484127 |
| 701528 | **SW** RR | 480128 | 481128 | 482128 | 483128 | 484128 |
| 701529 | **SW** RR | 480129 | 481129 | 482129 | 483129 | 484129 |
| 701530 | **SW** RR | 480130 | 481130 | 482130 | 483130 | 484130 |

# CLASS 707          DESIRO CITY          SIEMENS

South Western Railway suburban units. Built with the capability to be easily converted to dual-voltage units. Due to transfer to Southeastern (on sub-lease from SWR) during 2021.

**Formation:** DMS–TS–TS–TS–DMS.
**Systems:** 750 V DC third rail but with 25 kV AC overhead capability.
**Construction:** Aluminium.
**Traction Motors:** Four Siemens asynchronous of 200 kW.
**Wheel Arrangement:** Bo-Bo + 2-2 + 2-2 + 2-2 + Bo-Bo.
**Braking:** Disc, tread & regenerative.   **Dimensions:** 20.00/20.16 m x 2.80 m.
**Bogies:** Siemens SF7000 inside-frame. **Couplers:** Dellner 12.
**Gangways:** Within unit.           **Control System:** IGBT Inverter.
**Doors:** Sliding plug.              **Maximum Speed:** 100 mph.
**Heating & ventilation:** Air conditioning.
**Seating Layout:** 2+2/2+1 facing/unidirectional.
**Multiple Working:** Within class and with Classes 700 and 717.

**DMS(A).** Siemens Krefeld 2015–17. –/46. 37.9 t.
**TS.** Siemens Krefeld 2015–17. –/64. 28.3 t.
**TS.** Siemens Krefeld 2015–17. –/53(+4) 2W. 28.5 t.
**TS.** Siemens Krefeld 2015–17. –/62. 27.7 t.
**DMS(B).** Siemens Krefeld 2015–17. –/46. 37.9 t.

| | | | | | | | | | |
|---|---|---|---|---|---|---|---|---|---|
| 707 001 | **SS** | A | *SW* | WD | 421001 | 422001 | 423001 | 424001 | 425001 |
| 707 002 | **SS** | A | *SW* | WD | 421002 | 422002 | 423002 | 424002 | 425002 |
| 707 003 | **SS** | A | *SW* | WD | 421003 | 422003 | 423003 | 424003 | 425003 |
| 707 004 | **SS** | A | *SW* | WD | 421004 | 422004 | 423004 | 424004 | 425004 |
| 707 005 | **SS** | A | *SW* | WD | 421005 | 422005 | 423005 | 424005 | 425005 |
| 707 006 | **SS** | A | *SW* | WD | 421006 | 422006 | 423006 | 424006 | 425006 |
| 707 007 | **SS** | A | *SW* | WD | 421007 | 422007 | 423007 | 424007 | 425007 |
| 707 008 | **SS** | A | *SW* | WD | 421008 | 422008 | 423008 | 424008 | 425008 |
| 707 009 | **SS** | A | *SW* | WD | 421009 | 422009 | 423009 | 424009 | 425009 |
| 707 010 | **SS** | A | *SW* | WD | 421010 | 422010 | 423010 | 424010 | 425010 |
| 707 011 | **SS** | A | *SW* | WD | 421011 | 422011 | 423011 | 424011 | 425011 |
| 707 012 | **SS** | A | *SW* | WD | 421012 | 422012 | 423012 | 424012 | 425012 |
| 707 013 | **SS** | A | *SW* | WD | 421013 | 422013 | 423013 | 424013 | 425013 |
| 707 014 | **SS** | A | *SW* | WD | 421014 | 422014 | 423014 | 424014 | 425014 |
| 707 015 | **SS** | A | *SW* | WD | 421015 | 422015 | 423015 | 424015 | 425015 |
| 707 016 | **SS** | A | *SW* | WD | 421016 | 422016 | 423016 | 424016 | 425016 |
| 707 017 | **SS** | A | *SW* | WD | 421017 | 422017 | 423017 | 424017 | 425017 |
| 707 018 | **SS** | A | *SW* | WD | 421018 | 422018 | 423018 | 424018 | 425018 |
| 707 019 | **SS** | A | *SW* | WD | 421019 | 422019 | 423019 | 424019 | 425019 |
| 707 020 | **SS** | A | *SW* | WD | 421020 | 422020 | 423020 | 424020 | 425020 |
| 707 021 | **SS** | A | *SW* | WD | 421021 | 422021 | 423021 | 424021 | 425021 |
| 707 022 | **SS** | A | *SW* | WD | 421022 | 422022 | 423022 | 424022 | 425022 |
| 707 023 | **SS** | A | *SW* | WD | 421023 | 422023 | 423023 | 424023 | 425023 |
| 707 024 | **SS** | A | *SW* | WD | 421024 | 422024 | 423024 | 424024 | 425024 |
| 707 025 | **SS** | A | *SW* | WD | 421025 | 422025 | 423025 | 424025 | 425025 |
| 707 026 | **SS** | A | *SW* | WD | 421026 | 422026 | 423026 | 424026 | 425026 |
| 707 027 | **SS** | A | *SW* | WD | 421027 | 422027 | 423027 | 424027 | 425027 |
| 707 028 | **SS** | A | *SW* | WD | 421028 | 422028 | 423028 | 424028 | 425028 |
| 707 029 | **SS** | A | *SW* | WD | 421029 | 422029 | 423029 | 424029 | 425029 |
| 707 030 | **SS** | A | *SW* | WD | 421030 | 422030 | 423030 | 424030 | 425030 |

# CLASS 710     AVENTRA    BOMBARDIER DERBY

These suburban 4-car Aventras are being used by London Overground on Gospel Oak–Barking, London Euston–Watford Junction and Liverpool Street local services. There are a mix of AC only and dual-voltage units.

Originally 45 4-car units were ordered. In 2018 an extra three 4-cars and six 5-cars were ordered.

**Formation:** DMS–MS–PMS–DMS or DMS–MS–PMS–MS–DMS.
**Systems:** Class 710/1 25 kV AC overhead only. Class 710/2 25 kV AC overhead and 750 V DC third rail.
**Construction:** Aluminium.
**Traction Motors:** Two Bombardier asynchronous of 265 kW.
**Wheel Arrangement:** Bo-2 + 2-Bo + Bo-2 (+ 2-Bo) + 2-Bo.
**Braking:** Disc & regenerative. **Dimensions:** 21.45/19.99 m x 2.78 m.
**Bogies:** FLEXX B5000 inside-frame. **Couplers:** Dellner 12.
**Gangways:** Within unit. **Control System:** IGBT Inverter.
**Doors:** Sliding plug. **Maximum Speed:** 75 mph.
**Heating & ventilation:** Air conditioning.
**Seating Layout:** Longitudinal ("tube style") low density.
**Multiple Working:** Within class.

**Class 710/1.** 25 kV AC only 4-car units.

**DMS(A).** Bombardier Derby 2017–19. –/40(+6).     t.
**MS.** Bombardier Derby 2017–19. –/46.     t.
**PMS.** Bombardier Derby 2017–19. –/45(+6) 2W.     t.
**DMS(B).** Bombardier Derby 2017–19. –/40(+6).     t.

| | | | | | | | |
|---|---|---|---|---|---|---|---|
| 710 101 | **LD** | RF | *LO* | WN | 431101 | 431201 | 431301 | 431501 |
| 710 102 | **LD** | RF | *LO* | WN | 431102 | 431202 | 431302 | 431502 |
| 710 103 | **LD** | RF | *LO* | WN | 431103 | 431203 | 431303 | 431503 |
| 710 104 | **LD** | RF | *LO* | WN | 431104 | 431204 | 431304 | 431504 |
| 710 105 | **LD** | RF | *LO* | WN | 431105 | 431205 | 431305 | 431505 |
| 710 106 | **LD** | RF | *LO* | WN | 431106 | 431206 | 431306 | 431506 |
| 710 107 | **LD** | RF | *LO* | WN | 431107 | 431207 | 431307 | 431507 |
| 710 108 | **LD** | RF | *LO* | WN | 431108 | 431208 | 431308 | 431508 |
| 710 109 | **LD** | RF | *LO* | WN | 431109 | 431209 | 431309 | 431509 |
| 710 110 | **LD** | RF | *LO* | WN | 431110 | 431210 | 431310 | 431510 |
| 710 111 | **LD** | RF | *LO* | WN | 431111 | 431211 | 431311 | 431511 |
| 710 112 | **LD** | RF | *LO* | WN | 431112 | 431212 | 431312 | 431512 |
| 710 113 | **LD** | RF | *LO* | WN | 431113 | 431213 | 431313 | 431513 |
| 710 114 | **LD** | RF | *LO* | WN | 431114 | 431214 | 431314 | 431514 |
| 710 115 | **LD** | RF | *LO* | WN | 431115 | 431215 | 431315 | 431515 |
| 710 116 | **LD** | RF | *LO* | WN | 431116 | 431216 | 431316 | 431516 |
| 710 117 | **LD** | RF | *LO* | WN | 431117 | 431217 | 431317 | 431517 |
| 710 118 | **LD** | RF | *LO* | WN | 431118 | 431218 | 431318 | 431518 |
| 710 119 | **LD** | RF | *LO* | WN | 431119 | 431219 | 431319 | 431519 |
| 710 120 | **LD** | RF | *LO* | WN | 431120 | 431220 | 431320 | 431520 |
| 710 121 | **LD** | RF | *LO* | WN | 431121 | 431221 | 431321 | 431521 |
| 710 122 | **LD** | RF | *LO* | WN | 431122 | 431222 | 431322 | 431522 |
| 710 123 | **LD** | RF | *LO* | WN | 431123 | 431223 | 431323 | 431523 |

| 710124 | **LD** | RF | *LO* | WN | 431124 | 431224 | 431324 | 431524 |
| 710125 | **LD** | RF | *LO* | WN | 431125 | 431225 | 431325 | 431525 |
| 710126 | **LD** | RF | *LO* | WN | 431126 | 431226 | 431326 | 431526 |
| 710127 | **LD** | RF | *LO* | WN | 431127 | 431227 | 431327 | 431527 |
| 710128 | **LD** | RF | *LO* | WN | 431128 | 431228 | 431328 | 431528 |
| 710129 | **LD** | RF | *LO* | WN | 431129 | 431229 | 431329 | 431529 |
| 710130 | **LD** | RF | *LO* | WN | 431130 | 431230 | 431330 | 431530 |

**Class 710/2.** 25 kV AC/750 V DC 4-car units.

**DMS(A).** Bombardier Derby 2017–19. –/40(+6). 43.5 t.
**MS.** Bombardier Derby 2017–19. –/46. 32.3 t.
**PMS.** Bombardier Derby 2017–19. –/45(+6) 2W. 38.5 t.
**DMS(B).** Bombardier Derby 2017–19. –/40(+6).43.5 t.

| 710256 | **LD** | RF |      |    | 432156 | 432256 | 432356 | 432556 |
| 710257 | **LD** | RF | *LO* | WN | 432157 | 432257 | 432357 | 432557 |
| 710258 | **LD** | RF | *LO* | WN | 432158 | 432258 | 432358 | 432558 |
| 710259 | **LD** | RF | *LO* | WN | 432159 | 432259 | 432359 | 432559 |
| 710260 | **LD** | RF | *LO* | WN | 432160 | 432260 | 432360 | 432560 |
| 710261 | **LD** | RF | *LO* | WN | 432161 | 432261 | 432361 | 432561 |
| 710262 | **LD** | RF | *LO* | WN | 432162 | 432262 | 432362 | 432562 |
| 710263 | **LD** | RF | *LO* | WN | 432163 | 432263 | 432363 | 432563 |
| 710264 | **LD** | RF | *LO* | WN | 432164 | 432264 | 432364 | 432564 |
| 710265 | **LD** | RF | *LO* | WN | 432165 | 432265 | 432365 | 432565 |
| 710266 | **LD** | RF | *LO* | WN | 432166 | 432266 | 432366 | 432566 |
| 710267 | **LD** | RF | *LO* | WN | 432167 | 432267 | 432367 | 432567 |
| 710268 | **LD** | RF | *LO* | WN | 432168 | 432268 | 432368 | 432568 |
| 710269 | **LD** | RF | *LO* | WN | 432169 | 432269 | 432369 | 432569 |
| 710270 | **LD** | RF |      |    | 432170 | 432270 | 432370 | 432570 |
| 710271 | **LD** | RF | *LO* | WN | 432171 | 432271 | 432371 | 432571 |
| 710272 | **LD** | RF | *LO* | WN | 432172 | 432272 | 432372 | 432572 |
| 710273 | **LD** | RF | *LO* | WN | 432173 | 432273 | 432373 | 432573 |

**Class 710/2.** 25 kV AC/750 V DC 5-car units.

**DMS(A).** Bombardier Derby 2019–20. –/40(+6).     t.
**MS.** Bombardier Derby 2019–20. –/46.     t.
**PMS.** Bombardier Derby 2019–20. –/45(+6) 2W.     t.
**MS.** Bombardier Derby 2019–20.     t.
**DMS(B).** Bombardier Derby 2019–20. –/40(+6).     t.

| 710274 | **LD** | RF | 432174 | 432274 | 432374 | 432474 | 432574 |
| 710275 | **LD** | RF | 432175 | 432275 | 432375 | 432475 | 432575 |
| 710276 | **LD** | RF | 432176 | 432276 | 432376 | 432476 | 432576 |
| 710277 | **LD** | RF | 432177 | 432277 | 432377 | 432477 | 432577 |
| 710278 | **LD** | RF | 432178 | 432278 | 432378 | 432478 | 432578 |
| 710279 | **LD** | RF | 432179 | 432279 | 432379 | 432479 | 432579 |

# CLASS 717 DESIRO CITY SIEMENS

New dual-voltage 6-car units used on Great Northern services from London Moorgate. The design is based on Classes 700/707, but has emergency end doors for tunnel operation. Fitted with tripcocks for operation between Moorgate and Drayton Park.

**Formation:** DMS–TS–TS–MS–PTS–DMS.
**Systems:** 25 kV AC overhead and 750 V DC third rail.
**Construction:** Aluminium.
**Traction Motors:** Four Siemens asynchronous of 200 kW.
**Wheel Arrangement:** Bo-Bo + 2-2 + 2-2 + Bo-Bo + 2-2 + Bo-Bo.
**Braking:** Disc, tread & regenerative. **Dimensions:** 20.00 x 2.80 m.
**Bogies:** Siemens SF7000 inside-frame. **Couplers:** Dellner 12.
**Gangways:** Within unit + end doors. **Control System:** IGBT Inverter.
**Doors:** Sliding plug. **Maximum Speed:** 85 mph.
**Heating & ventilation:** Air conditioning.
**Seating Layout:** 2+2 facing/unidirectional.
**Multiple Working:** Within class and with Classes 700 and 707.

**DMS(A).** Siemens Krefeld 2017–18. –/52(+4). 38.8 t.
**TS.** Siemens Krefeld 2017–18. –/68. 28.8 t.
**TS.** Siemens Krefeld 2017–18. –/61(+4) 2W. 28.7 t.
**MS.** Siemens Krefeld 2017–18. –/68. 35.5 t.
**PTS.** Siemens Krefeld 2017–18. –/61(+3). 33.9 t.
**DMS(B).** Siemens Krefeld 2017–18. –/52(+4). 38.8 t.

| | | | | | | | | | |
|---|---|---|---|---|---|---|---|---|---|
| 717001 | **TL** | RR | *GN* | HE | 451001 | 452001 | 453001 | 454001 | 455001 456001 |
| 717002 | **TL** | RR | *GN* | HE | 451002 | 452002 | 453002 | 454002 | 455002 456002 |
| 717003 | **TL** | RR | *GN* | HE | 451003 | 452003 | 453003 | 454003 | 455003 456003 |
| 717004 | **TL** | RR | *GN* | HE | 451004 | 452004 | 453004 | 454004 | 455004 456004 |
| 717005 | **TL** | RR | *GN* | HE | 451005 | 452005 | 453005 | 454005 | 455005 456005 |
| 717006 | **TL** | RR | *GN* | HE | 451006 | 452006 | 453006 | 454006 | 455006 456006 |
| 717007 | **TL** | RR | *GN* | HE | 451007 | 452007 | 453007 | 454007 | 455007 456007 |
| 717008 | **TL** | RR | *GN* | HE | 451008 | 452008 | 453008 | 454008 | 455008 456008 |
| 717009 | **TL** | RR | *GN* | HE | 451009 | 452009 | 453009 | 454009 | 455009 456009 |
| 717010 | **TL** | RR | *GN* | HE | 451010 | 452010 | 453010 | 454010 | 455010 456010 |
| 717011 | **TL** | RR | *GN* | HE | 451011 | 452011 | 453011 | 454011 | 455011 456011 |
| 717012 | **TL** | RR | *GN* | HE | 451012 | 452012 | 453012 | 454012 | 455012 456012 |
| 717013 | **TL** | RR | *GN* | HE | 451013 | 452013 | 453013 | 454013 | 455013 456013 |
| 717014 | **TL** | RR | *GN* | HE | 451014 | 452014 | 453014 | 454014 | 455014 456014 |
| 717015 | **TL** | RR | *GN* | HE | 451015 | 452015 | 453015 | 454015 | 455015 456015 |
| 717016 | **TL** | RR | *GN* | HE | 451016 | 452016 | 453016 | 454016 | 455016 456016 |
| 717017 | **TL** | RR | *GN* | HE | 451017 | 452017 | 453017 | 454017 | 455017 456017 |
| 717018 | **TL** | RR | *GN* | HE | 451018 | 452018 | 453018 | 454018 | 455018 456018 |
| 717019 | **TL** | RR | *GN* | HE | 451019 | 452019 | 453019 | 454019 | 455019 456019 |
| 717020 | **TL** | RR | *GN* | HE | 451020 | 452020 | 453020 | 454020 | 455020 456020 |
| 717021 | **TL** | RR | *GN* | HE | 451021 | 452021 | 453021 | 454021 | 455021 456021 |
| 717022 | **TL** | RR | *GN* | HE | 451022 | 452022 | 453022 | 454022 | 455022 456022 |
| 717023 | **TL** | RR | *GN* | HE | 451023 | 452023 | 453023 | 454023 | 455023 456023 |
| 717024 | **TL** | RR | *GN* | HE | 451024 | 452024 | 453024 | 454024 | 455024 456024 |
| 717025 | **TL** | RR | *GN* | HE | 451025 | 452025 | 453025 | 454025 | 455025 456025 |

# CLASS 720     AVENTRA   BOMBARDIER DERBY

This large fleet of Aventra EMUs was ordered by Greater Anglia in 2016 to replace its entire Class 317, 321, 360 and 379 fleets on outer suburban and medium-distance services. In 2020 the order was amended – originally it was to be for 89 5-car units and 22 10-car units, but this has now been changed so that the whole order consists of 5-car units (133 5-cars in total). The additional 5-car units will still be numbered in the 720/1 series.

The units were more than a year late entering service owing to Bombardier Aventra software issues, finally being launched in autumn 2020. All are expected to be in service by summer 2022.

The Class 720/6 units are 10-car sets on order by c2c.

**Formation:** See class headings.
**Systems:** 25 kV AC overhead.
**Construction:** Aluminium.
**Traction Motors:** Two Bombardier asynchronous of 265 kW.
**Wheel Arrangement:**
**Braking:** Disc & regenerative                **Dimensions:** 24.54/24.21 x 2.77 m.
**Bogies:** FLEXX B5000 inside-frame.  **Couplers:** Dellner 12.
**Gangways:** Within unit.                      **Control System:** IGBT Inverter.
**Doors:** Sliding plug.                         **Maximum Speed:** 100 mph.
**Heating & ventilation:** Air conditioning.
**Seating Layout:** 3+2 facing/unidirectional.
**Multiple Working:** Within class.

**Class 720/1.** Greater Anglia 5-car units.
**Formation:** DMS–PMS–MS–MS–DTS.

**DMS.** Bombardier Derby 2018–21.              t.
**PMS.** Bombardier Derby 2018–21.              t.
**MS(A).** Bombardier Derby 2018–21.           t.
**MS(B).** Bombardier Derby 2018–21.           t.
**DTS.** Bombardier Derby 2018–21.              t.

| | | | | | | | |
|---|---|---|---|---|---|---|---|
| 720 101 | **GR** | A | 450101 | 451101 | 452101 | 453101 | 454101 |
| 720 102 | **GR** | A | 450102 | 451102 | 452102 | 453102 | 454102 |
| 720 103 | **GR** | A | 450103 | 451103 | 452103 | 453103 | 454103 |
| 720 104 | **GR** | A | 450104 | 451104 | 452104 | 453104 | 454104 |
| 720 105 | **GR** | A | 450105 | 451105 | 452105 | 453105 | 454105 |
| 720 106 | **GR** | A | 450106 | 451106 | 452106 | 453106 | 454106 |
| 720 107 | **GR** | A | 450107 | 451107 | 452107 | 453107 | 454107 |
| 720 108 | **GR** | A | 450108 | 451108 | 452108 | 453108 | 454108 |
| 720 109 | **GR** | A | 450109 | 451109 | 452109 | 453109 | 454109 |
| 720 110 | **GR** | A | 450110 | 451110 | 452110 | 453110 | 454110 |
| 720 111 | **GR** | A | 450111 | 451111 | 452111 | 453111 | 454111 |
| 720 112 | **GR** | A | 450112 | 451112 | 452112 | 453112 | 454112 |
| 720 113 | **GR** | A | 450113 | 451113 | 452113 | 453113 | 454113 |
| 720 114 | **GR** | A | 450114 | 451114 | 452114 | 453114 | 454114 |
| 720 115 | **GR** | A | 450115 | 451115 | 452115 | 453115 | 454115 |
| 720 116 | **GR** | A | 450116 | 451116 | 452116 | 453116 | 454116 |

| | | | | | | | | | |
|---|---|---|---|---|---|---|---|---|---|
| 720117 | **GR** | A | | | 450117 | 451117 | 452117 | 453117 | 454117 |
| 720118 | **GR** | A | | | 450118 | 451118 | 452118 | 453118 | 454118 |
| 720119 | **GR** | A | | | 450119 | 451119 | 452119 | 453119 | 454119 |
| 720120 | **GR** | A | | | 450120 | 451120 | 452120 | 453120 | 454120 |
| 720121 | **GR** | A | | | 450121 | 451121 | 452121 | 453121 | 454121 |
| 720122 | **GR** | A | | | 450122 | 451122 | 452122 | 453122 | 454122 |
| 720123 | **GR** | A | | | 450123 | 451123 | 452123 | 453123 | 454123 |
| 720124 | **GR** | A | | | 450124 | 451124 | 452124 | 453124 | 454124 |
| 720125 | **GR** | A | | | 450125 | 451125 | 452125 | 453125 | 454125 |
| 720126 | **GR** | A | | | 450126 | 451126 | 452126 | 453126 | 454126 |
| 720127 | **GR** | A | | | 450127 | 451127 | 452127 | 453127 | 454127 |
| 720128 | **GR** | A | | | 450128 | 451128 | 452128 | 453128 | 454128 |
| 720129 | **GR** | A | | | 450129 | 451129 | 452129 | 453129 | 454129 |
| 720130 | **GR** | A | | | 450130 | 451130 | 452130 | 453130 | 454130 |
| 720131 | **GR** | A | | | 450131 | 451131 | 452131 | 453131 | 454131 |
| 720132 | **GR** | A | | | 450132 | 451132 | 452132 | 453132 | 454132 |
| 720133 | **GR** | A | | | 450133 | 451133 | 452133 | 453133 | 454133 |
| 720134 | **GR** | A | | | 450134 | 451134 | 452134 | 453134 | 454134 |
| 720135 | **GR** | A | | | 450135 | 451135 | 452135 | 453135 | 454135 |
| 720136 | **GR** | A | | | 450136 | 451136 | 452136 | 453136 | 454136 |
| 720137 | **GR** | A | | | 450137 | 451137 | 452137 | 453137 | 454137 |
| 720138 | **GR** | A | | | 450138 | 451138 | 452138 | 453138 | 454138 |
| 720139 | **GR** | A | | | 450139 | 451139 | 452139 | 453139 | 454139 |
| 720140 | **GR** | A | | | 450140 | 451140 | 452140 | 453140 | 454140 |
| 720141 | **GR** | A | | | 450141 | 451141 | 452141 | 453141 | 454141 |
| 720142 | **GR** | A | | | 450142 | 451142 | 452142 | 453142 | 454142 |
| 720143 | **GR** | A | | | 450143 | 451143 | 452143 | 453143 | 454143 |
| 720144 | **GR** | A | | | 450144 | 451144 | 452144 | 453144 | 454144 |
| | | | | | | | | | |
| 720501 | **GR** | A | | | 450501 | 451501 | 452501 | 453501 | 459501 |
| 720502 | **GR** | A | | | 450502 | 451502 | 452502 | 453502 | 459502 |
| 720503 | **GR** | A | | | 450503 | 451503 | 452503 | 453503 | 459503 |
| 720504 | **GR** | A | | | 450504 | 451504 | 452504 | 453504 | 459504 |
| 720505 | **GR** | A | | | 450505 | 451505 | 452505 | 453505 | 459505 |
| 720506 | **GR** | A | | | 450506 | 451506 | 452506 | 453506 | 459506 |
| 720507 | **GR** | A | | | 450507 | 451507 | 452507 | 453507 | 459507 |
| 720508 | **GR** | A | | | 450508 | 451508 | 452508 | 453508 | 459508 |
| 720509 | **GR** | A | | | 450509 | 451509 | 452509 | 453509 | 459509 |
| 720510 | **GR** | A | | | 450510 | 451510 | 452510 | 453510 | 459510 |
| 720511 | **GR** | A | *GA* | IL | 450511 | 451511 | 452511 | 453511 | 459511 |
| 720512 | **GR** | A | | | 450512 | 451512 | 452512 | 453512 | 459512 |
| 720513 | **GR** | A | | | 450513 | 451513 | 452513 | 453513 | 459513 |
| 720514 | **GR** | A | | | 450514 | 451514 | 452514 | 453514 | 459514 |
| 720515 | **GR** | A | *GA* | IL | 450515 | 451515 | 452515 | 453515 | 459515 |
| 720516 | **GR** | A | | | 450516 | 451516 | 452516 | 453516 | 459516 |
| 720517 | **GR** | A | *GA* | IL | 450517 | 451517 | 452517 | 453517 | 459517 |
| 720518 | **GR** | A | | | 450518 | 451518 | 452518 | 453518 | 459518 |
| 720519 | **GR** | A | | | 450519 | 451519 | 452519 | 453519 | 459519 |
| 720520 | **GR** | A | | | 450520 | 451520 | 452520 | 453520 | 459520 |
| 720521 | **GR** | A | | | 450521 | 451521 | 452521 | 453521 | 459521 |
| 720522 | **GR** | A | | | 450522 | 451522 | 452522 | 453522 | 459522 |

| | | | | | | | | | |
|---|---|---|---|---|---|---|---|---|---|
| 720 523 | GR | A | | | 450523 | 451523 | 452523 | 453523 | 459523 |
| 720 524 | GR | A | | | 450524 | 451524 | 452524 | 453524 | 459524 |
| 720 525 | GR | A | | | 450525 | 451525 | 452525 | 453525 | 459525 |
| 720 526 | GR | A | | | 450526 | 451526 | 452526 | 453526 | 459526 |
| 720 527 | GR | A | | | 450527 | 451527 | 452527 | 453527 | 459527 |
| 720 528 | GR | A | | | 450528 | 451528 | 452528 | 453528 | 459528 |
| 720 529 | GR | A | | | 450529 | 451529 | 452529 | 453529 | 459529 |
| 720 530 | GR | A | | | 450530 | 451530 | 452530 | 453530 | 459530 |
| 720 531 | GR | A | | | 450531 | 451531 | 452531 | 453531 | 459531 |
| 720 532 | GR | A | | | 450532 | 451532 | 452532 | 453532 | 459532 |
| 720 533 | GR | A | | | 450533 | 451533 | 452533 | 453533 | 459533 |
| 720 534 | GR | A | | | 450534 | 451534 | 452534 | 453534 | 459534 |
| 720 535 | GR | A | | | 450535 | 451535 | 452535 | 453535 | 459535 |
| 720 536 | GR | A | GA | IL | 450536 | 451536 | 452536 | 453536 | 459536 |
| 720 537 | GR | A | GA | IL | 450537 | 451537 | 452537 | 453537 | 459537 |
| 720 538 | GR | A | GA | IL | 450538 | 451538 | 452538 | 453538 | 459538 |
| 720 539 | GR | A | GA | IL | 450539 | 451539 | 452539 | 453539 | 459539 |
| 720 540 | GR | A | GA | IL | 450540 | 451540 | 452540 | 453540 | 459540 |
| 720 541 | GR | A | | | 450541 | 451541 | 452541 | 453541 | 459541 |
| 720 542 | GR | A | | | 450542 | 451542 | 452542 | 453542 | 459542 |
| 720 543 | GR | A | GA | IL | 450543 | 451543 | 452543 | 453543 | 459543 |
| 720 544 | GR | A | | | 450544 | 451544 | 452544 | 453544 | 459544 |
| 720 545 | GR | A | | | 450545 | 451545 | 452545 | 453545 | 459545 |
| 720 546 | GR | A | | | 450546 | 451546 | 452546 | 453546 | 459546 |
| 720 547 | GR | A | | | 450547 | 451547 | 452547 | 453547 | 459547 |
| 720 548 | GR | A | GA | IL | 450548 | 451548 | 452548 | 453548 | 459548 |
| 720 549 | GR | A | | | 450549 | 451549 | 452549 | 453549 | 459549 |
| 720 550 | GR | A | GA | IL | 450550 | 451550 | 452550 | 453550 | 459550 |
| 720 551 | GR | A | | | 450551 | 451551 | 452551 | 453551 | 459551 |
| 720 552 | GR | A | | | 450552 | 451552 | 452552 | 453552 | 459552 |
| 720 553 | GR | A | | | 450553 | 451553 | 452553 | 453553 | 459553 |
| 720 554 | GR | A | | | 450554 | 451554 | 452554 | 453554 | 459554 |
| 720 555 | GR | A | | | 450555 | 451555 | 452555 | 453555 | 459555 |
| 720 556 | GR | A | GA | IL | 450556 | 451556 | 452556 | 453556 | 459556 |
| 720 557 | GR | A | | | 450557 | 451557 | 452557 | 453557 | 459557 |
| 720 558 | GR | A | | | 450558 | 451558 | 452558 | 453558 | 459558 |
| 720 559 | GR | A | | | 450559 | 451559 | 452559 | 453559 | 459559 |
| 720 560 | GR | A | | | 450560 | 451560 | 452560 | 453560 | 459560 |
| 720 561 | GR | A | | | 450561 | 451561 | 452561 | 453561 | 459561 |
| 720 562 | GR | A | | | 450562 | 451562 | 452562 | 453562 | 459562 |
| 720 563 | GR | A | | | 450563 | 451563 | 452563 | 453563 | 459563 |
| 720 564 | GR | A | | | 450564 | 451564 | 452564 | 453564 | 459564 |
| 720 565 | GR | A | | | 450565 | 451565 | 452565 | 453565 | 459565 |
| 720 566 | GR | A | | | 450566 | 451566 | 452566 | 453566 | 459566 |
| 720 567 | GR | A | | | 450567 | 451567 | 452567 | 453567 | 459567 |
| 720 568 | GR | A | | | 450568 | 451568 | 452568 | 453568 | 459568 |
| 720 569 | GR | A | | | 450569 | 451569 | 452569 | 453569 | 459569 |
| 720 570 | GR | A | | | 450570 | 451570 | 452570 | 453570 | 459570 |
| 720 571 | GR | A | | | 450571 | 451571 | 452571 | 453571 | 459571 |
| 720 572 | GR | A | | | 450572 | 451572 | 452572 | 453572 | 459572 |
| 720 573 | GR | A | | | 450573 | 451573 | 452573 | 453573 | 459573 |

| 720574 | **GR** | A | 450574 | 451574 | 452574 | 453574 | 459574 |
| 720575 | **GR** | A | 450575 | 451575 | 452575 | 453575 | 459575 |
| 720576 | **GR** | A | 450576 | 451576 | 452576 | 453576 | 459576 |
| 720577 | **GR** | A | 450577 | 451577 | 452577 | 453577 | 459577 |
| 720578 | **GR** | A | 450578 | 451578 | 452578 | 453578 | 459578 |
| 720579 | **GR** | A | 450579 | 451579 | 452579 | 453579 | 459579 |
| 720580 | **GR** | A | 450580 | 451580 | 452580 | 453580 | 459580 |
| 720581 | **GR** | A | 450581 | 451581 | 452581 | 453581 | 459581 |
| 720582 | **GR** | A | 450582 | 451582 | 452582 | 453582 | 459582 |
| 720583 | **GR** | A | 450583 | 451583 | 452583 | 453583 | 459583 |
| 720584 | **GR** | A | 450584 | 451584 | 452584 | 453584 | 459584 |
| 720585 | **GR** | A | 450585 | 451585 | 452585 | 453585 | 459585 |
| 720586 | **GR** | A | 450586 | 451586 | 452586 | 453586 | 459586 |
| 720587 | **GR** | A | 450587 | 451587 | 452587 | 453587 | 459587 |
| 720588 | **GR** | A | 450588 | 451588 | 452588 | 453588 | 459588 |
| 720589 | **GR** | A | 450589 | 451589 | 452589 | 453589 | 459589 |

**Class 720/6.** c2c 10-car units.
**Formation:** DMS–PMS–MS–MS–TS–MS–PMS–MS–MS–DTS.

**DMS.** Bombardier Derby 2021.          t.
**PMS(A).** Bombardier Derby 2021.          t.
**MS(A).** Bombardier Derby 2021.          t.
**MS(B).** Bombardier Derby 2021.          t.
**TS.** Bombardier Derby 2021.          t.
**MS(C).** Bombardier Derby 2021.          t.
**PMS(B).** Bombardier Derby 2021.          t.
**MS(D).** Bombardier Derby 2021.          t.
**MS(E).** Bombardier Derby 2021.          t.
**DTS.** Bombardier Derby 2021.          t.

| 720601 | P | 450601 | 451601 | 452601 | 453601 | 454601 |
| | | 455601 | 456601 | 457601 | 458601 | 459601 |
| 720602 | P | 450602 | 451602 | 452602 | 453602 | 454602 |
| | | 455602 | 456602 | 457602 | 458602 | 459602 |
| 720603 | P | 450603 | 451603 | 452603 | 453603 | 454603 |
| | | 455603 | 456603 | 457603 | 458603 | 459603 |
| 720604 | P | 450604 | 451604 | 452604 | 453604 | 454604 |
| | | 455604 | 456604 | 457604 | 458604 | 459604 |
| 720605 | P | 450605 | 451605 | 452605 | 453605 | 454605 |
| | | 455605 | 456605 | 457605 | 458605 | 459605 |
| 720606 | P | 450606 | 451606 | 452606 | 453606 | 454606 |
| | | 455606 | 456606 | 457606 | 458606 | 459606 |

## CLASS 730    AVENTRA    BOMBARDIER DERBY

West Midlands Trains has a mixed fleet of 3- and 5-car Aventra EMUs on order from Bombardier. The 3-car units will be used on suburban services around Birmingham, mainly on the Cross City line, while the 5-car units will be used on outer suburban and inter urban services from London Euston and in the West Midlands. Both types are due to enter service in 2021–22. Full details awaited.

**Formation:** DMS–PMS–DMS or DMC–MS–PMS–MS–DMS.
**Systems:** 25 kV AC overhead.
**Construction:** Aluminium.
**Traction Motors:** Two Bombardier asynchronous of 250 kW.
**Wheel Arrangement:**
**Braking:** Disc & regenerative.          **Dimensions:** 24.47/24.21 x 2.78 m.
**Bogies:** FLEXX B5000 inside-frame.   **Couplers:** Dellner 12.
**Gangways:** End gangways.              **Control System:** IGBT Inverter.
**Doors:** Sliding plug.
**Maximum Speed:** 730/0: 90 mph; 730/1 and 730/2: 110 mph.
**Heating & ventilation:** Air conditioning.
**Seating Layout:**
**Multiple Working:** Within class.

**Class 730/0.** 3-car West Midlands area units.

**DMS(A).** Bombardier Derby 2020–21.          t.
**PMS.** Bombardier Derby 2020–21.        t.
**DMS(B).** Bombardier Derby 2020–21.          t.

| | | | | |
|---|---|---|---|---|
| 730001 | CO | 490001 | 492001 | 494001 |
| 730002 | CO | 490002 | 492002 | 494002 |
| 730003 | CO | 490003 | 492003 | 494003 |
| 730004 | CO | 490004 | 492004 | 494004 |
| 730005 | CO | 490005 | 492005 | 494005 |
| 730006 | CO | 490006 | 492006 | 494006 |
| 730007 | CO | 490007 | 492007 | 494007 |
| 730008 | CO | 490008 | 492008 | 494008 |
| 730009 | CO | 490009 | 492009 | 494009 |
| 730010 | CO | 490010 | 492010 | 494010 |
| 730011 | CO | 490011 | 492011 | 494011 |
| 730012 | CO | 490012 | 492012 | 494012 |
| 730013 | CO | 490013 | 492013 | 494013 |
| 730014 | CO | 490014 | 492014 | 494014 |
| 730015 | CO | 490015 | 492015 | 494015 |
| 730016 | CO | 490016 | 492016 | 494016 |
| 730017 | CO | 490017 | 492017 | 494017 |
| 730018 | CO | 490018 | 492018 | 494018 |
| 730019 | CO | 490019 | 492019 | 494019 |
| 730020 | CO | 490020 | 492020 | 494020 |
| 730021 | CO | 490021 | 492021 | 494021 |
| 730022 | CO | 490022 | 492022 | 494022 |
| 730023 | CO | 490023 | 492023 | 494023 |

| | | | | | |
|---|---|---|---|---|---|
| 730024 | CO | 490024 | 492024 | 494024 | |
| 730025 | CO | 490025 | 492025 | 494025 | |
| 730026 | CO | 490026 | 492026 | 494026 | |
| 730027 | CO | 490027 | 492027 | 494027 | |
| 730028 | CO | 490028 | 492028 | 494028 | |
| 730029 | CO | 490029 | 492029 | 494029 | |
| 730030 | CO | 490030 | 492030 | 494030 | |
| 730031 | CO | 490031 | 492031 | 494031 | |
| 730032 | CO | 490032 | 492032 | 494032 | |
| 730033 | CO | 490033 | 492033 | 494033 | |
| 730034 | CO | 490034 | 492034 | 494034 | |
| 730035 | CO | 490035 | 492035 | 494035 | |
| 730036 | CO | 490036 | 492036 | 494036 | |

**Class 730/1.** 5-car outer suburban units.

**DMC.** Bombardier Derby 2020–21.     t.
**MS.** Bombardier Derby 2020–21.     t.
**PMS.** Bombardier Derby 2020–21.     t.
**MS.** Bombardier Derby 2020–21.     t.
**DMS.** Bombardier Derby 2020–21.     t.

| | | | | | | |
|---|---|---|---|---|---|---|
| 730101 | CO | 490101 | 491101 | 492101 | 493101 | 494101 |
| 730102 | CO | 490102 | 491102 | 492102 | 493102 | 494102 |
| 730103 | CO | 490103 | 491103 | 492103 | 493103 | 494103 |
| 730104 | CO | 490104 | 491104 | 492104 | 493104 | 494104 |
| 730105 | CO | 490105 | 491105 | 492105 | 493105 | 494105 |
| 730106 | CO | 490106 | 491106 | 492106 | 493106 | 494106 |
| 730107 | CO | 490107 | 491107 | 492107 | 493107 | 494107 |
| 730108 | CO | 490108 | 491108 | 492108 | 493108 | 494108 |
| 730109 | CO | 490109 | 491109 | 492109 | 493109 | 494109 |
| 730110 | CO | 490110 | 491110 | 492110 | 493110 | 494110 |
| 730111 | CO | 490111 | 491111 | 492111 | 493111 | 494111 |
| 730112 | CO | 490112 | 491112 | 492112 | 493112 | 494112 |
| 730113 | CO | 490113 | 491113 | 492113 | 493113 | 494113 |
| 730114 | CO | 490114 | 491114 | 492114 | 493114 | 494114 |
| 730115 | CO | 490115 | 491115 | 492115 | 493115 | 494115 |
| 730116 | CO | 490116 | 491116 | 492116 | 493116 | 494116 |
| 730117 | CO | 490117 | 491117 | 492117 | 493117 | 494117 |
| 730118 | CO | 490118 | 491118 | 492118 | 493118 | 494118 |
| 730119 | CO | 490119 | 491119 | 492119 | 493119 | 494119 |
| 730120 | CO | 490120 | 491120 | 492120 | 493120 | 494120 |
| 730121 | CO | 490121 | 491121 | 492121 | 493121 | 494121 |
| 730122 | CO | 490122 | 491122 | 492122 | 493122 | 494122 |
| 730123 | CO | 490123 | 491123 | 492123 | 493123 | 494123 |
| 730124 | CO | 490124 | 491124 | 492124 | 493124 | 494124 |
| 730125 | CO | 490125 | 491125 | 492125 | 493125 | 494125 |
| 730126 | CO | 490126 | 491126 | 492126 | 493126 | 494126 |
| 730127 | CO | 490127 | 491127 | 492127 | 493127 | 494127 |
| 730128 | CO | 490128 | 491128 | 492128 | 493128 | 494128 |
| 730129 | CO | 490129 | 491129 | 492129 | 493129 | 494129 |

**Class 730/2.** 5-car long distance units.

**DMC.** Bombardier Derby 2020–21.        t.
**MS.** Bombardier Derby 2020–21.         t.
**PMS.** Bombardier Derby 2020–21.        t.
**MS.** Bombardier Derby 2020–21.         t.
**DMS.** Bombardier Derby 2020–21.        t.

| | | | | | | |
|---|---|---|---|---|---|---|
| 730 201 | CO | 490201 | 491201 | 492201 | 493201 | 494201 |
| 730 202 | CO | 490202 | 491202 | 492202 | 493202 | 494202 |
| 730 203 | CO | 490203 | 491203 | 492203 | 493203 | 494203 |
| 730 204 | CO | 490204 | 491204 | 492204 | 493204 | 494204 |
| 730 205 | CO | 490205 | 491205 | 492205 | 493205 | 494205 |
| 730 206 | CO | 490206 | 491206 | 492206 | 493206 | 494206 |
| 730 207 | CO | 490207 | 491207 | 492207 | 493207 | 494207 |
| 730 208 | CO | 490208 | 491208 | 492208 | 493208 | 494208 |
| 730 209 | CO | 490209 | 491209 | 492209 | 493209 | 494209 |
| 730 210 | CO | 490210 | 491210 | 492210 | 493210 | 494210 |
| 730 211 | CO | 490211 | 491211 | 492211 | 493211 | 494211 |
| 730 212 | CO | 490212 | 491212 | 492212 | 493212 | 494212 |
| 730 213 | CO | 490213 | 491213 | 492213 | 493213 | 494213 |
| 730 214 | CO | 490214 | 491214 | 492214 | 493214 | 494214 |
| 730 215 | CO | 490215 | 491215 | 492215 | 493215 | 494215 |
| 730 216 | CO | 490216 | 491216 | 492216 | 493216 | 494216 |

# CLASS 745        FLIRT ELECTRIC        STADLER

This fleet of 20 12-car articulated Stadler EMUs was ordered by Greater Anglia in 2016 to replace its locomotive-hauled sets on Liverpool Street–Norwich services and Class 379s on the Liverpool Street–Stansted Airport route. The 12-car units are formed of two 6-car half units formed of three coupled articulated pairs.

**Formations (745/0):** DMF–PTF–TS–TS–TS–MS–MS–TS–TS–TS–PTS–DMS or **(745/1):** DMS–PTS–TS–TS–TS–MS–MS–TS–TS–TS–PTS–DMS.
**Systems:** 25 kV AC overhead.
**Construction:** Aluminium.
**Traction Motors:** Four TSA of 325 kW.
**Wheel Arrangement:** Bo-2-2 + 2-2-2 + 2-2-Bo + Bo-2-2 + 2-2-2 + 2-2-Bo.
**Braking:** Disc & regenerative    **Dimensions:**
**Bogies:** Stadler/Jacobs.         **Couplers:** Dellner 10.
**Gangways:** Within unit.          **Control System:** IGBT Inverter.
**Doors:** Sliding plug (one per vehicle). **Maximum Speed:** 100 mph.
**Heating & ventilation:** Air conditioning.
**Seating Layout:** 1: 2+1 facing/unidirectional, 2: 2+2 unidirectional/facing.
**Multiple Working:** Within class.

**Class 745/0.** Fitted with First Class and café bar and used on the London Liverpool Street–Norwich route.

**DMF.** Stadler Bussnang/Szolnok 2018–19.  36/–        t.
**PTF.** Stadler Bussnang/Szolnok 2018–19. 44/– 1T        t.
**TSMB.** Stadler Bussnang/Szolnok 2018–19. –/26(+9) 1TD 2W        t.
**TS.** Stadler Bussnang/Szolnok 2018–19. –/66(+12)        t.
**TS.** Stadler Bussnang/Szolnok 2018–19. –/70(+4) 1T        t.
**MS.** Stadler Bussnang/Szolnok 2018–19. –/58(+4)        t.
**MS.** Stadler Bussnang/Szolnok 2018–19. –/58(+4)        t.
**TS.** Stadler Bussnang/Szolnok 2018–19. –/70(+4) 1T        t.
**TS.** Stadler Bussnang/Szolnok 2018–19. –/74(+4)        t.
**TS.** Stadler Bussnang/Szolnok 2018–19. –/74(+4)        t.
**PTS.** Stadler Bussnang/Szolnok 2018–19. –/70(+4) 1T        t.
**DMS.** Stadler Bussnang/Szolnok 2018–19. –/58(+4)        t.

| 745001 | **GR** | RR | *GA* | NC | 413001 426001 332001 343001 341001 301001 |
| | | | | | 302001 342001 344001 346001 322001 312001 |
| 745002 | **GR** | RR | *GA* | NC | 413002 426002 332002 343002 341002 301002 |
| | | | | | 302002 342002 344002 346002 322002 312002 |
| 745003 | **GR** | RR | *GA* | NC | 413003 426003 332003 343003 341003 301003 |
| | | | | | 302003 342003 344003 346003 322003 312003 |
| 745004 | **GR** | RR | *GA* | NC | 413004 426004 332004 343004 341004 301004 |
| | | | | | 302004 342004 344004 346004 322004 312004 |
| 745005 | **GR** | RR | *GA* | NC | 413005 426005 332005 343005 341005 301005 |
| | | | | | 302005 342005 344005 346005 322005 312005 |
| 745006 | **GR** | RR | *GA* | NC | 413006 426006 332006 343006 341006 301006 |
| | | | | | 302006 342006 344006 346006 322006 312006 |
| 745007 | **GR** | RR | *GA* | NC | 413007 426007 332007 343007 341007 301007 |
| | | | | | 302007 342007 344007 346007 322007 312007 |
| 745008 | **GR** | RR | *GA* | NC | 413008 426008 332008 343008 341008 301008 |
| | | | | | 302008 342008 344008 346008 322008 312008 |
| 745009 | **GR** | RR | *GA* | NC | 413009 426009 332009 343009 341009 301009 |
| | | | | | 302009 342009 344009 346009 322009 312009 |
| 745010 | **GR** | RR | *GA* | NC | 413010 426010 332010 343010 341010 301010 |
| | | | | | 302010 342010 344010 346010 322010 312010 |

**Class 745/1.** Standard Class only units mainly for use between London Liverpool Street and Stansted Airport and for selected services to/from Norwich for maintenance purposes

**DMS.** Stadler Bussnang/Szolnok 2018–19. –/48(+6)        t.
**PTS.** Stadler Bussnang/Szolnok 2018–19. –/68 1T        t.
**TS(A).** Stadler Bussnang/Szolnok 2018–19. –/50(+9) 1TD 2W        t.
**TS(B).** Stadler Bussnang/Szolnok 2018–19. –/64(+8)        t.
**TS(C).** Stadler Bussnang/Szolnok 2018–19. –/68 1T        t.
**MS(A).** Stadler Bussnang/Szolnok 2018–19. –/56        t.
**MS(B).** Stadler Bussnang/Szolnok 2018–19. –/56        t.
**TS(D).** Stadler Bussnang/Szolnok 2018–19. –/68 1T        t.
**TS(E).** Stadler Bussnang/Szolnok 2018–19. –/64(+8)        t.
**TS(F).** Stadler Bussnang/Szolnok 2018–19. –/64(+8)        t.
**PTS.** Stadler Bussnang/Szolnok 2018–19. –/68 1T        t.
**DMS.** Stadler Bussnang/Szolnok 2018–19. –/48(+6)        t.

| 745 101 | **GR** | RR | *GA* | NC | 313101 326101 332101 343101 341101 301101 |
|         |        |    |      |    | 302101 342101 344101 346101 322101 312101 |
| 745 102 | **GR** | RR | *GA* | NC | 313102 326102 332102 343102 341102 301102 |
|         |        |    |      |    | 302102 342102 344102 346102 322102 312102 |
| 745 103 | **GR** | RR | *GA* | NC | 313103 326103 332103 343103 341103 301103 |
|         |        |    |      |    | 302103 342103 344103 346103 322103 312103 |
| 745 104 | **GR** | RR | *GA* | NC | 313104 326104 332104 343104 341104 301104 |
|         |        |    |      |    | 302104 342104 344104 346104 322104 312104 |
| 745 105 | **GR** | RR | *GA* | NC | 313105 326105 332105 343105 341105 301105 |
|         |        |    |      |    | 302105 342105 344105 346105 322105 312105 |
| 745 106 | **GR** | RR | *GA* | NC | 313106 326106 332106 343106 341106 301106 |
|         |        |    |      |    | 302106 342106 344106 346106 322106 312106 |
| 745 107 | **GR** | RR | *GA* | NC | 313107 326107 332107 343107 341107 301107 |
|         |        |    |      |    | 302107 342107 344107 346107 322107 312107 |
| 745 108 | **GR** | RR | *GA* | NC | 313108 326108 332108 343108 341108 301108 |
|         |        |    |      |    | 302108 342108 344108 346108 322108 312108 |
| 745 109 | **GR** | RR | *GA* | NC | 313109 326109 332109 343109 341109 301109 |
|         |        |    |      |    | 302109 342109 344109 346109 322109 312109 |
| 745 110 | **GR** | RR | *GA* | NC | 313110 326110 332110 343110 341110 301110 |
|         |        |    |      |    | 302110 342110 344110 346110 322110 312110 |

# CLASS 755        FLIRT BI-MODE        STADLER

This fleet of 3- and 4-car articulated Stadler bi-mode units was ordered by Greater Anglia in 2016 to replace all of its older DMU fleets. The first units entered service in summer 2019. The design features a "power pack" in the middle that houses two diesel engines for the 3-car units and four diesel engines for the 4-car units. This has been given its own number, effectively making the units 4- and 5-car, although there is no passenger accommodation in the power pack car.

**Formation**: DMS–PP–PTS–DMS or DMS–PTS–PP–PTS–DMS.
**Systems**: Diesel/25 kV AC overhead.
**Construction**: Aluminium.
**Engines**: (4-car): Four Deutz V8 of 480 kW (645 hp), (3-car): Two Four Deutz V8 of 480 kW (645 hp).
**Traction Motors**: 4 x TSA of 325 kW.
**Wheel Arrangement**: Bo-2-2-2-Bo or Bo-2-2-2-2-Bo.
**Braking**: Disc & regenerative.
**Dimensions**: 20.81/15.22/6.69 (PP) m x 2.72/2.82 (PP) m.
**Bogies**: Stadler/Jacobs.                **Couplers**: Dellner 10.
**Gangways**: Within unit.                **Control System**: IGBT Inverter.
**Doors**: Sliding plug (one per vehicle). **Maximum Speed**: 100 mph.
**Heating & ventilation**: Air conditioning.
**Seating Layout**: 2+2 unidirectional/facing.
**Multiple Working**: Within class.

**Class 755/3.** 3-car (plus power pack) units.

**DMS(A).** Stadler Szolnok/Siedlce/Bussnang/Valencia 2018–19. –/60(+4). 43.4 t.
**PP.** Stadler Bussnang/Valencia 2018–19. 25.4 t.
**PTS.** Stadler Szolnok/Siedlce/Bussnang/Valencia 2018–19. –/32(+7) 1TD 1T 2W. 24.2 t.
**DMS(B).**Stadler Szolnok/Siedlce/Bussnang/Valencia2018–19.–/52(+12).42.1t.

| | | | | | | | |
|---|---|---|---|---|---|---|---|
| 755 325 | **GR** | RR *GA* | NC | 911325 | 971325 | 981325 | 912325 |
| 755 326 | **GR** | RR *GA* | NC | 911326 | 971326 | 981326 | 912326 |
| 755 327 | **GR** | RR *GA* | NC | 911327 | 971327 | 981327 | 912327 |
| 755 328 | **GR** | RR *GA* | NC | 911328 | 971328 | 981328 | 912328 |
| 755 329 | **GR** | RR *GA* | NC | 911329 | 971329 | 981329 | 912329 |
| 755 330 | **GR** | RR *GA* | NC | 911330 | 971330 | 981330 | 912330 |
| 755 331 | **GR** | RR *GA* | NC | 911331 | 971331 | 981331 | 912331 |
| 755 332 | **GR** | RR *GA* | NC | 911332 | 971332 | 981332 | 912332 |
| 755 333 | **GR** | RR *GA* | NC | 911333 | 971333 | 981333 | 912333 |
| 755 334 | **GR** | RR *GA* | NC | 911334 | 971334 | 981334 | 912334 |
| 755 335 | **GR** | RR *GA* | NC | 911335 | 971335 | 981335 | 912335 |
| 755 336 | **GR** | RR *GA* | NC | 911336 | 971336 | 981336 | 912336 |
| 755 337 | **GR** | RR *GA* | NC | 911337 | 971337 | 981337 | 912337 |
| 755 338 | **GR** | RR *GA* | NC | 911338 | 971338 | 981338 | 912338 |

**Class 755/4.** 4-car (plus power pack) units.

**DMS(A).** Stadler Szolnok/Siedlce/Bussnang/Valencia 2018–19. –/60(+4). 41.4 t.
**PTS(A).** Stadler Szolnok/Siedlce/Bussnang/Valencia 2018–19. –/58(+4). 25.0 t.
**PP.** Stadler Bussnang/Valencia 2018–19. 28.5 t.
**PTS(B).** Stadler Szolnok/Siedlce/Bussnang/Valencia 2018–19. –/32(+7). 1TD 1T 2W. 26.4 t.
**DMS(B).** Stadler Szolnok/Siedlce/Bussnang/Valencia 2018–19. –/52(+12). 42.2 t.

| | | | | | | | | |
|---|---|---|---|---|---|---|---|---|
| 755 401 | **GR** | RR *GA* | NC | 911401 | 961401 | 971401 | 981401 | 912401 |
| 755 402 | **GR** | RR *GA* | NC | 911402 | 961402 | 971402 | 981402 | 912402 |
| 755 403 | **GR** | RR *GA* | NC | 911403 | 961403 | 971403 | 981403 | 912403 |
| 755 404 | **GR** | RR *GA* | NC | 911404 | 961404 | 971404 | 981404 | 912404 |
| 755 405 | **GR** | RR *GA* | NC | 911405 | 961405 | 971405 | 981405 | 912405 |
| 755 406 | **GR** | RR *GA* | NC | 911406 | 961406 | 971406 | 981406 | 912406 |
| 755 407 | **GR** | RR *GA* | NC | 911407 | 961407 | 971407 | 981407 | 912407 |
| 755 408 | **GR** | RR *GA* | NC | 911408 | 961408 | 971408 | 981408 | 912408 |
| 755 409 | **GR** | RR *GA* | NC | 911409 | 961409 | 971409 | 981409 | 912409 |
| 755 410 | **GR** | RR *GA* | NC | 911410 | 961410 | 971410 | 981410 | 912410 |
| 755 411 | **GR** | RR *GA* | NC | 911411 | 961411 | 971411 | 981411 | 912411 |
| 755 412 | **GR** | RR *GA* | NC | 911412 | 961412 | 971412 | 981412 | 912412 |
| 755 413 | **GR** | RR *GA* | NC | 911413 | 961413 | 971413 | 981413 | 912413 |
| 755 414 | **GR** | RR *GA* | NC | 911414 | 961414 | 971414 | 981414 | 912414 |
| 755 415 | **GR** | RR *GA* | NC | 911415 | 961415 | 971415 | 981415 | 912415 |
| 755 416 | **GR** | RR *GA* | NC | 911416 | 961416 | 971416 | 981416 | 912416 |
| 755 417 | **GR** | RR *GA* | NC | 911417 | 961417 | 971417 | 981417 | 912417 |
| 755 418 | **GR** | RR *GA* | NC | 911418 | 961418 | 971418 | 981418 | 912418 |
| 755 419 | **GR** | RR *GA* | NC | 911419 | 961419 | 971419 | 981419 | 912419 |
| 755 420 | **GR** | RR *GA* | NC | 911420 | 961420 | 971420 | 981420 | 912420 |
| 755 421 | **GR** | RR *GA* | NC | 911421 | 961421 | 971421 | 981421 | 912421 |

| 755422 | **GR** | RR *GA* | NC | 911422 | 961422 | 971422 | 981422 | 912422 |
| 755423 | **GR** | RR *GA* | NC | 911423 | 961423 | 971423 | 981423 | 912423 |
| 755424 | **GR** | RR *GA* | NC | 911424 | 961424 | 971424 | 981424 | 912424 |

# CLASS 756        FLIRT TRI-MODE            STADLER

This fleet of articulated FLIRT tri-mode diesel/electric/battery units is on order for Transport for Wales for use on the Cardiff Valley Lines (Rhymney, Coryton, Vale of Glamorgan, Penarth and Barry Island) from 2022. The units will look similar to Greater Anglia's Class 755s.

**Formation:** DMS–PP–PTS–DMS or DMS–PTS–PP–PTS–DMS.
**Systems:** Diesel/25 kV AC overhead/battery.
**Construction:** Aluminium.
**Engines:** (4-car): Four Deutz V8 of 480 kW (645 hp), (3-car): Two Four Deutz V8 of 480 kW (645 hp).
**Traction Motors:** 4 x TSA of 325 kW.
**Battery:** 1300 kW.
**Wheel Arrangement:** Bo-2-2-2-Bo or Bo-2-2-2-2-Bo.
**Braking:** Disc & regenerative.
**Dimensions:**
**Bogies:** Stadler/Jacobs.                **Couplers:** Dellner 10.
**Gangways:** Within unit.                 **Control System:** IGBT Inverter.
**Doors:** Sliding plug.                    **Maximum Speed:** 75 mph.
**Heating & ventilation:** Air conditioning.
**Seating Layout:** 2+2 unidirectional/facing.
**Multiple Working:** Within class.

**Class 756/0.** 3-car (plus power pack) units. Full details awaited.

| 756001 | 911001 | 971001 | 981001 | 912001 |
| 756002 | 911002 | 971002 | 981002 | 912002 |
| 756003 | 911003 | 971003 | 981003 | 912003 |
| 756004 | 911004 | 971004 | 981004 | 912004 |
| 756005 | 911005 | 971005 | 981005 | 912005 |
| 756006 | 911006 | 971006 | 981006 | 912006 |
| 756007 | 911007 | 971007 | 981007 | 912007 |

**Class 756/1.** 4-car (plus power pack) units. Full details awaited.

| 756101 | 911101 | 961101 | 971101 | 981101 | 912101 |
| 756102 | 911102 | 961102 | 971102 | 981102 | 912102 |
| 756103 | 911103 | 961103 | 971103 | 981103 | 912103 |
| 756104 | 911104 | 961104 | 971104 | 981104 | 912104 |
| 756105 | 911105 | 961105 | 971105 | 981105 | 912105 |
| 756106 | 911106 | 961106 | 971106 | 981106 | 912106 |
| 756107 | 911107 | 961107 | 971107 | 981107 | 912107 |
| 756108 | 911108 | 961108 | 971108 | 981108 | 912108 |
| 756109 | 911109 | 961109 | 971109 | 981109 | 912109 |
| 756110 | 911110 | 961110 | 971110 | 981110 | 912110 |
| 756111 | 911111 | 961111 | 971111 | 981111 | 912111 |
| 756112 | 911112 | 961112 | 971112 | 981112 | 912112 |

| 756 113 | 911113 | 961113 | 971113 | 981113 | 912113 |
| 756 114 | 911114 | 961114 | 971114 | 981114 | 912114 |
| 756 115 | 911115 | 961115 | 971115 | 981115 | 912115 |
| 756 116 | 911116 | 961116 | 971116 | 981116 | 912116 |
| 756 117 | 911117 | 961117 | 971117 | 981117 | 912117 |

## CLASS 769          FLEX          BREL YORK/BRUSH

In December 2016 it was announced that Porterbrook would be converting eight Class 319s into bi-mode "Flex" units for Northern, with two new diesel engines being fitted (one under each of the driving trailer cars) to drive ABB alternators. Four years on and the units are still to enter service with Northern, the project having been beset by problems and then delayed by the Covid-19 pandemic. Subsequently orders were placed by Transport for Wales for nine units (which started to enter service in 2020) and Great Western Railway for 19 units. The GWR units will be "tri-mode", with both AC overhead and DC third rail capability. Rail Operations Group has also ordered five units for its Orion logistics subsidiary.

Work on the conversions is taking place at Brush Loughborough, with Gemini Rail Group at Wolverton responsible for the refurbishment of the GWR units. All conversions are from Class 319/0 or 319/4 Phase 1 units. Full details awaited.

**Formation:** DMC–MS–TS–DMS.
**Systems:** Diesel/25 kV AC overhead/750 V DC third rail (GWR units only).
**Construction:** Steel.
**Engines:** Two MAN D2876 of 390 kW (523 hp).
**Traction Motors:** Four GEC G315BZ of 268 kW.
**Wheel Arrangement:** 2-2 + Bo-Bo + 2-2 + 2-2.
**Braking:** Disc.                         **Dimensions:** 20.17/20.16 x 2.82 m.
**Bogies:** P7-4 (MS), T3-7 (others).      **Couplers:** Tightlock.
**Gangways:** Within unit + end doors.    **Control System:** GTO chopper.
**Doors:** Sliding.
**Maximum Speed:** 100 mph (electric); 85 mph (diesel).
**Seating Layout:** 1: 2+1 facing (declassified); 2: 2+2/3+2 facing.
**Multiple Working:** Within class and with Class 319.

**77291–381. DMC.** Lot No. 31022 (odd nos.) 1987–88.
**77431–457. DMC.** Lot No. 31038 (odd nos.) 1988.
**62891–936. MS.** Lot No. 31023 1987–88.
**62961–974. MS.** Lot No. 31039 1988.
**71772–817. TS.** Lot No. 31024 1987–88.
**71866–879. TS.** Lot No. 31040 1988.
**77330–380. DMS.** Lot No. 31025 (even nos.) 1987–88.
**77430–456. DMS.** Lot No. 31041 (even nos.) 1988.

**Class 769/0.** Transport for Wales bi-mode units.

| 769002 | (319002) | TW | P | TW | CF | 77293 | 62892 | 71773 | 77292 |
| 769003 | (319003) | TW | P | TW | CF | 77295 | 62893 | 71774 | 77294 |
| 769006 | (319006) | TW | P | TW | CF | 77301 | 62896 | 71777 | 77300 |
| 769007 | (319007) | TW | P | TW | CF | 77303 | 62897 | 71778 | 77302 |
| 769008 | (319008) | TW | P | TW | CF | 77305 | 62898 | 71779 | 77304 |

**Class 769/4.** Northern and Transport for Wales bi-mode units.

| | | | | | | | | |
|---|---|---|---|---|---|---|---|---|
| 769421 | (319421) | **TW** | P | | CF | 77331 | 62911 | 71792 | 77330 |
| 769424 | (319424) | **NR** | P | | AN | 77337 | 62914 | 71795 | 77336 |
| 769426 | (319426) | **TW** | P | | CF | 77341 | 62916 | 71797 | 77340 |
| 769431 | (319431) | **NR** | P | | AN | 77351 | 62921 | 71802 | 77350 |
| 769434 | (319434) | **NR** | P | | AN | 77357 | 62924 | 71805 | 77356 |
| 769442 | (319442) | **NR** | P | | AN | 77373 | 62932 | 71813 | 77372 |
| 769445 | (319445) | **TW** | P | | CF | 77379 | 62935 | 71816 | 77378 |
| 769448 | (319448) | **NR** | P | | AN | 77433 | 62962 | 71867 | 77432 |
| 769450 | (319450) | **NR** | P | | AN | 77437 | 62964 | 71869 | 77436 |
| 769452 | (319452) | **TW** | P | | CF | 77441 | 62966 | 71871 | 77440 |
| 769456 | (319456) | **NR** | P | | AN | 77449 | 62970 | 71875 | 77448 |
| 769458 | (319458) | **NR** | P | | AN | 77453 | 62972 | 71877 | 77452 |

**Class 769/9.** Great Western Railway tri-mode units.

| | | | | | | | |
|---|---|---|---|---|---|---|---|
| 769922 | (319422) | | P | 77333 | 62912 | 71793 | 77332 |
| 769923 | (319423) | | P | 77335 | 62913 | 71794 | 77334 |
| 769925 | (319425) | | P | 77339 | 62915 | 71796 | 77338 |
| 769927 | (319427) | | P | 77343 | 62917 | 71798 | 77342 |
| 769928 | (319428) | | P | 77345 | 62918 | 71799 | 77344 |
| 769930 | (319430) | **GW** | P | 77349 | 62920 | 71801 | 77348 |
| 769932 | (319432) | | P | 77353 | 62922 | 71803 | 77352 |
| 769935 | (319435) | | P | 77359 | 62925 | 71806 | 77358 |
| 769936 | (319436) | **GW** | P | 77361 | 62926 | 71807 | 77360 |
| 769937 | (319437) | | P | 77363 | 62927 | 71808 | 77362 |
| 769938 | (319438) | | P | 77365 | 62928 | 71809 | 77364 |
| 769939 | (319439) | | P | 77367 | 62929 | 71810 | 77366 |
| 769940 | (319440) | | P | 77369 | 62930 | 71811 | 77368 |
| 769943 | (319443) | **GW** | P | 77375 | 62933 | 71814 | 77374 |
| 769944 | (319444) | | P | 77377 | 62934 | 71815 | 77376 |
| 769946 | (319446) | **GW** | P | 77381 | 62936 | 71817 | 77380 |
| 769947 | (319447) | | P | 77431 | 62961 | 71866 | 77430 |
| 769949 | (319449) | | P | 77435 | 62963 | 71868 | 77434 |
| 769959 | (319459) | | P | 77455 | 62973 | 71878 | 77454 |

# CLASS 777                                         STADLER

This fleet of articulated 4-car units was ordered from Stadler in 2017 by Merseytravel for the DC third rail Merseyrail suburban network, to replace Classes 507 and 508 in 2021–22. An option exists for up to a further 60 units.

**Formation:** DMS–MS–MS–DMS.
**System:** 750 V DC third rail.
**Construction:** Aluminium.
**Traction Motors:** Six TSA of 350 kW (470 hp) per unit.
**Wheel Arrangement:** 2-Bo-Bo-Bo-2.

**Braking:** Tread & regenerative.
**Bogies:** Jakobs.
**Gangways:** Within unit.
**Doors:** Sliding plug.

**Dimensions:** 19.00/13.50 x 2.82 m.
**Couplers:** Dellner 12.
**Control System:** IGBT Inverter.
**Maximum Speed:** 75 mph.

**Heating & ventilation:** Air conditioning.
**Seating Layout:** 2+2 facing/unidirectional.
**Multiple Working:** Within class.

**DMS(A).** Stadler Szolnok/Siedlce/Altenrhein 2018–20. –/53.      t.
**MS(A).** Stadler Szolnok/Siedlce/Altenrhein 2018–20. –/38(+1) 1W.    t.
**MS(B).** Stadler Szolnok/Siedlce/Altenrhein 2018–20. –/38(+1) 1W.    t.
**DMS(B).** Stadler Szolnok/Siedlce/Altenrhein 2018–20. –/53.      t.

| | | | | | |
|---|---|---|---|---|---|
| 777001 | MT | 427001 | 428001 | 429001 | 430001 |
| 777002 | MT | 427002 | 428002 | 429002 | 430002 |
| 777003 | MT | 427003 | 428003 | 429003 | 430003 |
| 777004 | MT | 427004 | 428004 | 429004 | 430004 |
| 777005 | MT | 427005 | 428005 | 429005 | 430005 |
| 777006 | MT | 427006 | 428006 | 429006 | 430006 |
| 777007 | MT | 427007 | 428007 | 429007 | 430007 |
| 777008 | MT | 427008 | 428008 | 429008 | 430008 |
| 777009 | MT | 427009 | 428009 | 429009 | 430009 |
| 777010 | MT | 427010 | 428010 | 429010 | 430010 |
| 777011 | MT | 427011 | 428011 | 429011 | 430011 |
| 777012 | MT | 427012 | 428012 | 429012 | 430012 |
| 777013 | MT | 427013 | 428013 | 429013 | 430013 |
| 777014 | MT | 427014 | 428014 | 429014 | 430014 |
| 777015 | MT | 427015 | 428015 | 429015 | 430015 |
| 777016 | MT | 427016 | 428016 | 429016 | 430016 |
| 777017 | MT | 427017 | 428017 | 429017 | 430017 |
| 777018 | MT | 427018 | 428018 | 429018 | 430018 |
| 777019 | MT | 427019 | 428019 | 429019 | 430019 |
| 777020 | MT | 427020 | 428020 | 429020 | 430020 |
| 777021 | MT | 427021 | 428021 | 429021 | 430021 |
| 777022 | MT | 427022 | 428022 | 429022 | 430022 |
| 777023 | MT | 427023 | 428023 | 429023 | 430023 |
| 777024 | MT | 427024 | 428024 | 429024 | 430024 |
| 777025 | MT | 427025 | 428025 | 429025 | 430025 |
| 777026 | MT | 427026 | 428026 | 429026 | 430026 |
| 777027 | MT | 427027 | 428027 | 429027 | 430027 |
| 777028 | MT | 427028 | 428028 | 429028 | 430028 |
| 777029 | MT | 427029 | 428029 | 429029 | 430029 |
| 777030 | MT | 427030 | 428030 | 429030 | 430030 |
| 777031 | MT | 427031 | 428031 | 429031 | 430031 |
| 777032 | MT | 427032 | 428032 | 429032 | 430032 |
| 777033 | MT | 427033 | 428033 | 429033 | 430033 |
| 777034 | MT | 427034 | 428034 | 429034 | 430034 |
| 777035 | MT | 427035 | 428035 | 429035 | 430035 |
| 777036 | MT | 427036 | 428036 | 429036 | 430036 |
| 777037 | MT | 427037 | 428037 | 429037 | 430037 |
| 777038 | MT | 427038 | 428038 | 429038 | 430038 |
| 777039 | MT | 427039 | 428039 | 429039 | 430039 |
| 777040 | MT | 427040 | 428040 | 429040 | 430040 |
| 777041 | MT | 427041 | 428041 | 429041 | 430041 |
| 777042 | MT | 427042 | 428042 | 429042 | 430042 |
| 777043 | MT | 427043 | 428043 | 429043 | 430043 |

| 777044 | MT | 427044 | 428044 | 429044 | 430044 |
| 777045 | MT | 427045 | 428045 | 429045 | 430045 |
| 777046 | MT | 427046 | 428046 | 429046 | 430046 |
| 777047 | MT | 427047 | 428047 | 429047 | 430047 |
| 777048 | MT | 427048 | 428048 | 429048 | 430048 |
| 777049 | MT | 427049 | 428049 | 429049 | 430049 |
| 777050 | MT | 427050 | 428050 | 429050 | 430050 |
| 777051 | MT | 427051 | 428051 | 429051 | 430051 |
| 777052 | MT | 427052 | 428052 | 429052 | 430052 |

# CLASS 799          HYDROFLEX     BRELYORK/BRUSH

This hydrogen demonstrator unit was converted in 2019 from a Class 319 as part of a partnership between Porterbrook and the University of Birmingham. It started main line testing in 2020.

The Class 799 MS has been heavily modified and is now fitted with batteries, a hydrogen fuel cell and four hydrogen tanks. Hydrogen is stored in tanks at high pressure, from where it is piped into fuel cells where it is mixed with oxygen to create electricity to power the motors. The energy can also be stored in the batteries, these being used at times of high demand.

**Formation:** DMC–MS–TS–DMS.
**Systems:** Hydrogen/25 kV AC overhead/750 V DC third rail.
**Construction:** Steel.
**Traction Motors:** Four GEC G315BZ of 268 kW.
**Wheel Arrangement:** 2-2 + Bo-Bo + 2-2 + 2-2.
**Braking:** Disc.                        **Dimensions:** 20.17/20.16 x 2.82 m.
**Bogies:** P7-4 (MS), T3-7 (others).     **Couplers:** Tightlock.
**Gangways:** Within unit + end doors.  **Doors:** Sliding.
**Maximum Speed:** 75 mph.
**Seating Layout:** 1: 2+1 facing (declassified); 2: 2+2/3+2 facing.

**Non-standard livery:** HydroFlex (green, grey and white).

**77291. DMC.** Lot No. 31022. 1987–88.
**62891. MS.** Lot No. 31023 1987–88.
**71772. TS.** Lot No. 31024 1987–88.
**77290. DMS.** Lot No. 31025 1987–88.

799001   (319001)    **0**   P   *RO*      LM   77291   62891   71772   77290

# 4.4. HITACHI IEP UNITS

## CLASS 800 INTERCITY EXPRESS PROGRAMME
## BI-MODE                                            HITACHI

In 2012 Agility Trains, a consortium of Hitachi and John Laing, signed a deal with the DfT to design, build, finance and maintain the next generation of InterCity rolling stock for the Great Western and East Coast Main Lines, principally to replace ageing High Speed Trains on these routes. A follow-on order in 2013 was placed for 30 9-car trains to replace the Class 91 and Mark 4 carriages on the ECML. This brought the total number of vehicles ordered to 866. Both GWR and LNER were originally planned to have a mix of 5-car and 9-car units which will be bi-mode and straight electric trains (although the EMUs also have one diesel engine fitted to each set). However, owing to delays with electrification works on the GWML, in 2016 it was announced that the 21 9-car electric Class 801 units for GWR would be built as 21 9-car bi-mode units, numbered instead in the Class 800/3 series.

The units are broadly based on the Southeastern Class 395s, but have 25–25.35 m length bodyshells. They are numbered in the Class 800 (bi-mode) and Class 801 (EMU) number series'. 12 trains (76 vehicles) were fully manufactured at Kasado in Japan before the new Hitachi factory at Newton Aycliffe, County Durham was up and running. The remaining trains are being assembled at either Newton Aycliffe or Kasado. New maintenance depots for the trains have been built at Stoke Gifford (Bristol), Swansea and North Pole (London, the former Eurostar depot) for the GWR sets and at Doncaster for the LNER units.

The first trains arrived for testing in 2015. 5-car units entered service on the Great Western Main Line in autumn 2017 and the fleet of Class 800s and 801s entered service on the East Coast Main Line in 2019–20.

In 2015 GWR ordered a further 22 5-car and seven 9-car IEPs, designated Class 802/0 (5-car) and Class 802/1 (9-car). These are mainly used on Paddington–West of England services.

In 2016 GWR ordered a further seven 9-car Class 802s, TransPennine Express ordered 19 5-car Class 802s and Hull Trains ordered five 5-car Class 802s, for delivery 2019–20. The majority of the Class 802s were constructed at Pistoia in Italy, with some at Kasado.

Subsequent orders for derivatives of this type of train have come from First Group for its ECML open access service, Avanti West Coast and East Midlands Railway.

**Formation:** Various, see class headings for details.
**Systems:** Diesel/25 kV AC overhead electric.
**Construction:** Aluminium.
**Diesel engines:** In the 5-car sets diesel engines are located in cars 2, 3 and 4. In the 9-car sets diesel engines are located in cars 2, 3, 5, 7 and 8.
**Engines:** MTU 12V 1600 R80L of 700 kW (940 hp).

**Traction Motors:** Four Hitachi asynchronous of 226 kW.
**Wheel Arrangement:** 2-2 + Bo-Bo + Bo-Bo + 2-2 or
2-2 + Bo-Bo + Bo-Bo + 2-2 + Bo-Bo + Bo-Bo + 2-2.
**Braking:** Disc & regenerative.          **Dimensions:** 25.35/25.00 m x 2.74 m.
**Bogies:** Hitachi.                        **Couplers:** Dellner 10.
**Gangways:** Within unit.                  **Control System:** IGBT Inverter.
**Doors:** Single-leaf sliding.             **Maximum Speed:** 125 mph.
**Heating & ventilation:** Air conditioning.
**Seating Layout:** 1: 2+1 facing/unidirectional; 2+2 facing/unidirectional.
**Multiple Working:** Within class and with all Classes 8xx.

**Class 800/0.** 5-car Great Western Railway units.
**Formation:** PDTS–MS–MS–MC–PDTRBF.

**PDTS.** Hitachi Newton Aycliffe/Kasado 2013–17. –/56 1TD. 47.8 t.
**MS.** Hitachi Newton Aycliffe/Kasado 2013–17. –/88. 50.1 t.
**MS.** Hitachi Newton Aycliffe/Kasado 2013–17. –/88 2T. 50.3 t.
**MC.** Hitachi Newton Aycliffe/Kasado 2013–17. 18/58 1T. 50.6 t.
**PDTRBF.** Hitachi Newton Aycliffe/Kasado 2013–17. 18/– 1TD 2W. 51.7 t.

| | | | | | | | | |
|---|---|---|---|---|---|---|---|---|
| 800001 | **GW** | AT | *GW* | NP | 811001 | 812001 | 813001 | 814001 | 815001 |
| 800002 | **GW** | AT | *GW* | NP | 811002 | 812002 | 813002 | 814002 | 815002 |
| 800003 | **GW** | AT | *GW* | NP | 811003 | 812003 | 813003 | 814003 | 815003 |
| 800004 | **GW** | AT | *GW* | NP | 811004 | 812004 | 813004 | 814004 | 815004 |
| 800005 | **GW** | AT | *GW* | NP | 811005 | 812005 | 813005 | 814005 | 815005 |
| 800006 | **GW** | AT | *GW* | NP | 811006 | 812006 | 813006 | 814006 | 815006 |
| 800007 | **GW** | AT | *GW* | NP | 811007 | 812007 | 813007 | 814007 | 815007 |
| 800008 | **GW** | AT | *GW* | NP | 811008 | 812008 | 813008 | 814008 | 815008 |
| 800009 | **GW** | AT | *GW* | NP | 811009 | 812009 | 813009 | 814009 | 815009 |
| 800010 | **GW** | AT | *GW* | NP | 811010 | 812010 | 813010 | 814010 | 815010 |
| 800011 | **GW** | AT | *GW* | NP | 811011 | 812011 | 813011 | 814011 | 815011 |
| 800012 | **GW** | AT | *GW* | NP | 811012 | 812012 | 813012 | 814012 | 815012 |
| 800013 | **GW** | AT | *GW* | NP | 811013 | 812013 | 813013 | 814013 | 815013 |
| 800014 | **GW** | AT | *GW* | NP | 811014 | 812014 | 813014 | 814014 | 815014 |
| 800015 | **GW** | AT | *GW* | NP | 811015 | 812015 | 813015 | 814015 | 815015 |
| 800016 | **GW** | AT | *GW* | NP | 811016 | 812016 | 813016 | 814016 | 815016 |
| 800017 | **GW** | AT | *GW* | NP | 811017 | 812017 | 813017 | 814017 | 815017 |
| 800018 | **GW** | AT | *GW* | NP | 811018 | 812018 | 813018 | 814018 | 815018 |
| 800019 | **GW** | AT | *GW* | NP | 811019 | 812019 | 813019 | 814019 | 815019 |
| 800020 | **GW** | AT | *GW* | NP | 811020 | 812020 | 813020 | 814020 | 815020 |
| 800021 | **GW** | AT | *GW* | NP | 811021 | 812021 | 813021 | 814021 | 815021 |
| 800022 | **GW** | AT | *GW* | NP | 811022 | 812022 | 813022 | 814022 | 815022 |
| 800023 | **GW** | AT | *GW* | NP | 811023 | 812023 | 813023 | 814023 | 815023 |
| 800024 | **GW** | AT | *GW* | NP | 811024 | 812024 | 813024 | 814024 | 815024 |
| 800025 | **GW** | AT | *GW* | NP | 811025 | 812025 | 813025 | 814025 | 815025 |
| 800026 | **GW** | AT | *GW* | NP | 811026 | 812026 | 813026 | 814026 | 815026 |
| 800027 | **GW** | AT | *GW* | NP | 811027 | 812027 | 813027 | 814027 | 815027 |
| 800028 | **GW** | AT | *GW* | NP | 811028 | 812028 | 813028 | 814028 | 815028 |
| 800029 | **GW** | AT | *GW* | NP | 811029 | 812029 | 813029 | 814029 | 815029 |
| 800030 | **GW** | AT | *GW* | NP | 811030 | 812030 | 813030 | 814030 | 815030 |
| 800031 | **GW** | AT | *GW* | NP | 811031 | 812031 | 813031 | 814031 | 815031 |
| 800032 | **GW** | AT | *GW* | NP | 811032 | 812032 | 813032 | 814032 | 815032 |

| | | | | | | | | | |
|---|---|---|---|---|---|---|---|---|---|
| 800033 | **GW** | AT | *GW* | NP | 811033 | 812033 | 813033 | 814033 | 815033 |
| 800034 | **GW** | AT | *GW* | NP | 811034 | 812034 | 813034 | 814034 | 815034 |
| 800035 | **GW** | AT | *GW* | NP | 811035 | 812035 | 813035 | 814035 | 815035 |
| 800036 | **GW** | AT | *GW* | NP | 811036 | 812036 | 813036 | 814036 | 815036 |

**Names (one on each driving car):**

| | |
|---|---|
| 800009 | Sir Gareth Edwards/John Charles |
| 800010 | Michael Bond/Paddington Bear |
| 800014 | Megan Lloyd George CH/Edith New |
| 800019 | Joy Lofthouse/Johnny Johnson MBE DFM |
| 800020 | Bob Woodward/Elizabeth Ralph |
| 800023 | Firefighter Fleur Lombard QGM/Kathryn Osmond |
| 800025 | Captain Sir Tom Moore |
| 800026 | Don Cameron |
| 800036 | Dr Paul Stephenson OBE |

**Class 800/1.** 9-car LNER units.
**Formation:** PDTS–MS–MS–TSRB–MS–TS–MC–MF–PDTRBF.

**PDTS.** Hitachi Kasado/Newton Aycliffe 2013–18. –/48 1TD 2W. 47.7 t.
**MS.** Hitachi Kasado/Newton Aycliffe 2013–18. –/88 1T. 50.5 t.
**MS.** Hitachi Kasado/Newton Aycliffe 2013–18. –/88 2T. 50.3 t.
**TSRB.** Hitachi Kasado/Newton Aycliffe 2013–18. –/72. 41.0 t.
**MS.** Hitachi Kasado/Newton Aycliffe 2013–18. –/88 2T. 50.3 t.
**TS.** Hitachi Kasado/Newton Aycliffe 2013–18. –/88 2T. 38.3 t.
**MC.** Hitachi Kasado/Newton Aycliffe 2013–18. 30/38. 49.1 t.
**MF.** Hitachi Kasado/Newton Aycliffe 2013–18. 56/– 1T. 50.6 t.
**PDTRBF.** Hitachi Kasado/Newton Aycliffe 2013–18. 15/– 1TD 2W. 51.7 t.

| | | | | | | | | | |
|---|---|---|---|---|---|---|---|---|---|
| 800101 | **LZ** | AT | *LN* | DN | 811101 | 812101 | 813101 | 814101 | 815101 |
| | | | | | 816101 | 817101 | 818101 | 819101 | |
| 800102 | **LZ** | AT | *LN* | DN | 811102 | 812102 | 813102 | 814102 | 815102 |
| | | | | | 816102 | 817102 | 818102 | 819102 | |
| 800103 | **LZ** | AT | *LN* | DN | 811103 | 812103 | 813103 | 814103 | 815103 |
| | | | | | 816103 | 817103 | 818103 | 819103 | |
| 800104 | **LZ** | AT | *LN* | DN | 811104 | 812104 | 813104 | 814104 | 815104 |
| | | | | | 816104 | 817104 | 818104 | 819104 | |
| 800105 | **LZ** | AT | *LN* | DN | 811105 | 812105 | 813105 | 814105 | 815105 |
| | | | | | 816105 | 817105 | 818105 | 819105 | |
| 800106 | **LZ** | AT | *LN* | DN | 811106 | 812106 | 813106 | 814106 | 815106 |
| | | | | | 816106 | 817106 | 818106 | 819106 | |
| 800107 | **LZ** | AT | *LN* | DN | 811107 | 812107 | 813107 | 814107 | 815107 |
| | | | | | 816107 | 817107 | 818107 | 819107 | |
| 800108 | **LZ** | AT | *LN* | DN | 811108 | 812108 | 813108 | 814108 | 815108 |
| | | | | | 816108 | 817108 | 818108 | 819108 | |
| 800109 | **LZ** | AT | *LN* | DN | 811109 | 812109 | 813109 | 814109 | 815109 |
| | | | | | 816109 | 817109 | 818109 | 819109 | |
| 800110 | **LZ** | AT | *LN* | DN | 811110 | 812110 | 813110 | 814110 | 815110 |
| | | | | | 816110 | 817110 | 818110 | 819110 | |
| 800111 | **LZ** | AT | *LN* | DN | 811111 | 812111 | 813111 | 814111 | 815111 |
| | | | | | 816111 | 817111 | 818111 | 819111 | |
| 800112 | **LZ** | AT | *LN* | DN | 811112 | 812112 | 813112 | 814112 | 815112 |
| | | | | | 816112 | 817112 | 818112 | 819112 | |

800 113    **LZ**  AT  *LN*  DN    811113  812113  813113  814113  815113
                                    816113  817113  818113  819113

**Class 800/2.** 5-car LNER units.
**Formation:** PDTS–MSRB–MS–MC–PDTRBF.

**PDTS.** Hitachi Newton Aycliffe/Kasado 2018–19. –/56 1TD. 47.8 t.
**MSRB.** Hitachi Newton Aycliffe/Kasado 2018–19. –/72. 50.1 t.
**MS.** Hitachi Newton Aycliffe/Kasado 2018–19. –/88 2T. 50.3 t.
**MC.** Hitachi Newton Aycliffe/Kasado 2018–19. 30/38 1T. 50.6 t.
**PDTRBF.** Hitachi Newton Aycliffe/Kasado 2018–19. 18/– 1TD 2W. 51.7 t.

| | | | | | | | | | |
|---|---|---|---|---|---|---|---|---|---|
| 800 201 | **LZ** | AT | *LN* | DN | 811201 | 812201 | 813201 | 814201 | 815201 |
| 800 202 | **LZ** | AT | *LN* | DN | 811202 | 812202 | 813202 | 814202 | 815202 |
| 800 203 | **LZ** | AT | *LN* | DN | 811203 | 812203 | 813203 | 814203 | 815203 |
| 800 204 | **LZ** | AT | *LN* | DN | 811204 | 812204 | 813204 | 814204 | 815204 |
| 800 205 | **LZ** | AT | *LN* | DN | 811205 | 812205 | 813205 | 814205 | 815205 |
| 800 206 | **LZ** | AT | *LN* | DN | 811206 | 812206 | 813206 | 814206 | 815206 |
| 800 207 | **LZ** | AT | *LN* | DN | 811207 | 812207 | 813207 | 814207 | 815207 |
| 800 208 | **LZ** | AT | *LN* | DN | 811208 | 812208 | 813208 | 814208 | 815208 |
| 800 209 | **LZ** | AT | *LN* | DN | 811209 | 812209 | 813209 | 814209 | 815209 |
| 800 210 | **LZ** | AT | *LN* | DN | 811210 | 812210 | 813210 | 814210 | 815210 |

**Class 800/3.** 9-car Great Western Railway units. Originally to be built as electric trains and numbered in the Class 801/0 series.
**Formation:** PDTS–MS–MS–TS–MS–TS–MS–MF–PDTRBF.

**PDTS.** Hitachi Newton Aycliffe/Kasado 2017–18. –/48 1TD 2W. 47.8 t.
**MS.** Hitachi Newton Aycliffe/Kasado 2017–18. –/88 1T. 50.1 t.
**MS.** Hitachi Newton Aycliffe/Kasado 2017–18. –/88 2T. 50.3 t.
**TS.** Hitachi Newton Aycliffe/Kasado 2017–18. –/88. 41.0 t.
**MS.** Hitachi Newton Aycliffe/Kasado 2017–18. –/88 2T. 50.3 t.
**TS.** Hitachi Newton Aycliffe/Kasado 2017–18. –/88 2T. 38.3 t.
**MS.** Hitachi Newton Aycliffe/Kasado 2017–18. –/88. 49.1 t.
**MF.** Hitachi Newton Aycliffe/Kasado 2017–18. 56/– 1T. 50.6 t.
**PDTRBF.** Hitachi Newton Aycliffe/Kasado 2017–18. 15/– 1TD 2W. 51.7 t.

| | | | | | | | | | |
|---|---|---|---|---|---|---|---|---|---|
| 800 301 | **GW** | AT | *GW* | NP | 821001 | 822001 | 823001 | 824001 | 825001 |
| | | | | | 826001 | 827001 | 828001 | 829001 | |
| 800 302 | **GW** | AT | *GW* | NP | 821002 | 822002 | 823002 | 824002 | 825002 |
| | | | | | 826002 | 827002 | 828002 | 829002 | |
| 800 303 | **GW** | AT | *GW* | NP | 821003 | 822003 | 823003 | 824003 | 825003 |
| | | | | | 826003 | 827003 | 828003 | 829003 | |
| 800 304 | **GW** | AT | *GW* | NP | 821004 | 822004 | 823004 | 824004 | 825004 |
| | | | | | 826004 | 827004 | 828004 | 829004 | |
| 800 305 | **GW** | AT | *GW* | NP | 821005 | 822005 | 823005 | 824005 | 825005 |
| | | | | | 826005 | 827005 | 828005 | 829005 | |
| 800 306 | **GW** | AT | *GW* | NP | 821006 | 822006 | 823006 | 824006 | 825006 |
| | | | | | 826006 | 827006 | 828006 | 829006 | |
| 800 307 | **GW** | AT | *GW* | NP | 821007 | 822007 | 823007 | 824007 | 825007 |
| | | | | | 826007 | 827007 | 828007 | 829007 | |
| 800 308 | **GW** | AT | *GW* | NP | 821008 | 822008 | 823008 | 824008 | 825008 |
| | | | | | 826008 | 827008 | 828008 | 829008 | |

| 800 309 | **GW** | AT | *GW* | NP | 821009 | 822009 | 823009 | 824009 | 825009 |
| | | | | | 826009 | 827009 | 828009 | 829009 | |
| 800 310 | **GW** | AT | *GW* | NP | 821010 | 822010 | 823010 | 824010 | 825010 |
| | | | | | 826010 | 827010 | 828010 | 829010 | |
| 800 311 | **GW** | AT | *GW* | NP | 821011 | 822011 | 823011 | 824011 | 825011 |
| | | | | | 826011 | 827011 | 828011 | 829011 | |
| 800 312 | **GW** | AT | *GW* | NP | 821012 | 822012 | 823012 | 824012 | 825012 |
| | | | | | 826012 | 827012 | 828012 | 829012 | |
| 800 313 | **GW** | AT | *GW* | NP | 821013 | 822013 | 823013 | 824013 | 825013 |
| | | | | | 826013 | 827013 | 828013 | 829013 | |
| 800 314 | **GW** | AT | *GW* | NP | 821014 | 822014 | 823014 | 824014 | 825014 |
| | | | | | 826014 | 827014 | 828014 | 829014 | |
| 800 315 | **GW** | AT | *GW* | NP | 821015 | 822015 | 823015 | 824015 | 825015 |
| | | | | | 826015 | 827015 | 828015 | 829015 | |
| 800 316 | **GW** | AT | *GW* | NP | 821016 | 822016 | 823016 | 824016 | 825016 |
| | | | | | 826016 | 827016 | 828016 | 829016 | |
| 800 317 | **GW** | AT | *GW* | NP | 821017 | 822017 | 823017 | 824017 | 825017 |
| | | | | | 826017 | 827017 | 828017 | 829017 | |
| 800 318 | **GW** | AT | *GW* | NP | 821018 | 822018 | 823018 | 824018 | 825018 |
| | | | | | 826018 | 827018 | 828018 | 829018 | |
| 800 319 | **GW** | AT | *GW* | NP | 821019 | 822019 | 823019 | 824019 | 825019 |
| | | | | | 826019 | 827019 | 828019 | 829019 | |
| 800 320 | **GW** | AT | *GW* | NP | 821020 | 822020 | 823020 | 824020 | 825020 |
| | | | | | 826020 | 827020 | 828020 | 829020 | |
| 800 321 | **GW** | AT | *GW* | NP | 821021 | 822021 | 823021 | 824021 | 825021 |
| | | | | | 826021 | 827021 | 828021 | 829021 | |

**Name (carried on alternative driving cars):**

| 800 306 | Allan Leonard Lewis VC/Harold Day DSC |
| 800 314 | Odette Hallowes GC MBE LdH |

# CLASS 801 INTERCITY EXPRESS PROGRAMME
## ELECTRIC                                      HITACHI

The Class 801s are electric units, but still have one diesel engine fitted per unit for emergency use or for use on diversionary routes when coupled to a Class 800.

**Formation:** Various, see class headings for details.
**Systems:** 25 kV AC overhead electric, plus one diesel engine per set.
**Construction:** Aluminium.
**Diesel engines:** In the 5-car sets the single diesel engine is located in car 2 and in the 9-car sets the diesel engine is located in car 8.
**Engines:** MTU 12V 1600 R80L of 700 kW (940 hp).
**Traction Motors:** Four Hitachi asynchronous of 226 kW.
**Wheel Arrangement:** 2-2 + Bo-Bo + Bo-Bo + Bo-Bo + 2-2 or
2-2 + Bo-Bo + Bo-Bo + 2-2 + Bo-Bo + 2-2 + Bo-Bo + Bo-Bo + 2-2.
**Braking:** Disc & regenerative.        **Dimensions:** 25.35/25.00 m x 2.74 m.
**Bogies:** Hitachi.                     **Couplers:** Dellner 10.

**Gangways:** Within unit.      **Control System:** IGBT Inverter.
**Doors:** Single-leaf sliding.      **Maximum Speed:** 125 mph.
**Heating & ventilation:** Air conditioning.
**Seating Layout:** 1: 2+1 facing/unidirectional; 2+2 facing/unidirectional.
**Multiple Working:** Within class and with all Classes 8xx.

**Class 801/1.** 5-car LNER units.
**Formation:** PDTS–MSRB–MS–MC–PDTRBF.

**PDTS.** Hitachi Newton Aycliffe/Kasado 2016–19. –/56 1TD. 47.8 t.
**MSRB.** Hitachi Newton Aycliffe/Kasado 2016–19. –/72. 52.1 t.
**MS.** Hitachi Newton Aycliffe/Kasado 2016–19. –/88 2T. 43.5 t.
**MC.** Hitachi Newton Aycliffe/Kasado 2016–19. 30/38 1T. 44.1 t.
**PDTRBF.** Hitachi Newton Aycliffe/Kasado 2016–19. 18/– 1TD 2W. 51.2 t.

| | | | | | | | | | |
|---|---|---|---|---|---|---|---|---|---|
| 801101 | LZ | AT | *LN* | DN | 821101 | 822101 | 823101 | 824101 | 825101 |
| 801102 | LZ | AT | *LN* | DN | 821102 | 822102 | 823102 | 824102 | 825102 |
| 801103 | LZ | AT | *LN* | DN | 821103 | 822103 | 823103 | 824103 | 825103 |
| 801104 | LZ | AT | *LN* | DN | 821104 | 822104 | 823104 | 824104 | 825104 |
| 801105 | LZ | AT | *LN* | DN | 821105 | 822105 | 823105 | 824105 | 825105 |
| 801106 | LZ | AT | *LN* | DN | 821106 | 822106 | 823106 | 824106 | 825106 |
| 801107 | LZ | AT | *LN* | DN | 821107 | 822107 | 823107 | 824107 | 825107 |
| 801108 | LZ | AT | *LN* | DN | 821108 | 822108 | 823108 | 824108 | 825108 |
| 801109 | LZ | AT | *LN* | DN | 821109 | 822109 | 823109 | 824109 | 825109 |
| 801110 | LZ | AT | *LN* | DN | 821110 | 822110 | 823110 | 824110 | 825110 |
| 801111 | LZ | AT | *LN* | DN | 821111 | 822111 | 823111 | 824111 | 825111 |
| 801112 | LZ | AT | *LN* | DN | 821112 | 822112 | 823112 | 824112 | 825112 |

**Class 801/2.** 9-car LNER units.
**Formation:** PDTS–MS–MS–TSRB–MS–TS–MC–MF–PDTRBF.

**PDTS.** Hitachi Newton Aycliffe/Kasado 2018–20. –/48 1TD 2W. 47.7 t.
**MS.** Hitachi Newton Aycliffe/Kasado 2018–20. –/88 1T. 50.5 t.
**MS.** Hitachi Newton Aycliffe/Kasado 2018–20. –/88 2T. 43.5 t.
**TSRB.** Hitachi Newton Aycliffe/Kasado 2018–20. –/72. 43.0 t.
**MS.** Hitachi Newton Aycliffe/Kasado 2018–20. –/88 2T. 43.5 t.
**TS.** Hitachi Newton Aycliffe/Kasado 2018–20. –/88 2T. 38.3 t.
**MC.** Hitachi Newton Aycliffe/Kasado 2018–20. 30/38. 42.6 t.
**MF.** Hitachi Newton Aycliffe/Kasado 2018–20. 56/– 1T. 43.8 t.
**PDTRBF.** Hitachi Newton Aycliffe/Kasado 2018–20. 15/– 1TD 2W. 51.7 t.

| | | | | | | | | | |
|---|---|---|---|---|---|---|---|---|---|
| 801201 | LZ | AT | *LN* | BN | 821201 | 822201 | 823201 | 824201 | 825201 |
| | | | | | 826201 | 827201 | 828201 | 829201 | |
| 801202 | LZ | AT | *LN* | BN | 821202 | 822202 | 823202 | 824202 | 825202 |
| | | | | | 826202 | 827202 | 828202 | 829202 | |
| 801203 | LZ | AT | *LN* | BN | 821203 | 822203 | 823203 | 824203 | 825203 |
| | | | | | 826203 | 827203 | 828203 | 829203 | |
| 801204 | LZ | AT | *LN* | BN | 821204 | 822204 | 823204 | 824204 | 825204 |
| | | | | | 826204 | 827204 | 828204 | 829204 | |
| 801205 | LZ | AT | *LN* | BN | 821205 | 822205 | 823205 | 824205 | 825205 |
| | | | | | 826205 | 827205 | 828205 | 829205 | |
| 801206 | LZ | AT | *LN* | BN | 821206 | 822206 | 823206 | 824206 | 825206 |
| | | | | | 826206 | 827206 | 828206 | 829206 | |

| | | | | | | | | |
|---|---|---|---|---|---|---|---|---|
| 801207 | LZ | AT | LN | BN | 821207 | 822207 | 823207 | 824207 | 825207 |
| | | | | | 826207 | 827207 | 828207 | 829207 | |
| 801208 | LZ | AT | LN | BN | 821208 | 822208 | 823208 | 824208 | 825208 |
| | | | | | 826208 | 827208 | 828208 | 829208 | |
| 801209 | LZ | AT | LN | BN | 821209 | 822209 | 823209 | 824209 | 825209 |
| | | | | | 826209 | 827209 | 828209 | 829209 | |
| 801210 | LZ | AT | LN | BN | 821210 | 822210 | 823210 | 824210 | 825210 |
| | | | | | 826210 | 827210 | 828210 | 829210 | |
| 801211 | LZ | AT | LN | BN | 821211 | 822211 | 823211 | 824211 | 825211 |
| | | | | | 826211 | 827211 | 828211 | 829211 | |
| 801212 | LZ | AT | LN | BN | 821212 | 822212 | 823212 | 824212 | 825212 |
| | | | | | 826212 | 827212 | 828212 | 829212 | |
| 801213 | LZ | AT | LN | BN | 821213 | 822213 | 823213 | 824213 | 825213 |
| | | | | | 826213 | 827213 | 828213 | 829213 | |
| 801214 | LZ | AT | LN | BN | 821214 | 822214 | 823214 | 824214 | 825214 |
| | | | | | 826214 | 827214 | 828214 | 829214 | |
| 801215 | LZ | AT | LN | BN | 821215 | 822215 | 823215 | 824215 | 825215 |
| | | | | | 826215 | 827215 | 828215 | 829215 | |
| 801216 | LZ | AT | LN | BN | 821216 | 822216 | 823216 | 824216 | 825216 |
| | | | | | 826216 | 827216 | 828216 | 829216 | |
| 801217 | LZ | AT | LN | BN | 821217 | 822217 | 823217 | 824217 | 825217 |
| | | | | | 826217 | 827217 | 828217 | 829217 | |
| 801218 | LZ | AT | LN | BN | 821218 | 822218 | 823218 | 824218 | 825218 |
| | | | | | 826218 | 827218 | 828218 | 829218 | |
| 801219 | LZ | AT | LN | BN | 821219 | 822219 | 823219 | 824219 | 825219 |
| | | | | | 826219 | 827219 | 828219 | 829219 | |
| 801220 | LZ | AT | LN | BN | 821220 | 822220 | 823220 | 824220 | 825220 |
| | | | | | 826220 | 827220 | 828220 | 829220 | |
| 801221 | LZ | AT | LN | BN | 821221 | 822221 | 823221 | 824221 | 825221 |
| | | | | | 826221 | 827221 | 828221 | 829221 | |
| 801222 | LZ | AT | LN | BN | 821222 | 822222 | 823222 | 824222 | 825222 |
| | | | | | 826222 | 827222 | 828222 | 829222 | |
| 801223 | LZ | AT | LN | BN | 821223 | 822223 | 823223 | 824223 | 825223 |
| | | | | | 826223 | 827223 | 828223 | 829223 | |
| 801224 | LZ | AT | LN | BN | 821224 | 822224 | 823224 | 824224 | 825224 |
| | | | | | 826224 | 827224 | 828224 | 829224 | |
| 801225 | LZ | AT | LN | BN | 821225 | 822225 | 823225 | 824225 | 825225 |
| | | | | | 826225 | 827225 | 828225 | 829225 | |
| 801226 | LZ | AT | LN | BN | 821226 | 822226 | 823226 | 824226 | 825226 |
| | | | | | 826226 | 827226 | 828226 | 829226 | |
| 801227 | LZ | AT | LN | BN | 821227 | 822227 | 823227 | 824227 | 825227 |
| | | | | | 826227 | 827227 | 828227 | 829227 | |
| 801228 | LZ | AT | LN | BN | 821228 | 822228 | 823228 | 824228 | 825228 |
| | | | | | 826228 | 827228 | 828228 | 829228 | |
| 801229 | LZ | AT | LN | BN | 821229 | 822229 | 823229 | 824229 | 825229 |
| | | | | | 826229 | 827229 | 828229 | 829229 | |
| 801230 | LZ | AT | LN | BN | 821230 | 822230 | 823230 | 824230 | 825230 |
| | | | | | 826230 | 827230 | 828230 | 829230 | |

# CLASS 802          AT300                    HITACHI

These units are technically very similar to the Class 800s. The GWR units have modifications to the roof-mounted brake resistors for frequent operation along the Dawlish seawall.

**Formation:** Various, full details awaited.
**Systems:** Diesel/25 kV AC overhead electric.
**Construction:** Aluminium.
**Diesel engines:** In the 5-car sets diesel engines are located in cars 2, 3 and 4. In the 9-car sets diesel engines are located in cars 2, 3, 5, 7 and 8.
**Engines:** MTU 12V 1600 R80L of 700 kW (940 hp).
**Traction Motors:** Four Hitachi asynchronous of 226 kW.
**Wheel Arrangement:** 2-2 + Bo-Bo + Bo-Bo + 2-2 or
2-2 + Bo-Bo + Bo-Bo + 2-2 + Bo-Bo + 2-2 + Bo-Bo + Bo-Bo + 2-2.

| | |
|---|---|
| **Braking:** Disc & regenerative. | **Dimensions:** 25.35/25.00 m x 2.74 m. |
| **Bogies:** Hitachi. | **Couplers:** Dellner 10. |
| **Gangways:** Within unit. | **Control System:** IGBT Inverter. |
| **Doors:** Single-leaf sliding. | **Maximum Speed:** 125 mph. |

**Heating & ventilation:** Air conditioning.
**Seating Layout:** 1: 2+1 facing/unidirectional; 2+2 facing/unidirectional.
**Multiple Working:** Within class and with all Classes 8xx.

**Class 802/0.** 5-car Great Western Railway units. Pre-series units 802 001/002 were built at Kasado and the remainder at Pistoia.
**Formation:** PDTS–MS–MS–MC–PDTRBF.

**PDTS.** Hitachi Pistoia/Kasado 2017–18. –/56 1TD. 48.0 t.
**MS.** Hitachi Pistoia/Kasado 2017–18. –/88. 50.9 t.
**MS.** Hitachi Pistoia/Kasado 2017–18. –/88 2T 51.1 t.
**MC.** Hitachi Pistoia/Kasado 2017–18. 18/58 1T. 51.5 t.
**PDTRBF.** Hitachi Pistoia/Kasado 2017–18. 18/– 1TD 2W. 51.3 t.

| | | | | | | | | | |
|---|---|---|---|---|---|---|---|---|---|
| 802 001 | **GW** | E | *GW* | NP | 831001 | 832001 | 833001 | 834001 | 835001 |
| 802 002 | **GW** | E | *GW* | NP | 831002 | 832002 | 833002 | 834002 | 835002 |
| 802 003 | **GW** | E | *GW* | NP | 831003 | 832003 | 833003 | 834003 | 835003 |
| 802 004 | **GW** | E | *GW* | NP | 831004 | 832004 | 833004 | 834004 | 835004 |
| 802 005 | **GW** | E | *GW* | NP | 831005 | 832005 | 833005 | 834005 | 835005 |
| 802 006 | **GW** | E | *GW* | NP | 831006 | 832006 | 833006 | 834006 | 835006 |
| 802 007 | **GW** | E | *GW* | NP | 831007 | 832007 | 833007 | 834007 | 835007 |
| 802 008 | **GW** | E | *GW* | NP | 831008 | 832008 | 833008 | 834008 | 835008 |
| 802 009 | **GW** | E | *GW* | NP | 831009 | 832009 | 833009 | 834009 | 835009 |
| 802 010 | **GW** | E | *GW* | NP | 831010 | 832010 | 833010 | 834010 | 835010 |
| 802 011 | **GW** | E | *GW* | NP | 831011 | 832011 | 833011 | 834011 | 835011 |
| 802 012 | **GW** | E | *GW* | NP | 831012 | 832012 | 833012 | 834012 | 835012 |
| 802 013 | **GW** | E | *GW* | NP | 831013 | 832013 | 833013 | 834013 | 835013 |
| 802 014 | **GW** | E | *GW* | NP | 831014 | 832014 | 833014 | 834014 | 835014 |
| 802 015 | **GW** | E | *GW* | NP | 831015 | 832015 | 833015 | 834015 | 835015 |
| 802 016 | **GW** | E | *GW* | NP | 831016 | 832016 | 833016 | 834016 | 835016 |
| 802 017 | **GW** | E | *GW* | NP | 831017 | 832017 | 833017 | 834017 | 835017 |
| 802 018 | **GW** | E | *GW* | NP | 831018 | 832018 | 833018 | 834018 | 835018 |
| 802 019 | **GW** | E | *GW* | NP | 831019 | 832019 | 833019 | 834019 | 835019 |

| 802 020 | **GW** | E | *GW* | NP | 831020 | 832020 | 833020 | 834020 | 835020 |
|---------|--------|---|------|----|--------|--------|--------|--------|--------|
| 802 021 | **GW** | E | *GW* | NP | 831021 | 832021 | 833021 | 834021 | 835021 |
| 802 022 | **GW** | E | *GW* | NP | 831022 | 832022 | 833022 | 834022 | 835022 |

**Names (one on each driving car):**

| 802 006 | Harry Billinge MBE LdH |
|---------|------------------------|
| 802 008 | Rick Rescorla/RNLB Solomon Browne |
| 802 010 | Corporal George Sheard |
| 802 011 | Sir Joshua Reynolds PRA/Capt. Robert Falcon Scott RN CVO |
| 802 013 | Michael Eavis CBE |

**Class 802/1.** 9-car Great Western Railway units. Pre-series unit 802 101 was built at Kasado and the remainder at Pistoia.
**Formation:** PDTS–MS–MS–TS–MS–TS–MC–MF–PDTRBF.

**PDTS.** Hitachi Pistoia/Kasado 2017–18. –/48 1TD 2W. 47.7 t.
**MS.** Hitachi Pistoia/Kasado 2017–18. –/88 1T. 50.1 t.
**MS.** Hitachi Pistoia/Kasado 2017–18. –/88 2T. 50.3 t.
**TS.** Hitachi Pistoia/Kasado 2017–18. –/88. 41.0 t.
**MS.** Hitachi Pistoia/Kasado 2017–18. –/88 2T. 50.3 t.
**TS.** Hitachi Pistoia/Kasado 2017–18. –/88 2T. 38.3 t.
**MS.** Hitachi Pistoia/Kasado 2017–18. –/88. 50.3 t.
**MF.** Hitachi Pistoia/Kasado 2017–18. 56/– 1T. 50.6 t.
**PDTRBF.** Hitachi Pistoia/Kasado 2017–18. 15/– 1TD 2W. 51.7 t.

| 802 101 | **GW** | E | *GW* | NP | 831101 | 832101 | 833101 | 834101 | 835101 |
|---------|--------|---|------|----|--------|--------|--------|--------|--------|
|         |        |   |      |    | 836101 | 837101 | 838101 | 839101 |        |
| 802 102 | **GW** | E | *GW* | NP | 831102 | 832102 | 833102 | 834102 | 835102 |
|         |        |   |      |    | 836102 | 837102 | 838102 | 839102 |        |
| 802 103 | **GW** | E | *GW* | NP | 831103 | 832103 | 833103 | 834103 | 835103 |
|         |        |   |      |    | 836103 | 837103 | 838103 | 839103 |        |
| 802 104 | **GW** | E | *GW* | NP | 831104 | 832104 | 833104 | 834104 | 835104 |
|         |        |   |      |    | 836104 | 837104 | 838104 | 839104 |        |
| 802 105 | **GW** | E | *GW* | NP | 831105 | 832105 | 833105 | 834105 | 835105 |
|         |        |   |      |    | 836105 | 837105 | 838105 | 839105 |        |
| 802 106 | **GW** | E | *GW* | NP | 831106 | 832106 | 833106 | 834106 | 835106 |
|         |        |   |      |    | 836106 | 837106 | 838106 | 839106 |        |
| 802 107 | **GW** | E | *GW* | NP | 831107 | 832107 | 833107 | 834107 | 835107 |
|         |        |   |      |    | 836107 | 837107 | 838107 | 839107 |        |
| 802 108 | **GW** | E | *GW* | NP | 831108 | 832108 | 833108 | 834108 | 835108 |
|         |        |   |      |    | 836108 | 837108 | 838108 | 839108 |        |
| 802 109 | **GW** | E | *GW* | NP | 831109 | 832109 | 833109 | 834109 | 835109 |
|         |        |   |      |    | 836109 | 837109 | 838109 | 839109 |        |
| 802 110 | **GW** | E | *GW* | NP | 831110 | 832110 | 833110 | 834110 | 835110 |
|         |        |   |      |    | 836110 | 837110 | 838110 | 839110 |        |
| 802 111 | **GW** | E | *GW* | NP | 831111 | 832111 | 833111 | 834111 | 835111 |
|         |        |   |      |    | 836111 | 837111 | 838111 | 839111 |        |
| 802 112 | **GW** | E | *GW* | NP | 831112 | 832112 | 833112 | 834112 | 835112 |
|         |        |   |      |    | 836112 | 837112 | 838112 | 839112 |        |
| 802 113 | **GW** | E | *GW* | NP | 831113 | 832113 | 833113 | 834113 | 835113 |
|         |        |   |      |    | 836113 | 837113 | 838113 | 839113 |        |

| 802 114 | **GW** | E | *GW* | NP | 831114 | 832114 | 833114 | 834114 | 835114 |
|---------|--------|---|------|----|--------|--------|--------|--------|--------|
|         |        |   |      |    | 836114 | 837114 | 838114 | 839114 |        |

**Name:** 802 101    Nancy Astor CH

**Class 802/2.** TransPennine Express units.
**Formation:** PDTS–MS–MS–MS–PDTF.

**PDTS.** Hitachi Pistoia/Kasado 2018–19. –/56 1TD. 48.0 t.
**MS.** Hitachi Pistoia/Kasado 2018–19. –/86. 50.9 t.
**MS.** Hitachi Pistoia/Kasado 2018–19. –/88 2T 51.1 t.
**MS.** Hitachi Pistoia/Kasado 2018–19. –/88 1T 51.3 t.
**PDTRBF.** Hitachi Pistoia/Kasado 2018–19. 24/– 1TD 2W. 50.2 t.

| 802 201 | **TP** | A | *TP* | DN | 831201 | 832201 | 833201 | 834201 | 835201 |
|---------|--------|---|------|----|--------|--------|--------|--------|--------|
| 802 202 | **TP** | A | *TP* | DN | 831202 | 832202 | 833202 | 834202 | 835202 |
| 802 203 | **TP** | A | *TP* | DN | 831203 | 832203 | 833203 | 834203 | 835203 |
| 802 204 | **TP** | A | *TP* | DN | 831204 | 832204 | 833204 | 834204 | 835204 |
| 802 205 | **TP** | A | *TP* | DN | 831205 | 832205 | 833205 | 834205 | 835205 |
| 802 206 | **TP** | A | *TP* | DN | 831206 | 832206 | 833206 | 834206 | 835206 |
| 802 207 | **TP** | A | *TP* | DN | 831207 | 832207 | 833207 | 834207 | 835207 |
| 802 208 | **TP** | A | *TP* | DN | 831208 | 832208 | 833208 | 834208 | 835208 |
| 802 209 | **TP** | A | *TP* | DN | 831209 | 832209 | 833209 | 834209 | 835209 |
| 802 210 | **TP** | A | *TP* | DN | 831210 | 832210 | 833210 | 834210 | 835210 |
| 802 211 | **TP** | A | *TP* | DN | 831211 | 832211 | 833211 | 834211 | 835211 |
| 802 212 | **TP** | A | *TP* | DN | 831212 | 832212 | 833212 | 834212 | 835212 |
| 802 213 | **TP** | A | *TP* | DN | 831213 | 832213 | 833213 | 834213 | 835213 |
| 802 214 | **TP** | A | *TP* | DN | 831214 | 832214 | 833214 | 834214 | 835214 |
| 802 215 | **TP** | A | *TP* | DN | 831215 | 832215 | 833215 | 834215 | 835215 |
| 802 216 | **TP** | A | *TP* | DN | 831216 | 832216 | 833216 | 834216 | 835216 |
| 802 217 | **TP** | A | *TP* | DN | 831217 | 832217 | 833217 | 834217 | 835217 |
| 802 218 | **TP** | A | *TP* | DN | 831218 | 832218 | 833218 | 834218 | 835218 |
| 802 219 | **TP** | A | *TP* | DN | 831219 | 832219 | 833219 | 834219 | 835219 |

**Class 802/3.** Hull Trains units.
**Formation:** PDTS–MS–MS–MS–PDTF.

**PDTS.** Hitachi Pistoia 2018–19. –/50 1TD 1W. 48.0 t.
**MS.** Hitachi Pistoia 2018–19. –/88. 49.6 t.
**MS.** Hitachi Pistoia 2018–19. –/88 2T 50.4 t.
**MC.** Hitachi Pistoia 2018–19. 18/58 1T 50.4 t.
**PDTRBF.** Hitachi Pistoia 2018–19. 25/– 1TD 2W. 49.6 t.

| 802 301 | **HT** | A | *HT* | BN | 831301 | 832301 | 833301 | 834301 | 835301 |
|---------|--------|---|------|----|--------|--------|--------|--------|--------|
| 802 302 | **HT** | A | *HT* | BN | 831302 | 832302 | 833302 | 834302 | 835302 |
| 802 303 | **HT** | A | *HT* | BN | 831303 | 832303 | 833303 | 834303 | 835303 |
| 802 304 | **HT** | A | *HT* | BN | 831304 | 832304 | 833304 | 834304 | 835304 |
| 802 305 | **HT** | A | *HT* | BN | 831305 | 832305 | 833305 | 834305 | 835305 |

# CLASS 803                                              HITACHI

Five 5-car electric-only units under construction for First Group for its planned open access service on the East Coast Main Line from King's Cross to Edinburgh, due to start in autumn 2021. Full details awaited.

**Formation:** PDTS–MS–MS–MS–PDTS.
**Systems:** 25 kV AC overhead electric.
**Construction:** Aluminium.
**Traction Motors:**
**Wheel Arrangement:** 2-2 + Bo-Bo + Bo-Bo + Bo-Bo + 2-2.
**Braking:** Disc & regenerative.     **Dimensions:**
**Bogies:** Hitachi.                  **Couplers:** Dellner 10.
**Gangways:** Within unit.            **Control System:** IGBT Inverter.
**Doors:** Single-leaf sliding.       **Maximum Speed:** 125 mph.
**Heating & ventilation:** Air conditioning.
**Seating Layout:**
**Multiple Working:** Within class and with all Classes 8xx.

**PDTS.** Hitachi Kasado/Newton Aycliffe 2020–21.
**MS.** Hitachi Kasado/Newton Aycliffe 2020–21.
**MS.** Hitachi Kasado/Newton Aycliffe 2020–21.
**MS.** Hitachi Kasado/Newton Aycliffe 2020–21.
**PDTF.** Hitachi Kasado/Newton Aycliffe 2020–21.

| | | | | | | |
|---|---|---|---|---|---|---|
| 803001 | FG | 841001 | 842001 | 843001 | 844001 | 845001 |
| 803002 | FG | 841002 | 842002 | 843002 | 844002 | 845002 |
| 803003 | FG | 841003 | 842003 | 843003 | 844003 | 845003 |
| 803004 | FG | 841004 | 842004 | 843004 | 844004 | 845004 |
| 803005 | FG | 841005 | 842005 | 843005 | 844005 | 845005 |

# CLASS 805                                              HITACHI

These 13 5-car bi-mode units are on order for Avanti West Coast and will enter service in 2022, replacing the Class 221 Voyagers and operating services such as Euston–Chester–Holyhead, allowing the elimination of long-distance diesel operation on the West Coast Main Line. Full details awaited.

**Formation:** PDTS–MS–MS–MS–PDTF.
**Systems:** Diesel/25 kV AC overhead electric.
**Construction:** Aluminium.
**Engines:**
**Construction:** Aluminium.
**Traction Motors:**
**Wheel Arrangement:** 2-2 + Bo-Bo + Bo-Bo + Bo-Bo + 2-2.
**Braking:** Disc & regenerative.     **Dimensions:**
**Bogies:** Hitachi.                  **Couplers:** Dellner 10.
**Gangways:** Within unit.            **Control System:** IGBT Inverter.
**Doors:** Single-leaf sliding.       **Maximum Speed:** 125 mph.
**Heating & ventilation:** Air conditioning.
**Seating Layout:**

**Multiple Working:** Within class and with all Classes 8xx.

**PDTS.** Hitachi Kasado/Newton Aycliffe 2020–21.
**MS.** Hitachi Kasado/Newton Aycliffe 2020–21.
**MS.** Hitachi Kasado/Newton Aycliffe 2020–21.
**MS.** Hitachi Kasado/Newton Aycliffe 2020–21.
**PDTF.** Hitachi Kasado/Newton Aycliffe 2020–21.

| | | | | | | |
|---|---|---|---|---|---|---|
| 805 001 | RR | 861 001 | 862 001 | 863 001 | 864 001 | 865 001 |
| 805 002 | RR | 861 002 | 862 002 | 863 002 | 864 002 | 865 002 |
| 805 003 | RR | 861 003 | 862 003 | 863 003 | 864 003 | 865 003 |
| 805 004 | RR | 861 004 | 862 004 | 863 004 | 864 004 | 865 004 |
| 805 005 | RR | 861 005 | 862 005 | 863 005 | 864 005 | 865 005 |
| 805 006 | RR | 861 006 | 862 006 | 863 006 | 864 006 | 865 006 |
| 805 007 | RR | 861 007 | 862 007 | 863 007 | 864 007 | 865 007 |
| 805 008 | RR | 861 008 | 862 008 | 863 008 | 864 008 | 865 008 |
| 805 009 | RR | 861 009 | 862 009 | 863 009 | 864 009 | 865 009 |
| 805 010 | RR | 861 010 | 862 010 | 863 010 | 864 010 | 865 010 |
| 805 011 | RR | 861 011 | 862 011 | 863 011 | 864 011 | 865 011 |
| 805 012 | RR | 861 012 | 862 012 | 863 012 | 864 012 | 865 012 |
| 805 013 | RR | 861 013 | 862 013 | 863 013 | 864 013 | 865 013 |

# CLASS 807                                    HITACHI

These ten 7-car electric units for Avanti West Coast will be similar to Class 801s, in that they will have one diesel engine. They are planned to be used on services between Euston, the Midlands and Liverpool from 2022. Full details awaited.

**Formation:** PDTS–MS–MS–TS–MS–MC–PDTF.
**Systems:** 25 kV AC overhead electric, plus one diesel engine per set.
**Construction:** Aluminium.
**Engines:**
**Construction:** Aluminium.
**Traction Motors:**
**Wheel Arrangement:**
**Braking:** Disc & regenerative.           **Dimensions:**
**Bogies:** Hitachi.                        **Couplers:** Dellner 10.
**Gangways:** Within unit.                  **Control System:** IGBT Inverter.
**Doors:** Single-leaf sliding.             **Maximum Speed:** 125 mph.
**Heating & ventilation:** Air conditioning.
**Seating Layout:**
**Multiple Working:** Within class and with all Classes 8xx.

**PDTS.** Hitachi Kasado/Newton Aycliffe 2020–21.
**MS.** Hitachi Kasado/Newton Aycliffe 2020–21.
**MS.** Hitachi Kasado/Newton Aycliffe 2020–21.
**TS.** Hitachi Kasado/Newton Aycliffe 2020–21.
**MS.** Hitachi Kasado/Newton Aycliffe 2020–21.
**MC.** Hitachi Kasado/Newton Aycliffe 2020–21.
**PDTF.** Hitachi Kasado/Newton Aycliffe 2020–21.

| 807 001 | RR | 871001 | 872001 | 873001 | 874001 | 875001 |
|         |    | 876001 | 877001 |        |        |        |
| 807 002 | RR | 871002 | 872002 | 873002 | 874002 | 875002 |
|         |    | 876002 | 877002 |        |        |        |
| 807 003 | RR | 871003 | 872003 | 873003 | 874003 | 875003 |
|         |    | 876003 | 877003 |        |        |        |
| 807 004 | RR | 871004 | 872004 | 873004 | 874004 | 875004 |
|         |    | 876004 | 877004 |        |        |        |
| 807 005 | RR | 871005 | 872005 | 873005 | 874005 | 875005 |
|         |    | 876005 | 877005 |        |        |        |
| 807 006 | RR | 871006 | 872006 | 873006 | 874006 | 875006 |
|         |    | 876006 | 877006 |        |        |        |
| 807 007 | RR | 871007 | 872007 | 873007 | 874007 | 875007 |
|         |    | 876007 | 877007 |        |        |        |
| 807 008 | RR | 871008 | 872008 | 873008 | 874008 | 875008 |
|         |    | 876008 | 877008 |        |        |        |
| 807 009 | RR | 871009 | 872009 | 873009 | 874009 | 875009 |
|         |    | 876009 | 877009 |        |        |        |
| 807 010 | RR | 871010 | 872010 | 873010 | 874010 | 875010 |
|         |    | 876010 | 877010 |        |        |        |

# CLASS 810     AT300 SXR     HITACHI

East Midlands Railway has ordered this fleet of 33 5-car bi-mode units for use on the Midland Main Line, principally between St Pancras and Sheffield/Nottingham, from 2023. They will have shorter 24 m bodies to better match platforms on the route. Full details awaited.

**Formation:** PDTRBF–MC–TS–MS–DPTS.
**Systems:** Diesel/25 kV AC overhead electric.
**Construction:** Aluminium.
**Diesel engines:** Diesel engines are located in cars 1, 2, 4 and 5.
**Engines:** MTU of 735 kW (985 hp).
**Construction:** Aluminium.
**Traction Motors:** Four Hitachi asynchronous of 250 kW.
**Wheel Arrangement:**
**Braking:** Disc & regenerative.
**Bogies:** Hitachi.
**Gangways:** Within unit.
**Doors:** Single-leaf sliding.
**Heating & ventilation:** Air conditioning.
**Seating Layout:** 1: 2+1 facing/unidirectional; 2+2 facing/unidirectional.
**Multiple Working:** Within class and with all Classes 8xx.

**Dimensions:**
**Couplers:** Dellner 10.
**Control System:** IGBT Inverter.
**Maximum Speed:** 125 mph.

**PDTRBF.** Hitachi Newton Aycliffe 2021–22.
**MS.** Hitachi Newton Aycliffe 2021–22.
**TS.** Hitachi Newton Aycliffe 2021–22.
**MS.** Hitachi Newton Aycliffe 2021–22.
**DPTS.** Hitachi Newton Aycliffe 2021–22.

| | | | | | |
|---|---|---|---|---|---|
| 810001 | RR | 851001 | 852001 | 853001 | 854001 | 855001 |
| 810002 | RR | 851002 | 852002 | 853002 | 854002 | 855002 |
| 810003 | RR | 851003 | 852003 | 853003 | 854003 | 855003 |
| 810004 | RR | 851004 | 852004 | 853004 | 854004 | 855004 |
| 810005 | RR | 851005 | 852005 | 853005 | 854005 | 855005 |
| 810006 | RR | 851006 | 852006 | 853006 | 854006 | 855006 |
| 810007 | RR | 851007 | 852007 | 853007 | 854007 | 855007 |
| 810008 | RR | 851008 | 852008 | 853008 | 854008 | 855008 |
| 810009 | RR | 851009 | 852009 | 853009 | 854009 | 855009 |
| 810010 | RR | 851010 | 852010 | 853010 | 854010 | 855010 |
| 810011 | RR | 851011 | 852011 | 853011 | 854011 | 855011 |
| 810012 | RR | 851012 | 852012 | 853012 | 854012 | 855012 |
| 810013 | RR | 851013 | 852013 | 853013 | 854013 | 855013 |
| 810014 | RR | 851014 | 852014 | 853014 | 854014 | 855014 |
| 810015 | RR | 851015 | 852015 | 853015 | 854015 | 855015 |
| 810016 | RR | 851016 | 852016 | 853016 | 854016 | 855016 |
| 810017 | RR | 851017 | 852017 | 853017 | 854017 | 855017 |
| 810018 | RR | 851018 | 852018 | 853018 | 854018 | 855018 |
| 810019 | RR | 851019 | 852019 | 853019 | 854019 | 855019 |
| 810020 | RR | 851020 | 852020 | 853020 | 854020 | 855020 |
| 810021 | RR | 851021 | 852021 | 853021 | 854021 | 855021 |
| 810022 | RR | 851022 | 852022 | 853022 | 854022 | 855022 |
| 810023 | RR | 851023 | 852023 | 853023 | 854023 | 855023 |
| 810024 | RR | 851024 | 852024 | 853024 | 854024 | 855024 |
| 810025 | RR | 851025 | 852025 | 853025 | 854025 | 855025 |
| 810026 | RR | 851026 | 852026 | 853026 | 854026 | 855026 |
| 810027 | RR | 851027 | 852027 | 853027 | 854027 | 855027 |
| 810028 | RR | 851028 | 852028 | 853028 | 854028 | 855028 |
| 810029 | RR | 851029 | 852029 | 853029 | 854029 | 855029 |
| 810030 | RR | 851030 | 852030 | 853030 | 854030 | 855030 |
| 810031 | RR | 851031 | 852031 | 853031 | 854031 | 855031 |
| 810032 | RR | 851032 | 852032 | 853032 | 854032 | 855032 |
| 810033 | RR | 851033 | 852033 | 853033 | 854033 | 855033 |

# 4.5. EUROSTAR UNITS

The original Eurostar Class 373 units were built for and are normally used on services between Britain and continental Europe via the Channel Tunnel. SNCF-owned units 3225/26 and 3227/28 have been removed from the Eurostar pool and withdrawn. As they are not now permitted through the Channel Tunnel these units are not listed here.

The trailers from SNCF set 3203/04 were refurbished and renumbered to run with power cars 3211/12 (original power cars 3203/04 have been scrapped, as have the trailers from 3211/12).

Each Class 373 train consists of two 10-car units coupled, with a motor car at each driving end. All units are articulated with an extra motor bogie on the coach adjacent to the motor car.

All Class 373 sets can be used between London St Pancras and Paris, Brussels and Disneyland Paris. Certain sets (shown *) are equipped for 1500 V DC operation and are used for the winter service to Bourg Saint Maurice and the summer service to Avignon. All eight refurbished units are fitted for operation on 1500 V DC.

Seven 8-car Class 373 sets were built for Regional Eurostar services, but apart from power cars 3304 and 3308 which have been preserved, the rest have been scrapped.

The second generation Eurostar trains, the Siemens Class 374s, have now been introduced and have replaced most of the Class 373s. Eight sets have been fully refurbished and will be retained as part of Eurostar's long-term fleet – 3007/08, 3015/16, 3205/06, 3209/10, 3211/12, 3219/20, 3221/22 and 3229/30. However, at the time of writing the whole Class 373 fleet was mothballed following the reduction in services as a result of the Covid-19 pandemic.

## CLASS 373     "THREE CAPITALS" EUROSTARS

**10-car half-sets.** Built for services starting from or terminating in London Waterloo (now St Pancras). Individual vehicles in each set are allocated numbers 373xxx0 + 373xxx1 + 373xxx2 + 373xxx3 + 373xxx4 + 373xxx5 + 373xxx6 + 373xxx7 + 373xxx8 + 373xxx9, where 3xxx denotes the set number.

**Formation:** DM–MS–4TS–RB–2TF–TBF. Gangwayed within pair of units. Air conditioned.
**Construction:** Steel.
**Supply Systems:** 25 kV AC 50 Hz overhead or 3000 V DC overhead
(* also equipped for 1500 V DC overhead operation).
**Control System:** GTO–GTO Inverter on UK 750 V DC and 25 kV AC, GTO Chopper on SNCB 3000 V DC.
**Continuous rating:** 12 x 240 kW (25 kV AC); 5700 kW (1500 and 3000 V DC).
**Wheel Arrangement:** Bo-Bo + Bo–2–2–2–2–2–2–2–2–2.
**Lengths:** 22.15 m (DM), 21.85 m (MS & TBF), 18.70 m (other cars).
**Couplers:** Schaku 10S at outer ends, Schaku 10L at inner end of each DM and outer ends of each sub set.

**Maximum Speed:** 186 mph (300 km/h).
**Built:** 1992–93 by GEC-Alsthom/Brush/ANF/De Dietrich/BN Construction/ACEC.

DM vehicles carry the set numbers indicated below.

**Non-standard livery:** 3213 and 3224 – Izy (green, white & purple).

† Refurbished.

At the time of writing the following sets were misformed: 3213 with 3224 and 3214 with 3223.
3213/24 is on hire to Thalys for the Paris–Brussels "Izy" service.

**373xxx0 series. DM.** Lot No. 31118 1992–95. 68.5 t.
**373xxx1 series. MS.** Lot No. 31119 1992–95. –/48 2T. 44.6 t.
**373xxx2 series. TS.** Lot No. 31120 1992–95. –/56 1T. 28.1 t.
**373xxx3 series. TS.** Lot No. 31121 1992–95. –/56 2T. 29.7 t.
**373xxx4 series. TS.** Lot No. 31122 1992–95. –/56 1T. 28.3 t.
**373xxx5 series. TS.** Lot No. 31123 1992–95. –/56 2T. 29.2 t.
**373xxx6 series. RB.** Lot No. 31124 1992–95. 31.1 t.
**373xxx7 series. TF.** Lot No. 31125 1992–95. 39/– 1T. 29.6 t.
**373xxx8 series. TF.** Lot No. 31126 1992–95. 39/– 1T. 32.2 t.
**373xxx9 series. TBF.** Lot No. 31127 1992–95. 25/– 1TD. 39.4 t.

| | | | | | |
|---|---|---|---|---|---|
| 3007 | †* **ES** | EU | *EU* | TI | |
| 3008 | †* **ES** | EU | *EU* | TI | |
| 3015 | †* **ES** | EU | *EU* | TI | |
| 3016 | †* **ES** | EU | *EU* | TI | |
| 3205 | †* **ES** | SF | *EU* | LY | |
| 3206 | †* **ES** | SF | *EU* | LY | |
| 3209 | †* **ES** | SF | *EU* | LY | |
| 3210 | †* **ES** | SF | *EU* | LY | |
| 3211 | †* **ES** | SF | *EU* | LY | |
| 3212 | †* **ES** | SF | *EU* | LY | |
| 3213 | * | **0** | SF | *EU* | LY |
| 3214 | * | **EU** | SF | | LY |

| | | | | | |
|---|---|---|---|---|---|
| 3215 | * | **EU** | SF | | TI |
| 3216 | * | **EU** | SF | | TI |
| 3217 | | **EU** | SF | | TI |
| 3218 | | **EU** | SF | | TI |
| 3219 | †* **ES** | SF | *EU* | LY | |
| 3220 | †* **ES** | SF | *EU* | LY | |
| 3221 | †* **ES** | SF | *EU* | LY | |
| 3222 | †* **ES** | SF | *EU* | LY | |
| 3223 | * | **EU** | SF | | LY |
| 3224 | * | **0** | SF | *EU* | LY |
| 3229 | †* **ES** | SF | *EU* | LY | |
| 3230 | †* **ES** | SF | *EU* | LY | |

**Spare DM:**

3999    **ES**    EU    *EU*    TI

# CLASS 374                          SIEMENS VELARO e320

**8-car half-sets.** These units are similar to the DB Class 407 ICE sets, with distributed power rather than a power car at either end like the Class 373s. The first sets entered service in November 2015, operating initially on the St Pancras–Paris route. They have also been used on the new St Pancras–Amsterdam service from 2018.

The initial order was for ten units (4001–20) and this was then increased by another seven (4021–34) in 2014. An option exists for a further six units.

**Formation:** DMF–TBF–MS–TS–TS–MS–TS–MSRB.
Gangwayed within pair of units. Air conditioned.
**Construction:** Aluminium.          **Control System:** IGBT Inverter.
**Supply Systems:** 25 kV AC 50 Hz overhead, 1500 V DC overhead and 3000 V DC overhead.
**Continuous rating:** 8000 kW (25 kV AC), 4200 kW (1500 and 3000 V DC).
**Wheel Arrangement:** Bo-Bo + 2-2 + Bo-Bo + 2-2 + 2-2 + Bo-Bo + 2-2 + Bo-Bo.
**Lengths:** 26.035 m (DMF), 24.775 m (other cars).
**Couplers:** Dellner 12.          **Maximum Speed:** 200 mph (320 km/h).
**Built:** 2012–17 by Siemens, Krefeld, Germany.

DM vehicles carry the full 12-digit EVNs as indicated below. For example set 4001/02 carries the numbers 93 70 3740 011-9 + 93 70 3740 012-7 + 93 70 3740 013-5 + 93 70 3740 014-3 + 93 70 3740 015-0 + 93 70 3740 016-8 + 93 70 3740 017-6 + 93 70 3740 018-4 + 93 70 3740 028-3 + 93 70 3740 027-5 + 93 70 3740 026-7 + 93 70 3740 025-9 + 93 70 3740 024-2 + 93 70 3740 023-4 + 93 70 3740 022-6 + 93 70 3740 021-8.

**93 70 3740 xx1-c series. DMF.** Siemens Krefeld 2012–17. 40/–. 58.0 t.
**93 70 3740 xx2-c series. TBF.** Siemens Krefeld 2012–17. 36/– 2T. 59.0 t.
**93 70 3740 xx3-c series. MF.** Siemens Krefeld 2012–17. 34/–(+2) 2T. 59.0 t.
**93 70 3740 xx4-c series. TS.** Siemens Krefeld 2012–17. –/76 2T. 53.0 t.
**93 70 3740 xx5-c series. TS.** Siemens Krefeld 2012–17. –/76 2T. 53.0 t.
**93 70 3740 xx6-c series. MS.** Siemens Krefeld 2012–17. –/76 2T. 1TD 2W. 58.0 t.
**93 70 3740 xx7-c series. TS.** Siemens Krefeld 2012–17. –/76 2T. 57.0 t.
**93 70 3740 xx8-c series. MSRB.** Siemens Krefeld 2012–17. –/32 2T. 58.0 t.

| | | | | | | | | |
|---|---|---|---|---|---|---|---|---|
| 4001 | **ES** | EU | *EU* | TI | 4018 | **ES** | EU | *EU* | TI |
| 4002 | **ES** | EU | *EU* | TI | 4019 | **ES** | EU | *EU* | TI |
| 4003 | **ES** | EU | *EU* | TI | 4020 | **ES** | EU | *EU* | TI |
| 4004 | **ES** | EU | *EU* | TI | 4021 | **ES** | EU | *EU* | TI |
| 4005 | **ES** | EU | *EU* | TI | 4022 | **ES** | EU | *EU* | TI |
| 4006 | **ES** | EU | *EU* | TI | 4023 | **ES** | EU | *EU* | TI |
| 4007 | **ES** | EU | *EU* | TI | 4024 | **ES** | EU | *EU* | TI |
| 4008 | **ES** | EU | *EU* | TI | 4025 | **ES** | EU | *EU* | TI |
| 4009 | **ES** | EU | *EU* | TI | 4026 | **ES** | EU | *EU* | TI |
| 4010 | **ES** | EU | *EU* | TI | 4027 | **ES** | EU | *EU* | TI |
| 4011 | **ES** | EU | *EU* | TI | 4028 | **ES** | EU | *EU* | TI |
| 4012 | **ES** | EU | *EU* | TI | 4029 | **ES** | EU | *EU* | TI |
| 4013 | **ES** | EU | *EU* | TI | 4030 | **ES** | EU | *EU* | TI |
| 4014 | **ES** | EU | *EU* | TI | 4031 | **ES** | EU | *EU* | TI |
| 4015 | **ES** | EU | *EU* | TI | 4032 | **ES** | EU | *EU* | TI |
| 4016 | **ES** | EU | *EU* | TI | 4033 | **ES** | EU | *EU* | TI |
| 4017 | **ES** | EU | *EU* | TI | 4034 | **ES** | EU | *EU* | TI |

# 4.6. EMU VEHICLES IN INDUSTRIAL SERVICE

This list comprises EMU vehicles that have been withdrawn from active service but continue to be used in industrial service or for emergency training.

| Cl. 390 | 69133 | 69833 |       | Avanti West Coast Training Centre, Westmere Drive, Crewe, Cheshire (ex-unit 390033) |
|---------|-------|-------|-------|---|
| Cl. 390 | 69633 | 69733 |       | The Fire Service College, Moreton-in-Marsh, Gloucestershire (ex-unit 390033) |
| Cl. 390 | 69933 |       |       | Safety & Accident Investigation Centre, Cranfield University, Cranfield, Bedfordshire (ex-unit 390033) |
| Cl. 508 | 64649 | 64712 |       | Emergency Services Training Centre, Seacombe, Merseyside (ex-units 508201/209) |
| Cl. 508 | 64681 | 71511 | 64724 | The Fire Service College, Moreton-in-Marsh, Gloucestershire (unit 508212) |

# 4.7. EMUS AWAITING DISPOSAL

This list comprises former main line EMU vehicles which are awaiting disposal.

## 25 kV AC 50 Hz OVERHEAD UNITS:

| Cl. 309 | **RR** | WC | CS | 71758 |
|---------|--------|----|----|-------|
| Cl. 365 | **N**  | X  | ZN | 65919 |

# 5. ON-TRACK MACHINES

These machines are used for maintaining, renewing and enhancing the infrastructure of the national railway network. With the exception of snowploughs all can be self-propelled, controlled either from a cab mounted on the machine or remotely. They are permitted to operate either under their own power or in train formations throughout the network both within and outside engineering possessions. Machines only permitted to be used within engineering possessions, referred to as On-Track Plant, are not included. Also not included are wagons included in OTM consists and overseas based machines that might make occasional short visits.

For each machine its GB operational number, owner or responsible custodian and type is given, plus its name if carried. In addition, for snow clearance equipment the berthing location is given. Actual operation of each machine is undertaken by either the owner/responsible custodian or a contracted responsible custodian.

Machines were numbered by British Rail with either six-digit wagon series numbers or in the CEPS (Civil Engineers Plant System) series with five prefixed digits. Machines delivered from 2013 onwards carry 12-digit EVN series numbers, most additionally carrying a shorter GB operational number. In most cases the later resemble CEPS numbers. Machines are listed here by GB operational number, which in some cases is also the EVN number. Anomalies in such numbering mean this is not strictly numeric, but the order they would have been if allocated CEPS numbers correctly. Machines that carry additional identifying numbers have these shown "xxxx".

(S) after the registered number designates a machine that is currently stored (the storage location of each is given at the end of this section).

# DYNAMIC TRACK STABILISERS

| | | |
|---|---|---|
| DR 72211 | BB | Plasser & Theurer DGS 62-N |
| DR 72213 | BB | Plasser & Theurer DGS 62-N |

# TAMPERS

### Plasser & Theurer 09 Series

| | | | |
|---|---|---|---|
| DR 73109 | SK | Plasser & Theurer 09-3X-RT | |
| DR 73110 | SK | Plasser & Theurer 09-3X-RT | PETER WHITE |
| DR 73111 | NR | Plasser & Theurer 09-3X-Dynamic | |
| DR 73113 | NR | Plasser & Theurer 09-3X-Dynamic | |
| DR 73114 | NR | Plasser & Theurer 09-3X-Dynamic | Ron Henderson |
| DR 73115 | NR | Plasser & Theurer 09-3X-Dynamic | |
| DR 73116 | NR | Plasser & Theurer 09-3X Dynamic | |
| DR 73117 | NR | Plasser & Theurer 09-3X Dynamic | |
| DR 73118 | NR | Plasser & Theurer 09-3X Dynamic | |
| DR 73120 | NR | Plasser & Theurer 09-3X Dynamic | "99 70 9123 120-6" |

| DR 73121 | NR | Plasser & Theurer 09-2X Dynamic | "99 70 9123 121-4" |
| DR 73122 | NR | Plasser & Theurer 09-2X Dynamic | "99 70 9123 122-2" |
| 928001 | SK | Plasser & Theurer Unimat 09-4x4/4S Dynamic | "99 70 9128 001-3" |
| DR 74002 | SK | Plasser & Theurer Unimat 09-4x4/4S Dynamic | "99 70 9128 002-1" |
| DR 75008 | CS | Plasser & Theurer 09-4x4/4S Dynamic | "99 70 9123 008-3" |
| DR 75009 | CS | Plasser & Theurer 09-4x4/4S Dynamic | "99 70 9123 009-1" |
| DR 75010 | CS | Plasser & Theurer 09-4x4/4S Dynamic | "99 70 9123 010-9" |
| DR 75011 | CS | Plasser & Theurer 09-4x4/4S Dynamic | "99 70 9123 011-7" |
| DR 75012 | SK | Plasser & Theurer 09-4x4/4S Dynamic | "99 70 9123 012-5" |
| DR 75013 | SK | Plasser & Theurer 09-4x4/4S Dynamic | "99 70 9123 013-3" |
| DR 75014 | SK | Plasser & Theurer 09-4x4/4S Dynamic | "99 70 9123 014-1" |
| DR 75015 | SK | Plasser & Theurer 09-4x4/4S Dynamic | "99 70 9123 015-8" |

**Names:**

DR 75010 Roger Nicholas       |     DR 75011     Andrew Smith

**Plasser & Theurer 08 Series and 08 Series (compact)**

| DR 73803 | SK | Plasser & Theurer 08-32U-RT | Alexander Graham Bell |
| DR 73804 | SK | Plasser & Theurer 08-32U-RT | James Watt |
| DR 73805 (S) | CS | Plasser & Theurer 08-16/32U-RT | |
| DR 73806 | CS | Plasser & Theurer 08-16/32U-RT | Karine |
| DR 73904 | SK | Plasser & Theurer 08-4x4/4S-RT | Thomas Telford |
| DR 73905 | CS | Plasser & Theurer 08-4x4/4S-RT | |
| DR 73906 | CS | Plasser & Theurer 08-4x4/4S-RT | Panther |
| DR 73907 | CS | Plasser & Theurer 08-4x4/4S-RT | |
| DR 73908 | CS | Plasser & Theurer 08-4x4/4S-RT | |
| DR 73909 | CS | Plasser & Theurer 08-4x4/4S-RT | Saturn |
| DR 73910 | CS | Plasser & Theurer 08-4x4/4S-RT | Jupiter |
| DR 73911 | CS | Plasser & Theurer 08-16/4x4C-RT | Puma |
| DR 73912 | CS | Plasser & Theurer 08-16/4x4C-RT | Lynx |
| DR 73913 | CS | Plasser & Theurer 08-12/4x4C-RT | |
| DR 73914 | SK | Plasser & Theurer 08-4x4/4S-RT | Robert McAlpine |
| DR 73915 | SK | Plasser & Theurer 08-16/4x4C-RT | William Arrol |
| DR 73916 | SK | Plasser & Theurer 08-16/4x4C-RT | First Engineering |
| DR 73917 | BB | Plasser & Theurer 08-4x4/4S-RT | |
| DR 73918 | BB | Plasser & Theurer 08-4x4/4S-RT | |
| DR 73919 | CS | Plasser & Theurer 08-16/4x4C100-RT (with trailer) | |
| DR 73920 | CS | Plasser & Theurer 08-16/4x4C80-RT | |
| DR 73921 | CS | Plasser & Theurer 08-16/4x4C80-RT | |
| DR 73922 | CS | Plasser & Theurer 08-16/4x4C80-RT | John Snowdon |
| DR 73923 | CS | Plasser & Theurer 08-4x4/4S-RT | Mercury |
| DR 73924 | CS | Plasser & Theurer 08-16/4x4C100-RT | |
| DR 73925 | CS | Plasser & Theurer 08-16/4x4C100-RT | Europa |
| DR 73926 | BB | Plasser & Theurer 08-16/4x4C100-RT | Stephen Keith Blanchard |
| DR 73927 (S) | BB | Plasser & Theurer 08-16/4x4C100-RT | |
| DR 73929 | CS | Plasser & Theurer 08-4x4/4S-RT | |
| DR 73930 | CS | Plasser & Theurer 08-4x4/4S-RT | |
| DR 73931 | CS | Plasser & Theurer 08-16/4x4C100-RT | |
| DR 73932 | SK | Plasser & Theurer 08-4x4/4S-RT | |
| DR 73933 | SK | Plasser & Theurer 08-16/4x4/C100-RT (with trailer) | |

| DR 73934 | SK | Plasser & Theurer 08-16/4x4/C100-RT (with trailer) | |
| DR 73935 | CS | Plasser & Theurer 08-4x4/4S-RT | |
| DR 73936 | CS | Plasser & Theurer 08-4x4/4S-RT | |
| DR 73937 | BB | Plasser & Theurer 08-16/4x4C100-RT | |
| DR 73938 | BB | Plasser & Theurer 08-16/4x4C100-RT | |
| DR 73939 | BB | Plasser & Theurer 08-16/4x4C100-RT Pat Best | |
| DR 73940 | SK | Plasser & Theurer 08-4x4/4S-RT | |
| DR 73941 | SK | Plasser & Theurer 08-4x4/4S-RT | |
| DR 73942 | CS | Plasser & Theurer 08-4x4/4S-RT | |
| DR 73943 | BB | Plasser & Theurer 08-16/4x4C100-RT | |
| DR 73944 | BB | Plasser & Theurer 08-16/4x4C100-RT | |
| DR 73945 | BB | Plasser & Theurer 08-16/4x4C100-RT | |
| DR 73946 | VO | Plasser & Theurer Euromat 08-4x4/4S | |
| DR 73947 | CS | Plasser & Theurer 08-4x4/4S-RT | |
| DR 73948 | CS | Plasser & Theurer 08-4x4/4S-RT | |
| DR 73949 | BB | Plasser & Theurer 08-4x4/4S-RT | "99 70 9123 016-6" |
| DR 73950 | BB | Plasser & Theurer 08-4x4/4S-RT | "99 70 9123 017-4" |

**Matisa**

| DR 75301 | VO | Matisa B 45 UE | | |
| DR 75302 | VO | Matisa B 45 UE | Gary Wright | |
| DR 75303 | VO | Matisa B 45 UE | | |
| DR 75401 | VO | Matisa B 41 UE | | |
| DR 75402 | VO | Matisa B 41 UE | | |
| DR 75404 | VO | Matisa B 41 UE | | |
| DR 75405 | VO | Matisa B 41 UE | | |
| DR 75406 | CS | Matisa B 41 UE | Eric Machell | |
| DR 75407 | CS | Matisa B 41 UE | Gerry Taylor | |
| DR 75408 | BB | Matisa B 41 UE | | |
| DR 75409 | BB | Matisa B 41 UE | | |
| DR 75410 | BB | Matisa B 41 UE | | |
| DR 75411 | BB | Matisa B 41 UE | | |
| DR 75501 | BB | Matisa B 66 UC | | |
| DR 75502 | BB | Matisa B 66 UC | | |
| DR 75503 | VO | Matisa B 66 UC | "Gill Cowling" | "99 70 9124 001-7" |
| DR 75504 | VO | Matisa B 66 UC | | "99 70 9124 002-5" |

# BALLAST CLEANERS

| DR 76501 | NR | Plasser & Theurer RM-900-RT | |
| DR 76502 | NR | Plasser & Theurer RM-900-RT | |
| DR 76503 | NR | Plasser & Theurer RM-900-RT | |
| DR 76504 | NR | Plasser & Theurer RM-900 | "99 70 9314 504-0" |

# VACUUM PREPARATION MACHINES

| DR 76701 | NR | Plasser & Theurer VM80-NR |
| DR 76703 (S) | NR | Plasser & Theurer VM80-NR |

# RAIL VACUUM MACHINES

| 99 70 9515 002-2 | RC | Railcare 16000-480-UK RailVac OTM |
| 99 70 9515 003-0 | RC | Railcare 16000-480-UK RailVac OTM |
| 99 70 9515 004-8 | RC | Railcare 16000-480-UK RailVac OTM |
| 99 70 9515 005-5 | RC | Railcare 16000-480-UK RailVac OTM |

# BALLAST FEEDER MACHINE

| 99 70 9552 020-8 | RC | Railcare Ballast Feeder UK |

# BALLAST TRANSFER MACHINES

| DR 76750 NR | Matisa D75 | *(works with DR 78802/DR 78812/ DR 78822/DR 78832)* |
| DR 76751 NR | Matisa D75 | *(works with DR 78801/DR 78811/ DR 78821/DR 78831)* |

# CONSOLIDATION MACHINES

| DR 76801 | NR | Plasser & Theurer 09-CM-NR |
| DR 76802 | NR | Plasser & Theurer 09-2X-CM "99 70 9320 802-0" |

# FINISHING MACHINES & BALLAST REGULATORS

| DR 77001 | SK | Plasser & Theurer AFM 2000-RT Finishing Machine | Anthony Lou Phillips |
| DR 77002 | SK | Plasser & Theurer AFM 2000-RT Finishing Machine | |
| DR 77010 | NR | Plasser & Theurer USP 6000 Regulator "99 70 9125 010-7" | |
| DR 77322 (S) | BB | Plasser & Theurer USP 5000C Regulator | |
| DR 77327 | CS | Plasser & Theurer USP 5000C Regulator | |
| DR 77336 (S) | BB | Plasser & Theurer USP 5000C Regulator | |
| DR 77801 | VO | Matisa R 24 S Regulator | |
| DR 77802 | VO | Matisa R 24 S Regulator | |
| DR 77901 | CS | Plasser & Theurer USP 5000-RT Regulator | |
| DR 77903 | NR | Plasser & Theurer USP 5000-RT Regulator | |
| DR 77904 | NR | Plasser & Theurer USP 5000-RT Regulator | |
| DR 77905 | NR | Plasser & Theurer USP 5000-RT Regulator | |
| DR 77906 | NR | Plasser & Theurer USP 5000-RT Regulator | |
| DR 77907 | NR | Plasser & Theurer USP 5000-RT Regulator | |
| DR 77908 | SK | Plasser & Theurer USP 5000-RT Regulator | |
| DR 77909 | NR | Plasser & Theurer USP 5000 Regulator "99 70 9125 909-0" | |

# TWIN JIB TRACK RELAYERS

| DRP 78213 | VO | Plasser & Theurer Self-Propelled Heavy Duty |
| DRP 78215 | BA | Plasser & Theurer Self-Propelled Heavy Duty |

| DRP 78216     | BB | Plasser & Theurer Self-Propelled Heavy Duty |
| DRP 78217 (S) | BA | Plasser & Theurer Self-Propelled Heavy Duty |
| DRP 78219     | BA | Plasser & Theurer Self-Propelled Heavy Duty |
| DRP 78221     | BB | Plasser & Theurer Self-Propelled Heavy Duty |
| DRP 78222     | BB | Plasser & Theurer Self-Propelled Heavy Duty |
| DRC 78226     | CS | Cowans Sheldon Self-Propelled Heavy Duty |
| DRC 78229 (S) | NR | Cowans Sheldon Self-Propelled Heavy Duty |
| DRC 78231 (S) | NR | Cowans Sheldon Self-Propelled Heavy Duty |
| DRC 78234 (S) | NR | Cowans Sheldon Self-Propelled Heavy Duty |
| DRC 78235     | CS | Cowans Sheldon Self-Propelled Heavy Duty |

# NEW TRACK CONSTRUCTION
# TRAIN PROPULSION MACHINES

| DR 78701 | BB | Harsco Track Technologies NTC-PW |
| DR 78702 | BB | Harsco Track Technologies NTC-PW |

# TRACK RENEWAL MACHINES

**Matisa P95 Track Renewals Trains**
DR 78801+DR 78811+DR 78821+DR 78831 NR *(works with DR 76751)*
DR 78802+DR 78812+DR 78822+DR 78832 NR *(works with DR 76750)*

# RAIL GRINDING TRAINS

**Loram C21**
| DR 79231 + DR 79232 + DR 79233 + DR 79236 + DR 79237 | | LO |
| DR 79241 + DR 79242 + DR 79243 + DR 79244 + DR 79245 + DR 79246 + DR 79247 | | NR |
| DR 79251 + DR 79252 + DR 79253 + DR 79254 + DR 79255 + DR 79256 + DR 79257 | | NR |

**Names:**  DR 79231          Pete Erwin
         DR 79241/247     Roger South *(one plate on opposite sides of each)*
         DR 79251/257     Martin Elwood *(one plate on opposite sides of each)*

**Harsco Track Technologies RGH20C**
DR 79261 + DR 79271   NR
DR 79262 + DR 79272   NR
DR 79263 + DR 79273   NR
DR 79265 + DR 79264 +DR 79274   NR
DR 79267 + DR 79277   NR

**Loram C44**
| DR 79301 + DR 79302 + | NR | 99 70 9427 038-3 + 99 70 9427 039-1+ |
| DR 79303 + DR 79304 | | 99 70 9427 040-9 + 99 70 9427 041-7 |
| DR 79401 + DR 79402 + | NR | 99 70 9427 042-5 + 99 70 9427 043-3+ |
| DR 79403 + DR 79404 | | 99 70 9427 044-1 + 99 70 9427 045-8 |
| DR 79501 + DR 79502 + | NR | 99 70 9427 046-6 + 99 70 9427 047-4 + |
| DR 79503 + DR 79504 + | | 99 70 9427 048-2 + 99 70 9427 049-0+ |
| DR 79505 + DR 79506 + | | 99 70 9427 050-8 + 99 70 9427 051-6 + |
| DR 79507 | | 99 70 9427 052-4 |

# RAIL MILLING MACHINES

| DR 79101 | XR | Linsinger MG31-UK Milling Machine | "99 70 9127 006-3" |
|---|---|---|---|
| DR 79102 | NR | Linsinger SF06-UK Milling Machine<br>+ trailer DR 79103 | "99 70 9127 007-1" |
| DR 79104 | NR | Linsinger SF06-UK Milling Machine<br>+ trailer DR 79105 | "99 70 9127 008-9" |

| DR 79601 + DR 79602 + | SC | 99 70 9427 063-1 + 99 70 9427 064-9 |
|---|---|---|
| DR 79603 + DR 79604 | | 99 70 9427 065-6 + 99 70 9527 005-1 |
| | Schweerbau High Speed Milling Machine | |

# STONEBLOWERS

| DR 80200 (S) | HR | Pandrol Jackson Plain Line | |
|---|---|---|---|
| DR 80201 | NR | Pandrol Jackson Plain Line | |
| DR 80202 (S) | HR | Pandrol Jackson Plain Line | |
| DR 80203 (S) | HR | Pandrol Jackson Plain Line | |
| DR 80204 (S) | HR | Pandrol Jackson Plain Line | |
| DR 80205 | NR | Pandrol Jackson Plain Line | |
| DR 80206 | NR | Pandrol Jackson Plain Line | |
| DR 80208 | NR | Pandrol Jackson Plain Line | |
| DR 80209 | NR | Pandrol Jackson Plain Line | |
| DR 80210 | NR | Pandrol Jackson Plain Line | |
| DR 80211 | NR | Pandrol Jackson Plain Line | |
| DR 80213 | NR | Harsco Track Technologies Plain Line | |
| DR 80214 | NR | Harsco Track Technologies Plain Line | |
| DR 80215 | NR | Harsco Track Technologies Plain Line | |
| DR 80216 | NR | Harsco Track Technologies Plain Line | |
| DR 80217 | NR | Harsco Track Technologies Plain Line | |
| DR 80301 | NR | Harsco Track Technologies Multi-purpose | Stephen Cornish |
| DR 80302 | NR | Harsco Track Technologies Multi-purpose | |
| DR 80303 | NR | Harsco Track Technologies Multi-purpose | |

# CRANES

| DRP 81505 | BB | Plasser & Theurer 12 tonne Heavy Duty Diesel Hydraulic |
|---|---|---|
| DRP 81508 | BB | Plasser & Theurer 12 tonne Heavy Duty Diesel Hydraulic |
| DRP 81513 | BB | Plasser & Theurer 12 tonne Heavy Duty Diesel Hydraulic |
| DRP 81517 | BB | Plasser & Theurer 12 tonne Heavy Duty Diesel Hydraulic |
| DRP 81525 | BB | Plasser & Theurer 12 tonne Heavy Duty Diesel Hydraulic |
| DRP 81532 | BB | Plasser & Theurer 12 tonne Heavy Duty Diesel Hydraulic |
| DRK 81601 | VO | Kirow KRC 810UK 100 tonne Heavy Duty Diesel Hydraulic |
| DRK 81602 | BB | Kirow KRC 810UK 100 tonne Heavy Duty Diesel Hydraulic |
| DRK 81611 | BB | Kirow KRC 1200UK 125 tonne Heavy Duty Diesel Hydraulic |
| DRK 81612 | CS | Kirow KRC 1200UK 125 tonne Heavy Duty Diesel Hydraulic |
| DRK 81613 | VO | Kirow KRC 1200UK 125 tonne Heavy Duty Diesel Hydraulic |

| DRK 81621 | VO | Kirow KRC 250UK 25 tonne Diesel Hydraulic |
| DRK 81622 | VO | Kirow KRC 250UK 25 tonne Diesel Hydraulic |
| DRK 81623 | SK | Kirow KRC 250UK 25 tonne Diesel Hydraulic |
| DRK 81624 | SK | Kirow KRC 250UK 25 tonne Diesel Hydraulic |
| DRK 81625 | SK | Kirow KRC 250UK 25 tonne Diesel Hydraulic |
| DRK 81626 | SK | Kirow KRC 250S 25 tonne Diesel Hydraulic "99 70 9319 012-9" |

99 70 9319 013-7  NR  Kirow KRC 1200UK 125 tonne Heavy Duty Diesel Hydraulic

**Names:**

| DRK 81601 | Nigel Chester | | DRK 81611 | Malcolm L. Pearce |

# LONG WELDED RAIL TRAIN PROPULSION MACHINES

| DR 89005 | NR | Cowans Boyd PW |
| DR 89007 | NR | Cowans Boyd PW |
| DR 89008 | NR | Cowans Boyd PW |

# BALLAST SYSTEM PROPULSION MACHINES

| DR 92285 | NR | Plasser & Theurer PW-RT | |
| DR 92286 | NR | Plasser & Theurer NPW-RT | |
| DR 92331 | NR | Plasser & Theurer PW-RT | |
| DR 92332 | NR | Plasser & Theurer NPW-RT | |
| DR 92431 | NR | Plasser & Theurer PW-RT | |
| DR 92432 | NR | Plasser & Theurer NPW-RT | |
| DR 92477 | NR | Plasser & Theurer PW | "99 70 9310 477-3" |
| DR 92478 | NR | Plasser & Theurer NPW | "99 70 9310 478-1" |

# BREAKDOWN CRANES

| ADRC 96710 (S) | NR | Cowans Sheldon 75 tonne Diesel Hydraulic |
| ADRC 96713 (S) | NR | Cowans Sheldon 75 tonne Diesel Hydraulic |
| ADRC 96715 (S) | NR | Cowans Sheldon 75 tonne Diesel Hydraulic |

# HIGH SPEED 1 MAINTENANCE TRAIN VEHICLES

| DR 97001 | H1 | Eiv de Brieve DU94BA TRAMM with Crane | "DU 94 B 001 URS" |
| DR 97011 | H1 | Windhoff MPV (Modular) | |
| DR 97012 | H1 | Windhoff MPV (Modular) | Geoff Bell |
| DR 97013 | H1 | Windhoff MPV (Modular) | |
| DR 97014 | H1 | Windhoff MPV (Modular) | |

## MOBILE MAINTENANCE TRAINS

**Robel Type 69.70 Mobile Maintenance System**
DR 97501/601/801 NR "99 70 9481 001-4 + 99 70 9559 001-1 + 99 70 9580 001-4"
DR 97502/602/802 NR "99 70 9481 002-2 + 99 70 9559 002-9 + 99 70 9580 002-2"
DR 97503/603/803 NR "99 70 9481 003-0 + 99 70 9559 003-7 + 99 70 9580 003-0"
DR 97504/604/804 NR "99 70 9481 004-8 + 99 70 9559 004-5 + 99 70 9580 004-8"
DR 97505/605/805 NR "99 70 9481 005-5 + 99 70 9559 005-2 + 99 70 9580 005-5"
DR 97506/606/806 NR "99 70 9481 006-3 + 99 70 9559 006-0 + 99 70 9580 006-3"
DR 97507/607/807 NR "99 70 9481 007-1 + 99 70 9559 007-8 + 99 70 9580 007-1"
DR 97508/608/808 NR "99 70 9481 008-9 + 99 70 9559 008-6 + 99 70 9580 008-9"

## ELIZABETH LINE MAINTENANCE TRAIN VEHICLES

| DR 97509 | XR | Robel Power Car A | "99 70 9481 009-7" |
|----------|-----|-------------------|--------------------|
| DR 97510 | XR | Robel Power Car B | "99 70 9481 010-5" |
| DR 97511 | XR | Robel Power Car B | "99 70 9481 011-3" |
| DR 97512 | XR | Robel Power Car E | "99 70 9481 012-1" |

## ELECTRIFICATION VEHICLES

| DR 76901 | NR | Windhoff MPV with Piling Equipment | "99 70 9131 001-8" |
|----------|-----|------------------------------------|--------------------|
| DR 76903 | NR | Windhoff MPV with Piling Equipment | "99 70 9131 003-4" |
| DR 76905 | NR | Windhoff MPV with Piling Equipment | "99 70 9131 005-9" |
| DR 76906 | NR | Windhoff MPV with Concrete Equipment | "99 70 9131 006-7" |
| DR 76910 | NR | Windhoff MPV with Concrete Equipment | "99 70 9131 010-9" |
| DR 76911 | NR | Windhoff MPV with Structure Equipment | "99 70 9131 011-7" |
| DR 76913 | NR | Windhoff MPV with Structure Equipment | "99 70 9131 013-3" |
| DR 76914 | NR | Windhoff MPV with Overhead Line Equipment | "99 70 9131 014-1" |
| DR 76915 | NR | Windhoff MPV with Overhead Line Equipment | "99 70 9131 015-8" |
| DR 76918 | NR | Windhoff MPV with Overhead Line Equipment | "99 70 9131 018-2" |
| DR 76920 | NR | Windhoff MPV with Overhead Line Equipment | "99 70 9131 020-8" |
| DR 76921 | NR | Windhoff MPV with Overhead Line Equipment | "99 70 9131 021-6" |
| DR 76922 | NR | Windhoff MPV with Final Works Equipment | "99 70 9131 022-4" |
| DR 76923 | NR | Windhoff MPV with Final Works Equipment | "99 70 9131 023-2" |

| DR 98001 | NR | Windhoff MPV with Piling Equipment |
|----------|-----|------------------------------------|
| DR 98002 | NR | Windhoff MPV with Overhead Line Renewal Equipment |
| DR 98003 | NR | Windhoff MPV with Overhead Line Renewal Equipment |
| DR 98004 | NR | Windhoff MPV with Overhead Line Renewal Equipment |
| DR 98005 | NR | Windhoff MPV with Overhead Line Renewal Equipment |
| DR 98006 | NR | Windhoff MPV with Overhead Line Renewal Equipment |
| DR 98007 | NR | Windhoff MPV with Piling Equipment |
| DR 98009 | NR | Windhoff MPV with Overhead Line Renewal Equipment |
| DR 98010 | NR | Windhoff MPV with Overhead Line Renewal Equipment |
| DR 98011 | NR | Windhoff MPV with Overhead Line Renewal Equipment |
| DR 98012 | NR | Windhoff MPV with Overhead Line Renewal Equipment |
| DR 98013 | NR | Windhoff MPV with Overhead Line Renewal Equipment |
| DR 98014 | NR | Windhoff MPV with Overhead Line Renewal Equipment |

| 99 70 9231 001-7 | AM | SVI RT250 with crane & access platform |
| 99 70 9231 004-1 | AM | SVI PT500 with wire manipulator & access platform |
| 99 70 9231 005-8 | AM | SVI RSM9 with access platform |
| 99 70 9231 006-6 | AM | SVI RSM9 with access platform |
| 99 70 9231 007-4 | AM | APV250 with access platform |

**Names:**

| DR 76901 | BRUNEL |
| DR 76923 | GAVIN ROBERTS |
| DR 98003 | ANTHONY WRIGHTON 1944–2011 |
| DR 98004 | PHILIP CATTRELL 1961–2011 |
| DR 98006 | JASON MCDONNELL 1970–2016 |
| DR 98009 | MELVYN SMITH 1953–2011 |
| DR 98010 | BENJAMIN GAUTREY 1992–2011 |
| DR 98012 | TERENCE HAND 1962–2016 |
| DR 98013 | DAVID WOOD 1951–2015 |
| DR 98014 | WAYNE IMLACH 1955–2015 |

# GENERAL PURPOSE VEHICLES

| DR 98215A + DR 98215B | BB | Plasser & Theurer GP-TRAMM with Trailer |
| DR 98216A + DR 98216B | BB | Plasser & Theurer GP-TRAMM with Trailer |
| DR 98217A + DR 98217B | BB | Plasser & Theurer GP-TRAMM with Trailer |
| DR 98218A + DR 98218B | BB | Plasser & Theurer GP-TRAMM with Trailer |
| DR 98219A + DR 98219B | BB | Plasser & Theurer GP-TRAMM with Trailer |
| DR 98220A + DR 98220B | BB | Plasser & Theurer GP-TRAMM with Trailer |

| DR 98307A (S) | CS | Geismar GP-TRAMM VMT 860 PL/UM |
| DR 98307B* | CS | Geismar GP-TRAMM Trailer |
| DR 98308A + DR 98308B (S) | CS | Geismar GP-TRAMM VMT 860 PL/UM with Trailer |

* In use as a propelling control vehicle at Baglan Bay Yard.

| DR 98901 + DR 98951 | NR | Windhoff MPV Master & Slave |
| DR 98902 + DR 98952 | NR | Windhoff MPV Master & Slave |
| DR 98903 + DR 98953 | NR | Windhoff MPV Master & Slave |
| DR 98904 + DR 98954 | NR | Windhoff MPV Master & Slave |
| DR 98905 + DR 98955 | NR | Windhoff MPV Master & Slave |
| DR 98906 + DR 98956 | NR | Windhoff MPV Master & Slave |
| DR 98907 + DR 98957 | NR | Windhoff MPV Master & Slave |
| DR 98908 + DR 98958 | NR | Windhoff MPV Master & Slave |
| DR 98909 + DR 98959 | NR | Windhoff MPV Master & Slave |
| DR 98910 + DR 98960 | NR | Windhoff MPV Master & Slave |
| DR 98911 + DR 98961 | NR | Windhoff MPV Master & Slave |
| DR 98912 + DR 98962 | NR | Windhoff MPV Master & Slave |
| DR 98913 + DR 98963 | NR | Windhoff MPV Master & Slave |
| DR 98914 + DR 98964 | NR | Windhoff MPV Master & Slave |
| DR 98915 + DR 98965 | NR | Windhoff MPV Master & Slave |
| DR 98916 + DR 98966 | NR | Windhoff MPV Master & Slave |
| DR 98917 + DR 98967 | NR | Windhoff MPV Master & Slave |
| DR 98918 + DR 98968 | NR | Windhoff MPV Master & Slave |
| DR 98919 + DR 98969 | NR | Windhoff MPV Master & Slave |

| DR 98920 + DR 98970 | NR | Windhoff MPV Master & Slave |
| DR 98921 + DR 98971 | NR | Windhoff MPV Master & Slave |
| DR 98922 + DR 98972 | NR | Windhoff MPV Master & Slave |
| DR 98923 + DR 98973 | NR | Windhoff MPV Master & Slave |
| DR 98924 + DR 98974 | NR | Windhoff MPV Master & Slave |
| DR 98925 + DR 98975 | NR | Windhoff MPV Master & Slave |
| DR 98926 + DR 98976 | NR | Windhoff MPV Master & Powered Slave |
| DR 98927 + DR 98977 | NR | Windhoff MPV Master & Powered Slave |
| DR 98928 + DR 98978 | NR | Windhoff MPV Master & Powered Slave |
| DR 98929 + DR 98979 | NR | Windhoff MPV Master & Powered Slave |
| DR 98930 + DR 98980 | NR | Windhoff MPV Master & Powered Slave |
| DR 98931 + DR 98981 | NR | Windhoff MPV Master & Powered Slave |
| DR 98932 + DR 98982 | NR | Windhoff MPV Master & Powered Slave |

**Names:**

DR 98914+DR 98964 Dick Preston | DR 98923+DR 98973 Chris Lemon
DR 98915+DR 98965 Nigel Cummins | DR 98926+DR 98976 John Denyer

# INFRASTRUCTURE MONITORING VEHICLES

"950 001" is a purpose-built Track Assessment Unit based on the BREL Class 150/1 design.

| DR 98008 | NR | Windhoff MPV Twin-cab with surveying equipment |
| 999600+999601 | NR | BREL York Track Assessment Unit "950 001" |
| 999800 | NR | Plasser & Theurer EM-SAT 100/RT Track Survey Car |
| 999801 | NR | Plasser & Theurer EM-SAT 100/RT Track Survey Car |

# SNOWPLOUGHS

| ADB 965203 | NR | Independent Drift Plough | Carlisle Kingmoor Depot |
| ADB 965206 | NR | Independent Drift Plough | Leeman Road Sidings, York |
| ADB 965208 | NR | Independent Drift Plough | Norwich Thorpe Yard |
| ADB 965209 | NR | Independent Drift Plough | Motherwell Depot |
| ADB 965210 | NR | Independent Drift Plough | West Yard, Tonbridge |
| ADB 965211 | NR | Independent Drift Plough | Tonbridge West Yard |
| ADB 965217 | NR | Independent Drift Plough | Leeman Road Sidings, York |
| ADB 965219 | NR | Independent Drift Plough | Norwich Thorpe Yard |
| ADB 965223 | NR | Independent Drift Plough | Fairwater Yard, Taunton |
| ADB 965224 | NR | Independent Drift Plough | Millburn Yard, Inverness |
| ADB 965230 | NR | Independent Drift Plough | Millburn Yard, Inverness |
| ADB 965231 | NR | Independent Drift Plough | Motherwell Depot |
| ADB 965234 | NR | Independent Drift Plough | Millburn Yard, Inverness |
| ADB 965235 | NR | Independent Drift Plough | Fairwater Yard, Taunton |
| ADB 965236 | NR | Independent Drift Plough | West Yard, Tonbridge |
| ADB 965237 | NR | Independent Drift Plough | Tonbridge West Yard |
| ADB 965240 | NR | Independent Drift Plough | York North Yard Sidings |
| ADB 965241 | NR | Independent Drift Plough | York Yard North Sidings |
| ADB 965242 | NR | Independent Drift Plough | Carlisle Kingmoor Depot |

| ADB 965243 | NR | Independent Drift Plough | Millburn Yard, Inverness |
|---|---|---|---|
| ADB 965576 | NR | Beilhack Type PB600 Plough | West Yard, Doncaster |
| ADB 965577 | NR | Beilhack Type PB600 Plough | West Yard, Doncaster |
| ADB 965578 | NR | Beilhack Type PB600 Plough | Kingmoor Yard, Carlisle |
| ADB 965579 | NR | Beilhack Type PB600 Plough | Kingmoor Yard, Carlisle |
| ADB 965580 | NR | Beilhack Type PB600 Plough | Crewe Gresty Bridge Depot |
| ADB 965581 | NR | Beilhack Type PB600 Plough | Crewe Gresty Bridge Depot |
| ADB 966098 | NR | Beilhack Type PB600 Plough | West Yard, Doncaster |
| ADB 966099 | NR | Beilhack Type PB600 Plough | West Yard, Doncaster |

## SNOWBLOWERS

| ADB 968500 | NR | Beilhack Self-Propelled Rotary | Edinburgh Slateford Depot |
|---|---|---|---|
| ADB 968501 | NR | Beilhack Self-Propelled Rotary | Edinburgh Slateford Depot |

## ON-TRACK MACHINES AWAITING DISPOSAL

**Tampers**

| DR 73105 | Plasser & Theurer 09-32 CSM | Cardiff Canton Depot |
|---|---|---|
| DR 75403 | Matisa B 41 UE | France/Eastleigh Works |

**Twin Jib track relayer**

DRB 78123 British Hoist & Crane Non-Self-Propelled    Polmadie DHS

## LOCATIONS OF STORED ON-TRACK MACHINES

The locations of machines shown above as stored (S) are shown here.

| DR 73805 | Rugby Depot | DR 80200 | Thuxton, Mid Norfolk Railway |
|---|---|---|---|
| DR 73927 | Ashford OTM Depot | DR 80202 | Leeds Holbeck Depot |
| DR 76703 | Fairwater Yard, Taunton | DR 80203 | Leeds Holbeck Depot |
| DR 77322 | Colchester OTM Depot | DR 80204 | Thuxton, Mid Norfolk Railway |
| DR 77336 | Hither Green Depot | ARDC 96710 | Burton-upon-Trent |
| DRP 78217 | Glasgow Rutherglen Depot | ARDC 96713 | Wigan Springs Branch Depot |
| DRC 78229 | Beeston Sidings | ARDC 96715 | Wigan Springs Branch Depot |
| DRC 78231 | Beeston Sidings | DR 98307A | Darley Dale |
| DRC 78234 | Beeston Sidings | DR 98308A+ | |
| DR 79234+ | | DR 98308B | Barry Rail Centre |
| DR 79235 | RTC Business Park, Derby | | |

# 6. CODES

## 6.1. LIVERY CODES

Livery codes are used to denote the various liveries carried. It is impossible to list every livery variation which currently exists. In particular items ignored for this publication include:

* Minor colour variations.
* Omission of logos.
* All numbering, lettering and brandings.

Descriptions quoted are thus a general guide only. Logos as appropriate for each livery are normally deemed to be carried. The colour of the lower half of the bodyside is generally stated first.

*Code Description*

**AB**  Arriva Trains Wales/Welsh Government sponsored all over dark blue.
**AG**  Arlington Fleet Services (green).
**AI**  Aggregate Industries (green, light grey & blue).
**AL**  Advertising/promotional livery (see class heading for details).
**AR**  Anglia Railways (turquoise blue with a white stripe).
**AT**  Avanti West Coast (dark green, dark grey, white, cream & orange).
**AV**  Arriva Trains (turquoise blue with white doors & a cream "swish").
**AW**  Arriva Trains Wales/Welsh Government sponsored dark & light blue.
**AZ**  Advenza Freight (deep blue with green Advenza brandings).
**B**   BR blue.
**BG**  BR blue & grey lined out in white.
**BL**  BR Revised blue with yellow cabs, grey roof, large numbers & logo.
**C2**  c2c (white with dark blue doors).
**CA**  Caledonian Sleeper (dark blue).
**CC**  BR Carmine & Cream.
**CD**  Cotswold Rail (silver with blue & red logo).
**CE**  BR Civil Engineers (yellow & grey with black cab doors & window surrounds).
**CH**  BR Western Region/GWR (chocolate & cream lined out in gold).
**CL**  Chiltern Railways Mainline Class 168 (white & silver).
**CM**  Chiltern Railways Mainline loco-hauled (two-tone grey/white & silver with blue stripes).
**CN**  Connex/Southeastern (white with black window surrounds & grey lower band).
**CR**  Chiltern Railways (blue & white with a red stripe).
**CS**  Colas Rail (yellow, orange & black).
**CU**  Corus (silver with red logos).
**DB**  DB Cargo (Deutsche Bahn red with grey roof & solebar).
**DC**  Devon & Cornwall Railways (metallic silver).
**DG**  BR Departmental (dark grey with black cab doors & window surrounds).
**DI**  New DRS {Class 68 style} (deep blue & aquamarine with large compass logo).
**DR**  Direct Rail Services (dark blue with light blue or dark grey roof).
**DS**  Revised Direct Rail Services (dark blue, light blue & green. "Compass" logo).

**E**    English Welsh & Scottish Railway (maroon bodyside & roof with a broad gold bodyside band).

**EA**    East Midlands Trains revised HST (dark blue, orange & red).

**EB**    Eurotunnel (two-tone grey with a broad blue stripe).

**EG**    "EWS grey" (as **F** but with large yellow & red EWS logo).

**EI**    East Midlands Railway {interim} (white with deep purple swish at unit ends).

**EP**    European Passenger Services (two-tone grey with dark blue roof).

**EM**    East Midlands Trains {Connect} (blue with red & orange swish at unit ends).

**ER**    East Midlands Railway (two-tone purple with white lower bodyside lining and doors).

**ES**    Revised Eurostar (deep blue & two-tone grey).

**EU**    Eurostar (white with dark blue & yellow stripes).

**EX**    Europhoenix (silver, blue & red).

**F**    BR Trainload Freight (two-tone grey with black cab doors & window surrounds. Various logos).

**FA**    Fastline Freight (grey & black with white & orange stripes).

**FB**    First Group dark blue.

**FD**    First Great Western "Dynamic Lines" (dark blue with thin multi-coloured lines on the lower bodyside).

**FE**    Railfreight Distribution International (two tone-grey with black cab doors & dark blue roof).

**FER**    Fertis (light grey with a dark grey roof & solebar).

**FF**    Freightliner grey (two-tone grey with black cab doors & window surrounds. Freightliner logo).

**FG**    New Freightliner Genesee & Wyoming style (orange with black & yellow lower bodyside stripes).

**FH**    Revised Freightliner {PowerHaul} (dark green with yellow cab ends & grey stripe/buffer beam).

**FL**    Freightliner (dark green with yellow cabs).

**FO**    BR Railfreight (grey bodysides, yellow cabs & red lower bodyside stripe, large BR logo).

**FR**    Fragonset Railways (black with silver roof & a red bodyside band lined out in white).

**FS**    First Group (indigo blue with pink & white stripes).

**FU**    First Group "Urban Lights" (varying blue or uniform indigo blue with pink, white & blue markings on the lower bodyside).

**G¹**    BR Green (plain green, with white stripe on main line locomotives).

**G²**    BR Southern Region/SR or BR DMU green.

**GA**    Greater Anglia (white with red doors & black window surrounds).

**GB**    GB Railfreight (blue with orange cantrail & solebar stripes, orange cabs).

**GC**    Grand Central (all over black with an orange stripe).

**GG**    BR two-tone green.

**GL**    First Great Western locomotives (green with a gold stripe).

**GR**    New Greater Anglia (white/grey with black window surrounds & red & dark grey on the lower bodyside).

**GV**    Gatwick Express Class 442 (red, white & indigo blue with mauve & blue doors).

**GW**    Great Western Railway (TOC) dark green.

**GY**    Eurotunnel (grey & yellow).

**GX**    Gatwick Express Class 387 (red with white lining and grey doors).

| | |
|---|---|
| **HA** | Hanson Quarry Products (dark blue/silver with oxide red roof). |
| **HB** | HSBC Rail (Oxford blue & white). |
| **HC** | Heathrow Connect (grey with a broad deep blue bodyside band & orange doors). |
| **HE** | Heathrow Express (silver with purple doors and black window surrounds. |
| **HN** | Harry Needle Railroad Company (orange with a black roof and solebar). |
| **HT** | New Hull Trains (First Group dark blue with a multi-coloured band on lower bodyside depicting images from the route). |
| **HU** | Hunslet Engine Company (dark blue & orange). |
| **HX** | New Heathrow Express (silver, grey & purple). |
| **IC** | BR InterCity (dark grey/white/red/white). |
| **K** | Black. |
| **KB** | Knorr-Bremse Rail UK (blue, white & light green). |
| **LD** | New London Overground (black upper bodyside with white, orange & blue lower bodyside stripes & orange doors). |
| **LH** | BR Loadhaul (black with orange cabsides). |
| **LI** | London Northwestern Railway {interim} (dark green at unit ends and doors applied on **LM** light grey/black livery). |
| **LM** | London Midland (light grey & green with black stripe around the windows). |
| **LN** | London Northwestern Railway (light grey, dark green & light green). |
| **LO** | London Overground (all over white with a blue solebar & black window surrounds and orange doors). |
| **LT** | London Transport maroon & cream. |
| **LZ** | LNER Azuma (white with red window surrounds). |
| **M** | BR maroon (maroon lined out in straw & black). |
| **ML** | BR Mainline Freight (aircraft blue with a silver stripe). |
| **MP** | Midland Pullman (nanking blue & white). |
| **MT** | Maritime (blue with white lettering). |
| **MY** | Merseyrail (all over yellow or all over grey (alternate sides). |
| **N** | BR Network SouthEast (white & blue with red lower bodyside stripe, grey solebar & cab ends). |
| **NB** | Northern all over dark blue. |
| **NC** | National Express white (white with blue doors). |
| **NO** | Northern (deep blue, purple & white). |
| **NR** | New Northern (white & purple). |
| **NX** | National Express (white with grey ends). |
| **O** | Non-standard (see class heading for details). |
| **PB** | Porterbrook Leasing Company (blue). |
| **PC** | Pullman Car Company (umber & cream with gold lettering lined out in gold). |
| **RB** | Riviera Trains Oxford blue. |
| **RL** | RMS Locotec (dark blue with light grey cabsides). |
| **RM** | Royal Mail (all over red). |
| **RO** | Rail Operations Group (dark blue). |
| **RP** | Royal Train (claret, lined out in red & black). |
| **RR** | Regional Railways (dark blue & grey with light blue & white stripes, three narrow dark blue stripes at vehicle ends). |
| **RS** | Railway Support Services (grey with a red solebar). |
| **RV** | Riviera Trains Great Briton (Oxford blue & cream lined out in gold). |
| **RX** | Rail Express Systems (dark grey & red with or without blue markings). |
| **RZ** | Royal Train revised (plain claret, no lining). |
| **SB** | Southeastern blue (all over blue with black window surrounds). |

**SD** Stagecoach/South West Trains outer suburban {Class 450 style} (deep blue with red doors & orange & red cab sides).

**SE** Southeastern suburban (all over white with black window surrounds, light blue doors and (on some units) dark blue lower bodyside stripe).

**SI** ScotRail InterCity HST (light grey & dark blue with INTER7CITY branding).

**SL** Silverlink (indigo blue with white stripe, green lower body & yellow doors).

**SN** Southern (white & dark green with light green semi-circles at one end of each vehicle. Light grey band at solebar level).

**SR** ScotRail – Scotland's Railways (dark blue with Scottish Saltire flag & white/light blue flashes).

**SS** South West Trains inner suburban {Class 455 style} (red with blue & orange flashes at unit ends).

**ST** Stagecoach {long-distance stock} (white & dark blue with dark blue window surrounds and red & orange swishes at unit ends).

**SW** South Western Railway (two-tone grey with a yellow lower bodyside stripe).

**TF** TfL Rail (white with blue doors and lower bodyside stripe).

**TG** Govia Thameslink interim {Class 387} (white with dark green doors).

**TL** Govia Thameslink Railway (light grey & white with blue doors).

**TP** TransPennine Express (silver, grey, blue & purple).

**TT** Transmart Trains (all over green).

**TW** Transport for Wales (white with a broad red stripe at cantrail level & red doors).

**U** Plain white or grey undercoat.

**V** Virgin Trains (red with black doors extending into bodysides, three white lower bodysides stripes).

**VE** Virgin Trains East Coast (red & white with black window surrounds).

**VP** Virgin Trains shunters (black with a large black & white chequered flag on the bodyside).

**VN** Northern Belle (crimson lake & cream lined out in gold).

**VT** Virgin Trains silver (silver, with black window surrounds, white cantrail stripe & red roof. Red swept down at unit ends).

**VI** Vivarail (white & green).

**VW** New Virgin Trains {unbranded} (all over white).

**WA** Wabtec Rail (black).

**WC** West Coast Railway Company maroon.

**WI** West Midlands Railway {interim} (gold at unit ends & gold doors applied on **LM** light grey/black livery).

**WM** West Midlands Railway (gold & metallic purple).

**XC** CrossCountry (two-tone silver with deep crimson ends & pink doors).

**XR** Crossrail (white with black window surrounds and a purple lower bodyside).

**Y** Network Rail yellow.

## 6.2. OWNER CODES

The following codes are used to define the ownership details of the locomotives or rolling stock listed in this book. Codes shown indicate either the legal owner or "responsible custodian" of each vehicle.

| | |
|---|---|
| 125 | 125 Group |
| 20 | Class 20189 |
| 37 | Scottish Thirty-Seven Group |
| 40 | Class 40 Preservation Society |
| 47 | Stratford 47 Group |
| 50 | Class 50 Alliance |
| 56 | Class 56 Locomotives |
| 70 | 7029 Clun Castle |
| 71 | 71A Locomotives |
| 2L | Class 20 Locomotives |
| A | Angel Trains |
| AD | AV Dawson |
| AF | Arlington Fleet Services |
| AK | Akiem |
| AM | Alstom |
| AT | Agility Trains |
| AV | Arriva UK Trains |
| BA | Babcock Rail |
| BB | Balfour Beatty Rail Infrastructure Services |
| BD | Bardon Aggregates |
| BE | Belmond (UK) |
| BN | Beacon Rail |
| BR | Brodie Leasing |
| BT | Bombardier Transportation |
| CD | Crewe Diesel Preservation Group |
| CL | Caledonian Rail Leasing |
| CO | Corelink Rail Infrastructure |
| CT | Cross London Trains |
| CS | Colas Rail |
| D0 | D05 Preservation Group |
| DA | Data Acquisition & Testing Services |
| DB | DB Cargo (UK) |
| DC | DC Rail |
| DP | Deltic Preservation Society |
| DR | Direct Rail Services |
| DT | The Diesel Traction Group |
| E | Eversholt Rail (UK) |
| EE | English Electric Preservation |
| EL | Electric Traction Limited |
| EM | East Midlands Railway |
| EO | ElectroMotive Diesel Services |
| EP | Europhoenix |
| ER | Eastern Rail Services |
| ET | Eurotunnel |
| EU | Eurostar International |

EY   European Metal Recycling
FG   First Group
FL   Freightliner
GB   GB Railfreight
GW   Great Western Railway (assets of the Greater Western franchise)
H1   Network Rail (High Speed)
HD   Hastings Diesels
HE   Heathrow Airport Holdings
HH   Hanson & Hall Rail Services
HN   Harry Needle Railroad Company
HR   Harsco Track Technologies
HT   Hanson Traction
HU   Hunslet Engine Company
LF   Lombard North Central
LN   London Overground
LO   LORAM (UK)
LS   Locomotive Services
LU   London Underground
ME   Meteor Power
MR   Mendip Rail
MT   Merseytravel
NB   Boden Rail Engineering
NM   National Museum of Science & Industry
NN   North Norfolk Railway
NR   Network Rail
NS   Nemesis Rail
NY   North Yorkshire Moors Railway Enterprises
P   Porterbrook Leasing Company
PO   Other private owner
PP   Peter Pan Locomotive Company
PR   The Princess Royal Class Locomotive Trust
QW   QW Rail Leasing
RC   RailCare UK
RF   Rail for London (Transport for London)
RL   Rail Management Services (trading as RMS Locotec)
RM   Royal Mail
RO   Rail Operations Group
RP   Rampart Engineering
RR   Rock Rail
RS   Railway Support Services
RU   Russell Logistics
RV   Riviera Trains
SB   Steve Beniston
SC   Schweerbau (UK)
SF   SNCF (Société Nationale des Chemins de fer Français)
SI   Speno International
SK   Swietelsky Babcock Rail
SP   The Scottish Railway Preservation Society
SR   ScotRail
ST   Shaun Wright
SU   SembCorp Utilities UK

SW  South Western Railway
SY  South Yorkshire Passenger Transport Executive
TF  Train Fleet (Department for Transport)
TT  Transmart Trains
TW  Transport for Wales
UR  UK Rail Leasing
VG  Victoria Group
VI  Vivarail
VO  VolkerRail
VT  Vintage Trains
WA  Wabtec Rail Group
WC  West Coast Railway Company
WM  West Midlands Trains
X   Sold for scrap/further use and awaiting collection

# 6.3. LOCOMOTIVE POOL CODES

Locomotives are split into operational groups ("pools") for diagramming and maintenance purposes. The codes used to denote these pools are shown in this publication.

AWCA  West Coast Railway Company operational locomotives.
AWCX  West Coast Railway Company stored locomotives.
CFOL  Class 50 Operations locomotives.
CFSL  Class 40 Preservation Society Locomotives.
COFS  Colas Rail Class 56.
COLO  Colas Rail Classes 66 & 70.
COLS  Colas Rail stored locomotives.
COTS  Colas Rail Classes 37, 43 & 67.
DCRO  DC Rail Class 50 & 56.
DCRS  DC Rail Class 60.
DFGI  Freightliner Class 70.
DFHG  Freightliner Class 59.
DFHH  Freightliner Class 66/6.
DFIM  Freightliner Class 66/5.
DFIN  Freightliner low emission Class 66.
DFLC  Freightliner Class 90.
DFNC  Freightliner Class 86/6.
DHLT  Freightliner locomotives awaiting maintenance/repair/disposal.
EFOO  Great Western Railway Class 57.
EFPC  Great Western Railway 43.
EHPC  CrossCountry Class 43.
EMPC  East Midlands Railway Class 43.
EPEX  Europhoenix locomotives for export.
EPUK  Europhoenix UK locomotives.
GBBR  GB Railfreight Class 73 for possible rebuilding.
GBBT  GB Railfreight Class 66. Large fuel tanks.
GBCS  GB Railfreight Class 73/9. Caledonian Sleeper.
GBCT  GB Railfreight Class 92. Channel Tunnel traffic.
GBDF  GB Railfreight Class 47.

| | |
|---|---|
| GBEB | GB Railfreight Class 66. Ex-European, large fuel tanks. |
| GBED | GB Railfreight Class 73. |
| GBEL | GB Railfreight Class 66. New build, small fuel tanks. |
| GBFM | GB Railfreight Class 66. RETB fitted. |
| GBGD | GB Railfreight Class 56. Operational locomotives. |
| GBGS | GB Railfreight Class 56. Stored locomotives. |
| GBLT | GB Railfreight Class 66. Small fuel tanks. |
| GBNB | GB Railfreight Class 66. New build. |
| GBNR | GB Railfreight Class 73/9. Network Rail contracts. |
| GBOB | GB Railfreight Class 66. Former DB Cargo locomotives; large fuel tanks and buckeye couplers. |
| GBSD | GB Railfreight. Stored locomotives. |
| GBSL | GB Railfreight Class 92. Caledonian Sleeper. |
| GBST | GB Railfreight Class 92. Caledonian Sleeper & Channel Tunnel. |
| GBTG | GB Railfreight Class 60. |
| GBYH | GB Railfreight Class 59. |
| GROG | Rail Operations Group operational locomotives. |
| HAPC | ScotRail Class 43. |
| HNRL | Harry Needle Railroad Company hire locomotives. |
| HNRS | Harry Needle Railroad Company stored locomotives. |
| HTLX | Hanson & Hall Rail Services locomotives. |
| HYWD | South Western Railway Class 73. |
| IECA | London North Eastern Railway Class 91. |
| IECP | London North Eastern Railway Class 43. |
| LSLO | Locomotive Services operational locomotives. |
| LSLS | Locomotive Services stored locomotives. |
| MBDL | Non TOC-owned diesel locomotives. |
| MBED | Non TOC-owned electro-diesel locomotives. |
| MBEL | Non TOC-owned electric locomotives. |
| MOLO | Class 20189 Ltd Class 20. |
| NRLO | Nemesis Rail locomotives. |
| QADD | Network Rail locomotives. |
| QCAR | Network Rail New Measurement Train Class 43. |
| QETS | Network Rail Class 37. |
| RAJV | Scottish Railway Preservation Society Class 37. |
| SAXL | Eversholt Rail off-lease locomotives. |
| SBXL | Porterbrook Leasing Company stored locomotives. |
| SCEL | Angel Trains stored locomotives. |
| SROG | Rail Operations Group locomotives under overhaul. |
| TPCF | TransPennine Express Class 68 locomotives (commissioning). |
| TPEX | TransPennine Express Class 68 locomotives. |
| UKRL | UK Rail Leasing. Operational locomotives. |
| UKRM | UK Rail Leasing. Locomotives for overhaul. |
| UKRS | UK Rail Leasing. Stored locomotives. |
| WAAC | DB Cargo Class 67. |
| WAWC | DB Cargo Class 67 for hire to Transport for Wales. |
| WBAE | DB Cargo Class 66. Locomotives fitted with "stop-start" technology. |
| WBAR | DB Cargo Class 66. Fitted with remote monitoring equipment. |
| WBAT | DB Cargo Class 66. |
| WBBE | DB Cargo Class 66. RETB fitted and fitted with "stop-start" technology. |
| WBBT | DB Cargo Class 66. RETB fitted. |

| | |
|---|---|
| WBLE | DB Cargo Class 66. Dedicated locomotives for Lickey Incline banking duties. Fitted with "stop-start" technology. |
| WBLT | DB Cargo Class 66. Dedicated locomotives for Lickey Incline banking duties. |
| WCAT | DB Cargo Class 60. |
| WCBT | DB Cargo Class 60. Extended-range fuel tanks. |
| WEAC | DB Cargo Class 90. |
| WEDC | DB Cargo Class 90. Modified for operation with Mark 4s. |
| WFBC | DB Cargo Class 92 with TVM430 cab signalling equipment for use on High Speed 1. |
| WQAA | DB Cargo stored locomotives Group 1A (short-term maintenance). |
| WQAB | DB Cargo stored locomotives Group 1B. |
| WQBA | DB Cargo stored locomotives Group 2 (unserviceable). |
| WQCA | DB Cargo stored locomotives Group 3 (unserviceable). |
| WQDA | DB Cargo stored locomotives Group 4 (awaiting disposal). |
| XHAC | Direct Rail Services Classes 37/4 & 57/3. |
| XHCE | Direct Rail Services Class 68 for hire to Chiltern Railways. |
| XHCK | Direct Rail Services Classes 20 & 57/0. |
| XHIM | Direct Rail Services locomotives – Intermodal traffic. |
| XHNC | Direct Rail Services locomotives – nuclear traffic/general. |
| XHSS | Direct Rail Services stored locomotives. |
| XHVE | Direct Rail Services Classes 68 & 88. |
| XHVT | Direct Rail Services Class 57/3 for hire to Avanti West Coast. |

# 6.4. OPERATOR CODES

Operator codes are used to denote the organisation that facilitates the use of that vehicle, and may not be the actual Train Operating Company which runs the train. Where no operator code is shown, vehicles are currently not in use.

| | |
|---|---|
| AW | Avanti West Coast |
| BP | Belmond British Pullman |
| C2 | c2c |
| CA | Caledonian Sleeper |
| CR | Chiltern Railways |
| CS | Colas Rail |
| DB | DB Cargo (UK) |
| DR | Direct Rail Services |
| EM | East Midlands Railway |
| EU | Eurostar (UK) |
| GA | Greater Anglia |
| GB | GB Railfreight |
| GC | Grand Central |
| GN | Great Northern (part of Govia Thameslink Railway) |
| GW | Great Western Railway |
| HD | Hastings Diesels |
| HE | Heathrow Express |
| HT | Hull Trains |
| LN | London North Eastern Railway |
| LO | London Overground |

| | |
|---|---|
| *LS* | Locomotive Services |
| *ME* | Merseyrail |
| *NO* | Northern |
| *NY* | North Yorkshire Moors Railway |
| *PR* | The Princess Royal Class Locomotive Trust |
| *RO* | Rail Operations Group |
| *RS* | The Royal Scotsman (Belmond) |
| *RT* | Royal Train |
| *RV* | Riviera Trains |
| *SE* | Southeastern |
| *SN* | Southern (part of Govia Thameslink Railway) |
| *SP* | The Scottish Railway Preservation Society |
| *SR* | ScotRail |
| *SW* | South Western Railway |
| *SY* | Stagecoach Supertram |
| *TL* | Thameslink (part of Govia Thameslink Railway) |
| *TP* | TransPennine Express |
| *TW* | Transport for Wales |
| *VT* | Vintage Trains |
| *WC* | West Coast Railway Company |
| *WM* | West Midlands Trains |
| *XC* | CrossCountry |
| *XR* | TfL Rail |

# 6.5. ALLOCATION & LOCATION CODES

Allocation codes are used in this publication to denote the normal maintenance base ("depots") of each operational locomotive, multiple unit or coach. However, maintenance may be carried out at other locations and may also be carried out by mobile maintenance teams. Location codes are used to denote common storage locations whilst the full place name is used for other locations. The designation (S) denotes stored.

| Code | Depot | Depot Operator |
|---|---|---|
| AD | Ashford (Kent) | Hitachi |
| AK | Ardwick (Manchester) | Siemens |
| AL | Aylesbury | Chiltern Railways |
| AN | Allerton (Liverpool) | Northern |
| BD | Birkenhead North | Stadler Rail Service UK |
| BF | Bedford Cauldwell Walk | Govia Thameslink Railway |
| BH | Barrow Hill (Chesterfield) | Barrow Hill Engine Shed Society |
| BI | Brighton Lovers Walk | Govia Thameslink Railway |
| BK | Bristol Barton Hill | Arriva TrainCare |
| BL | Shackerstone, Battlefield Line | *Storage location only* |
| BM | Bournemouth | South Western Railway |
| BN | Bounds Green (London) | Hitachi |
| BO | Bo'ness (West Lothian) | The Bo'ness & Kinneil Railway |
| BQ | Bury (Greater Manchester) | East Lancashire Railway Trust |
| BR | MoD Bicester | *Storage location only* |
| BU | Burton-upon-Trent | Nemesis Rail |

| | | |
|---|---|---|
| BY | Bletchley | West Midlands Trains |
| CB | Crewe Basford Hall | Freightliner Engineering |
| CE | Crewe International | DB Cargo (UK) |
| CF | Cardiff Canton | Transport for Wales/Colas Rail |
| CH | Chester | Alstom |
| CK | Corkerhill (Glasgow) | ScotRail |
| CL | Crewe LNWR Heritage | LNWR Heritage Company |
| CN | Castle Donington RFT | *Storage location only* |
| CO | Coquelles (France) | Eurotunnel |
| CP | Crewe Carriage Shed | Arriva TrainCare |
| CR | Crewe Gresty Bridge | Direct Rail Services |
| CS | Carnforth | West Coast Railway Company |
| CT | Cheriton (Folkestone) | Eurotunnel |
| CY | Crewe South Yard | *Storage location only* |
| CZ | Central Rivers (Barton-under-Needwood) | Bombardier Transportation |
| DE | East Dereham (Norfolk) | Mid Norfolk Railway |
| DN | Doncaster Carr | Hitachi |
| DR | Doncaster Belmont Yard/RMT | *Storage location only* |
| DU | Dundee West Sidings | *Storage location only* |
| DY | Derby Etches Park | East Midlands Railway |
| EC | Edinburgh Craigentinny | Hitachi |
| EH | Eastleigh | Arriva TrainCare |
| EM | East Ham (London) | c2c |
| EP | Ely Papworth Sidings | *Storage location only* |
| EX | Exeter | Great Western Railway |
| FA | Fawley (Hampshire) | *Storage location only* |
| GA | Gascoigne Wood Sidings (South Milford) | *Storage location only* |
| GW | Glasgow Shields Road | ScotRail |
| HA | Haymarket (Edinburgh) | ScotRail |
| HE | Hornsey (London) | Govia Thameslink Railway |
| HJ | Hoo Junction (Kent) | Colas Rail |
| HL | Hellifield | *Storage location only* |
| HM | Healey Mills (Wakefield) | *Storage location only* |
| HN | Hamilton (Glasgow) | Assenta Rail |
| HO | Hope Cement Works | Breedon Hope Cement |
| HT | Heaton (Newcastle-upon-Tyne) | Northern |
| IL | Ilford (London) | Greater Anglia/TfL Rail |
| IS | Inverness | ScotRail |
| KK | Kirkdale (Liverpool) | Stadler Rail Service UK |
| KM | Carlisle Kingmoor | Direct Rail Services |
| KR | Kidderminster | Severn Valley Railway |
| LA | Laira (Plymouth) | Great Western Railway |
| LB | Loughborough Works | Brush Traction |
| LD | Leeds Midland Road | Freightliner Engineering |
| LE | Landore (Swansea) | Chrysalis Rail |
| LM | Quinton Rail Technology Centre (Long Marston, Warwickshire) | Motorail Logistics |
| LR | Leicester | UK Rail Leasing |
| LT | Longport (Stoke-on-Trent) | ElectroMotive Diesel Services |
| LW | MoD Longtown (Cumbria) | *Storage location only* |
| LY | Le Landy (Paris) | SNCF |

| | | |
|---|---|---|
| MA | Longsight (Manchester) | Alstom |
| MD | Merehead | Mendip Rail |
| ME | Mossend Yard | *Storage location only* |
| MH | Millerhill (Edinburgh) | *Storage location only* |
| MN | Machynlleth | Transport for Wales |
| MS | Milford Sidings (South Milford) | *Storage location only* |
| NC | Norwich Crown Point | Greater Anglia |
| NG | New Cross Gate (London) | London Overground |
| NH | Newton Heath (Manchester) | Northern |
| NL | Neville Hill (Leeds) | East Midlands Railway/Northern |
| NM | Nottingham Eastcroft | East Midlands Railway/Boden Rail |
| NN | Northampton King's Heath | Siemens |
| NO | Weybourne (Norfolk) | North Norfolk Railway |
| NP | North Pole (London) | Hitachi |
| NT | Northam (Southampton) | Siemens |
| NU | Sheffield Nunnery | Stagecoach Supertram |
| NY | Grosmont (North Yorkshire) | North Yorkshire Moors Railway Enterprises |
| OC | Old Oak Common Crossrail (London) | TfL Rail |
| OH | Old Oak Common Heathrow | Heathrow Express |
| PM | St Philip's Marsh (Bristol) | Great Western Railway |
| PO | Polmadie (Glasgow) | Alstom |
| PZ | Penzance Long Rock | Great Western Railway |
| RG | Reading | Great Western Railway |
| RM | Ramsgate | Southeastern |
| RJ | Rectory Junction (Nottingham) | Data Acquisition & Testing Services |
| RO | Rowsley (Derbyshire) | Peak Rail |
| RR | Doncaster Roberts Road | ElectroMotive Diesel Services |
| RS | Ruislip (London) | London Underground |
| RU | Rugby | Colas Rail |
| RY | Ryde (Isle of Wight) | South Western Railway |
| SA | Salisbury | South Western Railway |
| SC | Scunthorpe Steelworks | British Steel |
| SE | St Leonards (Hastings) | St Leonards Railway Engineering |
| SG | Slade Green (London) | Southeastern |
| SH | Southall (London) | West Coast Rly Co/Locomotive Services |
| SJ | Stourbridge Junction | Parry People Movers |
| SK | Swanwick West (Derbyshire) | The Princess Royal Locomotive Trust |
| SL | Stewarts Lane (London) | Govia Thameslink Railway/Belmond |
| SO | Soho (Birmingham) | West Midlands Trains |
| SP | Springs Branch (Wigan) | DB Cargo (UK) |
| SU | Selhurst (Croydon) | Govia Thameslink Railway |
| SW | Swanage | Swanage Railway |
| TB | Three Bridges (Crawley) | Siemens |
| TI | Temple Mills (London) | Eurostar International |
| TJ | Tavistock Junction Yard (Plymouth) | *Storage location only* |
| TM | Tyseley Locomotive Works | Vintage Trains |
| TO | Toton (Nottinghamshire) | DB Cargo (UK) |
| TS | Tyseley (Birmingham) | West Midlands Trains |
| TY | Tyne Yard (Newcastle) | *Storage location only* |
| WB | Wembley (London) | Alstom |
| WD | Wimbledon (London) | South Western Railway |

| WE | Willesden Brent sidings | *Storage location only* |
|----|----|----|
| WN | Willesden (London) | Bombardier Transportation |
| WO | Wolsingham, Weardale Railway | RMS Locotec |
| WS | Worksop (Nottinghamshire) | Harry Needle Railroad Company |
| YA | Great Yarmouth | Eastern Rail Services |
| YK | National Railway Museum (York) | National Museum of Science & Industry |
| YO | Yoker (Glasgow) | ScotRail |
| XW | Crofton (Wakefield) | Bombardier Transportation |
| | | |
| ZA | RTC Business Park (Derby) | LORAM (UK) |
| ZB | Doncaster Works | Wabtec Rail |
| ZC | Crewe Works | Bombardier Transportation UK |
| ZD | Derby Works | Bombardier Transportation UK |
| ZG | Eastleigh Works | Arlington Fleet Services |
| ZH | Springburn Depot (Glasgow) | *Closed, storage location only* |
| ZI | Ilford Works | Bombardier Transportation UK |
| ZJ | Stoke-on-Trent Works | Axiom Rail (Stoke) |
| ZK | Kilmarnock Caledonia Works | Brodie Engineering |
| ZM | Kilmarnock Bonnyton Works | Brodie Engineering |
| ZN | Wolverton Works | Gemini Rail Group |
| ZR | Holgate Works (York) | Network Rail |

# 6.6. ABBREVIATIONS

**The following general abbreviations are used in this book:**

| AC | Alternating Current (ie Overhead supply) |
|----|----|
| AFD | Air Force Department |
| BAA | British Airports Authority |
| BR | British Railways |
| BSI | Bergische Stahl Industrie |
| CRDC | Component Recovery & Disposal Centre |
| C&W | Carriage & Wagon |
| DC | Direct Current (ie Third Rail) |
| DEMU | Diesel Electric Multiple Unit |
| DERA | Defence Evaluation & Research Agency |
| DfT | Department for Transport |
| Dia | Diagram number |
| DMU | Diesel Multiple Unit (general term) |
| DSDC | Defence Storage & Distribution Centre |
| DRS | Direct Rail Services |
| ETS | Electric Train Supply |
| EMU | Electric Multiple Unit (general term) |
| GWR | Great Western Railway |
| FLT | Freightliner Terminal |
| HB | Hunslet-Barclay |
| hp | Horse power |
| HNRC | Harry Needle Railroad Company |
| Hz | Hertz |
| kN | Kilonewtons |
| km/h | Kilometres per hour |

| kW | Kilowatts |
| lbf | Pounds force |
| LT | London Transport |
| LUL | London Underground Limited |
| m | Metres |
| mm | Millimetres |
| mph | Miles per hour |
| NPCCS | Non Passenger Carrying Coaching Stock |
| PTE | Passenger Transport Executive |
| RCH | Railway Clearing House |
| RMT | Royal Mail Terminal |
| rpm | Revolutions per minute |
| RR | Rolls Royce |
| RSL | Rolling Stock Library |
| SR | BR Southern Region and Southern Railway |
| t | Tonnes |
| T | Toilet |
| TD | Toilet suitable for use by disabled passengers |
| TDM | Time Division Multiplex |
| TOPS | Total Operations Processing System |
| V | Volts |
| W | Wheelchair space |

# 6.7 BUILDERS

Builders are shown in the class headings. The workshops of British Railways and the pre-nationalisation and pre-grouping companies were first transferred to a wholly-owned subsidiary called British Rail Engineering Ltd (BREL). These workshops were later privatised, BREL then becoming BREL Ltd. Some of the works were then taken over by ABB, which was later merged with Daimler-Benz Transportation to become Adtranz. This was later taken over by Bombardier Transportation, which now operates the important works at Derby Litchurch Lane. Bombardier also built vehicles for the British market in Brugge, Belgium.

Other workshops were the subject of separate sales, Springburn, Glasgow and Wolverton becoming "Railcare" and Eastleigh becoming "Wessex Traincare". All three were sold to GEC-Alsthom (now Alstom) but Eastleigh closed in 2006, although the site is now used as a storage and refurbishment location, now operated by Arlington Fleet Services.

Part of Doncaster Works was sold to RFS Engineering, which became insolvent and was bought out and renamed RFS Industries. Doncaster Works now forms part of Wabtec Rail Group.

A number of companies still manufacture or assemble trains in Great Britain, with others planning to open new plants. Bombardier builds trains at its Derby Works and Hitachi at Newton Aycliffe, County Durham. In 2018 CAF opened a new manufacturing and assembly plant at Llanwern, near Newport, and Siemens is building a new plant at Goole, which will initially manufacture trains for London Underground.

The builder details in the class headings show the owner at the time of vehicle construction followed by details of the works as follows:

| | |
|---|---|
| Ashford | Ashford Works (now Ashford Rail Plant depot, not the same location as the Ashford Chart Leacon Works). |
| Birmingham | The former Metro-Cammell works at Saltley, Birmingham, later operated by Alstom. |
| Cowlairs | Cowlairs Works, Glasgow. |
| Derby | Derby Carriage Works (also known as Litchurch Lane). |
| Doncaster | Doncaster Works. |
| Eastleigh | Eastleigh Works |
| Swindon | Swindon Works. |
| Wolverton | Wolverton Works. |
| York | York Carriage Works. |

Other builders are:

| | |
|---|---|
| Alexander | Walter Alexander, Falkirk. |
| Alstom | Valencia, Spain (later sold to Vossloh and then Stadler) and Savigliano (Italy). |
| Barclay | Andrew Barclay, Caledonia Works, Kilmarnock (now Wabtec). |
| BRCW | Birmingham Railway Carriage & Wagon, Smethwick. |
| CAF | Construcciones y Auxiliar de Ferrocarriles (works in Newport, UK and Zaragoza, Beasain, Castejon and Irun in Spain). |
| Cravens | Cravens, Sheffield. |
| Gloucester | Gloucester Railway Carriage & Wagon, Gloucester. |
| Hitachi | Hitachi Rail Europe (Newton Aycliffe, UK, Kasado, Japan and Pistoia, Italy). |
| Hunslet-Barclay | Hunslet-Barclay, Caledonia Works, Kilmarnock (later Wabtec, now Brodie Engineering). |
| Hunslet TPL | Hunslet Transportation Projects, Leeds. |
| Lancing | SR, Lancing Works. |
| Leyland Bus | Leyland Bus, Workington. |
| Metro-Cammell | Metropolitan-Cammell, Saltley, Birmingham |
| Pressed Steel | Pressed Steel, Linwood. |
| Charles Roberts | Charles Roberts, Horbury Junction, Wakefield (later Bombardier). |
| SGP | Simmering-Graz-Pauker, Austria (now owned by Siemens). |
| Siemens | Siemens Transportation Systems (principal works is in Krefeld (Germany) with others in Vienna (Austria) and Prague (Czech Republic, now closed). A new plant is under construction at Goole, UK. |
| SRP | Specialist Rail Products Ltd (A subsidiary of RFS). |
| Stadler | Stadler Rail Group. Principal works building rolling stock for the UK market at Altenrhein and Bussnang (Switzerland), Siedlce (Poland), Szolnok (Hungary) and Valencia, Spain (the former Alstom plant). |
| Vossloh | Vossloh Rail Vehicles, Valencia, Spain (sold to Stadler in 2015). |